C0-AQX-828

MODULARITY AND THE MOTOR THEORY OF SPEECH PERCEPTION

Proceedings of a Conference
to Honor Alvin M. Liberman

MODULARITY AND THE MOTOR THEORY OF SPEECH PERCEPTION

Proceedings of a Conference
to Honor Alvin M. Liberman

Edited by

Ignatius G. Mattingly
Michael Studdert-Kennedy

Haskins Laboratories
New Haven, Connecticut

LEA LAWRENCE ERLBAUM ASSOCIATES, PUBLISHERS

1991   Hillsdale, New Jersey   Hove and London

QP
399
·M63
1991

Copyright © 1991 by Lawrence Erlbaum Associates, Inc.
All rights reserved. No part of this book may be reproduced in
any form, by photostat, microform, retrieval system, or any other
means, without the prior written permission of the publisher.

Lawrence Erlbaum Associates, Inc., Publishers
365 Broadway
Hillsdale, New Jersey 07642

Library of Congress Cataloging-in-Publication Data

Modularity and the motor theory of speech perception / edited by Ignatius G. Mattingly,
   Michael Studdert-Kennedy.
      p.   cm.
      "Proceedings of a conference to honor Alvin M. Liberman."
      Includes bibliographical references and index.
      ISBN 0-8058-0331-9
      1. Speech perception—Congresses.   2. Liberman, Alvin M. (Alvin Meyer)—
Congresses.   I. Mattingly, Ignatius G.   II. Studdert—Kennedy, Michael.
III. Liberman, Alvin M. (Alvin Meyer)
QP399.M63   1991
612.7'8—dc20   90-44718
                                                                     CIP

Printed in the United States of America
10 9 8 7 6 5 4 3 2 1

3 3001 00761 6112

Contents

Contributors and Participants

Ursula Bellugi
The Salk Institute
San Diego, California

Paul Bertelson
Laboratoire de Psychologie
  expérimentale
Université Libre de Bruxelles
Brussels, Belgium

Sheila Blumstein
Department of Linguistics
Brown University
Providence, Rhode Island

Albert Bregman
Department of Psychology
McGill University
Montreal, Quebec

Catherine Browman
Haskins Laboratories
New Haven, Connecticut

J. C. Catford
Department of Linguistics
University of Michigan
Ann Arbor, Michigan

Franklin S. Cooper
Haskins Laboratories
New Haven, Connecticut

Stephen Crain
Haskins Laboratories
New Haven, Connecticut

C. J. Darwin
Laboratory of Experimental
  Psychology
University of Sussex
Brighton, England

Beatrice de Gelder
Laboratoire de Psychologie
  expérimentale
Université Libre de Bruxelles
Brussels, Belgium

Peter Eimas
Department of Psychology
Brown University
Providence, Rhode Island

Janet Fodor
Department of Linguistics
The Graduate School, City
   University of New York
New York, New York

Jerry Fodor
Department of Philosophy
The Graduate School, City
   University of New York
New York, New York

Carol Fowler
Haskins Laboratories
New Haven, Connecticut

Lyn Frazier
Department of Linguistics
University of Massachusetts
Amherst, Massachusetts

Osamu Fujimura
Division of Speech and Hearing
   Research
Ohio State University

Merrill Garrett
Department of Psychology
University of Arizona
Tucson, Arizona

Lila Gleitman
Department of Psychology
University of Pennsylvania
Philadelphia, Pennsylvania

Louis Goldstein
Haskins Laboratories
New Haven, Connecticut

Paul Gorrell
Linguistics Program
University of Maryland
College Park, Maryland

Mark Haggard
Institute of Hearing Research
Medical Research Council
University of Nottingham
Nottingham, England

Daniel Holender
Laboratoire de Psychologie
   expérimentale
Université Libre de Bruxelles
Brussels, Belgium

James J. Jenkins
Department of Psychology
University of South Florida
Tampa, Florida

Peter Jusczyk
Department of Psychology
University of Oregon
Eugene, Oregon

Dennis Klatt (deceased)
Research Laboratory of Electronics
Massachusetts Institute of Technology
Cambridge, Massachusetts

Edward S. Klima
Department of Linguistics
University of California
San Diego, California

Masakazu Konishi
Division of Biology
California Institute of Technology
Pasadena, California

Harlan Lane
Department of Psychology
Northeastern University
Boston, Massachusetts

Alvin M. Liberman
Haskins Laboratories
New Haven, Connecticut

Mark Liberman
AT&T Bell Laboratories
Murray Hill, New Jersey

Björn Lindblom
Department of Linguistics
University of Texas
Austin, Texas

Peter MacNeilage
Department of Linguistics
University of Texas
Austin, Texas

Virginia Mann
Department of Cognitive Sciences
University of California
Irvine, California

Daniel Margoliash
Department of Anatomy
University of Chicago
Chicago, Illinois

Ignatius G. Mattingly
Haskins Laboratories
New Haven, Connecticut

Jacques Mehler
Laboratoire de Psychologie
Paris, France

Joanne Miller
Department of Psychology
Northeastern University
Boston, Massachusetts

Helen Neville
The Salk Institute
San Diego, California

Fernando Nottebohm
Rockefeller University
New York, New York

David Pisoni
Department of Psychology
Indiana University
Bloomington, Indiana

Howard Poizner
Center for Molecular and Behavioral
    Neuroscience
Rutgers University
Newark, New Jersey

Robert Remez
Department of Psychology
Barnard College
New York, New York

Bruno H. Repp
Haskins Laboratories
New Haven, Connecticut

Lawrence Rosenblum
Department of Psychology
University of California
Riverside, California

Arthur Samuel
Department of Psychology
Yale University
New Haven, Connecticut

Donald Shankweiler
Haskins Laboratories
New Haven, Connecticut

Kenneth N. Stevens
Research Laboratory of Electronics
Massachusetts Institute of Technology
Cambridge, Massachusetts

Michael Studdert-Kennedy
Haskins Laboratories
New Haven, Connecticut

Quentin Summerfield
Institute of Hearing Research
Medical Research Council
University of Nottingham
Nottingham, England

Marilyn Vihman
Haverford College
Haverford, Pennsylvania

Janet Werker
Department of Psychology
University of British Columbia
Vancouver, British Columbia

Preface

This book is the proceedings of a conference held in New Haven, Connecticut, June 5–8, 1988, sponsored by Haskins Laboratories, and entitled "Modularity and the Motor Theory of Speech Perception." The purpose of the conference was to honor Alvin Meyer Liberman for his outstanding contributions to research in speech perception since he joined the Laboratories in 1944.

Liberman's first contribution, in collaboration with Franklin Cooper, Pierre Delattre, and others, was to invent a way to do speech perception research. Natural speech signals are extremely complex: Their perceptually significant components cannot be readily isolated by filtering or by temporal segmentation. But early work at Haskins with the Pattern Playback synthesizer had shown that spectrotemporal patterns modeled on those of natural utterances, but highly simplified, could be used to synthesize intelligible speech. Liberman and his colleagues demonstrated that valid and reliable conclusions about speech perception could be based on naive subjects' judgments of such synthetic speech, generated from carefully controlled patterns.

Using this method, Liberman and his colleagues proceeded to identify and describe the speech cues, the acoustic events that support the perception of particular phonetic categories. During the 1940s and 1950s, they studied the sounds of English, manner class by manner class, opening up the field of acoustic phonetics and laying the foundation for speech synthesis by rule.

Spurred by the observation that speech was far more efficiently perceived than the nonphonetic acoustic substitutes for letters they had hoped to use in a reading machine for the blind, Liberman and his colleagues also investigated differences between the perception of speech and the perception of other acoustic signals. Over the years, they discovered a range of effects, from categorical perception and right-ear advantages in dichotic listening to trading relations and duplex perception, that could not be readily explained on psychoacoustic grounds.

Such findings as these encouraged Liberman to develop the Motor Theory, an account of the psychology of speech perception that had been adumbrated in some of the earliest Haskins papers. As currently formulated, the theory makes two related claims: First, that the entities perceived are not acoustic or auditory events as such, but articulatory gestures; second, that the perception of speech, together with other psycholinguistic processes, is the business of a special neural mechanism—a module, in Jerry Fodor's sense. These ideas have developed over many years. In earlier formulations, it was the listeners' own articulatory productions that guided their perceptions of speech; more recently, it is suggested that an abstract vocal tract model determines both speech production and speech perception. Again, it was proposed earlier that "speech is special," with the implication that speech perception was totally different from any other perceptual process; more recently, speech perception, though still having its own peculiar domain, is seen as one of a class of modular perceptual processes. Finally, and perhaps most importantly, Liberman's perspective has become increasingly biological; on his present view, speech perception has more in common with echolocation in the bat than with perception of Morse code in the human.

It would perhaps have been nice to say, at this point in Liberman's career, that these views of his had found widespread acceptance. Such, however, is far from the case. Liberman's ideas were controversial when first proposed and have remained controversial ever since. What *can* be said is that they have been extraordinarily influential, in the sense that a large fraction of the research in speech perception during the past 30 years has consisted of attempts to corroborate or disprove them.

Under these circumstances, the customary procedures for honoring a distinguished scholar on the occasion of his retirement seemed to us inappropriate. We could, indeed, have planned a conference in which all the participants agreed with Liberman. But surely the best way to honor a controversial figure is to continue the controversies he has provoked. Therefore, we decided to invite both critics and supporters to comment on Liberman's ideas and their implications, not only for speech perception and production but for such arguably related areas at the production and perception of sign language, perception in nonhuman animals, lipreading, language acquisition, sentence processing, reading, and learning to read. An introduction by Franklin Cooper was followed by presentations from fourteen speakers. Each of these presentations was commented on briefly by another speaker. There were also three panel discussions; one member of each panel acted as reporter. A summary by James Jenkins concluded the conference. All this material is included here, except for a few of the comments, written versions of which were not received by our deadline. Finally, it seemed only fair to give Liberman an opportunity to react to the conference after seeing the written versions of the papers and comments; his reflections appear at the end of the book.

The editors would like to thank Yvonne Manning, Joan Martinez, Nancy O'Brien, and Zefang Wang for their generous assistance in preparing the manuscript, and Diana Fish for her skillful indexing. We are particularly grateful to Alice Dadourian not only for editorial advice and assistance, but also for the efficiency and enthusiasm with which she handled the logistics of the conference itself.

I.G.M.
M.S.-K.

Chapter 1

Introduction: Speech Perception

Franklin S. Cooper
Haskins Laboratories

Welcome to the Conference on Modularity and the Motor Theory of Speech Perception. It is a real pleasure to see so many old friends and to greet those of you whom I have known only by reputation—a pleasure, too, to welcome you graduate students on whom the future of speech research depends. If you are wondering about the viability of a field of research that is already honoring one of its pioneers, the papers you are about to hear will make it clear, I think, that there are more problems ahead of you than there are solutions behind us grey-beards. For example: Modularity and the Motor Theory. So welcome to the intellectual challenges as well as to this conference!

To Al Liberman, who is himself an old hand at conferences, this one must be something of a novelty: It was arranged *for* him, not *by* him! It is entirely appropriate that Haskins Laboratories should wish to honor him. Al has been a co-worker and a cobeliever in Haskins Laboratories ever since he joined it in 1944 and a continuing inspiration to all of us, both personally and intellectually. He still wanders the halls asking, "What have you discovered today?" It is doubly appropriate that he be honored by a conference on Modularity and the Motor Theory of Speech Perception, since these ideas have been central to his own work and to the many contributions he has made to speech research. I could say more—much more—in the same vein but will limit it to one personal comment: To me, Al has been a friend, and I am the one honored.

Let me consider with you some simple-minded questions. How does it happen that we are here to talk about the Motor Theory of Speech Perception? (I shall leave Modularity aside for a moment.) Part of the answer lies in the history of the field, and as we probe that history—for the benefit of you younger people—we shall find even prior questions. Thus, talking about a theory implies some kind of

1

problem for that theory to explain. Was there such a problem? This may seem a strange thing to ask, since the question of how speech is perceived has been a thorny problem for as long as most of you can remember. Nearly as ancient is the Motor Theory as a proposed solution.

But there was a time when even the problem did not exist—or was not known to be a problem. In the same sense, gravity was not a problem before Newton's time: Everybody knew that apples fell down just as everything else did. So likewise the perception of speech posed no special problem; it and other sounds were heard and recognized all in the same general way.

Let me press the parallel a little farther: Neither Isaac Newton nor Alvin Liberman *discovered* his problem until it fell on him. Newton can now be dismissed, though we should note that it is not every man of science who provides his own problem as well as its solution.

Back to Al and how he discovered *his* problem: Namely, how is speech perceived? He did not begin with speech. The problem that he and I were working on at the end of World War II was the practical one of designing a reading machine for blinded veterans. Our approach was simple and direct: The machine would scan a line of type and convert the distinctive letter shapes into distinctive sound shapes which the blind reader would, with practice, come to recognize—and so to read printed books by ear.

The difficulty that we encountered—as did others before and after us—was that the reading rates were so painfully slow, even after hours and hours of practice, that no one would use the device. We tried many things to make the sounds more distinctive and more easily learned, but reading rates were no better and often worse. Most frustrating was that the performance of our subjects when identifying our machine-made words was much poorer than their performance when identifying nonsense words, spoken by a person.

Thus did Al's problem come down upon him: Finally, he realized that the right question was not why machine-made sounds are so poor but rather why man-made sounds are so good. What is so special about speech that makes its perception so easy?

He then supposed that speech was just a better acoustic alphabet—that it took the phonetic string of a sentence and spelled it out with unit sounds that could be heard easily and rapidly, because they flowed together into words. By studying these unit sounds of speech, he might be able to design a better set of sounds for the reading machine.

But by this time, the Potter, Kopp, and Green (1947) collection of spectrograms had been published, and one could see that finding acoustic invariants for the phonemes would not be so easy. One could pick out some of the acoustic consequences of articulation, but where in all this complex pattern were the acoustic cues for perceiving the individual speech sounds known to be lurking there?

This search for the acoustic cues was the task that Al, Pierre Delattre, and I undertook in the early 1950s using spectrograph and pattern playback. What we found was well known at the time and is still available in the literature. Cues there were—in abundance and extreme diversity. Before the end of the decade, most of them had been found and organized into rules for synthesis that generated quite intelligible speech (Liberman, Ingemann, Lisker, Delattre, & Cooper, 1959).

But it was the diversity and curious character of the cues that needed a better explanation than current auditory theories of perception could provide. The cues for a particular speech sound seemed to make sense only when one considered how that sound had been articulated. Al made these arguments explicit in his 1957 (Liberman, 1957) review paper and offered a motor theory to explain why speech is so exceptionally efficient as a carrier of messages.

Thus history, not logic, is the principal reason we are here to talk about a motor theory of speech *perception* rather than a motor theory of speech *production.*

There were other reasons, too. There was then a bias—which still persists—toward thinking about speech as "that which goes into the ear" rather than "that which comes out of the mouth." Little wonder, since the ear and its roots in the brain are so much more elegant and mysterious than the mouth's crossed-up plumbing and ventilating systems, which can't even breathe and swallow at the same time! Then, too, instrumentation was largely lacking for research on production.

Let me add as an aside that although Al continued to focus on the perception of speech and its many unique characteristics, there were some of us here who did start, in the late 1950s, to look for phonological structure on the production side. The Laboratories still has a major program ongoing in this area, and we are by no means alone.

Now, what would be different if we were talking about a motor theory of speech production instead of a motor theory of speech perception? Surely there must be close linkages between the two processes and their mechanisms unless, indeed, a single mechanism performs both functions. But whatever the internal structure of the speech module (or modules), the input and output signals are very different in kind and structure. This calls for a restructuring operation somewhere in the sequence—one that may put tighter constraints on a model for the speech module than do either perception or production.

So another question: Should we perhaps be talking about a motor theory of speech *per se,* where "speech" stands for "communication by voice?" This would emphasize the communicative function that is served by *both* perception and production. Moreover, it would give central place to the operation that ensures error-free regeneration of spoken messages, even when repeated many times.

You may object to so much emphasis on the relaying of spoken messages from person to person, since it is so rarely done. The point is that it can be done; the mechanism is in place and in use for other purposes. Long ago, this kind of relaying was common; indeed, speech—aided by rhyme—served to repeat epic poems intact across the ages. The trick, just as with long-distance telephony now that it has gone digital, is to regenerate the signal each time it is relayed. The incoming signal, contaminated with noise and distortion, is replaced by a shiny new signal in canonical form. For humans, the regenerated signals serve a further purpose: They are just what is needed for memory, since the bit rate for identifying the message units is so much less than for describing the incoming sounds.

Regeneration is only one of several names for the function I have been talking about. Categorization is an essential part of the function, and with labeling included it provides the recognition stage in models of speech perception. Restructuring, or recoding, are also closely related terms. In models of speech production, the generative part of regeneration corresponds to setting up motor plans or coordinative structures. I have used the term "regeneration," because it relates to both input and output and implies the communicative function of which it is an essential part.

Clearly, regeneration also implies *units*. In their canonical form, these would be the "intended gestures" of the motor theory. But surely these are only a subset of all possible gestures, so what constrains the choice? Speed of execution is one requirement. In fact, people can and do talk at rates of up to fifteen or so units per second—which seems impossibly high for such slow machinery as tongue and jaw. So we should not expect speech gestures to conform to our usual notion of a completed movement such as a nod of the head or a wave of the hand. No amount of coarticulation between such gestures (i.e., overlap along the time line), would crowd them into the time allowed.

But coarticulation across the time line could do it. Given the several articulators that we have and their potential for independent and concurrent action, the total system could achieve a succession of discrete states—nameable as phonemes or intended gestures—and so attain a kind of phase velocity much higher than that of the individual articulators. It may be comforting to note that this way of looking at speech—searching for coincidences and alignments during ongoing gesturing—conforms to the cosmic strategy whereby astrologers seek our destinies in planetary alignments.

Another constraint on the choice of gestures is the fairly obvious one that they must have acoustic consequences. Preferably, the consequences would be as strong and distinctive as they are for [s] and [ʃ], but given the nature of the gestures, most of the sounds are necessarily variable with context and some, to round out the inventory, are even as feeble and confusable as [f] and [θ].

A more demanding requirement is that the units be *permutable*. Thus, assuming speech to be a succession of discrete states that progresses from one intended gesture to the next, then the set of possible "next gestures" from any particular state is small and sharply constrained. It is limited—not by phonological rules—but by circumstances such as that some of the articulators are already in mid-movement and must, therefore, continue moving in the next gesture. In a more general way, one of the prices of parallelism is that there is no way to extract a time slice without leaving rough edges, so shuffling its position means finding a place where the edges will match.

It might be useful to turn this argument on its head and use the permutability requirement to reinterpret our knowledge of how real phonemic units combine and recombine. That could help us to arrive at physiological descriptions of the "intended gestures."

Much of what I have been saying has dealt with the constraints that particular processes put on models for speech. Let me now try a different tack and ask about *minimal* constraints on the speech signal at various stages of the communicative process: Thus, what requirements at the very least must the unit signals of speech meet, if they are to be useful in perception, in production, and in such intermediate processing as may be needed to link perception and production? And, having asked these questions, let me propose answers: For perception, the signals must at the very least be audible; for production, they must be utterable; and for the intermediate processing, they must be both regenerable and permutable; it would help, if they were also memorable. The moral I would draw is obvious: The constraints that really bind are the need to regenerate and the need to permute the signal units.

Finally, let me return to my original question, slightly sharpened: We are, in fact, met here to talk about Modularity and the Motor Theory of Speech Perception. Does that emphasis on perception mean that we are "barking up the wrong tree?" Like most simple-minded questions, this one has two answers: YES, if we suppose that perception is all-important, or that it can be dealt with in isolation. NO, if we consider that perception by itself is a very large topic for a single conference, and if we remember that the models we build for perception must be compatible with the rest of the communicative process; that is, they must honor the Throughput Principle: That which goes in at the ear, and out from the mouth, must somehow go through the head.

References

Liberman, A. M. (1957). Some results of research on speech perception. *Journal of the Acoustical Society of America, 29,* 117–123.

Liberman, A. M., Ingemann, F., Lisker, L., Delattre, P. C., & Cooper, F. S. (1959). Minimal rules for synthesizing speech. *Journal of the Acoustical Society of America, 31,* 1490–1499.

Potter, R. K., Kopp, G. A., & Green, H. (1947). *Visible speech.* New York: Von Nostrand.

Chapter 2

The Status of Phonetic Gestures

Björn Lindblom

Department of Linguistics, University of Texas, and University of Stockholm

Abstract

In this chapter, I shall argue that speakers adaptively tune phonetic gestures to the various needs of speaking situations (the plasticity of phonetic gestures) and that languages make their selection of phonetic gesture inventories under the strong influence of motor and perceptual constraints that are language independent and in no way special to speech (the functional adaptation of phonetic gestures). These points have implications for a number of issues on which the Motor Theory takes a stance. In particular, the evidence reviewed challenges two assumptions that are central to the Motor Theory—that of modularity and gestural invariance. First, if phonetic gestures possess invariance at the level of motor commands, and listeners are able to perceive such gestural invariance, why is speech production so often nevertheless under output-oriented control? Second, the Motor Theory assumes that speech perception is a biologically specialized process that bypasses the auditory mechanisms responsible for the processing of nonspeech sounds. It also assumes that the motor system for vocal tract control exhibits specialized adaptations. If so, why do inventories of vowels and consonants nevertheless show evidence of being optimized with respect to motoric and perceptual limitations that must be regarded as biologically general and not at all special to speaking and listening?

There are two aspects of phonetic gestures that merit special attention in the context of the Motor Theory (MT), (Liberman & Mattingly, 1985). One striking fact comes from observations of how speech is produced: A large body of experimental evidence suggests that phonetic gestures are highly malleable and adaptive. They exhibit *plasticity*.

The second point emerges from cross-linguistic data on how languages select gestures to build segment inventories: Phonologies are "quantal" in that they use similar gestures drawn from a remarkably small universal set (Stevens, 1989). Moreover, in individual languages, the selection of vowel and consonants from this set is systematic and lawful. It is governed by certain "implicational laws" (Jakobson, 1968; Lindblom & Maddieson, 1988).

As we try to explain why systems of phonetic gestures exhibit these quantal and implicational properties, we are led to argue that they are selected so as to meet collectively a demand for "sufficient perceptual contrast." Developing this point, we shall suggest that phonetic gestures can be seen as *adaptations* to constraints on motoric and perceptual mechanisms that are language independent and not special to speech.

The plasticity of phonetic gestures is a phenomenon that any theory aimed at resolving the issue of *phonetic invariance* (Perkell & Klatt, 1986) must account for. The MT addresses this issue by claiming as Liberman and Mattingly (1985) wrote: "The objects of speech perception are the intended phonetic gestures of the speaker, represented in the brain as invariant motor commands" (p. 2). Furthermore, viewing phonetic gesture inventories as adaptations to nonspecial input/output mechanisms poses another interesting problem for the MT that argues that both the production and the perception of speech are "modular," biologically specialized processes. Let us see where contrasting these views will lead us.

The Plasticity of Phonetic Gestures

The MT Model of Speech Production

Liberman and Mattingly (1985) took the following stance on the invariance issue:

> Phonetic perception is perception of gesture. . . . [They further state] the invariant source of the phonetic percept is somewhere in the processes by which the sounds of speech are produced. (pp. 21–23)

The authors recognized the complexity and variability that phonetic gestures exhibit in instrumental analyses but claimed (Liberman & Mattingly, 1985):

> It is nonetheless clear that, despite such variation, the gestures have a virtue that the acoustic cues lack: Instances of a particular gesture always have certain topological properties not shared by any other gesture. [They conclude that] the gestures do have characteristic invariant properties, as the motor theory requires, though these must be seen, not as peripheral movements, but as the more remote structures that control the movements. These structures correspond to the speaker's intentions. (p. 23)

Vowel Reduction

We can illustrate this theory of invariance with some examples of the so-called *undershoot* phenomenon (Lindblom, 1963). Figure 2.1 shows spectrograms of three English words containing one, two, and three syllables: *muse, music, musically*. The increase in word length is correlated with a shortening of the initial, stressed vowel. This durational variation is associated with shifts in the extent to which mid-vowel formant patterns approach a hypothetical target. Note the extent of the F2 contour, which shows a clear dependence on vowel duration. The tongue, initially in a palatal position, undershoots its velar /u/ target more and more as the vowel becomes shorter. Note that these samples are all from syllables carrying lexical main stress. Therefore, we are justified in calling the phenomenon illustrated in Fig. 2.1 *duration-dependent* undershoot.

In conformity with the Liberman–Mattingly model of speech production, it seems possible to suggest that the undershoot effect is due to the spatial and temporal overlap of adjacent motor commands. The durational variations induced by changing word length cause differences in timing of the motor commands, and, provided that the time constants of the articulators are assumed not to change, the MT makes the correct prediction that in a particular context reaching the target configuration of the stressed vowel is a function of the duration of the vowel. Because undershoot is lawfully related to the duration and the context of the vowel gestures, it is possible to claim that something nonetheless remains invariant: the underlying intention, or "Lautabsicht" (Lindblom, 1963). On this view of speech, therefore, the task of the listener becomes that of inferring the intended gestures from highly encoded and indirect acoustic information.

For biomechanical reasons, the simple undershoot model may still be said to have a certain validity. However, there are complications. Mainly they arise from the fact that in natural speech a speaker's intentions go far beyond that of merely producing a sequence of invariant phonetic gestures. We begin to see these complications as soon as we broaden the scope of our inquiry and approach slightly more ecological speaking conditions than those normally studied in our laboratories.

Apparently speakers are free to vary degree of undershoot somewhat independently of vowel duration. This is evident from studies indicating on the one hand that in fast speech, articulatory and acoustic goals can be attained *despite* short segment durations (Engstrand, 1988; Gay, 1978; Kuehn & Moll, 1976) and on the other hand that reductions can occur *despite* adequate duration (Nord, 1986). How talkers go about varying degree of undershoot is not known. One possibility is that deviations from duration-dependent undershoot might be due to processes such as "overarticulating" and "underarticulating" (cf. discussion of "clear speech" following). The observed deviations of duration-dependence obviously constitute an embarrassment for the simplest version of the undershoot model

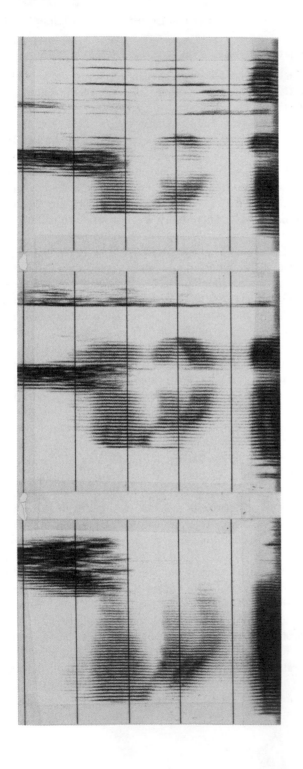

MUSE   MUSIC   MUSICALLY

FIG. 2.1. Vowel reduction and 'duration-dependent formant undershoot'' (Lindblom, 1963). Spectrograms of three English words (from left to right): *muse, music, musically*. Note the variation in the duration of the initial vowel and the associated changes in the frequency contours of F2.

(Lindblom, 1963). An improved model is clearly needed capable of capturing the malleability of phonetic gestures.

Compensatory Articulation

Speakers are in fact capable of reorganizing phonetic gestures so as to reach constant acoustic and perceptual goals. This has been shown most clearly by experiments on *compensatory articulation* in which atypical jaw positions are induced by means of so-called "bite blocks" (Lindblom, Lubker, & Gay, 1979; Lindblom, Lubker, Lyberg, Branderud, & Holmgren, 1987). The relative ease with which speakers adapt to an unnatural bite block can be accounted for by assuming also that normal speech motor control is intrinsically compensatory. Although the bite block must be overcome by invoking rather extreme articulations, the compensation occurs effortlessly, because not only speech but motor behavior in general is organized to be compensatory. For the sake of those who take a dim view of bite block experiments and remain unconvinced by claims that bite block speech tells us anything at all about normal speech, let us examine another case of compensation, but one found in a more ecological speaking situation.

Loud Speech

Consider the control of vowel duration in *loud speech*. Speakers have been shown to use larger jaw openings when speaking louder. The effect is independent of vowel identity and has been demonstrated for several languages (Schulman, 1989). Now this raises a problem for the production of loud vowel duration in the following way. Recall the Extent of Movement Hypothesis proposed by Fischer-Jørgensen (1964). It explains why, everything else being equal, open vowels universally tend to be longer than close vowels. The main effect is that in an open vowel occurring in a CVC environment, the jaw moves further than in a close vowel in the same context. Using a quantitative articulatory model formalizing Fischer-Jørgensen's idea, I showed for /ibVbi/-utterances (Lindblom, 1967) that owing to these differences in jaw movement, the release of the first /b/ will occur more and more prematurely, and the implosion of the second /b/ will be increasingly delayed as the degree of opening of the vowel is increased. In addition to supporting the Extent of Movement Hypothesis, these model experiments indicate that the effect can in fact be so drastic that unless the lip gestures for the /b/:s are reorganized to compensate for the jaw movement, unacceptably large durational differences between open and close vowels will result. The need for such compensation was indeed substantiated by the lip and jaw measurements of the same study (Lindblom, 1967, e.g., Fig. I-A-14).

Because loud speech uses more open jaw positions, the Extent of Movement Hypothesis applies also to that style of speech. Experimental data (Schulman,

1989; Lindblom, 1987) show that the increased jaw openings of loud vowels are compensated for by other articulators in order to make vowel durations of loud and normal conditions more similar than they would have been without compensatory maneuvers.

Clear Speech

We recently began a series of studies aiming at describing the acoustic properties of clear speech. Presumably when people speak more clearly, they do so in an effort to become more intelligible. One issue is whether this speaking style differs from more neutral speech mainly in that its signal-to-noise ratio is better or whether it also involves a reorganization of phonetic gestures and acoustic patterns. There is evidence indicating that such reorganization does indeed take place and can be rather extensive (Picheny, Durlach, & Braida, 1986; Uchanski, Durlach, & Braida, 1987).

We have preliminary data on American English vowels (Moon & Lindblom, 1989) produced in contexts that meet the following conditions:

1. The vowels and their consonantal environments should be chosen so as to maximize large "locus-to-target" distances (e.g., front vowels occurring in a labio-velar environment: *wheel, will, well, wail*)
2. The vowels should carry lexical main stress
3. They should vary in duration.

The latter two requirements were met by making use of the so-called "word length effect." The length of the test words was varied by adding *-ing* and *-ingham* to the CVC sequence under analysis, which produced series such as *will, willing, Willingham,* and so forth. Subjects were asked to read randomized lists of such tokens. Initially they were instructed to adopt a comfortable tempo and vocal effort but received no specific instructions otherwise. We refer to these speech samples as citation form speech (CF). In the second half of the recordings, they read similar lists but were now explicitly told to overarticulate and to speak as clearly as possible (CS lists). Measurements were made of vowel duration and of formant frequencies at points of minimum rate of change in the vowels and of the locus pattern of the consonants.

Plots of formant frequencies versus vowel duration were prepared for all the test items. The vowel formant patterns of both CF and CS samples were found to exhibit duration-dependent undershoot. For both styles, the data points tended to cluster in ways that could be described in terms of exponential curves similar to those used in Lindblom (1963). However, there were significant differences: Overarticulated vowels were consistently of longer duration, and for every vowel examined, the CS undershoot curve was different from the corresponding CF curve. These differences can be summarized by saying that for each individual vowel the asymptotes of the exponentials tend to be located much closer to the formant values observed for null-context environments such as /h–d/. Plotting the data on an F1/F2 vowel chart, we observe that the CS vowel space invokes values that are more peripheral and closer to the /h–d/ targets than the CF tokens, which are more context-sensitive and, hence, more centralized in the formant space.

The analysis of the investigation from which these observations are taken is still in progress. In the near future, we expect to be able to give a more comprehensive report on the robustness and generality of the observed effects across a wide range of speakers and contexts. Nevertheless, a trend fully compatible with previous work on CS acoustics (Picheny et al., 1986, Uchanski et al., 1987) is evident in the patterning of the data, which so far suggest that it does not merely improve the S/N ratio. Clear speech is a transform that tends to enhance the acoustic contrast among vowel phonemes, making their formant patterns less dependent on context and more widely dispersed.

If our preliminary results are further corroborated, we must ask: Why should there be such a thing as clear speech? Why do talkers bother to make extensive adjustments of their phonetic gestures and the associated acoustic patterns? Is it because in so doing they facilitate the listener's access to the distal objects of perception: the underlying phonetic gestures (cf. the Motor Theory)? Instead, is it because they thereby make acoustically stable and salient properties of the signal easier to identify (cf. the Quantal Theory of Speech)? Finally, is it —as we prefer to argue— because lexical access is based on "sufficient contrast" (cf. the Theory of Adaptive Dispersion as presented in the following)?

Is Invariance Necessarily Phonetic?

How do we account for the variance of phonetic gestures that we observe in compensatory articulations, in loud speech, and in clear speech? No doubt proponents of the MT would pin their hopes on future research demonstrating how the speech system succeeds in computing a family of gestures that, in spite of substantial surface variability, topologically share certain unique properties and nevertheless manage to remain *motorically* invariant.

However, faced with a rather impressive body of evidence on the plasticity of motor gestures in general and phonetic gestures in particular, we are easily persuaded by an alternative vision according to which invariants will ultimately have to be defined in terms of the *purpose* and *primary ecological function* of the gestures, namely lexical access, comprehension, and social interaction. On this view, phonetic gestures should not be expected to be motorically invariant, because they are merely adaptive and malleable means to more global communicative ends.

Why then are we looking for phonetic invariance? Is it not needed for satisfactory lexical access? Here is a summary of an argument that leads us to conclude that in principle it is indeed dispensable.

We begin by noting that the structure of all languages exhibits redundancy and that the perception of speech is the product of two types of information: signal-driven and signal-independent information. As a consequence of redundancy, the words and phonemes of individual utterances show short-term variations in predictability. Consider the following two utterances[1]:

Utterance A: *A stitch in time saves* _____.
Utterance B: *The next number is* _____.

A reduced, articulatorily simplified pronunciation of *nine* would stand a better chance of being correctly identified in utterance A than in utterance B. Whether reduced or not, any phonetic form that is correctly identified would by definition be perceptually adequate (sufficiently rich). From the viewpoint of lexical access, such a form can be said to exhibit sufficient perceptual contrast.

These considerations lead us to conclude that phonetic invariance is not necessarily essential for lexical access. Speech signals will be adequate for lexical access as long as they are rich enough to match in a complementary fashion the listener's running access to signal-independent information. According to this theory, therefore, the critical condition that phonetic gestures must meet is that they be *perceptually sufficiently contrastive.*

Coarticulation

With the idea of "sufficient perceptual contrast" in mind, let us take a new look at some well-known measurements often referred to in discussions of consonant–vowel coarticulation. Early work on the acoustic patterns of synthetic speech led Haskins researchers to conclude that the objects of speech perception were not to be found at the acoustic surface but might be sought in upstream invariant motor processes. In 1966, Öhman published his spectrographic measurements on V_1CV_2 sequences. His results give a vivid demonstration of massive coarticulation effects and seem at least at first glance to lend strong support to the Haskins idea that there is simply no way to define a phonetic category in purely acoustic terms.

To make this point, we reproduce one of Öhman's diagrams in Fig. 2.2, an illustration, as good as any, of the observation that place information for a given consonant is carried by a rising transition in one vowel context and a falling

---

[1]In my choice of these examples I am indebted to Lieberman (1963).

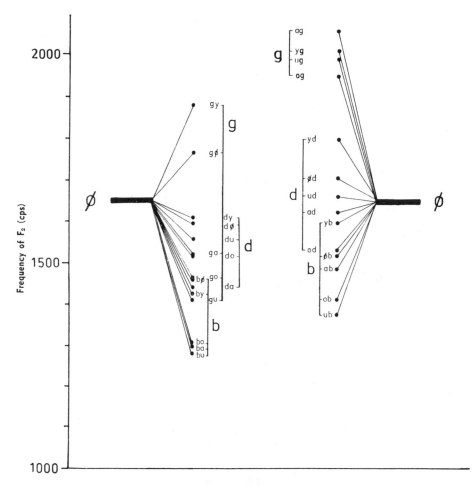

FIG. 2.2. Formant transitions and consonant-vowel coarticulation.
Stylized second-formant transitions observed in VCV utterances. The
symbols at transition endpoints identify the following and preceding
contexts respectively (adapted from Öhman, 1966, with permission).

transition in another (Liberman, Delattre, Cooper, & Gertsman 1954).

However, although admittedly complex, do acoustic patterns of this kind
really justify the conclusion that there is simply no way to define a phonetic
category in purely acoustic terms? Let us replot the Öhman data as shown in Fig.
2.3.

The data points pertain to F2 and F3 of the CV_2-boundary (x- and y-axes) and

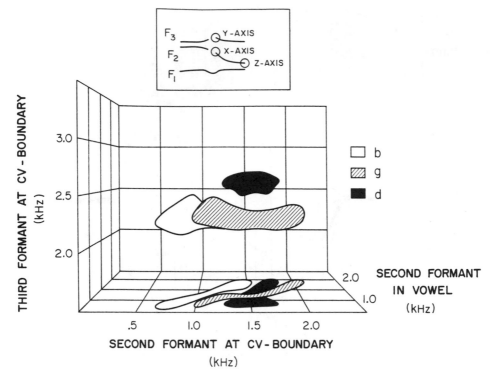

FIG. 2.3. A three-dimensional representation of formant measurements at CV-boundary of VCV sequences (Öhman 1966). The "clouds" of the diagram includes all the data in Tables II and IV of the Öhman (1966) article. X-axis: Second formant at CV-boundary. Y-axis: Third formant at CV-boundary. Y-axis: Second formant in final vowel.

to F2 of the V_2 vowel (z-axis) and are from his Tables II and IV (Öhman, 1966). We see a three-dimensional view of three "clouds" that correspond to samples of V_1bV_2, V_1dV_2 and $V_1g_2V_2$ utterances, respectively, and that, in spite of all the vowel–consonant coarticulation, do not overlap and hence, are sufficiently distinct from each other.

The implication of this result is this: If we make the reasonable assumption that perception has access to (at least) these three parameters of the VCV utterances, the information available in the acoustic signal should be sufficient to disambiguate the place of the consonants. Needless to say, the three dimensions selected here do not by any means exhaust the signal attributes that might carry place information. One obvious omission is the spectral dynamics of the stop releases. Spectra for /b/ would be relatively weak and flat whereas those for /d/ and /g/ would show distinct stronger energy concentrations of mainly front cavity dependence (Stevens, 1968). Adding such dimensions to the consonant space would be an effective means of further increasing the separation of the three clouds and thus enhancing their distinctiveness.

Please note the following: Given the preceding analysis, we do not, unlike proponents of the MT, need to postulate that a specialized mechanism evolved to handle coarticulation in CV syllables. Phonetic categories are "polymorphous" phenomena (Kluender, Diehl, & Killeen, 1987) that, if sufficiently contrastive perceptually, do the job of differentating lexical items from each other. Their polymorphous nature and the notion of sufficient contrast imply that there is no single necessary or sufficient cue that must always be present for category membership.

This analysis is supported by work on speech perception by animals. Most recently Kluender et al. (1987) demonstrated the ability of Japanese quail to learn to discriminate place in stop consonants and to generalize their judgments to new vowel contexts. These birds are also capable of using cues for voicing, vowel height, and sex of talker. These findings strongly suggest that quail perform well on the discrimination tasks not because they are equipped with a specialized processor for speech, but because they are able to exploit the stimulus properties, and because these properties are acoustically sufficiently rich.

The Linguistic Selection of Phonetic Gesture Inventories: Adaptation to Non-specialized Input/Output Constraints

It appears reasonable to assume that the factors that shape the vowel and consonant inventories of the languages of the world originate in the interactive behavior of speakers and listeners. What is the nature of the selection criteria that might govern the evolution of phonetic systems?

The Quantal Theory of Speech (Stevens, 1989) hypothesizes that languages tend to seek out regions of high *acoustic* and *auditory stability* in the universal phonetic space and that these regions represent the physical correlates of the distinctive features of phonological systems. Both talker-oriented and listener-oriented factors motivate the choice of acoustic stability as a basis for selections.

An alternative theory, the Theory of Adaptive Dispersion (Lindblom, Mac-Neilage, & Studdert-Kennedy, forthcoming), shares with the Quantal Theory the assumption that the factors shaping phonetic inventories originate in on-line speaker–listener interactions but differs in that it explores the consequences of adopting another selection criterion, namely *sufficient perceptual contrast*. Some of the results obtained within that paradigm bear on the present discussion.

Perceptual Contrast

Let us first look at dispersion and the notion of perceptual contrast. Typological studies of vowel systems (Crothers, 1978; Maddieson, 1984) show that the most favored inventories are drawn from a small subset of the total set of observed qualities. The data of Table 2.1 are from Crothers (1978).

It is evident that languages favor peripheral vowels and that there is a tendency to use many more sonority (open/close) contrasts than chromaticity (front/back and rounded/unrounded) contrasts.

Suppose we approach these observations from the following point of view: *If vowels systems were seen as adaptations to the universal auditory constraints of human hearing, what would they be like?* This is essentially the question that we have addressed in a number of studies. Here is a brief summary of some of the results.

Three studies explore the notion of "maximal perceptual contrast." In Liljencrants and Lindblom (1972), a formant-based distance metric was used to quantify the notion of perceptual contrast and to predict the phonetic values of vowel systems as a function of inventory size. The predictions were successful in reflecting the patterns of *dispersion* clearly evident in the typological data. Their major failure was that, in large systems, too many high vowels were generated.

In Lindblom (1986), the simulations were repeated with a psychoacoustically better-motivated distance metric (Bladon & Lindblom, 1981). This revision led to clear improvements, implying that as our description of the auditory constraints becomes better, so will our predictions. A third study (Lindblom, in press) combines the 1986 model with the results of experiments using Direct Magnitude Estimation (DME). The DME technique was used to compare subjects' judgments of movement along the dimensions of jaw opening and anterior–posterior positioning of the tongue. The results indicated that jaw movements appeared subjectively more extensive than tongue movements, although displacements were equal in terms of physical measures (Lindblom & Lubker, 1985). Incorporating those results into the simulations, we revised the optimization criterion to encompass also articulatory discriminability, departing from the

TABLE 2.1
Most Favored Vowel Systems Observed in a Corpus of Over 200 Languages (Crothers, 1978)

Inventory Size	Vowel Qualities	No of LG's
3	i a u	23
4	i a u ɛ	13
4	i a u ɨ	9
5	i a u ɛ ɔ	55
5	i a u ɛ ɨ	5
6	i a u ɛ ɔ ɨ	29
6	i a u ɛ ɔ e	7
7	i a u e o ɨ ə	14
7	i a u ɛ ɔ e o	11
9	i a u ɛ ɔ e o ɨ ə	7

TABLE 2.2
Predicted Vowel Systems Derived From Quantitative
Simulations (Adapted from Lindblom, MacNeilage &
Studdert-Kennedy, forthcoming).

Inventory Size	Vowel Qualities
3	i a u
4	i a u ɛ
5	i a u ɛ ɔ
6	i a u ɛ ɔ ʉ
7	i a u ɛ ɑ ʉ ɤ
9	i a u ɛ ɑ e o ʉ ə

assumption that vowels tend to evolve so as to both sound and feel sufficiently different.

Evaluating the results, two things should be noted. The probability of selecting a correct system by pure chance is less than 10^{-3}, irrespective of system size. The predictions are perfect, if we measure agreement between model and data in terms of the number of sonority and chromaticity contrasts. Bearing these points in mind, we see from Table 2.2 that the simulations achieve an extremely close agreement with the typological data.

Adaptive Dispersion

In the three studies reviewed above, articulatory factors play a role in delimiting the phonetic space of "possible vowels" (Lindblom & Sundberg, 1971), but beyond that they are essentially neglected. There is a great deal of evidence (Lindblom et al., forthcoming) indicating that articulation plays an important role and that production constraints tend to counterbalance demands for perceptual contrast. Briefly let us mention a single example due to Maddieson (1984). The optimal five-vowel system is / i e a o u/ not /iː ẽ a̰ o̰ uˤ/. He suggested that a principle of "sufficient contrast," rather than of maximal contrast, may underlie such patterns.

Recent work (Lindblom et al., forthcoming) indicates that both vowel and consonant systems appear to be organized so as to meet a demand for "sufficient contrast." This becomes clear, once we begin to examine the contents of phonetic systems in relation to inventory size.

Our source of information is the UPSID database (Maddieson, 1984), which contains typological data on the segment inventories of 317 languages. Figure 2.4 exemplifies the results of sorting the consonant segments of UPSID into three categories—Basic, Elaborated, and Complex articulations—and then plotting the number of segments that a language uses in each category as a function of the total

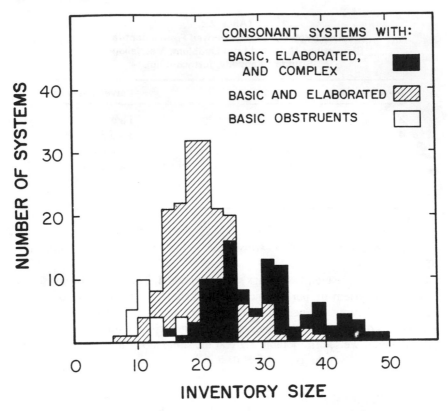

FIG. 2.4.   Inventory size as a determinant of the contents of obstruent systems. Small inventories invoke Basic articulations, medium systems Basic and Elaborated segments and large inventories recruit Basic, Elaborated as well as Complex articulations. Data from the UPSID database (Maddieson, 1984).

number of consonants in that language[2]. Figure 2.4 shows a histogram plot describing the distribution of obstruents in the UPSID corpus. The diagram tells us that the contents of UPSID inventories is determined by inventory size. First, they invoke Basic articulations, then Basic and Elaborated, and ultimately all three types, including the Complex.

This Size Principle makes sense, if we assume that, in small systems, elemen-

---

[2]Elaborated articulations are place, source, and manner mechanisms that can be seen as elaborated versions of more elementary, or Basic, articulations. Segments containing combinations of Elaborated articulations are classified as Complex.

Basic: b, m, t, i, a . . .
Elaborated: p', ɗ, ɹ, mb, ʈ, q, pʲ, . . .
Complex: qh, ãũ, q', ʰʈ, . . .

tary articulations achieve sufficient contrast, whereas in larger systems, demands for greater intrasystemic distinctiveness cause additional dimensions (elaborations) to be recruited and combined to form complex segments. Data of this sort lend support to the Theory of Adaptive Dispersion (Lindblom & Maddieson, 1988; Lindblom et al., forthcoming) and suggest that the Size Principle, combined with quantitative measures of perceptual distinctiveness and articulatory complexity, should play a significant role in accounting for the contents of phonetic inventories.

The conclusions relevant to the present context are as follows: The results are compatible with claiming that inventories of phonetic gestures are selected so as to optimize both the distinctiveness and the pronounceability of individual segments. Phonetic gestures can, thus, be seen as *adaptations* to motoric and perceptual constraints that are language-independent and in no way special to speech. Facts about the way humans respond to psychophysical, nonspeech stimuli are sufficient to enable us to predict with good accuracy the essential contents of vowel inventories in a large number of languages. If human speech perception is a biologically specialized process that bypasses nonspeech hearing, why do vowel system patterns show such clear adaptations to auditory constraints not special to speech?

Conclusions

Plasticity and Invariance

Our interpretations are in agreement with the MT in that the distal object of speech perception is the speaker's intention. However, we differ by claiming that a speaker's intentions go beyond the production of phonetic gestures. We see the gestures as no more than a variable and adaptive means to the more global, ecologically more primary ends of speech acts: lexical access, comprehension, and social interaction. On this view, phonetic gestures are not strong candidates for the invariant units of speech. In fact, we argue that phonetic invariance is not necessary at all for adequate lexical access, because successful speech understanding presupposes gestures that are sufficiently contrastive but not necessarily physically constant.

Modularity and Phonological Adaptations

Assuming that speech perception is modular and operates by by-passing the general-purpose mechanisms of auditory perception, we face the question: Why are the fossilized gestures of phonological inventories so well adapted to biological properties of production and perception not special to speech? There appears to be a clear problem here for the MT.

Consider also the quantal and implicational nature of sound structure, which is the fact that languages tend to use similar gestures drawn from a very limited universal set and that the subsets they select show a strongly hierarchical organization internally. How does the MT account for such facts?

One possibility would be to suggest that all of these properties reflect the way that the "speech-processing module" works. We might assume that the module accepts only a limited number of gestures and that it somehow imposes an implicational structure on phonological systems. If so, we are led to ask: How did the speech-processing module get that way in the first place? It seems clear that if at an early stage of the game we claim that "speech is special," we shall *a priori* deprive ourselves of all opportunities to provide performance-based explanations of phonological facts. Consequently, we are forced to conclude that suggesting that the quantal and implicational organization of sound systems reflects the way that the speech-processing module works is a solution that completely begs the question on an issue that must be regarded as central to linguistic theory.

Speech Evolution

Admittedly, postulating biologically specialized systems for the production and perception of speech—as the MT does—appears not only reasonable but necessary in the light of a great deal of evidence. Claiming that linguistic perception does not in some sense presuppose specialized neural architecture would clearly be counter-factual. Why then have we pursued a line of reasoning that consistently sets out to deny the existence of such specializations? The answer is that denying the existence of specializations is not the expression of a belief or a conviction. It simply reflects a methodological strategy.

As we compare spoken language with the input and output structures underlying its use, we note that the motoric and perceptual mechanisms were in place long before language entered the stage. An initial task on the agenda of an evolutionary research program on spoken language would, therefore, seem to be to investigate how the newcomers, speech and language, could acquire some of their properties by adapting to the phylogenetically older structures rather than the other way around. The question would be: If language were seen as a set of adaptations to the constraints of early man's vocal, auditory, and cognitive systems, what would it be like?

The MT reverses this query completely, responding instead to: If speech production and speech perception were seen as adaptations to language what would they be like? Consider the following statements (Liberman & Mattingly 1985):

> Adaptations of the motor system for controlling the organs of the vocal tract took precedence in the evolution of speech. These adaptations made it possible, not only to produce phonetic gestures, but also to coarticulate them so that they could be

produced rapidly. A perceiving system, specialized to take account of the complex acoustic consequences, developed concomitantly. (p. 7)

Perhaps Liberman and Mattingly were correct in saying that their theory "is neither logically meaningless nor biologically unthinkable" (Liberman & Mattingly 1985, p. 3). Once evolved, language could conceivably continue to develop in coevolution with the input/output mechanisms.

However, this approach has a methodological problem. How do we go about reconstructing the path of development towards specialization and uniqueness without running the risk of prejudging the issue? One possible answer—the one favored here—is that we can minimize this risk, if, in attempting to derive language from nonlanguage, we first make the most of the non-special mechanisms.

Acknowledgments

The author is indebted to Randy Diehl and Peter MacNeilage for helpful comments on this manuscript.

References

Bladon, R. A. W., & Lindblom, B. (1981). Modeling the judgment of vowel quality differences. *Journal of the Acoustical Society of America, 69,* 1414–1422.

Crothers, J. (1978). Typology and universals of vowel systems. In J. H. Greenberg, C. A. Ferguson, & E. A. Moravcsik (Eds.), *Universals of human language* (vol. 2, pp. 99–152). Stanford, CA: Stanford University Press.

Engstrand, O. (1988). Articulatory correlates of stress and speaking rate in Swedish VCV utterances. *Journal of the Acoustical Society of America, 83,* 1863–1875.

Fischer-Jørgensen, E. (1964). Sound duration and place of articulation. *Zeitschrift für Sprachwissenschaft und Kommunikationsforschung, 17,* 175–207.

Gay, T. (1978). Effect of speaking rate on vowel formant movements. *Journal of the Acoustical Society of America, 63,* 223–230.

Jakobson, R. (1968). *Child language, aphasia, and phonological universals.* The Hague: Mouton.

Kluender, K. R., Diehl, R. L., & Killeen, P. R. (1987). Japanese quail can learn phonetic categories. *Science, 237,* 1195–1197.

Kuehn, D. P., & Moll, K. L. (1976). A cineradiographic study of VC and CV articulatory velocities. *Journal of Phonetics, 4,* 303–320.

Liberman, A. M., Delattre, P. C., Cooper, F. S., & Gerstman, L. J. (1954). The role of consonant–vowel transitions in the perception of the stop and nasal consonants. *Psychological Monographs, 68,* 1–13.

Liberman, A. M., & Mattingly, I. G. (1985). The motor theory of speech perception revised. *Cognition, 21,* 1–36.

Lieberman, P. (1963). Some effects of semantic and grammatical context on the production and perception of speech. *Language and Speech, 6,* 172–187.

Liljencrants, J., & Lindblom, B. (1972). Numerical simulation of vowel quality systems: The role of perceptual contrast. *Language, 48,* 839–862.

Lindblom, B. (1963). Spectrographic study of vowel reduction. *Journal of the Acoustical Society of America, 35,* 1773–1781.

Lindblom, B. (1967). Vowel duration and a model of lip mandible coordination. *Quarterly Progress and Status Report, 4,* 1–29.

Lindblom, B. (1986). Phonetic universals in vowel systems. In J. J. Ohala & J. J. Jaeger (Eds.), *Experimental phonology* (pp. 13–44). Orlando, FL: Academic Press.

Lindblom, B. (1987). Absolute constancy and adaptive variability: Two themes in the quest for phonetic invariance. *Proceedings of the XIth International Congress of Phonetic Sciences* (vol. 3, pp. 1–18), Tallinn: Academy of Sciences of the Estonian S.S.R.

Lindblom, B. (in press). A model of phonetic variation and selection and the evolution of vowel systems. In W. S.-Y. Wang (Ed.), *Language transmission and change.* New York: Blackwell.

Lindblom, B., & Lubker, J. (1985). The speech homunculus and a problem of phonetic linguistics. In V. A. Fromkin (Ed.), *Phonetic linguistics* (pp. 169–192). Orlando, FL: Academic Press.

Lindblom, B., Lubker, J., & Gay, T. (1979). Formant frequencies of some fixed-mandible vowels and a model of speech motor programming by predictive simulation. *Journal of Phonetics, 7,* 147–161.

Lindblom, B., Lubker, J., Lyberg, B., Branderud, P., & Holmgren, K. (1987). The concept of target and speech timing. In R. Channon & L. Shockey (Eds.), *In honor of Ilse Lehiste* (pp. 161–182). Dordrecht, Holland: Foris.

Lindblom, B., MacNeilage, P., & Studdert-Kennedy, M. (forthcoming). *Evolution of spoken language.* Orlando, FL: Academic Press.

Lindblom, B., & Maddieson, I. (1988). Phonetic universals in consonant systems. In L. M. Hyman & C. N. Li (Eds.), *Language, speech and mind* (pp. 62–78). New York: Routledge.

Lindblom, B., & Sundberg, J. (1971). Acoustical consequences of lip, tongue, jaw and larynx movement. *Journal of the Acoustical Society of America, 50,* 1166–1179.

Maddieson, I. (1984). *Patterns of sound.* Cambridge: Cambridge University Press.

Moon, S.-J., & Lindblom, B. (1989). Formant undershoot in clear and citation-form speech: A second progress report. *Quarterly Progress and Status Report, 1,* 121–123. Stockholm: Department of Speech Communication, RIT.

Nord, L. (1986). Acoustic studies of vowel reduction in Swedish. *Quarterly Progress and Status Report, 4,* 19–36.

Öhman, S. (1966). Coarticulation in VCV utterances: Spectrographic measurements. *Journal of the Acoustical Society of America, 39,* 151–168.

Perkell, J., & Klatt, D. (1986). *Invariance and variability in speech processes.* Hillsdale, NJ: Lawrence Erlbaum Associates.

Picheny, M. A., Durlach, N. I., & Braida, L. D. (1986). Speaking clearly for the hard of hearing II: Acoustic characteristics of clear and conversational speech. *Journal of Speech and Hearing Research, 29,* 434–446.

Schulman, R. (1989). Articulatory dynamics of loud and normal speech. *Journal of the Acoustical Society of America, 85,* 295–312.

Stevens, K. N. (1968). Acoustic correlates of place of articulation for stop and fricative consonants. *Quarterly Progress Report, 89,* 199–205. Cambridge, MA: Research Laboratory of Electronics, MIT.

Stevens, K. N. (1989). On the quantal nature of speech. *Journal of Phonetics, 17,* 3–45.

Uchanski, R. M., Durlach, N. I., & Braida, L. D. (1987, November). *Clear speech.* Paper presented as part of a seminar on "Hearing-aid processed speech" at a meeting of the American Speech-Language-Hearing Association, New Orleans.

Comment: Beyond the Segment

Osamu Fujimura

The Division of Speech and Hearing Science, Ohio State University

Segmentalism

Lindblom gives an intriguing argument that the linguistic system for speech communication is largely determined by biological constraints that are not speech specific and by the requirement that the verbal communication be efficient. Such conditions can be shown to be satisfied by the sound patterns of existing natural languages, he argues, when we examine the observable characteristics of acoustic signals or their auditory perceptual values that represent the phonetic units of those languages. Phonetic units such as vowels and consonants form a system of segmental units in such a way that their auditory effects are maximally distinct under the peripheral perceptual constraints. Therefore, if I understand his point correctly, the reference to motor gestures, which Al Liberman and his colleagues' motor theory assumes as the basic principle of speech perception, should not necessarily be of primary concern for us; what we need is to assume that perception sorts distinct signals into categories of patterns segment by segment.

From my point of view, the segment inventory is only a part of language as a system of verbal codes. The human competence in verbal communication processes goes well beyond what a theory of phonemes can describe. What one has to depend on in perceiving speech messages is not limited to the capability of identifying isolated segmental units, even if that constitutes part of the actual process. As for the "segmental aspects" of speech, furthermore, a more interesting question would be to ask to what extent the concatenation-coarticulation approach would work, if we took syllables or demisyllables instead of the phonemic segments as the categories, because we know segment-by-segment identification simply does not work in the way the phonemic theory would prescribe. At best, such a system would involve very complex and abstract processes. As a concatenative unit, if we take the concept literally in analysing acoustic or auditory signals as they are, we will probably need to consider some rather large phonetic phrases, something like the stress group or foot in English (for some relevant observations about cognitive programming of motor execution, see Sternberg, Knoll, Monsell, & Wright, 1978, 1988) or an intonation phrase at some level (Pierrehumbert, 1980). This situation may be in some sense realistic, when we discuss initial exposures of infants to the surrounding language, where, for example, crucial parts of utterances, such as key words in focus, are marked with readily accessible prosodic cues, and those materials are drawn from a relatively limited vocabulary of simple words or phrases. Within such a prosodically coherent phrasal unit (including single words under certain environments), I think the organization is multidimensionally interwoven in the sense that there are no internal breakpoints in time that strictly synchronize phonetic events in different dimensions, such as voice pitch, movements of the mandible, tongue body, lips, velum, and so forth, and, depending on the descriptive scheme, temporal modulation (Fujimura, 1987b; Edwards & Beckman, 1988). To decompose such a phonetically coherent unit into constituent phonetic elements normally requires a complex procedure to map signals into abstract structures. A straightforward and transparent principle like concatenation and smoothing does not govern the phenomena under such circumstances.

I do not think any of the organizational issues such as temporal organization principles of speech, either within or among such phonetic phrases, can be accounted for by the biological/physical principles as we know them, except their rather peripheral constraints, such as declination and smoothing, pausing or decelerating for preparing the next phrase in the cognitive process, and, of course, some aspects of local characteristics of articulatory dynamics (see Browman & Goldstein, chapter 13 this volume). There are many linguistic structural choices that have to be made for producing or identifying specific structures. The choices are made lawfully within a very specifically selected framework, as we all know, but all we can say at present from a biological or physical point of view about the principles governing the rule systems of language seems to be that they are often (but not necessarily always) crucially specific to humans.

There are cases where sophisticated and careful consideration of necessary conditions can narrow down possibilities to a striking extent within a very limited domain. Lindblom's explanation of existing vowel systems may be cited as such a case, assuming that his demonstration holds for phonetic substances rather than the symbols used by linguists for transcribing different languages, as Mark Liberman aptly questioned in the conference. Local phonetic characteristics such as the "target values" of vowels are presumably the most likely aspects of speech phenomena that are significantly dictated by biological/physical constraints.

However, that there are such aspects of speech phenomena does not mean that that *is* the primary principle.

We should not be confused about the distinction between necessary conditions and sufficient conditions. It is obvious that both production and perception have to be under given physical and biological constraints as necessary conditions for any human activity. Given that Lindblom clearly admits that postulating specialized systems appears not only reasonable but also necessary, there is no disagreement about this. It may be, as he asserts, a matter of methodological strategy of research that he advocates a different characterization of the process of speech perception. However, I think it is also a matter of focus of interest (i.e. whether we are interested in the mental representation and a synchronic description of language or in providing ecological accounts of language evolution). I accept his assertion that general biological apparatus had developed before speech functions were needed. However, the highly evolved speech processing functions and mechanisms still can be special, because clearly there are needed functions other than swallowing and breathing, in order to utter and understand speech. That some phonetic capabilities are observed in animals does not lead us to the conclusion, as Lindblom appears to suggest, that biological principles commonly applicable to animals can account for phonetic capabilities. The respiratory mechanism, for example, is clearly a necessary component of speech production, and it does give some relevant constraints about what language must be like, but nobody argues that the characteristics of this biological mechanism are sufficient to account for the characteristics of speech.

I believe that it is important to distinguish the principles governing the real-time process of speech production and perception from those prescribing the evolution of linguistic systems. The process of evolution must respect a number of factors, and it is a slow (quasi-static) process that can balance out all different types of influences into an equilibrium of a synchronic system. The process is slow in reference to the time constant of developing and adapting the biological neural network. Speech production and perception are not such slow processes. It is a process of selecting elements of information to be conveyed according to a fixed and recognized framework of coding messages. Fixed elemental patterns can be organized into a seemingly variable component of the whole of an utterance. In my understanding, it is the issue of how listeners identify such organizational structures of utterances, rather than how elemental units evolve as the ingredients of phonetic forms, that the motor theory is or should be primarily concerned with.

Likewise, it is important to distinguish what a speaker or hearer can do under special circumstances from what he or she usually or typically does. Whatever a speaker makes use of as the program for generating specific utterances, it must be readjustable according to various situations and disturbances, and the perceptual system also must be able to conform to and recover from the variable effects of such disturbances and readjustments. Such readjustments may occur in part in anticipation of specific effects that are assessable by nonspeech measures, such as sensing the bite block via tactile, proprioceptive, and other means. However, in any case, such readjustability should not be taken as a proof that speaking strategies are not composed of fixed components of control programs. The entire configuration of control may well be formed out of fixed patterns involving adjustable parameters based on a certain framework of representation.

In order to understand the general characteristics of how speech is organized, uttered, and perceived, we need to identify speech organization principles that handle inherently multidimensional temporal structures. I think Sven Öhman was correct, when he proposed the consonantal perturbation theory (1967) as the result of encountering some difficulty in acoustic data interpretation using the concept of coarticulation. It is remarkable that he did it twenty years ago; the current nonlinear theory of phonology, its reference to articulatory organs (McCarthy, 1988), and many new observations in speech articulation, all are consistent with his insight. Obviously what he did was only a beginning. We now know much more about the abstract representation of sound patterns. The currently emerging multidimensional (multi-tier) theory of phonology may or may not succeed, and any model reflecting such representations will be inevitably complex. The mapping between abstract phonological representations onto observable speech phenomena must be rather opaque, in spite of the theory's direct reference to physiological apparatus.

I think pursuing a theory of perception as well as production referring to articulatory gestures is promising not only to understand what a speaker actually does and how signals are characterized accordingly but also given the independent linguistic justifications of phonological rules referring to such gestures. The classical concept of coarticulation as *the* principle of speech organization by concatenation is necessary but far from sufficient. There are more than assimilatory effects in phonological representations and the temporal organization of speech. As the first step, however, the question we need to ask may be what other principles we will have to introduce after generalizing the concept of coarticulation to inherently multidimensional representations, where smoothing works in different dimensions separately. In such a model, timing relations among elemental gestures in different articulatory dimensions seem to provide critical information (Fujimura, 1986).

Nonlinearity in the Sense of Superposition Principle

Suppose the mapping relation between the two representations of speech messages at the output of the production description (say, patterns of motor control) and the input to the perceptual system (say, auditory patterns) were described by a linear transformation in the sense of superpositionality. Then we would specify a message at the production output level by a set X of entities x_i in the form of a linear combination, and the same message can be represented as a linear combination based on a set Y of input patterns y_j. Each entity, for example y_j, could be an elemental time function, and overlapping signals could be decomposed into the constituent elements and their contributions to the given composite signal. Such a system would allow us to analyze many data of utterances by automatic statistical processing to derive a set of effective constituent elements empirically (Atal, 1983; van Dijk-Kappers & Marcus, 1988). Between such descriptive systems, based on X and Y for input and output, respectively (if they were available for speech descriptions), there would be no point in arguing which system is primary and which is secondary as Liberman and Mattingly (1985) aptly cautioned. The causal primacy of the production description is clearly valid, but that simply says that speech is physically produced and only then is heard.

It is the lack of linearity, in the sense of additivity or the applicability of the superposition principle, that makes motor theory a nontrivial theory. Either articulatory or auditory description may be formulated as a mostly linear process by choosing appropriate input–output levels and a framework of description. However, the mapping relation between the two levels representing the motor commands on the one hand and the auditory patterns on the other cannot be superpositional in any significant sense. This difficulty is there, whichever levels of representation we may choose for production and perception, as long as we take the production representation at a level reasonably transparently related to what we know as phonetic units, such as distinctive features, and the perceptual representation similarly transparent to phonetic units. Because the mapping is not linear, the usual and the most powerful reasoning method, first treating two factors of the problem separately and then combining them to predict the result for more general and complex situation, simply does not work. In my interpretation, the motor theory is an attempt to represent the auditory or some cognitive perceptual patterns of speech in terms of units in the motor-level representation of the message. The claim is in essence, if I am correct, that the information at this level is representable in such a way that a phonological representation has an approximately linear mapping into this motor-level representation. If this claim can be maintained, it seems at least to me that our study of speech organization can be reduced to components of tractable forms.

We wish to describe the principles of phonetic organization through a composition of effects of features. According to the classical theory (Jakobson, Fant, & Halle, 1963), each distinctive feature has its inherent phonetic target pattern, and each segment is represented by a simultaneous bundle of distinctive features. However, when we bundle up a set of distinctive feature values, each of which is evaluated under a certain condition of other feature values, all of a sudden the component values may change. A combination of elementary articulatory gestures does not necessarily result in a combination of acoustic or auditory characteristics, if the individual effects are evaluated separately under certain conditions that are not satisfied for the particular combination in question. Here we are talking about the mapping between phonological representations and articulatory or motor command representations. We do not know yet how we can describe the entire system based on invariant manifestations of elemental phonological units and simple and effective organizational principles to organize a phonetic material to be uttered.

My argument is that the system linearity is the critical issue for a successful endeavor in this area, and whether the system is linear or not depends crucially on the choice of the descriptive framework. Furthermore my conjecture, based on articulatory observations, is that certain organizational processes expressed in terms of articulatory or motor events are more nearly linearly related to the phonological description than most other descriptions (see Fujimura, 1987a). This would mean that a certain framework of articulatory representation with respect to temporal organization processes more or less allows a composition of complex cases out of a superposition of elemental mapping relations between a phonological representation and the articulatory characterization. More specifically, a correspondence between phonological features and elemental gestures must be representable by an approximately linear relation by appropriately choosing both the phonological and articulatory frameworks of representation. In the case of prosodic modulation, features representing phrase boundaries and stress/emphasis, and so on, or, in other words, configurational as well as prosodic specificatory features in the sense of Jakobson, Fant, and Halle, must be shown to have linear relations with, say, timing values of gesture organization control (cf. the gesture score in Browman & Goldstein, chapter 13 this volume, and Fujimura, 1987b).

The general framework of the phonological specifications for a message is inherently multidimensional, as theorists of nonlinear phonology advocate, and it is now becoming clear that specifications cannot be fully provided to be complete for each segment in terms of feature values. The phonetic implementation process has to consider both partial specifications of "segmental" features and "suprasegmental" features simultaneously. In such an opaque and complex system as the multidimensional representations with partial specifications and dimension-by-dimension implementation rules with linking constraints, the need for an explicit model of temporal organization is immense. Browman and Goldstein's work aims at such a model, working at the moment within a very limited local domain. A nonlinear model (in the sense of superposition) of this type eventually has to incorporate all factors that affect speech utterances under various circumstances, at least to first-order approximation, so that the setting is roughly correct for all the feature values, for the entire stretch of the phrasal unit that is approximately independent. It also must contain parameters that are sensitive to the context external to such a phrasal unit. Only then we can assume local superpositionality, so that we can reason the effects of different features involved, one by one, implicating their general phonetic significance.

I hope we will be able to achieve this stage of study soon. Our capability is probably not limited by the computational complexity. We need good insights into the problem, and the best insight, apart from intuition, can be obtained only through observations and interpretations of direct articulatory facts. Such observations will not automatically lead us to a good model; but they will delimit the domain of search, and we need such a guidance as much as possible, along with insights about other cognitive behaviors than speech production.

I do not believe we can understand speech and language only by statistical processing of observable data, nor by any elementary inference of automatic learning, based on a less than minimal descriptive framework that is inherent to language. I highly appreciate Lindblom's pointing out very interesting observations about some elements of language, but I also need more information about its inherent structure and organization.

References

Atal, B. S. (1983). Efficient coding of LPC parameters by temporal decomposition. *ICASSP Proceedings* (Vol. 2, 81–84). New York: IEEE Acoustics, Speech and Signal Processing Society.

Edwards, J., & Beckman, M. E. (1988). Articulatory timing and the prosodic interpretation of syllable duration. In O. Fujimura (Ed.), Articulatory organization—from phonology to speech signal [Special issue]. *Phonetica, 45,* 140–155.

Fujimura, O. (1986). Relative invariance of articulatory movements: An iceberg model. In J. S. Perkell & D. H. Klatt (Eds.), *Invariance and variability in speech processes* (pp. 226–242). Hillsdale, NJ: Lawrence Erlbaum Associates.

Fujimura, O. (1987a). Fundamentals and applications in speech production research. *Proceedings of the XIth International Congress of Phonetic Sciences* (Vol. 6, 10–27). Tallinn: Academy of Sciences of the Estonian S.S.R.

Fujimura, O. (1987b). A linear model of speech timing. In R. Channon & L. Shockey (Eds.), *In honor of Ilse Lehiste* (pp. 109–123). Dordrecht: Foris.

Jakobson, R., Fant, G., & Halle, M. (1963). *Preliminaries to speech analysis.* Cambridge, MA: MIT Press.

Liberman, A. M., & Mattingly, I. G. (1985). The motor theory of speech perception revised. *Cognition, 21,* 1–36.

McCarthy, J. J. (1988). Feature geometry and dependency: A review. In O. Fujimura (Ed.), Articulatory organization—from phonology to speech signal [Special issue]. *Phonetica, 45,* 84–108.

Öhman, S. E. G. (1967). Numerical model of coarticulation. *Journal of the Acoustical Society of America, 41,* 310–320.

Pierrehumbert, J. B. (1980). *The phonology and phonetics of English intonation.* Unpublished doctoral dissertation, Massachusetts Institute of Technology.

Sternberg, S., Knoll, R. L., Monsell, S., & Wright, C. E. (1988). Motor programs and hierarchical organization in the control of rapid speech. In O. Fujimura (Ed.), Articulatory organization—from phonology to speech signal [Special issue]. *Phonetica, 45,* 175–197.

Sternberg, S., Monsell, S., Knoll, R. L., & Wright, C. E. (1978). The latency and duration of rapid movement sequences: Comparisons of speech and typewriting. In G. E. Stelmach (Ed.), *Information processing in motor control and learning* (pp. 117–152). New York: Academic Press.

van Dijk-Kappers, A., & Marcus, S. (1988). Temporal decomposition in speech. Manuscript submitted for publication.

Chapter 3

The Perception of Phonetic Gestures

Carol A. Fowler

Haskins Laboratories and Dartmouth College

Lawrence D. Rosenblum

University of California, Riverside

Abstract

Evidence in the literature on speech perception shows very clearly that listeners recover a talker's phonetic gestures from the acoustic speech signal. Throughout most of its history, the Motor Theory has been the only theory to confront this evidence and to provide an explanation for it. Specifically, the Motor Theory proposes that the dimensions of a listener's percept of a speech utterance conform more closely to those of a talker's phonetic gestures than to those of the acoustic speech signal, because, according to the theory, listeners access their speech motor systems in perception. Accordingly, their experience hearing a speech utterance conforms to processes that their own motor systems would engage in to produce a signal like the one they are perceiving. If the Motor Theory is correct, speech perception is quite unlike general auditory perception where access to a motor system could not be involved and where motor theorists claim perception is "homomorphic"—conforming to dimensions of the acoustic signal directly. Recently, motor theorists have suggested that speech perception is "modular." A major source of evidence in favor of a distinct speech module is the phenomenon of duplex perception.

We offer some challenges to the Motor Theory. First, we suggest an alternative explanation for listeners' recovery of phonetic gestures. In particular, we suggest that phonetic gestures are "distal events," and that perception involves recovery of distal events from proximal stimulation. This holds for perception of other acoustic stimuli and for visual stimuli where access to the motor system cannot be invoked to explain distal-event perception. Accordingly, we suggest that speech perception is not special in its recovery of phonetic gestures; all perception is "heteromorphic," not homomorphic. We also provide evidence that the phenomenon of duplex perception does not reveal modularity of speech perception

(although speech perception may yet be modular). Nonspeech sounds, not remotely likely to be perceived by a specialized module, may be perceived
duplexly.

We have titled our chapter "The perception of phonetic gestures," as if phonetic
gestures *are* perceived. By phonetic gestures, we refer to organized movements
of one or more vocal-tract structures that realize phonetic dimensions of an
utterance (cf. Browman & Goldstein, 1986; in press). An example of a gesture is
closure for a bilabial stop, which includes contributions by the jaw and the upper
and lower lips. Gestures are organized into larger segmental and suprasegmental
groupings, and we do not intend to imply that these larger organizations are not
perceived as well. We focus on gestures to emphasize a claim that in speech
perceptual objects are fundamentally articulatory as well as linguistic.

That is, in speech perception, articulatory events have a status quite different
from that of their acoustic products. The former are perceived, whereas the latter
are the means (or one of the means) by which they are perceived.

A claim that phonetic gestures are perceived is not uncontroversial, of course,
and there are other points of view (e.g., Massaro, 1987; Stevens & Blumstein,
1981). We do not intend to consider these other views here, however, but instead
to focus on agreements and disagreements between two theoretical perspectives
from which the claim is made. Accordingly, we begin by summarizing some of
the evidence that in our view justifies it.

Phonetic Gestures are Perceived:
Three Sources of Evidence

Correspondence Failures between Acoustic
Signal and Percept: Correspondences between
Gestures and Percept

Perhaps the most compelling evidence that gestures, and not their acoustic products, are perceptual objects is the failure of dimensions of speech percepts to
correspond to obvious dimensions of the acoustic signal and their correspondence instead to phonetically organized articulatory behaviors that produce the
signal. We offer three examples, all of them implicating articulatory gestures as
perceptual objects, and the third showing most clearly that the perceived gestures
are not surface articulatory movements but rather linguistically organized
gestures.

Synthetic /di/ *and* /du/.   One example from the early work at Haskins
Laboratories (Liberman, Cooper, Shankweiler, & Studdert-Kennedy, 1967) is of
synthetic /di/ and /du/. Monosyllables, such as those in Fig. 3.1, can be

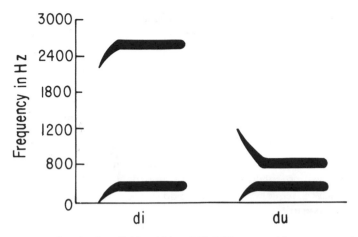

FIG. 3.1. Synthetic syllables /di/ and /du/. The second formant transitions identify the initial consonant as /d/ rather than as /b/ or /g/. (Adapted from Liberman, Cooper, Shankweiler, & Studdert-Kennedy, 1967, copyright, 1967, by American Psychological Association).

synthesized that consist only of two formants. The information specifying /d/ (rather than /b/ or /g/) in both syllables is the second-formant transition. These transitions are very different in the two syllables, and, extracted from their syllables, they sound very different. Each sounds more or less like the frequency glide it resembles in the visible display. Neither sounds like /d/. In the context of their respective syllables, however, they sound alike, and they sound like /d/.

The consonantal segments in /di/ and /du/ are produced alike by a constriction and release gesture of the tongue tip against the alveolar ridge. When listeners perceive the synthetic /di/ and /du/ syllables of Fig. 3.1, their percepts correspond to the implied constriction and release gestures, not, it seems, to the context-sensitive acoustic signal.

Functional Equivalence of Acoustic "Cues".   We expect listeners to be very good at distinguishing an interval of silence from nonsilence—from a set of frequency glides, for example. Furthermore, we expect them to distinguish acoustic signals that differ in two ways more readily than signals that differ in just one of the two ways. Both of these expectations are violated—another example of noncorrespondence—if the silence and glides are joint acoustic products of a common constriction and release gesture for a stop consonant.

Fitch, Halwes, Erickson, and Liberman (1980) created synthetic syllables identified as *slit* or *split* by varying the duration of a silent interval following the fricative and manipulating the presence or absence of transitions for a bilabial stop following the silent interval. A relatively long silent interval and the presence of transitions both signal a stop, the silent interval cueing the closure and the transitions—the release. Fitch and colleagues found that pairs of syllables differing on both cue dimensions, duration of silence, and presence/absence of transitions were either more discriminable than pairs differing in one of these ways or less discriminable depending on how the cues were combined. A syllable with a long silent interval and transitions was highly discriminable from a syllable with a shorter silent interval and no transitions; the one was identified as *split* and the other as *slit*. A syllable with a short silent interval and transitions was nearly indiscriminable from one with a longer interval and no transitions; both were identified as *split*. Syllables differing in two ways are indiscriminable just when the acoustic cues that distinguish them are "functionally equivalent"— that is, they cue the same articulatory gesture. A long silent interval does not normally sound like a set of frequency glides but it does in a context in which both specify a consonantal constriction.

Perception of Intonation.   The findings just summarized, among others, reveal that listeners perceive gestures. Apparently, listeners do not perceive the acoustic signal *per se*.

Nor, however, do they perceive "raw" articulatory motions as such. Rather, they perceive linguistically organized (phonetic) gestures. Research on the various ways in which fundamental frequency (henceforth, FO) is perceived shows this most clearly.

Perceived intonational peak height will not in general correspond to the absolute rate at which the vocal folds open and close during production of the peak. Instead, perception of the peak corresponds to just those influences on the rate of opening and closing that are caused by gestures intended by the talker to affect intonational peak height. (Largely, intonational melody is implemented by contraction and relaxation of muscles of the larynx that tense the vocal folds; see, e.g., Ohala, 1978). There are other influences on the rate of vocal fold opening and closing that may either decrease or increase FO. Some of these influences due to lung deflation during an expiration ("declination", Gelfer, Harris, Collier, & Baer, 1985; Gelfer, Harris, & Baer, 1987) or to segmental perturbations reflecting vowel height (e.g., Lehiste & Peterson, 1961) and obstruent voicing (e.g., Ohde, 1984) are largely or entirely automatic consequences of other things that talkers are doing: producing an utterance on an expiratory airflow, producing a close or open vowel (Honda, 1981), producing a voiced or voiceless obstruent (Ohde, 1984; Löfqvist, Baer, McGarr, & Story, 1988). They do not sound like changes in pitch; rather, they sound like what they are: information for early-to-late serial position in an utterance in the case of declination (Pierrehumbert, 1979; see also Lehiste, 1982), and information for vowel height (Silverman, 1987; Reinholt Peterson, 1986) or consonant voicing (e.g., Silverman, 1986) in the case of segmental perturbations.

As we will suggest following, listeners apparently use configurations of changes in different acoustic variables to recover the distinct, organized articulatory systems that implement the various linguistic dimensions of talkers' utterances. By using acoustic information in this way, listeners can recover what Liberman (1982) has called the talker's "phonetic intents."

Audio-visual Integration of Gestural Information

A video display of a face mouthing /ga/ synchronized with an acoustic signal of the speaker saying /ba/ is heard most typically as /da/ (MacDonald & McGurk, 1978). Subjects' identifications of syllables presented in this type of experiment reflect an integration of information from the optical and acoustic sources. Furthermore, as Liberman (1982) pointed out, the integration affects what listeners experience *hearing* to the extent that they cannot tell what contribution to their perceptual experience is made by the acoustic signal and what by the video display.[1]

Why does integration occur? One answer is that both sources of information, the optical and the acoustic, apparently provide information about the same event of talking, and they do so by providing information about the talkers' phonetic gestures.

Shadowing

Listeners' latency to repeat a syllable they hear is very short—in Porter's research (Porter, 1978; Porter & Lubker, 1980), around 180 ms on average. Although these latencies are obtained in a choice reaction-time procedure (in which the vocal response required is different for different stimuli to respond), latencies approach simple reaction times (in which the same response occurs to any stimulus to respond), and they are much shorter than choice reaction times using a button press.

Why should these particular choice reaction times be so fast? Presumably, the compatibility between stimulus and response explains the fast response times. Indeed, it effectively eliminates the element of choice. If listeners perceive the talker's phonetic gestures, then the only response requiring essentially no choice at all is one that reproduces those gestures.

The Motor Theory

Throughout most of its history, the motor theory (e.g., Liberman, Cooper, Harris, & MacNeilage, 1963; Liberman et al., 1967; Liberman & Mattingly, 1985; see also Cooper, Delattre, Liberman, Borst, & Gerstman, 1952) has been the

---

[1]There is a small qualification to the claim that listeners cannot tell what contributions visible and audible information each have to their perceptual experience in the McGurk effect. Massaro (1987) showed that effects of the video display can be reduced but not eliminated by instructing subjects to look at but to ignore the display.

only theory of speech perception to identify the phonetic gesture as an object of perception. Here we describe the motor theory by discussing what precisely the motor theorists have considered to be the object of perception, how they characterize the process of speech perception, and why recently they have introduced the idea that speech perception is accomplished by a specialized module.

What is Perceived for the Motor Theorist?

Coarticulation is the reason why the acoustic signal appears to correspond so badly to the sequences of phonemes that talkers intend to produce. Due to coarticulation, phonemes are produced in overlapping time frames so that the acoustic signal is everywhere (or nearly everywhere: see, e.g., Stevens & Blumstein, 1981) context-sensitive. This makes the signal a complex "code" on the phonemes of the language, not a cipher (e.g., an alphabet).[2] In "Perception of the speech code" (1967), Liberman and his colleagues speculated that coarticulatory "encoding" is in part a necessary consequence of properties of the speech articulators (their sluggishness, for example). However, in their view, coarticulation is also promoted both by the nature of phonemes themselves—that they are realized by sets of subphonemic features[3]—and by the listener's short-term memory, which would be overtaxed by the slow transmission rate of an acoustic cipher.

In producing speech, talkers exploit the fact that the different articulators—the lips, velum, jaw, and so forth—can be independently controlled. Subphonemic features, such as lip rounding, velum lowering, and alveolar closure each use subsets of the articulators—often just one. Therefore, more than one feature can be produced at a time. Speech can be produced at rapid rates by allowing "parallel transmission" of the subphonemic features of different phonemes. This increases the transmission rates for listeners, but it also creates much of the encoding that is considered responsible for the apparent lack of invariance between acoustic and phonetic segments.

The listener's percept corresponds it seems neither to the encoded cues in the acoustic signal nor even to the encoded succession of vocal tract shapes during speech production but instead to a sequence of discrete, unencoded phonemes, each composed of its own component subphonemic features. To explain why "perception mirrors articulation more closely than sound" (Liberman, Cooper, Shankweiler, & Studdert-Kennedy, 1967, p. 453) and yet achieves recovery of discrete unencoded phonemes, the motor theorists proposed as a first hypothesis

---

[2]Liberman and colleagues identified a cipher as a system in which each unique unit of the message maps onto a unique symbol. In contrast, in a code, the correspondence between message unit and symbol is not 1:1.

[3]Liberman and colleagues proposed to replace the more conventional view of the features of a phoneme (for example, that of Jakobson, Fant, & Halle, 1972) with one of features as "implicit instructions to separate and independent parts of the motor machinery" (p. 446).

that perceivers somehow access their speech-motor systems in perception and that the percept they achieve corresponds to a stage in production before encoding of the speech segments takes place. In "Perception of the speech code," (Liberman et al., 1967) the stage was one in which "motor commands" to the muscles were selected to implement subphonemic features. In "The motor theory revised," (Liberman & Mattingly, 1985), a revision to the theory reflects developments in our understanding of motor control. Evidence suggests that activities of the vocal tract are products of functional couplings among articulators (e.g., Folkins & Abbs, 1975, 1976; Kelso, Tuller, Vatikiotis-Bateson, & Fowler, 1984) that produce gestures as defined earlier, not independent movements of the articulators identified with subphonemic features as in "Perception of the speech code." In "The motor theory revised," control structures for gestures have replaced motor commands for subphonemic features as invariants of production and as objects of perception for listeners.[4] Like subphonemic features, control structures are abstract, prevented by coarticulation from making public appearances in the vocal tract. Liberman and Mattingly (1985) wrote of the perceptual objects of the revised theory:

> We would argue, then, that the gestures do have characteristic invariant properties, as the motor theory requires, though these must be seen, not as peripheral movements, but as the more remote structures that control the movements. These structures correspond to the speaker's intentions. (p. 23)

In recovering abstract gestures, processes of speech perception yield quite different kinds of perceptual objects than general auditory perception. In auditory perception, more generally, according to Liberman and Mattingly (1985), listeners hear the signal as "ordinary sound" (p. 6); that is, they hear the acoustic signal as such. In another paper (Mattingly & Liberman 1988), they referred to this apparently more straightforward perceptual object as "homomorphic," in contrast to objects of speech perception, which are "heteromorphic." An example they offer of homomorphic auditory perception is perception of isolated formant transitions, which sound like the frequency glides they resemble in a spectrographic display.

How Perception Takes Place in the Motor Theory

In the motor theory, listeners use "analysis by synthesis" to recover phonetic gestures from the encoded, informationally impoverished acoustic signal. This aspect of the theory has never been worked out in detail. However, in general, analysis by synthesis consists in analyzing a signal by guessing how the signal

---

[4]With one apparent slip: "The objects of speech perception are the intended phonetic gestures of the speaker, represented in the brain as invariant motor commands" (p. 2).

might have been produced (e.g., Stevens, 1960; Stevens & Halle, 1967). Liberman and Mattingly (1985) referred to an "internal, innately specified vocal-tract synthesizer that incorporates complete information about the anatomical and physiological characteristics of the vocal tract and also about the articulatory and acoustic consequences of linguistically significant gestures" (p. 26). The synthesizer computes candidate gestures and then determines which of those gestures in combination with others identified as ongoing in the vocal tract could account for the acoustic signal.

Speech Perception as Modular

If speech perception does involve accessing the speech-motor system, then it must indeed be special and quite distinct from general auditory perception. It is special in its objects of perception, in the kinds of processes applied to the acoustic signal, and presumably in the neural systems dedicated to those processes as well. Liberman and Mattingly had proposed that speech perception is achieved by a specialized module.

A module (Fodor, 1983) is a cognitive system that tends to be narrowly specialized ("domain specific"), using computations that are special ("eccentric") to its domain; it is computationally autonomous (so that different systems do not compete for resources) and prototypically is associated with a distinct neural substrate. In addition, modules tend to be "informationally encapsulated," bringing to bear on the processing they do only some of the relevant information the perceiver may have; in particular, processing of "input" (perceptual) systems—prime examples of modules—is protected early on from bias by "top-down" information.

The speech perceptual system of the motor theory has all of these characteristics. It is narrowly specialized and its perception-production link is eccentric; moreover, it is associated with a specialized neural substrate (e.g., Kimura, 1961). In addition, as the remarkable phenomenon of duplex perception (e.g., Rand, 1974; Liberman, Isenberg, & Rakerd, 1981) suggests, the speech perceiving system is autonomous and informationally encapsulated.

In duplex perception as it is typically investigated (e.g., Liberman et al., 1981; Mann & Liberman, 1983; Repp, Milburn, & Ashkenas, 1983), most of an acoustic CV syllable (the "base" at the left of Fig. 3.2) is presented to one ear, while the remainder, generally a formant transition (either of the "chirps" on the right side of Fig. 3.2), is presented to the other ear. Heard in isolation, the base is ambiguous between /da/ and /ga/, but listeners generally report hearing /da/. (It was identified as /da/ 87% of the time in the study by Repp, Milburn, & Ashkenas, 1983.) In isolation, the chirps sound like the frequency glides they resemble; they do not sound speech-like. Presented dichotically, listeners integrate the chirp and the base, hearing the integrated /da/ or /ga/ in the ear receiving the base. Remarkably, in addition, they hear the chirp in the other ear.

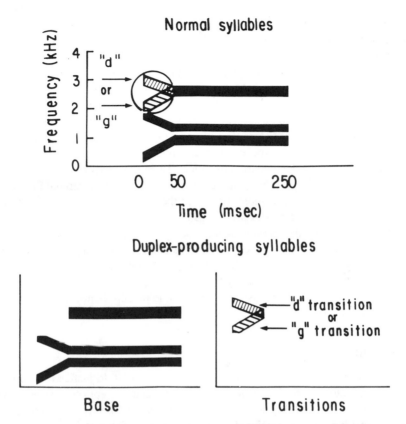

FIG. 3.2. Stimuli that yield duplex perception. The base is presented to one ear and the third formants to another. In the ear to which the base is presented, listeners hear the syllable specified jointly by the base and the transitions; in the other ear, they hear the transitions as frequency glides. (Adapted from Whalen & Liberman, 1987, copyright, 1987 by the AAAS).

Researchers who have investigated duplex perception describe it as perception of the same part of an acoustic signal in two ways simultaneously. If that characterization is correct, it implies strongly that the percepts are outputs of two distinct and autonomous perceptual systems, one specialized for speech and the other perhaps general to other acoustic signals.

A striking characteristic of speech perceptual systems that integrate syllable fragments presented to different ears is their imperviousness to information in the spatial separation of the fragments that they cannot possibly be part of the same spoken syllable—an instance perhaps of information encapsulation.

In recent work, Mattingly and Liberman (1988) revised, or expanded on, Fodor's view of modules by proposing a distinction between "closed" and "open" modules. Closed modules, including the speech module and a sound-localization module, for example, are narrowly specialized, as Fodor has characterized modules more generally. In addition (among other special properties), they yield heteromorphic percepts—that is, percepts whose dimensions are not those of the proximal stimulation. Although Mattingly and Liberman had characterized the heteromorphic percept in this way—in terms of what it does *not* conform to—it appears that the heteromorphic percept can be characterized in a more positive way as well. The dimensions of heteromorphic percepts are those of distal events, not of proximal stimulation. The speech module renders phonetic gestures; the sound-localization module renders location in space. By contrast, open modules are sort of "everything-else" perceptual systems. An open auditory-perceptual module is responsible for perception of most sounds in the environment. According to the theory, outputs of open modules are homomorphic.

In the context of this account of auditory perception, the conditions under which duplex perception is studied are seen as somehow tricking the open module into providing a percept of the isolated formant transition, although the transition is also being perceived by the speech module. Accordingly, two percepts are provided for one acoustic fragment; one percept is homomorphic, and the other is heteromorphic.

Prospectus

Our brief overview of the motor theory obviously cannot do justice to it. In our view, it is to date superior to other theories of speech perception in at least two major respects: in its ability to handle the full range of behavioral findings on speech perception—in particular, of course, the evidence that listeners recover phonetic gestures—and in having developed its account of speech in the context of a more general theory of biological specializations for perception.

Our purpose here, however, is not just to praise the theory but to challenge it as well, with the further aim of provoking the motor theorists either to buttress their theory where it appears to us vulnerable or else to revise it further.

We will raise three general questions from the perspective of our own, direct-realist theory (Fowler, 1986a, 1986b; Rosenblum, 1987). First, we question the inference from evidence that listeners recover phonetic gestures that the listener's own speech-motor system plays a role in perception. The nature of the challenge we mount to this inference leads to a second one. We question the idea that, whereas a specialized speech module—and other closed modules—render heteromorphic percepts, other percepts are homomorphic. Finally, we challenge the idea that duplex perception reveals that speech perception is achieved by a closed module.

Standing behind all of these specific questions we raise about claims of the motor theory is a general issue that needs to be confronted by all of us who study speech perception and for that matter perception more generally. The issue is one of determining when behavioral data warrant inferences being drawn about perceptual processes taking place inside perceivers and when the data deserve accounting instead in terms of the nature of events taking place publicly when something is perceived.

Does Perceptual Recovery of Phonetic Gestures Implicate the Listener's Speech Motor System?

In our view, the evidence that perceivers recover phonetic gestures in speech perception is incontrovertible,[5] and any theory of speech perception is inadequate, unless it can provide a unified account of those findings. However, the motor theorists have drawn an inference from these findings that we argue is not warranted by the general observation that listeners recover gestures. The inference is that recovery of gestures implies access by the perceiver to his own speech-motor system. It is notable, perhaps, that, in neither "Perception of the speech code" nor "The motor theory revised," do Liberman and his colleagues offer any evidence in support of this claim except evidence that listeners recover gestures—and that human left-cerebral hemispheres are specialized for speech, and especially for phonetic perception (e.g., Kimura, 1961; Liberman, 1974; Studdert-Kennedy & Shankweiler, 1970).

There is another way to explain why listeners recover phonetic gestures. It is that phonetic gestures are among the "distal events" that occur when speech is perceived and that perception universally involves recovery of distal events from information in proximal stimulation.

Distal Events Universally are Perceptual Objects: Proximal Stimuli Universally are Not.

Consider, first, visual perception observed from outside the perceiver.[6] Visual perceivers recover properties of objects and events in their environment ("distal events"). They can do so, in part, because the environment supplies information

---

[5]One can certainly challenge the idea that listeners recover the very gestures that occurred to produce a speech signal. Obviously there are no gestures at all responsible for most synthetic speech or for "sine-wave speech" (e.g., Remez, Rubin, Pisoni, & Carrell, 1981), and quite different behaviors underlie a parrot's or mynah bird's mimicking of speech. The claim that we argue is incontrovertible is that listeners recover gestures from speech-like signals, even those generated in some other way. We direct realists (Fowler, 1986a, 1986b) would also argue that "misperceptions" (hearing phonetic gestures where there are none) can only occur in limited varieties of ways—the most notable being signals produced by certain mirage-producing human artifacts, such as speech synthesizers or mirage-producing birds. Another possibly includes signals produced to mimic those of normal speakers by speakers with pathologies of the vocal tract that prevent normal realization of gestures.

[6]There are two almost orthogonal perspectives from which perception can be studied. On the one hand, investigators can focus on processes inside the perceiver that take place from the time that a

about the objects and events in a form that their perceptual systems can use. Light reflects from objects and events, which structure it lawfully; given a distal event and light from some source, the reflected light must have the structure that it has. To the extent that the structure in the light is also specific to the properties of a distal event that caused it, it can serve as information to a perceiver about its distal source. The reflected light ("proximal stimulation") has another property that permits it its central role in perception. It can stimulate the visual system of a perceiver and thereby impart its structure to this system. From there, the perceiver can use the structure as information for distal-event perception.

The reflected light does not provide information to the visual system by picturing the world. Information in reflected light for "looming" (that is, for an object on a collision course with the perceiver's head), for example, is a certain manner of expansion of the contours of the object's reflection in the light, that progressively covers the contours of optical reflections of immobile parts of the perceiver's environment. When an object looms, it does not grow; it approaches. However, its optical reflection grows, and, confronted with such an optic array, perceivers (from fiddler crabs to kittens to rhesus monkeys to humans (Schiff, 1965; Schiff, Caviness & Gibson, 1962) behave as if they perceive an object on a collision course; that is, they try to avoid it.

Two related conclusions from this characterization of visual perception are, first, that observers see distal events based on information about them in proximal stimulation, and, second, that, in Mattingly and Liberman's terms, visual perception, therefore, is quite generally heteromorphic. It is not merely heteromorphic in respect to those aspects of stimulation handled by closed modules (for example, one that recovers depth information from binocular disparity); it is *generally* the case that the dimensions of the percept correspond with dimensions of distal objects and events, and not necessarily with those of a distal-event-free description of the proximal stimulation.[7]

Auditory perception is analogous to visual perception in its general character,

---

sense organ is stimulated until a percept is achieved or a response is made to the input. On the other hand, they can look outside the perceiver and ask what in the environment the organism under study perceives, what information in stimulation to the sense organs allows perception of the things perceived, and finally, whether the organisms in fact use the postulated information. Here we focus on this latter perspective, most closely associated with the work of James Gibson (e.g., 1966, 1979; Reed & Jones, 1982).

[7]It is easy to find examples in which perception is heteromorphic with respect to the proximal stimulation and homomorphic with respect to distal events—looming, for example. We can also think of some examples in which perception appears homomorphic with respect to proximal stimulation, but in the examples we have come up with, they are homomorphic with respect to the distal event as well (perception of a line drawn by a pencil, for example), and, thus, there is no way to decide whether perception is of the proximal stimulation or of the distal event. We challenge the motor theorists to provide an example in which perception is homomorphic with structure in proximal stimulation that is not also homomorphic with distal event structure. These would provide convincing cases of proximal stimulation perception.

viewed, once again from outside the perceiver. Consider any sounding object, a ringing bell, for example. The ringing bell is a "distal event" that structures an acoustic signal. The structuring of the air by the bell is lawful and, to the extent that it also tends to be specific to its distal source, the structure can provide information about the source to a sensitive perceiver. Like reflected light, the acoustic signal (the proximal stimulation) in fact has two critical properties that allow it to play a central role in perception. It is lawfully structured by some distal event, and it can stimulate the auditory system of perceivers, thereby imparting its structure to it. The perceiver then can use the structure as information for its source.

As for structure in reflected light, structure in an acoustic signal does not resemble the sound-producing source in any way. Accordingly, if auditory perception works similarly to visual perception—that is, if perceivers use structure in acoustic signals to recover their distal sources—then auditory percepts like visual percepts will be heteromorphic.

Liberman and Mattingly (1985; Mattingly & Liberman, 1988) suggested, however, that in general, auditory perceptions are homomorphic. We agree that our intuitions are less clear here than they are in the case of visual perception. However, it is an empirical question whether dimensions of listeners' percepts are better explained in terms of dimensions of distal events or of a distal-event-free description of proximal stimulation. To date, the question is untested, however; for whatever reason, researchers who study auditory perception rarely study perception of natural sound-producing events (see, however, Repp, 1987; VanDerVeer, 1979; Warren & Verbrugge, 1984).

Now consider speech perception. In speech, the distal event—at least the event in the environment that structures the acoustic speech signal—is the moving vocal tract. If, as we propose, the vocal tract produces phonetic gestures, then the distal event is, at the same time, the set of phonetic gestures that compose the talker's spoken message. The proximal stimulus is the acoustic signal, lawfully structured by movement in the vocal tract. To the extent that the structure in the signal also tends to be specific to the events that caused it, it can serve as information about those events to sensitive perceivers. The information that proximal stimulation provides will be about the phonetic gestures of the vocal tract. Accordingly, if speech perception works like visual perception, then recovery of phonetic gestures is not eccentric and does not require eccentric processing by a speech module. It is, instead, yet another instance of recovery of distal events by means of lawfully generated structure in proximal stimulation.

The general point we hope to make is that, arguably, all perception is heteromorphic, with dimensions of percepts always corresponding to those of distal events, not to distal-event-free descriptions of proximal stimuli. Speech is not special in that regard. A more specific point is that even if evidence were to show that speech perceivers do access their speech-motor systems, that perceptual process would not be needed to provide the reason why listeners' percepts are heteromorphic. The reason percepts are heteromorphic is that perceivers universally use proximal stimuli as information about events taking place in the world; they do not use them as perceptual objects *per se*.

Are Phonetic Gestures Public or Private?

Although, in "Perception of the speech code" and "The motor theory revised," evidence that listeners recover gestures is the only *evidence* cited in favor of the view that perceivers access their speech motor systems, that evidence is not the only *reason* why the motor theorists and other theorists invoke a construct inside the perceiver rather than the proximal stimulation outside to explain why the percept has the character it does. A very important reason why, for the motor theorists, the proximal stimulation is not by itself sufficient to specify phonetic gestures is that, in their view, phonetic gestures are abstract control structures corresponding to the speaker's intentions but not to the movements actually taking place in the vocal tract. If phonetic gestures are not "out there" in the vocal tract, then they cannot be analogous to other distal events, because they cannot themselves lawfully structure the acoustic signal.

In our view, this characterization of phonetic gestures is mistaken, however. We can identify two considerations that appear to support it, but we find neither convincing. One is that any gesture of the vocal tract is merely a token action. Yet perceivers do not just recognize the token, they recognize it *as* a member of a larger linguistically significant category. That seems to localize the thing perceived in the mind of the perceiver, not in the mouth of the talker. More than that, the same collections of token gestures may be identified as tokens of different categories by speakers of different languages. (Thus, for example, speakers of English may identify a voiceless unaspirated stop in stressed syllable-initial position as a /b/, whereas speakers of languages in which voiceless unaspirated stops can appear stressed-syllable initially may identify it as an instance of a /p/.) Here, it seems, the information for category membership cannot possibly be in the gestures themselves or in the proximal stimulation; it must be in the head of the perceiver. The second consideration is that coarticulation, by most accounts, prevents nondestructive realization of phonetic gestures in the vocal tract. We briefly address both considerations.

Yet another analogy: There are chairs in the world that do not look very much like prototypical chairs. Recognizing them as chairs may require learning how people typically use them—learning their "proper function" in Millikan's terms (1984). By most accounts, learning involves some enduring change inside the perceiver. Notice, however, that even if it does, what makes the token chair a chair remains its properties and its use in the world prototypically as a chair. Too, whatever perceivers may learn about that chair and about chairs in general is only what they learn; the chair itself and the means by which its type-hood can be identified remain unquestionably out there in the world. Phonetic gestures and phonetic segments are like chairs (in this respect). Token instances of bilabial closure are members of a type, because the tokens all are products of a common coupling among jaw and lips, realized in the vocal tract of talkers who achieve bilabial closure. Instances of bilabial closure in stressed-syllable-initial position that have a particular timing relation to a glottal opening gesture are tokens of a phonological category, /b/, in some languages, and of a different category, /p/, in others, because of the different ways that they are deployed by members of the different language communities. That differential deployment is what allowed descriptive linguists to identify members of phonemic categories as such, and presumably it is also what allows language learners to acquire the phonological categories of their native language. By most accounts, when language learners discover the categories of their language, the learning involves enduring changes inside the learner. However, even if it does, it is no more the case that the phonetic gestures or the phonetic segments move inside the mind than it is that chairs move inside, when we learn how to recognize them as such. What we have learned is what we *know* about chairs and phonetic segments; it is not the chairs or the phonetic segments themselves. They remain outside.

Turning to coarticulation, it is described in the motor theory as "encoding," by Ohala (e.g., 1981) as "distortion," by Daniloff and Hammarberg (1973), as "assimilation" and by Hockett (1955) as "smashing" and "rubbing together" of phonetic segments (in the way that raw eggs would be smashed and rubbed together were they sent through a wringer). None of these characterizations is warranted, however. Coarticulation may instead by characterized as gestural layering—a temporally staggered realization of gestures that sometimes do and sometimes do not share one or more articulators.

In fact, this kind of gestural layering occurs commonly in motor behavior. When someone walks, the movement of his or her arm is seen as pendular. However, the surface movement is a complex (layered) vector including not only the swing of the arm but also movement of the whole body in the direction of locomotion. This layering is not described as "encoding," "distortion," or even as assimilation of the arm movement to the movement of the body as a whole. And for good reason: That is not what it is. The movement reflects a convergence of forces of movement on a body segment. The forces are separate for the walker, information in proximal stimulation allows their parsing (Johansson, 1973), and perceivers detect their separation.

There is evidence already suggesting that at least some of coarticulation is gestural layering (Carney & Moll, 1971; Öhman, 1966; see also Browman & Goldstein, in press), not encoding or distortion or assimilation. There is also convincing evidence that perceivers recover separate gestures more or less in the way that Johansson has suggested they recover separate sources of movement of body segments in perception of locomotion. Listeners use information for a coarticulating segment that is present in the domain of another segment as information for the coarticulating segment itself (e.g., Fowler, 1984; Mann, 1980; Whalen, 1984); they do not hear the coarticulated segment as assimilated or apparently as distorted or encoded (Fowler, 1981, 1984; Fowler & Smith, 1986).

Our colleagues Catherine Browman and Louis Goldstein (1985, 1986, in press; chapter 13 this volume) have proposed that phonetic primitives of languages are gestural, not abstract featural. Our colleague Elliot Saltzman (1986; Saltzman & Kelso, 1987; see also, Kelso, Saltzman, & Tuller, 1986) is developing a model that implements phonetic gestures as functional couplings among the articulators and that realizes the gestural layering characteristic of coarticulation. To the extent that these approaches both succeed, they will show that phonetic gestures—speakers' intentions—can be realized in the vocal tract nondestructively and, hence, can structure acoustic signals directly.

Do listeners need an innate vocal tract synthesizer to recognize acoustic reflections of phonetic gestures? Although it might seem to help, it cannot be necessary, because there is no analogous way to explain how observers recognize most distal events from their optical reflections. Somehow the acoustic and optical reflections of a source must identify the source on their own. In some instances, we begin to understand the means by which acoustic patternings can specify their gestural sources. We consider one such instance next.

How Acoustic Structure may Serve as Information for Gestures

We return to the example previously described of listeners' perception of those linguistic dimensions of an utterance that are cued in some way by variation in FO. A variety of linguistic and paralinguistic properties of an utterance have converging effects on FO. Yet listeners pull apart those effects in perception.

What guides the listeners' factoring of converging effects of FO? Presumably, it is the configuration of acoustic products of the several gestures that have effects, among others, on FO. Intonational peaks are local changes in an FO contour that are effected by means that, to a first approximation, only affect FO; they are produced, largely, by contraction and relaxation of muscles that stretch or shorten the vocal folds (e.g., Ohala, 1978). In contrast, declination is a global change in FO that, excepting the initial peak in a sentence, tracks the decline in subglottal pressure (Gelfer et al., 1985; Gelfer et al., 1987). Subglottal pressure affects not only FO, but amplitude as well, and several researchers have noticed that amplitude declines in parallel with FO, and resets when FO resets at major syntactic boundaries (e.g., Breckenridge, 1977; Maeda, 1976). The parallel decline in amplitude and FO constitutes information that pinpoints the mechanism behind the FO decline—gradual lung deflation, incompletely offset by expiratory-muscle activity. That mechanism is distinct from the mechanism by which intonational peaks are produced. Evidence that listeners pull apart the two effects on FO (Pierrehumbert, 1979; Silverman, 1987) suggests that they are sensitive to the distinct gestural sources of these effects on FO.

By the same token, FO perturbations due to height differences among vowels are not confused by listeners with information for intonational peak height, although FO differences due to vowel height are local, like intonational peaks, and are similar in magnitude to differences among intonational peaks in a sentence (Silverman, 1987). The mechanisms for the two effects on FO are different, and apparently listeners are sensitive to that. Honda (1981) showed a strong correlation between activity of the genioglossus muscle, active in pulling the root of the tongue forward for high vowels, and intrinsic FO of vowels. Posterior fibers of the genioglossus muscle insert into the hyoid bone of the larynx. Therefore, contraction of the genioglossus may pull the hyoid forward, rotating the thyroid cartilage to which the vocal folds attach, and thereby may stretch the vocal folds. Other acoustic consequences of genioglossus contraction, of course, are changes in the resonances of the vocal tract, which reflect movement of the tongue. These changes, along with those in FO (and perhaps others as well) pinpoint a phonetic gesture that achieves a vowel-specific change in vocal-tract shape. If listeners can use that configuration of acoustic reflections of tongue movement (or, more likely, of coordinated tongue and jaw movement) to recover the vocalic gesture, then they can pull apart effects on FO of the vocalic gesture from those of the intonation contour that co-occur with them.

Listeners do just that. In sentence pairs such as *They only feast before fasting* and *They only fast before feasting,* with intonational peaks on the *fVst* syllables, listeners require a higher peak on *feast* in the second sentence than on *fast* in the first sentence in order to hear the first peak of each sentence as higher than the second (Silverman, 1987). Compatibly, among steady-state vowels on the same FO, more open vowels sound higher in pitch than more closed vowels (Stoll, 1984). Intrinsic FO of vowels does not contribute to perception of an intonation contour or to perception of pitch. However, it is not thrown away by perceivers either. Rather, along with spectral information, it serves as information for vowel height (Reinholt Peterson, 1986).

We will not review the literature on listeners' use of FO perturbations due to obstruent voicing, except to say that it reveals the same picture of the perceiver as the literature on listeners' use of information for vowel height (for a description of the FO perturbations, see Ohde, 1984; for studies of listeners' use of the perturbations, see Abramson & Lisker, 1985; Fujimura, 1971; Haggard, Ambler & Callow, 1970; Silverman, 1986; for evidence that listeners can detect the perturbations when they are superimposed on intonation contours, see Silverman, 1986). As the Motor Theory and the theory of direct perception both claim, listeners' percepts do not correspond to superficial aspects of the acoustic signal. They correspond to gestures, signalled, we propose, by configurations of acoustic reflections of those gestures.

Does Duplex Perception Reveal a Closed Speech Module?

We return to the phenomenon of duplex perception and consider whether it does convincingly reveal distinct closed and open modules for speech perception and general auditory perception respectively. As noted earlier, duplex perception is obtained typically when most of the acoustic structure of a synthetic syllable is presented to one ear, and the remainder—usually a formant transition—is presented to the other ear (refer to Fig. 3.2). In such instances, listeners hear two things. In the ear that gets most of the signal, they hear a coherent syllable, the identity of which is determined by the transition presented to the other ear. At the same time, they hear a distinct, nonspeech chirp in the ear receiving the transition. The percept is duplex—the transition is heard as a critical part of a speech syllable, hypothetically as a result of its being processed by the speech module, and it is heard simultaneously as a nonspeech chirp, hypothetically as a result of its being processed also by an open auditory module (Liberman & Mattingly, 1985). Here we offer a different interpretation of the findings.

Whalen and Liberman (1987) recently showed that duplex perception can occur with monaural or diotic presentation of the base and transition of a syllable. In this case, duplexity is attained by increasing the intensity of the third formant transition relative to the base until listeners hear both an integrated syllable (/da/ or /ga/ depending on the transition) and a nonspeech whistle (sinusoids were used for transitions). In the experiment, subjects first were asked to label the isolated sinusoidal transitions as /da/ or /ga/. Although they were consistent in their labeling, reliably identifying one whistle as /da/ and the other as /ga/, their overall accuracy was not greater than chance. About half the subjects were consistently right, and the remainder were consistently wrong. The whistles are distinct, but they do not sound like /da/ or /ga/. Next, Whalen and Liberman determined "duplexity thresholds" for listeners. They presented the base and one of the sinusoids simultaneously and gave listeners control over the intensity of the sinusoid. Listeners adjusted its intensity to the point where they just heard a whistle. At threshold, subjects were able to match these duplex sinusoids to sinusoids presented in isolation. Finally, subjects were asked to identify the integrated speech syllables as /da/ or /ga/ at sinusoid intensities both 6 dB above and 4 dB below the duplexity threshold. Subjects were consistently good at these tasks, achieving accuracy scores well above 90%.

In the absence of any transition, listeners hear only the base and identify it as /da/ most of the time. When a sinusoidal transition is present, but at intensities below the duplexity threshold, subjects hear only the unambiguous syllable (/da/ or /ga/, depending on the transition). Finally, when the intensity of the transition reaches and exceeds the duplexity threshold, subjects hear the /da/ or /ga/ and they hear a whistle at the same time (i.e., the transition is duplexed).

This experiment reveals two new aspects of the duplex phenomenon. One is that getting a duplex percept requires a sufficiently high intensity of the transition. A second is that the transition integrates with the syllable at intensities below the duplexity threshold. Based on this latter finding, Whalen and Liberman concluded that processing of the sinusoid as speech has priority. It is as if a (neurally encoded) acoustic signal must first pass through the speech module at which point portions of the signal that specify speech events are peeled off. After the speech module takes its part, any residual is passed on to the auditory module, where it is perceived homomorphically. Mattingly and Liberman (1988) referred to this priority of speech processing as "pre-emptiveness," and Whalen and Liberman (1987) suggested that it reflects the "profound biological significance of speech."

There is another way to look at these findings, however. They suggest that duplex perception does not, in fact, involve the *same* acoustic fragment being perceived in two ways simultaneously. Rather *part* of the transition integrates with the syllable and the *remainder* is heard as a whistle or chirp.[8] As Whalen and Liberman (1987) themselves described it:

> The phonetic mode takes precedence in processing the transitions, using them for its special linguistic purposes until, having appropriated its share, it passes the *remainder* to be perceived by the nonspeech system as auditory whistles. (p. 171, our italics).

This is important, because in earlier reports of duplex perception, it was the apparent perception of the transition in two different ways at once that was considered strong evidence favoring two distinct perceptual systems, one for speech and one for general auditory perception. In addition, research to date has only looked for pre-emptiveness using speech syllables. Accordingly, it is premature to conclude that speech especially is pre-emptive. Possibly acoustic fragments integrate preferentially whenever the integrated signal specifies some coherent sound-producing event.

We have recently looked for duplex perception in perception of nonspeech sounds (Fowler & Rosenblum, in press). We predicted that it would be possible to observe duplex perception and pre-emptiveness whenever two conditions are met: a) a pair of acoustic fragments is presented that, integrated, specify a natural distal event; and b) one of the fragments is unnaturally intense. Under these conditions, the integrated event should be pre-emptive, and the intense fragment

---

[8]Bregman (1987) considered duplex perception to disconfirm his "rule of disjoint allocation" in acoustic scene analysis by listeners. According to the rule, each acoustic fragment is assigned in perception to one and only one environmental source. It seems, however, that duplex perception does not disconfirm the rule.

should be duplexed *regardless* of the type of natural sound-producing event that is involved, whether it is speech or nonspeech, and whether it is profoundly biologically significant or biologically trivial.

There have been other attempts to get duplex perception for nonspeech sounds. All the ones of which we are aware have used musical stimuli, however (e.g., Pastore, Schmuckler, Rosenblum, & Szczesuil, 1983; Collins, 1985). We chose not to use musical stimuli, because it might be argued that there is a music module. (Music is universal among human cultures, and there is evidence for an anatomical specialization of the brain for music perception—for example, Shapiro, Grossman, & Gardner, 1981). These considerations led us to choose a nonspeech event that evolution could not have anticipated. We chose an event involving a recent human artifact: a slamming metal door.

To generate our stimuli, we recorded a heavy metal door (of a sound-attenuating booth) being slammed shut. A waveform display of this sound can be seen in top left-hand panel of Fig. 3.3, and a spectral cross-section taken about 10 ms into the signal can be seen in the top right-hand panel. To produce our chirp, we high-pass filtered the signal at 3000 Hz. To produce a base, we low-passed filtered the original signal, also at 3000 Hz (see bottom panels of Fig. 3.3). To us, the high-pass-filtered chirp sounded like a can of rice being shaken, whereas the low-pass-filtered base sounded like a wooden door being slammed shut. (That is, the clanging of the metal door was largely absent.)

We asked 16 listeners to identify the original metal door, the base, and the chirp. The modal identifications of the metal door and the base included mention of a door; however, less than half the subjects reported hearing a door slam. Even so, essentially all of the identifications involved hard collisions of some sort (e.g., boots clomping on stairs, shovel banged on sidewalk). In contrast, no subject identified the chirp as a door sound, and no identifications described hard collisions. Most identifications of the chirp referred to an event involving shaking (tambourine, maracas, castinets, keys).

Given our metal-door chirp and another chirp made by high-pass filtering a wooden-door slam, subjects could not identify which was a filtered metal-door slam and which a filtered wooden-door slam. Subjects were consistent in their labeling judgments, identifying one of the chirps as a metal door and the other as a wooden door. However, overall, more of them were consistently wrong than right. On average, they identified the metal-door chirp as the sound of a metal door 31% of the time and the wooden-door chirp as a metal door sound 79% of the time.

To test for duplex perception and pre-emptiveness, we first trained subjects to identify the unfiltered door sound as a metal door, the base as a wooden door, and the upper frequencies of the door as a shaking sound. Next, we tested them on stimuli created from the base and the chirp. We created 15 different diotic stimuli. All included the base, and almost all included the metal-door chirp. The stimuli differed in the intensity of the chirp. The chirp was attenuated or amplified by multiplying its digitized voltages by the following values: 0, .05, .1, .15,

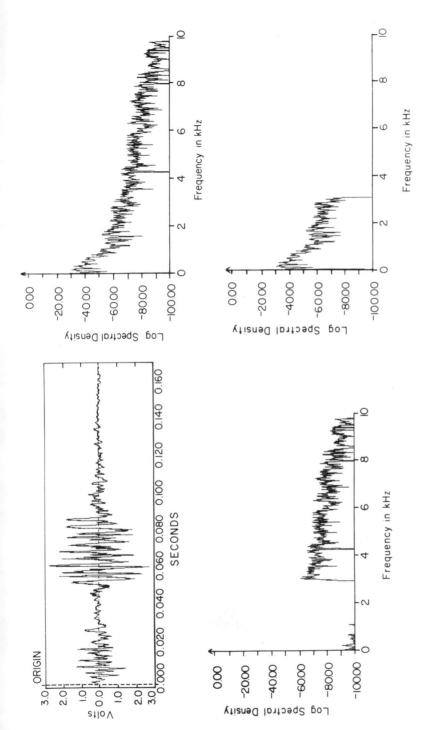

FIG. 3.3. Display of stimuli used to obtain duplex perception of closing-door sounds. Clockwise from top left: waveform of a slamming metal door, spectral cross-section of the door sound taken about 10 ms into the signal, spectral cross-section of the low-pass filtered door sound (the "base"), spectral cross-section of the high-pass filtered door sound (the "shaking sound").

.2, .9, .95, 1, 1.05, 1.1, 4, 4.5, 5, 5.5, and 6. That is, there were 15 different intensities falling into three ranges: Five were well below the natural intensity relationship of the chirp to the base; five were in the range of the natural intensity relation, and five were well above it. Three tokens of each of these stimuli were presented to subjects diotically in a randomized order. Listeners were told that they might hear one of the stimuli (metal door, wooden door, or shaking sound) or sometimes two of them simultaneously on each trial. They were to indicate what they heard on each trial by writing an identifying letter or pair of letters on their answer sheets.

In our analyses, we have grouped responses to the 15 stimuli into three blocks of five. In Fig. 3.4, we have labeled these Intensity Conditions low, medium, and high. Figure 3.4 presents the results as percentages of responses in the various response categories across the three intensity conditions. We show only the three most interesting (and most frequent) responses. The figure shows that the most frequent response for the low intensity condition is wooden door, the label we asked subjects to use, when they heard the base. The most frequent response for the medium condition is metal door, the label we asked subjects to use, when they heard the metal door slam. The preferred response for the high-intensity block of stimuli is overwhelmingly metal door + chirp, the response that indicates a duplex percept. The changes in response frequency over the three intensity conditions for each response type are highly significant.

Our results can be summarized as follows. First, at very low intensities of the upper frequencies of the door, subjects hear the base only. When the chirp is amplified to an intensity at or near its natural intensity relation to the base,

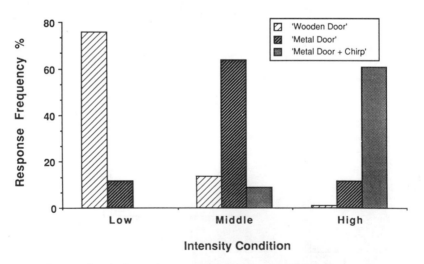

FIG. 3.4.   Percentage of responses falling in the three response categories, "wooden door," "metal door," and "metal door plus shaking sound" across three intensity ranges of the shaking sound.

subjects report hearing a metal door the majority of the time. Further amplification of the chirp leads to reports of the metal door and a separate shaking sound. The percept is duplex, and the metal door slam is pre-emptive.

There are several additional tests that we must run to determine whether our door slams, are in fact, perceived analogously to speech syllables in procedures revealing duplex perception. If we can show that they are, then we will conclude that an account of our findings that invokes a closed module is inappropriate. Evolution is unlikely to have anticipated metal door slams, and metal-door slams are not profoundly biologically significant. We suggest alternatively that pre-emptiveness occurs when a chirp fills a "hole" in a simultaneously presented acoustic signal so that together the two parts of the signal specify some sound-producing distal event. If anything is left over after the hole is filled, the remainder is heard as separate.

Summary and Concluding Remarks

We have raised three challenges to the motor theory. We challenge the inference from evidence that phonetic gestures are perceived that speech perception involves access to the talker's own motor system. The basis for our challenge is a claim that dimensions of percepts always conform to those of distal events, even in cases where access to an internal synthesizer for the events is unlikely. A second, related challenge is to the idea that only some percepts are heteromorphic—just those for which we have evolved closed modules. When Mattingly and Liberman had written that speech perception is heteromorphic, they had meant heteromorphic with respect to structure in proximal stimulation, but they have always meant as well that the percept is homomorphic with respect to dimensions of the distal source of the proximal stimulation. We argue that percepts are *generally* heteromorphic with respect to structure in proximal stimulation, but whether they are or not, they are always homomorphic with respect to dimensions of distal events. Finally, we challenge the interpretation of duplex perception that ascribes it to simultaneous processing of one part of an acoustic signal by two modules. We suggest instead that duplex perception reflects the listener's parsing of acoustic structure into disjoint parts that specify, insofar as the acoustic structure permits, coherent distal events.

Where (in our view) does this leave the motor theory? It is fundamentally correct in its claim that listeners perceive phonetic gestures, and also, possibly, in its claim that humans have evolved neural systems specialized for perception and production of phonetic gestures. It is wrong, we believe, specifically in its claims about what those specialized systems do and generally in the view that closed modules must be invoked to explain why distal events are perceived.

Obviously, we prefer our own, direct-realist theory, not so much because it handles the data better, but because, in our view, it fits better in a universal theory of perception. However our theory may be judged in relation to the motor theory, we recognize that we would not have developed it at all in the absence of the important discoveries of the motor theorists that gestures are perceived.

Acknowledgments

Preparation of this manuscript was supported by a fellowship from the John Simon Guggenheim Memorial Foundation to the first author and by grants NIH–NICHD HD–01994 and NINCDS NS–13617 to Haskins Laboratories.

References

Abramson, A., & Lisker, L. (1985). Relative power of cues: FO shift versus voice timing. In V. Fromkin (Ed.), *Phonetic linguistics: Essays in honor of Peter Ladefoged* (pp. 25–32). Orlando: Academic Press.

Breckenridge, J. (1977). *Declination as a phonological process.* Bell Laboratories Technological Memo. Murray Hill, NJ.

Bregman, A. (1987). The meaning of duplex perception. In M. E. H. Schouten (Ed.), *The psychophysics of speech perception* (pp. 95–111). Dordrecht: Martinus Nijhoff.

Browman, C., & Goldstein, L. (1985). Dynamic modeling of phonetic structure. In V. Fromkin (Ed.), *Phonetic linguistics: Essays in honor of Peter Ladefoged* (pp. 35–53). Orlando, FL: Academic Press.

Browman, C., & Goldstein, L. (1986). Towards an articulatory phonology. In C. Ewan & J. Anderson (Eds.), *Phonology yearbook* (vol. 3, pp. 219–254). Cambridge, England: Cambridge University Press.

Browman, C., & Goldstein, L. (in press). Tiers in articulatory phonology with some implications for casual speech. In J. Kingston & M. Beckman (Eds.), *Papers in laboratory phonology I. Between the grammar and the physics of speech.* Cambridge: Cambridge University Press.

Carney, P., & Moll, K. (1971). A cinefluorographic investigation of fricative-consonant vowel coarticulation. *Phonetica, 23,* 193–201.

Collins, S. (1985). Duplex perception with musical stimuli: A further investigation. *Perception & Psychophysics, 38,* 172–177.

Cooper, F., Delattre, P., Liberman, A., Borst, J., & Gerstman, L. (1952). Some experiments on the perception of synthetic speech sounds. *Journal of the Acoustical Society of America, 24,* 597–606.

Daniloff, R., & Hammarberg, R. (1973). On defining coarticulation. *Journal of Phonetics, 1,* 239–248.

Fitch, H., Halwes, T., Erickson, D., & Liberman, A. (1980). Perceptual equivalence of two acoustic cues for stop consonant manner. *Perception & Psychophysics, 27,* 343–350.

Fodor, J. (1983). *The modularity of mind.* Cambridge, MA: MIT Press.

Folkins, J., & Abbs, J. (1975). Lip and jaw motor control during speech: Responses to resistive loading of the jaw. *Journal of Speech and Hearing Research, 18,* 207–220.

Folkins, J., & Abbs, J. (1976). Additional observations on responses to resistive loading of the jaw. *Journal of Speech and Hearing Research, 19,* 820–821.

Fowler, C. (1981). Production and perception of coarticulation among stressed and unstressed vowels. *Journal of Speech and Hearing Research, 46,* 127–139.

Fowler, C. (1984). Segmentation of coarticulated speech in perception. *Perception & Psychophysics, 36,* 359–368.

Fowler, C. (1986a). An event approach to the study of speech perception from a direct-realist perspective. *Journal of Phonetics, 14,* 3–28.

Fowler, C. (1986b). Reply to commentators. *Journal of Phonetics, 14,* 149–170.

Fowler, C., & Rosenblum, L. (in press). Duplex perception: A comparison of monosyllables and slamming doors. *Journal of Experimental Psychology: Human Perception and Performance.*

Fowler, C., & Smith, M. (1986). Speech perception as "vector analysis": An approach to the problems of segmentation and invariance. In J. Perkell & D. Klatt (Eds.), *Invariance and variability of speech processes* (pp. 123–135). Hillsdale, NJ: Lawrence Erlbaum Associates.

Fujimura, O. (1971). Remarks on stop consonants: Synthesis experiments and acoustic cues. In L. Hammerich, R. Jakobson, & E. Zwirner (Eds.), *Form and substance* (pp. 221–232). Copenhagen: Akademisk Forlag.

Gelfer, C., Harris, K., Collier, R., & Baer, T. (1985). Is declination actively controlled? In I. Titze & R. Scherer (Eds.), *Vocal-fold physiology: Biomechanics, acoustics and phonatory control* (pp. 113–126). Denver: Denver Center for the Performing Arts.

Gelfer, C., Harris, K., & Baer, T. (1987). Controlled variables in sentence intonation. In T. Baer, C. Sasaki, & K. Harris (Eds.), *Laryngeal function in phonation and respiration* (pp. 422–432). Boston: College-Hill Press.

Gibson, J. J. (1966). *The senses considered as perceptual systems.* Boston: Houghton Mifflin.

Gibson, J. J. (1979). *The ecological approach to visual perception.* Boston: Houghton Mifflin.

Haggard, M., Ambler, S., & Callow, M. (1970). Pitch as a voicing cue. *Journal of the Acoustical Society of America, 47,* 613–617.

Hockett, C. (1955). *Manual of phonology.* (Publications in anthropology and linguistics, No. 11). Bloomington, IN: Indiana University Press.

Honda, K. (1981). Relationship between pitch control and vowel articulation. In D. Bless & J. Abbs (Eds.), *Vocal-fold physiology* (pp. 286–297). San Diego: College-Hill Press.

Jakobson, R., Fant, G., & Halle, M. (1972). *Preliminaries to speech analysis* (10th ed.). Cambridge, MA: MIT Press.

Johansson, G. (1973). Visual perception of biological motion. *Perception & Psychophysics, 14,* 201–211.

Kelso, J. A. S., Tuller, B., Vatikiotis-Bateson, E., & Fowler, C. (1984). Functionally-specific articulatory cooperation following jaw perturbations during speech: Evidence for coordinative structures. *Journal of Experimental Psychology: Human Perception and Performance, 10,* 812–832.

Kelso, J. A. S., Saltzman, E., & Tuller, B. (1986). The dynamical perspective on speech production: Data and theory. *Journal of Phonetics, 14,* 29–59.

Kimura, D. (1961). Cerebral dominance and the perception of verbal stimuli. *Canadian Journal of Psychology, 15,* 166–171.

Lehiste, I. (1982). Some phonetic characteristics of discourse. *Studia Linguistica, 36,* 117–130.

Lehiste, I., & Peterson, G. (1961). Some basic considerations in the analysis of intonation. *Journal of the Acoustical Society of America, 33,* 419–425.

Liberman, A. (1974). The specialization of the language hemisphere (pp. 43–56). In F. O. Schmitt & F. G. Worden (Eds.), *The neurosciences: Third study program.* Cambridge, MA: MIT Press.

Liberman, A. (1982). On finding that speech is special. *American Psychologist, 37,* 148–167.

Liberman, A., Cooper, F., Harris, K., & MacNeilage, P. (1963). A motor theory of speech perception. *Proceedings of the Speech Communication Seminar* (paper D3). Stockholm: Royal Institute of Technology.

Liberman, A., Cooper, F., Shankweiler, D., & Studdert-Kennedy, M. (1967). Perception of the speech code. *Psychological Review, 74,* 431–461.

Liberman, A., Isenberg, D., & Rakerd, B. (1981). Duplex perception of cues for stop consonants: Evidence for a phonetic module. *Perception & Psychophysics, 30,* 133–143.

Liberman, A., & Mattingly, I. (1985). The Motor Theory of Speech Perception Revised. *Cognition, 21,* 1–36.

Löfqvist, A., Baer, T., McGarr, N., & Seider Story, R. (1988). The cricothyroid muscle in voicing control. *Journal of the Acoustical Society of America, 83,* S111.

MacDonald, M., & McGurk, H. (1978). Visual influences on speech perception. *Perception & Psychophysics, 24,* 253–257.

Maeda, S. (1976). *A characterization of American English intonation.* Unpublished doctoral dissertation, Massachusetts Institute of Technology.

Mann, V. (1980). Influence of preceding liquid on stop consonant perception. *Perception & Psychophysics, 28,* 407–412.

Mann, V., & Liberman, A. (1983). Some differences between phonetic and auditory modes of perception. *Cognition, 14,* 211–235.

Massaro, D. (1987). *Speech perception by ear and eye: A paradigm for psychological inquiry.* Hillsdale, NJ: Lawrence Erlbaum Associates.

Mattingly, I., & Liberman, A. (1988). Specialized perceiving systems for speech and other biologically significant sounds. In G. Edelman, W. Gall, & W. Cowan (Eds.), *Auditory function: The neurological basis of hearing* (pp. 775–792). New York: Wiley.

Millikan, R. (1984). *Language and other biological categories.* Cambridge, MA: MIT Press.

Ohala, J. (1978). Production of tone. In V. Fromkin (Ed.), *Tone: A linguistic survey* (pp. 5–39). New York: Academic Press.

Ohala, J. (1981). The listener as a source of sound change. In C. Masek, R. Hendrick, & M. Miller (Eds.), *Papers from the parasession on language and behavior* (pp. 178–203). Chicago: Chicago Linguistics Society.

Ohde, R. (1984). Fundamental frequency as an acoustic correlate of stop consonant voicing. *Journal of the Acoustical Society of America, 75,* 224–240.

Öhman, S. (1966). Coarticulation in VCV utterances: Spectrographic measures. *Journal of the Acoustical Society of America, 39,* 151–168.

Pastore, R., Schmuckler, M., Rosenblum, L. D., & Szczesiul, R. (1983). Duplex perception with musical stimuli. *Perception & Psychophysics, 33,* 323–332.

Pierrehumbert, J. (1979). The perception of fundamental frequency. *Journal of the Acoustical Society of America, 66,* 363–369.

Porter, R. (1978). *Rapid shadowing of syllables: Evidence for symmetry of speech perceptual and motor systems.* Paper presented at the meeting of the Psychonomics Society, San Antonio.

Porter, R., & Lubker, J. (1980). Rapid reproduction of vowel-vowel sequences: Evidence for a fast and direct acoustic-motoric linkage in speech. *Journal of Speech and Hearing Research, 23,* 593–602.

Rand, T. (1974). Dichotic release from masking for speech. *Journal of the Acoustical Society of America, 55,* 678–680.

Reed, E., & Jones, R. (1982). *Reasons for realism: Selected essays of James J. Gibson.* Hillsdale, NJ: Lawrence Erlbaum Associates.

Reinholt Peterson, N. (1986). Perceptual compensation for segmentally-conditioned fundamental-frequency perturbations. *Phonetica, 43,* 31–42.

Remez, R., Rubin, P., Pisoni, D., & Carrell, T. (1981). Speech perception without traditional speech cues. *Science, 212,* 947–950.

Repp, B. (1987). The sound of two hands clapping: An exploratory study. *Journal of the Acoustical Society of America, 81,* 1100–1109.

Repp, B., Milburn, C., & Ashkenas, J. (1983). Duplex perception: Confirmation of fusion. *Perception & Psychophysics, 33,* 333–338.

Rosenblum, L. D. (1987). Towards an ecological alternative to the motor theory of speech perception. (Technical Report of Center for the Ecological Study of Perception and Action, University of Connecticut), *PAW Review 2*, 25–29.

Saltzman, E. (1986). Task dynamic coordination of the speech articulators. In H. Heuer & C. Fromm (Eds.), *Generation and modulation of action patterns* (Experimental Brain Research Series 15, pp. 129–144). New York: Springer.

Saltzman, E., & Kelso, J. A. S. (1987). Skilled actions: A task-dynamic approach. *Psychological Review, 94*, 84–106.

Schiff, W. (1965). Perception of impending collision. *Psychological Monographs, 79*, (604).

Schiff, W., Caviness, J., & Gibson, J. (1962). Persistent fear responses in rhesus monkeys to the optical stimulus of "looming." *Science, 136*, 982–983.

Shapiro, B., Grossman, M., & Gardner, H. (1981). Selective processing deficits in brain-damaged populations. *Neuropsychologia, 19*, 161–169.

Silverman, K. (1986). FO segmental cues depend on intonation: The case of the rise after voiced stops. *Phonetica, 43*, 76–92.

Silverman, K. (1987). *The structure and processing of fundamental frequency contours*. Unpublished doctoral dissertation, Cambridge University.

Stevens, K. (1960). Toward a model for speech recognition. *Journal of the Acoustical Society of America, 32*, 47–55.

Stevens, K., & Blumstein, S. (1981). The search for invariant correlates of acoustic features. In P. Eimas & J. Miller (Eds.), *Perspectives on the study of speech* (pp. 1–38). Hillsdale, NJ: Lawrence Erlbaum Associates.

Stevens, K., & Halle, M. (1967). Remarks on analysis by synthesis and distinctive features. In W. Wathen-Dunn (Ed.), *Models for the perception of speech and visual form* (pp. 88–102). Cambridge, MA: MIT Press.

Stoll, G. (1984). Pitch of vowels: Experimental and theoretical investigation of its dependence on vowel quality. *Speech Communication, 3*, 137–150.

Studdert-Kennedy, M., & Shankweiler, D. (1970). Hemispheric specialization for speech perception. *Journal of the Acoustical Society of America, 48*, 579–594.

VanDerVeer, N. (1979). *Ecological acoustics: Human perception of environmental sounds*. Unpublished doctoral dissertation, Cornell University.

Warren, W., & Verbrugge, R. (1984). Auditory perception of breaking and bouncing events: A case study in ecological acoustics. *Journal of Experimental Psychology: Human Perception and Performance, 10*, 704–712.

Whalen, D. (1984). Subcategorical mismatches slow phonetic judgments. *Perception & Psychophysics, 35*, 49–64.

Whalen, D., & Liberman, A. (1987). Speech perception takes precedence over nonspeech perception. *Science, 237*, 169–171.

Comment: The Gesture as a Unit in Speech Perception Theories

Peter F. MacNeilage

Department of Linguistics, University of Texas at Austin

For both the Motor Theory of Speech Perception (Liberman & Mattingly, 1985; Mattingly & Liberman, 1988) and the Direct-Realist theory of speech perception (Fowler, 1986a,b; Fowler & Rosenblum, chapter 3 this volume) a proposed unit of motor organization—the gesture—is postulated as a unit in the speech perception process. In the brief space available to me here, I wish to consider the concept of the gesture as a production unit in a historical perspective and relate my conclusion to these two perception theories. My conclusion is that the concept of gesture is not yet adequately defined and that this is a serious problem for both of these theories.

The first prominent theory regarding the control processes underlying speech *production* was the Motor Command Theory (Liberman, Cooper, Harris, & MacNeilage, 1962). In brief, the theory was that (with minor exceptions) the brain issues a single command for each phoneme and that the lack of invariance for a given phoneme at the surface level of speech production (which involves coarticulation, stress variations, and speaking style differences) was due to the sluggishness of the peripheral apparatus in carrying out the invariant commands. This theory is of course of special interest here, because it arose as part of the original Motor Theory of Speech Perception, according to which speech was perceived by reference to these motor commands. One important property of this theory, in the light of subsequent discussion, was that it made no distinction between surface and underlying levels as far as the neural control system itself is concerned. The neural events that reached the muscles were considered to have a 1 : 1 relation with commands. A great merit of the Motor Command Theory was that it was testable. Electromyographic studies by myself and others (for a summary of these studies, see MacNeilage, 1972) showed that rather than being invariant, the motor commands reaching the muscles for a given phoneme varied with the coarticulatory demands of both adjacent and nonadjacent segments, with stress levels and with speaking rate.

When it became clear that there was no invariance in the control signals to the muscles, I proposed an alternative control process that, like the subsequent proposal of the Revised Motor Theory (Liberman & Mattingly, 1985), added a distinction between surface (neuromuscular) control variability and underlying invariance (MacNeilage, 1970). I proposed that at the underlying level, invariant spatial targets were specified and that control variations were introduced at a subsequent stage. Like the Motor Command Theory, this theory had the merit of being testable. Folkins and Abbs (1975) provided disconfirming evidence by showing that when mandibular elevation was perturbed, subjects made lip closure in a different spatial position than the normal one. Electromyographic evidence showed that this difference in position was actively achieved, rather than being a passive mechanical consequence of the perturbation. Thus, the experiment showed the control system to be more versatile than the Spatial Target Theory implied.

In the Revised Motor Theory, Liberman and Mattingly responded to the disconfirmation of the Motor Command Theory as I did by postulating that invariance for production lay at an underlying level distinct from the surface level of neuromuscular control. In their words (Liberman & Mattingly, 1985), invariance became a property of "more remote structures that control the movements. These structures correspond to the speaker's intentions" (p. 23). Like me, they also changed the unit of production from the segmental to the subsegmental level. In their case, gestures, not phonemes, became the production entities to which the listener referred.

Liberman and Mattingly readily conceded that by postulating invariant underlying gestural control signals they were not providing a satisfactory new theory of speech production. They pointed out (Liberman & Mattingly, 1985) that "What is far from being understood is the nature of the system that computes the topologically appropriate version of a gesture in a particular context" (p. 23). However, Liberman and Mattingly were not concerned that they did not have a workable production theory. Liberman and Mattingly (1985) emphasized that "this problem is not peculiar to the Motor Theory; it is familiar to many who study the control and coordination of movement; for they, like us, must consider whether, given context-conditioned variability, at the surface, motor acts are nevertheless governed by invariants of some sort" (p. 23).

I would agree with Liberman and Mattingly that the way in which the production system solves the invariance problem is far from being understood. What I do not agree with is that this is a minor problem for the Motor Theory, because it is a shared problem. I see it as a crucial problem for the theory. What is at issue, as Liberman and Mattingly themselves pointed out, is no less than *"whether* (italics ours). . . motor acts are nevertheless governed by invariants of some sort." Thus, speech production theory cannot at present provide the answer to the central question of the Motor Theory: whether there are such things as invariant gestures. The lack of explication by the authors of the claim that there are invariant underlying gestural control signals makes the theory untestable, unlike the earlier motor command and target theories. This is particularly serious, because Liberman and Mattingly themselves point out that they see no straight-forward relation between the underlying level and the level of programmed contextual variation. Consequently, they provide no means whereby the listener apprehends the speaker's intentions when provided with a signal containing contextual variation. This is of course a longstanding problem of the Motor Theory. In 1978, Pick and Saltzman pointed out that "even if it could be shown that speech perception is specially mediated by reference to production, the pattern recognition problem must still be solved" (p. 53). This is what Fowler and Rosenblum (chapter 3 this volume) claim to have successfully addressed, as we will see later.

The uncertainty of the theoretical status of underlying gestural control signals seems particularly problematical for the Motor Theory, because such strong claims are made about them. In the Revised Theory, these gestures are consid-ered to be innate. In the 1985 paper, it was even claimed that innate, gesture-based perceptual ability was immune from effects of early experience. In 1967, Rootes, Chase, and I interpreted the categorical speech perception of a patient with congenital deficits in articulatory control as evidence against a motor theory of perception (MacNeilage, Rootes, & Chase, 1967). However, in the 1985 paper, the perceptual abilities of this patient were cited as evidence *for* the existence of innate motor gestures that were sufficient to mediate perception even in the absence of normal motor development. Liberman has informed me that he no longer holds this extreme view of the power of the innate endowment (person-al communication, June 1988). Consequently, the perceptual abilities of this patient remain a problem for the Motor Theory. In addition, the assumption of *innate* gestures still brings with it a new theoretical problem. The problem is raised in the following excerpt:

> Perhaps, then, the sensitivity of infants to the acoustic consequences of linguistic gestures includes all those gestures that could be phonetically significant in any language, acquisition of ones native language being a process of losing sensitivity to gestures it does not use. (Liberman & Mattingly, 1985, p. 24)

The problem is that the neonate is given a considerable capacity to do not only things that any one speaker is never called on to do, but also things that the ancestors of any one speaker were presumably never called on to do. That is, it includes a capacity to perceive and produce a large family of specific nonuniver-sal sounds. The question is, therefore, how could such capacities have been selected for, when no single line of descent ever exhibited them all?

An additional problem with the notion of innate gestures is that it seems ill-equipped to deal with the facts of speech acquisition. If we indeed possess such an efficient set of presumably equipotential capacities, why does it take the typical child 3.5 years to successfully produce the sounds of the language, and why are most (but interestingly not all) universal sounds mastered before non-universal ones? In addition, why does perceptual ability seem to develop so much more readily than production ability in infants?

The absence of an adequate specification of the putative underlying control units of the Motor Theory raises the question of where the concept of gesture came from. I do not know who first used this term in modern speech production theory. Informally, of course, its meaning is clear. There are as many gestures in a segment as there are degrees of freedom in the control apparatus. However, how many gestures are there in a given segment, and how do we identify them? This was also a problem for the target theory, but one that I did not come to grips with.

To her credit, Fowler has recognised that the explication of the gesture concept for *production* is central, if a theory of perception is to be based on it. Fowler and Rosenblum (chapter 3 this volume) provided the following definition of gestures: "organized movements of one or more vocal tract structures that realize phonetic dimensions of an utterance." Consider the details of this definition. What is value of denoting the movements as organized? How many vocal tract structures are involved in any given case? Consider here a couple of examples. First, in many speakers, elevation of the left and right sides of the tongue for a lateral such as [l] is asymmetrical. Is the control of the two sides of the tongue the task of two gestures or one, or just part of one? Second, the English rhotacized vowel is associated with a double hump in the tongue, one in the oral cavity and one in the pharyngeal cavity (see MacNeilage & Sholes, 1964, for an illustrative cine-fluorogram). How many gestures are involved in this sound? I would contend that examples of gestures given to date are ad hoc and, therefore, necessarily circular and that the concept cannot yet be given a definition with predictive power. The same considerations apply to the notion of "phonetic dimensions of an utterance." How can they be defined independently of what we already know from linguistic analysis, and if they cannot, how are they an advance on current linguistic analysis? I have no objection to the use of the notion of gesture as a place-holder, expressing the conviction that at some level speech production must have a finite set of control entities. However, at the present level of development of the concept, I do not see how it can have explanatory status in a view of how *perception* occurs.

This conclusion, that the concept of gesture has not yet been satisfactorily defined, is obviously at variance with Fowler and Rosenblum's contention that ". . . the evidence that perceivers recover phonetic gestures in speech perception is incontravertible." (For a controversy regarding this question, see Diehl & Kluender (1989) and attendant commentary). They present an extremely variegated set of results intended to support this extreme claim. These results range from old examples often used as evidence for the motor theory by Liberman and his colleagues, examples such as the [di]-[du] and [slɪt]-[splɪt], examples through perception of intonation and the McGurk effect to the ability to do rapid shadowing. I only have space here to respond very briefly to most of the examples. I find none of them force me to conclude that gestures must be perceived, especially in the face of the definitional problems I have already outlined. Some of the arguments are dealt with elsewhere. Lindblom (chapter 2 this volume) has suggested that F2–F3 relations could form the basis for invariant auditory categorization of stop consonants with the same place of articulation (including [di] and [du]). Kluender Diehl, and Killeen (1987) have shown that the Japanese Quail can form an equivalence group for [d]-vowel syllables including [di] and [du]. The complementary relation between silence and formant transitions in cueing the [slɪt]-[splɪt] distinction could be learned from auditory experience. The perception of "da" when presented with an optical [ga] and an auditory [ba] seems contradictory to the gestural theory as neither of the distal objects represented in the stimuli was an apical tongue gesture. The assertion that only gestural perception could allow shadowing with the observed rapidity is unsupported. I can make no brief response to the examples of perception of intonation but would note that the question takes us very far afield, when the central issue of the status of *subsegmental* gestures still seems so undecided.

Another problem with Fowler's direct-realist view, in my opinion, is the lack of evidence for her assumption that a distinction between underlying and surface levels of gestures is not necessary. Fowler's (1986a) view is summarized in the following excerpt:

An event theory of speech production must aim to characterize articulation of phonetic segments as overlapping sets of coordinated gestures, where each set of coordinated gestures conforms to a phonetic segment. By hypothesis, the organization of the vocal tract to produce a phonetic segment is invariant over variation in segmental and suprasegmental contexts. The segment may be realized differently in different contexts—because of competing demands on the articulators made by phonetic segments realized in an overlapping time frame. To the extent that a description of speech production along these lines can be worked out, the possibility remains that phonetic segments are literally uttered and therefore are available to be directly perceived if the acoustic signal is sufficiently informative. (p. 11)

Fowler appealed to the "task dynamic" approach to speech production (See Kelso, Saltzman, & Tuller, 1986, for a review of this approach) to provide evidence for her view that a distinction between surface and underlying levels is unnecessary. This approach is not in fact supportive of Fowler's position, as it involves a distinction between an underlying level of goal specification and a set of realization procedures. However, neither is it counterevidence to Fowler's unilevel view, as the choice of two levels was made by Kelso and colleagues on an ad hoc basis (Lindblom & MacNeilage, 1986).

A final problem for gestural theories is that in cases where different speakers of a single language produce a given distinction with different gestures, listeners ought to hear different gestures, but to my knowledge this does not occur. For example, in English, bunched [r] and retroflex [r] are considered to have equivalent status, as do apical [s] and laminal [s]. In my classes, I usually find about as many people use apical [s] as laminal [s]. (If gestures are innate, why is there such redundancy in the gestural inventory?) Presumably each variant differs acoustically in subtle ways from the other, but as the linguistically important factor is that *both* variants are distinct from the other sounds of the language, such differences are not salient to the listener. Auditory similarity is, therefore, presumably more important than gestural dissimilarity. Diehl and Kluender (1989) point out other cases in which auditory and gestural aspects of production go their separate ways, and the language system goes with the auditory dimension.

At this stage of the development of both the Motor Theory and the Direct Realist Theory, it would be extremely desirable, if predictions could be made based specifically on the respective gesture concepts. (Incidentally, I applaud the rather conclusive test of the Motor Theory prediction regarding duplex perception of nonspeech sounds, reported by Fowler and Rosenblum.) These predictions should be sufficient to allow a choice between the two uses of the gesture concept and a choice between gestural theories of perception and more orthodox theories based on conceptions of auditory function. Focal points from the standpoint of speech *production* would be the claim of the Motor Theory that the gestures are innate, and the claim of the Direct Realist Theory that there is only one level of gesture production. In the absence of such predictions, I see a continuation of the present confusing theoretical situation in this area—a situation not profitable for the field.

Conclusions

In both of the approaches to the theory of speech perception considered here, the Motor Theory and the Direct Realist Theory, a motor entity called the gesture is regarded as a unit of perception. Both approaches share the problem that the concept of gesture has not been adequately explicated, either at the underlying or the surface level of production. The lack of explication at the underlying level is a problem for the Motor Theory as it depends on innate underlying gestures as the control structures for perception. The Revised Motor Theory shares with the old theory the additional problem of not specifying how these structures, which in their opinion are not directly reflected at the surface level of production, are accessed by the perceiver. According to the Direct Realist Theory, a distinction between surface and underlying levels of gestures is not necessary. This claim has not been adequately established, and the primary assumption of the theory, that the gesture is available to the listener at the surface level of production, has not yet been substantiated. At this stage, I believe that it is incumbent upon the proponents of these theories to develop predictions, which, if confirmed, would establish their claims of unique solutions. An alternative, testable view of the status of phonetic gestures in both production and perception,—a view that I find preferable,—is given in chapter 2 of this volume by Lindblom.

Acknowledgments

I thank Randy Diehl, Bjorn Lindblom, and Michael Studdert-Kennedy for comments on this manuscript.

References

Diehl, R. L., & Kluender, K. R. (1989). On the objects of speech perception. *Ecological Psychology, 1,* 121–144.

Folkins, J. W., & Abbs, J. H. (1975). Lip and jaw motor control during speech: Responses to resistive loading of the jaw. *Journal of Speech and Hearing Research, 18,* 207–220.

Fowler, C. A. (1986a). An event approach to the study of speech perception from a direct-realist perspective. *Journal of Phonetics, 14,* 3–28.

Fowler, C. A. (1986b). Reply to commentators. *Journal of Phonetics, 14,* 149–170.

Kelso, J. A. S., Saltzman, E. L., & Tuller, B. (1986). The dynamical perspective on speech production: Data and theory. *Journal of Phonetics, 14,* 29–60.

Kluender, K. R., Diehl, R., & Killeen, P. R. (1987). Japanese quail can learn phonetic categories. *Science, 237,* 1195–1197.

Liberman, A. M., Cooper, F. S., Harris, K., & MacNeilage, P. F. (1962). A motor theory of speech perception. In *Proceedings of the Speech Communication Seminar.*(Vol. 2, D3) Stockholm: Royal Institute of Technology.

Liberman, A. M., & Mattingly, I. G. (1985). The motor theory of speech perception revised. *Cognition, 21,* 1–36.

Lindblom, B., & MacNeilage, P. F. (1986). Action theory: Problems and alternative approaches. *Journal of Phonetics, 14,* 117–132.

MacNeilage, P. F. (1970). Motor control of serial ordering of speech. *Psychological Review, 77,* 182–196.

MacNeilage, P. F. (1972). Speech physiology. In J. H. Gilbert (Ed.), *Speech and cortical functioning* (pp. 1–72). New York: Academic Press.

MacNeilage, P. F., Rootes, T. P., & Chase, R. A. (1967). Speech production and perception in a patient with severe impairment of somesthetic perception and motor control. *Journal of Speech and Hearing Research, 10,* 449–467.

MacNeilage, P. F., & Sholes, G. N. (1964). An electromyographic study of the tongue during speech production. *Journal of Speech and Hearing Research, 7,* 209–232.

Mattingly, I. G., & Liberman, A. M. (1988). Specialized perceiving systems for speech and other biologically significant sounds. In G. M. Edelman, W. E. Gall, & W. M. Cowan (Eds.), *Auditory function: The neurological bases of hearing* (pp. 775–792). New York: Wiley.

Pick, H. L., & Saltzman, E. (Eds.) (1978). *Modes of perceiving and processing information.* Hillsdale, NJ: Lawrence Erlbaum Associates.

Chapter 4
_____

Ontogeny of Phonetic Gestures: Speech Production

Marilyn May Vihman
Haverford College

Abstract

Each child must work out the speech gestures and their relation to acoustic patterns anew based on feed-back from his or her own production practice or babbling as well as on perception of the speech of others. Evidence that this is the case may be derived from three types of differences across first language learners.

1. Deaf infants differ from normally hearing infants at least from the onset of canonical babbling, which is considerably delayed and inconsistent in the hearing-impaired.

2. Individual children learning the same language show the greatest differences in many phonetic categories in the prelinguistic stage. As early words begin to be used, the influence of the language being learned exerts a unifying pressure on the infants' productions. Repeated syllable production in babbling leads to the development of articulatory plans (or "vocal motor schemes") particular to each child. These plans underlie the subsequent development of unique word production strategies, which reflect an intersection of phonetic preferences and ambient language constraints. The choice of words to produce reflects the matching of adult word targets as globally perceived against the child's pre-existing vocal motor schemes.

3. Differences across infants learning different languages are apparent at least from the beginnings of word production, again reflecting the influence of particular linguistic inventories and structures on the child's development of a repertoire of speech patterns.

Consider two sharply contrasting views as to the origin of phonetic gestures. On the one hand, the gestures are said to be genetically specified and special to speech with, as Liberman & Mattingly (1985) wrote, a "biologically based link between perception and production" (p. 6). On the other hand, each infant is seen as having to rediscover the relevant gestures through attention to the speech of others (Boysson-Bardies, Halle, Sagart, & Durand, 1989). In what follows, I will marshal evidence from infant vocal production to support a slightly modified version of the second, constructivist position: I will claim that each child must work out the speech gestures and their relation to acoustic patterns anew, based in the **first** instance on feed-back from the child's own production practice or babble and, secondarily, on perception of the speech of others. Crucial evidence in defense of either of the alternative positions is difficult to come by. The constructivist or cognitive position has been defended elsewhere, notably in Menn (1983) and Macken and Ferguson (1983), with evidence based largely on word phonology. I will restrict myself here to the earliest signs of influence from the environment, beginning with the emergence of canonical babbling and extending only as late as the development of a small lexicon. I will draw on three kinds of differences among first-language learners: a) deaf vs. hearing infants, b) individual children learning the same language, and c) children learning different languages.

Differences between Deaf and Hearing Infants

Until recently, the rare studies of deaf infants' vocalizations involved few subjects, chiefly because of the difficulty of reliably identifying hearing loss within the first months of life. Early studies suggested that deaf infants babble similarly to hearing infants but with a decrease in volubility over time. More recent investigators (e.g., Gilbert, 1982) have been critical of the data and the "myth . . . that deaf infants babble until six months and then their babbling decreases" (p. 511). Recent studies by Oller (1986) and Stoel-Gammon (1988) and their colleagues (Stoel-Gammon & Otomo, 1986; Oller, Eilers, Bull, & Carney, 1985; Oller & Eilers, 1988) have included longitudinal data collection and detailed discussion of the origin, timing, and gravity of their subjects' hearing impairment as well as individual rather than group results, and these studies reflect concern for careful operational definitions of "babbling," "age of onset," and other analytic categories. They come to the common conclusion that babbling in deaf infants differs both quantitatively and qualitatively from that of normally hearing infants.

Oller and Eilers (1988) stated clearly the issue that interests us here:

> If deaf infants babble in the same way and at the same age as their hearing counterparts, it would suggest that humans are born with a phonetic inheritance that unfolds without extensive auditory experience. On the other hand, if deaf infants'

vocalizations differ from those of hearing infants, it would suggest that auditory experience plays an important role in the timely emergence of speech-like sounds. (p. 441)

Oller and Eilers are at pains to define "babbling" in terms of consonant production. They take the occurrence of a .2 ratio of CV or VC syllables to total utterances to represent an operational definition of the canonical babbling stage, which applies in hearing infants at any point after the emergence of the first CV syllables. They emphasized (Oller & Eilers, 1988) that "the onset of the Canonical Stage is critical because it represents the point at which infants produce mature phonetic sequences (syllables) that can function as the phonetic building blocks of words" (pp. 441f).

Given this definition in terms of canonical syllable production, Oller and Eilers' results, based on longitudinal data from 9 singly handicapped deaf infants, are clear-cut. Whereas the 21 hearing infants in their study entered the canonical babbling stage at 6–10 months (mode: 7 months), the range for the deaf children was 11–25 months, despite early amplification and speech stimulation. Several of the deaf infants failed to produce canonical syllables in some samples after the onset of syllable production had been identified by clinical staff as well as parents. Analysis of the babbling ratio in six deaf infants 5 to 6 months after onset of canonical syllable production showed that just 3 produced vocalizations falling within the same range as hearing infants (see Fig. 4.1), with .7–.9 canonical syllables per utterance; these infants showed the beginnings of speech communication as well, whereas the remaining three did not.

Stoel-Gammon and Otomo (1986) compared variety of consonant types and proportion of multisyllabic sequences involving the use of true consonants (excluding glides, [h], and glottal stop) in normally hearing and hearing-impaired infants (six followed longitudinally from ages ranging from 4 to 11 months). The hearing-impaired produced fewer consonant types per session and showed a clear decrease in types used over time, whereas the normally hearing showed an increase. The hearing-impaired used a lower proportion of multisyllabic utterances, and some used no true consonants, whereas proportionate use of true consonants in multisyllabic utterances increased over time for the normally hearing. It is notable that in their more heterogenous hearing-impaired sample, Stoel-Gammon and Otomo reported that even subjects with moderate hearing loss performed differently than hearing subjects, and for those subjects who experienced a sudden hearing loss due to illness, "normal prelinguistic and early linguistic development is not only arrested . . . but . . . reverts to patterns resembling those predominating at earlier stages of development" (1986, p. 40). The divergence between impaired and normally hearing infants with respect to consonant-type use was first evident at 6 to 8 months.

In the recent literature on the differences between hearing and deaf infants, the focus on consonantal production is unmistakable. It seems reasonable to con-

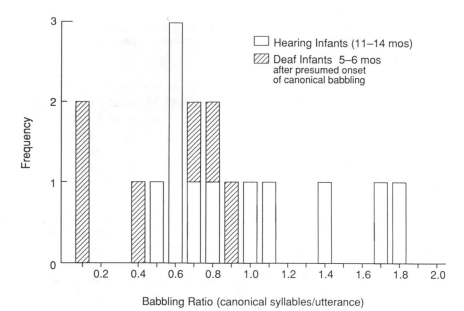

FIG. 4.1.   Babbling in canonical stage deaf and hearing infants. Adapted from Oller & Eilers (1988), with permission.

clude that auditory input is essential for the normal timely development of a repertoire of adult-like syllables including consonantal margins. The fact that at least some deaf infants do eventually enter the canonical stage of vocal production may be ascribed to the slow accumulation of relevant knowledge based on an extended period of limited auditory exposure.

Ample data are available to support the regularity of emergence of consonantal vocalizations among normal children, the ease and reliability with which this milestone may be identified (even by the untrained), and the steady increase in true consonant use throughout the period of transition to speech, both across different language groups and as viewed through widely varying methodological lenses (cf. Holmgren, Lindblom, Aurelius, Jalling, & Zetterström, 1986, and Roug, Landberg, & Lundberg, 1989 [Swedish], Koopmans-van Beinum & Van der Stelt, 1986 [Dutch], Kent & Murray, 1982, and Vihman, Ferguson, & Elbert, 1986 [English]). The embeddedness of canonical syllable production in a pre-occurring vocal rhythmicity has been demonstrated as well (Bickley, Lindblom, & Roug, 1986). The role of language input in leading the child to produce more consonantal vocalizations may be inferred from Vihman and Miller (1988), who showed that inclusion of at least one consonant is a stable feature of the majority of the children's early words. Finally, the important role played by consonantal production in language development may be inferred from the correlation of diversity and relative frequency of consonant use with lexical advance (McCune

& Vihman, 1987) and with later phonological advance (Vihman & Greenlee, 1987).

Differences among Children Learning the Same Language

The greatest differences in the use of many phonetic categories are found in the prelinguistic stage for children learning the same language (Vihman et al., 1986; cf. also Oller et al., 1985). For example, large standard deviations were found to obtain for 10 American children in relative frequency of use of different places of articulation and of true consonants in half-hour sessions in which no more than four different words were used spontaneously ("0-word" and "4-word" sampling points) (Vihman et al., 1986). In later sessions, in which a significantly larger number of words were used ("15-" and "25-word" points, corresponding to cumulative lexicons of 30–50 words altogether, by maternal account), the standard deviation dropped, which was taken to reflect the unifying influence of the common language being learned. Given the pattern of increasing uniformity with increasing lexical use, Vihman and colleagues predicted that the overall level of use of the phonetic categories analyzed would obtain at least at the early stages for children learning languages other than English.

The international Cross-linguistic Project on Infant Vocalizations, which was undertaken to test this and other hypotheses regarding early consonant use in four languages—English, French, Japanese, and Swedish, has reported data supporting this prediction (Boysson-Bardies & Vihman, in press). American, French and Japanese children all showed high levels of use of labials at the 0-word point, with a decrease in variability once adult word use had become established (25-word point). This increasing uniformity can be interpreted as reflecting two factors: (1) The common occurrence of labials in the adult language (the children acquiring Swedish, which has the least initial labials in target words, showed a lower level of use at 0-words and only a slight drop in variability by 25-words); (2) the visibility of labial articulation, which facilitates the mastery of word-shapes including labials (note the absence of labial bias in the early word phonology of blind children: Mulford, 1988, and the disproportionate use by hearing-impaired children: Smith, 1982, Stoel-Gammon, 1989). But how is the wide phonetic variability across children learning the same language brought into greater uniformity as the children's lexical output expands?

The relevance of babbling to the beginnings of speech production has to my mind nowhere been more clearly articulated than in Fry (1966). Fry began by noting that "when babbling is well-established, the utterances are characterized by frequent repetitions of the same syllable or sound. . . . The child is now uttering sounds for the pleasure they give him" (p. 188). (Fry's use of the term "babbling" may be taken to mean canonical and variegated babble, as described by Oller, 1980, and Stark, 1980.) Repeated babbling production or "practice" is essential for two reasons. First, as Fry (1966) wrote, it enables the child to explore "the possibilities inherent in the phonatory and articulatory muscle systems" (p. 189). In particular, Fry (1966) explained:

> The child is "getting the idea" of combining the action of the larynx with the movements of the articulators, of controlling to some extent the larynx frequency, of using the outgoing airstream to produce different kinds of articulation, and also the idea, which is quite important, of producing the same sound again by repeating the movements. (p. 189)

Second, this practice leads the child to establish an auditory feedback loop. Fry (1966) wrote:

> As sound-producing movements are repeated and repeated, a strong link is forged between tactual and kinesthetic impressions and the auditory sensations that the child receives from his own utterances. (p. 189)

The pleasure the child derives from the "sense of movement" experienced in babbling is enhanced by the accompanying auditory sensations (and perhaps by the predictability of their return, which may afford a sense of power or control).

In Fry's account, therefore, we see that it is in the practice gained through babbling that the child gradually begins to be able to produce certain sounds, syllables, and sequences of syllables at will. McCune and Vihman (1987) suggested that children through their babble:

> Establish a limited range of intentional vocal patterns prior to word use, with strong individual differences in the segmental basis of these patterns. . . . [These vocal motor schemes are] motor acts which are performed intentionally and are capable of variation and combination to form larger units. (p. 72)

(cf. also Locke, 1986: "Movement patterns that are frequent in babbling are available for speaking" p. 243.) In other words, within the bounds of broad physiological constraints (e.g., relatively great use of the more easily mastered stop, nasal, and glide gestures as compared with fricatives and liquids; more common production of open, CV syllables than of either final consonants or clusters as in Locke, 1983), each child develops a unique set of vocal motor schemes or particular repeated phonetic patterns ("favorite sounds" in Ferguson, 1979) stumbled on and then repeated in the course of articulatory exploration in babbling.

How do children put to good use their newly achieved mastery over a small number of phonetic plans? It has been established that the phonetic characteristics of a given child's early words will be highly similar to that child's contemporaneous babble (Vihman, Macken, Miller, Simmons, & Miller, 1985).

McCune and Vihman traced the origins of early word production strategies to vocal motor schemes pre-established in babbling by two highly vocal subjects. One subject, Aislinn, made unusually high proportionate use of the glide yod as early as the 9 and 10 month sessions with which analysis began (57% of her vocalizations included a syllable-initial yod; over all 8 sessions analyzed, sylla-ble-initial yod occurred in 13% of her vocalizations as compared to a mean for 9 other subjects of 5%). In the following months, related patterns including the same palatal gesture appeared (vowel + i-offglide, palatalized consonants, disyl-lables ending in [i]). These palatal articulations formed the basis for an articulato-ry pattern that dominated her word production (affecting 75%–85% of her word tokens from 13 months on, when word use was well established). At 14 months, for example, all four well-practiced manifestations of the palatal gesture were represented in her words:

- use of yod: *lady* → [jeiji]
- use of palatal consonants: *mommy* → [maːɲi]
- use of Vi: *eye, hi, bye*
- use of (CV) Ci: *bunny* → [bæŋːi]

This child chose as word targets a disproportionate number of diminutives (*Er-nie, Bonnie*) and baby-talk words ending in -y (*bunny, daddy, dolly*). McCune and Vihman (1987) wrote:

> We can speculate that these relatively high frequency English words attracted Aislinn because of her favorable predisposition toward palatal patterns, and that it was the interactive match between child scheme and adult phonological structure which produced Aislinn's extremely high frequency pattern. (p. 75)

The other child whose phonological profile was outlined in McCune and Vihman (1987), Molly, made uncommonly high use of final consonants at 12–13 months, when she had reached the 15-word point (23% use, as compared to a mean of 7% across 6 other subjects at that lexical level). Concentration on final consonants evolved at 13 months into phonetic emphasis involving extra-long aspirated release of stops, lengthening of final nasals, and in most cases the addition of a final vowel, [i] or [ə] (see Vihman & Velleman, 1989). The result was word production patterns that overlapped to a remarkable extent with Aislinn's, although arrived at by a very different route: for example, *bang* → [bæŋːi] ∼ [bæini], *clock* → [kakːɪ] (13 months). The prevalence in English of -y- final as well as consonant-final words is no doubt implicated in Molly's development as well as in Aislinn's.

Whereas Aislinn targeted many words that exhibit a palatal pattern in the adult language, Molly seemed to seek out consonant-final words to produce. How are we to interpret such phonological selection of word targets (a phenomenon reported in Ferguson, Peizer, & Weeks, 1973, and Ferguson & Farwell, 1975, further explored in Shibamoto & Olmsted, 1978, and experimentally confirmed by Schwartz & Leonard, 1982)? Recall Fry's account of the development of an auditory feedback loop or link between repeatedly practiced babble patterns and their acoustic consequences. We have observed that each child develops, in the months following the onset of canonical babbling, a small repertoire of phonetic patterns reproducible at will. At 9 or 10 months, or whenever adult words first begin to be responded to with comprehension, the child may be supposed to be using global recognition patterns (Jusczyk, 1986) to discriminate a small number of situationally and/or affectively salient words. At some point thereafter, the child will notice that some of these interesting words are not, in his or her broadly sketched recognitory scheme at least, distinct from some one of the child's own familiar articulatory schemes or potential production plans (Vihman & Miller, 1988). (See also Locke's (1986) suggestion that children at the early stage of word production "consult their store of available articulations in search of the closest matches" p. 241.) To use less conscious-sounding, metalinguistic terminology, we can state the same idea in Piagetian sensorimotor terms: Once a "circular reaction" has been established (i.e., Fry's auditory feedback loop), such that upon producing a sequence [baba], the child is stimulated to repeat it, the way is open: a) for the sound of an adult word such as *baby, bottle,* or *bye-bye* to produce the same effect, resulting in apparent imitation; and eventually b) for objects and events associated with those word forms to stimulate spontaneous production of the same phonetic sequence.

This would provide a plausible developmental origin for the perception-production link, creating "perceptual units of imitation"—or of production model-

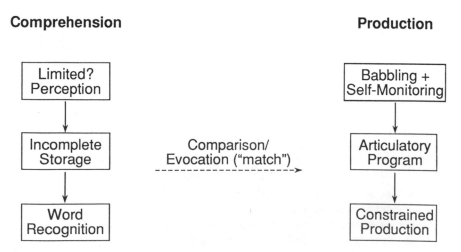

Comprehension   **Production**

Limited? Perception		Babbling + Self-Monitoring
Incomplete Storage	Comparison/ Evocation ("match")	Articulatory Program
Word Recognition		Constrained Production

FIG. 4.2.   Comprehension and production of early words.

led on adult targets—which, as Studdert-Kennedy (1987) wrote: "specify functional units of motor control, corresponding to actions of the articulators" (p. 71). According to this model, the child will actually attempt to produce an adult form only when it matches one of the child's more common babbled vocalizations, or is similar enough to evoke such a form. Thus, only words resembling the child's repertoire would be attempted. Figure 4.2 illustrates the proposed relationship between perception and production. The resulting early word forms, in addition to reflecting the particular inventory of sounds and syllables developed by the child, are typically quite accurate (Ferguson & Farwell, 1975; Vihman, 1987), the adult models as well as the child forms being restricted for the most part to simple syllable shapes and a small number of stops, nasals, and glides.

Differences across Children Learning Different Languages

Attempts to distinguish the vocalizations of infants from different language environments have been relatively unsuccessful (see the discouraging review in Locke, 1983, and also the negative results in Thevenin, Eilers, Oller, & La Voie, 1985). Perceptual judgments and the results of phonetic analyses were reportedly nonrandom in some studies, tending toward discrimination but without reaching statistical significance. In general, the categories on which children could be expected to differ, given differences in adult languages, are of low incidence in child vocalizations. Based on a phonetic comparison of the babbling of 12-month-old Spanish- and English-learning infants, Oller and Eilers (1982) concluded that "differences may be hard to find in the light of overwhelming similarities and rare production of non-universal phonetic elements" (p. 575), such as consonant clusters, final consonants, or fricatives.

To the extent that differences have appeared in the *earliest* babbling samples tested, those from infants less than a year old, they have typically involved prosody, or differences in intonation and largygeal production and control. Boysson-Bardies, Sagart, and Durand (1984) conducted two experiments using paired samples of babbling data from French and Arabic subjects. They suggest that the first language-specific differences in vocal production involve phonation types (expiratory respiration only in the French samples, rapidly alternated sequences of inspiratory and expiratory phonation in the Arabic) and in the organization of pitch and intensity contours (rhythmical weak–strong contrasts characterized the Arabic babbling only).

Boysson-Bardies and her colleagues also carried out instrumental analyses of possible cross-linguistic effects on vowel production at 10 months. Children learning French, English, Cantonese and Arabic were sampled. Plotting F1 and F2 values for each of the children yielded significantly stronger differences across children of differing ambient languages than within-language groups; the direction of the differences were shown to be characteristic of the respective ambient languages (Boysson-Bardies et al., 1989). These results may be taken to mean that global aspects of lip and tongue-root placement—that is, the "base of articulation" of the language—are adopted by infants in the course of the first year of life. This broad phonetic preadaptation would not generally affect infant consonant production, which has so far been shown to fall within universally specifiable limits in the first year, regardless of ambient language. (See, for example, the impressively consistent documentation of VOT, which appears to be set at "short lag," or voiceless unaspirated, in the majority of vocal productions of 12-month-old infants from a variety of linguistic backgrounds as reported by Preston, Yeni-Komshian, Stark, & Port, 1969; Enstrom, 1982; Eilers, Oller, & Benito-Garcia, 1984).

In the prelinguistic period there is, thus, some evidence of broad prosodic and phonatory differences across infants from different ambient languages. There is also evidence for a differing use of vowel space, although at the level of phonetic transcription of individual vowels, the differences have not been shown to reach significance (Oller & Eilers, 1982).

The likelihood of identifying cross-linguistic phonetic differences in early words and the babble vocalizations that co-occur with them has not been rejected on theoretical grounds, but it has not heretofore been specifically investigated, and the failure of adult judges to discriminate at a statistically significant level between the babbling of own- and other-language-learning infants even as late as 18 months (e.g., Atkinson, MacWhinney, & Stoel, 1968) casts doubt on the enterprise. Although such a finding may be seen as irrelevant to Brown's (1958) notion of "pre-linguistic" babbling drift, it is nevertheless of considerable independent interest in relation to the issues of the timing and nature of the earliest environmental influences on vocal production.

In addition to the results on consonant use referred to earlier, the Cross-linguistic Project on Infant Vocalizations also investigated the distribution of words of differing lengths. At this point analysis of the adult targets and child word production tokens is complete for the American, French and Japanese data. The results are shown in Table 1. Group means are characteristic: English target words are predominately monosyllabic, while disyllables dominate both French and Japanese targets. Polysyllabic targets are notably more frequent in the Japanese than in the English or French data. In production some differences are muted, with closer to even production of monosyllables and disyllables by French subjects and a higher mean for polysyllabic productions than for targets by all groups. The mean proportion of polysyllables produced by Japanese subjects is higher than that produced by the other groups. Furthermore, as a child-by-child comparison of polysyllabic targets and polysyllabic productions suggests, the Japanese long word tokens typically reflect long adult words (e.g., *oumachan*

Table 4.1
Distribution of Vocalization Length in Syllables (in percent).*

Adult word targets

American subjects

	Deborah	Emily	Molly	Sean	Timmy	mean
1	54	54	63	67	57	59
2	39	42	32	25	38	35
3+	7	4	6	8	5	5

French subjects

	Carole	Charles	Laurent	Marie	Noel	mean
1	26	37	25	17	34	25
2	72	62	72	68	66	68
3+	3	1	3	15	—	4

Japanese subjects

	Atsuko	Emi	Haruo	Kenji	Taro	mean
1	13	22	16	17	18	17
2	57	71	66	78	70	68
3+	30	7	18	5	12	14

Child productions

American subjects

	Deborah	Emily	Molly	Sean	Timmy	mean
1	52	51	51	74	40	54
2	40	40	42	19	48	38
3+	8	9	7	8	12	9

French subjects

	Carole	Charles	Laurent	Marie	Noel	mean
1	34	46	27	25	37	34
2	55	54	56	48	59	54
3+	11	—	17	28	4	12

Japanese subjects

	Atsuko	Emi	Haruo	Kenji	Taro	mean
1	14	35	18	21	30	24
2	52	64	60	70	61	61
3+	34	1	22	9	9	15

*All data based on 2 sessions each at the 4- and 15-word points and one session at the 25-word point, except for Emi, whose family returned to Japan after the first 15-word session. 1, 2, and 3+ indicate words of one, two, and three or more syllables, respectively.

'Mr. horsie', *owatchatta* 'it's over, all done', *oheso* 'navel', *ototo* 'fish'), whereas most of the long word tokens produced by American or French subjects involve "babbled" mono- or disyllabic words, such as *piggy-piggy-piggy* or *lapin-(la)pin* 'bunny-bunny'. Thus, word tokens reveal production differences, while adult target words suggest the origins of these differences in aspects of the structure of the adult language being acquired.

A Puzzle Regarding Perception

Little has been said here so far about the relation of perception to production in the period of transition to speech. Infant perceptual abilities are well known by now to be remarkable. In particular, they are far superior to that of adult speakers in dealing with nonnative contrasts (Trehub, 1976; Werker, Gilbert, Humphrey & Tees, 1981). A recent study by Werker and Tees (1984) suggested that the changeover from the infant's apparently universal discriminatory powers to the adult's pre-structured perceptual processing, which is heavily influenced by the phonological demands made by the language(s) acquired early in life, begins at around 11 months.

MacKain (1988) has explored some of the paradoxes involved in attempting to relate these results regarding early developmental changes in perception to current ideas about the origins of early (productive) lexical development, especially the view that the word, not the segment, is the unit around which early phonology is organized (Ferguson & Farwell, 1975; Ferguson, 1978, 1986). Specifically, she argued that because the evidence for experiential effects on perception toward the end of the first year of life was found through testing with nonsense syllables, the perceptual shift must be characterized as occurring on the level of the segment or syllable, not the word. She drew the conclusion (MacKain, 1988) that phonological organization of perceptual contrasts develops "quasi-independently" and in parallel with whole-word recognition in early lexical development, each being as follows:

> Directed toward distinctive teleological endpoints. At the phonetic-phonological level, the aim is to develop a system of phonemic relations and economize attention by limiting it to those attributes of speech which function phonologically, while at the lexical level the aim is to reproduce the word. (p. 56f)

She found parallel development of phonemic and lexical perceptual processing to be a way to reconcile Werker and Tees' (1984) results with Studdert-Kennedy's (1986) view of words as "sequential and coordinated articulatory gestures [which] can be reproduced without a concept of phonemic relations or an articulatory program in which individual segments are concatenated" (p. 58).

Alternatively, we may wonder just how the older, nondiscriminating infants in Werker and Tees' study processed the nonsense syllables on which they were tested. At 11 months or so, given normal babbling production and articulatory development, they may be supposed to have each begun to favor a particular subset of the articulatory gestures used in language, with perhaps a broad bias toward the prosodic and vocalic values characteristic of their language. Whereas at 8 or 9 months they were still able to process nonsense syllables naively, having as yet no investment in production so to speak, by 11 months they may be supposed to have begun the process of matching patterns heard against the vocal motor schemes they were constructing. The alien Hindi and Salish sounds could not be meaningfully processed at this point. Possibly sounds occurring in English but not yet available in the child's repertoire of articulatory gestures would have proven equally difficult to discriminate. The processing of the rarely occurring Hindi retroflex and Salish glottalized sounds by infants raised with those languages poses a problem for this account: Did such difficult and rare sounds occur in the productive repertoire of those infants at such an early age? Unfortunately, only three of five such infants proved amenable to testing; Werker and Tees did not mention whether the two (Salish) Thompson infants they located were among the three tested. Further work directly comparing production and perception in the same infants would undoubtedly shed some much-needed light on these issues.

Conclusions

To recapitulate briefly, differences between deaf and hearing children with regard to the onset of CV syllable production strongly suggest that the child requires both current and cumulative auditory experience to begin to build a system of articulatory plans. Differences between children learning the same language reveal a striking accord between preferred sound patterns produced in babbling and preferred forms of adult words to attempt to produce, as well as the child's own earliest word forms. This accord, along with the general tendency for wide variability at the outset of word production to be tamed with respect to most phonetic categories into relative uniformity by the time a 50-word lexicon has been achieved, I take to reflect the relevance of the child's knowledge of his or her own vocal motor schemes to the construction of viable word production patterns.

Production differences across children learning different languages, derived from the unitary system underlying early word production and contemporaneous babble, are a secondary reflection of the perceptible differences in target word characteristics as filtered through the infants' constrained productive capacities. Finally, the changeover from broad auditory or phonetic perceptual capacities to the more limited, prestructured perception characteristic of older language users I am tempted to interpret as reflecting the new relevance of the perception-production link the child constructs toward the end of the first year.

References

Atkinson, K., MacWhinney, B., & Stoel, C.(1968). *An experiment on the recognition of babbling* (Working Paper No. 14). Berkeley: University of California, Language Behavior Research Laboratory.

Bickley, C., Lindblom, B., & Roug, L. (1986). Acoustic measures of rhythm in infants' babbling, or "All God's Children Got Rhythm." *Twelfth International Congress of Acoustics* (Vol. 1, pp. A6-4). Toronto: Canadian Acoustical Society.

Brown, R. (1958). *Words and things*. Glencoe, IL: Free Press.

Boysson-Bardies, B. de, Halle, P., Sagart, L., & Durand, C. (1989). A cross-linguistic investigation of vowel formants in babbling. *Journal of Child Language, 16*, 1–17.

Boysson-Bardies, B. de, Sagart, L., & Durand, C. (1984). Discernible differences in the babbling of infants according to target language. *Journal of Child Language, 11*, 1–15.

Boysson-Bardies, B. de, & Vihman, M. M. (in press). Material evidence of infant selection from the target language: A cross-linguistic perspective. To appear in C. A. Ferguson, L. Menn, & C. Stoel-Gammon (Eds.), Phonological development: Models, research, implications. Parkton, MD: York Press.

Eilers, R. E., Oller, D. K., & Benito-Garcia, C. R. (1984). The acquisition of voicing contrast in Spanish and English learning infants and children: A longitudinal study. *Journal of Child Language, 11*, 313–336.

Enstrom, D. H. (1982). Infant labial, apical, and velar stop productions: A voice onset time analysis. *Phonetica, 39*, 47–60.

Ferguson, C. A. (1978). Learning to pronounce: The earliest stages of phonological development in the child. In F. D. Minifie & L. L. Lloyd (Eds.), *Communicative and cognitive abilities—early behavioral assessment* (pp. 273–297). Baltimore, MD: University Park Press.

Ferguson, C. A. (1979). Phonology as an individual access system: Some data from language acquisition. In C. J. Fillmore, D. Kempler, & W. S-Y. Wang (Eds.), *Individual differences in language ability and language behavior* (pp. 189–201). New York: Academic Press.

Ferguson, C. A. (1986). Discovering sound units and constructing sound systems: It's child's play. In J. S. Perkell & D. H. Klatt (Eds.), *Invariance and variability of speech processes* (pp. 36–51). Hillsdale, NJ: Lawrence Erlbaum Associates.

Ferguson, C. A., & Farwell, C. B. (1975). Words and sounds in early language acquisition. *Language, 15*, 419–439.

Ferguson, C. A., Peizer, D. B., & Weeks, T. A. (1973). Model-and-replica phonological grammar of a child's first words. *Lingua, 3*, 35–65.

Fry, D. B. (1966). The development of the phonological system in the normal and the deaf child. In F. Smith & G. Miller (Eds.), *The genesis of language: A psycholinguistic approach* (pp. 187–206). Cambridge, MA: MIT Press.

Gilbert, J. H. V. (1982). Babbling and the deaf child: A commentary on Lenneberg et al. (1965) and Lenneberg (1967). *Journal of Child Language, 9*, 511–515.

Holmgren, K., Lindblom, B., Aurelius, G., Jalling, B., & Zetterström, R. (1986). On the phonetics of infant vocalization. In B. Lindblom & R. Zetterström (Eds.), *Precursors of early speech* (pp. 51–66). Basingstoke, Hampshire: MacMillan.

Jusczyk, P. W. (1986). Toward a model of the development of speech perception. In J. S. Perkell & D. H. Klatt (Eds.), *Invariance and variability of speech processes* (pp. 1–19). Hillsdale, NJ: Lawrence Erlbaum Associates.

Kent, R. D., & Murray, A. D. (1982). Acoustic features of infant vocalic utterances at 3, 6, and 9 months. *Journal of the Acoustical Society of America, 72,* 353–365.

Koopmans-van Beinum, F. J., & Van der Stelt, J. M. (1986). Early stages in the development of speech movements. In B. Lindblom & R. Zetterström (Eds.), *Precursors of early speech* (pp. 37–50). Basingstoke, Hampshire: MacMillan.

Liberman, A. M., & Mattingly, I. G. (1985). The motor theory of speech perception revised. *Cognition, 21,* 1–36.

Locke, J. L. (1983). *Phonological acquisition and change.* New York: Academic Press.

Locke, J. L. (1986). Speech perception and the emergent lexicon: An ethological approach. In P. Fletcher & M. Garman (Eds.), *Language acquisition* (2nd ed., pp. 240–250). Cambridge: The University Press.

McCune, L., & Vihman, M. (1987). Vocal motor schemes. *Papers and Reports on Child Language Development, 26,* 72–79.

MacKain, K. S. (1988). Filling the gap between speech and language. In M. D. Smith & J. L. Locke (Eds.), *The emergent lexicon: The child's development of a linguistic vocabulary* (pp. 51–74). New York: Academic Press.

Macken, M. A., & Ferguson, C. A. (1983). Cognitive aspects of phonological development: Model, evidence and issues. In K. E. Nelson (Ed.), *Children's language, 4,* 255–282. Hillsdale, NJ: Lawrence Erlbaum Associates.

Menn, L. (1983). Development of articulatory, phonetic, and phonological capabilities. In B. Butterworth (Ed.), *Language Production, 2,* 3–50. London: Academic Press.

Mulford, R. (1988). First words of the blind child. In M. D. Smith & J. L. Locke (Eds.), *The emergent lexicon: The child's development of a linguistic vocabulary* (pp. 293–338). New York: Academic Press.

Oller, D. K. (1980). The emergence of the sounds of speech in infancy. In G. Yeni-Komshian, J. Kavanagh, & C. A. Ferguson (Eds.), *Child phonology, 2. Production* (pp. 93–112). New York: Academic Press.

Oller, D. K. (1986). Metaphonology and infant vocalizations. In B. Lindblom & R. Zetterström (Eds.), *Precursors of early speech* (pp. 21–36). Basingstoke, Hampshire: MacMillan.

Oller, D. K., & Eilers, R. E. (1982). Similarity of babbling in Spanish- and English-learning babies. *Journal of Child Language, 9,* 565–577.

Oller, D. K., & Eilers, R. E. (1988). The role of audition in infant babbling. *Child Development, 59,* 441–449.

Oller, D. K., Eilers, R. E., Bull, D. H., & Carney, A. E. (1985). Pre-speech vocalizations of a deaf infant: A comparison with normal metaphonological development. *Journal of Speech and Hearing Research, 28,* 47–63.

Preston, M. S., Yeni-Komshian, G. H., Stark, R. E., & Port, D. K. (1969, April). *Certain aspects of the development of speech production and perception in children.* Paper presented at the 77th Meeting of the Acoustical Society of America.

Roug, L., Landberg, I., & Lundberg, L.-H. (1989). Phonetic development in early infancy: A study of four Swedish children during the first 18 months of life. *Journal of Child Language, 16,* 19–40.

Schwartz, R., & Leonard, L. B. (1982). Do children pick and choose? An examination of phonological selection and avoidance in early lexical acquisition. *Journal of Child Language, 9,* 319–336.

Shibamoto, J. S., & Olmsted, D. L. (1978). Lexical and syllabic patterns in phonological acquisition. *Journal of Child Language, 5,* 417–456.

Smith, B. L. (1982). Some observations concerning pre-meaningful vocalizations of hearing-impaired infants. *Journal of Speech and Hearing Disorders, 47,* 439–442.

Stark, R. (1980). Stages of speech development in the first year of life. In G. Yeni-Komshian, J. Kavanagh, & C. A. Ferguson (Eds.), *Child phonology, 2. Production* (pp. 73–92). New York: Academic Press.

Stoel-Gammon, C. (1988). Prelinguistic vocalizations of hearing-impaired and normally hearing subjects: A comparison of consonantal inventories. *Journal of Speech and Hearing Disorders, 53*, 302–315.

Stoel-Gammon, C., & Otomo, K. (1986). Babbling development of hearing-impaired and normally hearing subjects. *Journal of Speech and Hearing Disorders, 51*, 33–41.

Studdert-Kennedy, M. (1986). Sources of variability in early speech development. In J. S. Perkell & D. H. Klatt (Eds.), *Invariance and variability of speech processes* (pp. 58–76). Hillsdale, NJ: Lawrence Erlbaum Associates.

Studdert-Kennedy, M. (1987). The phoneme as a perceptuo-motor structure. In A. Allport, D. MacKay, W. Prinz, & E. Scheerer (Eds.), *Language perception and production* (pp. 67–84). New York: Academic Press.

Thevenin, D. M., Eilers, R. E., Oller, D. K., & La Voie, L. (1985). Where's the drift in babbling drift? A cross-linguistic study. *Applied Psycholinguistics, 6,* 3–15.

Trehub, S. E. (1976). The discrimination of foreign speech contrasts by infants and adults. *Child Development, 44*, 466–472.

Vihman, M. M. (1987, October). *The interaction of production and perception in the transition to speech.* Paper presented at the Twelfth Annual Boston University Conference on Language Development.

Vihman, M. M., Ferguson, C. A., & Elbert, M. (1986). Phonological development from babbling to speech: Common tendencies and individual differences. *Applied Psycholinguistics, 7*, 3–40.

Vihman, M. M., & Greenlee, M. (1987). Individual differences in phonological development: Ages one and three years. *Journal of Speech and Hearing Research, 30*, 503–521.

Vihman, M. M., Macken, M. A., Miller, R., Simmons, H., & Miller, J. (1985). From babbling to speech: A reassessment of the continuity issue. *Language, 61*, 395–443.

Vihman, M. M., & Miller, R. (1988). Words and babble at the threshold of lexical acquisition. In M. D. Smith & J. L. Locke (Eds.), *The emergent lexicon: The child's development of a linguistic vocabulary* (pp. 151–183). New York: Academic Press.

Vihman, M. M., & Velleman, S. L. (1989). Phonological reorganization: A case study. *Language and Speech, 32*, 149–170.

Werker, J., Gilbert, J. H. V., Humphrey, K., & Tees, R. C. (1981). Developmental aspects of cross-language speech perception. *Child Development, 52*, 349–355.

Werker, J. F., & Tees, R. C. (1984). Cross-language speech perception: Evidence for perceptual reorganization during the first year of life. *Infant Behavior and Development, 7*, 49–63.

Comment: The Emergent Gesture

Michael Studdert-Kennedy

Haskins Laboratories

Marilyn Vihman contrasts two views of the origin of phonetic gestures. On the one hand is the proposal of Liberman and Mattingly (1985) that the speech perceptuomotor link is "biologically based" (p. 6), "not a learned association . . . but innately specified, requiring only epigenetic experience to bring it into play" (p. 3). On the other is the view developed by Vihman (chapter 4 this volume) that each infant has "to rediscover the relevant gestures through attention to the speech of others."

The two views are not entirely incompatible. Clearly the link is not arbitrary: It is not like the outcome of pairing the sound of a word with its meaning, for, as every feedback theory of speech motor control assumes, the speech signal is a necessary and lawful consequence of a speaker's articulations. Clearly, too, like every structure/function peculiar to a particular species, the link is biologically based: It is the product of a developmental process peculiar to humans. Finally, although we may balk at the slighting of experience implied by "*only* epigenetic experience" (my emphasis), it is precisely this experience with which Vihman's paper is concerned. What might surprise a reader inclined to accept innate specification is how important—indeed essential—that experience is. We see this, first, in the new view (elaborated by Vihman herself and by others) of the role of babbling in development.

Some twenty years ago, the English translation of Jakobson's *Kindersprache* (1968) was published, and the year before saw the publication of Lenneberg's *Biological Foundations of Language* (1967). Both these works viewed babbling as linguistically irrelevant and devoid of function. Jakobson, as is well known, believed that babbling was separated from the onset of true language by the developmental equivalent of a few moments of respectful silence and that the

85

phonetic content of infant babbling was essentially random. This notion has been disproved in several studies that Vihman reviews. Not only is there no silent gap, but babbling and early words overlap in both time and phonetic content. Indeed, it is precisely through perceptuomotor skills developed in babbling that the infant gains access to words in the surrounding language.

Lenneberg (1967) believed that the onset of babbling was independent of prior input and was not necessary for normal development. Among the bases for his belief were claims that: (a) the onset of babbling occurs at the normal time in deaf infants; and (b) a child tracheostomized and thus precluded from babbling, between the ages of 8 and 14 months, nonetheless a day after the tube had been removed produced the babbling sounds typical of its age (p. 140). The latter claim is difficult to assess, because the course of babbling had not been well described when Lenneberg wrote. However, the implication of the two claims is that the onset of speech is purely maturational and independent of experience in either hearing or producing speech sounds.

Yet, as Vihman has shown in her review, we now know that vocal babbling does not begin normally in the deaf. Moreover, "babbling" with the hands begins at around 5–6 months in deaf children exposed to American Sign Language (Newport & Meier, 1985; Petitto, 1989). The absence of vocal babbling and the presence of finger babbling in these children is evidence that communicative interaction with others is not only necessary but sufficient to induce babbling even in another modality.

To take Lenneberg's second claim, Locke and Pearson (1990), in a far more careful study than that of Lenneberg, have shown that a tracheostomized infant may be seriously delayed in development. They report on a child who was tracheostomized before babbling onset at 5 months and whose cannula was removed at 20 months, a period of enforced mutism that brackets the normal span of babbling. After decannulation, the frequency of the child's vocalizations increased dramatically, but the frequency of normal canonically babbled syllables (Oller, 1980) was initially no greater than in deaf infants 11–14 months of age. The child caught up with her peers by the beginning of her fifth year. But, as Locke and Pearson remarked, this may attest more to the plasticity of the young brain than to the lack of a role for babbling in normal development.

My next point concerns the gap between what a child recognizes and what a child produces. The gap is very much wider than the claim of an innately specified perceptuomotor link might lead us to expect. Eleven-month-old infants, well before they have begun to speak many words, are sensitive to word boundaries in infant-directed speech: They prefer to listen to a story in which pauses have been artificially inserted between words rather than within them (Kemler-Nelson, 1989). And a 15-month-old child with an output vocabulary of less than 10 words may have a recognition vocabulary of well over a hundred (Benedict, 1979).

Moreover, even if their earliest word percepts are "global" (Jusczyk, 1986, p.

11), children become sensitive to the internal structure of words as early as the second six months of life. In the studies of Werker and her colleagues, cited by Vihman (see also Werker, Chapter 5 this volume), infants of 10–12 months had already lost sensitivity to phonetic contrasts not used in the surrounding language. Apparently, the loss only occurs if the alien contrasting elements can be assimilated to a single phonological category in that language (Best, McRoberts, & Sithole, 1988). That these results were found with nonsense syllables does not contradict the hypothesis that the earliest unit of linguistic contrast in production is the word (Ferguson & Farwell, 1975; Ferguson, 1986; cf. MacKain, 1988). The results imply only that an 11-month-old infant, with a minimal output vocabulary, has already begun to perceive, sort, and store at least some words (including potential words or nonsense syllables) according to the phonetic functions of the elements that compose them.

Perceptual sensitivity to the internal structure of words that they cannot produce continues to be evident in the early speech of older children. Sometimes the error is largely a matter of gestural timing, as when Vihman's Molly says [itš] for *cheese,* suggesting that she has perceived the initial affricate correctly but has put it in the wrong place. At other times, the child is evidently striving to find the right gestures: Molly's attempts at *teeth* included [dɪts], [titstɪš] and [tɪtš] (Vihman & Velleman, 1989); for *thank-you,* Daniel Menn offered [geika], [dejdʌ], [gaita], [degʌ] and [gigu] (Menn, 1971). Idiosyncratic patterns of selection and avoidance tell the same story. Vihman's Aislinn liked to try words inviting a palatal articulation but did not always get them right. Menn's Jacob recognized and produced words with initial /d/, but recognized *ball, block,* and *box* for many months before he attempted any words with syllable-initial /b/ (Menn, 1976). In this and other instances of avoidance, the child seems to have a perceptual representation of a sound pattern but no corresponding articulatory representation.

All these and many more examples make it difficult to believe that, for a child learning to talk, "perception and production are only different sides of the same coin" (Liberman & Mattingly, 1985, p. 30) or that the child's perceptual representations "are computed by . . . an internal, innately specified vocal tract synthesizer" (p. 26). Two lines of argument might be offered to salvage these claims, but neither of them is compelling. First, we might propose that the child's difficulties are purely motoric and peripheral: Its percepts are "remote structures that . . . correspond to the speaker's intentions" (p. 23). Learning to talk would then be a matter of discovering how to actuate these remote control structures by linking them with their peripheral neuromotor mechanisms. The first difficulty with this proposal is that even if we are persuaded by the evidence for remote structures adduced from studies of adult speech perception, there is no corresponding evidence from studies of child speech perception. A more important objection, in my view, is that the proposal reverses the normal course of development both evolutionarily and ontogenetically: Behavior builds control structures; control structures do not build behavior (cf. Neville, chapter 11 this volume).

If we accept the latter objection, we might propose an alternative, epigenetic account of the origin of the perceptuomotor coin: Perhaps a child only achieves full perceptual representation of a word, when it discovers the corresponding motor control structures. Indeed, Vihman herself seems to have something like this in mind, when she proposes that the 11-month-old infants of Werker's study could not discriminate alien Hindi and Salish sounds, because they could not succeed in "matching patterns heard against the vocal motor schemes they were constructing. . . . Possibly sounds occurring in English but not yet available in the child's repertoire of articulatory gestures would have proven equally difficult to discriminate." As Vihman remarks, we do not yet have the data to test this hypothesis and its implications for the developmental mechanisms of early phonological organization. However, a general statement of the hypothesis might be the first premise of a motor theory: Listeners can only discriminate between speech sounds that they can distinguish in articulation. This premise has been refuted by several studies, including, for example, the work of Carney, Widin, and Viemeister (1977) on voice onset time, and the recent work of Best et al. (1988) on the discrimination of Zulu clicks by English adults and infants.

In any event, the account will not salvage the supposed identity of perceptual and motor representations, because it still requires that prior, independent perceptual representations (patterns heard) be available for comparison with items in the child's motor repertoire. These patterns heard and stored seem, in fact, to be precisely what keep a child on course in its dogged attempts to get a word right: They are the perceptual targets for which the child has not yet found the gestures.

In short, the evidence seems clear that the child initially has two independent systems, an input lexicon and an output lexicon (Menn, 1983), very much as Vihman proposes in her model (see Vihman's Fig. 4.2 this volume). At the same time, we should not let slip the central insight of Liberman and Mattingly (1985) that the structure of the speech signal is broadly isomorphic with the articulation that produced it: It is this isomorphism that permits the child to discover the correspondences between its babbling repertoire and the speech it hears, and so to forge the links between the two lexicons. Once the links are in place and a full phonological system established, we may indeed fairly characterize perception and production as two sides of the same coin. The reversible phonetic module, like other language universals, is then the outcome, not the innate, axiomatic *primum mobile* of development.

Finally, we should draw attention to the convergence between motor theory and child language studies in their use of motoric rather than conventional linguistic terminology to describe the speech of the learning child. Current discussions have at last begun to relinquish "phonemes" and "features." McCune and Vihman (1987) talk of "vocal motor schemes," Menn (1983) of "articulatory routines," Locke (1983) of "movement patterns," and Liberman and Mattingly (1985) of "gestures." A view of the child as a preformed adult endowed with specialized linguistic input and output devices is giving way to a view of the child as a creature equipped with ears and eyes and with various moving parts that can be harnessed to form the sounds and sights of its species' communicative signals.

One important consequence of the switch to motoric terminology is that we may finally be able to talk about the phonetics/phonology of speech and sign language in analogous terms. As is now generally recognized, oromanual sign languages are natural languages with a dual formational (phonological) and syntactic structure and a functional scope analogous to those of spoken languages (Klima & Bellugi, 1979; Poizner, Bellugi, and Klima, chapter 7 this volume). Moreover, studies of sign language aphasia have revealed striking correspondences between signed and spoken languages in patterns of breakdown and in their associated loci of brain lesion (Poizner, Klima, & Bellugi, 1987; cf. Neville, chapter 11 this volume). Evidently, structures in the left cerebral hemisphere have evolved and now develop ontogenetically to support the abstract, rule-governed processes of language, whatever its modality. But the basis for this development—the nature of the prelinguistic neural materials from which language is tinkered together (Jacob, 1977)—is far from clear.

Broadly, we may speculate that the evolution of spoken language entailed the replication and adaptation to vocal function of neural circuitry already evolved in the left hemisphere of prehominid primates for right-handed manipulation and bimanual coordination (MacNeilage, Studdert-Kennedy & Lindblom, 1987). "In other words, linguistic structure may emerge from, and may even be viewed as a special case of, motoric structure, the structure of action" (Studdert-Kennedy 1983, p. 5; cf. Turvey, 1980). The basic units of phonology would then be patterns of movement executed with communicative intent—that is, gestures— and these would be the elements from which the child builds its articulatory routines, whether vocal or manual. Of course, if this is so, we will have to grant the phonetic module a rather wider domain than Liberman and Mattingly (1985) proposed.

References

Benedict, H. (1979). Early lexical development: Comprehension and production. *Journal of Child Language, 6,* 183–200.

Best, C. T., McRoberts, G., & Sithole, N. (1988). Examination of perceptual reorganization for nonnative speech contrasts: Zulu click discrimination by English-speaking adults and infants. *Journal of Experimental Psychology: Human Perception and Performance, 14,* 345–360.

Carney, A. E., Widin, G. P., & Viemeister, N. F. (1977). Noncategorical perception of stop consonants differing in VOT. *Journal of the Acoustical Society of America, 62,* 961–970.

Ferguson, C. A. (1986). Words and sounds in early language acquisition. In J. S. Perkell & D. H.

Klatt (Eds.), *Invariance and variability of speech processes* (pp. 36–51). Hillsdale, NJ: Lawrence Erlbaum Associates.

Ferguson, C. A., & Farwell, C. B. (1975). Words and sounds in early language acquisition. *Language, 51*, 419–439.

Jacob, F. (1977). Evolution as tinkering. *Science, 196*, 1161–1166.

Jakobson, R. (1968). *Child language, aphasia and phonological universals.* The Hague: Mouton.

Jusczyk, P. W. (1986). Toward a model of the development of speech perception. In J. S. Perkell & D. H. Klatt (Eds.), *Invariance and variability of speech processes* (pp. 1–19). Hillsdale, NJ: Lawrence Erlbaum Associates.

Kemler-Nelson, D. G. (1989, April). *Developmental trends in infants' sensitivity to prosodic cues correlated with linguistic units.* Paper presented at Society for Research in Child Development, Kansas City, MO.

Klima, E. S., & Bellugi, U. (1979). *The signs of language.* Cambridge, MA: Harvard University Press.

Lenneberg, E. H. (1967). *Biological foundations of language.* New York: Wiley.

Liberman, A. M., & Mattingly, I. G. (1985). The motor theory of speech perception revised. *Cognition, 21*, 1–36.

Locke, J. L. (1983). *Phonological acquisition and change.* New York: Academic Press.

Locke, J. L., & Pearson, D. M. (1990). Linguistic significance of babbling: Evidence from tracheostomized infants. *Journal of Child Language, 17*, 1–16.

MacKain, K. S. (1988). Filling the gap between speech and language. In M. D. Smith & J. L. Locke (Eds.), *The emergent lexicon* (pp. 51–74). New York: Academic Press.

MacNeilage, P. F., Studdert-Kennedy, M., & Lindblom, B. E. F. (1987). Primate handedness reconsidered. *The Behavioral and Brain Sciences, 10*, 247–303.

McCune, L., & Vihman, M. (1987). Vocal motor schemes. *Papers and Reports on Child Language Development, 26*, 72–79.

Menn, L. (1971). Phonotactic rules in beginning speech. *Lingua, 49*, 11–49.

Menn, L. (1976). *Pattern, control, and contrast in beginning speech: A case study in the acquisition of word form and function.* Bloomington, IN: Indiana University Linguistics Club.

Menn, L. (1983). Development of articulatory, phonetic and phonological capabilities. In B. Butterworth (Ed.), *Language production* (vol. 2, pp. 3–50). London: Academic Press.

Newport, E. L., & Meier, R. P. (1985). The acquisition of American Sign Language. In D. I. Slobin, (Ed.), *The cross linguistic study of language acquisition* (vol. 1, pp. 881–938). Hillsdale, NJ: Lawrence Erlbaum Associates.

Oller, D. K. (1980). The emergence of the sounds of speech in infancy. In G. Yeni-Komshian, J. Kavanagh, & C. A. Ferguson (Eds.), *Child phonology. vol. 2: Production* (pp. 93–112). New York: Academic Press.

Petitto, L. A. (1989, April). *The equipotentiality of speech and gesture for language: Evidence from deaf children's babbling in sign.* Paper presented at Society for Research in Child Development, Kansas City, MO.

Poizner, H., Klima, E. S., & Bellugi, U. (1987). *What the hands reveal about the brain.* Cambridge, MA: MIT Press.

Studdert-Kennedy, M. (Ed.). (1983). *Psychobiology of language.* Cambridge, MA: MIT Press.

Turvey, M. T. (1980). Clues from the organization of motor systems. In U. Bellugi & M. Studdert-Kennedy (Eds.), *Signed and spoken language: Biological constraints on linguistic form* (pp. 41–56). Weinheim: Verlag Chemie GmbH.

Vihman, M. M., & Velleman, S. L. (1989). Phonological reorganization: A case study. *Language and Speech, 32*, 149–170.

Chapter 5

The Ontogeny of Speech Perception

Janet Werker

Department of Psychology,
University of British Columbia

Abstract

There is considerable evidence that speech is perceived by a specialized phonetic module in adults. However, it is still very unclear whether young infants show a similar specialization. Understanding developmental changes in the phonetic specificity of speech perception will clarify the theoretical understanding of modularity. This paper reviews research examining the ontogenetic origin and developmental progression of phonetic perception. Although the focus will be on the study of developmental changes in cross-language speech perception, other recent evidence suggesting early phonetic specialization will also be reviewed.

The cross-language research indicates that young infants can discriminate (and also apparently categorize) nearly every speech sound contrast on which they have been tested, including those that do not occur (or are not used contrastively) in their language-learning environment. However, older children and adults often show more difficulty discriminating nonnative contrasts, particularly those which are assimilated to a single phoneme in their native language. Research has shown that this developmental change is evident by the end of the first year of life, suggesting that some important reorganization has occurred by this time. The implications of initial phonetically relevant perception to theoretical models of speech perception will be discussed. As well, several alternative explanations for why the developmental reorganization begins to occur around one year of age will be outlined, and new data assessing one of these possibilities will be presented.

Contributing a chapter to a book honoring Alvin M. Liberman is both a privilege and an opportunity. It is a privilege to help honor the person who has been the central figure in the field of speech perception for the last 30 years. It is an opportunity to show the breadth of his influence; in particular, to show how my own work on developmental aspects of cross-language speech perception has been influenced directly and repeatedly by Al Liberman.

One of the first indications that speech perception is mediated by a specialized phonetic module was provided in early studies by Al Liberman and his colleagues. They showed that adult listeners typically perceive speech and speechlike stimuli categorically (Liberman, Cooper, Shankweiler, & Studdert-Kennedy, 1967). Subsequent research, beginning with the work by Peter Eimas and his colleagues, revealed that infants as young as one month of age also show categorical-like perception for speech stimuli (Eimas, Siqueland, Jusczyk, & Vigorito, 1971). This indicated that the specialization for speech perception may be present quite early in life. This chapter examines the ontogenetic origin and developmental progression of phonetic perception with a focus on the study of developmental changes in cross-language speech perception.

Phonetic possibilities are not infinite, but rather they are restricted in highly regular and systematic ways (Jakobson, Fant, & Halle, 1967). In a series of studies examining cross-language differences in VOT (voice onset time) values produced by speakers of 11 languages, Leigh Lisker and Arthur Abramson discovered that, rather than being random across the world's languages, the distribution of VOT values clusters around three points (Lisker & Abramson, 1964). Of special significance to cross-language research, their studies of speech perception indicated that adults often have difficulty discriminating between voicing categories that are not used phonemically in their native language (Lisker & Abramson, 1970). For example, an English speaker will initially have difficulty perceiving the difference between a prevoiced and a voiced /p/ as realized in Thai or Spanish but not English (Lisker & Abramson, 1964). In related research, it was shown that Japanese adults have difficulty perceiving the English /r/ vs. /l/ (Goto, 1971; MacKain, Best, & Strange, 1981; Miyawaki, Strange, Verbrugge, Liberman, Jenkins, & Fujimura, 1975) and English-speaking adults have difficulty with the Czech stridency contrast, /za/ versus /řa/ (Trehub, 1976). (For a summary of the early cross-language research, see Strange & Jenkins, 1978).

The finding that adults might have difficulty discriminating nonnative contrasts led to a reevaluation of the infant work. That is, the possibility was raised that both infants and adults might have to learn to discriminate phonetic contrasts and that by 1–4 months of age infants have already had enough experience to have acquired this ability. According to this interpretation, phonetic perception could still require specialized processing in the adult, but it would be an acquired phonetic specialization. This is a weaker form of biological specialization than would be evidence of phonetic perception that is apparent prior to experience with a language.

Tests of young infants prior to their first exposure to a particular contrast could help clarify the ontogeny of phonetic perception. In this endeavor, Streeter (1976) showed that Kikuyu-learning infants aged 2–3 months can discriminate the voiced versus voiceless distinction that is used in English (but not in Kikuyu). Similar results were reported for Spanish-learning infants aged 4–6 months of age by Lasky, Syrdal-Lasky, and Klein (1975). Results with regard to English-learning infants and the (non-English) lead boundary in VOT were initially equivocal (Butterfield & Cairns, 1974; Eilers, Gavin, & Wilson, 1979), but recent research clarifies that naive infants can also discriminate this lead boundary (Aslin, Pisoni, Hennessy, & Perey, 1981).

This pattern of broad-based phonetic sensitivities in the young infant and more limited (language-specific) capabilities in the adult led Peter Eimas (1975) to suggest that infants may have a biological predisposition to perceive speech and speech-like stimuli according to the universal set of phonetic categories and that there is a decline in this universal phonetic sensitivity as a function of acquiring a particular language. Support for this hypothesis was provided in a study by Sandra Trehub (1976), in which English-learning infants aged 1–5 months and English-speaking adults were compared on their ability to discriminate a phonetic contrast that is used in Czech (/za/–/řa/) but not English. Using very different testing procedures with the infants and the adults rendered the results somewhat difficult to interpret but nevertheless indicated that the young infants but not the adults could discriminate this nonnative contrast.

At this point, we began a series of experiments examining the effect of age and experience on cross-language speech perception. To begin, we selected a testing procedure—the Head Turn Procedure—which could be used with infants, children of all ages, and adults. This procedure is a variant on the class play audiometric procedure developed by Dix and Hallpike (1947) to test hearing in young children and in the 1970s was modified for use with infants as young as 5.5 months of age (Kuhl, 1979; Wilson, Moore, & Thompson, 1976).

The basic logic of this procedure is to condition the infant to turn her head when she detects a change in the speech stimulus. In the experimental set-up (see Fig. 5.1a), the infant sits on her parent's lap in a sound-attenuated chamber. An experimental assistant sits across the table from the mother and infant and shows the infant toys to keep her entertained. In the background, speech stimuli from a single phonetic category are presented at regular intervals. When the infant exhibits a "state of readiness" (quietly watching the assistant manipulate the toys), the computer is signalled. During the conditioning phase, this triggers the presentation of a stimulus from a contrasting phonetic category. Simultaneous with the presentation of the contrasting phone, the plexiglass box to the side of the infant is illuminated, and the toy animals inside are activated (see Fig. 5.1b). The infant turns her head to see the animals perform. After several pairings, the infant forms an association between the change in phonetic category and activation of the visual reinforcer, and consequently turns her head as soon as the sound changes in anticipation of seeing the toy animals.

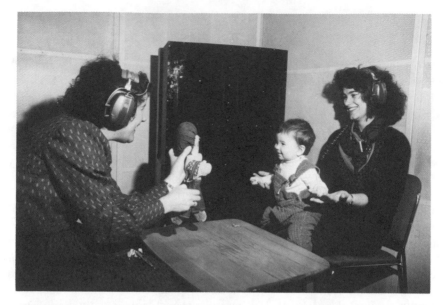

FIG. 5.1a. An infant attending to the experimental assistant during the "no-change" intervals in the Head Turn Procedure.

FIG. 5.1b. An infant turning her head toward the visual reinforcer upon detecting a change in the speech sound. (Notice that the correct head turn is "reinforced" by the activation of the toy animals as well as by clapping and praise by the experimental assistant.)

Once conditioning is successful (we currently use a criterion of three consecutive correct anticipatory head turns), the testing phase begins. During this phase, approximately half the trials are test trials (change to a contrasting phone), and half are control trials (no change). An observer who is unaware of the selection the infant hears presses a button if he/she detects a 90° head turn during an observation interval. Correct head turns (which are called "Hits") are reinforced with the activation of the visual reinforcer as well as with clapping and praise. Incorrect head turns ("False positives") and "Misses" are not reinforced, but are counted. In addition, "correct rejections" (the failure to turn the head in a control trial) are noted. Data are analyzed according to the number of infants reaching a pre-established criterion (e.g., 9 out of 10 correct responses in a row) and/or to the proportion of either correct responses or simply of hits within a set number of trials.

Our use of this procedure was taken in large part from the work of Patricia Kuhl (1979, 1987) who modified the procedure to make it more like a perceptual constancy task. In our implementation, we include several exemplars from the same phonetic category as background and several exemplars from the contrasting phonetic category as potential "test" stimuli, making the task to some extent, a phonetic constancy task. The infants have to show evidence not only of discriminating between two categories but also of not discriminating between stimulus tokens from within either category.

The Effect of Experience

To begin to assess the effect of experience on cross-language speech perception, we compared English-speaking adults, English-learning infants aged 6–8 months, and Hindi-speaking adults on their ability to discriminate the English /ba/–/da/ distinction (which is also used in Hindi), as well as two pairs of syllables that are phonemic contrasts in Hindi but not in English. These two nonnative contrasts were chosen to vary on potential difficulty. The first Hindi contrast involved a place-of-articulation distinction between a voiceless dental and a voiceless retroflex stop consonant (/ṭa/–/ṭa/). The second and potentially easier Hindi pair involved a contrast between a voiceless aspirated and breathy voiced dental stop; /tʰ/ and /dʰ/. The vowel /a/ was used in all cases. Naturally produced exemplars from each phonetic category were recorded from a native Hindi speaker. Several stimuli from each category were selected such that the distribution of nonphonetic acoustic cues (duration, intensity, fundamental frequency, etc.) overlapped between categories. In this way, only phonetically relevant cues could be used to discriminate between the two categories.

Figure 5.2 shows the results from the first study. As is evident, virtually all the infants reached discrimination criterion on both Hindi contrasts, as did Hindi-

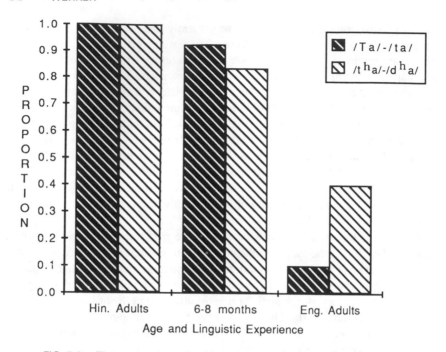

FIG. 5.2. The proportion of subjects per group reaching discrimination criterion on the two Hindi (non-English) phonetic contrasts.

speaking adults, but most of the English-speaking adults initially failed both non-English contrasts. That is, young infants were able to discriminate nonnative contrasts, whereas English-speaking adults failed. A second group of English adults was given 25 training trials on the Hindi contrasts, and although this was sufficient to improve performance on the Hindi voicing distinction, it did not affect performance on the retroflex/dental contrast (Werker, Gilbert, Humphrey, & Tees, 1981). In subsequent studies, we found that neither 500 training trials nor one year of Hindi study at the university level was sufficient to improve the performance of many English speaking adults on the Hindi retroflex/dental contrast (Tees & Werker, 1984).

The developmental change between infancy and adulthood was replicated using a non-English contrast from Inslekampx (Thompson), an Interior Salish Northwest Indian language. The contrast tested was a glottalized uvular versus a glottalized velar distinction /k̓i/–/q̓/. Again, English-learning infants aged 6–8 months and native Inslekampx-speaking adults were able to discriminate this distinction, but the majority of English-speaking adults were not (Werker & Tees, 1984a).

What is the Meaning of this Perceptual Decline?

The studies reviewed above are all consistent with the hypothesis that infants can discriminate the universal set of phonetic distinctions and that this universal sensitivity changes as a function of learning a particular language. The next series of experiments was designed to clarify the meaning of this developmental change.

To the extent that speech perception is processed by a special linguistic mechanism, we originally (incorrectly) predicted that the developmental change in the ability to discriminate nonnative phonetic contrasts would occur around puberty, the age at which Lenneberg (1967) claimed that the flexibility to learn a foreign language without an accent declines. However, contrary to expectation, our work indicated that 12-year-old and even 8- and 4-year-old English-speaking children were no more capable of discriminating the non-English syllables than were English speaking adults. This was the case, although these same 4-year-olds could easily discriminate the English /ba/–/da/ distinction in this procedure, and Hindi-learning 4-year-olds could easily discriminate both Hindi contrasts. Even more surprising, the 4-year-olds actually showed *more* difficulty on the perceptually *easier* Hindi voicing contrast than did the older children or the adults (Werker & Tees, 1983). Four out of ten subjects aged 8 and 12 years as well as adults were able to spontaneously reach discrimination criterion on the perceptually easier Hindi voicing distinction. However, none of the 4-year-old English-speaking children reached criterion on this contrast.

Why did the children aged 4 perform so poorly? We know from other psychological research that when children first begin to develop a rule system, they use it much more rigidly than older children or adults. For example, a child, 4–6 years of age will evidence much more rigid sex-role stereotypes than an older child (Carter & Patterson, 1982). This result with the 4-year-olds suggested that rather than explaining the age-related change in nonnative speech perception as a decline from lack of exposure to the speech sounds in question, it might more properly be explained as a reorganization.

If the developmental change in cross-language speech perception is best conceptualized as a reorganization rather than a loss, then one would predict that adult English speakers should be able to discriminate even the difficult nonnative distinctions under some testing conditions. Several experiments were run to address this question. Very briefly, in one experiment, adult English-speakers were shown to be able to discriminate truncated portions of both the retroflex/dental and glottalized velar/uvular nonnative syllables when they were presented in isolation (Werker & Tees, 1984b). This reveals that the ear's ability to discriminate the acoustic cues differentiating these nonnative contrasts has not disappeared, but that it is only easily accessed, when the stimuli are not language-like sounds.

In a further set of experiments, John Logan and I showed that adult English-speakers can even discriminate the full-syllable retroflex/dental contrast, if tested in a more sensitive testing procedure and if given enough practice (Werker & Logan, 1985). By varying the ISI and the amount of practice, we showed that subjects will demonstrate very different data patterns. At a long ISI (1500 msec), and without practice, subjects cannot discriminate nonnative contrasts. We called this a phonemic pattern of responding. When tested at a very short ISI (250 msec), subjects can discriminate a retroflex from a dental sound. We called this a (universal) phonetic pattern. Interestingly, when tested at an intermediate ISI (500 msec) and/or after several blocks of training trials at either of the other ISI's, subjects will begin to discriminate any differences between stimuli, including within phonetic category differences such as those between two different retroflex exemplars. We called this an auditory pattern of responding.

That subjects show three very different response patterns under different testing conditions is consistent with the view that the apparent decline in the ability to discriminate nonnative phonetic distinctions is evidence of a reorganization within the language system rather than an absolute loss or decline of sensitivity. These three differential patterns of responding may also help explain the inconsistent findings from other cross-language experiments with adults (Burnham, 1986; MacKain et al., 1981; Pisoni, Aslin, Perey, & Hennessy, 1982; Polka, 1987). It may be that subjects will show evidence of discriminating nonnative contrasts in some but not other testing procedures.

Nevertheless, there is no question that some nonnative contrasts are easier to discriminate than others. Denis Burnham (1986) suggested that those contrasts that are rare across the world's languages and particularly those that are acoustically less distinct will be the hardest to discriminate. An alternative hypothesis, suggested by both Strange (1986) and Best, McRoberts, and Sithole (1988), is that the ease of discriminability will vary depending upon the role of the stimuli within the phonological system of the speaker's native language.

Specifically, Best and colleagues suggested four different types of nonnative contrasts: a) those in which both members are assimilable to a single phonemic category in the native language (single-category assimilation), b) those in which each member is assimilable to a contrasting native language phonological category (opposing category assimilation), c) those in which one member is easily assimilated to a native language phonological category and the other member is not (category-goodness difference), and d) those in which neither member is assimilable to a native language phonological category (nonassimilation). Best argued that nonnative contrasts that contain stimuli fitting the type 1 category (single-category assimilation) should be the most difficult to discriminate.

In an initial test of this hypothesis, Best, McRoberts, and Sithole (1988) recently compared English-speaking adults, Zulu-speaking adults, and English-learning infants of three different ages on their ability to discriminate the (nonnative, and nonassimilable) Zulu clicks. As they predicted, all subjects were able to discriminate all the Zulu clicks, even though they were acoustically quite similar. In related work, Polka (1987) recently reported that English adults can discriminate the Persian unglottalized velar/uvular distinction—a contrast that fits Best's category 3 (category goodness).

Clearly, the retroflex/dental distinction considered in our previous work fits type 1, because both stimuli are assimilable to the English alveolar category. However, the Hindi voiceless aspirated versus breathy voiced contrast more closely fits type 2, because there is a large VOT difference between the two classes of stimuli making them assimilable to the contrasting English voiced versus voiceless phonological categories. This could explain the relative difference in ease between these distinctions. The Inslekampx stimuli are a little more difficult to classify. In informal reports, most English subjects reported that they sounded like "funny" /k/s, but others reported that they did not sound speech-like at all, making them possibly fit type 1 for some listeners and type 4 for others. This could account for the fact that most English adults showed initial difficulty with this distinction, but some were able to discriminate it immediately.

Support for the notion that cross-language differences in speech perception can be explained by the phonological status of the stimuli is provided in a study recently completed by Harry McGurk, Paul Frost, and myself (Werker, McGurk, & Frost, 1987). This study shows there to be an effect of experience on the visual as well as the auditory aspects of speech perception. In this study, four groups of French-speaking adults differing in their English proficiency were compared to a group of English-speaking adults in a cross-language auditory-visual (AV) speech perception task (for a full description of the AV task, see McGurk & MacDonald, 1976). Subjects were shown a videotape of one of the authors (P. Frost) articulating six different syllables; /ba/, /va/, /ða/, /da/, /ʒa/ and /ga/. The acoustic signal /ba/ was dubbed onto each. In addition, there were three control conditions. In the visual-only control condition, the subjects viewed the videotape in silence. In one auditory-only condition, the subjects were presented with 10 /ba/s. In the other auditory-only control condition, each syllable was presented 10 times in random order without a visual display.

The English /ða/ was the critical cross-language comparison, because there is no interdental fricative in French. Results revealed that the French speakers *did* have difficulty perceiving the /ða/ in all conditions with particular difficulty in the AV condition. In this condition, English speakers perceived what they saw for all the frontal articulations, /ba/, /va/, /ða/ and /da/. For example, when presented with a visual /ða/ and an acoustic /ba/, they perceived a /ða/. In contrast, the French speakers consistently perceived this AV combination as a /ta/ or a /da/, and this effect was most pronounced in the French speakers who knew the least English. The visual interdental articulation clearly influenced the French speakers' perception because they did not report hearing a /ba/; instead they assimilated the syllable to the nearest place-of-articulation that has phonemic status in the French language. This evidence of the effect of experience on intermodal speech perception provides strong confirmatory evidence in support of a phonological-based reorganization.

When Does This Reorganization Occur?

The next series of experiments was designed to return to the question: When does this developmental reorganization occur? Having ascertained that children as young as age four were performing at least as poorly as adults on nonnative contrasts (Werker & Tees, 1983), we next (incorrectly) predicted that the reorganization would be apparent sometime around 18–24 months of age, when the child shows evidence of an explosion in productive vocabulary. However, in pilot-testing children between eight months and four years of age, it quickly became apparent that something was happening by the end of the first year of life.

At that point, we narrowed our investigation and concentrated on testing children up to one year of age. Three groups of infants aged 6–8, 8–10, and 10–12 months were compared on their ability to discriminate both the Hindi retroflex/dental /ṭa/–/ṭa/) and the Inslekampx glottalized velar/uvular (/k'i/–/q'i/) distinctions in a cross-sectional study. Each infant was first tested on the English /ba/–/da/ distinction to make sure they could (and would) perform in the procedure and was then tested on one of the nonnative contrasts. If they failed to discriminate the nonnative distinction within 25 trials, they were then retested on the /ba/–/da/ contrast to ensure they could perform in the task. As shown in Fig. 5.3a, virtually all the infants aged 6–8 months of age were able to discriminate both the nonnative contrasts, whereas among the infants aged 10–12 months, only one out of 10 was able to discriminate the Thompson and two out of 10 the Hindi contrast.

This experiment was replicated in a longitudinal design in which six infants were tested at three successive ages on their ability to discriminate the English /ba/–/da/, the Hindi /ṭa/–/ṭa/, and the Inslekampx /k'i/–/q'i/. Results were basically consistent with those obtained in the cross-sectional design, with all subjects discriminating both non-English contrasts at 6–8 months of age and not reaching criterion on either non-English contrast by 10–12 months of age (see Fig. 5.3b). Finally, to make sure that the decline at this time was not simply a general performance decline for difficult contrasts, we tested a few Hindi- and Inslekampx-learning infants aged 11–12 months on their ability to discriminate these contrasts. As shown in Fig. 5.3a, these infants reached discrimination criterion on their native contrast, and they did so within 10 change trials.

Chris Lalonde and I recently replicated this finding using a synthetic /ba/–/da/–/ḍa/ continuum where the differences within and between phonetic category could be precisely controlled. We synthesized a continuum by varying the starting frequency of the second and third formant transitions (for more synthesis

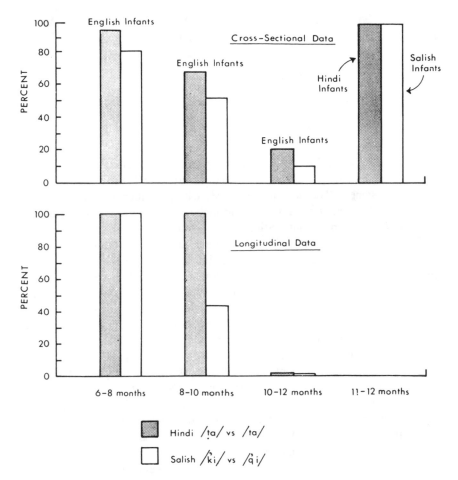

FIG. 5.3. The proportion of infants at three different ages able to discriminate the Hindi and Inslekampx (non-English) phonetic contrasts.
(From Werker & Tees, 1984a)

details, see Werker & Lalonde, 1988). English listeners divided this continuum
into two categories, /ba/ and /da/, and Hindi listeners divided it into three
categories, /ba/, dental /ḍa/, and retroflex /ḍa/ in both an identification and an
ABX discrimination task.

We then tested English-learning infants and Hindi- and English-speaking
adults on their ability to discriminate/categorize the stimuli according to both
phonetically relevant and nonrelevant boundary regions. Three exemplars from
either side of three boundary locations along this continuum were presented
using the Head Turn (Go/No–Go) Procedure. The continuum is shown in Fig.
5.4. The first boundary location was called Common; it corresponded to the
boundary between bilabial /ba/ and dental/alveolar /da/ for both the Hindi and

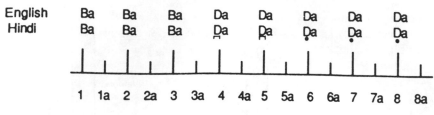

FIG. 5.4. The synthetic continuum.

the English listeners. The second boundary was called Hindi-only; it corresponded to the boundary location between dental /d̪a/ and retroflex /ḍa/ for the Hindi adult listeners. The third boundary we called Neither; it was at the /ḍa/ end of the continuum, at a point which no language is known to have a category distinction for stop consonants. Stimulus selections are shown in Table 5.1.

Infants aged 6–8 and 11–13 months were compared to both English- and Hindi-speaking adults. Results showed that infants aged 6–8 months and Hindi-speaking adults could discriminate the Common and Hindi-only pairings, but not the Neither, whereas older infants and English-speaking adults could discriminate only the Common pairing (Werker & Lalonde, 1988). This finding with the young infants confirms the phonetic specificity of infant perception, because the young infants could not correctly discriminate the Neither pairing. Although this research alone does not prove that there are special phonetic capacities in the young infant, when it is evaluated in the context of other work, it certainly strengthens this interpretation. For instance, Miller and Eimas substantiated that both context effects and trading relations operate in young infants (Miller & Eimas, 1979, 1983) and Hillenbrand showed there to be featural-level categorization by young infants (Hillenbrand, 1983, 1984). Most recently, Greiser and Kuhl (1989) showed that young human infants exhibit phonetic perceptual constancy for vowels and in fact generalize to novel instances of a single vowel category, but rhesus monkeys do not demonstrate this same phonetic perceptual constancy (Kuhl, 1989).

In addition, the comparison between the performance of younger and older infants in Werker and Lalonde (1988) replicates our previous finding (Werker & Tees, 1984a) of a change in cross-language speech perception sensitivity at around one-year of age. This demonstration with a new but related speech contrast confirms that an important change in phonetic perception is apparent by the end of

Table 5.1
Stimuli used in Werker and Lalonde (1988).

	Track 1	*Track 2*
Common	2a, 3, & 3a	4a, 5, & 5a
Hindi-only	4a, 5, & 5a	6a, 7, & 7a
Neither	5a, 6, & 6a	7a, 8, & 8a

the first year of life. Important developmental changes in other aspects of speech perception are also evident toward the end of the first year of life. For example, although 6-month-old infants are only sensitive to clause boundaries (Hirsch-Pasek, Kemler-Nelson, Jusczyk, Wright Cassidy, Druss, & Kennedy, 1987), 9-month-old infants are sensitive to both phrase and clause boundaries (Jusczyk, Hirsch-Pasek, Kemler-Nelson, Kennedy, Woodward, & Piwoz, 1990).

Of interest, changes in other aspects of speech perception have been shown to occur in even younger infants. For instance, cross-language studies indicate that English-learning infants are sensitive to both Polish and English clausal boundaries, but by 6 months of age, English-learning infants can no longer easily perceive the clause boundaries in Polish (Jusczyk, personal communication). Even more surprising is the recent evidence that within the first few months or even days after birth, infants show a preference for their native language (Mehler, Jusczyk, Lambertz, Halstead, Bertoncini, & Amiel-Tison, 1988), indicating that at the most global level, specific linguistic experience in utero may effect speech perception preferences by birth (also see DeCasper & Fifer, 1980).

Why Does the Reorganization Occur in the First Year of Life?

It is of interest to ask: "Why does the reorganization in phonetic perception begin so early in life? Before I start, I would like to note that although we have shown evidence of a reorganization for a small number of phonetic contrasts around one year of age, it is not at all clear (and probably not at all likely) that there will be an identical age-related function for all nonnative contrasts. Most likely, there will be different age functions for different types of contrasts. Categorization schemes such as those suggested by Best et al. (1988) or Burnham (1986) may ultimately be shown to account for early versus later reorganization. However, because it is clear that there is evidence of reorganization as early as one year of age, it becomes imperative to understand how such developmental change might occur. I would like to consider five possible explanations that have been proposed for why there may be changes in nonnative sensitivity and why such change may be evident as early as one year of life.

The five hypotheses are: a) the reorganization is an instance of the effect of experience on auditory/perceptual development, b) the reorganization is the result of a resetting of the parameters in the phonetic module, c) the reorganization is the result of perceptual abilities being mediated through the repertoire of sounds produced in canonical babbling, d) the reorganization is mediated by developing cognitive abilities, and e) the reorganization evidences the beginnings of a phonological system in the receptive lexicon.

According to the first possibility, the reorganization can be explained as an instance of the more general effect of experience on perceptual development. The

primary model for considering the effects of experience on perceptual development stems from the work of Gilbert Gottlieb (1976, 1981; see also Tees, 1976).
Gottlieb (1981) outlined several effects experience can have on perceptual development including: a) no effect, b) maintenance, c) facilitation (increase speed), d)
attunement (change end-point), or e) induction (all experience). Aslin (1987; see
also Aslin & Pisoni, 1980) extended this model to apply specifically to the
development of speech perception. Our previous research showing broad-based
initial abilities and subsequent decline without listening experience can be seen as
an instance of maintenance. However, the fact that adults can still discriminate the
nonnative contrasts under certain testing conditions indicates that maintenance is
operating at the level of linguistic categories rather than auditory abilities. The
construct, thus, requires some further elaboration to account for our data.

The second hypothesis is that age-related changes in cross-language speech
perception can be explained by a direct resetting of the parameters in the phonetic
module (Mattingly & Liberman, in press). According to this interpretation, the
initial universal phonetic sensitivities represent the default option in the phonetic
module. At some point in development, this encapsulated module becomes sensitive to the effects of linguistic experience and can be reset directly by the
phonetic parameters that have functional significance in the child's language
environment. This resetting is precognitive and takes place in much the same
way sound localization abilities are recalibrated as the child's head grows in size
across development.

The third possibility is that the reorganization occurs because of the child's
emerging productive abilities. According to this interpretation, the decline is
related to canonical babbling. That is, as the child begins to be able to produce
sounds intentionally, perception is filtered through production. This hypothesis is
discussed at greater length in the chapter by Vihman and Miller (chapter 4 this
volume). Although this interpretation is of interest, it must take into account the
fact that the Hindi- and Inslekampx-learning infants aged 11–12 months were
able to discriminate those same contrasts that English-learning infants could not
discriminate. For Vihman's interpretation to be correct, there would have to be
evidence that vocal production is already changing by this age in accordance with
relevant language-listening experience. There is, at present, little evidence to
support a language-specific shift in the repertoire of consonants this early (Eilers
& Oller, 1988; Locke, 1983). However, because present measurements of consonant production are so inaccurate, further research is needed to address this
hypothesis more directly.

The fourth possibility is that the reorganization is brought about through the
application of general cognitive abilities to the phonetic domain. There is considerable evidence that around 8–10 months of age, there are important changes in
the young infant's cognitive abilities. In particular, relevant changes include the
emergence of the ability to recall events over a delay without an immediate signi-
fier (Kagan & Hamburg, 1981) and the ability to form perceptual categories on

the basis of arbitrary (experimenter determined) sets of correlated attributes (Cohen, in press). According to this hypothesis, the reorganization in cross-language speech perception could be an instance of an initial, biologically based categorization ability (that might be phonetically relevant) coming under the mediation of cognitive control such that categories are reorganized to map onto those which have functional significance in the baby's language-learning environment.

It should be noted that the cognitive hypothesis is inconsistent with Liberman and Mattingly's hypothesis of modular recalibration. In this regard, Liberman and Mattingly (1985; Mattingly & Liberman, 1988) have argued that the phonetic module is impenetrable by other cognitive processes. If this is the case, there should be no influence of cognitive development on speech perception. However, Chris Lalonde has recently completed an experiment in which he has verified that at least one measure of cognitive development, performance on an object permanence task, is a better predictor of the decline in the ability to discriminate nonnative contrasts than is age (Lalonde, 1989). This raises the possibility that phonetic perception may be influenced by cognitive development. However, on the basis of current data, it is equally likely that developmental changes in cognition and phonetic perception are only coincidentally related.

The final possibility corresponds to that which we have suggested in previous work (Werker & Lalonde, 1988). We have argued that the reorganization may be related to the emergence of phonemic categories at this time; that is, it may reveal a shift from phonetic to phonemic processing.

A classic definition of a phoneme has two components: a) the child must show evidence of using a phone contrastively for it to be called a phoneme, and b) the use must be tied to meaning (Trubetskoy, 1969). Therefore, because a one-year-old child has only a very small productive vocabulary but a fairly large receptive vocabulary (cf. Benedict, 1979), we have begun a series of experiments investigating whether word forms are stored according to some sort of primitive phonological system in the early receptive lexicon (Werker, 1988). For example, if a child understands the word *cup,* will he/she accept the production *tup* or even *bup* as referring to a cup? Hopefully our current series of experiments will help clarify whether there is any evidence of the emergence of a phonemic system around 1 year of age.

Conclusions

In this chapter, I review some of the work exploring the ontogeny of speech perception. The research to date suggests very strongly that speech perception is organized according to phonetically relevant parameters even in the very young infant, even before relevant listening experience. This is consistent with the possibility that a specialized phonetic module is present by birth. In addition, there is considerable evidence that there are age-related changes in the sensitivity to nonnative phonetic contrasts. This chapter argues that these developmental changes must be explained by a reorganization in initial capabilities rather than an absolute loss.

Researchers are only beginning to ask why the reorganization in cross-language speech perception occurs as early as one year of age. Five possible hypotheses that are currently guiding research were outlined at the end of this chapter. Each of these hypotheses requires further elaboration and experimentation. In addition, several of these hypotheses may be complementary rather than mutually exclusive, with a combination of processes happening at one point in time or different types of explanations accounting for early versus later developmental change. Hopefully, continuing research investigating these possibilities will help further our understanding of the ontogeny of the specialized speech processing ability first identified by Alvin M. Liberman and his colleagues.

References

Aslin, R. N. (1987). Visual and auditory development in infancy. In J. D. Osofsky (Ed.), *Handbook of infant development* (2nd ed., pp. 5–97). New York: Wiley.

Aslin, R. N., & Pisoni, D. B. (1980). Some developmental processes in speech perception. In G. H. Yeni-Komshian, J. Kavanaugh, & C. A. Ferguson (Eds.), *Child phonology: Vol. 2. Perception* (pp. 67–96). New York: Academic Press.

Aslin, R. N., Pisoni, D. B., Hennessy, B. L., & Perey, A. J. (1981). Discrimination of voice onset time by human infants: New findings and implications for the effect of early experience. *Child Development, 52,* 1135–1145.

Benedict, H. (1979). Early lexical development. Comprehension and production. *Journal of Child Language, 6,* 183–200.

Best, C. T., McRoberts, G. W., & Sithole, N. M. (1988). Examination of perceptual reorganization for nonnative speech contrasts: Zulu click discrimination by English speaking adults and infants. *Journal of Experimental Psychology: Human Perception and Performance, 14,* 345–360.

Burnham, D. K. (1986). Developmental loss of speech perception: Exposure to and experience with a first language. *Applied Psycholinguistics, 7,* 207–240.

Butterfield, E., & Cairns, G. (1974). Discussion summary—Infant reception research. In R. Schiefelbusch & L. Lloyds (Eds.), *Language perspectives: Acquisition, retardation & intervention* (pp. 75–102). Baltimore: University Park Press.

Carter, D. B., & Patterson, C. J. (1982). Sex-roles as social conventions: The development of children's conception of sex-role stereotypes. *Developmental Psychology, 18,* 812–824.

Cohen, L. B. (in press). An information processing approach to infant cognitive development. In L. Weiskrantz (Ed.), *Thought without language*. Oxford University Press.

DeCasper, A. J., & Fifer, W. (1980). Of human bonding: Newborns prefer their mothers' voices. *Science, 208,* 1174–1176.

Dix, M. R., & Hallpike, C. S. (1947, November 8). The peep show: A new technique for pure tone audiometry in young children. *British Medical Journal,* 719–723.

Eilers, R. E., & Oller, D. K. (1988). Precursors to speech: What is innate and what is acquired? *Annals of Child Development,* (vol. 5, pp. 1–32). New York: JAI Press.

Eilers, R. E., Gavin, W., & Wilson, W. R. (1979). Linguistic experience and phonemic perception in infancy: A cross-linguistic study. *Child Development, 51,* 113–117.

Eimas, P. D. (1975). Developmental studies in speech perception. In L. B. Cohen & P. Salapatek (Eds.), *Infant perception: From sensation to cognition* (pp. 193–231). New York: Academic Press.

Eimas, P. D., Siqueland, E. R., Jusczyk, P., & Vigorito, J. (1971). Speech perception in infants. *Science, 171,* 303–306.

Goto, H. (1971). Auditory perception by normal Japanese adults of the sounds "L" and "R." *Neuropsychologia, 9,* 317–323.

Gottlieb, G. (1976). The roles of experience in the development of behavior and the nervous system. In G. Gottlieb (Ed.), *Development of neural and behavioral specificity* (pp. 1–35). New York: Academic Press.

Gottlieb, G. (1981). Roles of early experience in species-specific perceptual development. In R. N. Aslin, J. R. Ablerts, & M. R. Petersen (Eds.), *Development of perception: Psychobiological perspectives. Vol. 1. Audition, somatic perception, and the chemical senses* (pp. 5–44). New York: Academic Press.

Greiser, D., & Kuhl, P. K. (1989). *Categorization of speech by infants: Support for speech sound prototypes. Developmental Psychology, 25,* 577–588.

Hillenbrand, J. (1983). Perceptual organization of speech sounds by infants. *Journal of Speech and Hearing Research, 26,* 268–282.

Hillenbrand, J. (1984). Speech perception by infants: Categorization based on nasal consonant place of articulation. *Journal of the Acoustical Society of America, 75,* 1613–1622.

Hirsch-Pasek, K., Kemler-Nelson, D. G., Jusczyk, P. W., Wright Cassidy, K., Druss, B., & Kennedy, L. (1987). Clauses are perceptual units for young infants. *Cognition, 26,* 269–286.

Jakobson, R., Fant, G., & Halle, M. (1967). Preliminaries to speech analysis: The distinctive features and their correlates. Cambridge, MA: MIT Press.

Jusczyk, P. W., Hirsch-Pasek, K., Kemler-Nelson, D. G., Kennedy, L. J., Woodward, A., & Piwoz, J. (1990). *Perception of acoustic correlates to major phrasal units by young infants.* Manuscript submitted for publication.

Kagan, J., & Hamburg, M. (1981). The enhancement of memory in the first year. *The Journal of Genetic Psychology, 138,* 3–14.

Kuhl, P. K. (1979). Speech perception in early infancy: Perceptual constancy for spectrally dissimilar vowel categories. *Journal of the Acoustical Society of America, 66,* 1669–1679.

Kuhl, P. K. (1987). Perception of speech and sound in early infancy. In P. Salapatek & L. Cohen (Eds.), *Handbook of infant perception* (vol. 2, pp. 275–382). New York: Academic Press.

Kuhl, P. K. (1989). *Human adults and human infants exhibit a prototype effect for phoneme categories. Monkeys do not.* Manuscript submitted for publication.

Lalonde, C. E. (1989). An investigation of the relations among object search skills, cross-language speech perception, and visual categorization in infancy. Unpublished Master's Thesis, University of British Columbia.

Lasky, R. E., Syrdal-Lasky, A., & Klein, R. E. (1975). VOT discrimination by four and six and a half month infants from Spanish environments. *Journal of Experimental Child Psychology, 20,* 215–225.

Lenneberg, E. H. (1967). *Biological foundations of language.* New York: Wiley.

Liberman, A. M., Cooper, F. S., Shankweiler, D. P., & Studdert-Kennedy, M. (1967). Perception of the speech code. *Psychological Review, 74,* 431–461.

Liberman, A. M., & Mattingly, I. G. (1985). The motor theory of speech perception revised. *Cognition, 21,* 1–36.

Lisker, L., & Abramson, A. S. (1964). A cross-language study of voicing in initial stops: Acoustical measurements. *Word, 20,* 384–422.

Lisker, L., & Abramson, A. S. (1970). The voicing dimension: Some experiments in Comparative Phonetics. In B. Hála, M. Romportl, & P. Janota (Eds.), *Proceedings of the 6th International Congress of Phonetic Sciences* (pp. 563–567). Prague: Academia.

Locke, J. (1983). *Phonological acquisition and change.* New York: Academic Press.

MacKain, K. S., Best, C. T., & Strange, W. (1981). Categorical perception of English /r/ and /l/ by Japanese bilinguals. *Applied Psycholinguistics, 2,* 368–390.

Mattingly, I. G., & Liberman, A. M. (1988). Specialized perceiving systems for speech and other biologically significant sounds. In G. M. Edelman, W. E. Gall, & W. M. Cowan (Eds.), *Auditory function: The neurobiological bases of hearing* (pp. 775–792). New York: Wiley.

Mattingly, I. G., & Liberman, A. M. (in press). Speech and other auditory modules. In G. M. Edelman, W. E. Gall, & W. M. Cowan (Eds.). *Signal and sense: Local and global order in perceptual maps.* New York: Wiley.

McGurk, H., & MacDonald, J. (1976). Hearing lips and seeing voices. *Nature, 264,* 746–748.

Mehler, J., Jusczyk, P. W., Lambertz, G., Halsted, N., Bertoncini, J., & Amiel-Tison, C. (1988). A precursor of language acquisition in young infants. *Cognition, 29,* 143–178.

Miller, J. L., & Eimas, P. D. (1979). Organization in infant speech perception. *Canadian Journal of Psychology, 33,* 353–367.

Miller, J. L., & Eimas, P. D. (1983). Studies on the categorization of speech by infants. *Cognition, 13,* 135–165.

Miyawaki, K., Strange, W., Verbrugge, R. R., Liberman, A. M., Jenkins, J. J., & Fujimura, O. (1975). An effect of linguistic experience: The discrimination of (r) and (l) by native speakers of Japanese and English. *Perception & Psychophysics, 18,* 331–340.

Pisoni, D. B., Aslin, R. N., Perey, A. J., & Hennessy, B. L. (1982). Some effects of laboratory training on identification and discrimination of voicing contrasts in stop consonants. *Journal of Experimental Psychology: Human Perception and Performance, 8,* 279–314.

Polka, L. (1987). Perception of Persian uvular and velar stops by speakers of American English. *Journal of the Acoustical Society of America,* Suppl. 83, K6C(A).

Strange, W. (1986). Speech input and the development of speech perception. In J. F. Kavanagh (Ed.), *Otitis media and child development* (pp. 12–26). Parkton, MD: Yorkton Press.

Strange, W., & Jenkins, J. J. (1978). Role of linguistic experience in the perception of speech. In R. D. Walk & H. L. Pick (Eds.), *Perception and experience* (pp. 125–169). New York: Plenum.

Streeter, L. A. (1976). Language perception of 2-month-old infants shows effects of both innate mechanisms and experience. *Nature, 259,* 39–41.

Tees, R. C. (1976). Perceptual development in mammals. In G. Gottlieb (Ed.), *Development of neural and behavioral specificity* (pp. 281–326). New York: Academic Press.

Tees, R. C., & Werker, J. F. (1984). Perceptual flexibility: Maintenance or recovery of the ability to discriminate nonnative speech sounds. *Canadian Journal of Psychology, 38,* 579–590.

Trehub, S. E. (1976). The discrimination of foreign speech contrasts by infants and adults. *Child Development, 47,* 466–472.

Trubetskoy, N. S. (1969). *Principles of phonology.* (Christiane A. M. Baltaxe, Trans.) Berkeley and Los Angeles: University of California Press.

Werker, J. F. (1988, April). *Speech perception and the acquisition of word meaning.* Paper presented at the International Conference on Infant Studies, Washington, DC. (Abstract published in *Infant Behavior and Development, 11,* 357)

Werker, J. F., & Lalonde, C. E. (1988). Cross-language speech perception: Initial capabilities and developmental change. *Developmental Psychology, 24,* 1–12.

Werker, J. F., & Logan, J. (1985). Cross-language evidence for three factors in speech perception. *Perception & Psychophysics, 37,* 35–44.

Werker, J. F., Gilbert, J. H. V., Humphrey, G. K., & Tees, R. C. (1981). Developmental aspects of cross-language speech perception. *Child Development, 52,* 349–355.

Werker, J. F., McGurk, H., & Frost, P. E. (1987). *Cross-language differences in bimodal speech perception.* Paper presented at the combined English and Canadian Psychological Association Meeting, Oxford, England.

Werker, J. F., & Tees, R. C. (1983). Developmental changes across childhood in the perception of nonnative sounds. *Canadian Journal of Psychology, 37,* 278–286.

Werker, J. F., & Tees, R. C. (1984a). Cross-language speech perception: Evidence for perceptual reorganization during the first year of life. *Infant Behavior and Development, 7,* 49–63.

Werker, J. F., & Tees, R. C. (1984b). Phonemic and phonetic factors in adult cross-language speech perception. *Journal of the Acoustical Society of America, 75,* 1866–1878.

Wilson, W. R., Moore, J. M., & Thompson, G. (1976). *Sound field auditory thresholds of infants utilizing visual reinforcement audiometry (VRA).* Paper presented at The American Speech and Hearing Association, Houston, TX.

Comment: Some Effects of Language Acquisition on Speech Perception

Peter D. Eimas

Department of Psychology, Brown University

The research of Janet Werker has provided us with a rich body of data on how experience with the parental language alters our initial capacities to perceive the sounds of speech. Her writings and presentation have made it clear that if we are to understand the effects of linguistic experience, we must consider the specific acoustic information that is or is not experienced, as well as how acoustic information is used linguistically by the parental language. This is to say that we must recognize that the effects on perception of our earliest experience with language may have both auditory and linguistic origins.

The findings and ideas of Werker fit nicely with my own views, or biases depending on your point of view, on the perception of speech and its ontogenesis. These include the belief that there is an innately given, universal set of phonetic categories together with a set of procedures that enable the infant listener to map acoustic variants onto categorical representations. These views also include the idea that experience with the parental language acts as a means of selection (cf. Edelman, 1987); the initial, relatively large set of phonetic categories is reduced to a smaller set that is specific to the parental language. In support of these ideas, Werker, among others (see Eimas, Miller, & Jusczyk, 1987, for a review), has shown that infants about six months of age and younger are apparently able to discriminate all phonetic distinctions, even those that are not found in the parental language. Moreover, the discriminative process is categorical. However, as Werker has uniquely shown, the ability to discriminate some of the universal phonetic distinctions that are not part of the parental language begins to decline just after eight months of age and is nearly absent by ten to twelve months of age—a surprisingly early effect of experience with the parental language. Of interest, of course, is the nature of this loss and the specific factors in a language and in the acoustics per se that drive the phenomenon.

Werker's research with adult listeners informs us that the loss is most likely not perceptual; that is, it probably does not arise from a loss of sensitivity at the level of auditory processing. Under some experimental circumstances, and perhaps always when the critical acoustic information is presented in a nonlinguistic context, adult listeners are able to discriminate the sounds that define a nonnative phonetic contrast. The loss would, thus, seem to be phonetic or perhaps phonemic in nature (Werker & Logan, 1985; Werker & Tees, 1984).

This view is not complete, however. It needs elaboration, if we are to accommodate recent data by Best and her associates (Best, McRoberts, & Sithole, 1988), who found that infants born into English-speaking families did not lose the ability to hear a phonetic distinction based on the click sounds of Zulu by 14 months of age. Moreover, adult native speakers of English also showed no evidence of a loss in the ability to discriminate a number of these contrasts. Indeed, their performance did not differ reliably from that of native speakers of Zulu. Best et al. (1988) and Werker (chapter 5 this volume) have provided some beginnings into how we might accommodate these seemingly contradictory findings.

Consider the following three types of nonnative phonetic distinctions, with English as the parental language for the sake of the present discussion. The first is one in which both nonnative categories are assimilated into (or resemble) a single phonetic category in the parental language. This type is exemplified by the contrasts based on place of articulation that were investigated by Werker (Tees & Werker, 1984; Werker & Tees, 1984). The second class is one in which there is no assimilation into the parental categories. There is, for these contrasts, no resemblance to the categories of the parental language—a set of conditions that match the distinctions based on the click sounds found in Zulu. The third type consists of those distinctions that resemble contrasting categories in the parental language in that some of the acoustic characteristics that define the nonnative contrast are used productively in the native language. The voicing distinction in Hindi, studied by Werker and Tees (1984; Tees & Werker, 1984) is an example of this type of nonnative distinction. A variant of this class of nonnative contrasts is one in which either or both members of the nonnative contrast appear as allophonic variants in the native language. The ability of native speakers of English to discriminate prevoiced from voiced stops in syllable-initial position (e.g., Pisoni, Aslin, Perey, & Hennessy, 1982) may reflect this form of variation in English (cf. Tees & Werker, 1984).

In the case of the first distinction, it is easy to imagine how attentional processes would lead the infant to ignore a phonetic distinction that was not used to contrast meaning in the parental language. Of course, for this to occur, the infant must have knowledge of some words and how they contrast phonologically. In other words, the infant must have reached the point in language acquisition where at least some phonetic distinctions have come to signal contrasts in meaning (cf. MacKain, 1982), and more specifically, knowledge of how the native language uses the phonetic category into which the nonnative contrast has been assimilated must be available to the infant. As a result, when acoustic information signaling this form of nonnative contrast is encountered in a linguistic context, it is no longer discriminated, inasmuch as there is simply no phonetic distinction on which to base the discrimination.

However, this leaves us with an interesting question: Why is it that the physical information, once discriminable, is not heard as two different acoustic events? We can also ask: Why has a lack of differentiation at the phonetic or phonemic level resulted in a failure to detect a distinction at the auditory level, except possibly when the information is presented in a nonspeech context? After all, the critical information was once differentiated and surely has continued to be experienced as a consequence of the natural variation in the production of speech or as a consequence of other natural events that have acoustic consequences, and, thus, it is unlikely that the mechanisms of auditory perception for this information have atrophied. I do not have the answer but offer the following speculation. Higher levels of linguistic representation take precedence over lower levels, and lower levels of linguistic representation, the phonetic for purposes of this discussion, take precedence over auditory representations. By this I mean that, all other things being equal, representations that take precedence are those that we are most immediately aware of and that first determine behavior. Thus, the single phonetic representation onto which the nonnative contrast is mapped prevents discrimination of the acoustic difference that defines the nonnative contrast. One might now ask why the precedence effect works in this direction. My belief, once more speculative, is that representations from species-specific, biologically important functions take precedence over representations from functions that are more general, provided of course that the competition involves functions on a roughly comparable level.

With regard to the second type of nonnative contrasts, those that do not resemble any native contrasts, there is no loss of discriminative capacity according to the findings of Best et al. (1988). However, as they noted, discrimination is most likely occurring at an auditory level, at least in the case of their adult listeners, and I agree. I would argue, as would Best et al. for adult listeners, that a loss has occurred but that it is at the phonetic level. That is to say, the phonetic categories that are defined by the acoustic characteristics of clicks would not exist as phonetic in languages such as English, where they are not used productively. In my view of phonological development, phonetic distinctions that are not used to distinguish meaning are not retained beyond some as yet unspecifiable age. However, inasmuch as the acoustically differing clicks are not mapped into phonetic representations in the parental language, there can be no effects of linguistic precedence, in this case phonetic or phonemic precedence, and discrimination of the click sounds occurs. The discrimination that is made, however, is not between two linguistic entities but rather between two nonlinguistic, auditory events, at least for adult listeners. At what age the discrimination shifts from being based on innate phonetic categories to being based on acoustic properties alone remains to be determined. If this is true, we would not expect native adult speakers of English to perceive these sounds categorically by reference to their phonetic properties. Nor would we expect them to show trading relations or an equivalence of cues for the multiple acoustic properties that define these phonetic categories (Best, Morrongiello, & Robson, 1981). Finally, we would expect no evidence of orderly judgments of phonetic goodness for acoustic variants of a click category as Miller, Connine, Schermer, and Kluender (1983) found for differences in VOT in English speakers.

On this view, it is reasonable, I believe, to predict that nonnative distinctions that are assimilated into a single phonetic category will be lost as phonetic categories before distinctions that have no resemblance to the categories of the parental language. In the former case, there is evidence in the parental language that the nonnative distinctions do not signal contrasts in meaning. However, in the latter case, there can be no such evidence. The child must at some point in time infer their lack of productivity from the fact that no evidence has been found for productivity. Surely this process must take longer than one based on consistent evidence. As for the third class of nonnative contrasts, those that resemble opposing members of a native phonological distinction, these might be expected to be lost as phonetic categories at some intermediate point in development inasmuch as there is evidence in the parental language for their lack of productivity, but it is (at least in cases involving allophonic variation) inconsistent.

For any given language, there should be a number of nonnative contrasts that fit into each of the three types. It will be of interest to learn whether the ages at which they are lost as phonetic categories varies as I have suggested. Although the research necessary to test these ideas is inherently difficult, if it is possible to implement, it may yield more sensitive measures of phonological development than are presently available as well as provide new data on the differences between auditory and phonetic processing of speech signals.

Given the theme of this conference, I would like to conclude with a few remarks on the relevance of the infant data in general to the modularity hypothesis. In my view, there is nothing in the infant data as yet that compels a view that the system for speech perception constitutes a submodule of the input system for human language. Nevertheless, the data in many respects are compatible with this hypothesis. For example, a number of earlier studies have shown marked differences in perception, when a given acoustic contrast is presented in a linguistic as opposed to a nonlinguistic context (e.g., Eimas, 1974). Similarly, earlier work of Miller and myself (Miller & Eimas, 1983) showing trading relations and an equivalence of cues is compatible with a modularity hypothesis. Furthermore, recent unpublished results of Miller and myself showing that formant transitions that are sufficient to signal the distinction between /sṭa/ and /ska/ are no longer discriminable, when the silent interval between the initial /s/ and the vocalic segment is reduced from 100 to 20 msec are in accord with a modular perceptual system that is highly constrained by knowledge of the processes of articulation. Finally, the fact that the perception of speech is altered by our experience with the parental language and the fact that this alteration is linguistic and not auditory in nature also fit with a modularity hypothesis. The speech module is penetrable, as it must be early in life, if a selection is to occur at the phonetic level. However, the penetration involves linguistic information, and, furthermore, it is confined to the speech module. It does not spread to auditory processing systems.

Of course, knowing that speech is governed by a modular system is but a first step in theory construction. It remains for us to determine how the conversion from sound to a phonetic representation occurs and how knowledge of the processes of production are realized in the mechanisms of perception. In light of the history of our field, solutions to these problems will not be easily discovered, and they will be controversial.

Acknowledgment

Preparation of this discussion was supported in part by Grant HD 05331 from the National Institute of Child Health and Human Development. I thank Joanne L. Miller for her comments on an earlier version.

References

Best, C. T., McRoberts, G. W., & Sithole, N. N. (1988). The phonological basis of perceptual loss of nonnative contrasts: Maintenance of discrimination among Zulu Clicks by English-speaking adults and infants. *Journal of Experimental Psychology: Human Perception and Performance, 14,* 245–260.

Best, C. T., Morrongiello, B., & Robson, R. (1981). Perceptual equivalence of acoustic cues in speech and nonspeech perception. *Perception & Psychophysics, 29,* 191–211.

Edelman, G. (1987). *Neural Darwinism.* New York: Basic Books.

Eimas, P. D. (1974). Auditory and linguistic processing of cues for place of articulation by infants. *Perception & Psychophysics, 16,* 513–521.

Eimas, P. D., Miller, J. L., & Jusczyk, P. W. (1987). On infant speech perception and the acquisition of language. In S. Harnad (Ed.), *Categorical perception: The groundwork of cognition* (pp. 161–195). New York: Cambridge University Press.

MacKain, K. S. (1982). On explaining the role of experience on infants' speech discrimination. *Journal of Child Language, 9,* 527–542.

Miller, J. L., Connine, C. M., Schermer, T. M., & Kluender, K. R. (1983). A possible auditory basis for internal structure of phonetic categories. *Journal of the Acoustical Society of America, 73,* 2124–2133.

Miller, J. L., & Eimas, P. D. (1983). Studies on the categorization of speech by infants. *Cognition, 13,* 135–165.

Pisoni, D. B., Aslin, R. N., Perey, A. J., & Hennessy, B. L. (1982). Some effects of laboratory training on identification and discrimination of voicing contrasts in stop consonants. *Journal of Experimental Psychology: Human Perception and Performance, 8,* 297–314.

Tees, R. C., & Werker, J. L. (1984). Perceptual flexibility: Maintenance or recovery of the ability to discriminate nonnative speech sounds. *Canadian Journal of Psychology, 38,* 579–590.

Werker, J. F., & Logan, J. S. (1985). Cross-language evidence for three factors in speech perception. *Perception & Psychophysics, 37,* 35–44.

Werker, J. F., & Tees, R. C. (1984). Cross-language speech perception: Evidence for perceptual reorganization during the first year of life. *Infant Behavior & Development, 7,* 49–63.

Chapter 6

Visual Perception of Phonetic Gestures

Quentin Summerfield

MRC Institute of Hearing Research,
University of Nottingham, UK

Abstract

The vast majority of people benefit from seeing the face of the talker, and, thus, the visible movement of the lips, teeth, tongue, and jaw, when speech perception is difficult because of acoustical distortions such as noise or reverberation, but they do so to markedly varying extents. The benefit received correlates highly with the ability to lipread without acoustical information. Although such measures can be reliable, correlations with performance on other perceptual and cognitive tasks are inconsistent and surprisingly low. These observations mesh neatly with Alvin Liberman's suggestions that phonetic perception is subserved by a biologically (and, thus, perceptually and cognitively) distinct system specialized for recovering the articulatory gestures produced by talkers. A key issue in understanding how such a system might operate is to describe the process of audio-visual integration and in particular the representations of the auditory and visual streams of information at their conflux. This chapter will consider the merits of several representations including: a) vectors describing the magnitudes of independent acoustical and optical parameters of the speech waveform and the visible shape of the mouth, and b) time-varying kinematic patterns providing evidence of articulatory dynamics. The aim is not so much to list the empirical evidence for and against each representation as to clarify the essential differences between them, and to specify the contexts in which each has application and explanatory power.

Among the central tenets of the Revised Motor Theory of Speech Perception (Liberman & Mattingly, 1985) are two key suggestions: First, listeners are not primarily interested in the patterns of sound that talkers create but in the articulatory gestures that generate the sounds. Second, the recovery of these phonetic gestures is accomplished by a specialized perceptual module. It can be quite tricky to persuade a sceptical audience of the truth of these claims. However, the evident ability of people to lipread and to perceive speech audio-visually can come to the persuader's aid. All sighted people benefit from seeing the face of the talker, when the acoustical speech signal is distorted by, for example, noise, reverberation, or filtering. Therefore, setting the issue of modularity aside, surely this is clear evidence that the perception of speech can involve the perception of phonetic gestures?

My overall aim in this paper is to examine the extent to which this conclusion can be sustained by data. I shall do that by asking what properties must be possessed by the system that perceives speech, given that it can lipread and perceive audio-visually. My second aim is to determine whether these properties are consistent with the properties claimed for perceptual modules. In each case, I shall start by reviewing the facts briefly before considering their implications; although many of the established facts of lipreading and audio-visual speech perception are compatible with what is known about speech production and auditory speech perception, they may not be familiar.

Lipreading

If we attempt to answer to the question "How well can the phonetic module identify vowels and consonants by lipreading alone?" we might conclude: "Not very well." Difficulties arise, because the acoustical differences that distinguish many consonants are generated by the activity of articulators that are hidden within the mouth and cannot easily be seen. Thus, phonemes differing only in nasality (e.g., /b/ vs. /m/) or voicing (e.g., /b/ vs. /p/) that are distinguished by different states of the velum or larynx look the same. However, some other phonetic distinctions between consonants have visible correlates. In some cases, the constriction and release at the place of articulation can itself be seen (e.g., in /b/, /v/, /ð/, and /w/). In other cases, a consonant's manner of articulation can involve a characteristic degree of liprounding, proximity of the teeth, or speed of movement of the tongue (e.g., in /dʒ/, /l/, and /r/). As a result, nine or so categories of consonant can be distinguished with a reliability exceeding 75% correct (Walden, Prosek, Montgomery, Scherr & Jones, 1977) (e.g. (/b/, /p/, /m/), /w/, (/v/, /f/), (/ð/, /θ/), (/d/, /t/, /n/, /g/, /k/, /j/), (/s/, /z/), (/ʒ/, /zʒ/, /ʃ/, /tʃ/), /r/, /l/). However, performance at this level is achieved only when subjects are familiar with the task and the talker, the lighting illuminates the tip of the tongue, and the stimuli are articulated carefully but naturally in the context of open vowels (e.g., /ɑ/–consonant–/ɑ/) (Benguerel & Pichora-Fuller, 1982) so that the positions of the teeth and tongue can be seen. Thus, to summarize, although some phonetic distinctions among consonants cannot be distinguished by lipreading, others can, if the conditions are right.

The situation with vowels is rather different. Under optimal conditions, all English vowels are visibly distinct. This claim may seem surprising, given that a major determinant of the acoustical structure of vowels is the position of the body of the tongue (e.g., Stevens & House, 1955), which is often hard to see. However, in English, the height of the tongue in the mouth is rather highly correlated with the vertical separation of the lips. As a result, in the speech of a single talker, most stressed vowels are quite well specified by different degrees of horizontal and vertical separation of the lips, coupled with different durations (Fromkin, 1964; Montgomery & Jackson, 1983). Differences in the visibility of the teeth play a limited but systematic additional role (McGrath, 1985) as illustrated in Fig. 6.1. By using these cues, good lipreaders can identify English monophthongal vowels nearly perfectly, provided that the stimuli are produced carefully in a consonantal context that demarcates the duration of the syllable and does not impede the display of a wide range of lip shapes (Montgomery, Walden, & Prosek, 1987) (i.e., /d/–vowel–/d/ is preferable to /f/–vowel–/f/ or /ʃ/–vowel–/ʃ/). Thus, an alternative answer to the question "How well can the phonetic module lipread consonants and vowels?" could reasonably be given as "Quite well, given the limited evidence available to it."

In fluent speech, the optimal conditions of minimal coarticulation described above are rarely found. Thus, because of this, it might seem that sentences would be impossible to lipread: Many are. Of a corpus of 336 presented for identification by Rosen and Corcoran (1982), some were not identified correctly by any subject. Others, however, were identified perfectly by over 90% of the subjects. MacLeod (1987) determined some of the factors that affect the ease with which the content words in this corpus of sentences can be lipread. She confirmed expectations drawn from studies of the corresponding factors in acoustically presented sentences (e.g., Cole & Jakimik, 1980). Briefly, content words are more likely to be lipread correctly if: (a) they are familiar, (b) they are initiated by a consonant whose articulation visibly defines the start of the word, and (c) they look similar to few other words (i.e., the size of their visual cohort is small). Thus, *The boy forgot his book* is easy to lipread, whereas *The tea-towel's by the sink* is nearly impossible.

These analyses jointly suggest that lexical access in lipreading must generally be made directly from the visible pattern of articulation without individual consonants and vowels being identified at an intermediate stage. The corresponding idea that listeners may invoke the option of achieving lexical access directly from the acoustical speech signal received impetus from Klatt's analysis (1979) of the problems faced by designers of automatic speech recognizers. Klatt argued that the variability in the acoustical forms of phonemes means that decisions about acoustical properties such as the frequencies of particular formants are prone to error and, therefore, provide a poor basis for decisions about phonetic identity. As a result, decisions about phonemes provide a poor basis for decisions about words. These problems are compounded by the general absence of acoustical

A. 77.8% (12.4)

B. 56.1% (10.3)

C. 50.3% (12.0)

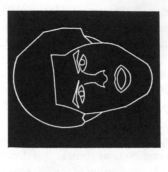

D. 56.7% (15.5)　　E. 51.1% (10.0)

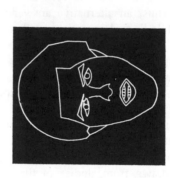

[F. 58.6% (12.6)]　　[G. 52.9% (12.1)]

markers of word boundaries. Overall, it is difficult to specify analytic rules to undo the phonological recoding that occurs within and between words in fluent speech. As a result, a sensible design would have a recognizer determine word boundaries by applying lexical and syntactic constraints to an unfolding acoustical input rather than first seeking evidence of word boundaries to define strings of phonemes that constitute words. The problem for speech recognition by lipreading is similar but greater. The visual evidence of individual consonants and vowels is less constraining than the acoustical evidence, and the visible markers of word boundaries are even fewer than the acoustical markers. Accordingly, strategies for exploiting lexical constraints in interpreting acoustical speech signals are likely to be at least as relevant in lipreading, if not more so.

Lipreading: A Module within a Module?

Although there is no fully developed account of lexical access in lipreading, teachers of lipreading have long acknowledged that people differ hugely in their ability. Laboratory evidence bears out the observation; in this section, I relate it to Fodor's (1983) suggestion that perceptual modules are encapsulated.

Encapsulation implies that the language-processing module possesses a knowledge of its own domain in order to carry out its function of identifying the words in utterances and their grammatical roles but that it neither requires nor is able to call upon general intellectual resources. Contrast that idea with the early and intuitively reasonable belief expressed by Kitson (1915) and Nitchie (1917), among others, that lipreading is a complex skill whose proficient performance is likely to depend on competence in many intellectual subskills. Clearly, if this were the case, lipreading would not coexist happily with the other properties of the language-processing module.

However, by the 1950s, research had confirmed the experiences of teachers of the deaf working in the oral tradition: lipreading was different from other intellectual skills in that it was (disturbingly) difficult to teach and learn. Individual differences among deaf children in the ability to lipread are large, but of this variance only small and often inconsistent proportions are related to individual differences in general intelligence, chronological age, or the amount of training

---

FIG. 6.1. Single frames extracted from video-recordings of normal (A), made-up (B, C), and synthetic (D, and E) faces during the vowel nucleus of the syllable /bib/. Percentages show the accuracy with which monopthongal vowels were identified by lipreading in each condition. Conditions F and G (not illustrated) were similar to D and E, except that the facial frame was excluded. Without the teeth, high front vowels, such as /i/ and /ɪ/, were confused with vowels articulated with similar lip shapes but with the jaw lower and the tongue further back in the mouth, such as /ɜ/ and /ɛ/. Synthetic vowels (D, E, F, G) in which the lips and teeth were animated were lipread as accurately as natural but made-up vowels in which only the lips and teeth were visible.

given. The conclusion that "good lipreaders are born, not made" is reinforced by finding a similar diversity of ability among adults with normal hearing; this variability forms a pattern of generally low and often nonsignificant correlations with other sensory, perceptual and cognitive abilities. (See Heider & Heider, 1940, and Utley, 1946, for influential studies. See Jeffers & Barley, 1971, and Farwell, 1976, for reviews.)

Unconvincing patterns of correlations are found in the first two lines of Fig. 6.2. The figure shows correlations between the ability to lipread words in sentences and five other measures. The first two lines summarize the results of studies reviewed by Jeffers and Barley (1971). These studies are a heterogeneous mixture; some involved adults, others children; some involved hearing-impaired subjects, others normal-hearing subjects. Line 1 shows the pattern of correlations with 18 measures of general and performance intelligence, such as the Weschler-Bellevue intelligence scales, from Tables 4–XI and 4–XII in Jeffers and Barley's book. Line 2 shows the pattern of correlations with scores on 13 tests of verbal reasoning from their Table 4-XXV. None of the studies involving adults with normal hearing found significant correlations. When studies with hearing-im-

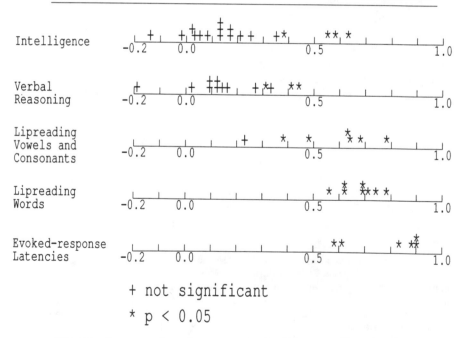

FIG. 6.2. Patterns of product-moment correlations between the ability to lipread words in sentences and five other measures. [+ not significant, * p < 0.05]

paired adults and children are included as well, then of the 18 attempts to link I.Q. and lipreading ability, only four found a significant relationship, with correlations ranging from the marginal (r = 0.38) to the moderate (r = 0.63). Considering the 13 studies that sought correlations between lipreading and skill in verbal reasoning, only three were successful, with a highest correlation of only 0.44. We may reasonably conclude that good lipreading depends on a minimal level of intelligence and verbal ability, but provided this is attained, further ability is not important.

An explanation for this absence of significant correlations would be found, if lipreading skills were generally poor with little systematic variation to be explained by individual differences in other factors. However, this is not the case. The distribution of lipreading skills in both the normal-hearing and hearing-impaired populations is broad. Indeed, it is to be lamented that excellence in lipreading is not related to the need to perform well, because in formal laboratory tests (which admittedly do not call upon the full range of tactics relevant to successful lipreading in everyday life), the best totally deaf and hearing-impaired subjects often perform only as well as the best subjects with normal hearing. Therefore, the failure to find significant correlations between lipreading and many other abilities can not be ascribed to a lack of variation among subjects in the ability to lipread.

To consolidate this argument, consider Fig. 6.3. It shows the relationship between two measures of lipreading ability obtained from 20 undergraduates with normal hearing and vision by MacLeod and Summerfield (1990). The vertical axis shows the percentage of content words that the subjects correctly identified in sentences by lipreading alone. Scores range from 0% to over 70%. The horizontal axis indicates the *difference* in dB between the minimal signal-to-noise ratios at which the subjects could report the content words correctly when only listening and when also viewing the talker. The first of these thresholds can be called an Auditory Speech Reception Threshold for sentences in Noise (A-SRTN); the second is the corresponding Audio-visual Speech Reception Threshold (AV-SRTN). The size of the difference between the two types of threshold ranges from less than 3dB to over 11dB, with an average of about 6dB. Its product-moment correlation with lipreading ability is 0.89 (n = 20, p < 0.01). Thus, there is a strong correlation between the ability to lipread and to use vision to supplement auditory speech perception, and there are large individual differences in those abilities even among a population of homogeneous age and intelligence screened to have normal hearing and vision.

Now consider the possibility that the large individual differences in lipreading stem from variation in the ability to use linguistic context or to reason verbally. If there were such differences, we should not expect a high correlation between the ability to lipread and to use vision to supplement hearing. This follows, because in computing the difference between a subject's A-SRTN and AV-SRTN, we would be partialling out effects of verbal and intellectual abilities. The task for

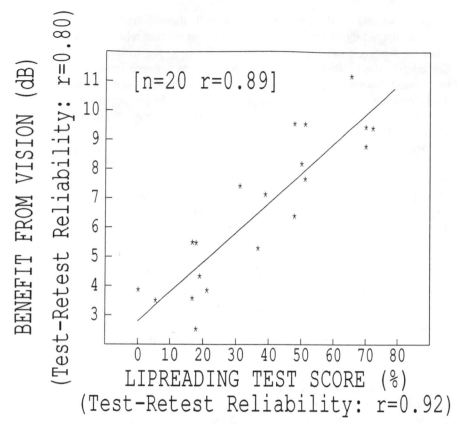

FIG. 6.3. The relationship between the ability to lipread words in sentences with no acoustical information (horizontal axis) and the additional amount of noise (in dB) that can be tolerated, when auditory speech perception was supplemented by vision (vertical axis). Data from 20 young adults with normal hearing and vision.

the subject is the same in each case—to identify words in sentences at a disadvantageous SNR—and would be expected to make similar demands on skills in verbal reasoning. Yet, these difference scores still correlate strongly with the ability to lipread visually presented sentences. Therefore, individual differences in the ability to lipread can reflect variation in general verbal and intellectual skills only to a minimal extent. Note that this is different from saying that the ability to use linguistic knowledge forms *no* part of lipreading. It says only that the ways in which subjects differ in linguistic ability are not relevant to the massive differences that are found in their ability to lipread.

What factors *do* correlate with the ability of normally hearing adults to lipread sentences? Two have been implicated systematically, one expected, the other more surprising. The first is simply the ability to lipread other types of utterance, such as vowels or consonants in nonsense syllables (shown in Line 3 of Fig. 6.2), or isolated words (shown in Line 4 of Fig. 6.2). Some of these results come from Jeffers and Barley, others from MacLeod (1987). Provided that the items within such a test cover a sufficiently wide range of difficulty to allow the best lipreaders to display their virtuosity, moderately high correlations with the ability to lipread sentences are found in the range from 0.6 to 0.8.

The second and more surprising measure that has been found to correlate with the ability to lipread is the latency of components of the electrical potentials recorded from the scalp in response to a bright flash of light (Shepherd, De-Lavergne, Frueh, & Clobridge, 1977; Shepherd, 1982; Samar & Sims, 1983). In each of these studies, a correlation of the order of −0.9 has been found, as shown in Line 5 of Fig. 6.2. The absolute size of the correlations is comparable with the test–retest reliability of lipreading tests themselves. It is, therefore, as high as is generally likely to be found between lipreading and performance on any other task. Some caution is warranted, because the results are not completely consistent. In different studies, high correlations have involved either a very early component of the visual-evoked response occurring within the first 20ms after the stimulus (Samar & Sims, 1983) or a later component occurring at about 120 ms (Shepherd et al., 1977; Shepherd, 1982). Nonetheless, analogous correlations have not been reported between the latency of evoked responses and the ability to perform other perceptual or cognitive skills (Shepherd, 1982). Thus, individual differences in the ability to lipread may reflect differences in the speed of neural processing in relatively early stages of visual analysis. Possibly a short evoked-response latency means that the subject's visual nervous system can accomplish more processing per second and that particular operations can be carried out faster. This suggests that the roots of good lipreading are to be found in a subject's hardwired physiology. If this interpretation is correct, it would not be surprising to find that lipreading is difficult to teach and to learn, that good lipreaders are "born and not made," and that ability is not related to complex conceptual cognitive abilities nor to those sensory and perceptual ones that have been examined so far.

Therefore, to summarize: There is wide variation in the ability to lipread, even within populations screened to have normal hearing and vision. The individual differences correlate consistently with other measures of the ability to lipread and with neurophysiological measures of speed of visual neural processing. They do not correlate systematically with other sensory, perceptual, or cognitive abilities. Provided, therefore, that we can interpret the degree of correlation between lipreading and X as evidence of the degree of involvement of X in lipreading, we are left with lipreading as a special skill, dependent only on unspecified and possibly hardwired aspects of visual analysis—precisely how we expect an input module to be organized.

Does this mean that we should regard lipreading as being subserved by an input module in its own right? I think not. The facility with which subjects use vision and hearing together, and the high correlation between the benefit they obtain and their ability to lipread, suggest that lipreading is not distinct from the linguistic-processing module but part of it: a submodule within a module, perhaps.

In concluding this section, two final questions must be answered. First, why are individual differences in the ability to lipread found? Second, why is there a less impressive range of individual differences in the ability to perceive speech auditorily? Possibly the answers are interrelated. The evolutionary pressures on mammals to develop refined hearing, and in particular to develop a refined ability to detect biologically significant sounds in noise, have been (and presumably continue to be) very strong. The result is a uniformly highly developed auditory ability in human beings. This is simply not true of lipreading. It is useful particularly as people grow old, and their hearing deteriorates, and it is useful, when speech must be understood in noise. However, given generally good hearing in a preindustrial population, these are not factors that will exert selective evolutionary pressure. (To be blunt, in early man, congenital deafness must have been a bar to survival and, thus, reproduction, whereas skills in lipreading in old age would have come too late to be selective.) Therefore, in comparing the ability of a group to understand speech by audition and by lipreading, we are comparing the performance of a biologically essential skill with the performance of a biological dispensable skill. It seems reasonable to expect greater variability in the performance of the biologically dispensable skill.

Audio-Visual Speech Perception

Lipreading would be worthy of study, even if it were as different from auditory speech perception as is Sign language, entailing its own modes of perceptual and linguistic analysis. However, what distinguishes lipreading from the perception of Sign is the tight relationship between the ability to lipread and to perceive speech audio-visually. It implies a close coupling between the auditory and visual analyses of speech and should, therefore, allow the phenomena of each to constrain theories about the other. In this section, I discuss the major phenomena of audio-visual speech perception and sketch a unifying account for them. In the following section, I shall consider their implications for the process of speech perception.

The phenomena of audio-visual speech perception can be placed on a continuum of effects ranging from clear evidence of the resonances of the talker's vocal tract in the acoustical signal, or its auditory representation along with low dependency on vision, to the inverse combinations. We can distinguish four landmarks on this continuum. They are distinguished by differences in the nature of the acoustical speech signal that accompanies the image of the talker's face: a) a broad-band signal spoken in a quiet anechoic environment; b) a signal distorted externally in the communication channel or internally during peripheral auditory analysis; c) a signal of reduced dimensionality that is not intelligible on its own but which successfully supplements lipreading; and d) a signal that is prosodically compatible but phonetically incompatible with the signal specified by the talker's lip movements.

We start with a broad-band speech signal spoken in a quiet anechoic environment. This is perfectly intelligible through audition alone to listeners with normal hearing. Nonetheless, the redundancy between vision and audition can be shown to be useful. If subjects are stressed, for example, by requiring them to shadow complex text rapidly, performance improves, if it is possible to see as well as hear the talker (Reisberg, McLean, & Goldfield, 1987).

At the next point on the continuum are found the natural distortions to an acoustic speech signal or its auditory representation that blur its spectral structure and so reduce but do not eliminate its intelligibility. Noise, reverberation, and low-pass filtering are three that are external to the listener; loss of sensitivity, impaired frequency selectivity, and impaired temporal resolution are three that are internal to the listener. For some subjects and some degrees of distortion, lipreading can restore near-perfect intelligibility, whereas the vast majority of subjects obtain some benefit from seeing the face of the talker. With a cooperative talker, the average benefit is equivalent to improving the signal-to-noise ratio (SNR) by between 5 and 10 dB, as shown in Fig. 6.3. (See also Middleweerd & Plomp, 1987, and MacLeod & Summerfield, 1987.) This difference can correspond to an increase in intelligibility of about 60 percentage points and is sufficiently large to have motivated speech technologists to explore the possibility of using automatic lipreading to bolster the performance of speech recognizers in noise (e.g., Petajan, 1984) where the accuracy of acoustical recognizers generally declines precipitously (Dautricht, Rabiner, & Martin, 1983).

Why does such benefit occur? Two factors are likely to be involved. First, in noise, vision shows when the talker is speaking and may also help to indicate which of the sounds arriving at the listener's ears constitute the talker's voice. For example, rapid movements of the articulators generate rapid changes in the frequency content of speech; the formation of constrictions lowers the overall amplitude whereas their release raises the overall amplitude, and changes in the direction of movement of an articulator tend to be accompanied by maxima or minima in the frequency or amplitude of a spectral component. The fact that these changes are occurring on the same time scale in the two modalities may allow vision to direct auditory attention to the relevant aspects of the acoustical signal and thus help to segregate the talker's speech from background sounds.

Second, benefit occurs because there is a complementary relationship between the robustness of acoustical speech features and the visibility of the articulatory gestures that produce them. Briefly, the spectral cues that reflect the shape of the mouth and the positions of the articulators are easily masked by noise or echoes, and they are difficult to detect and resolve in cases of cochlear hearing impairment. These cues indicate the place of articulation of consonants, and accordingly this feature is the first to be confused in noise, reverberation, or hearing impairment. (See Summerfield, 1987a, for a review.) However, as we have noted, the shape of the mouth and the positions of the articulators can be seen in lipreading. Therefore, in this case, visual distinctiveness can compensate for auditory ambiguity. Conversely, the temporal patterns of amplitude changes in the low-frequency region that indicate the rhythm and syllabicity of utterances and the nasality and voicing of consonants are intense and long-lasting. Accordingly they are resistant to masking and can be detected in spite of background noises, echoes, and impaired hearing. This is fortunate, because these features originate in the energy generated by the vibration of the vocal folds in the larynx and are difficult or impossible to lipread. One way of thinking of the complementary relationship is that hearing provides evidence of the excitation source for the talker's vocal tract whereas vision provides evidence of the filter that shapes the spectral envelope of the sound radiated from the lips.

This relationship is exploited in several types of aids to lipreading, which define the third point on the continuum of audio-visual phenomena. Designers of these devices acknowledge that a limited channel capacity is inevitable with electrical stimulation of the cochlea, with tactile stimulation, or with profoundly impaired hearing. Aids to lipreading generally convey a simplified signal of low dimensionality that indicates the behavior primarily of the source, leaving lipreading to provide evidence of the filter. The minimal requirement of such a signal is that its amplitude should indicate whether or not the vocal folds are vibrating. Typically, a few other features are also conveyed, for example, the rate of vibration of the vocal folds (Rosen, Fourcin, & Moore, 1981; Rosen, Walliker, Fourcin, & Ball, 1987), the detailed fluctuations of the overall amplitude contour (Grant, Ardell, Kuhl, & Sparks, 1985), or the energy fluctuations in one or two restricted frequency bands (Breeuwer & Plomp, 1984).

These first three points on the continuum of audio-visual phenomena involve a progressive reduction of the amount of spectral contrast in the acoustical signal. At the third point, the signal that supplements lipreading in some aids to lipreading is neutral as to the behavior of the vocal-tract filter. Logically, the next point on the continuum would be found, if conflicting evidence of the filter function were presented in the two modalities. Such a conflict was contrived by Summerfield and McGrath (1984). They synchronized a video recording of a talker speaking one /b/–vowel–/d/ syllable with an audio recording of a different /b/–vowel–/d/ syllable. Subjects could often detect the incompatibility between the modalities but nonetheless reported hearing a vowel whose spectral structure was a compromise between the spectral structures defined by the acoustical and visual vowels. This result is an instance of a class of audio-visual phenomena originally demonstrated with conflicting consonants by McGurk (McGurk & MacDonald, 1976; MacDonald & McGurk, 1978). (See Massaro, 1988, for a review.) To cite one familiar example, if a video recording of a talker saying /bɑ/ is presented in synchrony with an audio recording of the talker saying /gɑ/, many subjects do not perceive the incompatibility between the modalities and report hearing a syllable presented in neither individual modality: typically /dɑ/ or /ðɑ/.

I have argued elsewhere (Summerfield, 1987b) that such effects and all other phenomena in audio-visual speech perception are manifestations of two general principles: a) subjects know implicitly the audio-visual structure of the phonemes of their language; and b) when an audio-visual stimulus is presented, be it natural or artificial, subjects perceive the phoneme or sequence of phonemes whose audio-visual representation is most like the one that is presented. Accordingly, the "illusory" percept most likely to occur when conflicting evidence of consonants is presented in the two modalities is the consonant that simultaneously and best satisfies the following two criteria: a) being easily confused auditorily with the acoustical consonant and b) being visually compatible with the visible consonant.

Fig. 6.4 illustrates the application of the two criteria with a sketch of a very simple audio-visual speech recognizer. The recognizer distinguishes the five nonsense syllables /bɑ/, /vɑ/, /ðɑ/, /dɑ/, and /gɑ/. It operates in such a manner by sampling the stimulus every 10 ms. In Fig. 6.4, these points have been restricted to three for the sake of economy: before the initiation of the consonant, at the release of the consonant, and during the nucleus of the vowel. The recognizer seeks the route through the network shown in the figure that achieves the best match between the samples. Each template consists of a two-dimensional image of a mouth linked to the auditory spectrum (Moore & Glasberg, 1987) of the acoustical signal sampled at the release. The model recognizes syllables by finding the best *conjoint* match to the visual and auditory patterns.

Normally the model would do an adequate job of distinguishing the five consonants. The different mouth shapes that accompany /bɑ/, /vɑ/, /ðɑ/, and /dɑ/ would compensate for the similarity of their auditory spectra, for example. Consider now what would happen, if we presented a contrived audio-visual stimulus that consisted of an audio-recording of /bɑ/ in synchrony with a video-recording of /gɑ/. The best conjoint match could well be to the /dɑ/ template, and this is what some subjects perceive. In accordance with the two principles, /dɑ/ is auditorily quite similar to /bɑ/ (they are regularly confused in cases of noise, reverberation, or hearing impairment, for example), whereas visually /dɑ/ looks very similar to /gɑ/ (places of articulation within the mouth are difficult to distinguish).

The analysis can be taken one stage further. Acoustically, /bɑ/ is more similar to /ðɑ/ than /dɑ/, as reflected in confusions in noise, for example. In addition, the visible appearance of /gɑ/ is also compatible with /ðɑ/, provided the viewer knows that /ðɑ/ can be and normally is articulated without the tongue-tip appear-

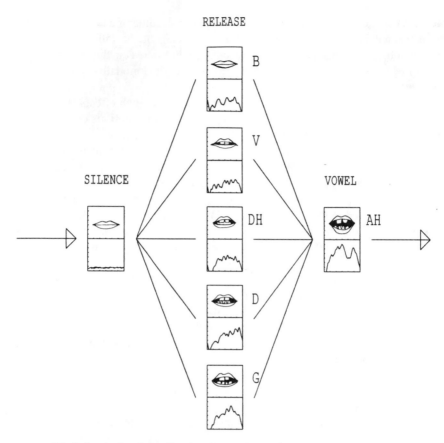

FIG. 6.4. A simple audio-visual speech recognizer which distinguishes the nonsense syllables /bɑ/, /vɑ/, /ðɑ/, /dɑ/, and /gɑ/ by finding the
route through a network of audio-visual templates which achieves the
best match to paired auditory and visual samples of the stimulus taken
at a sequence of points in time, restricted here for economy to three.
Each template consists of an image of the talker's mouth and the
auditory spectrum of the accompanying acoustical signal (intensity in
dB vertically, frequency in critical bandwidths horizontally).

ing prominently below the upper set of teeth. As a result, of the five templates,
/ðɑ/ is most compatible conjointly with the sound of /bɑ/ and the appearance of
/gɑ/, and this is what sophisticated subjects report.

This is not a surprising interpretation. It serves to state the obvious conclusions:

1. An audio-visual stimulus is perceived as an instance of category X, if it
   looks and sounds like X. However, it also relies on the two less obvious
   statements that follow.

2. There is a trade-off between looking and sounding like a particular phoneme.

3. A large part of likeness resides in the ability of neutral stimulus information where articulatory features are not evident in the input to be overridden by even quite weak information from another modality.

This account establishes a logical relationship between the laboratory contrivance of the McGurk Effect and the more natural cases where lipreading assists speech perception in cases of noise or hearing impairment. Therefore, because vision is beneficial to speech perception in these naturally occurring circumstances, audio-visual integration occurs easily and impressively in the laboratory. However, it should be noted that to obtain effects such as these, it is necessary to pit the *most* robust visual evidence of articulation against the *least* robust acoustical evidence.

The Perception of Phonetic Gestures

Within its very limited domain, the recognizer shown in Fig. 6.4 would perceive speech audio-visually and would generate McGurk Effects. I do not offer it as a complete model of audio-visual speech perception, although by analogy with LAFS (Klatt, 1979), it might be elaborated into something approaching a complete model. Instead it illustrates answers to two questions that any account of audio-visual speech perception must address: First, does integration occur before or after linguistic categorization of the auditory and visual streams of information, and, second, what form do the two streams take at their conflux?

An assured answer can be given only to the first question. Integration occurs before phonetic or lexical categorization. Three pieces of evidence establish this. First, it is possible to perceive speech audio-visually in conditions where lexical classification of the acoustical signal is impossible and where phonetic classification is difficult. These are conditions where the signal-to-noise ratio is very disadvantageous or where the acoustical signal has been replaced by one of the simplified signals shown clinically to aid lipreading: an F0-modulated pulse train, for example. Second, Massaro (1988) has shown that a mathematical description of precategorical integration predicts subjects' responses to audio-visual speech stimuli (presented at favorable signal-to-noise ratios) more accurately than does a postcategorical model. Third, Green and Miller (1985) demonstrated that a visual specification of the duration of a syllable provided by a video recording of a talker uttering the syllable could influence the listener's decision as to whether its initial consonant was voiced or voiceless. Thus, in this last example, information used to make a phonetic decision is derived from both modalities; the information must be combined before the decision is made. These demonstrations establish that audio-visual integration occurs before phonetic categorization; thus, they rule out the possibility that audio-visual integration involves the integration of categorized units.

What form does the precategorical representation take? Need it be the same for the two modalities? There are many possible answers, because every distinguishable account of auditory speech perception can be expanded into an account of audio-visual speech perception. (See Summerfield, 1987b, for a catalogue.) Some rationalization of the set of possibilities can be achieved by adopting the reasonable principle that compatible information processing is applied to the evidence of the two modalities.

We start with the model shown in Fig. 6.4. Recognition occurs by computing sequences of auditory spectra and two-dimensional images from the stimulus and matching them conjointly to stored sequences. A practical implementation would emphasize those aspects of spectra and images that are known to be perceptually relevant: peaks in auditory spectra (e.g., Assmann & Summerfield, 1989) and the inner margin of the lips in the image of a face (Brooke & Petajan, 1986). Such a strategy for recognition might achieve engineering adequacy in particular applications. However, this would be an inadequate perceptual model, because it would have great difficulty with several problems that human listener-viewers solve easily. For example, talkers can be lipread successfully from many viewing angles, ranging from front-face to profile (Erber, 1974). In addition, different talkers have differently shaped mouths, and they produce the same phoneme by adopting somewhat different configurations of the visible articulators, in part because the configuration of the lips can be traded for the configuration of the tongue (Stevens & House, 1955). Nevertheless, such talkers can be equally lipreadable (Montgomery & Jackson, 1983). The strategy of matching representations of front-facial images would not be able to accommodate these types of variation.

How might these problems be overcome? A possible strategy would entail defining a set of visible cues that can be extracted from all talkers and viewing angles and using them rather than the front-facial image as the basis for pattern matching. Candidate cues might be the horizontal and vertical separation of the lips, the extent of lip protrusion, and the vertical distances between the inner margins of the lips and teeth (see Fig. 6.1). To sustain the principle of compatible information processing, the acoustical speech signal would also be represented as a set of cues: voice-onset times, the gross shape of the spectrum at moments of abrupt amplitude change, the frequencies and movements of spectra peaks. Recognition would occur by matching acoustical and visual cues extracted from the stimulus to lists of such cues describing canonical instances of phonemes or words. Just as the success of the purely acoustical version of this strategy hinges on finding acoustical cues that are invariant over changes in context, so the success of the audio-visual version rests on finding visual cues that are similarly invariant. At present, the viability of the approach cannot be judged, because there are not sufficient data on the variation of candidate visual cues over changes in viewing angle and talker.

The move to a cue-based visual metric brings us closer to describing articulatory states and changes in those states; that is, the cue-based account implies that viewers determine what articulation the talker has performed. If the compatibility principle is to be sustained, we must assume that the reason for extracting acoustical cues is similarly to work out what articulations have occurred. Therefore, this option is essentially the motor theory in its modern form. I have much sympathy for it. It seems intuitively reasonable that what interests listeners and viewers are the articulatory gestures produced by talkers and that these can be determined both from listening and viewing. However, this conclusion is not an account of speech perception. It simply defines the outstanding questions as, first, what aspects of articulation constitute phonetic gestures, and, second, what computation recovers them from the acoustic signal. These problems are not trivial, because invariant articulatory states are not achieved (e.g., Abbs, 1986), possibly because there is sufficient independence of the muscle systems responsible for consonants and vowels to allow consonantal gestures to be superimposed on vowel-producing gestures (Öhman, 1967; Perkell, 1969; Fowler & Smith, 1986). I do not have a solution to the mathematical problem of disentangling gestures. All I can offer is a qualitative analogy (discussed quantitatively in Summerfield, 1987b) of which the further analysis might prove rewarding.

Imagine a hypothetical talker who speaks by oscillating his lips while vibrating his vocal folds with his velum lowered and his tongue back and low in his mouth. He produces a sequence of /mɑ/ sounds. He communicates by varying independently the frequency of his lip movements and their maximum velocity. Both these parameters can be seen. They are also conveyed in the acoustical signal that he generates. They can be found there as the modulation rate and peak rate of change of several parameters including the overall amplitude and the frequency of the first formant. Thus, in this hypothetical case, the parameters of modulation rate and velocity would represent a modality-independent description of the attributes of the talker's speech in which the listener-viewer would be interested. No doubt some of us would be better at lipreading these parameters than others; we would rely more heavily on vision in noise than in quiet, and a psychologist, by cross-splicing video recordings and audio recordings of the talker, might be able to fool us into believing that we had heard a lower velocity or faster modulation rate than was present in the acoustical signal.

At a somewhat deeper level of analysis, we could ask how the talker was controlling the oscillation of his lips, given that kinematic parameters such as modulation rate and velocity describe the behavior of mechanical systems, but are not controlled as such. The parameters that generate the kinematic behavior, and whose values have to be altered to change that behavior, are dynamic parameters such as mass, viscosity, and stiffness. Therefore, if we wished to establish the parameters over which the talker was exercising control, we should need to define a mechanical model of lip oscillations and determine the values of its dynamic parameters.

This idea is not quite as far-fetched as it may seem. In reiterant speech (Liberman & Streeter, 1978), where talkers preserve the prosody of an utterance but eliminate phonetic variation by producing each syllable as for example /mɑ/, lip movements are sinusoidal (Kelso, Vatikiotis-Bateson, Saltzman, & Kay, 1985). Lip movement can be modelled by assuming that the lips are configured functionally as a "periodic attractor;" this is a mass-spring system under forced vibration in which the energy supplied by the forcing function exactly compensates for the energy dissipated in friction (Browman & Goldstein, 1985). Changes in the amplitude and frequency of oscillation, with maximum velocity held constant, can be achieved by changing the stiffness parameter. Changes in the amplitude of oscillation and the maximum velocity, with the frequency of oscillation held constant, can be achieved by changing the resting length of the system. Thus, from the surface structure of these kinematic variables, listener-viewers would be able to unscramble the variation of modulation rate, maximum velocity, and maximum amplitude so as to determine the deep structure of the underlying dynamics. Within the domain of this simple system, they would have a modality-free metric in which to describe the phonetic intentions of the talker; this assumes that phonetic intentions signify the variables over which control is exercised in speech production.

Thus far, these ideas are intriguing rather than compelling. If talkers spoke purely by oscillating their lips sinusoidally, then it would be straightforward to model speech perception. The problem is, of course, that they also move their tongues, among other articulators. The challenge for the dynamic approach is to determine whether its mathematics can dissociate the consequences of the over-laid oscillations of the multiple articulators. As with much else in speech perception, it remains to be seen whether this will prove to be possible.

Conclusions

In this chapter, I have tried to show that there is much about lipreading and audio-visual speech perception that is compatible with the ideas of modularity and the motor theory. Equally, I hope that I have conveyed some of my doubts about whether the evidence is conclusive. People evidently find it easy and natural, even unavoidable, to combine vision and hearing when perceiving speech. Therefore, the role of vision should be integral to accounts of speech perception. In this respect, Alvin Liberman's ideas come closer to prompting a unifying account than most others.

References

Abbs, J. H. (1986). Invariance and variability in speech production: A distinction between linguistic intent and its neuromotor implementation. In J. S. Perkell & D. H. Klatt (Eds.), *Invariance and variability in speech processes* (pp. 202–218). Hillsdale, NJ: Lawrence Erlbaum Associates.

Assmann, P. F., & Summerfield, Q. (1989). Modelling the perception of concurrent vowels: Vowels with the same fundamental frequency. *Journal of the Acoustical Society of America, 85*, 327–338.

Benguerel, A. P., & Pichora-Fuller, M. K. (1982). Coarticulation effects in lipreading. *Journal of Speech and Hearing Research, 25*, 600–607.

Breeuwer, M., & Plomp, R. (1984). Speechreading supplemented with frequency-selective sound-pressure information. *Journal of the Acoustical Society of America, 76*, 686–691.

Brooke, N. M., & Petajan, E. D. (1986). Seeing speech: Investigations into the synthesis and recognition of visible speech movements using automatic image processing and computer graphics. *Proceedings of an International Conference on Speech Input/Output: Techniques and Applications, 258*, 104–109. London: Institute of Electrical Engineers.

Browman, C. P., & Goldstein, L. M. (1985). Dynamic modeling of phonetic structure. In V. A. Fromkin (Ed.), *Phonetic linguistics: Essays in honor of Peter Ladefoged* (pp. 35–53). New York: Academic Press.

Cole, R. A., & Jakimik, J. (1980). A model of speech perception. In R. A. Cole (Ed.), *Perception and production of fluent speech* (pp. 133–164). Hillsdale, NJ: Lawrence Erlbaum Associates.

Dautricht, B. A., Rabiner, L. R., & Martin, T. B. (1983). The effects of selected signal-processing techniques on the performance of a filter-bank based isolated word recognizer. *Bell Systems Technical Journal, 62*, 1311.

Erber, N. P. (1974). Effects of angle, distance, and illumination on visual reception of speech by profoundly deaf children. *Journal of Speech and Hearing Research, 17*, 99–112.

Farwell, R. M. (1976). Speech reading: A research review. *American Annals of the Deaf, 121*, 19–30.

Fodor, J. A. (1983). *The Modularity of Mind.* Cambridge, MA: MIT Press.

Fowler, C. A., & Smith, M. R. (1986). Speech perception as "Vector Analysis": An approach to the problem of invariance and segregation. In J. S. Perkell & D. H. Klatt (Eds.), *Invariance and variability in speech processes* (pp. 123–139). Hillsdale, NJ: Lawrence Erlbaum Associates.

Fromkin, V. (1964). Lip positions in American English. *Language and Speech, 7*, 215–225.

Grant, K. W., Ardell, L. H., Kuhl, P. K., & Sparks, D. W. (1985). The contribution of fundamental frequency, amplitude envelope, and voicing duration cues to speechreading in normal-hearing subjects. *Journal of the Acoustical Society of America, 77*, 671–677.

Green, K. P., & Miller, J. L. (1985). On the role of visual rate information in phonetic perception. *Perception & Psychophysics, 38*, 269–276.

Heider, F., & Heider, G. (1940). An experimental investigation of lipreading. *Psychological Monographs, 232*, 124–153.

Jeffers, J., & Barley, M. (1971). *Speechreading (Lipreading).* Springfield, IL: Thomas.

Kelso, J. A. S., Vatikiotis-Bateson, E., Saltzman, E. L., & Kay, B. (1985). A qualitative dynamic analysis of reiterant speech production: Phase portraits, kinematics, and dynamic modeling. *Journal of the Acoustical Society of America, 77*, 266–280.

Kitson, H. D. (1915). Psychological tests for lip-reading ability. *Volta Review, 17*, 471–476.

Klatt, D. H. (1979). Speech perception: A model of acoustic-phonetic analysis and lexical access. *Journal of Phonetics, 7*, 279–312.

Liberman, A. M., & Mattingly, I. G. (1985). The Motor Theory of Speech Perception Revised. *Cognition, 21*, 1–36.

Liberman, M. Y., & Streeter, L. A. (1978). Use of nonsense-syllable mimicry in the study of prosodic phenomena. *Journal of the Acoustical Society of America, 63*, 231–233.

MacDonald, J. W., & McGurk, H. (1978). Visual influences on speech perception processes. *Perception & Psychophysics, 4,* 253–257.

MacLeod, A. (1987). *Effective methods for measuring lipreading skills.* Unpublished doctoral dissertation, University of Nottingham, Nottingham, UK.

MacLeod, A., & Summerfield, Q. (1987). Quantifying the contribution of vision to speech perception in noise. *British Journal of Audiology, 21,* 131–141.

MacLeod, A., & Summerfield, Q. (1990). A procedure for measuring auditory and audio-visual speech-reception thresholds for sentences in noise: Rationale, evaluation, and recommendations for use. *British Journal of Audiology, 24,* 29–43.

Massaro, D. W. (1988). *Speech perception by ear and by eye: A paradigm for psychological inquiry.* Hillsdale, NJ: Lawrence Erlbaum Associates.

McGrath, M. (1985). *An examination of cues for visual and audio-visual speech perception using natural and computer-generated faces.* Unpublished doctoral dissertation, University of Nottingham, Nottingham, UK.

McGurk, H., & MacDonald, J. W. (1976). Hearing lips and seeing voices. *Nature, 264,* 746–748.

Middleweerd, M. J., & Plomp, R. (1987). The effect of speechreading on the speech-reception threshold of sentences in noise. *Journal of the Acoustical Society of America, 82,* 2145–2147.

Montgomery, A. A., & Jackson, P. L. (1983). Physical characteristics of the lips underlying vowel lipreading performance. *Journal of the Acoustical Society of America, 73,* 2134–2144.

Montgomery, A. A., Walden, B. E., & Prosek, R. A. (1987). Effects of consonantal context on vowel lipreading. *Journal of Speech and Hearing Research, 30,* 50–59.

Moore, B. C. J., & Glasberg, B. R. (1987). Formulae describing frequency selectivity as a function of frequency and level, and their use in calculating excitation patterns. *Hearing Research, 28,* 209–226.

Nitchie, E. B. (1917). Tests for determining skill in lipreading. *Volta Review, 19,* 222–223.

Öhman, S. E. G. (1967). Numerical model of coarticulation. *Journal of the Acoustical Society of America, 41,* 310–320.

Perkell, J. S. (1969). *Physiology of speech production: Results and implications of a quantitative cineradiographic study.* Cambridge, MA: MIT Press.

Petajan, E. D. (1984). Automatic lipreading to enhance speech recognition. *Proceedings of the global telecommunications conference, Atlanta, Georgia, U.S.A.* IEEE Communications Society, 265–272.

Reisberg, D., McLean, J., & Goldfield, A. (1987). Easy to hear but hard to understand: A lip-reading advantage with intact auditory stimuli. In, B. Dodd & R. Campbell (Eds.), *Hearing by eye: The psychology of lip-reading* (pp. 97–114). Hillsdale, NJ: Lawrence Erlbaum Associates.

Rosen, S. M., & Corcoran, T. (1982). A video-recorded test of lipreading for British English. *British Journal of Audiology, 16,* 245–254.

Rosen, S. M., Fourcin, A. J., & Moore, B. C. J. (1981). Voice pitch as an aid to lipreading. *Nature, 291,* 150–152.

Rosen, S. M., Walliker, J. R., Fourcin, A. J., & Ball, V. (1987). A microprocessor-based acoustic hearing aid for the profoundly impaired listener. *Journal of Rehabilitation Research and Development, 24,* 39–260.

Samar, V. J., & Sims, D. G. (1983). Visual evoked-response correlates of speechreading performance in normal-hearing adults: A replication and factor analytic extension. *Journal of Speech and Hearing Research, 26,* 2–9.

Shepherd, D. C., DeLavergne, R. W., Frueh, F. X., & Clobridge, C. (1977). *Journal of Speech and Hearing Research, 20,* 752–765.

Shepherd, D. C. (1982). Visual-neural correlate of speechreading ability in normal-hearing adults: Reliability. *Journal of Speech and Hearing Research, 25,* 521–527.

Stevens, K. N., & House, A. S. (1955). Development of a quantitative description of vowel articulation. *Journal of the Acoustical Society of America, 27,* 484–493.

Summerfield, Q. (1987a). Speech perception in normal and impaired hearing. *British Medical Bulletin, 43,* 909–925.

Summerfield, Q. (1987b). Some preliminaries to a comprehensive account of audio-visual speech perception. In, B. Dodd & R. Campbell (Eds.), *Hearing by eye: The psychology of lip-reading* (pp. 3–52). Hillsdale, NJ: Lawrence Erlbaum Associates.

Summerfield, Q., & McGrath, M. (1984). Detection and resolution of audio-visual incompatibility in the perception of vowels. *Quarterly Journal of Experimental Psychology, 36A,* 51–74.

Utley, J. (1946). A test of lipreading ability. *Journal of Speech and Hearing Disorders, 11,* 109–116.

Walden, B. E., Prosek, R. A., Montgomery, A. A., Scherr, C. K., & Jones, C. J. (1977). Effects of training on the visual recognition of consonants. *Journal of Speech and Hearing Research, 20,* 130–145.

Comment: Bimodal Speech Perception and the Motor Theory

Joanne L. Miller

Department of Psychology, Northeastern University

There is currently much debate and controversy concerning the nature of the acoustic information that is critical for speech perception and the nature of the processing mechanisms that map the relevant acoustic properties onto phonetic representations. However, even if these issues were to be resolved, we still would not have a complete account of phonetic perception. This is because, as Quentin Summerfield clearly describes (chapter 6 this volume), the perception of speech does not involve only the processing of acoustic information. Even in cases where neither the acoustic signal nor the listener's hearing is impoverished, observable articulatory movements on the talker's face provide phonetically relevant optic information that is used by the listener when perceiving speech.

In other words, any complete account of phonetic perception must accommodate the phenomenon of bimodal, auditory-visual speech perception. Although this might seem to complicate the task of understanding phonetic perception, bimodal speech perception may in fact provide some useful constraints on the way in which we conceptualize the speech perception process.

In my remarks, I will follow Summerfield's lead in considering how bimodal speech perception might bear specifically on the motor theory of speech perception as set forth by Liberman and his colleagues (Liberman, Cooper, Shankweiler, & Studdert-Kennedy, 1967; Liberman & Mattingly, 1985). I will focus on two aspects of the motor theory. First, I will highlight some of Summerfield's remarks concerning domain specificity. Next, I will consider an issue not explicitly raised by Summerfield, the issue of innateness—and I will suggest how the two aspects of the theory might be related.

Let me begin with domain specificity. According to the motor theory, speech perception is accomplished by a specialized module that has as its domain phonetic perception. The module operates mandatorily and with great speed so as to recover the intended gestures of the speaker. The proper objects of perception, thus, are phonetic gestures. The module is specific to phonetic perception and uses all relevant stimulus information to recover the phonetic structure of the utterance. If the phonetic processing system is indeed domain-specific in this way, it should be possible to show that the perceiver takes account not only of relevant acoustic information for phonetic structure but relevant information from outside the auditory modality. That is, the module should operate across traditional modalities, and, indeed, the various phenomena of bimodal speech perception reviewed by Summerfield, in particular the familiar "McGurk effect" (McGurk & MacDonald, 1976) are fully in accord with this prediction. Note further that these phenomena indicate that a purely auditory account of speech perception cannot in and of itself be complete.

However, using the existence of bimodal speech perception as evidence for the motor theory, and in particular the domain specificity of the proposed module, is not entirely straightforward. The reason, as suggested by Summerfield's comments, is the following: As far as we know, there are no significant individual differences in the ability of normal speaker/hearers of a language to perceive speech on the basis of the acoustic signal of speech. For all perceivers, the processing system seems to operate in a fast, mandatory fashion when confronted with the acoustic signal. Moreover, there is evidence to suggest that the system mandatorily uses all phonetically relevant acoustic properties of the speech signal when deriving the phonetic structure of the utterance. Any acoustic property that is the systematic consequence of a phonetically relevant articulatory movement appears to have linguistic significance for the perceiver, even if, in psychoacoustic terms, the property is not particularly salient (see Liberman & Mattingly, 1985).

However, as we have learned from Summerfield, the use of optic information from the talker's face during phonetic perception contrasts sharply with this picture. There are large individual differences in the ability to use the potential information provided by visible articulatory movements for speech perception. As Summerfield tells us, these individual differences are not correlated with measures of sensory, perceptual, or cognitive functioning; this is especially intriguing, for it suggests that the use of optic information may be a very specialized ability. Furthermore, as Summerfield notes, that is just what it would be, if performed by a phonetic processing module. However, if performed by the module, why do the individual differences in the use of optic information occur, given no such differences in the use of acoustic information? Summerfield proposes that the answer might lay in an evolutionary account; specifically, that there was evolutionary pressure to develop refined auditory abilities for biologically significant sounds but not to develop lipreading abilities.

However, whether or not this turns out to be the case, the asymmetry in the use of acoustic and optic information remains. This is problematic, for if the module truly has as its domain phonetic perception and is modality-independent, it should make use of relevant information about phonetic structure regardless of the modality in which the information is presented. Thus, if we are going to use the phenomenon of bimodal speech perception as evidence for a domain-specific phonetic module, we need a rationalization within the theory itself for the apparent mandatory use by all individuals of phonetically relevant acoustic but not optic information.

Let me turn now to the innateness issue and its relation to domain specificity. According to the motor theory, the specialized processing system for phonetic perception is innately given—it is part of our biological heritage as humans. Furthermore, this innately given system is operative early in infancy; that is, infants come to the world with tacit knowledge of articulation that allows them to perceive the phonetic structure of an utterance. In other words, according to the theory, we do not have to learn to map properties of the speech signal onto phonetic categories, although clearly the initial mappings of early infancy will be altered through appropriate experience with the parental language.

As is clear from the chapters in this volume (see, especially, chapter 5 by Werker with comments by Eimas), there is now considerable evidence that young infants do indeed have remarkably sophisticated speech processing abilities. There is some evidence that infants respond differently to speech and nonspeech signals, that is, signals that could have been the result of linguistically significant articulatory movements and signals that could not have been the result of such movements (e.g., Best, Hoffman, & Glanville, 1982). This, of course, is just what would be predicted by the motor theory. There is also evidence suggesting that when listening to speech, infants treat the acoustic information in a linguistically relevant manner. For example, infants show evidence of perceptual trading relations when processing acoustic properties of speech, relations that can be rationalized by how these properties covary in the production of speech (e.g., Miller & Eimas, 1983).

The infant data, thus, are in accord with the claim of an innately given phonetic processing mechanism for speech. However, notice that the results I have mentioned so far only address the infant's processing of the acoustic signal of speech. If the phonetic module is truly domain-specific and modality-independent, in the sense I discussed earlier, then infants should treat not only the acoustic consequences but also the optic consequences of speech in a linguistically relevant manner. That is, on a strong reading of the motor theory, young infants should show evidence of bimodal speech perception.

Although a direct test of such bimodal phenomena as the McGurk effect has not been reported for very young infants, we do have evidence that, by at least four to five months of age, infants appreciate the correspondence between the acoustic and optic consequences of articulation. Elegant studies by Kuhl and

Meltzoff (1982) and MacKain, Studdert-Kennedy, Spieker, and Stern (1983) have shown that infants prefer to look at a video display of a face that is articulating the syllables they are hearing rather than at a face that is articulating different syllables. It will be especially important to determine whether such abilities are present in very early infancy, and, in particular, whether the very young infant shows evidence of mapping optic information onto phonetically relevant categories. I should note that very young infants can perceive facial, nonspeech movements; in fact, at one to two days of age, infants are able to imitate facial movements that they see (Field, Woodson, Greenberg, & Cohen, 1982). What we do not know as yet is whether infants treat linguistically relevant movements differently from other movements, and, moreover, treat them in terms of phonetic structure.

If it turns out to be the case that very young infants are sensitive to both the acoustic and optic consequences of linguistically significant articulations and recognize the correspondence across modalities at a very early age, we will indeed have strong evidence in support of an innately specified, domain-specific but modality-independent module. Recall, however, that for adults there appears to be an asymmetry in the use of acoustic and optic information for phonetic perception: The use of acoustic but not optic information appears to be mandatory for all individuals. Perhaps a similar asymmetry will be revealed in development. Although very young infants—as young as one month of age—treat acoustic information in a linguistically relevant manner, maybe the same is not true for optic information. It could be that the mapping between the optic consequences of articulation and phonetic structure takes time to develop, is contingent on certain types of experience, or even proceeds, for a variety of possible reasons, somewhat differently in different individuals. That is to say, perhaps there is a primacy for the use of acoustic information for phonetic structure in development as there seems to be in adult perception. Such a result would constrain the notion of domain specificity as applied to speech.

As I said at the outset of my remarks, any complete theory of speech perception must be able to account for the fact that optic as well as acoustic information can be used for deriving the phonetic structure of the utterance. By examining further the nature of bimodal speech perception in adults and by charting its course in development, we should gain insight into the nature of the processing system that underlies our abilities to perceive speech and the extent to which the system truly has phonetic perception as its domain as proposed by the motor theory.

Acknowledgments

I thank Peter D. Eimas for his comments on an earlier version of this chapter. Support was provided by NIH Grant NS 14394 and NIH BRSG RR 07143.

References

Best, C. T., Hoffman, H., & Glanville, B. B. (1982). Development of infant ear asymmetries for speech and music. *Perception & Psychophysics, 31*, 75–85.

Field, T. M., Woodson, R., Greenberg, R., & Cohen, D. (1982). Discrimination and imitation of facial expressions by neonates. *Science, 218*, 179–181.

Kuhl, P. K., & Meltzoff, A. N. (1982). The bimodal perception of speech in infancy. *Science, 218*, 1138–1141.

Liberman, A. M., & Mattingly, I. G. (1985). The motor theory of speech perception revised. *Cognition, 21*, 1–36.

Liberman, A. M., Cooper, F. S., Shankweiler, D. P., & Studdert-Kennedy, M. (1967). Perception of the speech code. *Psychological Review, 74*, 431–461.

MacKain, K. S., Studdert-Kennedy, M., Spieker, S., & Stern, D. (1983). Infant intermodal speech perception is a left hemisphere function. *Science, 219*, 1347–1349.

McGurk, H., & MacDonald, J. (1976). Hearing lips and seeing voices. *Nature, 264*, 746–748.

Miller, J. L., & Eimas, P. D. (1983). Studies on the categorization of speech by infants. *Cognition, 13*, 135–165.

Chapter 7

Brain Function for Language: Perspectives from Another Modality

Howard Poizner

*Center for Molecular and Behavioral Neuroscience,
Rutgers University*

Ursula Bellugi

The Salk Institute

Edward S. Klima

*Department of Linguistics, University of California,
San Diego*

Abstract

The left cerebral hemisphere provides the neural substrate for language in hearing-speaking individuals. The underlying basis of the specialization of the left hemisphere for language, however, has not been clearly understood. The study of sign languages of deaf individuals provides a unique opportunity for investigating brain function for language, because sign language displays complex linguistic structures by manipulating spatial relations. It, thus, exhibits properties for which each of the hemispheres of hearing individuals shows a differing specialization. Understanding brain organization for sign languages is allowing us to uncover basic principles underlying hemispheric specialization.

We have been investigating the language, visual-spatial, and motor abilities of profoundly deaf signers who have acquired lesions of either the left or the right cerebral hemisphere. Remarkably, the signers with right hemisphere lesions were not aphasic for sign language. This preserved signing stood in the face of marked deficits the right-hemisphere damaged signers showed in processing nonlanguage spatial relations. In contrast, the signers with left-hemisphere damage showed frank sign language aphasias (and relatively preserved nonlanguage spatial functions). Importantly, the sign language impairments were not uniform, but rather cleaved along lines of linguistically relevant components. Taken together, the data indicate that the left hemisphere has an innate predisposition for language.

Furthermore, the underlying basis of the specialization of the left hemisphere for language seems related to linguistic functions and the processing operations required, rather than to properties of the signal itself.

Al Liberman has pioneered investigations into many areas central to the relation of brain, mind, and language. Liberman's elegant experiments on the acoustic and physiological basis for speech perception, on the grammars of speech and language, and on the specializations of the human brain have provided challenges and inspiration for all interested in language and brain function (Liberman, 1974, 1979, 1982; Liberman & Mattingly, 1985; Mattingly & Liberman, 1988). Our own research has benefited greatly from his insightful thinking and clear focus on the biological foundations of language, for this is a topic which we too have pursued, but from the particular perspective of signed languages of the deaf.[1]

Over the past several years, we have been investigating the functional organization of the brain for language across language modalities. We are naturally led to the study of visual-gestural languages, because they present a truly unusual opportunity to delve into the human capacity for language and to uncover for language in general how the brain is organized for language, how modifiable that organization is, and how that organization develops. There clearly has been an evolution of language in conjunction with speech. The shape of the vocal tract and mechanisms of breath control have changed from nonhuman primates to man, shaping the vocal apparatus into a more efficient transmission system for the production of a variety of sounds (Lenneberg, 1967; Lieberman, 1975). Furthermore, no known hearing society has a sign language as a primary mode of communication, and there exists a tight neurological linkage between the primary language mediating areas of the brain and the speech channel. These facts make remarkable the discoveries that there exist natural, fully developed, autonomous sign languages that show the kinds of complexities of linguistic structure found in spoken languages (Bellugi, 1988; Klima & Bellugi, 1979; Lane & Grosjean,

---

[1]Notational conventions used in this paper: Words in capital letters, e.g., SIGN represent English glosses for ASL signs. The gloss represents the meaning of the unmarked, unmodulated, basic form of a sign out of context. Morphological processes may be indicated by the specification of grammatical category of change or by the meaning of the inflected form: GIVE[Exhaustive] or GIVE['to each']. As part of the spatialized syntax of ASL, a horizontal plane in signing space is used for abstract spatial loci. Nouns, indexible verbs, pronouns, classifiers, size and shape specifiers can be associated with abstract spatial loci, and these are indicated by subscripts. Subscripts from the beginning of the alphabet are used to indicate spatial loci. Nouns, pronouns, and verbs of location are marked with a subscript to indicate the locus at which they are signed ($INDEX_a$, BOY_a, $AT-X_a$) in planes of signing space. Inflected verbs are marked with an initial subscript to mark origin location and/or a final subscript indicate the endpoint location ($_aGIVE_b$). Subscripts from the middle of the alphabet are used to indicate abstract indices; reference as well as coreference, (e.g., $_iSIGN_j$).

1980; Liddell, 1980; Studdert-Kennedy & Lane, 1980; Wilbur, 1987). American Sign Language (ASL) is one of those autonomous linguistic systems.

Language in the Visuospatial Modality

ASL has been forged into an autonomous language with its own internal mechanisms for relating visual form with meaning. Like spoken languages, ASL exhibits formal structuring at two distinct levels, one involving internal structure to the lexical units and a second involving rules governing the relations between signs in sentences. The structure of ASL is likewise similar to that of spoken languages in terms of hierarchically organized rules, rules based on underlying forms, and recursive grammatical processes. ASL has evolved linguistic mechanisms that are not derived from those of English (or any spoken language), thus offering a new perspective on the determinants of language form. We have been specifying the extent to which the formal properties of languages are shaped by the modalities involved in their perception and production and have found that for the form of its grammatical devices, the modality in which a language develops makes a crucial difference.

The use of space is a unique resource afforded by the modality of signed languages. The inflectional and derivational devices of ASL, for example, make structured use of space and movement, nesting the basic sign stem in spatial patterns and complex dynamic contours of movement (Bellugi, Klima & Poizner, 1988). In ASL grammatical morphology, root, derivational patterns and inflectional patterns co-occur as layered in the final surface form, and forms can be spatially nested within one another (see Fig. 7.1a). Furthermore, many syntactic functions fulfilled in spoken languages by word order or case marking are expressed in ASL by essentially spatial mechanisms (see Fig. 7.1b). For example, nominals introduced into ASL discourse may be assigned to arbitrary loci in a plane of signing space. A pronominal sign directed to a specific locus clearly refers back to the previously mentioned nominal, even with many other signs intervening. The ASL system of verb agreement is also essentially spatialized. Verb signs for a large class of verbs move between the abstract loci in signing space, bearing obligatory markers for person (and number) via spatial indices, thereby specifying subject and object. This spatialized system, thus, allows explicit reference through pronominals and agreement markers to multiple distinct third-person referents (Lillo-Martin & Klima, in press). The use of spatial loci for referential indexing, verb agreement, and complex embedded structures is clearly a unique property of visual-gestural systems. ASL is, thus, markedly different in surface form from English and from spoken languages in general. Although ASL is the most thoroughly analyzed of the signed languages of the world to date, other signed languages examined suggest that these characteristics

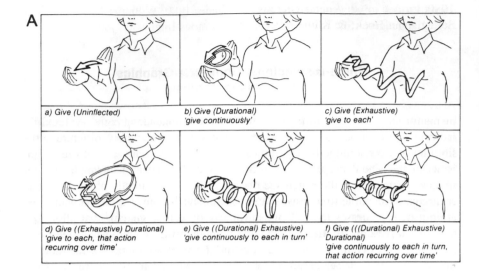

a) Give (Uninflected)

b) Give (Durational)
'give continuously'

c) Give (Exhaustive)
'give to each'

d) Give ((Exhaustive) Durational)
'give to each, that action
recurring over time'

e) Give ((Durational) Exhaustive)
'give continuously to each in turn'

f) Give (((Durational) Exhaustive)
Durational)
'give continuously to each in turn,
that action recurring over time'

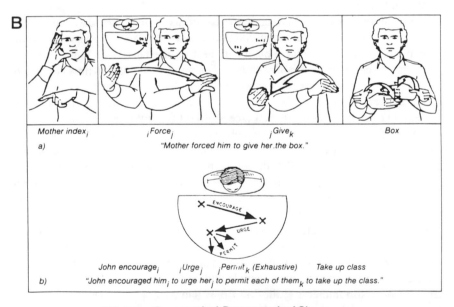

Mother index$_i$　　　　$_i$Force$_j$　　　　$_j$Give$_k$　　　　Box

a)　　　　　　　"Mother forced him to give her.the box."

John encourage$_i$　　$_i$Urge$_j$　　$_j$Permit$_k$ (Exhaustive)　　Take up class

b)　　"John encouraged him$_i$ to urge her$_j$ to permit each of them$_k$ to take up the class."

FIG. 7.1.　Grammatical Processes in ASL.
(a) Recursive nesting of morphological processes.
(b) Syntactic spatial mechanisms.

may turn out to be general characteristics of primary signed languages (Fok, Bellugi, van Hoek, & Klima, 1988).

Three-Dimensional Computer Graphics and Linguistic Analysis

In many ways, the transmission system of sign languages (visual-gestural) is radically different from that of speech and offers remarkably different possibilities and constraints. In our studies, we take advantage of a basic difference between the signal properties of sign and speech. In sign languages, unlike spoken language, the movements of the articulators are directly observable and are, thus, susceptible to noninvasive measurement. To investigate the nature of grammatical processes in ASL, we have developed new systems that allow the realtime, three-dimensional tracking and computergraphic analysis of hand and arm movements (Poizner, Wooten, & Salot, 1986; Poizner, Klima, Bellugi, & Livingston, 1986; Jennings & Poizner, 1988). Two optoelectronic cameras directly sense the positions of infra-red emitting diodes that are attached to the hands and arms (see Fig. 7.2). A microcomputer synchronizes the sequential flashing of the diodes with the digitizing of the camera signals. The three-dimensional coordinates are then computed from the two sets of camera data. Finally, the movement is reconstructed in three dimensions on a computergraphic system for interactive analysis. Figure 7.3 presents three-dimensional reconstructions of the sequence of hand and arm positions for three grammatically inflected ASL signs.

Figure 7.3 illustrates the structured use of spatial contrasts within ASL's rich morphological system. The Apportionative Internal inflection contrasts minimally with the Seriated Internal inflection in trajectory shape: The former inflection is made with a circular path shape in the vertical plane of signing space, whereas the latter inflection is made with a linear path shape (these inflections and the Seriated External inflection convey different class membership distinctions, as described in Klima & Bellugi, 1979). The Seriated Internal inflection, however, contrasts minimally with the Seriated External inflection, not in trajectory shape but in planar locus. Variation in planar locus for a variety of ASL inflections for temporal aspect, number, and distributional aspect are presented in Fig. 7.4. These movements were digitized and the best fitting plane of the hand motion computed. Figure 7.4 shows several groupings of movements. Movements conveying temporal aspect distinctions (points H, J, and K) are grouped together in a sagittal plane, whereas those for number and distributional aspect (points A, B, C, D, E, and L) cluster in either the horizontal or vertical plane relative to the body. These clusterings based on the spatial properties of the movements markedly correspond to the independent linguistic classifications of these forms (Poizner, 1983).

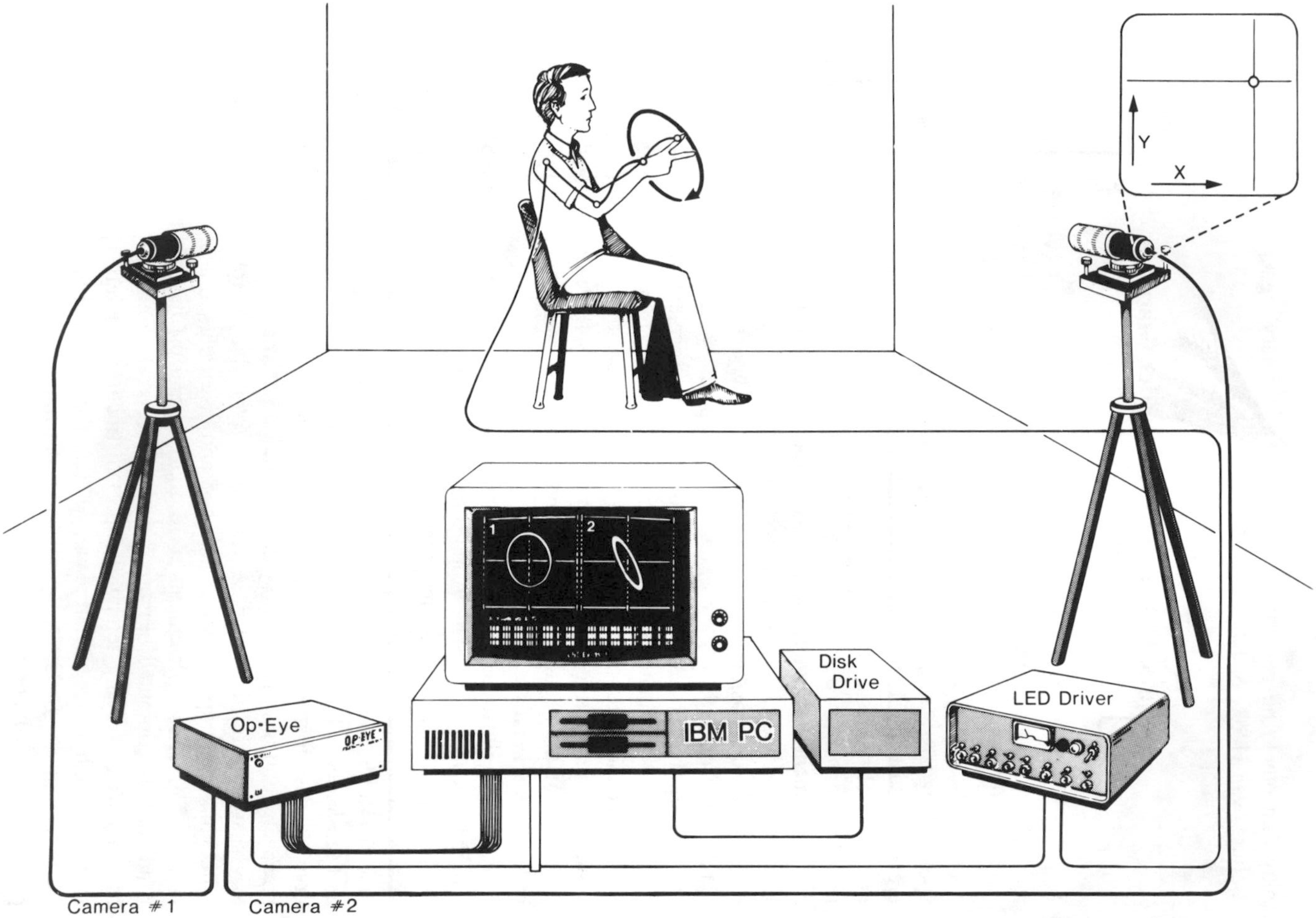

FIG. 7.2. Three-dimensional movement monitoring system. The main hardware com-

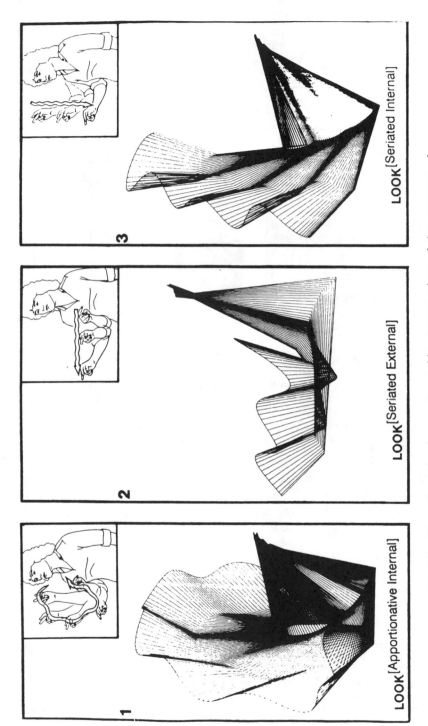

LOOK[Apportionative Internal]

LOOK[Seriated External]

LOOK[Seriated Internal]

FIG. 7.3. Three-dimensional computergraphic reconstructions of the sequence of arm positions for three grammatically inflected ASL signs.

151

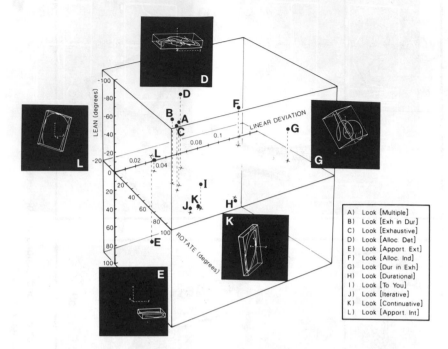

FIG. 7.4. Three-dimensional visual-phonetic analysis of the linguistic
dimension Planar Locus. The two axes Lean and Rotate provide two
angles (elevation and azimuth) that specify the particular plane of motion of the hand. The third axis, Linear Deviation, specifies how planar
a motion was.

Thus, such spatial contrasts as trajectory shape and planar locus are key
formational building blocks of ASL's morphology. Furthermore, as stated previously, space in ASL is actively manipulated for syntax and discourse. Nominals are assigned spatial loci in the horizontal plane of signing space, pronoun
signs are directed toward those loci, and verb signs move among the spatial loci
to convey grammatical subject and object. Because the left cerebral hemisphere
in man has been considered specialized for linguistic functions, and the right, for
visuospatial functions, ASL exhibits properties for which each of the hemispheres of hearing people shows a differing specialization.

FIG. 7.5. Three-dimensional reconstructions of two ASL inflections.
(a) Line drawings.
(b) The entire reconstructed movement of the hands with time pointers 'windowing'
one movement cycle.
(c) Characteristics of one movement cycle. Tangential velocity is given in meters per
second and acceleration in meters per second.[2]

A

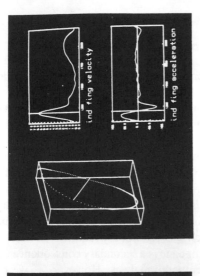

B

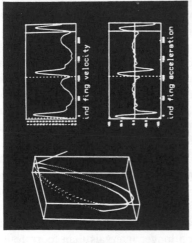

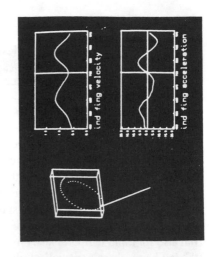

C

ind fing velocity

ind fing acceleration

LOOK [Continuative]

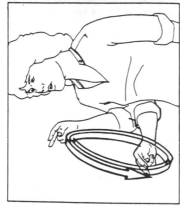

ind fing velocity

ind fing acceleration

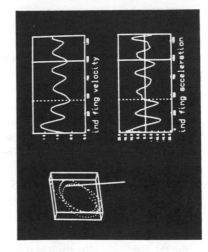

ind fing velocity

ind fing acceleration

LOOK [Durational]

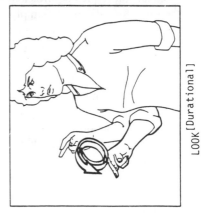

ind fing velocity

ind fing acceleration

The Nature of Hemispheric Specialization

Understanding how sign language is represented in the brain should allow us to uncover the basic principles underlying hemispheric specialization. In the first place, such data will allow us to test alternate theories of the nature of hemispheric specialization. The left cerebral hemisphere is closely connected with speech. A neuroanatomical difference between the hemispheres is in the planum temporale—a portion of *auditory* association cortex known to mediate language—which is, even at birth, larger in the left hemisphere than in the right. The finer auditory analysis that this area may allow has been suggested as a possible underlying basis for the left hemisphere's specialization for language. A related theory links the fact that the left hemisphere is specialized not only for language but also for rapid temporal analysis, which speech strongly requires. In this view, the left hemisphere's specialization for language is a secondary consequence of its more primary specialization for rapid temporal analysis. However, as we have seen, sign language relies heavily on spatial contrasts rather than on temporal contrasts. Furthermore, the temporal contrasts that do occur in ASL do not require the same degree of rapid temporal analysis as those of speech.

Figure 7.5 presents computer-graphic reconstructions for two grammatical inflections in ASL, the Continuative and Durational, which are minimally contrasted by their temporal qualities and serve to elucidate a difference in timing between signed and spoken language. The Continuative inflection, meaning "action for a long time," is made with a tense, rapid outward movement with an elliptical slow return to the starting point. The Durational inflection, meaning "continuous action," is made with a smooth, circular, even movement that is repeated. The panels of Fig. 7.5 present for each inflection the reconstructed movement of the hand along with the associated velocity and acceleration profiles both for the entire movement and for a single movement cycle. We find that the temporal contrasts underlying these inflections, as well as those for ASL in general, are typically stretched over much longer intervals than those found in speech. Sign language simply does not use the extremely rapid 40–50 msec temporal intervals found in spoken languages to contrast forms (Poizner, Klima, & Bellugi, 1987). Rather, temporal variation in sign language occurs over much longer intervals, and sign language heavily uses spatial contrasts. Thus, theories basing the specialization of the left hemisphere for language in all its aspects on superior capacities for auditory processing and rapid temporal analysis would not predict left hemisphere specialization for sign language. Sign language pits linguistic function against stimulus form in very strong way, because, in large part, it conveys grammatical relations through spatial relations.

Evidence from Brain-lesioned Signers

In a series of studies, we have been examining the effects of brain-damage on language and nonlanguage performance in deaf signers with left-hemisphere or right-hemisphere damage. Our general program includes an array of probes: a) our adaptation, for ASL, of the Boston Diagnostic Aphasia Examination (BDAE) (Goodglass & Kaplan, 1983), b) linguistic tests we designed for processing the structural levels of ASL (sublexical, semantic, morphological, and syntactic), c) an analysis of production of ASL at all linguistic levels, and d) tests of non-language spatial processing and motor control. The battery of language and non-language tasks was administered to deaf brain-lesioned subjects and to matched deaf controls (Poizner et al., 1987; 1990; Bellugi et al., 1988; Klima, Bellugi, & Poizner, 1988; Poizner, Kaplan, Bellugi, & Padden, 1984; Poizner, Bellugi, & Iragui, 1984).

We report here on studies of six brain-lesioned signers: Three have left-hemisphere damage (Paul D., Gail D., and Karen L.); three have right-hemisphere damage (Brenda I., Sarah M., and Gilbert G.). All subjects were members of deaf communities, had been educated in residential schools for deaf

LEFT HEMISPHERE DAMAGED SIGNERS

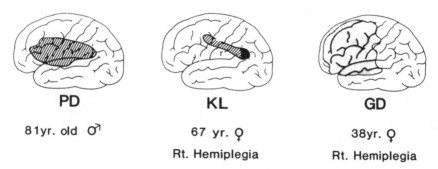

PD	KL	GD
81yr. old ♂	67 yr. ♀	38yr. ♀
	Rt. Hemiplegia	Rt. Hemiplegia

RIGHT HEMISPHERE DAMAGED SIGNERS

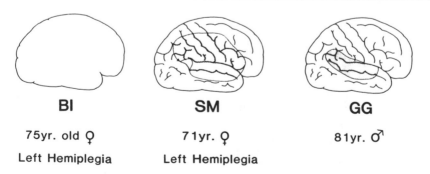

BI	SM	GG
75yr. old ♀	71yr. ♀	81yr. ♂
Left Hemiplegia	Left Hemiplegia	

FIG. 7.6. Lateral reconstructions of brain lesions of the brain-damaged signers.

children, and had deaf or hard-of-hearing spouses. All were right-handed before their strokes. For each subject, the primary form of communication with family and friends was ASL.

Figure 7.6 presents lateral reconstructions of brain lesions and summary characteristics of the six deaf, brain-lesioned subjects. In brief, Paul D. has a subcortical lesion in his left hemisphere, with an anterior focus deep to Broca's area and including major portions of the basal ganglia. The lesion extends posteriorly into the white matter underlying the left supramarginal and, to a lesser extent, angular gyri. Gail D. has a large left-hemisphere lesion that involved most of the convexity of the frontal lobe, including Broca's area and the anterior portions of the superior and middle temporal gyri. This lesion is typical of those that produce agrammatic aphasia in hearing-speaking individuals. Finally, Karen L. has a circumscribed cortical lesion in the region of the left inferior parietal lobule that extended subcortically into the postcentral and precentral gyri, as well as into the posterior portion of the middle frontal gyrus. Both the traditional Broca's area and Wernicke's area were spared.

As for the right-lesioned signers, Sarah M. had a massive lesion involving most of the territory of the right middle cerebral artery. The lesion extends from the frontal operculum, the area of the right hemisphere homologous to Broca's area, involves premotor, motor, and somatosensory areas, to include the inferior parietal lobule, superior parietal lobule, and the middle and superior temporal gyri. Large critical areas of the right hemisphere were, thus, damaged. Gilbert G.'s lesion involves the cortex and underlying white matter in the superior temporal gyrus, extending inferiorly to partially involve the middle temporal gyrus. Posteriorly, the lesion extends into the lower portion of the inferior parietal lobule. Unfortunately, no CT scan was available for Brenda I., but, like Sarah M., she showed a dense paralysis of her left arm and hand (see Poizner et al., 1987 for more detailed neurological information on the six signers).

Preserved Language in Right-lesioned Signers

Quite remarkably, the signers with right-hemisphere damage were not aphasic for sign language. They exhibited fluent, grammatical, virtually error-free signing. Figure 7.7 (top) shows the rating-scale profiles from the ASL adaptation of the BDAE for the three left-lesioned signers. The middle part of the figure presents the rating scale profiles of three matched deaf control subjects, showing normal performance. Performance of the right-lesioned signers is shown in the bottom

FIG. 7.7.   Rating scale profiles form the ASL adaptation of the Boston Diagnostic Aphasia Examination for left- and right-lesioned signers and controls. Note that performance of the right-lesioned signers is similar to that of the controls.

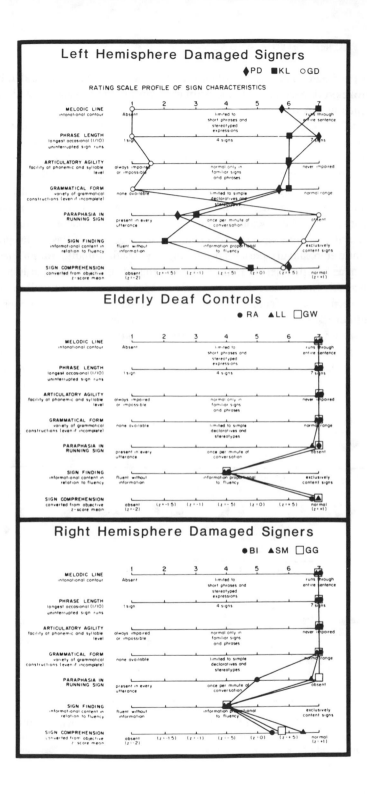

panel of the figure. The rating scale profiles of their sign characteristics, shown in the lower portion of the figure, reflect their grammatical (nonaphasic) signing; in fact, their profiles are much like those of the control subjects. Furthermore, the right-lesioned signers, but not those with left-hemisphere damage, were unimpaired on our tests for processing the various levels of structure of ASL.

Importantly, this preserved signing was in the face of marked deficits the right-hemisphere damaged signers showed in processing nonlanguage spatial relations. Across a range of tests, including drawing, block design, attention to visual space, perception of line orientation, facial recognition, and visual closure, right-lesioned signers showed many of the classic visuospatial impairments seen in hearing patients with right-hemisphere damage. In contrast, left-lesioned signers showed relatively preserved nonlanguage spatial functioning. Figure 7.8 presents example performance on a block design test in which subjects must assemble either four or nine three-dimensional blocks to match a two-dimensional model of the top surface. The left-hemisphere damaged signers (upper row) produced correct constructions on the simple block designs and made only featural errors on the more complex designs; in contrast, the right-hemisphere damaged signers (lower row) produced erratic and incorrect constructions and tended to break the overall configurations of the designs. The severe spatial

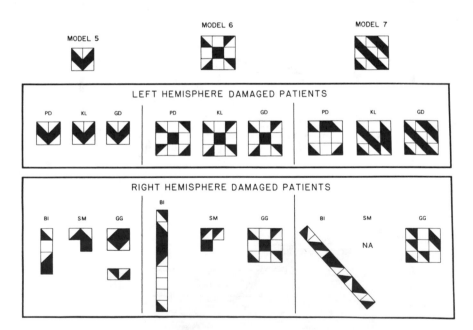

FIG. 7.8.   Performance of left- and right-lesioned signers on the WAIS-R block design task, a nonlanguage visuospatial task. Note the broken configurations and severe spatial disorganization of the right-lesioned signers.

disorganization of the constructions of the right-lesioned signers provides one reflection of their severe spatial loss. These nonlanguage data show that the right hemisphere in deaf signers can develop cerebral specialization for nonlanguage visuospatial functions (Poizner, Kaplan, et al., 1984). However, despite their nonlanguage spatial deficits, the sign language (including spatially expressed syntax) of the right-lesioned signers was unimpaired. The correct use of the spatial mechanisms for syntax in right-lesioned signers points to the abstract nature of these mechanisms in ASL.

Sign Language Aphasias in Left-lesioned Signers

The three signers with left-hemisphere damage show clear sign language impairments, as indicated by their results on the sign language adaptation of the BDAE, on tests for processing the structural levels of ASL, and on a linguistic analysis of their signing. Figure 7.7 (middle) presents the rating scale profiles from the sign adaptation of the BDAE for the three left-lesioned signers, contrasted with right-lesioned signers and controls. On each scale, the scores of the left-lesioned signers are scattered, spanning virtually the entire range of values. These profiles reflect frank sign language aphasias. These aphasias contrast with the overall preserved nonlanguage spatial functions of the left-lesioned signers. Moreover, the sign language impairments are not uniform but rather diverge along lines of linguistically relevant components.

Gail D: Agrammatic Sign Aphasia

One left-lesioned signer, Gail D., is agrammatic for ASL. She is severely aphasic, with her signing faltering and often reduced to single-sign utterances. She uses hardly any indexic pronouns (the spatially indexed "pointing" sign forms that have pronominal function in ASL), and her verbs are without any spatial indices whatever. In fact, her signing is devoid of any of the syntactic and morphological marking required in ASL (i.e., her signing is what would be classified as *agrammatic* in speech-aphasics). Her language profile is very much like that of hearing patients classified as Broca's aphasics.

Gail D.'s description of the Cookie Theft picture from the BDAE (shown in Figure 7.9) is characteristic of her signing output and stands in marked contrast to the responses of the other two patients. Her complete description of the picture was the following:

Gail D.: THREE...MOTHER...BROTHER...WHAT?...F-E-F-A-L-L...TURN-OFF.
"Three...(Examiner prompts)...Mother...(E prompts)...Brother...(E prompts)...
What?...(E prompts)...Fall...(E prompts)...Turn off."

Gail D.'s sparse description is not due to any reluctance to communicate on her part but to the extreme effort her signing seems to require; she is clearly frustrated in her attempts to communicate. She tried to produce not just signs but also gestures, mimes, fingerspelling, and the mouthing of English words: However, she is no better at producing these other means of communication than she is at signing. Gail D. can at times make single signs fluently and with little hesitation, for example, as single sign responses to comprehension tests. In expository conversation, however, she experiences great difficulty in expression. Her narratives are severely limited, effortfully produced, and without any of the grammatical apparatus of ASL.

The most salient characteristic of Gail D.'s signing is that it is agrammatic and effortful, composed of short utterances that consist largely of single, open-class items. She omits all grammatical formatives, including most pronouns, all inflectional and derivational processes, and all aspects of spatially organized syntax. Importantly, this nearly complete absence in Gail D.'s signing of any of ASL's inflectional morphology occurred, even although such inflectional morphology is not conveyed "horizontally" through a linear sequence of units, but rather "vertically" through the layering of form components. Gail G. was able to concatenate gestures, but few of her multisign utterances give any indication of having a sentence structure, whereby the meaning of the sentence as a whole is derived in a principled way from the meanings of the parts and their function in the sentence. Gail D.'s utterances lack any hierarchical combination of separate meaningful components. Thus, the basis for such combination, whether it is linear, as in many spoken languages, or layered, as in ASL, does not seem to be a crucial factor. Gail D.'s case shows the devastating effect that left-hemisphere damage can have on a visual-gestural language.

Karen L: Grammatical but Underspecified Signing and Impaired Sign Comprehension

Another left-hemisphere damaged patient (Karen L.) retained fluent output in signing after her stroke but shows impairment within sublexical structure (the equivalent of phonemic paraphasias in spoken language); however, she has relatively preserved grammar. In free conversation, Karen L. uses the spatialized syntactic mechanisms of ASL abundantly, including pronominal indices and verb indexing (the spatial device for indicating grammatical relations through verb agreement). Her language output is highly irregular, however, in that she characteristically fails to specify the nominals associated with these spatial indices; that is, the antecedents of the referentially functioning indices of her inflecting verbs and of her indexic pronouns are very often missing. These omissions give rise to an impression of vagueness and lack of content in her signing. Furthermore, Karen L. has a marked and lasting sign comprehension loss.

Karen L. communicates well and freely, carrying on a conversation (indeed, a monologue) with normal rate, flow, and with a wide range of grammatical structures. Karen L. signs freely without prompting. What follows is a sample of her signing that relates some incident in her past.

Karen L: THERE$_a$ NOT-YET SEE. *THEY$_{b-c}$ SAY PRETTY *THERE$_a$. THIS[+ to front] BETTER THAN *THAT$_d$. TROUBLE *THERE$_d$ THAN HERE. QUIET HERE, *THERE$_e$ TROUBLE. RIOTS[Allocative] DRINK[Habitual].

An English equivalent is:

Karen L: I have not yet seen what's over there. They [unspecified] say it is pretty there [unspecified]. This is better than that [unspecified]. There was more trouble over there [unspecified] than here. It's quiet here. Over there [unspecified] was trouble—riots in different places and regular boozing.
Examiner: Where was the trouble?
[Examiner is lost in terms of the referents of the conversation.]

As this exchange indicates, it was often impossible to tell what Karen L. was talking about, because she used pronominal indexes so freely without specifying in any way their antecedents. Her signing, however, is grammatical with appropriate morphological inflections, including those for indexing, which she frequently used. Yet her signing shows two specific deficits: paraphasias in ongoing signing, involving substitutions within the parameters of signs, and failure to specify the nominals associated with her indexes. Furthermore, her comprehension of ASL is markedly impaired.

Paul D.: Paragrammatic Signing

A third left-hemisphere damaged patient (Paul D.), whose signing is also fluent and unfaltering in delivery after his stroke, shows a linguistic impairment with respect to the appropriate selection of lexical signs and also with respect to the selection and combination of the morphological operations that "modulate" the meaning of signs. His signing includes many substituted or added inflectional and derivational morphemes as well as lexical substitutions. Moreover, he fails to use the spatialized syntax of ASL (pronominal indexes and verb agreement markers). His signing is marked by an overabundance of nominals, a lack of pronominal indexes and the failure to mark verb agreement correctly at all. This appears to be an impairment of spatially organized syntax and discourse. Thus, two left-hemisphere lesioned patients have primary impairment at the *grammatical* level, the one agrammatic (Gail D.) and the other *paragrammatic* (Paul D.).

Paul D. presents a particularly interesting pattern of language breakdown. We have found that he shows parallel errors in ASL signing and in written English with respect to morphology. However, he appears to have a sign language specific breakdown in syntax. We asked Paul D. to describe the Cookie Theft picture in ASL and in written English. Figure 7.9 presents Paul D.'s written version of the story and an error from his signed version. His written description is:

I see a kitchen where a girl washes *his dishes and a big cookie jar *jarring a boy in the kitchen and a young girl *outstretching her arms *at the cookie and *jar the cover and I notice the *award of the water washing toward the floor.

Paul D. was asked to describe the scene in ASL, and part of his response is:

Paul D.: GIRL SPILL (THERE) [points to woman in picture]. WATER OVER-FLOW, WATER. (SHE)[points to woman] *CARELESS[Predispositional]. (HE) [points to boy] *FALL-LONG-DISTANCE-DOWN. (SHE)[points to woman] *GIGGLING. (SHE)[points to woman] WORK, THERE. (SHE)[points to woman] *SPILL-ALL-OVER-SELF.

Paragrammatisms in each passage are starred (*) and include a number of forms that are inappropriate or ungrammatical for the context. An English translation of Paul D.'s signing is:

The girl spilled there [pointing to the woman]. The water overflowed, the water. She is always careless by nature. He [referring to the boy] fell in a double somer-sault to the ground. She [referring to the woman] is giggling. She [the woman] is working; she spilled water all over her dress.

Both Paul D.'s writing and his signing display errors of selection at the lexical and morphological levels. His written description contained inappropriate selections, such as "jar *jarring," "girl *outstretching her arms," and "*jar the cover," and "the *award of the water." Similarly, instead of a sign meaning "starting to fall," he used a form that means "fall a long distance;" instead of a sign form meaning "spill on the floor," he signed a form that means "spilled all over herself," and so forth. Figure 7.9 presents one error from his signed description. He used the morphologically complex form meaning "characteristically careless," when the sign form that would have been appropriate for the context is the uninflected form CARELESS. Thus, his signing, like his writing, showed paragrammatisms and inappropriate morphological augmentations.

Therefore, these data indicate a parallel breakdown at the morphological level in Paul D.'s signing and writing. This demonstrates that morphological breakdown in aphasia can be independent of language modality. Sign language, however, in a striking way shows its roots in the visual modality through the special

(A)

(B)

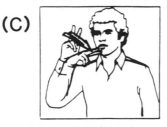

Correct form for context

*CARELESS (Uninflected)

Paul D.'s Morphological Augmentation

*CARELESS [Predispositional]

FIG. 7.9.   Paul D.'s written English and ASL errors.
(a) The Cookie Theft elicitation card from the Boston Diagnostic Aphasia Examination. Copyright © 1972 by Lea and Febiger.
(b) Paul D.'s written description of the cookie theft picture.
(c) An error from Paul D.'s signed description. Note the morphological errors in both his writing and signing.

spatialized organization underlying its syntax. We have found that Paul D. has problems with the spatialized syntax of ASL that differ from his impairment in English syntax. This sign-specific syntactic breakdown may be intimately related to requirements of a syntax that is specifically spatially organized.

Although Paul D. makes many incorrect selections of lexical items, the syntactic structures of English are generally well preserved in his writing. In English, verbs are appropriately inflected for tense and number, and Paul D. makes few noticeable omissions. In contrast, Paul D.'s signing shows a pronounced irregularity in those aspects of syntax and discourse that are spatialized in ASL. Recall that pronominal reference in ASL is realized *spatially*—by means of "pointing" *indexic* pronoun forms; similarly, verb agreement (specifying grammatical relations on the basis of indexing) is a part of the spatialized system. An analysis of Paul D.'s signing suggests that he tends to avoid indexic pronouns (part of the spatialized system) and to overuse nouns—more than five times as many nouns as indexic pronouns in a stretch of discourse, which is highly irregular when compared to the noun/pronoun ratio in the signing of the age-matched, deaf controls. Moreover, he made errors in the spatially organized verb agreement system. For example, in signing the ASL equivalent of "We arrived (in Jerusalem) and stayed there," Paul D. produced a syntactically well-formed sentence consisting of the three signs: ARRIVE, STAY, THERE. However, each of the three signs was indexed to a different locus, when all three signs should have been indexed to the same locus. This is typical of Paul D.'s errors of indexic verb agreement in ASL's spatialized syntax.

Such problems may well be related to the organizational requirements of spatial planning and spatial memory involved in planning discourse. In ASL, the formal means for indicating pronominal reference is negotiated on-line and is spatialized. One aspect of this processing is that the signer has to negotiate the placement of points as he or she goes along, because there are no predefined points to choose from in sign. Furthermore, a signer must plan ahead to establish abstract loci so that they are suitably placed for subsequent reference. In addition, of course, a signer must remember where each locus exists in the signing plane. As we have seen, Paul D. has difficulty with the entire system of spatial indexes in ASL. He underuses the spatial indexes for purposes of pronominal reference and verb agreement, and he incorrectly indexes verbs. He also performed poorly on a test of the comprehension of nominals and their associated spatial loci and on a test of spatially organized syntax. Paul D.'s difficulties here may be due in part to the special requirements of spatially organized syntax in sign—spatial memory, spatial planning, and syntactic and discourse structure.

Brain, Language, and Modality

Patterns of language breakdown and preservation in left- as opposed to right-lesioned signers lead us to the following conclusions. Because the left-lesioned signers show frank sign language aphasias, and the right-lesioned signers show preserved language function, it appears that it is indeed the left cerebral hemisphere that is specialized for Sign language. This provides support for the proposition that the left cerebral hemisphere in humans has an innate predisposition for language. Thus, there appear to be anatomical structures within the left hemisphere that emerge as spacial-purpose linguistic processors in persons who have profound and lifelong auditory deprivation and who communicate with a linguistic system that uses radically different channels of reception and transmission from that of speech. In this crucial respect, brain organization for language in deaf signers parallels that in hearing, speaking individuals.

Furthermore, our data indicate that differential damage within the left hemisphere produces different forms of sign aphasia and suggest the possibility that those anatomical structures within the left hemisphere that subserve visual-gestural language differ in part from those that subserve auditory-vocal language. Gail D. has a massive lesion to the left hemisphere that in hearing persons is typically associated with a lasting agrammatic aphasia. Her lesion involves not only the traditional Broca's area but also much of the surrounding cortex of the frontal lobe. Gail D. has a severe agrammatic aphasia for sign language. Her case points to the fact that there is an anterior region of the left hemisphere that is important for sign language. Whether or not this will turn out to be the same as the anterior region for speech is not clear, because her lesion is so large that it includes not only Broca's area but also much of the surrounding cortex. Broca's area is adjacent to that part of motor cortex that controls movement of the vocal tract. An analogous area that controls movement of the hands is located just superior to Broca's area, and Gail D.'s broad lesion includes both of these areas. Whether or not the same sign symptomatology would appear, if one or the other were spared cannot be answered from this case. Gail D.'s case is an important one, however, because a comparable lesion in hearing people is typically associated with agrammatic aphasia. Indeed, she has a clearcut aphasia for sign language that is remarkably similar to that of hearing agrammatics.

The case of Karen L. points to a possible difference between those neural structures that may underlie spoken language and signed language. Her lesion is in the left parietal lobe (supramarginal and angular gyri) with a subcortical extension into the frontal lobe. Her lesion is well circumscribed and spares the traditional Broca's and Wernicke's areas. Although a hearing patient with this lesion might have some initial speech comprehension difficulties and suffer from word-finding difficulties, we would not expect a lasting speech comprehension deficit. Karen L., however, has such a pronounced and lasting deficit in the comprehension of sign language. It may well be that anatomical structures of the inferior parietal lobule of the left hemisphere play a greater role for sign language than for spoken language. These structures are intimately involved with higher order spatial analysis as well as with gestural control and may have been recruited in the service of sign language, because in sign language grammatical relations and spatial relations are so intertwined.

There is other evidence that indicates that brain structures are not indelibly and unalterably wired for particular functions but rather that the brain optimizes particular processing tasks. For example, Merzenich and his colleagues (Merzenich, Nelson, Stryker, Cynader, Schoppmann, & Zook, 1984; Merzenich, Kass, Wall, Sur, Nelson, & Felleman, 1983; Merzenich & Kaas, 1982) have studied the cortical reorganization that occurs in the central representation of the body's skin surface after peripheral nerve injury. These investigators cut the peripheral nerves of monkeys that provide the brain with sensory input from skin surfaces, and they found that the brain's map of these surfaces was dramatically reorganized. In that reorganization, the representation of skin surfaces in cortical areas adjacent to deprived areas expanded to occupy the deprived cortical zones. Furthermore, this reorganization (and optimization) of brain function occurred after only relatively brief periods of altered somatosensory input to the brain.

It is important to note that we are not implying that sign language (or sign language processing) is localized in the left parietal lobe (or in a left anterior region). There are a number of cortical and subcortical brain regions that are intimately involved with spoken language processing (Damasio & Geschwind, 1984), and there is undoubtedly a similarly large number of brain structures on whose integrated performance sign language functioning crucially depends on. The parietal (and frontal) lobes are heavily and reciprocally interconnected with many other cortical and subcortical structures, making them important nodes in a number of distributed systems (Mountcastle, Motter, Steinmetz, & Duffy, 1984). It may well be that the brain's execution of the complex linguistic functions of sign language are carried out by neuronal processing mechanisms of those distributed systems. It is important to note that our data lead to the view that those distributed brain systems that underlie visual-gestural languages differ in part from those that subserve language in the vocal-auditory mode.

Hemispheric Specialization

All six of our patients, before their strokes, were skilled signers who had used ASL as their primary mode of communication throughout their lives. Although the left-lesioned patients were able to process visuospatial relations well, and the although right-lesioned patients were extremely impaired, the language behavior of these patients was quite the opposite. An especially dramatic finding is the contrast between right-lesioned Sarah M. and left-lesioned Gail D. Gail D. suffered massive damage to the left frontal lobe and was the most severely aphasic of all the subjects. Her signing was reduced to very short effortful utterances that consisted largely of single, open-class items. She omitted all grammatical formatives, including most pronouns, all inflectional and derivational processes, and all aspects of spatially organized syntax. However, her capacity for nonlanguage visuospatial processing was the most intact of any of the six subjects. She had excellent performance on drawing and constructional tasks, and she scored in the normal range on tests of facial recognition, perception of line orientation, and judgement of dot localization. Gail D.'s case is striking, because it shows the separation that can occur in brain organization for linguistic and for visuospatial capacity, even for a visuospatial language.

The case of Sarah M. stands in marked contrast. Her case is a dramatic one, because she had been an accomplished artist before her stroke, with superior nonlanguage visuospatial capacities. After her stroke, Sarah M.'s visuospatial nonlanguage functioning showed profound impairment. Even when copying simple line drawings after her stroke, she showed profound impairment. Even when copying simple line drawings after her stroke, she showed spatial disorganization, massive left-hemispatial neglect, and failure to indicate perspective. Her performance on other constructional tasks was likewise extremely impoverished, although these tasks were ones she excelled at prior to her stroke. However, Sarah M. was not aphasic for sign language.

Sarah M.'s lesion was a massive one to the right hemisphere that included most of the territory of the right middle cerebral artery. The lesion included areas that would be crucial to language, if the lesion occurred in the left hemisphere of a hearing patient. In all likelihood, Sarah M. would be globally aphasic had this lesion been in the *left* hemisphere in a hearing person. Thus, there is more than ample possibility for aphasic symptomatology to occur following the particular lesion in this case due to its size and location. Yet astonishingly no aphasia for sign language resulted. Despite Sarah M.'s profound visuospatial impairment, her signing was virtually impeccable. This underscores the complete separation in function that can occur between the specializations of the right and the left cerebral hemispheres in congenitally deaf signers. This result is particularly revealing, because, in sign language, language and spatial relations participate in one and the same channel.

Conclusions

Patterns of breakdown of a visuospatial language in deaf signers, thus, allow new perspectives on the nature and determinants of cerebral specialization for language. First, these data show that hearing and speech are not necessary for the development of hemispheric specialization. Sound is *not* crucial. Second, the data show that the two cerebral hemispheres of congenitally deaf signers can develop separate functional specializations for nonlanguage spatial processing and for language processing, even though sign language is conveyed in large part via spatial manipulation. Furthermore, it is the left cerebral hemisphere that is dominant for sign language. Thus, the left cerebral hemisphere in man appears to have an innate predisposition for language, independent of language modality. It therefore appears that linguistic functions and the processing operations required, rather than the form of the signal, promotes left hemisphere specialization for language.

Acknowledgments

This research was supported in part by the National Science Foundation grant #BNS-9000407 and National Institutes of Health grants, #NS25149 to Rutgers University, and by National Insititues of Health grants #NS19096, #NS 15175, and #HD 13249 to the Salk Institute for Biological Studies. We thank Robbin Battison, David Corina, Karen van Hoek, Diane Lillo-Martin, Maureen O'Grady, Lucinda O'Grady, Carol Padden, Dennis Schemenauer, and James Tucker for their help in these studies. We also thank the subjects and their families who participated. Line drawing illustrations of signs by Frank A. Paul, copyright, Ursula Bellugi, The Salk Institute.

References

Bellugi, U. (1988). The acquisition of a spatial language. In F. Kessell (Ed.), *The development of language and language researchers, essays in honor of Roger Brown.* (pp. 153–185). Hillsdale, NJ: Lawrence Erlbaum Associates.

Bellugi, U., Klima, E. S., & Poizner, H. (1988). Sign language and the brain. In F. Plum (Ed.), *Language, communication, and the brain* (pp. 39–56). New York: Raven Press.

Damasio, A., & Geschwind, N. (1984). The neural basis of language. *Annual Review of Neuroscience, 7,* 127–147.

Fok, Y. Y. A., Bellugi, U., van Hoek, K., & Klima, E. S. (1988). The formal properties of Chinese languages in space. In M. Liu, H. C. Chen, & M. J. Chen (Eds.), Cognitive aspects of the Chinese language (pp. 187–205). Hong Kong: Asian Research Service.

Goodglass, H., & Kaplan, E. (1972/1983). *The assessment of aphasia and related disorders.* (Rev. ed.). Philadelphia: Lea & Febiger.

Jennings, P., & Poizner, H. (1988). Computergraphic modelling and analysis II: Three dimensional reconstruction and interactive analysis. *Journal of Neuroscience Methods, 24,* 45–55.

Klima, E. S., & Bellugi, U. (1979). *The signs of language.* Cambridge, MA: Harvard University Press.

Klima, E. S., Bellugi, U., & Poizner, H. (1988). Grammar and space in sign aphasiology. *Aphasiology, 2,* 319–328.

Lane, H., & Grosjean, F. (Eds.). (1980). *Recent perspectives on American Sign Language.* Hillsdale, NJ: Lawrence Erlbaum Associates.

Lenneberg, E. (1967). *Biological foundations of language.* New York: Wiley.

Liberman, A. M. (1974). The specialization of the language hemisphere. In F. O. Schmitt & F. G. Worden (Eds.), *The neurosciences: Third study program* (pp. 43–56). Cambridge, MA: MIT Press.

Liberman, A. M. (1979). Duplex perception and integration of cues: Evidence that speech is different from nonspeech and similar to language. In E. Fischer-Jorgensen, J. Rischel, & N. Thorsen (Eds.), *Proceedings of the IXth International Congress of Phonetic Sciences, 2* 468–473. Copenhagen: University of Copenhagen.

Liberman, A. M. (1982). On finding that speech is special. *American Psychologist, 37,* 148–167.

Liberman, A. M., & Mattingly, I. G. (1985). The Motor Theory of Speech Perception Revised. *Cognition, 21,* 1–36.

Liddell, S. K. (1980). *American Sign Language syntax.* The Hague: Mouton.

Lieberman, P. (1975). *On the origins of language.* New York: Macmillan.

Lillo-Martin, D., & Klima, E. S. (in press). Pointing out differences: American Sign Language pronouns in syntactic theory. In S. Fischer & P. Siple (Eds.), *Theoretical issues in sign language research.* Chicago: University of Chicago Press.

Mattingly, I. G., & Liberman, A. M. (1988). Specialized perceiving systems for speech and other biologically significant sounds. In G. M. Edelman, W. E. Gall, & W. M. Cowan (Eds.), *Auditory function: The neurological bases of hearing* (pp. 775–792). New York: Wiley.

Merzenich, M. M., & Kaas, J. H. (1982). Reorganization of mammalian somatosensory cortex following peripheral nerve injury. *Trends in Neuroscience, 5* (12), 434–436.

Merzenich, M. M., Kaas, J. H., Wall, J. T., Sur, M., Nelson, R. J., & Felleman, D. J. (1983). Progression of change following median nerve section in the cortical representation of the hand in Areas 3b and 1 in adult owl and squirrel monkeys. *Neuroscience, 10,* 639–665.

Merzenich, M. M., Nelson, R. J., Stryker, M. P., Cynader, M. S., Schoppmann, A., & Zook, J. M. (1984). Somatosensory cortical map changes following digit amputation in adult monkeys. *The Journal of Comparative Neurology, 224,* 591–605.

Mountcastle, V. B., Motter, B. C., Steinmetz, M. A., & Duffy, C. J. (1984). Looking and seeing: Visual functions of the parietal lobe. In G. Edelman, W. Gall, & W. Cowan (Eds.), *Dynamic aspects of neocortical function* (pp. 159–193). New York: Wiley.

Poizner, H. (1983, April). *Motion analysis of grammatical processes in a visual gestural language.* Paper presented at SIGGRAPH/SIGART Interdisciplinary Workshop on Motion: Representation and Perception, Toronto, Canada.

Poizner, H., Bellugi, U., & Iragui, V. (1984). Apraxia and aphasia for a visual-gestural language, *American Journal of Physiology: Regulatory, Integrative and Comparative Physiology, 246,* R868–R883.

Poizner, H., Bellugi, U., & Klima, E. S. (1990). 'Biological Foundations of Language: Clues from Sign Language.' In W. Maxwell Cowan, (Ed.), *Annual Review of Neuroscience.* Palo Alto, CA: Annual Reviews Inc., *13,* 283–307.

Poizner, H., Kaplan, E., Bellugi, U., & Padden, C. (1984). Visual-spatial processing in deaf brain-damaged signers. *Brain and Cognition, 3,* 281–306.

Poizner, H., Klima, E. S., & Bellugi, U. (1987). *What the hands reveal about the brain.* Cambridge, MA: MIT Press.

Poizner, H., Klima, E. S., Bellugi, U., & Livingston, R. (1986). Motion analysis of grammatical processes in a visual-gestural language. In G. Balzano & V. McCabe (Eds.), *Event cognition* (pp. 155–174). Hillsdale, NJ: Lawrence Erlbaum Associates.

Poizner, H., Wooten, E., & Salot, D. (1986). Computergraphic modeling and analysis: A portable system for tracking arm movements in three-dimensional space [Special issue on computers and vision]. *Behavior Research Methods, Instruments, and Computers, 18,* 427–433.

Studdert-Kennedy, M., & Lane, H. (1980). Clues from the differences between signed and spoken language. In U. Bellugi & M. Studdert-Kennedy (Eds.), *Signed and spoken language: Biological constraints on linguistic form* (pp. 29–39). Weinheim: Verlag Chemie.

Wilbur, R. B. (1987). *American Sign Language linguistic and applied dimensions.* Boston: College Hill Press.

Comment: Dr. Harlan and Mr. Lane

Harlan Lane

Department of Psychology, Northeastern University

The first job I ever had was at Haskins Labs, washing test tubes for protozoologist Seymour Hutner. I also tried in vain for several months to culture *Euglena Klebsii* in the laboratory. After my desperate final attempt using chicken soup also ended in failure, I took a more lively interest in the strange sounds emanating from the floor below. What sort of people would endlessly drone, "These days a chicken leg is a rare dish," when countless chickens, each possessing two legs, were stacked high in local butcher shops and supermarkets?

One evening, on my way downstairs, I penetrated the floor below despite loudly brayed admonitions that I should "Never kill a snake with your bare hands!" and I asked what it was all about. A genial, tall, soft-spoken man responded in terms I could understand and in ways that captured my imagination my life long. His name was Alvin Liberman. Not long after, I found myself employed at Haskins as a kind of song-and-dance man, doing the Do-To one-step, two-step, and three-step. It led to my first publication.

So you will understand my allegiance to Haskins Labs and to Alvin Liberman in particular. As a young psychologist, however, I was led to question in print the argument that led from categorical perception to the motor theory. That left me with a certain skepticism about the theory. There is still a debate in my mind between that iconoclastic young psychologist, call him Harlan, and Lane, scion of Haskins. Here is what they said last night concerning the motor theory and the relevance of the research by Poizner, Bellugi, and Klima.

HARLAN: Well, Lane, you and other proponents of the motor theory should be delighted with the findings on brain function and American Sign Language. Recall that the ASL speakers with right hemisphere lesions had grave difficulty in spatial perception but apparently none in perceiving spatial language. When visual perception goes one way, visual-manual language goes another. There seem to be two distinct processing mechanisms operating in parallel, one perceptual, the other linguistic, for if a perceptual stage fed a linguistic one, the disruption of spatial perception would have led to a disruption of Sign language perception. As Liberman and Mattingly (1985) put it: "[Speech] perception requires no . . . arbitrary progression from an auditory stage to a superseding phonetic label" (p. 18).

Just as the signers with right hemisphere lesions had poor spatial perception but good sign perception, so, too, two signers with left hemisphere lesions had *good* spatial perception but poor sign perception. Both populations testify to a dissociation between visual perception and linguistically significant perception of visual cues.

LANE: Yes, I am interested to see that the distinction between auditory and speech perception is mirrored by one between visual and sign perception, but I fear you are about to propose that the same mechanism is involved in both cases.

HARLAN: Well, doesn't it stand to reason? In Sign as in speech, the objects of perception are, as Liberman and Mattingly (1985) put it, "the intended phonetic gestures of the speaker, represented in the brain as invariant motor commands that call for movements of the articulators through certain linguistically significant configurations" (p. 2). Both speech and sign involve a rapid and precise peripheral mechanism with a high degree of central neural coordination. If speech and sign do share a common mechanism, they may share a common neural substrate. In that event, a left hemisphere lesion with a locus that disrupts spoken language in hearing adults may disrupt Sign language in deaf adults— just what Poizner, Bellugi, and Klima have demonstrated.

LANE: Hold on now. Some of their ASL speakers with left hemisphere lesions had comprehension difficulty, but it was not necessarily due to a failure of the phonetic module. The commonalities between the aphasias in the two different language modes were higher order—breakdowns in morphology and syntax. There was no disruption in the control and perception of gesture. Besides, how can you make inferences from the cortical organization of the deaf patients to that of ordinary users of spoken language? The deaf people may have had an abnormal cortical organization for language on five counts: They had suffered prolonged auditory deprivation; they acquired their first language late in life; they had long-standing lesions; they were in varying degrees bilingual; and their most fluent language was manual-visual rather than oral-aural.

HARLAN: Yet the effects of their lesions were generally comparable to those reported in the literature for hearing monolinguals. You must concede that hearing and speech are not necessary for the specialization of the left hemisphere. The signers with left hemisphere lesions had impaired perception not of gestures—true—but of linguistically significant gestures, of ASL. And that's just my point.

Look, Lane, every culture has a creation myth, and you can't imagine revising yours. Suppose, in the beginning, there were neural networks developed for the hierarchical control of motor behavior. If spoken and signed languages share a common mechanism and substrate, perhaps this is because the neurological specialization that evolved exploited those networks, not for recovering spoken language gestures in particular, but linguistic gestures in general, whether spoken or signed. In that event, speech gestures should be recoverable by eye as well as by ear—and so they seem to be.

LANE: What you have never understood about the phonetic module is that it is required precisely because of the complex encoding of speech in the acoustic wave. It evolved hand-in-hand—or rather concomitantly with the evolution of the motor system that allowed coarticulated phonetic gestures; thus, they could be produced rapidly. In your paper with Michael Studdert-Kennedy (1981) you pointed out that the gestures comprising signs have many more degrees of freedom, they are more numerous and more extensively layered; there is less need for concatenation and rapid switching from one to the next. Hence, there is no complex decoding problem—there is no need for a phonetic module. Moreover, I'm not convinced there is one at work in ASL perception. The deficits in spatial perception of the ASL users with right hemisphere lesions were not shown to be just those required for ASL perception. Perhaps the precise visual perceptual capacities required for ASL perception were still intact, even if perception of block arrays was impaired. And one of these subjects did show some difficulty in comprehending some spatial aspects of sign (Poizner, Kaplan, Bellugi, & Padden, 1984).

HARLAN: Our disagreement is clear. For you, the raison d'etre of the phonetic module is the complex encoding of gesture in the acoustic wave. Therefore, you must challenge the evidence that in sign, as in speech, the perception of linguistically significant signals is conducted differently from the perception of nonlinguistic signals. Or you must accept the evidence, and postulate two different mechanisms that have this result in common. For me, the evidence points to a single mechanism.

As in the case of speech, the same distal stimulus can give rise to two different perceptions: Poizner (1981) has shown that nonsense words in ASL are assigned to different perceptual spaces by subjects ignorant of ASL and native speakers of ASL. As in speech perception and depth perception, there seems to be a biologically specialized perceiving module, which leads the observer effortlessly from the visual signal to the perception of an intended phonetic gesture, thanks to neuromuscular information available to observer and signer. Both observer and signer know the motor invariances that lead fingers, hands, and arms to move together to the right place at the right time; in short, both have a model of linguistically significant limb movement.

When a native signer looks at ASL presented in a point-light display with just some of the normal visual cues available, what he sees is not an arbitrary fireworks of points of light nor something from which he can deduce a sign: He sees the sign itself. Native signers who become visually impaired soon learn to understand Sign by placing their hands over the signing hands of their interlocutor. I daresay there is a McGurk effect that can be demonstrated here.

Now that the two parties had come upon an experiment to conduct, they suspended their debate and retired for the night.

References

Liberman, A. M., & Mattingly, I. G. (1985). The motor theory of speech perception revised. *Cognition, 21,* 1–36.

Poizner, H. (1981). Visual and "phonetic" encoding of movement: Evidence from American Sign Language. *Science, 212,* 691–693.

Poizner, H., Kaplan, E., Bellugi, U., & Padden, C. (1984). Visual-spatial processing in deaf brain-damaged signers. *Brain and Cognition, 3,* 281–306.

Studdert-Kennedy, M., & Lane, H. L. (1981). Clues from the differences between signed and spoken language. In U. Bellugi & M. Studdert-Kennedy (Eds.), *Signed and spoken language: Biological constraints on linguistic form* (pp. 29–39). Weinheim: Verlag Chemie.

Chapter 8

Panel Discussion: The Motor Theory and Alternative Accounts

J. C. Catford
Department of Linguistics, University of Michigan

Peter W. Jusczyk
Department of Psychology, University of Oregon

Dennis H. Klatt (Chairman)
Research Laboratory of Electronics, Massachusetts Institute of Technology

Alvin M. Liberman
Haskins Laboratories

Robert E. Remez (Reporter)
Department of Psychology, Barnard College

Kenneth N. Stevens
Research Laboratory of Electronics, Massachusetts Institute of Technology

KLATT: Let me begin by spending one or two minutes with a few thoughts of my own on this subject. Some of you may have noticed a brief review paper in our *Working Papers, VI,* (Klatt, 1988), which discusses some of the recent models of speech perception. It is relatively easy to list candidate models, and I am not going to spend any time trying to define them or to apologize for those left off the list. The only observation I want to make at this point is that the most recent revised Motor Theory has changed from its original conception (a sort of analysis by synthesis module involving the articulators) to something that is not particularly well specified. One of my hopes this afternoon is that someone will say exactly what they think the revised Motor Theory would look like, if it were incorporated in a speech recognition device. Maybe most of you in the audience have a general idea of what that would look like, but perhaps not.

175

Evidence from Phonetic Training and Diachrony

CATFORD: As a linguistic phonetician, my experience predisposed me many years ago to some kind of motor theory of speech perception. First, in dealing with many exotic languages, I often found that I could identify exotic sounds more easily, regularly, and certainly, after I learned to produce them and not before. I am sure others have had that experience, both phoneticians and learners of languages.

Second, again as a phonetician, in the teaching of phonetics I have devoted a great deal of attention with students to developing the motor aspects of what they are doing and, following the precepts of Henry Sweet (1877) more than a century ago, to teaching people to produce sounds silently. We spend many, many minutes sitting in class silently mouthing vowels so that people can become conscious of the proprioceptive and tactile sensations that accompany them. Thereafter, they tend to perform rather well on tests of ability to identify vowel sounds. Of course, this is purely anecdotal evidence that people can identify sounds more easily after they have learned to mouth them. Incidentally, the technique of silent practice of sounds in the teaching of phonetics is motivated by my experience that auditory sensations mask the proprioceptive sensations, and in order to get at the latter, you have to eliminate the auditory sensations.

Nearly twenty years ago, I carried out a very primitive experiment with a very small number of subjects and with the assistance of a young graduate student at the University of Michigan named David Pisoni (who probably would like to forget about it). We did a little experiment in which I taught a very small group of linguistically naive students to produce a number of exotic sounds. One group was instructed purely auditorily without revealing anything about producing the sounds and without even letting them see my lips or my face. I talked to them through a grid—a colander, as a matter of fact. The other group was taught purely articulatorily, and individuals were told very precisely what to do and encouraged to do it but as far as possible were not allowed to hear the sound until each finally produced it. Finally, both groups were given an identification test for the exotic sounds that they had been taught, including some other novel sounds for purposes of contrast. They were also given a production test that was rated by myself and another phonetician, Kenneth Hill. The net result of this was that the group that had been taught on the articulatory basis performed better in all tests than the group that had been taught auditorily, including the auditory identification test. This was a very simplistic and small pilot experiment that I regret to say was never replicated, but it tended to support what I knew perfectly well from my own experience about the perceptual role in articulation.

Now, most of the discussions today have been about segments, but in every language there are phonological units of higher rank than the segment. In the kind of linguistics that I subscribe to, systemic linguistics (Catford, 1985), we recognize the following ranks of units in English: the tone group or intonation group, the foot or rhythmic group, the syllable, and finally the segmental phoneme. One characteristic of English speakers is their tendency to imagine that they produce isochronous feet. Yet when people measure the duration of feet or rhythmic units in English, these units do not turn out to be strictly isochronous, although there is undoubtably a tendency in that direction. In other words, the duration of a foot is not proportional to the number of syllables in it, not by any means; the metrical feet, thus, tend to be isochronous but are far from strict isochrony. I have long held the view that although there may be only this approximate isochrony in production, there certainly is *isodynamism*. We tend in English to deliver each foot or rhythmic group with roughly the same amount of energy, the same amount of muscular activity. What people perceive when they listen to English and say, "That sounds isochronous," is possibly a kind of appreciation of the motor side of this, a kind of motor isodynamism.

On other matters, I wanted to introduce some relevant evidence from diachronic phonetics. Although there are many sound changes that have an obvious acoustic or auditory basis, there are many that have not. I will mention one that is rather striking, because it has often been put forward erroneously as a typical example of an acoustically based sound change. I refer to the supposed change of the velar fricative /x/ to the labiodental fricative /f/ in the development of a word like *laugh,* which was assumed to have been originally something like [lɑːx]. As a matter of fact, this is not the case, because there was no simple velar [x] in *laugh* at the time when the change occurred. It was a strongly labialized velar [xʷ], or better [xɸ], the strong progressive labialization terminating in a pure labial. We know this from seventeenth century descriptions and from modern dialects, particularly in the south of Scotland, where people pronounce *laugh* and *cough* as [lɑːxɸ] and [kɔxɸ], exemplifying the strongly labialized [x] and suggesting an articulatory principle at work in the diachronic effect. In other words, it is not a case of a purely acoustically based switch from /x/ to /f/ motivated by the presence of the acoustic feature *grave,* common to both sounds, but rather a perpetuation of the kinaesthetically conspicuous labial articulation (Dobson, 1968).

There are many other changes of this sort, like the development of Semitic emphatics, particularly in Arabic, from what were presumably formerly glottalic sounds in proto-Semitic (i.e., sounds for which the airstream is initiated not by the lungs but by an upward thrust of the larynx with the glottis closed). Thus, sounds like [tʼ] and [tsʼ] became pharyngealized [tˤ] and [sˤ]. What is left is a trace of the former initiatory gesture—a pharyngeal compression, as a result of the upward movement of the larynx.

Such examples suggest that an articulatory emphasis in perception—the perception of a motor event—may influence diachronic processes in language.

The Speech Mode and Motor Agnosticism

JUSCZYK: I think it was about twenty years ago, when, as an undergraduate, I first came into contact with the Motor Theory of Speech Perception. Peter Eimas handed me the 1967 paper and said something like, "Here, read this about four or five times. By the time you get done you will know all about speech perception." I struggled with that paper for a long time, but I learned a lot, and I want to say here and to Al that even today, this is still the bible that we start the students on. It is a tribute to Al that this paper, which he wrote along with Frank Cooper, Don Shankweiler, and Michael Studdert-Kennedy (1967), shaped our thoughts on speech and perception and is still a very important paper in the field.

To begin, I will ask: If the Motor Theory of Speech Perception is correct, then how can we explain the fact that there are so many agnostics out there? It seems to me that there may be some reasons to explain this, and I would like to offer a few.

One reason stems from the fact that, for most of us who are concerned with internal workings of perceptual processes, the most obvious aspect of speech perception is the acoustic signal that strikes the ear. One who adopts that literal-minded perspective probably would look at speech perception beginning with the acoustic signal striking the ear. That may not be the most prominent reason for agnosticism about motor theory, but it is one possibility.

Then, there are other kinds of questions that we can trace to the research that has been done on Motor Theory over the years. Most of this research I regard as very important and interesting research, a lot of which has been devoted to showing the difficulty in accounting for speech perception according to an acoustic view. The classic examples that have been cited here today concern things like the perceptual effects of removing a cue from its context and then revealing that it is not perceived in the same way that it is within the speech signal itself. That line of research was very important in directing all of us in the field to treat the speech signal in terms of its overall context, although it falls short of warranting a specifically motor account of contextual variation.

The most convincing evidence that there has to be a phonetic mode of speech perception—I am not going to go so far as saying that I believe the Motor Theory, but simply that there has to be a phonetic mode of speech perception—concerns the later research also done in this vein, looking at sinewave speech perception (Remez, Rubin, Pisoni, & Carrell, 1981). I think it is very difficult to explain how it is that you can have exactly the same physical signal perceived in two different ways simply by varying instructions to the subject or at least by suggesting that in one case the sounds are produced by a musical synthesizer, in another case produced by a lousy speech synthesizer. That suggests the existence of at least a couple of available perceptual organizations, only one of which is actually geared to perceiving the speech signal.

It is another question entirely whether this capacity for perceptual organization in a speech mode is in place in very young infants. When we look at the beginnings of speech perception, our problem is to determine whether we observe sensitivity to the linguistic properties of speech. The development of perception that occurs while learning a particular language—namely, the apparent shifts in sensitivity that occur for certain phonetic contrasts—makes the assessment of the role of articulation difficult.

To convert me from my agnosticism with respect to the Motor Theory of Speech Perception would require an account of just how it is, if indeed we are perceiving gestures, that the acoustic signal is recast as the gestures of production. In other words, an explicit account must be produced detailing the decoding process by which the gestures, or better still, the intentions behind the gestures, are recovered from the acoustic signal. At the very least, this will employ some kind of mapping between the sound structure and the gestures. That has been the fundamental problem in speech perception, as Frank Cooper said, ever since the early attempts to build reading machines for the blind. It is also important in this line of research not to lose sight of the fact that the ultimate goal here, the kind of description that we are looking for, has to be a description that is sufficient for perception of fluent speech. I think we have to be sensitive to this sort of thing and not always think in terms of recovering a complete phonetic description.

A Less-Specifically-Motor Theory

REMEZ: One virtue of the Motor Theory—that it links so many important aspects of speech and language, and does so appealingly—puts the panelist at a disadvantage. Because there is more to it than the individual findings that it rationalizes, one cannot simply review the familiar facts, or scrutinize particular discrimination results, or test techniques, or explanations of release-burst effects and the like. To adopt such a narrow focus seems to me to mistake the fine grain of the Motor Theory for its motivating themes and, thus, to miss the overarching virtue of the model. However, it is so much to deal with altogether!

I want only to raise two points with the panel and you. For one, I think it is clear that the Motor Theory is *false*. For the other, I think the evidence indicates no less that the Motor Theory is essentially, fundamentally, primarily, and basically *true*. Here are the arguments.

First, to put a sharper point on my claim that the Motor Theory is false, I need to say that the theory in its recent version now presumes a rather modest mediating role for the nerve-muscle components of speech production, or covert articulatory inferences, and this follows the important, recent noncognitive development of the perceptual account. The authors convince me, too, that this version of the model is justified. After all, ordinary listeners know little about speech production, and certainly they know less than they should, if the perception of an utterance were to produce representations of its motoric cause. In this newer version of the motor theory, the actual details of articulation that are said to mediate perception are correspondingly remote from perceptual experience—encapsulated and shielded from cognitive inspection.

My description here of this less specifically Motor Theory is taken from

Liberman & Mattingly in their 1985 reconsideration of Motor Theory. They set the perceiver's focus on the linguistic *intentions* of the talker rather than on the imbricated gestures that actually compose the coarticulated acts of sound production. In this way, perception is said to occur without promoting a cognitive representation of the action, and the role of gestures is left completely preperceptual. This lets the Motor Theory preserve the explanatory emphasis on the causes of speech sounds as it admits that simple listening fails to produce explicit knowledge of the gestures of production. However, this less specifically Motor Theory is motor only in a figurative sense. It is because such an account unmistakably differs from one which exploits anticipated proprioceptive return, or articulatory reference, or perception of gestures, or analysis by synthesis—but does not differ substantially from a model in which phonetic significance is projected from auditory representations by analytic means—that I say it is false: At least it is less true now to call it a *motor* theory. This is not exactly claiming that the Motor Theory is false, I know, but it does urge its proponents and detractors to measure how much the account has evolved as a description of perception.

My second point is that the Motor Theory is true, and true in many deep aspects. I want to choose one facet that perhaps has special significance for psychologists: Its consistent assertion that the causes of stimulation—and not the patterns of stimulation themselves—constitute the objects and events of perceptual experience. This doctrine is not original in the Motor Theory, of course, but it is the case that over the past two decades the Motor Theory has usually offered the clearest empirical setting of the distinction in psychology, and it is at least for this reason that most students of psychology know about it. In speech, it reduces to the problem of explaining the existence of phonetic categories whose instances are not rationalized by means of stimulus similarity, neither superficial nor, as far as anyone knows, higher-order. The Motor Theory refers this problem to articulation because of the independent premise that the perceiver experiences a talker's act and not simply the sounds incident at the ear that issue from a vocal tract. This step is axiomatic in the respect that it sets the problem for the theorist. It says that no account of perception may fail to acknowledge the listener's experience of speech as phonetic in nature and suggests a theorem to guide the investigation.

The authors themselves say that the "Motor Theory does not provide a complete explanation, certainly not in its present state, but it does head the theoretical enterprise in the right direction." They might have said "directions" really, for the challenge to improve the individual parts of the model, unified under a biological rubric, is an aspect of its appeal and a clue to understanding its perennial value. In other words, it is not just this year's psychological mini-theory pitched to explain the assortment of phonetic categories in a language. I am sure I speak for many of us, now that I return from the adventures that the

Motor Theory has sent me off on, to say how important the Motor Theory has been.

Acoustic Links to Phonetic Units

STEVENS: I want to begin by noting aspects of speech perception theory that most but perhaps not all researchers would agree on. The first aspect is that there is a single lexicon that serves both production and perception. The primitives are units that are used to specify items in the lexicon, whether they be features, gestures, acoustic patterns, or phonemic segments, and these units must have links to both the acoustic material that describes the speech signal and to the articulatory activity that produces the speech signal. In perception, the acoustic patterns are transformed into these units, and the result can be used to access the lexical items. In production, this pattern of units in the lexicon is transformed into articulatory movements. There might be some disagreement concerning the nature of these units that specify lexical items.

The second point of agreement is that special mechanisms are brought into play for the processing of speech. One cannot deny the fact that in order to access these lexical items during continuous speech, it is necessary to derive from the speech signal a representation in terms of units with similar dimensionality to the lexical representation. The transformation of the acoustic signal so that it is in a form that permits accessing the lexicon is special for speech. One of Alvin Liberman's contributions to this field is his eloquent and persistent statement of this view that there is a special mode for processing speech. Few would disagree with this proposition, although there may be different opinions as to what form this special type of processing takes.

What is the nature of the representation that is derived from the acoustic signal to allow access to the lexicon? We can only speculate at present, I think, as we attempt to refine our understanding of speech production, speech acoustics, and speech perception. One of the arguments for leaning toward gestures or intended gestures as the units of representation is the apparent lack of straightforward relations between acoustic patterns and gestures. The acoustic patterns that show apparent variability with context are simple measures that can be made on an intensity-frequency-time representation—measures such as the frequency of a burst, the direction of the transition of a particular formant, the duration of a silent interval, and so forth.

With a redefinition of the relevant acoustic measures together with attention to the transformation of the sound by the peripheral auditory system, one might argue that the apparent variability with context is reduced and may even disappear. Take, for example, the frequently cited case of place of articulation for a stop consonant such as an alveolar stop. Where an alveolar stop is produced by placing the tongue tip in the vicinity of the alveolar ridge, building up pressure, and then releasing the consonant, there is a well defined sequence of acoustic events. Thus, because the tongue tip is located 1.5–2.5 cm from the lip opening, the sound produced has a broad spectral peak at high frequencies, and the spectrum amplitude in this frequency range shows a decrease immediately following the release. An example is given in Fig. 8.1a for a male speaker producing the syllable /di/. This figure shows two spectra: The solid curve is the smoothed spectrum sampled at the burst (with a time window indicated on the waveform below), and the dotted line is the spectrum sampled at 14 ms later in the vowel. For the burst spectrum, the high-frequency amplitude exceeds that in the following vowel. This simple property, which occurs in a frequency range above that which is normally relevant for vowel perception, is observed consistently and is not influenced by properties of the adjacent vowel, such as its rounding. It is true that the exact frequency of the high-frequency peak can be affected by the adjacent vowel, as can the exact starting frequencies of the formants, such as the onset of F2 at the beginning of the adjacent vowel. However, the overall property of a diffuse rising spectrum that contrasts with the spectrum of the adjacent vowel remains. This particular property defines the alveolar gesture. Whether one regards this acoustic property as leading to a representation in terms of a gesture, or whether the acoustic property itself can be used to access the lexicon, is a matter of preference. The gesture defines the acoustic property and vice versa.

Consider now the acoustic consequence of producing a velar consonant. The distinguishing characteristic of a velar consonant is that the length of the acoustic cavity in front of the constriction is such that its resonance corresponds to the second or the third formant of the adjacent vowel. For a high front vowel, it may be the fourth formant actually corresponding to F2'. When the velar consonant is released, the resulting noise burst shows a compact spectral peak. This peak is contiguous with F2 or F3 of the following vowel. Smoothed spectra sampled at the burst and at the vowel onset are shown in Fig. 8.1b, for a female speaker producing /gɔ/. The burst spectrum has a midfrequency peak that is contiguous with F2 of the vowel, with an amplitude that is a few dB above that of the F2 prominence in the vowel spectrum. The exact frequency of the peak is influenced by the vowel context, but the general property of a compact peak continuous with a vowel formant is always there. There is a requirement that the spectrum amplitude of the burst cannot be substantially less than the amplitude of the corresponding spectral peak in the adjacent vowel. The spectral compactness disappears as we move into the adjacent vowel. It can be noted, in passing, that this particular sequence of acoustic events is dependent on the properties of the vocal tract walls as well as on the rate of release. Similar statements are possible for other places of articulation and for other manners of articulation, although in some cases, particularly for combinations in languages that have not been thoroughly studied, the acoustic-articulatory relations are not yet worked out.

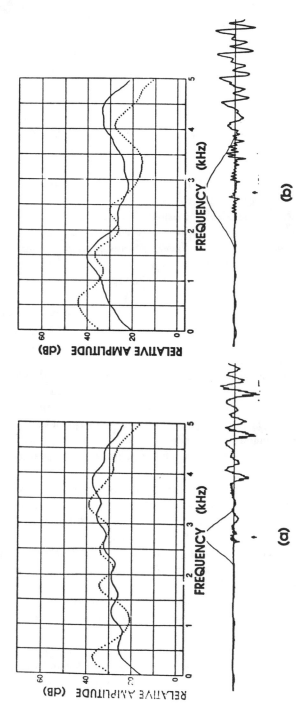

FIG. 8.1. Smoothed spectra sampled in the burst (solid lines) and near the onset of voicing (dotted lines) at the release of two stop consonants. In (a), the utterance is /di/ produced by a male speaker, and in (b), the utterance is /gɔ/ produced by a female speaker. Waveforms and time windows (centered on the burst) are shown at the bottom of each panel. Spectra are preemphasized.

The situation is slightly different, when one examines the acoustic manifestations of manner distinctions among consonants: for example, between stop and continuant consonants, or between sonorant and nonsonorant consonants. Here the acoustic correlates of the distinctions are fairly straightforward, whereas the articulatory or gestural description requires specification of aerodynamic variables rather than specification of instructions to particular articulatory structures. For example, a stop consonant is characterized by a particular degree of abruptness in the sound at the release over some frequency regions, or more precisely, in the auditory representation of the sound. This abruptness in the representation on the auditory nerve is influenced by the duration of silence preceding the release because of the effects of auditory adaptation, as well as by the physical characteristics of the onset consistent with the observations of Fitch and her colleagues on the *slit–split* distinction (Fitch, Halwes, Erickson, & Liberman, 1980). Sonorancy, on the other hand, requires continuity of the spectrum amplitude at very low frequencies around the first one or two harmonics, because no pressure is built up behind a consonantal constriction. Lack of sonorancy implies a reduction in the low frequency amplitude.

These acoustic properties are different from the ones that have been traditionally called cues. A cue, as the term has been used, might be the frequency of a burst, or the transition of a particular formant, or the duration of the silence, and so forth. All are entities that correspond to simple measurements on a spectrographic representation. These cues are certainly context-dependent as well as speaker-dependent and cannot provide a simple link to the units that specify the lexical items. The properties I am talking about are relational. They involve assessing spectral shapes, sometimes in particular frequency ranges. In examining these shapes in relation to immediately adjacent shapes, these properties have been shown to demonstrate independence of context and speaker when properly defined.

To some, these types of properties may appear to be too abstract. Furthermore, as we see at this meeting, there are those who prefer to postulate a direct transformation between these acoustic or auditory patterns and a gestural representation. To others, these acoustic or auditory patterns sampled at the appropriate points in time may well provide a relatively direct link to the units that describe the lexical items. It is my understanding that even at the level of a cochlear nucleus, the kinds of relational properties described here may well be taking form. My suggestion is that we should tread slowly rather than jumping to the conclusion that the acoustic material cannot provide a relatively direct link to the underlying phonetic units.

LIBERMAN: First, about Björn [Lindblom]'s presentation: We heard some very elegant data, and it was very eloquently presented. They are very important data, as well, though I am not sure what their relevance is to questions about specialization. I think what I heard Bjorn say was that there are but two necessary and sufficient conditions for the selection of articulatory gestures used in speech. One is a normal auditory system, and the other is a motor system obedient to something we might call the Law of Least Effort, but other primates have auditory systems very much like ours, and I assume their motor systems obey the Law of Least Effort, yet they do not talk.

I would rather reinterpret Bjorn's very interesting presentation this way: Given a set of gestures that for some reason evolved, then those that are least effortful are used more frequently. As for the auditory constraints, I point out also that many of them could be very low level, for no matter how separate the modules are, the systems for ordinary auditory perception and for phonetic perception must share many structures and much physiology. They have the same basilar membrane, the same hair cells, the same auditory nerve, the same cochlear nucleus, and so on, and some of these auditory constraints could very well originate at the level of the basilar membrane.

I think what is omitted from Björn's discussion has to do with coarticulation, which is the heart of the speech production process as I see it, and I would guess that those gestures were selected which lent themselves more or less effectively to being coarticulated. Otherwise, I have no reservations about what Bjorn said. It is terribly interesting and important, and the data are very impressive.

Carol Fowler and Larry Rosenblum, as always, gave us a very lucid, thoughtful, scholarly, and totally fair presentation. I have just a couple of small comments about it. Carol and Larry said that acoustic events structure the sound, and the listener then responds to that structure or resonates to that structure. That is certainly true for what Ignatius [Mattingly] and I have called the open modules, the systems that Mark Konishi (in press) has described as those which can have a direct projection from the sensory epithelium to some perceptual map. It does not apply, however, to the so-called closed modules, for example, to sound localization, which Carol talked about. There the relevant information is, for example, interaural disparities of time, but these are not produced by the acoustic event out there. They are a consequence of the fact that our ears are separated and a consequence of the fact that we have a highly specialized module in our heads that converts the time disparity into location. We do not know exactly how this works in the human being, and I refer you to the beautiful work of Mark Konishi on the barn owl for a plausible model (Konishi, Takahashi, Wagner, Sullivan, & Carr, 1988). Of these systems—stereopsis, echo-ranging in the bat, sound localization, at the very least—it is simply not true that the relevant information is structured by the acoustic event. Otherwise, I certainly agree with Carol and Larry that a distal event is perceived in speech, and the distal event is a gesture. I also agree that in general the nervous system tries to do this whenever it can. I think the real question is: How does it do it?

I will say just a word about one aspect of what Peter MacNeilage had to say. He remarked that there is apparently no very direct test of the Motor Theory, that we have hidden all of our assumptions very nicely, that we have made them very abstract, and so on. Well, I think that is not quite true. I think there is already a neurobiological test. The data are not very clear, and there are not many data, but I think those data will increase at a very rapid rate in the next ten or fifteen years. What the Motor Theory says is that there ought to be a more or less common locus for perception and production. Now, it is very hard to do the relevant experiments in the phonetic system. There have been several done by a neurosurgeon named Ojemann (1983), and the results so far certainly do indicate a more or less common locus. Then, of course, there are the experiments by the neuroethologists like Mark Konishi, Dan Margoliash, and Fernando Nottebohm, which also indicate in general that there is something like a common locus for perception and production in the communication systems of animals. My point, putting aside the question of what the data say right now, is that the theory is testable in that sense. Ultimately, many aspects of the motor theory and modularity have to be neurobiological, and there is some hope that we will be able to make those kinds of tests.

As I told him after his very interesting comments, I agree with Harlan and with Lane. I see no contradiction between them. I also want to say that Howard [Poizner]'s data and presentation were very interesting. My point is that there is a language module which has various components. One of those components is a phonetic system. Sign, fortunately for the signers, does not need a phonetic component, because this part of the system is so much richer than what goes on in this ridiculous plumbing in our vocal tracts, to use Frank [Cooper]'s description.

It is amazing that nature chose to put something like language through the ear and out of the mouth, instead of having it evolve, indeed, as sign. As I have suggested to some of the sign people, one has to think in this connection about what the situation would be like, if language had evolved originally to be sign and all the normal people were signers, and then we had to worry about the blind. Suppose somebody said, "Well, you know, if we make gestures with the tongue, we can modulate sound and make them hear the sound." I suggest to you that it would not work, because there are just too many constraints on such a system. That is exactly the circumstance in which you need a phonetic module and not just a tendency to build a lexicon out of phonologic units and then to go on to syntax.

CAROL FOWLER: When Al first suggested to me that sound localization was one clear instance in which the information was not really out there but was created by the interactions of the two ears, I accepted his comment and thought it was right. On further reflection, I have to come to another way of thinking about it, and I wanted to tell him and you about it.

If I stand here and speak, and we take any two points in this room, the acoustic energy created by my speaking is going to arrive at those two places at different times and with different intensities. We could use those paired arrival-time and intensity differences to locate me in space. The information is out there, after all. It happens that we have two ears, and we happen to intercept the different arrival times and intensity differences that arrive at the two ears. In fact, at any two points in the room that information is available. I will not conclude from this that we do not have a neural specification for sound localization, because we obviously do. Likewise, I suspect we have a neural specialization for speech perception, but my argument is that we do not have one because the information out there is inadequate.

In the case of sound localization, we are dealing with tiny time-of-arrival differences and tiny intensity differences, and it may be very useful to dedicate a neurological system to that job and to nothing else. Likewise in speech, as I attempted to create some stimuli to use in a duplex perception experiment, I found that there are not a lot of signals that look much like speech acoustically, and it may be useful to devote a neurologically specialized system to just those kinds of acoustic signals, but my analysis indicates that specializations do not evolve because the information is inadequate. They evolve to take advantage of existing information.

JUSCZYK: Following up on Fowler's comment, it seems that we should be able to specify what it is that turns on this speech module. At least, we should attempt to define the properties of a signal that allow it to engage a special mode of perception. For instance, some of the work with sinewave speech is one way of trying to take apart the signal and to look closely at the acoustic properties which allow the use of whatever the phonetic module brings with it. Actually, sinewave speech may so unlike speech in its short-term spectra that the auditory analysis overrides the speech analysis initially, at least for some listeners, and then, once listeners are given the additional information that the sinewave signal is phonetic in nature, they are able to achieve the alternative phonetic organization of the signal. Whatever that specific case turns out to be, though, I think that if we grant that there are multiple perceptual organizations, then we have to come up next with an account that specifies how the phonetic system takes priority in some situations.

LILA GLEITMAN: I think it is getting late enough so at least some of the laymen can reveal their real bewilderment here. I was particularly bewildered by two things. I heard Al give a very good account of why Sign language does not have a phonetics, and that surprised me very much. It also surprised me that the Sign language people did not leap up to oppose this claim. So, either Al better say something to support his claim, or the sign people better tell me that they agree with him.

LIBERMAN: I did not mean to say that Sign language lacks phonetics. What I meant to say was that the phonetics is transparent and that nothing special is required to process it, for much the same reason that nothing special is required to read the letters of the alphabet or the characters of a logography. The visual system is perfectly adequate for the job. There is just so much richness there that the gestures in Sign or the characters in written language have only to conform to the most general principles that govern the visual perception of shapes.

Obviously, in the ordinary sense there are phonetic variations in Sign as a function of context, as a function of all kinds of things. My point is simply that in these visually based instances, the phonetics is perfectly transparent, permitting immediate recourse to the phonologic system used as a basis for the lexicon. In speech, there is a phonetic level in addition to the phonologic. The corroborating evidence is very simply that narrow phonetic transcriptions fail to work well in a reading system. Anybody who has ever tried this found it terribly difficult, and the closer the transcription got to the real phonetics, the harder it became for the reader, inasmuch as the separation between words is eliminated in that case. The only orthographies that seem to work are relatively abstract phonologic representations, which presumably come fairly close to the forms words take, when they are stored in the head.

MICHAEL STUDDERT-KENNEDY: I am going to raise an issue that I think relates to this. First of all, I should just remark in passing that I doubt whether a narrow phonetic transcription of Sign would be very easy to read either, but I do not think it has anything to do with language. I think it would be very difficult to read a narrow phonetic transcription of a tennis stroke.

I also think that coarticulation must be ubiquitous in Sign. It has not actually been deeply studied from that point of view, but I very much doubt whether there are invariances that could be easily specified in sign patterns to be picked up by an automatic sign recognizer.

Overall, I think coarticulation is grossly overestimated as an important factor in motivating a specialization for speech perception. The reason for this is, quite simply, that it is backwards to argue that the phonetic module exists in order to form coarticulated phonetic segments in production and to undo the obscuring effect of coarticulation on segments in perception. In that framework, the talker must start with the units to be coarticulated, but where do those units come from?

One would expect children to begin by coarticulating segments maximally and to learn to talk by acquiring the ability to resist coarticulation. They would eventually reach a point where they are sufficiently not coarticulating for us to understand what they are talking about. In actual fact, early speech is incomprehensible, when children are really laying everything on top of one another, and a complete muddle results. So, the whole notion of speech sounds evolving in order to be coarticulated is absolutely backwards and leaves us without an account for the origin of the units.

LIBERMAN: I think perhaps the problem with the child who speaks unintelligibly is not necessarily that the child is coarticulating too much, whatever that means, but that he is not coarticulating properly. It is not just that there should be overlap and merging of gestures representing successive units in a string, but that at the same time the phonetic structure must be preserved. This is the faculty which develops.

EDWARD KLIMA: It has always seemed sort of an interesting tactic to say that Sign has no phonetics, though the intention is really to say that there is no perceptual necessity for signers to have a sign module. The necessity for a special psychological mechanism for decoding the phonetics of the signal and the necessity for a linguistic description to admit phonetic phenomena are utterly different issues.

American Sign Language certainly has a phonetics and certainly has phonetic determination of categories, which we would call phonemes. It has all those linguistic characteristics, but I quite agree that there is nothing to require special perceptual mechanisms.

HARLAN LANE: Wholly apart from whether there *ought* to be a specialized phonetic module for sign languages, I would like to consider whether there *is* one. It seems to me that some of the compelling arguments for the presence of a module in speech also apply in the case of Sign. In the case of speech, the evidence is the lack of analytical separation of the cues and the absence of anything inferential about arriving at the perceptual result. It is an argument for some that when speech and sound go their separate ways, speech perception goes the way of articulation. Well, these same things exist for Sign. The perception of the point-light displays is compelling for native signers, much as the Johansson (1973) walking display is compelling for me. The aphasia data suggest the same kind of dissociation between the sensory and perceptual functions on the one hand and linguistic ability on the other. This is not quite the issue that Al has spoken to, but I gather your position, Al, is that there is a module for Sign, but not a phonetic one—but it seems to complicate the picture a bit, if we propose that there is a module for Sign, even though there is no phonetic motivation for it and that there also is a module for speech, but one which is motivated on phonetic grounds. That seems to me to be a mild embarrassment for the theoretical position.

KLIMA: A lot of evidence has been presented here that the perception of speech is very different from the perception of other acoustic phenomena. I am convinced that for speech, a module is required for phonetics. It seems to be reasonable to conclude from our evidence on aphasia that there certainly is a module for the syntax of Sign. A module for visual phonetics, specifically for Sign, is probably not necessary, though it may be.

The evidence from the tests employing the point-light display is complicated to interpret. There, the subjects know that they are seeing signs. In the sign mode, they see those particular movements in a special way, though their mode of seeing, in general, is probably not changed in the sign mode.

IGNATIUS MATTINGLY: It is rather risky for me to argue about Sign with Ed Klima, but when I watch a signer, I am impressed by how much is going on. It is a little like watching the magician who moves his hands very fast and can fool you if you do not know what the trick is. I can follow any one part of the signer's articulation without difficulty in what I suppose is a purely visual mode, though to take it all in is a substantial challenge. On this basis, I think there is a good possibility that a special processor exists for the phonetic side of the gestures.

PETER MACNEILAGE: I would like to comment on Al's views about the testability of the Motor Theory in the neurobiological realm. First, the presently available data only offer equivocal support to modularity. In one case, Ojemann's (1983) work showed that electrical stimulation in the same location of the peri-Sylvian area of the left hemisphere produced deficits in phoneme perception and oral gesture repetition. The coincidence between the perceptual and the productive deficits offers support for the model, which holds that these functions are integral to each other. In addition, damage anywhere around the peri-Sylvian area may lead to impairment of speech perception, whether frontal, parietal, or temporal regions are involved, but rather different speech production effects can follow injury to different portions of the peri-Sylvian cortex. With damage to the frontal lobes, articulatory organization may suffer, as if there were problems with motor commands. With injury to parietal and temporal cortex, impairment of the organization of the underlying entities may ensue, and this does not indicate motor problems at all. As the evidence stands, one could argue there is partial support for modularity but no more, in these co-occurrences of perception and production problems.

To show that I am not entirely negative about this theory, I am going to try to give a little help here, finally, to the possibility that we might have such a module. In a recent paper, Galaburda and Pandya (1983) pointed out that the arcuate fasciculus does not exist in monkeys. In monkeys, the path from the temporal lobe to the frontal lobe is a direct tract, the unsinate fasciculus. Humans have the arcuate fasciculus, which makes a stop in the parietal lobe, so to speak. On this evidence, I want to suggest that humans have two capabilities attributable to the underlying anatomy. First, we still have that sort of throughput system, which is probably operative when we do very rapid shadowing. It rests on the polysensory reception center, which monkeys also possess in the area analogous to Broca's area. This looks like a relatively modular temporo-frontal subsystem with a fairly direct link between auditory and motor capabilities. Second, we also can undertake the short-term organization of the linguistic properties of utterances, drawing on thousands of items and concatenation possibilities, by relying on the parietal lobe. This second system is perhaps not nearly so modular as the first.

QUENTIN SUMMERFIELD: (To KLATT) Suppose that somebody started to implement Ken [Stevens]' view of lexical access on the computer, and simultaneously somebody attempted to form and to implement algorithms to recover the gestures produced in the vocal tract. Would either of them solve the problem? Which of them would succeed first?

KLATT: If, as I have claimed elsewhere, the revised Motor Theory does indeed imply a *black box* device that takes acoustic waveforms or auditory spectra as input and produces an intended articulatory-gesture score (not unlike a time-asynchronous distinctive feature matrix just described by Stevens) as output, then there are several ways one might approach the task of constructing a speech recognition algorithm that mimicked this transformation. Two obvious alternatives are: a) to use experts in acoustic-phonetics to study a body of natural speech data and to program a set of rules to go from acoustics to gestures (or from acoustics to articulatory shapes—and then to gestures); and b) to rely on one of the powerful new learning programs, such as a neural network or a hidden Markov process, to discover the appropriate mapping from acoustics to gestures from a body of hand-labeled training data. Given the paucity of qualified volunteers thus far to tackle the expert knowledge-based approach, I would advocate a serious effort to use the latter automated-training approach, in spite of the difficulties of amassing sufficient hand-labeled training data and of determining *how* the black box works, if it works. Therefore, because of the complexities of speech (cue trading, time asynchronies between articulators, variability within and across speakers, etc.) and the relative inefficiency with which present learning programs discover these kinds of dependencies, immense amounts of data are likely to be required, all with the output gestural score provided by a human transcriber. While I suspect the task is impractical and will fail in speech recognition performance terms, such a project would be very worthwhile to attempt, because it would force proponents of the revised Motor Theory to face real data and to specify more fully the nature of the inputs and outputs of such a theory.

SUMMERFIELD: Will Ken's scheme work? As he outlined it, it seemed so clear and reasonable that I am amazed that automatic speech recognizers work as badly as they do.

KLATT: Accessing a lexicon from a reasonably accurate featural score should be possible, but can an accurate featural score be computed from the acoustic input at this time? I guess I have two levels of optimism. The first is that if someone were to pursue the sorts of analysis that Ken is proposing for various features and to build them into a recognition device in the insightful way that he described, then real progress will be made. My guess is that such a recognition device would work much better than any phonetically based recognition device currently existing, but my second level of optimism is that this device will not touch a human listener. We just do not know enough yet. There are a lot of crucial things we do not know.

STEVENS: I would like to raise an issue that may transcend any of the problems that we have mentioned about extracting information for a particular word from acoustic structure. Consider the details of this analysis of an utterance of the word *advertisement,* spoken casually, in Fig. 8.2. There is very little evidence of a /d/; the /v/ is turned into a sonorant consonant; the /r/ extends its effects way back into the first vowel; and, the /t/ is fricated, not a stop.

Maybe we need to extract the underlying gestures to recognize this word from its acoustic pattern, but I think there is more to the task than that. Clearly, acoustic information for some phonetic properties is preserved, and other acoustic-phonetic information is lost. The real problem in building a speech recognizer is dealing with this loss of information. Perhaps this is an invariance problem too, but there is no way to recover anything about a /d/ from this signal. It is missing, and attempts to rely on rules, or on principles of local interaction that lead the /v/ seemingly to hide the /d/, do not go very far.

MEMBER OF THE AUDIENCE: There is a high-frequency burst up there!

STEVENS: No, I don't see evidence of a high-frequency burst for the /d/.

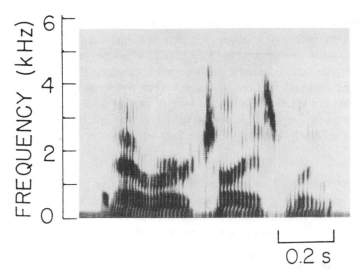

FIG. 8.2.   Spectrogram of a casually spoken version of the word *advertisement.* Of particular interest are the acoustic events between the first two vowels, which show considerable modification from the expected pattern. See discussion in text.

REMEZ: There really are two recognition problems here. The first is the familiar one, of the acoustic-to-phonetic projection. It seems reasonable to represent the talker's utterance as reduced, assimilated, or recoded, if the goal of this first recognition problem is a veridical description of the spoken forms. We would be happy with any recognizer that took the utterance depicted in the figure and returned as the transcription: [ævətsɑizmən?]. The second problem requires a lexical addressing scheme to accept probes that depart lawfully from citation form, permitting casually or informally spoken utterances to serve as legitimate representations despite missing or replaced segments. Only the first problem is the familiar invariance problem, treating the many-to-one and nonunique correspondence of acoustic structure and phonetic identity. The second, lexically motivated problem only begins once phonetic recognition concludes with a casually rendered instance of a word.

OSAMU FUJIMURA: I challenge Ken to visit Wisconsin and take the microbeam data of this particular kind of example. I also have had many experiences in which the acoustics led me to doubt that there were gestures for a consonant in a reduced syllable, but the microbeam revealed that the gestures were there. The present case may be an instance of this kind.

STUDDERT-KENNEDY: (To STEVENS) As I understand your position, you are really arguing for two lexicons. It is akin to a situation that appears to prevail in children, when they are first learning to talk, when they may have a very large receptive vocabulary and a quite small output vocabulary. (Incidentally, this also occurs in adult speakers of the language.) Your system of representation of the lexicon does not appear to have any way of getting from the acoustics to the gestural or motor output. Is it your assumption that this link is established by association in which babbling then becomes an important component?

STEVENS: Actually, I do not have a position on that. I would say that the lexicon is represented in abstract units that are neither directly articulatory nor directly acoustic. A relation projects these abstract units both to the acoustics and to the articulation. As you can see, I am taking the view of Jakobson, originally postulating something like features which have both acoustic correlates and articulatory correlates and must have both (Jakobson, Fant, & Halle, 1972).

KLATT: It sounds like we are beginning to wind down, and someone is going to have a chance to get the final word. Any takers?

TERRY NEAREY: Ready? Everyone knows how to do phonetic transcription? For the final word, I give you a nonsense word. [Ed: At this point, Nearey says something like: [mətɛilɪgʌp].] I will identify it for you tomorrow.

JUSCZYK: This example demonstrates the facility for phonetic perception independent of lexical access, which nobody here is denying. Some plans for automatic speech recognizers admit as much, as in Dennis [Klatt]'s LAFS system, for example, which employed SCRIBER to supply phonetic representations (Klatt, 1980). Psychologically, although it may not be plausible to suppose that phonetic analysis is performed on-line, given the speed with which we recognize fluent speech, there is no doubt that we can derive that sort of representation later on. Otherwise, any nonsense word or any new word would bring recognition to a halt.

References

Catford, J. C. (1985). "Rest" and "open transition" in a systemic phonology of English. In J. D. Bevan & W. S. Greaves (Eds.), *Systemic perspectives on discourse. Vol. 1: Selected theoretical papers from the Ninth International Systemic Workshop* (pp. 333–349). Norwood, NJ: Ablex.

Dobson, E. J. (1968). *English pronunciation 1500–1700* (2nd ed.). Oxford: Oxford University Press.

Fitch, H., Halwes, T., Erickson, D., & Liberman, A. M. (1980). Perceptual equivalence of two acoustic cues for stop consonant manner. *Perception & Psychophysics, 27,* 343–350.

Galaburda, A. M., & Pandya, D. N. (1983). The intrinsic architectonic and connectional organization of the superior temporal region of the rhesus monkey. *Journal of Comparative Neurology, 221,* 169–184.

Jakobson, R., Fant, G., & Halle, M. (1972). *Preliminaries to speech analysis* (10th ed.). Cambridge, MA: MIT Press.

Johansson, G. (1973). Visual perception of biological motion. *Perception & Psychophysics, 14,* 201–211.

Klatt, D. (1980). Speech perception: A model of acoustic phonetic analysis and lexical access. In R. A. Cole (Ed.), *Perception and production of fluent speech* (pp. 243–288). Hillsdale, NJ: Lawrence Erlbaum Associates.

Klatt, D. (1988). Review of selected models of speech perception. *Speech Communication Group Working Papers, 6,* 201–262. Research Laboratory of Electronics, MIT.

Konishi, M., Takahashi, T. T., Wagner, H., Sullivan, W. E., & Carr, C. E. (1988). Neurophysiological and anatomical substrates of sound localization in the owl. In G. M. Edelman, W. E. Gall, & W. M. Cowan (Eds.), *Auditory function: Neurological bases of hearing* (pp. 721–745). New York: Wiley.

Konishi, M. (in press). From stimulus to map. In G. M. Edelman, W. E. Gall, & W. M. Cowan, (Eds.), *Signal and sense: Local and global order in perceptual maps.* New York: Wiley.

Liberman, A. M., Cooper, F. S., Shankweiler, D., & Studdert-Kennedy, M. (1967). Perception of the speech code. *Psychological Review, 74,* 431–461.

Liberman, A. M., & Mattingly, I. G. (1985). The Motor Theory of Speech Perception Revised. *Cognition, 21,* 1–36.

Ojemann, G. (1983). Brain organization for language from the perspective of electrical stimulation mapping. *Behavioral and Brain Sciences, 6,* 189–230.

Remez, R. E., Rubin, P. E., Pisoni, D. B., & Carrell, T. D. (1981). Speech perception without traditional speech cues. *Science, 212,* 947–950.

Sweet, H. (1877). *A handbook of phonetics.* Oxford: Clarendon Press.

Chapter 9

The Compositional Process in Cognition with Applications to Speech Perception

Albert S. Bregman

Department of Psychology, McGill University

Abstract

The world has regularities at different scales of space and time. These interact to give us observable phenomena (encodedness). Epistemic mechanisms integrate across receptive mechanisms and cues, and the resulting perceptual descriptions represent the world regularities, not the sensory evidence. The transformation from evidence to description generally does not map local regions of stimulation onto underlying descriptions in a one-to-one fashion. A single piece of sensory evidence must be allowed to support more than one world regularity as long as the constructed descriptions are not contradictory (duplex perception); however, contradictions will be avoided (categorical perception). If a particular description uses up a piece of the evidence, it will be useful to form a remainder that can be used to support the descriptions of other regularities, either of the same or other types (pre-emptiveness). Human speech perception is subject to these principles, as is nonspeech auditory perception, visual perception, space perception, and the understanding of human nonspeech movements and social intentions.

In this chapter, I will take the position that although the research at Haskins Laboratories has often been taken as showing the special properties of a phonetic recognition module, it has really been encountering the general properties of schema-based recognition. These properties have been interpreted as belonging to speech perception for an interesting reason. It was discovered that simpler theories of pattern recognition could not explain the phonetic interpretation of speech sounds; thus, it was felt that speech must be special. However, I think that these simpler theories were equally wrong for all cases of recognition. Recognition, in general, displays the more complex properties attributed to speech perception.

Understanding as Composition

It seems that psychology keeps swinging back and forth between two positions. One is the uniformity view, the idea that the various capabilities of the mind are formed out of the same kind of basic computing element. The other is the modularity view, the idea that our different sorts of abilities are accomplished by distinct mechanisms that have different modes of operation. From Aristotle, with his distinct faculties, to the Associationists and Behaviorists, with their uniform principles of mental structure, and now back to modules again, the pendulum moves on. Clearly there must be strong motivations for both points of view. Although people like to satirize their intellectual opponents by accusing them of irrelevant motivations, such as attempting to support religion on the one side and play-acting at science on the other, I believe that the motivations for both views are empirical in nature. The modular view is supported by the uniqueness of the patterns employed by the mind in vision, in hearing, in language, in humor, and so on. The uniformity view is supported by observations that hold true in many areas of mental skill. These include the effects of practice, of interfering learning and of "set," and an organization in terms of separable schemas.

My aim in this chapter is to present some points of uniformity that cut across our mental capacities. I want to show that the phenomena of speech perception display properties that are characteristic of a broad class of mechanisms that humans use for understanding their world. I will use the term "epistemic systems" for them, referring to systems whose job it is to understand the world. Among these are the ones that understand physical properties of the world, such as space, the positions and shapes and colors of objects, what action has caused an event, and so on. Also included are those that understand the perceived actions of another person, such as struggling with a heavy load or skating, and that deal with social situations, such as wrestling or agreeing. The system or systems that understand language also fall into this class.

Epistemic systems all live in the same world. Furthermore, because this world has certain very general properties that influence all the things that we might want to know about it, it has forced a common set of strategies upon many different epistemic systems. The question of whether they have all incorporated these strategies by sharing some central biological mechanisms or by replicating similar ones for specialized use is a difficult one for which there is no answer at this time. The answer is unimportant for the present discussion; the importance of the similarity is that it makes it hard to distinguish innate systems from learned ones, and linguistic ones from nonlinguistic ones, just by looking at the way in which they function. What is the source of this similarity of function? I think it is the structure of the physical world.

If the scientific view is correct, the world has a very interesting structure, namely that all the complex phenomena that we encounter are generated by the interaction of relatively simple regularities. The regularities described by the concepts and laws of physics are beautiful examples of some of these underlying factors. However, there are others that physics rarely bothers to mention but are crucial in allowing humans to cope with the world. One of these is that enduring objects exist. Knowledge of this regularity confers power on the knower. For example, if we use a constellation of sensory evidence to derive the fact that an object is in front of us, we can predict, with a high degree of probability, that if we look away and then look back within a short time, the object will still be there, or that if part of the object moves away, the rest will also move away—crucial things to know. Another set of regularities concerns the fact that objects are laid out in space, that some are nearer to others, that they can move through this space, that despite its motion the position of an object has continuity from one moment to the next, and so forth.

Social phenomena are also the product of the interaction of basic behavioral regularities. Most of us believe that people's behaviors do not just happen but are generated by underlying factors such as motives, knowledge, interpretations of events, and the like. Our knowledge of these generative influences, inexact as it is, gives us the capacity to interact with others.

If the world's events (including the actions of people) are generated by the interaction of basic regularities, it stands to reason that the most powerful understanding of this world is one which captures the component regularities explicitly, together with the ways in which they can combine. Science is after this sort of understanding, but so is common sense. When we explain things to one another, we talk in terms of such regularities as causality, location, objects, motives, diseases, words, and so on, depending on the domain of interest. We combine concepts that describe basic regularities in order to explain complex experiences. If the world were not truly factorable into component regularities, we could never come to understand it by using concepts in this way.

Relation Between Concept and Vehicle is Very Indirect

Although we would like our understandings of phenomena to be based on a comprehension of the underlying regularities that generate them, it is not a straightforward matter to detect these regularities by using our senses. The regularities are not laid down end-to-end in the sensory evidence like beads on a string. When we hear a spoken utterance, for example, the phonemes that generate it are not presented end-to-end in the sound. This fact has been called the "encodedness" property of speech. Although S–R theory thought we made one response after another, we really do not. Neither does the physical world. There is a high level of encodedness in nature. The observed state of the world is the result of the interaction of many generative laws and regularities. Take, for example, the pattern of light coming off a flag waving in the wind. It encodes the strength of the wind, the lightness of the cloth, the connectedness of the cloth, the pattern printed on it, and the compactness of the light source (through the depth of shadows). I am not talking about perception here but about the world itself and how the light encodes basic aspects of objects and events. When we observe the interior of a room, the world does not present us with the color of the light, the reflective color of the surfaces, their slants, glossiness, their distances, and so on, all laid out individually end-to-end like a chain of stimulus beads in the sensory input. Similarly, when a child pretends to be an elephant, the pretending, the elephant, and the particular actions of the elephant are not laid out end-to-end in the behavior. When she pretends to be sipping tea, the substitution rule, "wooden box for teacup" is not explicitly written into the behavior; it is highly encoded. Yet we can only make sense of the behavior through our implicit understanding that this rule is temporarily active.

Meaning Depends on Context

The meaning of a piece of sensory evidence usually depends on its context. If we interpret a piece of a neighbor's behavior as pretending, we will be less inclined to telephone the neighborhood psychiatrist. Similarly, if we assume, in a heard utterance, that we are hearing a rapid (rather than a slow) sequence of articulations, the phonetic significance attributed to a silence of a certain duration will be different than if the assumed rate of articulation is slow. Consider another example: If we sense a sequence of acoustic elements and assume that they are coming from two different streams of events, the interpretation may be quite different than if they were assumed to all come from a single event stream. For example, we will hear two melodies instead of one. I have spoken of context. My use of the word does not refer to the *accompanying sense data* but to the set of generative influences (such as pretending, /b/, or two streams) that we assume to be present.

The Process of Assimilation

We can refer to the mental building blocks out of which our understanding of the world is constructed as schemas. Schemas can be thought of as specialists. Each one deals with a recurrent regularity in our world at some level of abstraction. Therefore, because any real-life situation can be understood in terms of the interaction of a large number of such regularities at different levels of abstraction, all active in the situation at once, the specialists must interconnect temporarily in any actual situation to create a structure that involves many schemas at the same time. (Let us call this a "description.") This requirement is most evident when we understand speech. Our understanding must deal with the intentions of speakers, their prior knowledge, what *they* assume *our* prior knowledge to be, the cardinal meanings of words, how word meanings are modified in context, how grammar tells us how to combine meanings, how phonemes combine to structure the sound that we hear, and much more.

The process whereby a particular set of schemas is activated in a situation is poorly understood, although it is the most important question in psychology. The best that psychology has been able to provide is a name—assimilation. Why does a person see a particular glance of a boss as expressing criticism whereas the boss has no critical intentions? How is it possible to set oneself to see human or animal figures in the clouds whereas one's neighbor, looking at the same clouds, sees a variety of types of clouds—cumulus, cirrus, and so on? How is it possible that one person will hear a set of simultaneous sine-wave glides as speech whereas another will not? We realize that the perceiver has assimilated the input into some particular set of schemas, but we do not understand why.

Evidence that There Are Separable Schemas

Thus far I have been using a necessity-based argument. It argues that because the world is built out of interacting generative principles, it would be *necessary* for an efficient perceiver to build up a particular kind of description of the world, one in which the elements that created the description corresponded to basic regularities in the world. But how do we know that our understanding *is* indeed a construction of basic elements? Confirmation comes from the phenomena of "biasing," "forcing," and "extensibility."

Biasing and Forcing

The fact that the schemas will sometimes apply themselves to a situation and sometimes will not do so gives us strong evidence that they exist as separable processes. Two people may see a situation in almost identical ways except for some glaringly different aspects. This suggests to us that the descriptive elements that differ are dissociable parts of the description.

Confirming evidence comes from the phenomena of biasing and forcing of interpretations. If we think that the interpretation of sensory input is created out of a composition of generative factors and that the resulting description is obliged to account for the sense data, then when we select one explanatory factor for inclusion, we will be forced to include others. We have special names for an exaggerated tendency to insert a certain descriptive concept into an interpretation. We call it "bias" or "set." When bias causes certain concepts to enter a description, it often forces other ones in as well. For example, if we assume that the accused is guilty, then when he tells us that he was somewhere else at the time of the crime, we will be forced to insert the generative principle of "lying" into our understanding of the data. If our retina registers an elliptical contour, and we insert "circle-shaped" as part of the interpretation, then the explanatory idea, "seen from an angle," has to be inserted. If we interpret one acoustic segment in speech as one particular phoneme, this may force an interpretation of the next segment so as to be consistent with what we know about coarticulation. The phenomena of bias and forcing are hard to explain except via the assumption that we are creating a description in which the elements are allowed to combine only in certain ways.

Consistency

The forcing is imposed by rules of consistency. Descriptions are allowed to be applied to data only in certain combinations. For example, we do not want to interpret one flat region as being in front of (and occluding) a second one and at the same time as being behind it (and, therefore, occluded). This is why the ambiguous vase-faces picture of the Gestalt psychologists cannot be seen as a vase and as faces at the same time. Because we are trying to impose a particular three-dimensional description onto the picture, we are prevented from imposing another one at the same time. If we were to change the picture so that it was less likely to engaged our schema for a three-dimensional scene and instead engaged the schema that deals with jigsaw puzzle pieces, we would be able to see the shapes of all three regions without any sense of having to flip the perceptual organization in order to do so.

Let us return to the speech-is-special debate. One of the ways in which it is possible to enforce rules for the permissible combination of descriptions is through a mental model of the physical process that we assume to be generating the sense data, because the model will tell us which descriptions of that data are compatible with which others. It has been claimed that consistency in the interpretation of an acoustic segment as a phonetic sequence is ensured by the listener's mental model of the vocal tract of the speaker. In the language that I introduced earlier, such a model is called a schema. Schemas probably apply themselves to sensory data by using "assimilation-formulas" of the following type: "If there is an X, a Y, and a Z in the data, then a pattern of the type that I represent is present." This statement also can be read in the inverse direction: "If there is a pattern that I represent in the data, and I detect an X and a Y, then that other, Z-like piece of data must actually be a Z." This inverse reading (some might want to call it "top-down processing") enforces consistency of interpretation.

Although we rarely think of their role in quite this way, consistency requirements allow an epistemic system to be flexible. An example would be the following: Suppose a person seems to be asserting something, and the syntax specialists have detected only a verb phrase, "refutes you," in the utterance. Suppose, in addition, that the grammar specifies that this type of verb phrase must be accompanied by a noun phrase. Suppose, as well, that there is a visual input, a pointing gesture, present at the time that the noun phrase would have been expected. The system may interpret this gesture as the missing noun phrase. It may receive support for this interpretation from the activation of a number of other schemas: (a) the schema that encodes the fact that *noun phrases refer*, (b) the "reference by pointing" schema, (c) the schema that understands that books contain print, (d) one that knows that print conveys ideas, (e) another that knows that ideas can refute. By using this network of schemas, it ultimately derives the following assertion: "<The idea content of the pointed-to book> refutes you." We know that the human mind is flexible in this way. The only explanation for this adaptability is that the schemas are temporarily coupled into networks by consistency requirements, but the coupling is loose and does not prevent a deviant piece of data from being assigned a role that it is not usually given as long as it is possible to construct an indirect path of support (a longer but consistent description).

I deliberately chose an example in which the consistency requirements operated across a set of schemas at different levels to show that the schemas that interact do not all have to be located within a single informationally encapsulated system.

Extensibility of the Set of Schemas

Perhaps a stronger reason for wanting to think in terms of a large set of interacting schemas rather than in terms of iron-clad modules is extensibility—the fact that the set of generalizations that we understand about the world can be expanded through learning. In the learning of their language, children gradually discover that there are different kinds of phrases with different privileges of occurrence and different roles. In baseball, they learn that there are different players with different roles. In reading, they learn that the "qu" letter cluster represents a single sound. And so on. The divisibility of any global competence (such as language) into competences at particular things supports our belief that separate epistemic specialists (schemas) exist.

How the Sense Data Affect the Assimilation

Categorical Perception

The phenomenon of categorical perception has been seen as a property of speech perception, but it can be best understood as showing how some forms of schemas assimilate sense data. These schemas seem to assimilate the input in the following way. A number of specialists receive the sensory evidence in parallel, look for the kind of evidence that they know about, and try to build the kind of description that they specialize in. However, because there are often rules that make two descriptions incompatible, specialists have to be able to inhibit or preempt one another. We assume that the ones that discover the evidence that they need with the least requirement for any relaxation of their assimilation rules will inhibit the specialists that are building incompatible descriptions.

One of the consequences of such winner-takes-all competitions is categorical perception. There are at least two kinds of schemas that our minds try to use in building descriptions. We can call them "configural" and "variational." Configural schemas are noun-like. They pick out natural kinds of structures in our experience. (Examples are trees, bosses, mothers, horns, dogs, the letter *e*, words, phonemes, contracts, etc.) When we talk about these matters, we usually refer to them by nouns. The variational type of descriptive element deals with the ways in which natural kinds can vary. We speak of how high the pitch of a voice is, how bright a light is, how honest a politician is, and so on. Often the English language deals with such concepts by adjectives, by expressions of degree or amount, or by the *-ness* construction (as in *brightness*).

It is the configural concepts rather than the variational ones that are responsible for categorical perception. The discovery of a natural kind in the sensory evidence is a leap of induction. Not every member of the class has identical properties. Occasionally, a dog may have three legs rather than four. Some individuals may not pronounce a syllable in exactly the usual way. In performing an assimilation, the schemas are allowed to stretch their rules of evidence. There seem to be rules for choosing the best description. They probably choose those that minimize the number of schemas needed (principle of parsimony) and those in which the schemas fit the evidence with the least requirement for stretching the rules (principle of minimum stress).

Categorical perception occurs in a most noticeable way when we shift the evidence slowly from favoring one configural concept to favoring another. An example is the continuum of synthesized sounds that gradually change from supporting the interpretation that the syllable is a /ba/ to supporting the syllable /da/. Another can be seen when tones of alternating high and low frequency are gradually moved further apart in frequency. A point is reached at which the one-stream interpretation suddenly gives way to a two-stream interpretation. Another example is the set of rotations of a drawing that changes from supporting the interpretation "rabbit's head" to "duck's head" (see Fig. 9.1). There is a point at which the alternative interpretation begins to dominate, and there is a sudden switch in the perceived identity. When the evidence is ambiguous but remains accessible for repeated observation, as in the visual case or in the case of continuously repeating tones, there is often a tendency for the interpretation to

FIG. 9.1.   Three rotations of a drawing. The first one favors a duck interpretation and the last a rabbit. The middle one is ambiguous, and its interpretation tends to alternate.

flip back and forth among the dominant alternatives. This shows that the battle of interpretations continues even after one has apparently prevailed. This flip-flop of interpretation in the face of constant evidence is a good indicator of categorical perception. Categorical perception, therefore, occurs when incompatible configural descriptions compete for the same evidence.

Stretching of Rules

The ability to stretch the rules for assimilation makes it possible for us to make use of other knowledge in interpreting a particular parcel of sensory evidence. For example, we do not usually assimilate clusters of gliding pure tones into the speech schemas, but if we are told that they are an analog for speech, and particularly if we are told what the words are, we can assimilate the sounds to phonetic schemas. The biasing that is derived from having been told to listen for speech will have allowed us not to miss the fact that the sounds have a speech-like structure.

A similar example occurs in listening to nonspeech sounds. If we hear a pure tone A just before hearing a complex tone that contains tone A as a partial, we will be able to hear out A from the complex tone better than if we had not been biased in this way. We will not miss the fact that A was part of the complex tone. Our use of the sensory evidence will have been affected. Similarly, if we are told that an argument between two men is actually a vying for the approval of a nearby woman, we will not miss the influence of that motive on the behavior of the men (e.g., the sudden loss of force in the argument, when the woman leaves the room). These examples show how the ability of the assimilation process to change under the influence of bias is a powerful tool for analyzing complex situations.

Can the mind be formed out of fairly large modules on the scale of a speech-interpretation module? To answer this question, we have to ask how isolated the schemas that accomplish limited perceptual tasks are from the influence of other ones.

Types of Schemas

It is important to ask about the form that the schemas can take. Just saying that a schema exists does not tell you how complex its form is. For example, one can think of the simple association between two ideas, described by the associationists as a schema that captures the fact that a certain sensory experience tends to be followed by a certain other one. At the other extreme of complexity, one could imagine a schema being a working model of physical space that permits experiments about spatial locomotions to be done in the mind. Piaget has argued that we have a range of schemas that have different degrees of complexity.

One of the difficulties for the idea that the mind is formed out of large modules is that many cases of recognition seem to involve the collaboration of schemas at different levels of complexity. Here are some examples. If I think of myself answering a question at a lecture and look at the schemas that govern my selection of words, I can observe constraints derived from my knowledge of syntax. Such constraints are organized into a complex system that acts as if it were a model of the syntactic structure of English. One might want to call this a module. On the other hand, I frequently find myself overusing a word that I normally use infrequently and that has perfectly good synonyms. I can trace my use of that particular word to the fact that a number of speakers before me have used it. The constraint affecting the choice of this word seems to be a simple association between the word and the context; there is no other good reason to choose it. Therefore, my speech behavior seems to be created by constraints of grossly different orders of complexity acting together to shape the behavior. I have used an example drawn from behavior rather than perception, because it is often easier to understand the influences. However, the same diversity of schemas can be observed in a single act of perception as well. For example, it is likely that both the syntactic structure of the sentence and the probability of a particular word in the current context will affect our perceptual restoration of a segment of the sentence masked by a cough.

We can conclude that a wide range of regularities of different orders of complexity concerning the world around us have been captured in our schemas. It is virtually impossible to imagine how schemas of such different orders of complexities, operating over different spans of time, could coexist and be coordinated in the same mind. It is even harder to imagine how a system formed of rather large modules could allow the kind of adding-up of constraints that seems to occur in these examples.

Can we Get Unequivocal Evidence for
or against a Motor Theory?

I would now like to turn to an important question facing the Motor Theory of Speech Perception: whether it can be confirmed by the gathering of behavioral data. I would like to point out some of the difficulties in this project.

It has been argued that the process of interpreting speech as phonemes uses the whole range of sensory effects that are typically produced whenever a speaker produces phonemes. It has been proposed that the multiplicity and equivalence of various acoustic cues derives from the fact that they are all typically affected by the act of speaking (see Liberman, 1982; Liberman & Mattingly, 1985; Mattingly & Liberman, 1988). The schema for a phoneme is presumed to encode the relation between the speech gesture and its typical acoustic consequences. This confers upon listeners the ability to do without many of the typical cues for the phonemes that might be masked in certain contexts and enables them to make use of the correlations in the acoustics that have been caused by the articulation.

One might think that a test of whether the perceiver refers the signal to a model of articulation might be obtained by determining whether a distortion of heard speech was easier to deal with, if it was created by a distorted form of articulation rather than by a distortion of the acoustic signal without concern for articulation. Confirming evidence might not prove the point for the following reason. The theory might not be true, and instead the listener's schemas might represent the covariations in the acoustic waveform that were typically created by articulation, representing them in a way that did not explicitly relate to articulation. Accordingly, the test would have to be careful not to violate these correlations that might be important for the alternative theory. However, even if this objection were to be met and results favoring an articulation-based schema were found in this way, it would only show that an articulatory schema supplied the listener with one method for interpreting the signal. It would not exclude the concurrent participation by other schemas of a more acoustic nature.

On the other hand, one might think that if listeners could actually understand speech that no human vocal tract could produce, this would show that the listener's modelling of the signal source as a human vocal tract was not absolutely essential for the interpretation of speech. Is this what is shown by the fact that listeners can interpret sine-wave analogs as speech? In such analogs (e.g., Bailey, Dorman, & Summerfield, 1977), pure tones are made to trace out the trajectories that are normally followed by resonances in the human vocal tract as it speaks a sentence. No human vocal tract could ever produce such speech; yet it is remarkable how much of such a sentence listeners can understand, if they are first biased to hear it as speech. There is unfortunately a problem with this argument against the Motor Theory. It is based on the idea that the sensory consequences of articulation must be received in highly specific acoustic forms.

We have seen earlier, however, that in the process of assimilating evidence to an abstract schema, the rules of evidence can be stretched (one of the phenomena that Piaget referred to as "accommodation"). Therefore we cannot conclude that the sense data derived from sine-wave speech was not assimilated to an articulatory model.

It is hard, then, to think of decisive evidence that would rule out the possibility that both articulation-based and acoustics-based factors play a role in speech perception.

Innate vs. Learned Schemas

Let us now consider another issue raised by the Haskins group. Are speech recognition schemas innate? I think a more important issue is how one could discover whether or not they were innate. In the field of perception in general, it is evident that some recognition schemas must be innate and others learned. Among the innate ones is undoubtedly the one that derives evidence about the spatial origin of a sound by comparing its time of arrival at the two ears. One that is clearly learned is the description of a rabbit or a duck. There are others whose learned status is the subject of debate. An example of one of these is the specialist that coordinates speech gestures with their acoustic consequences.

It would be nice if we could tell simply by observing how a schema worked whether it was innate or learned. However, I do not believe that this will be possible. The functional characteristics of the two types are likely to resemble one another for two important reasons. One is that the encodedness of the world's regularities at all levels of description has created pressure on the specialists to work in a common way—not simply reacting to individual features, but deriving evidence to support some underlying conceptual description of the world. Both innate and learned schemas must deal with encodedness.

A second reason for expecting the two types of schemas, innate and learned, to have similar functional characteristics is that they are required to cooperate in a seamless way both within and across types, a requirement that I have illustrated in earlier examples.

Speech research has faced us with the question of whether the detection of phonetic structure can be based on an innately given model of the speech apparatus of the speaker. This would account for how the listener could perceive the phonemes in a sound if we assume that invariant properties of a particular phoneme are most easily describable through its production rather than through the acoustic signal. There is no logical reason why we should not have such schemas or why they should not be innate. However, it appears to me that we cannot derive support for these assumptions, especially the one about the schemas being unlearned, by simply looking at the functional characteristics of speech, unless we can find characteristics that are present in speech perception that are never present when we use learned schemas. I do not believe that we know of any such touchstone characteristics at the present time. The rest of this chapter will look at some of the candidate characteristics proposed by the Haskins group as distinguishing speech perception from other forms of understanding to see whether these characteristics are actually unique.

It has to be admitted at this point that even if we were never able to discover unique functional characteristics, this would not necessarily prevent us forever from discovering whether or not a schema was innate and biologically specific to a particular function. It would merely mean that looking for distinctive functional properties was not the right way to sort the issue out. Instead, this would have to be accomplished by physiological and developmental investigation, not by a study of the functional properties of mature schemas.

Composition in the Generating and Reading of Behavior

Let us consider the question of whether the parallel extraction of apparently sequential events is unique to phoneme perception. Earlier we saw that parallel transmission of the regularities in a scene was generally true of sensory input. One important case is in the hearing of speech as a sequence of phonemes. The articulation of a phoneme will shape not only the immediate motor action but also some of the actions before and after it. Therefore, each temporal segment will bear the imprint of more than one phonetic gesture. To derive a description of each underlying phoneme, the description-building process of the listener must fit a phoneme schema to a local part of the signal by being able to account for the transformations in the acoustic evidence that have been caused by neighboring phonemes.

This interaction of underlying intentions to form a "surface" action is seen not just in language but in all aspects of human movement. Stephen Handel (1989, p. 135) gives the example of jumping over a puddle.

> You make the jump far before you leap: approaching the puddle you vary your stride and shuffle your feet to avoid obstacles and to make the takeoff foot fall at the right point in front of the puddle. Moreover, even during takeoff, you are making anticipatory corrections for the landing. Thus, the movements for takeoff, jump, and landing are occurring at the same time.

This example relates to production of behavior, not to perception. Let us proceed to the latter. To read the behavior of another person, the observer has to account for the local parts of the action as due partly to an underlying local action and also a transformation of it resulting from the effects of earlier or later actions being coordinated with it. The human observer is very good at noticing the modifications of ongoing actions and using this information to anticipate future actions. We have seen an example in phoneme perception, but it occurs in many other kinds of human actions—in sports, for instance. A boxer learns not to telegraph his punches—that is not to adjust his current behavior in preparation for an action to follow—because his opponent can read his next act from the preparation. We sometimes even interpret earlier actions in the light of later ones. Grunts that we might interpret as expressions of pain are instead taken as expressions of effort as soon as we see that the person who is uttering them is struggling to steady a heavy load on his shoulders.

Parallel Perception of Different Aspects

There is a converse side to the lack of a direct mapping. This is that the same body of sensory evidence has to support more than one type of analysis at the same time. For example, the pitch contour of a sentence encodes many things. It tells us which words are being spoken (in languages such as English that use pitch to distinguish words by their stress patterns), whether the sentence is a question, whether certain words are being emphasized, and whether the speaker is getting nervous. All these influences combine to affect the local parts of the pitch pattern. Therefore, the factors that combine to affect the pitch pattern must be detected in combination, and it is not obvious that they could be extracted form the data in a fixed order. It seems rather that the analyses go on in parallel. We should notice that not all these factors are linguistic in nature. If they must be extracted in parallel from the same bit of sense evidence by an interactive process in which one aspect of the interpretation lays constraints on the others, it is hard to see how this could work, if we had a large language module that was "informationally encapsulated" or even a smaller phonemic module with this property.

The use of the same sensory data by different schemas operating in parallel is a ubiquitous fact of mental life. The identification of the rabbit's head and the fact that it is a rotated version must go on in parallel. The only way that the observer could know that it was a rotated version was by knowing that it was a rabbit's head. The direction of deviation from the normal orientation (either towards the horizontal or the vertical) that we see in the ambiguous duck-rabbit drawing depends on whether we identify it as a rabbit or a duck.

Another case of joint participation of schemas is when we hear some speech not just as speech but as "controlled rage." Knowing that it is controlled requires an understanding of the particular words and the tone of voice, a job performed by one set of schemas; knowing that it is rage requires an understanding of the social context by other schemas.

Mandatory Operation

We never know in advance what forms of regularity may be discoverable in a signal, therefore, many epistemic specialists are called into action, not by specific intentions on the part of the person to find this or that regularity in the signal but by the pattern of sensory evidence itself. That is, they exhibit "mandatory operation" (Fodor, 1983). Speech recognition shows this property. Does this mean that it is a module in Fodor's sense? The recognition of all sorts of familiar things shows this same mandatory property. We cannot prevent ourselves from hearing a very familiar melody when we are presented with the sequence of notes. Similarly, we find it impossible to prevent ourselves from reading words (a fact that is exploited in the Stroop test), and we cannot prevent ourselves from recognizing an American flag when we see one.

The automaticity with which schemas apply themselves to a situation holds for well-practiced motor schemas as well as epistemic ones. As skilled drivers, we can drive a car with very little intervention of conscious intentions, with the occasional humorous result that we find ourselves somewhere other than where we wanted to go. Our highly practiced motor skills are on automatic pilot most of the time, in the same way that our highly practiced recognition skills are.

Different Modes of Judgment with Different Sensitivities

In duplex perception of speech, when the format transition is judged on its own, the difference between the rising and falling versions may be barely noticeable. However, when they are integrated together with the base, the effects on the resulting phoneme are much more noticeable. This has been taken as evidence that different biological systems are dealing with the data in the two cases. However, it seems to me that the different use of evidence merely means that two different schemas are dealing with the evidence. Sensory evidence is used in different ways by different schemas. For this reason the same physical feature may be more or less strong in its effects on the encoding. One schema may deal with more complex patterns and another with simpler ones. We may find a greater sensitivity to the physical properties of a piece of sense data in a more complex pattern than in a simpler one when we are more practiced in judging the complex pattern as a whole.

We encounter a similar case in our ability to judge a piece of sense data better when it occurs as part of in one complex pattern than when it occurs in another one. We can see an example in music recognition. If we present two instances of the sequence C–E–G–C to listeners with the G in one of them slightly mistuned, this will probably be easier to detect than in the sequence n1–n2–G–n3, where n1, n2, and n3 are atonal notes. The major triad provides a familiar reference frame in the first case, permitting more accurate listening to take place.

Levels of Description

Duplex and Triplex Perception

There are two ways in which evidence can be shared by different schemas. We have already seen the first way: The same evidence can be used to specify independent aspects of the description. An example occurs in vision. Often the retinally received hue participates in specifying both the color of an object and the color of the illuminating light. Although these two aspects are not independently represented in the sensory evidence, they are independent facts about the world and independent aspects of our mental descriptions of that world. Their descriptions, being about independent aspects, can coexist in any combination. One can think of our awareness of what a lecturer is saying and of her nervousness as independent in this way, although both descriptions are derived from the same pitch pattern. When we use the same evidence to construct different but not incompatible facts about a situation, we can call this "duplex" perception as long as there is no third description to which the two descriptions belong.

"Triplex perception" is a second way of having different schemas use the same evidence. Sometimes, when we use a single piece of data to specify more than one description of a situation, the resulting descriptions are related. For example, one description can be of a part and the second of a whole in which the part resides. An example would be the description of a sensory input as specifying both a finger and a hand, the finger being part of the hand. Presumably there are different schemas for the finger and the hand, but there is some constraint on how they can coexist. One must be part of the other, if the same data specifies both. Fingers and palm constitute a hand. The lack of independence of the descriptions "hand" and "finger" does not reside merely in the fact that the same sense data is used to specify both but in the fact that the descriptions participate in a structure. We call this triplex (or hierarchical) perception, because in addition to the descriptions of the finger and the palm, there is a third description (hand) to which they both belong.

Why are Certain Cases of Duplex Perception Puzzling?

Certain cases of duplex perception are puzzling, because according to our expectations, they ought to be triplex. One such case, duplex perception of speech, is induced in a listener when we take the acoustic signal for a speech sound and alter it so that part of the information stands out from the rest. For example, we can present most of the signal to our left ear and only a formant transition to the right. We will hear the complete speech sound appearing to come from the left ear. In addition, we will hear an isolated chirp at the right ear. We do not hear this in a triplex manner. If we did, we would hear the isolated material at the left ear as one sound, the isolated material at the right as a second, and somehow know that the two together made a third thing, a speech sound.

The reason that we do not hear this input in a triplex fashion seems to be that the schema for a speech sound does not have a hierarchical structure that represents a phoneme as a set of chirps that are hierarchically assembled to form a phoneme. Rather than creating a hierarchical description for this one particular case, our minds prefer to represent the isolated formant transition as a separate sound.

The avoidance of hierarchical descriptions in this way is not restricted to speech perception. Informal experimentation by Valter Ciocca has found that if a synthesized sound of a barking dog is divided into a left ear component and a spectrally more restricted right ear component, the listener will hear the isolated component on the right and a full barking dog sound on the left. Fowler and Rosenblum, in an experiment reported in chapter 3 in this volume, have shown that a recording of a metallic door being slammed can be divided so that the lower frequency components are presented to one ear and the higher ones to the other. As a result, listeners hear the full slam on one side of their heads accompanied by a rattling sound on the other side.

One of the ways in which we confuse ourselves when we think about the duplex perception experiment is by using the terms "fused" and "segregated." It seems as though the left and right ear information has been fused for purposes of deriving a description of a speech sound or a door slamming but has been segregated for purposes of describing two separate sounds in space. This contradiction simply tells us that we should not be using the terms fused and segregated. The acoustic information has neither been fused nor segregated. It has simply been used twice in two different ways.

Duplex perception was first noticed with speech perception. For this reason, it was thought that it was due to the speech system's running in parallel with the nonspeech auditory system, the former responsible for the phonetic integration across the ears and the latter responsible for the hearing of the isolated chirp. However, the finding of duplex perception of a door slamming shows that the two co-occurring percepts need not belong to domains of experience that are so different as to require different biological modules for their perception.

Alteration and Suppression of Descriptions of Included Evidence

Mattingly and Liberman (1988) commented on the fact that we do not hear the component formants in a speech sound as chirps, although they would be heard that way, if they were presented alone. This suppression of the formation of other auditory descriptions when a phoneme is heard is taken by these authors as evidence that the phonetic system cannot be part of the general auditory recognition system. However, it seems likely that this absence of lower-level descriptions when a higher-order description is formed may be a more general phenomenon.

The Gestalt psychologists were insistent on the fact that when a complex display was presented to a person, the perceived result was not necessarily a hierarchical description in which the experience of the parts was unchanged. I can think of cases in which the perception of the whole totally obliterates the parts. For example, we do not normally perceive the word *cover* as containing the word *over,* or a drawn letter *T* as containing the drawn letter *I.* The reasons may

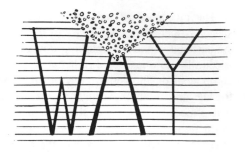

FIG. 9.2.   The center letters in WAY and WHY are retinally identical.

be no different from those that explain why we do not hear the speech sound /ba/ as containing the chirp quality that one of its formants would have, if played by itself, or the pure tone quality that one of its harmonics would have, if played by itself.

In other cases, descriptions *are* formed for the lower-level parts, but they are altered to be consistent with the more global description of which they are a part. In Fig. 9.2, the central letter in the word WHY is seen as an H, and in WAY, it is seen as A. However, the two shapes are identical when seen out of context. When it is seen as an H, the nonparallelness of its sides is "excused" by the general foreshortening of the display that results from a particular viewing angle. Similarly, when it is seen as an A, the absence of the apex of the A is excused by the assumption that it is being occluded by a nearer object.

Why does this loss or alteration of properties occur, when forms are embedded in larger ones? One possible explanation is that a higher-order description inhibits lower-order descriptions of the same sense data. Hence, the *cover* schema would inhibit the *over* schema in the previous example. Grossberg and his colleagues tried to give this a physiological interpretation via the concept of a "masking field" (see Grossberg, 1985; Cohen & Grossberg, 1986). This explanation, however, fails to deal with the fact that sometimes the lower-order description is not obliterated but incorporated as a part of the higher-order description as in the word *overcoat*. Clearly it must depend on which particular schemas are involved. Some schemas are built as hierarchies: In these schemas, certain parts retain their identities; other schemas are not built in this way.

It is interesting to consider the possibility that the ones that suppress or alter the perception of components work that way, because they are innate, whereas those that are hierarchical are learned. For example, when we look at a long line, we never see it as a succession of short lines, although any short segment seen in isolation would be seen as such. Similarly, in a collection of harmonics, we hear the global timbre of the whole spectrum rather than the timbre of the individual pure tones. Could it be that the uniformity of human experience in both these cases is due to the fact that the incorporation of the part into the whole is innately predetermined? It probably is, but the innateness explanation covers only some of the cases. Surely the incorporation of *over* into *cover* is not innately prearranged, nor is the incorporation that is seen in the following example. Let us take the case of the awareness of one's own behavior as an instance of perception and examine what happens as a skill is developed. When we first learn a new motor skill, we try to construct it out of movements that we already can do, and we are quite aware of the individual movements. When we reach a higher lever of skill, the movements blend together, and we no longer control them individually. Musicians report that if they do start to think about the individual movements that they are making, they disrupt their performance. This is an example of the loss of perceived properties of the components in a larger whole, and yet it is clearly a case where the larger whole is learned. I have not undertaken a thorough search for examples, but the ones I have found seem to imply that the loss or alteration of the properties of components is not restricted to innate processes.

Perhaps there is yet another factor involved in the disappearance of these properties. When we say that the word *over* is *hidden* inside *cover,* this statement may be misleading. Perhaps the definition of the word over is not "*o-v-e-r*" but rather "boundary–*o-v-e-r*–boundary." In ordinary printing, the spaces act as boundaries. In *cover,* there is no boundary before the *o.* Maybe there are boundaries in the case of *overcoat* as well. In compound words such as *overcoat,* the beginning or ending of another potential morpheme can provide the boundaries that each morpheme needs to fulfill its own definition (although the boundaries are only conceptual in nature). The nonoverlap of the scope of the two morphemes may permit boundaries to be hypothesized and a consistent two-morpheme description to be built. This supplying of boundaries by other morphemes may be the method by which the boundaries are supplied in fluent spoken language where there are no acoustic boundaries between words.

The same reasoning about boundaries can be used to explain why a speech sound is never heard as containing chirps, although they would be heard, if its formants were played alone. In a speech sound, there is no information that tells the ear that the chirp is a bounded entity and, hence, no separate description is built for it. Only when we differentiate it from the spectrum in which it is embedded, either by moving it to a different ear, making it much louder, or putting it on a different fundamental, are boundaries provided that allow a separate description to be built.

Relation between Conscious Experience and Schemas

Duplex perception raises another issue. Why does the listener think that the speech sound all came from one ear? Why are the true sources of the information not represented in the mind? Is this unique to speech perception? Mattingly and Liberman (1988) argued that it was. The phenomenon, however, is more widespread. Perceptual descriptions often encode the detected regularities but do not form descriptions for the separate pieces of sensory evidence. Many of the examples that I have given up to this point have demonstrated clearly that typically our consciousness does not represent the individual sensory components of an input. It makes what E. B. Titchener called the *stimulus error* (Titchener, 1910). It tells its story in terms of significant global units of description. It is obvious that this tendency makes its descriptions of the world more powerful. A description that says that a clarinet is present in a particular array of sound is likely to be more useful in predicting a future array than one that says that a frequency, 2045 Hz, is present in the array.

Frequently, individual components of the evidence do not receive explicit representation, even when they are derived from different mechanisms, different senses, or from memory as opposed to the sensory input itself. For example, McGurk and MacDonald (1976) showed that when we listen to a speaker, we incorporate the visual evidence derived from lip-reading into the percept seamlessly. There is no representation of how much has come from the eyes and how much from the ears. Listeners think they have *heard* the syllable even though they have partly derived its identity from visual evidence. This integration of information from different senses does not occur just with speech. A nonspeech example is the ventriloquism effect in which a sound seems to come from the direction of a visible source whose behavior is correlated with the sound; we have no awareness of the effect of the visual input. Yet another example is the seamless integration of descriptions derived from the signal and from memory in musical scale restoration. When a note from an ascending scale is replaced by a burst of white noise, listeners will often restore the note that fits the context but will have no awareness of the origins of their experience (perceptual versus mnemonic). They simply hear a whole scale. Consider another example: When we make sense of a story by mentally supplying missing logical links, we do not remember which facts were supplied explicitly by the words of the story and which by our assimilating them to our schemas. That is why eyewitness testimony is often so unreliable.

Trading Relations

The joint effect of different sources of evidence upon our conscious experience is often described in terms of "trading relations." If two parts of the sensory evidence both provide evidence for the same description, a bit more of one can often compensate for a bit less of the other. We see this in epistemic processes that range from the most primitive to the most sophisticated. For example, in our mental description of the spatial origin of a sound, we put together evidence from the relative intensity of the sound at our two ears, the relative time of arrival at the two ears, and the resemblance to earlier events. We can weaken the difference in time of arrival and compensate for it by a greater difference in intensity. Yet the listener is not aware that this is what happens. Similarly, in the perception of synthetic speech, we can change the acoustic evidence for the word *say* into that for the word *stay* by either lengthening the silence after the /s/ (to suggest the closure produced by the /t/) or by lowering the onset frequency of F1 (Best, Morrongiello, & Robson, 1981). The phonetic cues can trade off against one another, and the person's global impression of the derived experience may bear no specific mark of the factor that has led to the experience (see review by Repp, 1982). For example, it has been argued that it is hard for the listener to distinguish which factor has been used to suggest the /t/.

Mattingly and Liberman (1988) argued that perceiver's lack of awareness of the lower-level evidence that has led to the formation of a phonetic percept is the mark of a specialized phonetic perception system that is distinct from the more general auditory system. However, we can see it as the result of the fact that one sort of schema, a phonetic one, is being applied to the sensory evidence in preference to nonphonetic ones. Such a preference is not always present. If the listener applies a different schema to the sensory input, one which does not treat the two factors as specifying a single regularity in the world, the individual contributions of the two stimulus factors can be detected. Thus, for example, when sine-wave speech is not assimilated as speech, the different features that would combine to specify a speech sound can be heard individually.

There are some similar examples in vision. In the WAY versus WHY drawing, viewers do not know what evidence makes them think that the middle letter in WAY looks like an A. They are unaware of the trading relation between the drawn slope of the sides and the general foreshortening in producing their perceived slope. This example notwithstanding, it is usually harder in vision than in audition to show the complete absence of independent mental representation of the lower-level features. The stimulus for vision usually remains available so that we have time to inspect it and relate it to many different schemas. However, even in the visual cases one might still expect that the global interpretation would dominate the viewer's awareness. This sort of dominance is often found in social perception. For example, when we interpret an approach to us as unfriendly, we often cannot tell what it is about the actions that made them seem unfriendly. We just come away with the global impression.

Conscious global descriptions are usually not derived from *conscious* low-level descriptions, except when we are doing deliberate reasoning. On the contrary, even if they are derived from lower-level schemas operating on the evidence, the lower-level ones need not be represented consciously.

Order of Processing

I have described the description of regularity in our environments and in our commerce with it as deriving from the activity of specialists or schemas. Clearly there are schemas of different types, some concerned with regularities of primitive types and others with regularities of a high order of abstraction.

Constraint is not always from Bottom up

It is tempting to believe that these regularity-describing mechanisms apply themselves in a fixed order to the incoming sensory signal and that we can discover this order by looking for the constraints that early ones place on what can be detected by the later ones. However, the observations on this point are riddled with contradictions.

Here is an example. We think of spatial localization of sound as quite a primitive process. We could imagine how the detecting the spatial origin of a sound could affect how it might group with other ones, because we think of the grouping of sounds as something that happens *after* we know where they are coming from. However the opposite constraint is sometimes found. The grouping of sounds can influence where they appear to be coming from. Does this mean that grouping precedes localization in these cases?

Relation between Auditory Grouping and Phonetic Perception

There is some interest in how speech perception relates to auditory scene analysis. Scene analysis is the perceptual process that decides how to interpret an incoming time-varying spectrum as a number of distinct streams of sound with their individual locations, pitch motions, rhythms, and other qualities. I have often presented the view that the scene analysis processes act prior to auditory recognition processes so that the latter will not form descriptions for accidental combinations of sounds from unrelated acoustic events. In this view, phonetic perception builds on the results of the scene analysis process. A contrary view, offered by Mattingly and Liberman (1988), is that the mechanism for phonetic interpretation gets direct access to the unprocessed sensory input, removes what it needs, and then takes whatever is left over and passes it onward to the other auditory processes. This is referred to as pre-emptiveness.

Both these absolutist views are probably wrong. Phonetic interpretation cannot be first in line. There are plenty of examples of the fact that the recognition of phonemes takes advantage of scene analysis. For example, in a mixture of two voices, it is easier to recognize the phonemes of one voice, if the other is on a different pitch or comes from a different point in space.

Similarly, the assumption that scene analysis must always partition the incoming spectrum before phonetic perception can occur appropriately is supported in some cases but not in others. First, consider the favorable cases. It is supported by experiments from Darwin's laboratory at Sussex that show that scene analysis processes can determine whether or not a frequency component is used to specify the frequency of the first formant of a vowel (see Darwin, chapter 10 in this volume). Similarly, support comes from experiments by Ciocca and myself at McGill on duplex perception of speech. We have shown that in duplex perception

the use of the contralateral formant transition to specify the vowel can be reduced, when the segregation that occurs through scene analysis can be made
strong (Ciocca & Bregman, 1989).

However, there is also evidence that the partitioning of the auditory evidence
that is provided by scene analysis is not always necessary to the speech interpretation process. Even when two synthetic vowels are created with exactly
the same intensity, pitch, location in space, and duration, we can often hear both
of them in a mixture of the two. It appears that each vowel schema can select
what it needs out of the complex spectrum. Another example of this ability of a
schema to extract relevant evidence occurs in phonemic restoration. When a
noise burst replaces a phoneme in a sentence, the phoneme schema that is
activated by the context can select the frequencies that it needs out of the noise
burst. We know that it is selecting frequencies and not merely hallucinating,
because if the frequencies that it needs are not present in the noise, the phoneme
will not be "restored." A third example is duplex perception. Although the
scene-analysis process may be equivocating about the belongingness of the formant transition, the phonetic process has no qualms about incorporating it into
the phonetic interpretation.

Are we to conclude that neither scene analysis nor phoneme perception comes
first in the order of processing? I think that the more appropriate conclusion is
that it is hard to deduce very much about order of processing from data of the
type we have been considering. For example, auditory scene analysis might
indeed come first, but its function could be different from our usual conception of
it. Rather than absolutely partitioning the sensory evidence, it might just make
suggestions about the partitioning that later processes could overrule, if they had
strong evidence to the contrary. Yet another account could be constructed in
which the two processes acted concurrently, each able to benefit from constraints
created by the other. I cannot make up a story in which phonetic perception
comes first that still allows it to take advantage of the specialized capabilities of
the scene analysis system to partition the signal by its acoustic properties. This is
the only theoretical alternative that seems to be excluded both on theoretical and
empirical grounds.

Pre-Emptiveness Does not Imply Different Levels

Even when pre-emptiveness is found, it does not mean that the two schemas, the
pre-empting and the pre-empted one, reside in different modules in the brain or
operate at different levels of processing. Let us define preemptiveness as the
using up of evidence by one interpretation so that other interpretations cannot
also use it. Examples of this can be found in a variety of areas in which the
interpretations that are vying for the evidence do not seem to be at different levels
or in different systems. One familiar example is the Gestalt vase-faces illusion in
which the contour that separates the face region from the vase region is either

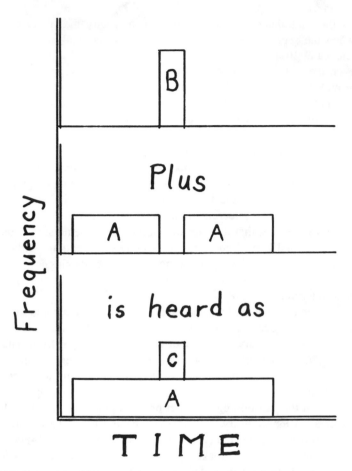

FIG. 9.3. A low frequency band of noise, A, captures its own frequencies out of a wide-band noise, B, allowing a high-pitched residual band to be heard.

allocated to the vase or the face but never to both at the same time. If the face gets the contour, the vase cannot have it. Yet the "faces-in-front-of-vase" and the "vase-in-front-of-faces" interpretations are obviously not in different modules.

There also are auditory examples in which an interpretation "uses up" evidence. One is diagrammed in Fig. 9.3. If we hear a wide-band noise burst (burst B), it has a particular perceptual quality. However, if the burst is preceded and followed by a long burst of noise that contains only the lower frequency components (burst A), the perception changes. We hear A continue right through B. Instead of hearing B as a wide-band noise, we hear burst A joined momentarily by a high-pitched noise burst (C). The stealing of the low frequencies out of B by A leaves a residual (C) that sounds like a high-pitched sound. B's low frequencies have been preempted by A. Yet we would not want to say that A and B were perceived by processes at different levels.

Another example of the using up of evidence happens in puzzles in which we are asked to detect words in strings of letters. Suppose we encounter this string.

FXKHXKCANNEDADVENTUREFYTKWL

On a particular attempt, we may detect the words CANNED and ADVENTURE, but not DAD and NED, which are there too. This is because the word schemas that are activated use up the letters that they account for and do not make them accessible to other word schemas. Again, the contending processes are not in different biological systems of analysis but wholly within the reading system.

We can also find examples in social perception in the interpretation of the intentions of another person. If I think that people of a particular group are exceedingly polite, then when one of them listens attentively to what I say, I am less likely to conclude that he or she has found what I have said very interesting. The "politeness" interpretation pre-empts the evidence, leaving less to be used to support the "interest" interpretation. Of course, if the display of interest is very strong, there may be enough apparent interest to satisfy the "politeness" schema and still leave some over for the "interest" schema. This example has the same formal structure as an experiment by Whalen and Liberman (1987) in which a weak sine tone was not heard as such but rather as helping to specify the identity of a speech sound. At greater intensities, the sine tone had enough energy to satisfy the phonetic schema with some energy left over to be heard as a separate whistle. This was taken as showing the precedence of speech perception over nonspeech perception. By analogy, my example drawn from social perception would be taken as showing that politeness perception had precedence over interest perception and, hence, was derived from an earlier-acting biological system.

Conclusions

Limitations of Functional Analysis

I have tried to show that many of the subtle properties of speech perception occur in a wide variety of other forms of human mental activity, both in activities that are probably innate and ones that are undoubtedly learned. We have been strongly impressed by the abstract nature of speech perception. We should be as strongly impressed by the abstract nature of all forms of human epistemic activity.

The fact that properties of learned and innate epistemic processes are so similar make it hard to tell what is learned and what is innate. Clearly everything that is learned has an innate basis; apes cannot learn in the ways that we do, and stones cannot learn at all. However, how our biological structures and our experiences interact to give us our powerful understandings of the world is a mystery that psychological science has not penetrated.

Contribution of the Haskins Research

The study of speech perception, especially the study of synthetic speech, about which we now know so much, has provided us with a wonderful *in vitro* preparation for the intensive study of human cognition. Liberman, Mattingly, Repp, Cooper, and the rest of group at Haskins Laboratories have done for phonetic perception what Chomsky did for syntax, what Piaget did for thought processes, and what the Gestalt psychologists did for perception in general. They have shown us that the objects of the human mind are quite different from what earlier formulations had imagined. They are not simple stimuli and responses that sit like beads on a chain, but abstract structures that are realized only indirectly in perception and action. All these theoreticians have emphasized the role played by complex relations spread out over time in determining the interpretation of events at local positions.

In What Way is Speech Special?

An argument has been made by Liberman and his colleagues that speech is special. We cannot really doubt that it is, because there are so many indications of its uniqueness. It plays a central role in all human affairs. One cannot imagine any human community that could survive as such without speech (if we include the sign language of the deaf as a special case of speech). Furthermore, it is most likely that there are biological specializations for speech in the human.

However, the exact nature of that specialness does not lie in its abstract properties, such as preemptiveness and encodedness. Such properties are widespread in human cognition. This fact is what leads me to believe that in the future, the contribution of the "speech-is-special" research will be seen to have been its role in challenging old ways of thinking and opening our eyes to the truly complex way in which speech perception proceeds. I think the question of whether these complexities are unique to speech perception or whether speech perception qualifies as a module in Fodor's sense will be seen in hindsight to have been much less important.

References

Bailey, P. J., Dorman, M. F., & Summerfield, A. Q. (1977). Identification of sine-wave analogs of CV syllables in speech and non-speech modes. *Journal of the Acoustical Society of America, 61,* 5(A).

Best, C. T., Morrongiello, B., & Robson, R. (1981). Perceptual equivalence of acoustic cues in speech and non-speech perception. *Perception & Psychophysics, 29,* 191–211.

Ciocca, V., & Bregman, A. S. (1989). The effects of auditory streaming on duplex perception. *Perception & Psychophysics, 46,* 39–48.

Cohen, M., & Grossberg, S. (1986). Neural dynamics of speech and language coding: Developmental programs, perceptual grouping, and competition for short-term memory. *Human Neurobiology, 5,* 1–22.

Fodor, J. (1983). *The modularity of mind.* Cambridge, MA: MIT Press.

Grossberg, S. (1985). The adaptive self-organization of serial order in behavior: Speech, language, and motor control. In E. C. Schwab & H. C. Nusbaum (Eds.), *Pattern recognition by humans and machines* (pp. 187–294). Orlando, FL: Academic Press.

Handel, S. (1989). *Listening: An introduction to the perception of auditory events.* Cambridge, MA: MIT Press.

Liberman, A. M. (1982). On finding that speech is special. *American Psychologist, 37,* 148–167.

Liberman, A. M., & Mattingly, I. G. (1985). The motor theory of speech perception revised. *Cognition, 21,* 1–36.

Mattingly, I.G., & Liberman, A. M. (1988). Speech and other auditory modules. In G. M. Edelman, W. E. Gall, & W. M. Cowan (Eds.), *Auditory function: the neurological basies of hearing* (pp. 775–792). New York: Wiley.

McGurk, H., & MacDonald, J. (1976). Hearing lips and seeing voices. *Nature, 264,* 746–748.

Repp, B. H. (1982). Phonetic trading relations and context effects: New experimental evidence for a speech mode of perception. *Psychological Bulletin, 92,* 81–110.

Titchener, E. B. (1910). *A textbook of psychology.* New York: Macmillan.

Whalen, D. H., & Liberman, A. M. (1987). Speech perception takes precedence over nonspeech perception. *Science, 237,* 169–171.

Comment: Modes of Processing Speech and Nonspeech Signals

David B. Pisoni

Department of Psychology, Indiana University

I am delighted to be here today to honor Al Liberman and talk about speech perception, particularly some findings that I know Al would be happy to hear about, given the theme of the conference: Motor Theory and Modularity. I feel a little awkward in talking to this audience about some of these findings, because I find myself in the rather uncomfortable position of disagreeing with the major conclusions of Al Bregman's talk, on the one hand, and defending Al Liberman's views about speech, on the other hand. This may seem a little curious to most of you in the audience, since I have always thought of myself as the "quiet" little gadfly off working in my Lab back in Indiana in the heartland of America, far away from Haskins Laboratories and all the day to day excitement that goes on there.

After reading Al Bregman's paper and thinking about his major claims, I began looking through my slide collection to find something to say about his arguments. As I thought more and more about what he said about speech perception and auditory perception, particularly "auditory scene analysis," I began to realize that maybe Al Liberman's arguments for "pre-emptiveness" of speech might *not* be as "bizarre" as I once thought they were, when I first read the Liberman and Mattingly *Cognition* paper a few years ago. When you think about things one way for a long time, it is often very difficult, if not impossible, to see them any other way!! Perhaps it takes a paper like Al Bregman's to get one to think a little like Al Liberman and to appreciate some of the very deep and unusual claims that Al has made over the years about speech.

In order to see how my thinking went over the last few weeks, I will begin by going back about 25 years to the days of the Pattern Playback synthesizer in the 1950s and 1960s, and briefly review some of the now "classic" experiments in

225

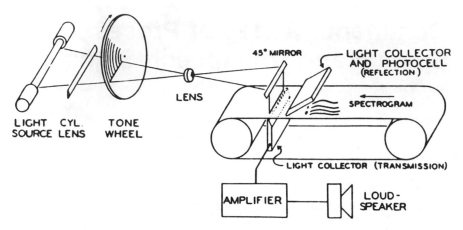

FIG. 1. A schematic representation of the Haskins Laboratories Pattern Playback speech synthesizer. Simplified spectrographic patterns of speech were painted by hand on an acetate belt to represent the important time-varying formant structure of an utterance. The device would convert these visual patterns into highly intelligible speech that could be used in perceptual experiments with human listeners. Photographs of spectrograms of natural speech could also be used as input to the device in order to reproduce utterances in synthetic form (from Cooper, Liberman, & Borst, 1951, with permission).

speech perception that form the knowledge base and early history of our field (see Fig. 1).

For a considerable number of years, Al Liberman and his collaborators at Haskins Laboratories have been interested in the differences in perception between speech and nonspeech signals. That such differences might exist was suggested by the report of the very first findings on categorical perception of stop consonants back in 1957 (Liberman, Harris, Hoffman, & Griffith, 1957). As is now well known to everyone, even introductory psychology students, the discrimination of most nonspeech continua is continuous and monotonic with changes in the physical scale. Observers are able to discriminate many more differences than they can reliably identify on an absolute basis. However, in the case of categorical perception, listeners can discriminate between two stimuli no better than they can identify them as different on an absolute basis, suggesting that discrimination of speech is in some way limited by absolute identification. Since categorical perception seemed to be restricted to speech stimuli, at least at that time in the late 1950s, particularly the perception of stop consonants, it became of some interest to determine the underlying basis for the nonmonotonic discrimination functions found for speech, as shown by the excellent discrimination observed at category boundaries and the relatively poor discrimination observed within categories.

It was with this general goal in mind that the first "nonspeech control" experiment was carried out by Al and his colleagues (Liberman, Harris, Kinney, & Lane, 1961). In this study, Liberman and colleagues wanted to determine whether the peaks in the discrimination function observed for stop consonants were a result of learning or whether they were given innately. If the peaks in discrimination could be attributed to learning, then an additional concern was to determine precisely what kind of learning was involved in the process. In order to answer both of these questions, Liberman and colleagues created a set of nonspeech stimuli by inverting the synthetic spectrographic patterns appropriate for the /do/–/to/ continuum before converting them to sound on the Pattern Playback. The aim of this manipulation was, at least in principle, to generate a set of nonspeech control stimuli that had all the properties of the speech stimuli but did not actually sound like speech. Examples of these stimuli are shown in Fig. 2.

The strategy of the Liberman et al. (1961) study was then to compare the discrimination functions for the speech signals with those obtained for their nonspeech controls in order to ascertain whether the nonspeech signals would

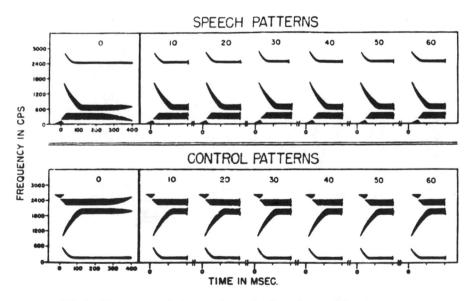

FIG. 2.   The top panel shows schematized spectrographic patterns appropriate for generating a continuum of synthetic speech stimuli ranging from /do/ to /to/. The bottom panel shows the set of control patterns that were created by inverting the speech patterns shown in the top panel. The control patterns contained all the timing information present in the original speech patterns, although they did not sound like speech (From Liberman, Harris, Kinney, & Lane, 1961. Copyright, 1961, American Psychological Association).

show comparable peaks and troughs in discrimination. At least two outcomes were possible from such an experiment. First, if discrimination peaks were present for the nonspeech stimuli, and they occurred in roughly the same regions as those found for the speech condition, the findings could then be attributed to the specific acoustic properties of the signals themselves, and not to any additional interpretative process whereby the signals were identified or encoded as speech. Liberman and colleagues suggested that this particular result would support an account of speech perception in terms of innate factors presumably involving some sort of psychophysical explanation.

The second possible outcome was quite different. Liberman and colleagues argued that if the discrimination peaks were absent from the nonspeech control stimuli, then a learning account would be appropriate. Moreover, depending upon the overall level of discrimination observed in the nonspeech condition, one of two possible learning explanations would be possible. These two learning explanations may be contrasted for the idealized cases as shown graphically in Fig. 3.

In both panels of this figure, a hypothetical ABX discrimination function for a selected speech continuum is shown by the solid lines and filled circles; the functions for the nonspeech control stimuli are shown as the dashed lines and open circles. Panel (a), on the left, illustrates the results predicted by a learning interpretation of the discrimination peak in terms of the concept of "acquired similarity." According to this view, the peak in the speech discrimination func-

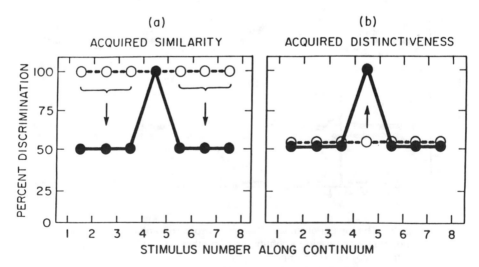

FIG. 3.   Idealized versions of ABX discrimination functions that would be expected from processes of acquired similarity (Panel a) or acquired distinctiveness (Panel b). These two functions illustrate how early linguistic experience might selectively modify speech discrimination capabilities.

tion arises from learning to *ignore* variations within phonological categories and learning to *attend* to variations across categories. Thus, discrimination of the relevant acoustic parameter underlying the speech contrast was originally presumed to be quite good, as shown by the high level of the nonspeech discrimination function. The effects of perceptual learning, therefore, serve to *attenuate* sensitivity selectively.

In contrast, Panel (b), on the right, illustrates the results predicted by an interpretation of the discrimination peak in terms of the concept of "acquired distinctiveness." According to this view, which was widely held by many psychologists back in the 1950s (see Gibson & Gibson, 1955), the peak in the discrimination function arises from learning to respond to stimuli that have somehow become more distinctive or salient to the listener through a process of *differentiation*. By this account, discrimination was originally assumed to be quite poor and the effects of perceptual learning were to make certain stimuli more *distinctive* by increasing the organism's sensitivity to them through exposure and feedback.

The results of the Liberman et al. (1961) /do/–/to/ control study did not reveal a peak in the ABX discrimination functions for the nonspeech stimuli, suggesting a learning explanation. In addition, the overall level of the discrimination function was quite low, very close to chance, suggesting that the peaks in the speech discrimination function were more likely to be the result of acquired distinctiveness than acquired similarity. At the time, Liberman and colleagues assumed that the distinctiveness for speech arose during the course of language learning, through mediation of the production system in the process of learning the relevant articulatory gestures needed to produce the same distinction, a position characterizing what would eventually become one of the earliest statements of the Motor Theory of Speech Perception. In the 1960s, these nonspeech results were often cited not only as evidence for the presence of important differences in perception between speech and nonspeech signals but also as additional support for the view that speech perception might have very close ties with speech production (Liberman, Cooper, Harris, & MacNeilage, 1963).

Numerous other speech–nonspeech comparisons have been carried out over the years at Haskins. All of these studies have revealed quite similar results, particularly with regard to comparisons involving the shape and relative level of the discrimination function (see Mattingly, Liberman, Syrdal, & Halwes, 1971; Miyawaki, Strange, Verbrugge, Liberman, Jenkins, & Fujimura, 1975). The nonspeech control signals have uniformly and consistently failed to show peaks in discrimination that were correlated with the peaks in the speech identification functions. Moreover, these nonspeech stimuli were typically discriminated at levels approaching chance responding. In more recent years, Liberman and his colleagues have tended to avoid explanations of these differences in terms of the older notions of "acquired similarity" and "acquired distinctiveness," preferring instead to characterize the differences in perception between speech and nonspeech as reflecting two basically different modes of perception, a speech mode and a nonspeech mode (Liberman, 1970). Until recently, the nonmonotonic discrimination functions observed for speech stimuli have typically been accounted for in terms of some additional, perhaps specialized, interpretative process involving phonetic categorization rather than a purely sensory-based process involving responses only to the psychophysical properties of the signals themselves (see Pisoni, 1977).

A number of criticisms can be leveled at these speech–nonspeech comparisons, particularly the results from the nonspeech control conditions, First, there is the question of whether the same psychophysical properties found in the original speech stimuli are indeed preserved in the nonspeech control stimuli. This criticism is appropriate for the original /do/–/to/ stimuli and the Mattingly et al. (1971) "chirp" and "bleat" controls, where the acoustic cues were removed from speech context and presented in isolation. This manipulation, while nominally preserving the speech cue, results in a marked change in the spectral context, which no doubt affects processing of the speech cue itself (see Stevens, 1980).

A second problem with these nonspeech control stimuli concerns the fact that subjects did not receive any experience or familiarization with these signals prior to the discrimination test. With complex multidimensional signals, it may be difficult for subjects to attend to the relevant attributes that distinguish different stimuli. Thus, a subject's performance may be no better than chance, if he is not attending selectively to the specific criterial attributes that distinguish these stimuli. Since all of the early nonspeech experiments were also run without feedback, a listener may focus his/her attention on one aspect or set of attributes on a given trial and an entirely different aspect of the stimulus on the next trial. As a result, the listener may respond to the same stimulus quite differently at different times during the course of the experiment, thus revealing a level of performance no better than chance, which is precisely what Liberman and his colleagues found in their early studies.

Finally, subjects in almost all of these nonspeech experiments never overtly labeled or identified these nonspeech stimuli into discrete perceptual categories before discrimination was measured, as is commonly done in the speech experiments. The prior labeling experience may tend to emphasize some aspects of the stimulus pattern and attenuate others in selective ways not known to the investigator. Some of these criticisms were specifically taken into account in the more recent nonspeech experiments, which may have been responsible for their more successful outcome compared to the earlier studies (see Pisoni, Carrell, & Gans, 1983).

Despite the methodological criticisms that can be leveled at these early nonspeech control experiments, a number of very general issues were identified at the time by Al Liberman and his colleagues, issues that still continue to occupy researchers today. Although discussion of concepts like "acquired distinctiveness" and "acquired similarity" in speech perception have faded away, there is currently a great deal of interest in the role of early linguistic experience in the development of speech perception in infants and young children and the effects of linguistic knowledge on speech perception in adults (see Aslin & Pisoni, 1980; Aslin, Pisoni, Hennessy, & Perey, 1981). Many of the theoretical issues touched upon in these early Haskins papers are still topics of great interest, although they have been modified to accommodate recent developments in cognitive psychology, linguistics, and neurobiology.

A period of some ten years elapsed between the Liberman et al. (1961) /do/–/to/ study and the first report by Peter Eimas and his colleagues on the discriminative abilities of young infants (Eimas, Siqueland, Jusczyk, & Vigorito, 1971). This well-known study not only showed categorical-like discrimination performance in infants, but it also demonstrated that infants are able to make very fine discriminations of relevant speech cues at an early age. In the years following this pioneering study, a great deal of data has been obtained in infant studies suggesting that the form of learning in speech perception is probably more nearly one of acquired similarity rather than acquired distinctiveness, at least with regard to the discrimination of speech sounds. Interest in the loss of discriminative abilities in language learning and the nature of the perceptual mechanisms underlying this loss is of course a topic of current interest and a great deal of research (Strange & Jenkins, 1978; Pisoni, Aslin, Perey, & Hennessy, 1982; Pisoni, Logan, & Lively, in press). Many people are now working on this problem with adults, infants, young children, and animals as well, following up on ideas and suggestions that Al Liberman made years ago.

Not only has there been recent interest and research on the nature and timecourse of the loss of discriminative abilities in infants and young children, but research has also continued in several directions on the perception of nonspeech signals having properties that are similar to speech. While the specific issues have changed somewhat since 1961, many of the fundamental theoretical questions still remain the same today. It is hard to think back to 1961 and imagine if anyone thought about the impact and importance the original /do/–/to/ study would have for the future of research in speech perception or for the interesting directions this work would take in the years to come. Indeed, it is rare in the field of experimental psychology for any set of issues to last for more than a few years. However, in the case of speech perception and more specifically with regard to differences in perception between speech and nonspeech signals, the fundamental questions have apparently endured for more than 25 years, and, what is more surprising, they are still prominent in current theoretical discussions today. Perhaps these issues have survived so long, because they deal with very deep and fundamental problems of perception and knowledge and their relation to the biology language. Perhaps they have endured simply because they have not as yet received any satisfactory theoretical account. Who really knows? Regardless of the final explanation, research continues on problems that were first identified by

Al Liberman back in 1961 using similar methodologies and experimental designs. Some of these recent findings have revealed important new properties about speech which lead some researchers to suppose that biologically specialized mechanisms are needed for perceptual analysis (see Liberman & Mattingly, 1985).

In addition to several prominent differences in the acoustic characteristics of speech and nonspeech sounds which set speech signals apart from other auditory signals in a listener's auditory environment, there are also a number of distinctive differences in the way in which speech and nonspeech sounds are encoded, recognized, and identified. Research by Al and his colleagues at Haskins has demonstrated that when human listeners are presented with speech signals, they typically respond to them as linguistic entities rather than as isolated auditory events in their environment. The set of labels used in responding to speech is not arbitrary—the labels are intimately associated with the function of speech as the signalling system used in spoken language. Speech signals are categorized and labeled almost immediately with reference to the listener's linguistic background and experience. Moreover, a listener's performance in identifying and discriminating a particular acoustic attribute is often a consequence of the functional role this property plays in the listener's own linguistic system. In some of my own studies, we have shown that it is possible to get human listeners to respond to the auditory properties of speech signals and to "hear out" certain components with extensive training and the use of very sensitive psychophysical procedures (Pisoni & Lazarus, 1974; Pisoni & Tash, 1974), but one of the fundamental differences in perception between speech and nonspeech sounds lies in the linguistic significance of the stimulus patterns to the listener and the context into which these patterns are subsequently integrated.

One very clear example of differences in mode of processing comes from a study carried out at Indiana by Mary Ellen Grunke and I several years ago on the perception of complex nonspeech auditory patterns that have properties that are similar to speech (Grunke & Pisoni, 1982). Subjects were required to identify auditory patterns with either acoustic or phonetic labels. No feedback was provided in this experiment, since we wanted to measure subjects' ability to categorize these auditory patterns solely on the basis of the acoustic or phonetic attributes implicit in these signals. Thus, we were not interested in the subjects' ability to learn an arbitrary sound-to-label association in the context of a particular test situation, as we had been in some of our previous experiments. The stimulus patterns were the single-, double-, and triple-tone signals shown in Fig. 4. Two conditions were examined. In the "phonetic" condition, subjects were told that the stimuli were distorted tokens of natural speech. The response labels provided to subjects were the syllables *ba, da, ab,* and *ad,* which were placed under four separate buttons on a response panel. In the "acoustic" condition, the subjects were told that the stimuli were frequency-modulated tones generated by a computer and that they consisted of a short interval with constant pitch, pre-

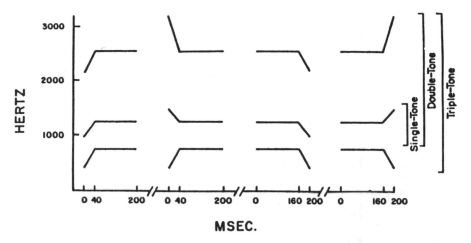

FIG. 4.   Schematic spectrographic patterns of the four nonspeech stimuli used in the Grunke and Pisoni (1982) pattern of learning experiments. Reprinted by permission of Psychonomic Society, Inc.

ceded or followed by a very rapid rise or fall in pitch. The response labels were schematic line drawings of the time course of the frequency change of each stimulus, ,,,.

Responses were scored as correct or incorrect depending on whether the indicated label was the most appropriate cue for the presented stimulus. Percent correct performance for both labeling conditions across the three stimulus sets is displayed in Fig. 5. For the single- and double-tone stimuli, the subjects were able to use acoustic labels more accurately than phonetic labels (single tones: 49.8% vs. 36.6% correct for acoustic and phonetic labels, respectively; double tones: 61.0% vs. 42.2%). However, with the triple tones, which contained energy in the first formant region, listeners assigned phonetic labels much more accurately than acoustic labels (62.7% correct for phonetic labels compared with 42.6% for acoustic labels). Subjects in the phonetic labeling condition were apparently able to hear these triple-tone patterns as speech, whereas subjects in the acoustic labeling condition had much more difficulty in focusing their attention on the individual components of the patterns. The decrement in performance for the acoustic labeling group can be accounted for by the presence of conflicting information in the F1 transition region for half the stimuli. In the triple-tone patterns, the F1 always rises in initial position and falls in final position. For stimuli containing rising transition in initial position (i.e., /ba/), or falling transitions in final position, such as /ab/, the information in F1 is *correlated* and *redundant* with the direction of the movements of F2 and F3, thus facilitating performance. However, for stimuli containing falling transitions in initial position i.e., /da/, and rising transitions in final position, such as /ad/, the F1

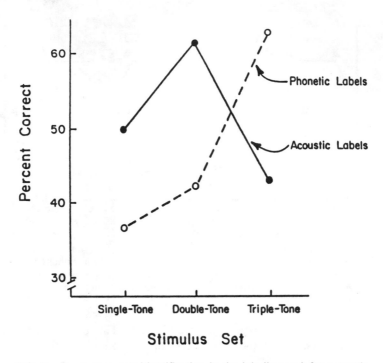

FIG. 5.   Percent correct identification in the labeling task for acoustic and phonetic labels. The data are shown separately for single-, double-, and triple-tone stimuli from each labeling condition (From Grunke & Pisoni, 1982. Reprinted by permission of Psychonomic Society, Inc.).

component conflicts with the direction of the transitions in the remainder of the pattern. Thus, listeners could attend to either the phonetic or acoustic properties of these signals with better-than-chance accuracy, but their overall level of performance varied with the complexity of the signal and the specific stimulus properties that were attended to under the two labeling conditions.

Examination of the labeling performance for the four separate stimuli shown in Fig. 6 indicated that, for acoustic labels, response accuracy was much greater for transition-final signals (/ab/, 69.44%; /ad/, 62.83%) than for transition-initial signals (/ab/, 38.94%; /da/, 33.39%). Interestingly however, when listeners assigned phonetic labels to these same signals, the differences between transition-initial and transition-final signals were reduced substantially and did not differ significantly from each other (/ba/, 45.17%; /da/, 43.00%; /ab/, 51.28%; /ad/, 49.27%). The data shown in FIG. 6 have been pooled across single, double, and triple tones, since the observed overall pattern of responses was essentially the same for each stimulus set. These results demonstrate a very marked dissociation in perception between auditory and phonetic categorization of the *same* acoustic signals.

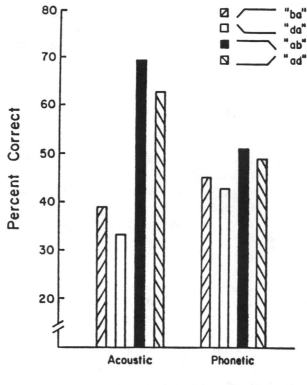

FIG. 6.   Percent correct identification for each of the individual stimuli used in the labeling task. Data are shown separately for acoustic and phonetic labeling conditions (From Grunke & Pisoni, 1982. Reprinted by permission of Psychonomic Society, Inc.).

Two other related findings obtained in Jim Sawusch's Lab at Buffalo have also demonstrated marked differences in perception between speech and nonspeech signals as a function of mode of processing. In one study, Eileen Schwab (1981) found substantial backward masking effects and upward spread of masking for sine-wave stimuli heard as nonspeech tonal patterns. However, both masking effects were subsequently eliminated when the same identical sine-wave patterns were heard by listeners as speech, and in a more recent study by Tomiak, Mullennix, and Sawusch (1987) using a Garner speeded classification task, subjects displayed evidence of processing separable dimensions with a set of noise-tone analogs of fricative-vowel syllables, when they were told the patterns were nonspeech sequences. Irrelevant variation in the noise spectra *did not* affect reaction times for the classification of the tones and vice versa. However, when subjects were told the patterns were fricative-vowel speech stimuli, the component dimensions were processed in an integral manner such that irrelevant variation in the fricative increased the reaction times to classify the vowels and vice versa. These results were obtained with a set of noise-tone analogs that did not contain any consonant-vowel transitions from the noise into the steady-state segments of the patterns. Thus, for the noise-tone analogs heard as speech, knowledge of coarticulation between adjacent segments appears to have been used even when the acoustic cues for coarticulation were absent from the stimulus pattern. Tomiak and colleagues suggested that the use of knowledge about coarticulation in speech perception is "mandatory," in Fodor's sense, and is automatically invoked whenever an auditory pattern is heard as speech and processed in the speech mode (Fodor, 1983).

It is clear from these three sets of results and other recent studies carried out at Haskins using nonspeech signals, which have properties similar to those found in speech, that differences in "mode of processing" can control *perceptual selectivity* quite substantially and can subsequently influence the perception of individual components of the stimulus pattern as well as the entire pattern itself (see Remez, Rubin, Pisoni, & Carrell, 1981). This can occur in quite different ways with the same stimulus patterns, depending primarily on whether the subject's attention in the task is directed toward coding either the auditory properties of the signals or the phonetic content of the overall patterns. In the former case, the process is more analytic, involving the processing or hearing out of the individual components of the stimulus, whereas in the latter case, the process is more nearly "holistic," insofar as the individual components may be combined to form well-defined and highly familiar perceptual (phonetic) categories. With regard to the perception of speech, these results imply that listeners probably do not isolate and then subsequently process only the distinctive speech cues in the stimulus. Rather, it seems very likely that listeners respond to these so-called "speech cues" as simply part of the configuration of a spectrally complex dynamic time-varying auditory pattern. In the case of speech, the patterns have certain well-defined distinctive properties and display spectral-temporal relations that elicit a qualitatively different mode of processing, a speech mode, that appears to be quite different from the way other nonspeech auditory signals are responded to under similar conditions. Such findings are probably not too surprising to anyone sitting in the audience today, but in thinking about these results and what they imply for theories of speech perception, we should not forget that it was Al Liberman who first raised these same questions more than 25 years ago in the now classic /do/–/to/ experiment, and it was Al Liberman who has relentlessly continued to pursue these and many other difficult and challenging problems in speech perception ever since. Let's just hope that it doesn't take us another 25 years to appreciate the many insights that Al has shown us about speech and language over the years. When this conference is over, maybe we can just go back to the lab with Al and get started working on some new experiments like many of us did years ago, when we first learned about speech from Al himself.

References

Aslin, R. N., & Pisoni, D. B. (1980). Some developmental processes in speech perception (pp. 67–96). In G. Yeni-Komshian, J. F. Kavanagh, & C. A. Ferguson (Eds.), *Child phonology: Perception & production.* New York: Academic Press.

Aslin, R. N., Pisoni, D. B., Hennessy, B. L., & Perey, A. J. (1981). Discrimination of voice onset time by human infants: New findings and implications for the effects of early experience. *Child Development, 52,* 1135–1145.

Cooper, F. S., Liberman, A. M., & Borst, J. M. (1951). The interconversion of audible and visible patterns as a basis for research in the perception of speech. *Journal of the Acoustical Society of America, 17,* 318–325.

Eimas, P. D., Siqueland, E. R., Jusczyk, P. W., & Vigorito, J. (1971). Speech perception in infants. *Science, 171,* 303–306.

Fodor, J. (1983). *The modularity of mind.* Cambridge, MA: MIT Press.

Gibson, J. J., & Gibson, E. J. (1955). Perceptual learning: Differentiation or enrichment? *Psychological Review, 62,* 32–41.

Grunke, M. E., & Pisoni, D. B. (1982). Some experiments on perceptual learning of mirror-image acoustic patterns. *Perception & Psychophysics, 31,* 210–218.

Liberman, A. M. (1970). Some characteristics of perception in the speech mode. In D. A. Hamburg (Ed.) *Perception and its disorders. Proceedings of the A.R.N.M.D.* (pp. 238–254). Baltimore: Williams & Wilkins.

Liberman, A. M., Cooper, F. S., Harris, K. S., & MacNeilage, P. F. (1963). A motor theory of speech perception. *Proceedings of the Stockholm Seminar* (Vol. 2, D3). Stockholm: Royal Institute of Technology.

Liberman, A. M., Harris, K. S., Hoffman, H. S., & Griffith, B. C. (1957). The discrimination of speech sounds within and across phoneme boundaries. *Journal of Experimental Psychology, 54,* 358–367.

Liberman, A. M., Harris, K. S., Kinney, J. A., & Lane, H. L. (1961). The discrimination of relative onset-time of the components of certain speech and non-speech patterns. *Journal of Experimental Psychology, 61,* 379–388.

Liberman, A. M., & Mattingly, I. G. (1985). The motor theory of speech perception revised. *Cognition, 21,* 1–36.

Mattingly, I., Liberman, A. M., Syrdal, A. K., & Halwes, T. (1971). Discrimination in speech and nonspeech modes. *Cognitive Psychology, 2,* 131–157.

Miyawaki, K., Strange, W., Verbrugge, R., Liberman, A. M., Jenkins, J. J., & Fujimura, O. (1975). An effect of linguistic experience: The discrimination of [r] and [l] by native speakers of Japanese and English. *Perception & Psychophysics, 18,* 331–340.

Pisoni, D. B. (1977). Identification and discrimination of the relative onset of two component tones: Implications for voicing perception in stops. *Journal of the Acoustical Society of America, 61,* 1352–1361.

Pisoni, D. B., Aslin, R. N., Perey, A. J., & Hennessy, B. L. (1982). Some effects of laboratory training on identification and discrimination of voicing contrasts in stop consonants. *Journal of Experimental Psychology: Human Perception and Performance, 8,* 297–314.

Pisoni, D. B., Carrell, T. D., & Gans, S. J. (1983). Perception of the duration of rapid spectrum changes in speech and nonspeech signals. *Perception & Psychophysics, 34,* 314–322.

Pisoni, D. B., & Lazarus, J. H. (1974). Categorical and noncategorical modes of speech perception along the voicing continuum. *Journal of the Acoustical Society of America, 55,* 328–333.

Pisoni, D. B., Logan, J. S., & Lively, S. (in press). Perceptual learning of nonnative speech contrasts: Implication for theories of speech perception. In H. C. Nusbaum and J. Goodman (Eds.) *Development of Speech Perception: The Transition from Recognizing Speech Sounds to Spoken Words.* Cambridge: MIT Press.

Pisoni, D. B., & Tash, J. B. (1974). Reaction times to comparisons within and across phonetic categories. *Perception & Psychophysics, 15,* 285–290.

Remez, R. E., Rubin, P. E., Pisoni, D. B., & Carrell, T. D. (1981). Speech perception without traditional speech cues. *Science, 212,* 947–950.

Schwab, E. C. (1981). *Auditory and phonetic processing for tone analogs of speech.* Unpublished doctoral dissertation, Department of Psychology, SUNY at Buffalo.

Stevens, K. N. (1980). Acoustic correlates of some phonetic categories. *Journal of the Acoustical Society of America, 68,* 836–842.

Strange, W., & Jenkins, J. J. (1978). Role of linguistic experience in the perception of speech. In R. D. Walk & H. L. Pick (Eds.), *Perception & experience* (pp. 125–169). New York: Plenum.

Tomiak, G. R., Mullennix, J. W., & Sawusch, J. R. (1987). Integral processing of phonemes: Evidence for a phonetic mode of perception. *Journal of the Acoustical Society of America, 81,* 755–764.

Chapter 10

The Relationship Between Speech Perception and the Perception of Other Sounds

C. J. Darwin

Laboratory of Experimental Psychology, University of Sussex

Abstract

Speech perception has evolved on a perceptual substrate that allows us to recognize complex sounds in a noisy and frequently reverberant environment. This substrate involves mechanisms that allow different sound sources to be separated and that allow sounds that are masked or spectrally changed to be heard for what they originally were. It is unlikely that speech sounds do not invoke them. Such mechanisms we can refer to as "auditory" in that they apply indiscriminately to speech and other sounds. They do not necessarily lead to a conscious percept but produce a representation of sound that can usefully make contact with knowledge about particular sound types and categories, be they speech or not. The speech module can apply its speech-specific knowledge to such a representation, as can processes or modules that lead to a conscious percept of sounds other than speech.

I will describe experiments on the perception of simple speech sounds in the presence of other sounds that demonstrate some of the auditory (in the previous sense) processes that might be used to construct such an abstract representation of sound. Properties such as local frequency continuity and onset-time constrain the alternatives that speech-specific knowledge considers.

In this chapter, I will not be concerned with the existence or the nature of a phonetic module. I am happy to agree with Mattingly and Liberman (1988) that we do have a special mechanism whose job it is to interpret sound phonetically. I will be concerned with the relationship between that module and our other auditory mechanisms. In particular, I will disagree with their view that the phonetic module is independent of those mechanisms of perceptual organization that Bregman has termed auditory scene analysis, and I will also argue against their view that the phonetic module preempts auditory processes (see also Whalen & Liberman, 1987).

First, we must make clear the scope of our discussion of mechanisms of perception. In particular, what are we taking as input? Papers on speech perception almost always describe their stimuli in terms of the control parameters of a synthesizer. Fundamental frequency, formant frequencies, and amplitudes and silence durations are typical of the descriptors used. Consequently, our theories of how sounds are perceived in terms of phonetic events take these properties as their starting point. For example, Mattingly & Liberman (in press) say that the phonetic module "tracks the changing center frequencies of formants"—a useful strategy, but it is one that begs the question of how the center frequencies of formants are obtained.

In the ideal world of the speech synthesiser and the sound-proof room, that problem is not practically important; a variety of mechanisms could recode the auditory spectrum of the sound into formant parameters. However, in the harsh acoustic conditions of our normal environment, the simple relationship between the auditory input and the abstract properties that the phonetic module requires breaks down. Reverberation fills silence and blurs onsets and offsets; objects and enclosed spaces in the environment change spectral balance through diffraction and resonance, and most seriously, extra sound sources add spectral peaks and mask existing ones.

A relevant question now is whether general auditory "scene analysis" (Bregman, 1978) mechanisms are involved in the process of producing from the raw auditory spectral analysis a more abstract description that involves such entities as formants, silence, rise-time, and so forth. I hope to demonstrate that they are.

A second concern of the chapter will be to examine the empirical data on the use of auditory scene analysis in organising the abstractly coded formant tracks into sources and phonetic percepts. I hope to show, again *pace* Mattingly and Liberman, that the phonetic module is not "independent of the modules for pitch and timbre." (Mattingly & Liberman, in press).

In this paper, I will draw predominantly on research done over the last seven or eight years at Sussex, much of which has benefited from the collaboration of my colleagues, Roy Gardner, Helen Pattison, and more recently, Denis McKeown.

Environmental Effects

A general problem facing the auditory system is how to recognise as similar sounds that have been produced under different environmental conditions: at different distances, round corners, in enclosed spaces with different reverberation times, in the presence of other sounds. Before the advent of speech, it seems plausible that auditory systems could have solved this very basic problem (although direct evidence appears to be lacking). If the perception of speech shows similar abilities, we might argue on grounds of parsimony that it is exploiting more ancient auditory mechanisms.

I will start by describing two sets of experimental results that draw attention to some of the issues that are raised by considering speech perception in a wider natural context.

Reverberation

A dramatic example of perceptual compensation for the adulterating effects of the environment comes from some recent work by Anthony J. Watkins of Reading University (Watkins, 1988) on the ability of the auditory system to compensate for the effects of reverberation. Reverberation increases a sound's duration, slowing rise/fall times and filling silent intervals. We would, thus, expect it to have a substantial effect on a phonetic distinction such as that between *dish* and *ditch,* which relies on just those properties. Watkins produced a continuum of sounds by splicing silence into a nonreverberant recording of *dish.* He then gave this continuum to listeners in each of four different listening conditions. In two of these conditions, the word was presented in isolation, but with either no reverberation or a reverberation time of about one second. In the other two, it was embedded in the carrier sentence, "I found it in the . . . . ," which in turn could be recorded either with or without reverberation. Watkins found that the boundary between *dish* and *ditch* was at the same point along the continuum for all the conditions except for the one in which the reverberant word was presented without its carrier sentence. Here subjects never perceive an unambiguous *ditch.* The carrier sentence is, thus, providing information about reverberation conditions that influences the way that the phonetic module interprets the acoustic cues. Do we then have a special module to tell us about reverberation? If we do, its deliberations seem to be available to the phonetic module.

Spectral Balance

Distant sounds and those produced out of the line of sight will have a different spectral balance from close direct sounds, but the changes in spectral tilt are generally small compared with the slope of formant peaks: Thus, the frequencies of spectral peaks due to formants remain relatively invariant. There are, however, marked changes in the relative amplitudes of formant peaks, and Denis McKeown, David Kirby and I (Darwin, McKeown & Kirby, 1989) have recently shown that these changes in the relative amplitudes of formants produce shifts in the F1 boundary between /bɪt/ and /bɛt/ that can be removed by embedding the word in a similarly filtered carrier sentence. The mechanisms responsible for this compensation are probably the same as those that allow us to recognise as similar nonspeech timbres produced under different listening conditions.

These two examples, reverberation and spectral balance, show first that natural listening conditions can distort or remove cues to phonetic categories. They also show that listeners can compensate for these changes provided they are given a sufficient context to allow them to estimate their extent.

Extraneous Sounds

The most pervasive characteristic of natural sound is that it is a mixture of the output from many different sound sources. The silent episodes of one source are filled by the sounds of the rest. Only the spectral peaks of a sound may emerge from the background, and they will be joined by those of other sources. To disentangle from this mixture a clear phonetic percept requires all the accumulated skill of our auditory and phonetic processes. The problem of extraneous sounds is not unique to speech any more than are the problems of reverberation and distance described previously, so there is at least a *prima facie* case for supposing that the prespeech auditory system has evolved methods for coping with the problem. The evolutionarily recent speech module could do worse than to take advantage of its forebear's talents. We will review experiments on this issue in some detail after we have looked more closely at the concept of sound source.

Sounds and Sources

What do we mean by a "sound source?" Just as in vision there is a hierarchy of objects to which our attention can be directed (e.g., a serif on a letter in a word on a label on a panel on a computer monitor), so the term "sound source" should be seen as hierarchical (the scratchy attack of the bottom note of the chord of the first violin in the string quartet). A well-known example is the sound of a bell, which at one level is a single source, but which can be heard as consisting of changing patterns of different groups of harmonics. Perception usually makes us aware of only the highest level of source, unless we listen analytically.

Speech itself can be regarded as consisting of multiple sound sources: plosive bursts, frication, aspiration, and voicing exciting different parts of a vocal tract that is subject to discontinuous changes in its transfer function. It is also particularly hard to listen to speech analytically. Helmholtz (1954/1885) commented for example, on the difficulty of hearing out the individual harmonics in a speech sound:

> The partial tones of the human voice are comparatively most difficult to distinguish . . . Nevertheless they were distinguished even by Rameau (1726) without the assistance of any apparatus. (p. 51)

Then he offered his explanation, which is based on experience rather than an innate mechanism:

> The reason for this difficulty is most probably that we have all our lives remarked and observed the tones of the human voice more than any other, and always with the sole purpose of grasping it as a whole and obtaining a clear knowledge and perception of its manifold changes of quality. (p. 104)

A parsimonious way of dealing with sound that is a mixture of such hierarchical sources would be to apply different levels of constraint at different places in the hierarchy (cf. Marr, 1982, for vision). Thus, for example, common onset-time, repetition, and continuity are sensible constraints to apply at the bottom of a hierarchy where we are concerned with primitive mechanical events of one object hitting another whose resonances remain steady or change smoothly. Such constraints could provide a preliminary grouping of spectral primitives that would make explicit spectral properties that were not apparent in the original sound. Thus, for example, if one component of a complex sound starts earlier than the remainder, it might be grouped separately from them, resulting in it being more easily heard out (Rasch, 1981) or more easily incorporated into a rhythmic grouping with other sounds (Dannenbring & Bregman, 1978), with a consequent reduction in the richness of the perceived timbre of the remaining complex (Bregman & Pinker, 1978). Such effects are readily demonstrated with nonspeech sounds, providing experimental evidence that primitive "scene analysis" operations exist. Our own experiments using simple speech sounds, which are described in the next section, indicate that these scene analysis mechanisms are not preempted by the specifically phonetic mechanisms of the phonetic module.

Perceptual Grouping Prior To Phonetic Categorization

The experiments described in this section attempt to extend to the perception of single speech sounds the findings of Bregman and his associates on the perceptual organization of repeated sequences of nonspeech sounds. The significance of the experiments for the present chapter is that they address directly the question of the relationship between mechanisms that are specifically phonetic—the speech module—and mechanisms that have a more general auditory function.

The phonetic module maps acoustic properties onto phonetic categories. However, as we have seen above, the normal listening conditions of the environment change the acoustic properties of a particular phone: Silences are filled by reverberation; spectral slopes are altered by the transfer function between the speaker and the listener, and existing spectral peaks are masked and new peaks added by extraneous sound sources. These perturbations apply to all sound, and must be overcome before sounds can be recognised in the normal environment.

Arguing along these lines leads us to suppose that there are general auditory mechanisms that have evolved to cope with the constancy problem posed by environmental effects on sound and that these mechanisms precede the phonetic module. This prediction is directly opposed to the claim by Whalen and Liberman (1987) and by Mattingly and Liberman (in press) that the phonetic module takes precedence over nonspeech perception. We have already seen in Watkins' experiments on reverberation and in our own on spectral balance that some adulterations produced by the environment can be compensated for. We now turn to the problem of additional sound sources. The following experiments provide a test of these opposing views by asking whether the phonetic category produced by the phonetic module can be influenced by auditory grouping mechanisms.

Onset-Time Differences and Continuity

Our experiments take the simplest case of a speech sound with an additional sound source—a single speaker intoning a steady vowel in the presence of a pure tone at the same frequency, amplitude, and phase as one of the harmonics of the vowel close to its first formant.

The effect on the vowel spectrum of adding this tone is to boost the intensity of that harmonic by 6dB. If the listener considers this energy increase to be part of the vowel, then there will be an apparent change in the first formant (F1) frequency. In our experiments, this shift in the apparent F1 frequency results in a change in the measured phoneme boundary along an F1 continuum between /ɪ/ and /ɛ/.

If, on the other hand, the listener is given some clue that the added tone is indeed an additional sound source, then we would hope that he would be able to recover the original vowel colour from the mixture, and the phoneme boundary would return to its original position.

In a number of experiments (Darwin, 1984a, 1984b; Darwin & Sutherland, 1984), we investigated the effects of varying the relative onset and offset times of the original vowel and the tone. We measured the /ɪ/–/ɛ/ phoneme boundary along the original F1 continuum both with no additional tone and under various conditions of added tone. When the added tone is strictly simultaneous with the vowel, it is taken by the listener to be part of the vowel[1], and there is a shift in the perceived F1 frequency detected as a change in the measured phoneme boundary.

However, consider now the case where the added energy starts or stops at a different time from the original vowel. This is illustrated in the top row of panels in Fig. 10.1. The physical spectrum during the vowel still has the energy of the 500 Hz component boosted by 6dB, but now there is a clue to the listener that

---

[1]There are limits to the increase in energy of a harmonic that can be heard as part of a vowel. If the energy of a single harmonic is boosted too much, it ceases to make any additional change to vowel quality and is heard as a separate sound (Darwin, 1984b). This effect is discussed following.

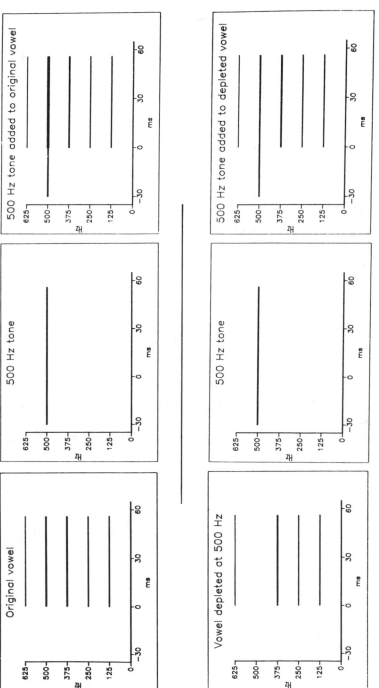

FIG. 10.1. Schematic narrow-band spectrograms of the F1 region of various sounds. The top row of panels illustrates the effect of adding a 500 Hz tone to a vowel near the /ɪ/–/ɛ/ phoneme boundary. The tone has the same amplitude and phase as the 500 Hz component in the vowel but starts thirty milliseconds earlier. The bottom row shows the effect of adding the same tone to a vowel that is similar but lacks the 500 Hz component.

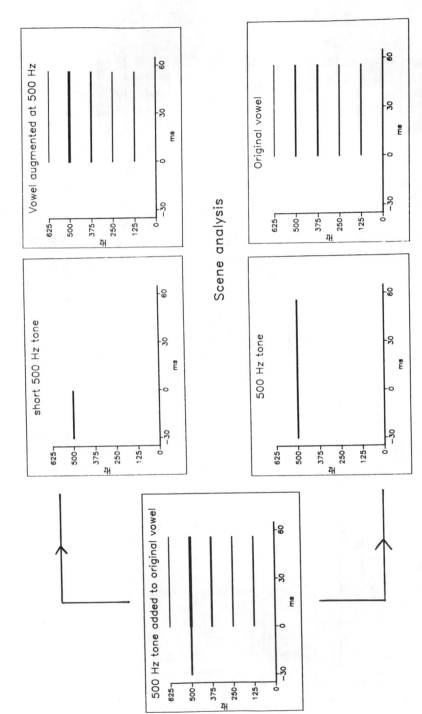

FIG. 10.2. Predictions of how listeners should perceive the stimulus constructed as in the top row of FIG. 10.1 according to the hypothesis that speech perception mechanisms pre-empt auditory perception (top) and according to the hypothesis that auditory scene analysis processes first limit the alternatives considered by the speech processing mechanism (bottom).

perhaps not all that energy originates from the vowel. Listeners do in fact exploit that clue and hear this sound as illustrated schematically in the lower panels of Fig. 10.2. They hear the 500 Hz tone continuing through the vowel, which now has a perceived F1 close to its original value. The perceived vowel is then not one that corresponds to the physically present spectrum, but rather one that corresponds to the physical spectrum minus the additional tone. This recovery of the original vowel occurs provided that the tone starts more than a few tens of milliseconds before the vowel, or (if the vowel is short) stops more than about 100 ms after it.

The experiment is simple, and the results seem intuitively plausible, if not obvious. However, the results are incompatible with the notion proposed by Whalen and Liberman (1987) that phonetic mechanisms preempt mechanisms of auditory perceptual organisation. The predictions of a pre-empting hypothesis are shown in the top row of panels in Fig. 10.2. If they did preempt, then having the tone lead the vowel should make no difference to the vowel quality; subjects should hear the vowel quality equivalent to a vowel with the boosted 500 Hz component plus a short tone that stops as the vowel starts.

The prediction of the pre-empting hypothesis is especially clear in another condition that we ran. Here we added the tone to a vowel that had already been depleted at the tone's frequency (Fig. 10.1, bottom row). The effect of adding the extra tone was then to produce a spectrum identical to the original vowel, that is, one produced by a serial formant synthesiser. So beautiful an example of a speech sound should be pounced on by the pre-empting phonetic module, leaving the additional percept of a short tone protruding from the front of the vowel and stopping as the vowel starts. However, that is not what we found. As in the first experiment, the leading tone is heard as continuing through the vowel, which is heard as having a quality equivalent to one depleted in energy at the tone's frequency (see Fig. 10.3).

The auditory grouping or scene analysis mechanisms are using onset-time differences to segregate a potential additional sound source and invoking a principle of continuity to extend it through the subsequent vowel. It then presents to the subsequent phonetic module a vowel that is less speech-like than the one that is present in the original spectrum.

A similar conclusion can also be drawn from one of the conditions of an earlier experiment (Darwin, 1981) whose main purpose was to investigate the role of pitch in the grouping of speech sounds. This experiment exploited the fact that a three-formant synthesis of the syllable /li/ can be changed to /ru/ by adding an extra formant track between /li/'s first and second formants (see Fig. 10.4). When all four formants are excited at the same pitch, and they start and stop simultaneously, then the dominant percept is /ru/. The condition of interest for present purposes extrapolates forwards the transition at the front of the added formant. This has the effect of reducing the /ru/ responses by about two-thirds and increasing the /li/ responses by half. Again, phonetic pre-empting should

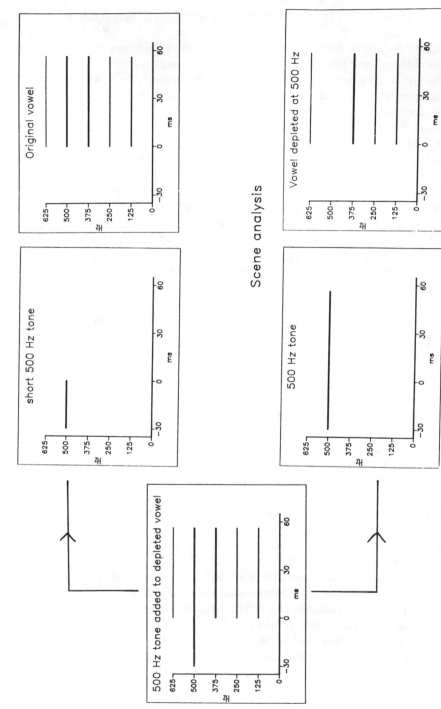

FIG. 10.3. Same as FIG. 10.2 but using the stimulus from the bottom row of FIG. 10.1.

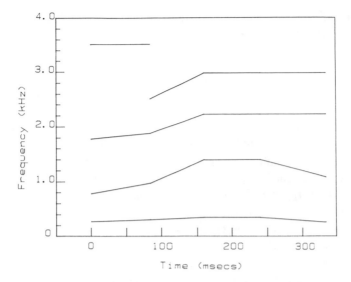

FIG. 10.4. Formant tracks of composite /ru/–/li/ syllable. F1, F2, and F3 come from /ru/; F1, F3, and F4 come from /li/.

predict no change, with the extrapolation being heard as a chirp that stops with the start of the remaining formants. What in fact happens is that continuity constraints between the extrapolated transition and its continuation into the syllable tend to remove it before the phonetic module can perceive it.

In summary, continuity of a particular frequency component or of the track of a formant peak is able to remove particular components or features from the ensemble that the phonetic module looks at. We also find similar effects with repetition of simple acoustic events.

Repetition

If a tone added at the frequency of one of the harmonics of a steady-state vowel can be removed by making it start or stop at a different time from the rest of the vowel, can we achieve a similar result by playing a sequence of tones before a vowel at the same frequency, intensity, and duration as a tone that has been added to the vowel? Three experiments performed with Roy Gardner and Helen Pattison (Pattison, Gardner, & Darwin, 1986; Darwin & Gardner, 1987; Darwin, Pattison, & Gardner, 1989) have addressed this question. We used a similar paradigm to that used for onset times, measuring the /ɪ/–/ɛ/ phoneme boundary for various F1 continua. Energy was added to each member of the original continuum at 500 Hz to produce a 6 dB increase in the energy of the 500 Hz component. This continuum was then embedded in various tone sequences and the phoneme boundary measured again. The experiments allow us to draw the following conclusions:

1. If a tone at the frequency of a harmonic of a vowel is repeated before the vowel (in our case 10 times a second), then it can remove added energy at its frequency. One token before the vowel works significantly; the effect asymptotes (with almost complete removal) by 4 repetitions before the vowel and is greater if the tone is also repeated after the vowel. This result is not expected according to phonetic pre-empting.

2. When a descending sequence of tones precedes the vowel, with the sequence designed to predict a tone in the vowel at the frequency of the added energy, we find results similar to those found with a steady sequence, though less strong.

3. However, an ascending sequence of tones that also predicts the appropriate frequency has almost no effect.

4. The effects of the ascending and descending tonal series can be predicted from the separate effects of their individual tones; we do not appear to use the contour of the tone sequence to predict the position of the tone embedded in the vowel.

Repetition of a simple tone, thus, leads to its being removed from the vowel percept. However, the mechanisms that produce this effect appear not to be able to exploit predictive effects of a sequence of rising or falling tones. This result fits nicely with the notion, adumbrated earlier, that perception exploits a hierarchy of constraints based on a hierarchy of sources.

Mechanisms at the lowest level organize sound according to very simple constraints such as onset-time, continuity, and repetition, providing a more abstract redescription of the incoming spectra. Following a principle of least commitment, more arbitrary constraints such as are present in our tone sequences should not be applied at this early stage. Once this low-level organization has been achieved, then constraints such as those of the phonetic module or those learned about specific nonspeech sounds can sensibly be applied.

Thus far in our discussion, we have not mentioned the role that pitch or a common harmonic structure plays in grouping speech sounds. The issue is complex, partly because the mechanisms of pitch perception themselves are still somewhat puzzling.

Pitch

Algorithms for separating the speech of two different speakers rely extensively on the two voices having instantaneously different fundamental frequencies (Assmann & Summerfield, 1987; Gardner, 1988; Parsons, 1976; Scheffers, 1983;

Stubbs & Summerfield, 1988; Weintraub, 1987) and different pitch contours (Parsons, 1976). It is also clear that human listeners find it easier to identify pairs of simultaneous vowels (Assmann & Summerfield, 1987; Scheffers, 1983; Zwicker, 1984) or indeed continuous speech from two speakers (Brokx & Nooteboom, 1982), when they are on different rather than the same fundamental frequency. The mechanisms responsible for this advantage are not yet understood, but it is likely that they share many properties with those of pitch perception, because both depend on the quasiperiodicity of the voiced signal.

Our own experiments on the separation of the speech of one speaker from other simultaneous sounds have demonstrated the use of harmonic structure both at the level of individual harmonics (Darwin & Gardner, 1986) and for individual formants (Darwin, 1981; Gardner, Gaskill & Darwin, 1989).

Both our own and others' experiments on this topic clearly show that components that do not share a common fundamental frequency are more likely to be excluded from the phonetic percept than those that do share a common fundamental. This conclusion goes against the claim of Mattingly and Liberman (in press) that "phonetic perception does not depend on the output representations of the module(s) for pitch." Their conclusion was based on the results of experiments on duplex perception. The observation here is that sounds on different fundamentals *can* contribute to the same phonetic percept: A chirp on one fundamental can combine with a base on a different fundamental to give a stop consonant percept. However, the conclusion exceeds the data. "May ignore," yes; "does not depend on," no! Take an analogous example from vision: We can readily perceive a square, if two of its sides are red and two blue. However, it is wrong to claim that form perception does not depend on the output of color mechanisms, because we can clearly see a square that is isoluminant with its background but a different hue. Mattingly and Liberman's claim would be justified, only if the pitch of a formant *never* influenced the extent to which it was incorporated into a phonetic percept. However, the evidence that formants, or indeed individual harmonics, can be excluded from a phonetic percept on the basis of differences in fundamental frequency is now indisputable. I will give two experimental examples from our own work.

The first is based on experiments from Brian Moore and his colleagues on pitch perception (Moore, Glasberg, & Peters, 1985). They discovered that if a single harmonic of a complex tone were mistuned by less than about 3%, it would continue to make a full contribution to the overall pitch. However, if it were mistuned by more than that, it made progressively less contribution, until by 8% it made little or no contribution to the pitch of the complex. A subsequent experiment (Moore, Peters, & Glasberg, 1985) also showed that listeners could hear out the mistuned harmonic at around 2% mistuning, so the harmonic starts to make a reduced contribution to pitch at around the degree of mistuning that is required for it to begin to be heard out. If a harmonic may be excluded from the calculation of pitch by virtue of being mistuned, can it also be excluded from the calculation of formant frequencies?

To answer this question, we (Darwin & Gardner, 1986) used the /ɪ/-/ɛ/ continuum described earlier. One of the harmonics of the vowel, near to the first formant frequency was progressively mistuned (see Fig. 10.5) and the resulting phoneme boundary between /ɪ/ and /ɛ/ measured. If the criterion for exclusion from the formant calculation is the same as that for exclusion from pitch, then we should find that mistuning the harmonic produces little effect on vowel perception until it exceeds 3%. Greater mistuning should have progressively more effect, until by around 8% the vowel quality should be the same, as if the mistuned component were physically absent. Our results showed that changes in vowel color did occur in the appropriate directions, although by 8% mistuning the effect was not complete.

The second experimental example (Gardner, Gaskill, & Darwin, 1989) looks at the effect of mistuning the harmonics within an entire formant region and uses the /ru/-/li/ paradigm described earlier (Darwin, 1981). Here a four-formant composite syllable is used whose percept can be changed from /ru/ to /li/ by changing the fundamental frequency of the second formant, thus causing it to be perceptually grouped out from the remaining formants (see Fig. 10.4). As the fundamental frequency of the second formant of the four-formant complex is changed from that of the remaining formants, two things happen. First, the formant with the different fundamental is heard as a separate sound, although it still contributes to the overall phonetic percept that stays predominantly at /ru/. This stage is equivalent to that of the duplex perception of chirps and base syllables. However, as the pitch difference increases, the odd formant contributes less and less to the phonetic percept that becomes entirely /li/. Duplex perception is, thus, an intermediate stage between full integration and full segregation.

In terms of a hierarchical view of auditory organization, grouping on the basis of a common fundamental identifies harmonically related sets of frequency components as two "sources." The phonetic module will be more likely to take together those components that share a common pitch, but its own phonetic constraints will, where necessary, override the separation induced by the pitch difference. In whispered or breathy voice, the phonetic module has to take together formants whose excitation is uncorrelated, although I know of no specifically phonetic reason why it should tolerate two distinct fundamentals in different parts of the spectrum.

Two points have emerged: First, subjects may be able to identify a formant or harmonic as separate by virtue of its different pitch whereas it continues to contribute to the phonetic category; second, a pitch difference can be a sufficient cue to segregate a formant or harmonic from others before phonetic classification. The first point confirms the empirical basis for Mattingly and Liberman's claim that the phonetic module is independent of the output of the pitch processor; the second disconfirms it.

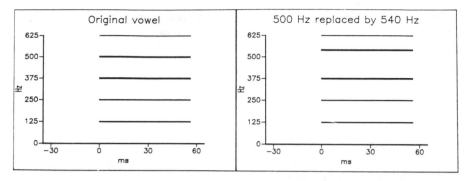

FIG. 10.5. Schematic narrow-band spectrogram of the F1 region of a vowel near the /ɪ/-/ɛ/ phoneme boundary (left) and the same vowel but with the 500 Hz component mistuned by 40 Hz (right).

The Relationship between Auditory and Speech Mechanisms

The main conclusion of the first part of this chapter was that there are some basic mechanisms of auditory organization that influence how the speech module categorises a particular sound. Thus, the relative onset-times of speech components and also their harmonic relations limit the interpretations that the speech module can make.

Beyond this bald conclusion, we can glimpse some of the complexities of the mechanisms involved by considering a little more closely two of the experiments that I have already described.

First, let us look more closely at the experiment in which one harmonic of a vowel starts before the rest. The basic result is that the unsynchronized harmonic is perceptually segregated from the vowel, and the simple interpretation is that the segregation is done on the basis of the relative onset-times of the harmonics. However, if a difference in onset-time always produced perceptual segregation, then normal fluent speech would lose its coherence: The leading higher formants of an aspirated stop would segregate from the delayed voiced first formant, and bursts would lose their aspirations. To prevent our perceptual world being so fragmented, the phonetic module must combine into a single phonetic whole the multiple auditory objects that the earlier primitive grouping mechanisms feed it. When those primitive groupings produce objects that the phonetic module cannot combine coherently, then we perceive additional sound sources.

However, we can also perceive additional sound sources even when the primitive auditory mechanisms have *not* segregated the input on the basis of timing or harmonicity. If one harmonic of a vowel is boosted substantially, it does not dominate the perception of formant frequency as it would if it continued to make a full contribution to vowel quality; rather, it is heard as a separate tone along with a vowel that has taken some but not all of its amplitude (Darwin, 1984b). Segregation has occurred, although the boosted harmonic is perfectly in tune and starts and stops at the same time as the other harmonics. Part of the energy of the boosted harmonic has been discounted by some mechanism (such as the phonetic module) that is aware of the likely formant bandwidths for speech.[2]

The perceptual segregation of sound into speech and other sounds is not something that can be achieved simply on the basis of primitive grouping operations. The phonetic module takes multiple primitive groupings and assembles them into a coherent phonetic interpretation. Therefore, what at a low level of grouping appears to be multiple sources becomes a single speech stream. The phonetic module is also capable of rejecting, on phonetic grounds, groupings that satisfy lower level constraints. Thus, part of the energy at a harmonic frequency can be discarded in order to obtain a phonetically plausible formant bandwidth.

However, as previous sections of this chapter were at pains to point out, the phonetic module is not unrestricted in the interpretations that it can impose on the raw auditory information. Primitive grouping operations that are sensitive to very simple constraints on sound production limit the interpretation that the phonetic module can make.

Contrasting Speech Constraints with General Auditory Constraints

In the final part of this chapter, I will illustrate the need for speech-specific mechanisms with some evidence that arose from combining two paradigms, one from Dannenbring (1976) on auditory continuity effects and the other from Strange's silent-centre syllable school of speech science (e.g., Strange, Verbrugge, Shankweiler, & Edman, 1976). The speech stimuli that we used derive from an older experiment by Lindblom and Studdert-Kennedy (1967) in which they found that rapidly articulated syllables were heard as having more extreme vowels than those actually reached by the formant tracks. The results drew attention to the importance of constraints on articulatory dynamics for speech perception.

Dannenbring found that if a sine wave whose frequency is modulated by a triangular waveform is masked by noise near the apex of the modulating triangle, subjects will hear the sine wave as continuing behind the noise. However, the maximum frequency heard will not exceed the maximum excursion of the un-

---

[2]It is important to realise that the process of segregation may involve *part* of the energy at a particular frequency (see Bregman, 1987). 80 dB of energy at a particular harmonic frequency is compatible with one source having around 80 dB of energy and any number of other sources having a few dB less at the same time. Therefore, the speech module has only to recognise that the available evidence is compatible with its expectations based on the amplitude of the other harmonics.

masked waveform. The perceptual system interpolates between the unmasked frequencies rather than extrapolating the slope at the point at which the masking starts or stops. We wanted to see whether similar results held for speech sounds.

The point of the experiment was to see whether Dannenbring's result, that interrupted frequency transitions are not extrapolated, also applied to the interpretation of speech sounds. We suspected that speech sounds might not give the same result as Dannenbring obtained for nonspeech, because our speech perceptual apparatus is very sensitive to the dynamic constraints of speech production. Lindblom and Studdert-Kennedy's subjects heard different vowels, depending on the dynamics of the formant transitions. Would our subjects interpret interrupted formant transitions in a way that suggested an extrapolation based on the dynamics of the formant transitions?

A speech analogue of Dannenbring's experiment was performed by Joe Hancock as an undergraduate project and subsequently refined by Susan Dye as part of her graduate work. The experiments used the syllables /jɪj/, /jæj/, and /jɛj/, whose formant transitions make U or inverted Us of decreasing depths. The formant tracks for the /jæj/ syllable are shown in Fig. 10.6. The /jɛj/ and /jɪj/

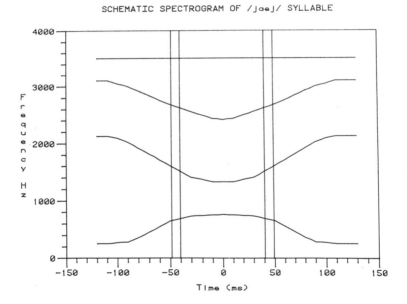

SCHEMATIC SPECTROGRAM OF /jɑej/ SYLLABLE

FIG. 10.6.   Formant tracks for synthetic /jæj/ syllable. The outer pair of vertical lines marks the position of the /jæj/–/jɛj/ phoneme boundary for the silent-center condition where different durations of silence replaced the center of the syllable. The inner pair of vertical lines marks the boundary for the interpolated condition where the formant tracks were interpolated between the values reached at the limits of the corresponding silent-center condition.

formants make less extreme excursions. We created various continua of sounds from these three basic syllables by replacing different durations of formant transition symmetrically about the center of the symmetrical synthetic stimuli either with silence, with noise, or with an interpolated (flat) formant track. As the centers of the syllables are removed, the vowel percept changes to a more closed vowel (/æ/ -> /ɛ/ -> /I/). The question we asked was whether the phoneme boundaries occurred at the same place for the different continua. Dannenbring's results with nonspeech frequency sweeps indicate that the auditory system does not extrapolate beyond the end of an interrupted sweep. If speech sounds behave like nonspeech, then the phoneme bondary would be in the same position for noise, silent, or interpolated centers. However, if subjects can use the dynamic properties of the formant transitions to interpret the vowel (as Strange et al.'s and Lindblom & Studdert-Kennedy's experiments suggest), then we might expect the noise-centered and the silent-centered syllables to be heard as more extreme (open) than the syllables in which the formant tracks have been interpolated across the center portion.

We asked the subjects to label the continua as /jɪj/, /jɛj/, or /jæj/. Hancock's experiment demonstrates no difference between the noise and the silent condition, thus, Dye's replication uses only the silent-center condition. Her results and Hancock's show that when the phoneme boundary lies at a point where the formant transition is moving rapidly (as with the /jæj/–/jɛj/ boundary on the /jæj/-based continuum), the interpolated condition gives a different phoneme boundary from the silent-center condition (see Fig. 10.7). The direction of the difference is that the silent-center condition is heard as more extreme (a more open vowel) than the interpolated condition.

The main result[3] then is to reveal an effect with speech sounds that Dannenbring did not find with simple frequency sweeps, namely that the speech-perceptual system behaves as if it extrapolated frequency contours. The silent-center syllables are heard as more open than the interpolated vowels. This apparent extrapolation is an indication that the phonetic module, being more specialized, can exploit more specific constraints than can the more primitive and eclectic mechanisms responsible for Dannenbring's continuity effect.

These experiments complement our work on grouping described in the previous part of the chapter. The grouping experiments demonstrate how low-level constraints that are common to speech and other sounds help to organize the auditory input for subsequent interpretation by a phonetic module. The present experiments illustrate the phonetic module at work, using constraints on speech production (that are not common to the production of other sounds) to interpret grouped auditory information.

---

[3]A subsidiary point made by these experiments is that vowel quality is not *just* determined by the formant transitions. If the steady-state made no contribution, then the phoneme boundaries in the silent-center and interpolated conditions should have been the same. They were not.

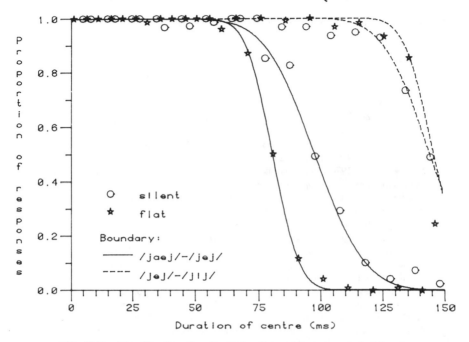

FIG. 10.7. Identification functions for the continua created either by replacing the centre of a /jæj/ syllable with silence (circles) or by interpolating a flat formant contour across the same duration interval (stars).

Conclusions

The chapter demonstrates that general auditory grouping principles do influence the way that we hear speech sounds. In auditory terms, speech can be thought of as a multiple source that has its own unique constraints. The speech module puts together those groupings of sound from an early stage in auditory processing that fulfill its own criteria and that are then interpreted in terms of constraints on the dynamics of vocal tract movement.

Acknowledgments

The research was supported by the UK SERC on grants GR/D 28768, GR/C 8522.1, and GR/D 65930.

References

Assmann, P., & Summerfield, Q. (1987). Perceptual segregation of concurrent vowels. *Journal of the Acoustical Society of America, 82*(S1), S120.

Bregman, A. S. (1978). The formation of auditory streams. In J. Requin (Ed.), *Attention and performance VII*. Hillsdale, NJ: Lawrence Erlbaum Associates.

Bregman, A. S. (1987). The meaning of duplex perception: Sounds as transparent objects. In M. E. H. Schouten (Ed.), *The psychophysics of speech perception* (pp. 95–111). NATO ASI Series. Dordrecht: M. Nijhoff.

Bregman, A. S., & Pinker, S. (1978). Auditory streaming and the building of timbre. *Canadian Journal of Psychology, 32,* 19–31.

Brokx, J. P. L., & Nooteboom, S. G. (1982). Intonation and perceptual separation of simultaneous voices. *Journal of Phonetics, 10,* 23–36.

Dannenbring, G. L. (1976). Perceived auditory continuity with alternately rising and falling frequency transitions. *Canadian Journal of Psychology, 30,* 99–114.

Dannenbring, G. L., & Bregman, A. S. (1978). Streaming vs. fusion of sinusoidal components of complex tones. *Perception and Psychophysics, 24,* 369–376.

Darwin, C. J. (1981). Perceptual grouping of speech components differing in fundamental frequency and onset-time. *Quarterly Journal of Experimental Psychology, 33A,* 185–208.

Darwin, C. J. (1984a). Auditory processing and speech perception. In H. Bouma and D. G. Bouwhuis (Eds.), *Attention and performance X: Control of language processes* (pp. 197–210). Hillsdale, NJ: Lawrence Erlbaum Associates.

Darwin, C. J. (1984b). Perceiving vowels in the presence of another sound: Constraints on formant perception. *Journal of the Acoustical Society of America, 76,* 1636–1647.

Darwin, C. J., & Gardner, R. B. (1986). Mistuning a harmonic of a vowel: Grouping and phase effects on vowel quality. *Journal of the Acoustical Society of America, 79,* 838–845.

Darwin, C. J., & Gardner, R. B. (1987). Perceptual separation of vowels from concurrent sounds. In M. E. H. Schouten (Ed.), *The psychophysics of speech perception* (pp. 112–124). Dordrecht: M. Nijhoff.

Darwin, C. J., McKeown, J. D., & Kirby, D. (1989). Compensation for transmission channel and speaker effects on vowel quality. *Speech Communication, 8,* 221–234.

Darwin, C. J., Pattison, H., & Gardner, R. B. (1989). Vowel quality changes produced by surrounding tone sequences. *Perception & Psychophysics, 45,* 333–342.

Darwin, C. J., & Sutherland, N. S. (1984). Grouping frequency components of vowels: When is a harmonic not a harmonic? *Quarterly Journal of Experimental Psychology, 36A*(2), 193–208.

Gardner, R. B. (1988, August). *An algorithm for separating simultaneous speech sounds.* Paper presented at 7th FASE Symposium, Edinburgh.

Gardner, R. B., Gaskill, S. A., & Darwin, C. J. (1989). Perceptual grouping of formants with static and dynamic differences in fundamental frequency. *Journal of the Acoustical Society of America, 85,* 1329–1337.

Helmholtz, H. (1954). *On the sensations of tone.* (A. J. Ellis, Trans.). New York: Dover. (Original work published 1885)

Lindblom, B. E. F., & Studdert-Kennedy, M. G. (1967). On the role of formant transitions in speech perception. *Journal of the Acoustical Society of America, 42,* 803–843.

Marr, D. (1982). *Vision.* New York: Freeman.

Mattingly, I. G., & Liberman, A. M. (in press). Speech and other auditory modules. In G. W. Edelman, W. E. Gall, & W. M. Cowan (Eds.), *Signal and sense: Local and global order in perceptual maps.* New York: Wiley.

Mattingly, I. G., & Liberman, A. M. (1988). Specialized perceiving systems for speech and other biologically significant sounds. In G. W. Edelman, W. E. Gall, & W. M. Cowan (Eds.), *Auditory function: The neurobiological bases of hearing* (pp. 775–793). New York: Wiley.

Moore, B. C. J., Glasberg, B. R., & Peters, R. W. (1985). Relative dominance of individual partials in determining the pitch of complex tones. *Journal of the Acoustical Society of America, 77*, 1853–1860.

Moore, B. C. J., Peters, R. W., & Glasberg, B. R. (1985). Thresholds for the detection of inharmonicity in complex tones. *Journal of the Acoustical Society of America, 77*, 1861–1868.

Parsons, T. W. (1976). Separation of speech from interfering speech by means of harmonic selection. *Journal of the Acoustical Society of America, 60*, 656–660.

Pattison, H., Gardner, R. B., & Darwin, C. J. (1986). Effects of acoustical context on perceived vowel quality. *Journal of the Acoustical Society of America, 80*(S1), S110–111.

Rasch, R. (1981). *Aspects of the perception and performance of polyphonic music.* Utrecht: Elinkwijk.

Scheffers, M. T. (1983). *Sifting vowels: Auditory pitch analysis and sound segregation.* Unpublished doctoral dissertation, Groningen University, The Netherlands.

Strange, W., Verbrugge, R., Shankweiler, D., & Edman, T. (1976). Consonant environment specifies vowel identity. *Journal of the Acoustical Society of America, 60*, 213–224.

Stubbs, R. J., & Summerfield, A. Q. (1988, August). *Separation of simultaneous voices.* Paper presented at the 7th FASE Symposium, Edinburgh.

Watkins, A. J. (1988, July). *Effects of room reverberation on the fricative/affricate distinction.* Paper presented at the Second Franco-British Speech Meeting, University of Sussex.

Weintraub, M. (1987). Sound separation and auditory perceptual organization. In M. E. H. Schouten (Ed.), *The psychophysics of speech perception* (pp. 125–134). NATO ASI Series. Dordrecht: M. Nijhoff.

Whalen, D. H., & Liberman, A. M. (1987). Speech perception takes precedence over nonspeech perception. *Science, 237*, 169–171.

Zwicker, U. T. (1984). Auditory recognition of diotic and dichotic vowel pairs. *Speech Communication, 3*, 265–277.

Comment: Around Duplex Perception

Bruno H. Repp

Haskins Laboratories

Darwin's interesting presentation was obviously stimulated by the recent writings of Mattingly and Liberman, particularly their latest paper entitled "Speech and other auditory modules" (Mattingly & Liberman, in press). My comments fall into three groups. The first few remarks concern differences in the experimental paradigms relied on by Darwin and by the Haskins researchers. Then I have a few comments on the duplex perception situation as interpreted by Mattingly and Liberman. Finally, I would like to speculate on the possible mechanism of dichotic integration in the duplex perception task. (For a description of that task in this volume, see Fowler & Rosenblum, chap. 3).

Darwin concluded on the basis of his evidence that speech perception is dependent on the outcome of auditory scene analysis, whereas Mattingly and Liberman have concluded exactly the opposite. These conclusions derive from different experimental situations, however. Many of Darwin's experiments concern the integration of a *single harmonic* into the overall spectral pattern of the stimulus. The Haskins experiments, on the other hand, rely exclusively on duplex perception where the integration of *formants* is at stake. Now, it is quite possible that auditory scene analysis does most of its work before the spectral pattern is recoded into more abstract auditory parameters, such as formant frequencies, which require integration across a number of harmonics (see, e.g., Darwin & Gardner, 1985). If so, the duplex perception paradigm may be less sensitive to factors that cause auditory source segregation. Note also that Darwin's task is set up to be highly sensitive to the perceived *intensity* of a particular harmonic, whereas the duplex perception paradigm is not similarly sensitive to the relative intensity of the critical formant—on the contrary, subjects' responses are unaffected by variations of relative intensities over a wide range (Rand, 1974;

Bentin & Mann, 1983). Thus, the subjects' responses in these tasks are controlled by different stimulus variables. Thus, Darwin's conclusion that auditory scene analysis occurs prior to phonetic perception still seems valid to me.

Another reason why some of Darwin's experiments were particularly sensitive to the auditory Gestalt laws governing scene analysis is that he manipulated continuity with preceding context. Darwin's most striking finding is that a tone whose onset precedes a vowel and that coincides with a harmonic of the vowel is perceptually subtracted from that harmonic. (In fact, Darwin anticipated this effect when he considered the tone to be present in the vowel, although it was not physically distinct from the vowel's harmonic.) No comparable manipulation of continuity with preceding context has been performed in the duplex perception paradigm (with the exception of a recent study by Ciocca & Bregman, 1989). Rather, most of the manipulations in that paradigm concerned parts of the stimulus that occurred simultaneously. Onset asynchrony may be a stronger segregating factor than differences in fundamental frequency, intensity, spectrum, or spatial location.

Moreover, although the experimental situations contrived by Darwin are highly artificial, they nevertheless isolate some aspects of speech perception in a noisy environment, and this may be precisely what our auditory systems are adapted for. The duplex perception paradigm, on the other hand, is not intended to simulate such a natural situation and, therefore, may confuse our auditory systems.

Darwin did refer to some of his other experiments that come closer to the duplex perception situation, those involving the /ru/-/li/ contrast. However, whereas the phonetic contrast in duplex perception experiments nearly always concerned two consonants in the same vocalic context, the /ru/-/li/ consonantal contrast is confounded with a vowel difference, and Darwin's other experiments relied solely on vowel quality distinctions. Since vowels are not perceived as categorically as consonants, this may also have contributed to the greater sensitivity of Darwin's subjects to certain stimulus variations. This is all speculative, but the bottom line is that Darwin's experiments were simply more apt to reveal the workings of auditory scene analysis than were the duplex perception experiments.

Now to some comments on duplex perception itself. Although the comments pertain primarily to the work of Mattingly and Liberman (in press), they are relevant to Darwin's presentation in so far as all these researchers are concerned with the relation between auditory processing and phonetic perception but arrive at quite different conclusions. By searching for potential weak spots in Mattingly and Liberman's impressive armor, I hope to find indirect support for Darwin's thesis that auditory processes are important in speech perception.

Mattingly and Liberman claim that the critical formant transition in the duplex stimulus is perceived in two ways at the same time: as nonspeech and as speech—that is, as a chirp and as a consonant. I concur, of course, that the chirp percept corresponds to the isolated transition as such, but I am uncomfortable with the suggestion that the transition *is* the consonant. Rather, I believe the consonant is an abstract category that is cued by the position of the critical formant in the larger spectro-temporal pattern of the speech signal (cf. Jusczyk, Smith, & Murphy, 1981). In other words, the chirp percept is analytic, whereas the speech percept is synthetic. From my perspective, therefore, the two percepts do *not* result from the same stimulus. There simply is no phonetic percept corresponding to the transition alone.

Laboratory experiments often require listeners to perceive complex auditory patterns analytically. Presenting listeners with speech, however, encourages synthetic perception, because the integrated auditory patterns of speech are familiar and meaningful. Moreover, some of the auditory patterns associated with speech, especially with stop consonants, are so complex that their components are very difficult to perceive analytically. Mattingly and Liberman are struck by the fact that the chirp-like transition of the critical formant is not heard in a regular syllable, and they conclude that, therefore, phonetic perception is not based on auditory features (or "homomorphic primitives", as they call them) but on dimensions of an entirely different sort. There are two possible objections to this conclusion: First, there may be purely auditory reasons why the transition is difficult to hear; no one has yet demonstrated that it is possible to focus on individual resonance frequencies when a complex of such frequencies changes simultaneously, often in divergent directions. These components may nevertheless be represented at some stage in auditory perception and, in principle, could act as auditory primitives. Second, instead of a collection of auditory features, a complex auditory pattern may present itself holistically to the phonetic classification mechanism. The immediate attachment of a phonetic label to this synthetic auditory percept in the perceiver's mind may suggest that nothing auditory was perceived but instead something more abstract—articulatory movements, the speaker's intention, or whatever seems closest to the phonetic units in awareness. The problem here is that *we don't know what speech (particularly a stop consonant) sounds like,* because we have no vocabulary to describe the complex auditory impression other than the phonetic labels themselves. This is the illusion of categorical perception. With these comments, I mean to challenge the assumption that phonetic perception *must* be based on primitives—that is, on *primitive* primitives. I am suggesting that, instead of heteromorphic primitives, *homomorphic complexes* may be the objects of phonetic perception (cf. Diehl & Kluender, 1989). Such complex auditory properties may bear a closer relationship to the articulatory gestures that are often said to be perceived "directly" (Mattingly & Liberman, in press; Fowler & Rosenblum, chapter 3 this volume).

The almost exclusive focus of Mattingly and Liberman on stop consonants, whose auditory correlates are particularly complex, may be responsible for some of their extreme views. Consider fricatives instead. As I showed some years ago (Repp, 1981), naive listeners perceive fricatives in vocalic contexts in terms of phonetic categories, but once their attention is drawn to the sound of the noise itself, they can make very accurate judgments about its pitch-like quality. Although I never tested this explicitly, I believe listeners can classify fricatives accurately into phonetic categories whether or not they are aware of the auditory quality of the noise. The same is most likely true for vowels, where it is not difficult to perceive timbre changes or even "hear out" individual formants while also being aware of phonetic category membership. Why should the same not be true for stop consonants? The only difference is that, because of their complex and transient nature, their auditory correlates can no longer be characterized in terms of simple dimensions such as fixed pitch or timbre; but the fact that we cannot describe the auditory quality in words does not mean it is not perceived.

Related to this observation is the question of whether the "base" in the duplex perception paradigm (that is, the ambiguous part of the syllable lacking the critical formant transition) is perceived as such. Mattingly and Liberman have emphasized that duplex perception is duplex, not triplex: Listeners do not "hear" the base, only the complete syllable and the chirp. However, subjects' verbal reports tell us only what they *think* they hear; their auditory experience is filtered through their conceptual and linguistic inventories. At the level of phonetic categories, where the listener's attention is focused, it is impossible to perceive two different syllables such as /da/ and /ga/ at the same time, especially if one of them is ambiguous. At the level of auditory perception, it is highly likely that there are only two percepts also (one of them being the chirp), but it should not be a foregone conclusion that the other auditory percept corresponds to the full syllable rather than the base. In principle, it should be possible to examine this interesting issue by means of analytic experimental techniques that somehow circumvent phonetic interpretation (e.g., selective adaptation; cf. Roberts & Summerfield, 1981).

I turn now to the final part of my comments, which concerns the possible mechanism of dichotic integration in the duplex perception situation. When duplex perception research started in earnest at Haskins Laboratories about ten years ago, the emphasis was on the simultaneous operation of two perceptual modes, speech and nonspeech. It became increasingly clear, however, that the really interesting part is the speech percept. It is not very surprising that the isolated transition is heard as a chirp, but to explain how it is perceptually integrated with the base in the other ear still poses a challenge. No corresponding types of fusion are known to occur with arbitrary nonspeech sounds, although Fowler and Rosenblum (chapter 3 this volume) have been able to obtain something similar with familiar environmental sounds. Perhaps it is the naturalness and familiarity of the complex auditory pattern that causes its reintegration when its components are split between the ears.

For the common experimental situation in which the distinction between /da/ and /ga/ is cued exclusively by the third-formant (F3) transition, it is known that the fusion is not caused by the continuity of energy in the F3 region across the two ears: Repp and Bentin (1984) showed that it makes little difference if the steady state of F3 is omitted in the base. More interestingly, the fusion is not caused by the absence of an F3 transition in the base: In unpublished follow-up research, Bentin and I pitted the isolated transition against a *full* syllable having a conflicting F3 transition. In that situation, the isolated transition competed effectively with the transition in the full syllable, and often overrode it. This situation is reminiscent of dichotic experiments conducted some years ago by Robert Porter and his colleagues in New Orleans, in which they pitted full syllables against a variety of "challenges", including isolated formants (e.g., Porter & Mirabile, 1977; Porter, Cullen, Whittaker, & Castellanos, 1981). All these studies, of course, are offspring of the standard dichotic listening paradigm in which two different full syllables are presented simultaneously (see, e.g., Halwes, 1969; Repp, 1977). The mechanism of dichotic integration in all these situations is likely to be the same.

I suspect this integration reflects not only auditory factors but spectral *relationships* and pattern coherence peculiar to natural auditory events. Several additional findings are of interest here. Repp and Bentin (1984) showed that the /da/–/ga/ distinction can be perceived when an ambiguous base is paired with just a brief steady-state F3 in the other ear. Thus, the formant onset frequency seems to be crucial, not so much the direction of the transition. Pastore, Szczesiul, Rosenblum, & Schmuckler (1982) discovered an effect whereby the syllable /pa/ in one ear was transformed into /ta/ when a burst of white noise was presented to the opposite ear. In subsequent, unpublished experiments (Pastore, personal communication), they employed a variety of filtered noises and showed that, for the effect to operate, the noise spectrum had to include the region characteristic of a /t/ release burst. It seems to have been the *relationship* between that noise and the syllable in the other ear that cued the /t/ percept.

All these examples concerned place of articulation distinctions for stop consonants. The most striking example of a relational dichotic effect, however, comes from some old dichotic research of mine (Repp, 1976) that involved the voicing distinction. When stop-consonant-vowel syllables varying in VOT were presented to one ear, and steady-state vowels of varying fundamental frequency were presented to the other ear at different stimulus-onset asynchronies (SOAs), the perception of the voicing category of the stops was affected: Stops tended to be perceived as voiced when the contralateral vowel onset preceded or lagged slightly behind the stop release, but as voiceless when the vowel lagged behind by more than about 30 ms. In other words, the SOA acted like a *cross-ear* VOT, which competed with the VOT within the stop-vowel syllable. Also, voiceless responses were increased when the fundamental frequency of the vowel in the other ear was raised. These forms of dichotic integration seem to be purely relational in character. Although we are still far from understanding their precise causes, they should draw our attention to the importance of relational variables for phonetic perception. Too often, phonetic cues have been regarded simply as independent acoustic parameters. Much significant information, however, may be contained in relational properties, and these properties may be much less sensitive to auditory factors that can segregate independent events, such as spatial separation or different fundamental frequencies. In other words, *meaningful spectral and temporal relationships may transcend the parsing mechanisms of auditory scene analysis,* and phonetic perception may rest in part on the processing of such relational information.

Acknowledgments

Preparation of these comments was supported by NICHD Grant HD–01994 and BRSG Grant RR–05596 to Haskins Laboratories. I am grateful to Alvin Liberman, Ignatius Mattingly, Lawrence Rosenblum, and Michael Studdert-Kennedy for helpful comments on an earlier draft.

References

Bentin, S., & Mann, V. A. (1983). Selective effects of masking on speech and nonspeech in the duplex perception paradigm. *Haskins Laboratories Status Report on Speech Research, SR–76,* 65–85.

Ciocca, V., & Bregman, A. S. (1989). The effects of auditory streaming on duplex perception. *Perception & Psychophysics, 46,* 39–48.

Darwin, C. J., & Gardner, R. B. (1985). Which harmonics contribute to the estimation of first formant frequency? *Speech Communication, 4,* 231–235.

Diehl, R. L., & Kluender, K. R. (1989). On the objects of speech perception. *Ecological Psychology, 1,* 121–144.

Halwes, T. G. (1969). *Effects of dichotic fusion on the perception of speech.* Unpublished doctoral dissertation, University of Minnesota.

Jusczyk, P. W., Smith, L. B., & Murphy, C. (1981). The perceptual classification of speech. *Perception & Psychophysics, 30,* 10–23.

Mattingly, I. G., & Liberman, A. M. (in press). Speech and other auditory modules. In G. M. Edelman, W. E. Gall, & W. M. Cowan (Eds.), *Signal and sense: Local and global order in perceptual maps.* New York: Wiley.

Pastore, R. E., Szczesiul, R., Rosenblum, L. D., & Schmuckler, M. (1982). When is a [p] a [t], and when is it not. *Journal of the Acoustical Society of America, 72*(Suppl. 1), S16 (Abstract).

Porter, R. J., Jr., Cullen, J. K., Whittaker, R. G., & Castellanos, F. X. (1981). Dichotic and monotic masking of CV syllables by CV second formants with different steady-state durations. *Phonetica, 38,* 252–259.

Porter, R. J., Jr., & Mirabile, P. J. (1977). Dichotic and monotic interactions between speech and nonspeech sounds at different stimulus onset asynchronies. *Perception & Psychophysics, 21,* 408–412.

Rand, T. C. (1974). Dichotic release from masking for speech. *Journal of the Acoustical Society of America, 55,* 678–680.

Repp, B. H. (1976). Dichotic "masking" of voice onset time. *Journal of the Acoustical Society of America, 59,* 183–194.

Repp, B. H. (1977). Dichotic competition of speech sounds: The role of acoustic stimulus structure. *Journal of Experimental Psychology: Human Perception and Performance, 3,* 37–50.

Repp, B. H. (1981). Two strategies in fricative discrimination. *Perception & Psychophysics, 30,* 217–227.

Repp, B. H., & Bentin, S. (1984). Parameters of spectral/temporal fusion in speech perception. *Perception & Psychophysics, 36,* 523–530.

Roberts, M., & Summerfield, Q. (1981). Audiovisual presentation demonstrates that selective adaptation in speech perception is purely auditory. *Perception & Psychophysics, 30,* 309–314.

Chapter 11

Whence the Specialization of the Language Hemisphere?

Helen J. Neville
The Salk Institute

Abstract

Employing a combined behavioral-electrophysiological approach, we have separately assessed the effects of auditory deprivation, the late and imperfect acquisition of English, and the early acquisition of American Sign Language (ASL) on cerebral organization in congenitally deaf adults. The results from sensory studies suggest that auditory deprivation alters the anterior/posterior organization of the visual system in a bilaterally symmetrical fashion. The results from language studies suggest that the acquisition of formal (i.e., grammatical) language early in development is necessary and sufficient to stabilize a genetically biased special role of the left hemisphere in language processing: Deaf subjects who have not fully acquired the grammar of English do not show specialization of the left anterior brain regions during the reading of English, but deaf subjects who score well on tests of English grammar do display the normal pattern. Similarly, deaf and hearing subjects who acquired ASL as a first language early in development display specialization of the left anterior regions for ASL, but those who acquired ASL late and imperfectly do not. Further results from nonlanguage cognitive studies suggest that the modality through which language is first acquired significantly impacts the fundamental specializations of the two hemispheres for nonlanguage processing. Together, this pattern of results suggests that there are biological constraints on the development of language-relevant brain systems, and that the mature pattern of organization is significantly impacted by specific aspects of early language input.

I had the great privilege and good fortune of meeting Alvin Liberman many years ago, when I was a graduate student struggling with the question of whether the complementary functional specializations of the hemispheres develop along with the acquisition of general cognitive abilities or with the acquisition of language per se. I had been studying cerebral specialization in congenitally deaf children of two types: those who had not acquired any language at all (but who had normal nonverbal verbal IQs) and a group who had acquired American Sign Language (ASL) from their parents. All the deaf children were in a residential school that employed the "oral" approach (i.e., their teachers were valiantly striving to teach them to produce speech). The results that I had obtained in my dissertation research were puzzling: On a picture perception task, normal children displayed right hemisphere specialization; deaf children without any language displayed no differences between the hemispheres, and deaf subjects (Ss) who knew ASL displayed left hemisphere specialization. In discussing these results with Professor Liberman, he suggested that perhaps a major clue in understanding the nature of hemispheric specializations might be the fact and the nature of the acquisition of a formal (i.e., a grammatical) language. A few years later, Professor Liberman (1974) published his ideas along these lines. He suggested that the unique function of the language hemisphere is to process grammatical recodings of linguistic information. The function of grammatical recodings is to restructure information so that it is appropriate for the mechanisms that transmit and store linguistic information. In this provocative and now classic article, Liberman discussed two types of grammatical conversions (a) that between acoustic input and the phonetic message—now known as the speech code—and (b) the grammar that links the phonetic and the semantic levels (i.e., syntax). In this chapter, I will present evidence that suggests the acquisition of competence in the second type of grammatical recoding (i.e., at the level of syntax) is both necessary and sufficient to stabilize a genetic bias for the left hemisphere to mediate language and that this occurs regardless of the modality through which language is acquired.

The approach that we have taken to these issues over the past several years has been to try to determine which factors in ontogeny are critical in setting up and stabilizing the ubiquitous specialization of the left hemisphere for language. To this end, we have studied different populations of individuals whose experience with language has or has not included the motor skills necessary for speech, the phonological decoding of language, and/or the acquisition of the grammar of a language. Following are described studies of language processing by individuals who have had specific alterations in one or more aspects of language experience. Following this is a brief summary of results from studies of nonlanguage processing that suggest that characteristics of the language first acquired (i.e., its structure and modality of transmission) determine the nature of hemispheric specializations for nonlanguage material.

Electrophysiological Method

Our approach to the study of cerebral organization in humans has been to obtain behavioral data employing standard measures of signal detection and reaction time, and to simultaneously record from electrodes placed over different regions of the scalp the electrical signals that are time-locked to discrete sensory or cognitive events such as the presentation of a flash of light or the correct recognition of a word. Averages of epochs of electrophysiological activity associated with similar stimuli or responses are termed "event-related brain potentials," or ERPs. Over the past two decades, this approach has proven to be valuable in assessing the integrity of neural systems and in elucidating the time course and subprocesses of several cognitive functions, including language (see Goff, Allison, & Vaughan, 1978; Hillyard, Picton, & Regan, 1978; Hillyard & Kutas, 1983; Kutas & Hillyard, 1984b, for reviews).

Subjects

We have employed the combined behavioral-electrophysiological approach in the study of individuals who have had a very extreme and highly specific form of altered experience. These are deaf individuals who have sustained total auditory deprivation since birth. All of our deaf subjects were born bilaterally and profoundly deaf, and they were born to deaf parents. The etiology of their deafness is genetic, in which case the cochlea does not differentiate normally. The CNS is not directly affected by the disease, and, thus, our subjects are otherwise neurologically normal (i.e., clinically) and tend to be college students as are our normally hearing control subjects.

In humans and probably in other animals as well, the impact of unimodal sensory deprivation extends well beyond the development of sensory functions. Thus, our deaf subjects, as a consequence of their auditory deprivation, have also had markedly abnormal language experience. None of them has acquired speech or any auditory language comprehension. Instead, they learned ASL from their deaf parents at the normal age for language acquisition. The perception of ASL relies heavily on peripheral vision, because in sign discourse, the eyes are typically focused on the eyes and face of the signer so that much of the signed information falls outside the foveal region. The vocabulary and grammar of ASL make extensive use of visual space and of modulations of hand movements. For example, the same handshape presented at different locations or with different motions can convey different semantic or grammatical information (Klima & Bellugi, 1979).

In several studies, we have compared cerebral organization in deaf and hearing subjects during different sensory, cognitive, and language tasks. In order to dissociate the influences of auditory deprivation and the acquisition of a visual sign language on the differences between deaf and hearing subjects, we compare these results with those from a third group of subjects: These are normal hearing individuals born to deaf parents (HD subjects). These people have acquired ASL as a first language like the deaf subjects but have not experienced any auditory deprivation. All of our hearing, deaf, and HD subjects are strongly and equally right-handed, as measured by the Edinburgh Inventory of Handedness.

Language Processing

Considerable controversy still surrounds the nature of the special function of the left hemisphere in language processing, the degree to which this function may be determined at birth, and the role that experience might play in the left hemisphere's development. Clinical studies of hemispherectomized patients show that early in development, each hemisphere has similar if not identical capabilities to sustain language and other cognitive skills. However, little is known about the role of language experience in reducing the redundancy and increasing the specificity of hemispheric function in ontogeny. If language experience does impact cerebral development, then aspects of cerebral specialization ought to be different in deaf and hearing Ss when they read English. Hearing people learn English first through the auditory modality, and they utilize this information in learning to read. According to several studies, when hearing Ss read, they translate the visual word to an auditory sound (so-called phonological decoding). On the other hand, deaf Ss apparently do not perform this visual-auditory phonological conversion (Conrad, 1977). Would these different experiences result in different patterns of cerebral activity during reading?

Hemifield Studies

English

To study this issue, we developed a paradigm that produced reliable evidence of cerebral specialization during reading in normal adults, and then compared the results from deaf subjects tested on the same paradigm. Briefly (see Neville, Kutas, & Schmidt, 1982a; Neville, Kutas, & Schmidt, 1984), words were projected to the left (LVF) or right (RVF) visual field or bilaterally for 100 ms, and, two seconds following word onset, Ss wrote the word. Every hearing S reported the words more accurately after they were presented to the RVF (i.e., to the left hemisphere), thus providing behavioral evidence for a greater role of the left hemisphere in this task. The simultaneously recorded ERPs to each word presentation displayed a different pattern of activity depending on where, within and between the hemispheres, they were recorded. ERPs from over left and right occipital regions reflected the anatomy of the visual system. For example, the sensory N1 (100 ms) component was larger from the hemisphere contralateral to the visual field in which the word was presented. By contrast, ERPs recorded over anterior temporal regions were asymmetrical in the same way regardless of where in the visual field a word appeared. In each case, the left-hemisphere response displayed a negative (410 ms)–positive (560 ms) shift that was absent or small in ERPs recorded from over the right hemisphere (see Fig. 11.1). This asymmetry, like the behavioral asymmetry, was evident in each of the hearing Ss. This asymmetry was evident neither in left-handed individuals nor in tasks employing nonlanguage stimuli, therefore, we interpreted it as an index of some aspect of the left hemisphere's greater role in this reading task.

The results from the congenitally deaf adults (all were bilaterally and profoundly deaf, had acquired ASL as a first language, and had not acquired speech) were markedly different from those of the hearing Ss (see Neville, Kutas, & Schmidt, 1982b). Neither the behavioral data nor the ERPs displayed evidence of left-hemisphere specialization in this task. The deaf subjects reported the words as accurately as the hearing Ss, but they were equally accurate when words were presented to the LVF and RVF. In addition, whereas over the left anterior temporal region ERPs from hearing Ss displayed a prominent negative–positive shift, ERPs from the deaf Ss did not (see Fig. 11.2). However, in contrast to results from the hearing Ss, deaf Ss displayed a negative potential over the right temporal region. Thus, these results suggest that deaf Ss do not display the normal pattern of left-hemisphere specialization for written English. If we knew why this is so, we would know something about the factor(s) that are important in the development of left-hemisphere specialization in normal hearing Ss.

There are several ways in which our deaf Ss' experience with English differed from that of hearing Ss that might account for the absence of left-hemisphere specialization. It could be, as has been proposed, that the left hemisphere is specifically specialized for the phonological decoding that characterizes reading by hearing Ss but not by deaf Ss. On the other hand, as mentioned previously, Liberman proposed that the special role of the left hemisphere for language arises in conjunction with the acquisition of the grammatical or propositional coding strategies that characterize language use (Liberman, 1974). Most deaf Ss do not acquire full grammatical competence in English, and this may be the reason they do not display left-hemisphere specialization during reading. Alternatively, a third possibility is that the acquisition of two languages by the deaf Ss (i.e., ASL first and then English) would account for these results. Indeed several lines of evidence suggest that hemispheric specialization differs in monolinguals and bilinguals. One way we investigated this third possibility was to test the hearing Ss born to deaf parents (HD) on this task. If the acquisition of two languages (ASL first) was an important variable in determining this pattern of results, their data should parallel those of the deaf Ss. On the other hand, if left hemisphere

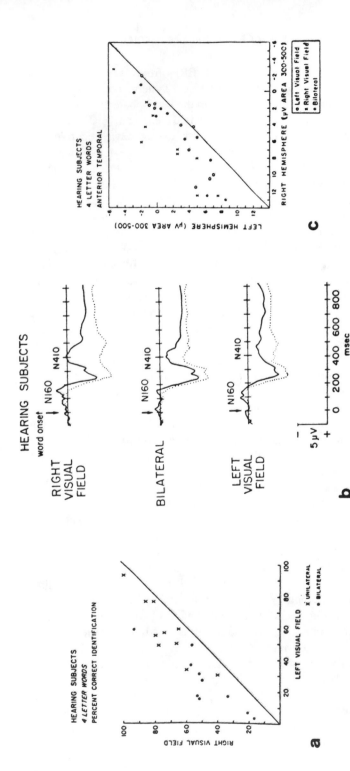

FIG. 11.1.   (a) Percent correct word identification for each hearing subject. Points fall above the diagonal, if accuracy was better after right visual field (left hemisphere) presentations. (b) ERPs averaged over all ten hearing subjects from left (—) and right (...) anterior temporal electrodes during right, bilateral, and left visual field word presentations. (c) Amplitude of N410 for each subject after words were presented to the left, right, or bilateral visual fields. Points fall above the diagonal, if the amplitude was greater from the left than from the right anterior temporal region (from Neville, Kutas, & Schmidt, 1984).

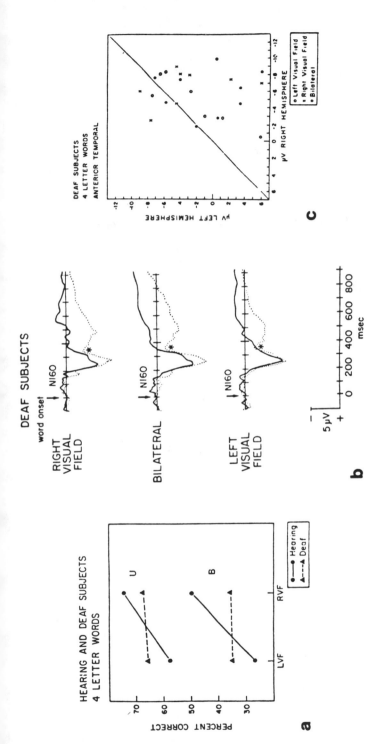

FIG. 11.2. (a) Percent accuracy of word identification after left and right visual field presentations (U = Unilateral; B = Bilateral) by hearing (—) and deaf (---) subjects. (b) ERPs averaged over all eight deaf subjects from left (—) and right (...) anterior temporal electrodes during right, bilateral, and left visual field word presentations. (c) Peak-to-peak amplitude of negative–positive shift for each deaf subject after left, right, or bilateral visual field word presentations. Points fall below the diagonal, if the right anterior temporal amplitude was greater than the left (from Neville, Kutas, & Schmidt, 1984).

specialization arises in conjunction with phonological decoding or grammatical encoding of English, then the HD Ss should display results similar to those of the hearing Ss.

The HD Ss reported the words more accurately after they were presented to the RVF than the LVF, suggesting, left-hemisphere specialization for the hearing Ss. As seen in Fig. 11.3, over the anterior temporal regions the ERPs from this group displayed an asymmetry similar to that observed in the hearing Ss. This pattern occurred independently of the visual field to which words were presented. These results suggest that the absence of left-hemisphere specialization in the deaf subjects was not attributable to the acquisition of ASL as a first language but may instead be linked to processes involved in either phonological or grammatical decoding.

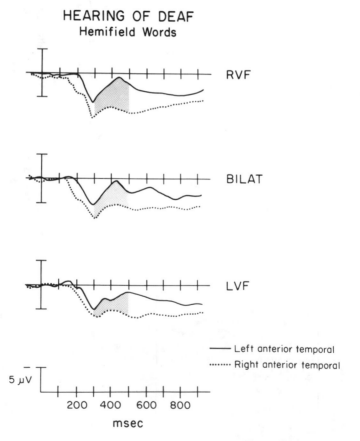

FIG. 11.3.   ERPs elicited by written English words presented to right or left visual fields (RVF and LVF) or bilaterally from hearing Ss born to deaf parents who acquired ASL as a first language.

American Sign Language

In order to assess the roles of phonological processing and/or grammatical recoding in producing left-hemisphere specialization for English (observed in the hearing but not the deaf subjects), we performed a version of this experiment with ASL. ASL is not phonological (i.e., in the sense of being sound-based), thus, if phonological decoding is an important variable in setting up left-hemisphere specialization, we would not expect to see this asymmetry when deaf Ss process ASL. On the other hand, because ASL is highly grammatical (Klima & Bellugi, 1979), if grammatical recoding is an important variable in the development of left-hemisphere specialization for a language (and if phonological decoding is not essential), deaf Ss should display left-hemisphere specialization in processing ASL. To test these hypotheses, we digitized filmed sequences of a person signing (6 frames per sign at 180 ms) and presented each sign once to the left and once to the right visual field just as the English words had been presented. Two seconds after sign onset, Ss made the sign just presented. These responses were videotaped and scored for accuracy of hand shape, location, and movement. Every deaf subject reported the signs more accurately after they were presented to the RVF, suggesting a greater role for the left hemisphere. This is what was observed when hearing Ss read English and contrasts with the results for deaf subjects reading English. Moreover, these signs—which are physically very dissimilar from printed words—elicited ERPs from over anterior regions that displayed a pattern of results similar to that seen when the hearing Ss read English. That is, they were characterized by a negative–positive shift that was larger from the left than the right hemisphere (see Fig. 11.4). Furthermore, this asymmetry occurred independently of where in the visual field a sign appeared, as we had observed in ERPs from hearing Ss reading English words. We also recorded ERPs to these stimuli from normally hearing subjects who did not know ASL. They were asked to mimic the signs as best they could. ERPs from these subjects did not display the asymmetrical negativity characteristic of the deaf Ss but instead displayed a prolonged positive shift that was symmetrical from the two hemispheres (see Fig. 11.5).

The results from these studies showing similar patterns of electrical activity 300–600 ms following the onset of information presented via English and ASL suggest that there may be substantial overlap in the identity of the neural systems utilized in the processing of signed and spoken languages. Moreover, with respect to the question we began with, the results showing that hearing but not deaf Ss display left-hemisphere specialization for English; deaf Ss, but not hearing Ss who do not know ASL, display left-hemisphere specialization for ASL suggest: (a) Experience with language presented in the auditory modality, or more specifically phonological decoding, is *not* necessary for the specialization of the language hemisphere, and (b) the special role of the left hemisphere may develop along with the acquisition of grammatical competence in a language, whether in the auditory or visual modality.

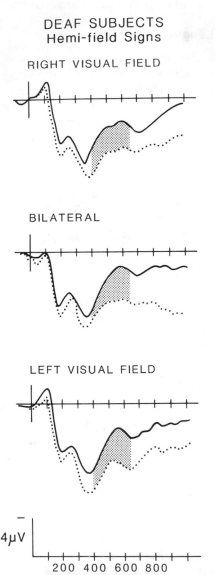

DEAF SUBJECTS
Hemi-field Signs

RIGHT VISUAL FIELD

BILATERAL

LEFT VISUAL FIELD

4µV

200 400 600 800
msec

——— LEFT BROCA'S
········ RIGHT BROCA'S

FIG. 11.4. ERPs from 9 congenitally deaf Ss recorded over left and right frontal regions (over Broca's area) to signs presented in the right or left visual field or to two different signs in each visual field (from Neville, in press).

HEARING SUBJECTS
Hemi-field Signs

RIGHT VISUAL FIELD

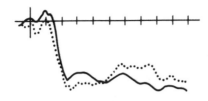

BILATERAL

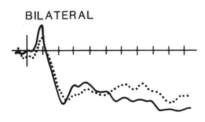

LEFT VISUAL FIELD

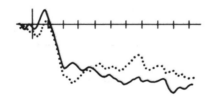

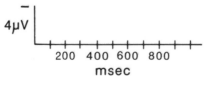

4µV

200 400 600 800
msec

——— LEFT BROCA'S
·········· RIGHT BROCA'S

FIG. 11.5. ERPs from 10 normally hearing Ss recorded over left and right frontal regions (over Broca's area) to signs presented in the right or left visual field or to two different signs in each visual field. (from Neville, in press).

Hearing Subjects/Deaf Parents
Early Acquisition ASL

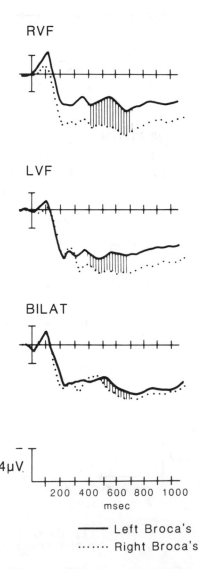

FIG. 11.6. ERPs elicited by ASL signs presented to the right or left visual fields (RVF, LVF) or bilaterally. Responses from hearing subjects born to deaf parents who acquired ASL as a first language. Recordings from over frontal (Broca's area) brain regions.

Hearing Interpreters
Late Acquistion ASL

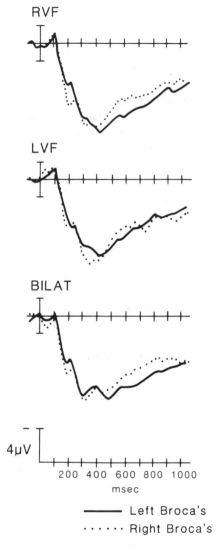

FIG. 11.7. ERPs elicited by ASL signs presented to the right or left visual fields (RVF, LVF) or bilaterally. Responses from hearing interpreters of ASL who acquired ASL after fifteen years of age. Recordings from over frontal (Broca's area) brain regions.

If these hypotheses are correct, then hearing Ss who learned ASL as a first language and have fully acquired the grammar of ASL should also display a pattern of asymmetries similar to that of the deaf Ss. We utilized this same paradigm to test ten HD Ss (hearing Ss who had deaf parents) who had learned ASL as a first language from their parents. Each of these subjects was more accurate at reporting the signs when they were presented to the RVF. Additionally, the ERPs from anterior regions displayed a similar pattern of asymmetries to that observed in the deaf Ss (see Fig. 11.6). Thus, these results are also in line with the hypothesis that grammatical recoding of linguistic information is necessary for specialization of the language hemisphere.

We also utilized this paradigm to test the hypothesis that there is a critical or sensitive period within which the acquisition of language can occur that is determined by the maturation of systems within the left hemisphere. Studies by Newport and colleagues (Newport, 1988) have reported behavioral evidence consistent with the critical period concept. Deaf Ss who were born to hearing parents and were exposed to ASL after 6 years of age do not attain native fluency in the grammar of ASL. We tested the hypothesis that these limits are imposed by systems within the left hemisphere by studying a group of hearing Ss who had learned ASL after the age of 15 years and who were certified interpreters of ASL for the deaf. This group certainly has a good command of ASL but were exposed only late in development. The ERPs from this group did not display the asymmetrical negative–positive shift over anterior regions, thus providing support for the hypothesis that the acquisition of grammar is limited by maturational constraints within the left hemisphere (see Fig. 11.7).

Sentence Processing

We wished to further test the hypothesized role of grammatical encoding in the specialization of the language hemisphere and also to compare and contrast the effects of early language experience on grammatical versus semantic processing. In addition, we wished to test the generality of the results presented previously, which were all for the presentation of isolated signs and words to the hemifields. Thus, we conducted a series of studies of sentence processing by deaf and hearing Ss, including sentences in both English and ASL.

English Sentences

Briefly, the English sentences were presented one word at a time (interword interval—700 ms) to the central two degrees of vision. ERPs to the words in the middle of the sentences were coded and averaged according to whether they were content or "open class" words (nouns, verbs, and adjectives, i.e., words that make reference to specific objects and events), or function or "closed class" words (pronouns, prepositions, articles, conjunctions, i.e., the small, "closed" set of words that specify the relations between content words). The closed class words are viewed as providing much of the syntactic structure to sentences, whereas the open class words carry semantic information. Clinical data documenting the effects of lesions suggest that nonidentical neural systems mediate these two aspects of language processing. Lesions to the anterior regions of the left hemisphere disrupt the use and comprehension of the closed class vocabulary, whereas lesions to posterior regions of the left hemisphere disrupt the use of open class words. Additionally, lesions to posterior areas of the right hemisphere diminish some aspects of semantic functioning (Wapner, Hamby, & Gardner, 1981).

The ERPs elicited by these sentences in normal hearing Ss provide further evidence that different systems are active in processing open and closed class words. As seen in Fig. 11.8, ERPs to the closed class words displayed a

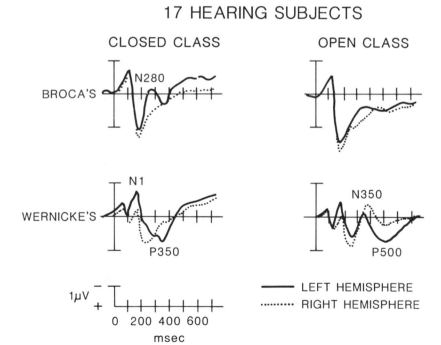

ENGLISH SENTENCES
17 HEARING SUBJECTS

FIG. 11.8. ERPs to open and closed class words within English sentences from normal hearing Ss recorded over anterior temporal (near Broca's area) and parietal (over Wernicke's area) sites of the left hemisphere and homologous positions over the right hemisphere (from Neville, in press).

negative peak around 280 ms (N280) that was most evident over the left hemisphere. This peak was evident over anterior brain regions but not over posterior cortex. By contrast, ERPs to the open class words did not display a prominent N280 in ERPs from the anterior areas, but from over parietal regions they displayed a negative component around 350 ms (N350) that was evident over both hemispheres. We determined that the different morphologies that characterized the ERPs to these different classes of words were not attributable to their different frequencies in the language, to their lengths, or to differences in their imageability scores and instead are likely to index their different functions in language processing.

If the asymmetrical response to the closed class words indexes functions germane to grammatical processing, then we might expect this response to be absent or small in deaf Ss who have not fully acquired the grammar of English.

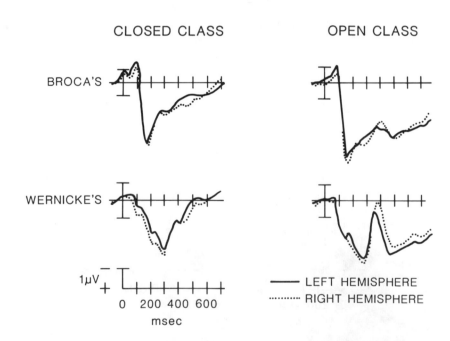

FIG. 11.9.   ERPs to open and closed class words within English sentences from congenitally deaf Ss recorded over anterior temporal (near Broca's area) and parietal (over Wernicke's area) sites of the left hemisphere and homologous positions over the right hemisphere (from Neville, in press).

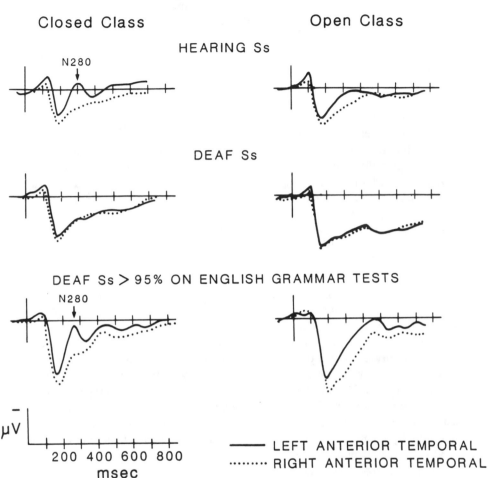

FIG. 11.10.   ERPs to open and closed class words recorded over left and right anterior temporal regions. Recordings from normal hearing Ss and from congenitally deaf Ss who scored poorly (middle) and well (bottom) on tests of English grammar (from Neville, in press).

We recorded ERPs to these same sentences from ten congenitally deaf adults, each of whom scored significantly lower on tests of English grammar than did our normally hearing Ss. As seen in Fig. 11.9, ERPs from these Ss to the closed class words, in contrast to those of the hearing Ss, did not display the N280 component nor any asymmetries in amplitude from anterior or posterior brain regions. We also studied a group of congenitally deaf Ss who scored virtually perfectly on the tests of English grammar (Fig. 11.10). These Ss, like the other deaf Ss, were congenitally, bilaterally, and profoundly deaf, had not acquired speech, and used ASL as their major form of communication. Nonetheless they did display a pattern of hemispheric specialization similar to that observed in the hearing Ss. Thus, these data strongly suggest that neither the motor skills involved in speech nor phonological decoding of acoustic information are necessary in the specialization of the language hemisphere but that the acquisition of grammatical competence in a language is both necessary and sufficient in the development of left-hemisphere specialization for that language.

We contrasted these results for grammatical processing with the data relevant to semantic processing. As seen in Fig. 11.8 and Fig. 11.9, in contrast to the group differences in ERPs to the closed class words, deaf and hearing Ss displayed similar ERPs to the open class words. In both groups, ERPs to these words displayed a prominent negative peak between 350–400 ms over left and right parietal regions. To the extent that this component reflects aspects of semantic processing, these results suggest that there are strong similarities in this aspect of language processing, the different early language experience of the deaf Ss notwithstanding. Further studies of semantic processing in deaf and hearing Ss are consistent with this view (Neville, 1985; Kutas, Neville, & Holcomb, 1987). For example, when hearing Ss are presented with sentences that are semantically inappropriate (e.g., "I have five fingers on my *moon*"), the anomalous word elicits a prominent negative wave around 400 ms after word onset (N400—Kutas & Hillyard, 1980; Neville, Kutas, Chesney, & Schmidt, 1986). The amplitude of this response, which is largest over parietal cortex bilaterally, is inversely related to predictability or "cloze probability" of a word and is, thus, an index of the degree to which a word has been activated or "primed" by the preceding context (Kutas & Hillyard, 1984a). We presented English sentences of this type, together with an equal number of semantically appropriate sentences, to a group of hearing and deaf Ss. Remarkably, the N400 response in the deaf and hearing Ss was virtually identical (see Fig. 11.11). These results for semantic processing stand in marked contrast to the results for grammatical processing.

These data suggest that the systems that mediate the acquisition of aspects of syntactic processing appear to be vulnerable to and dependent on specific types of early language experience. However, aspects of semantic processing may develop in a very similar fashion even after widely varying conditions of early language experience. This may be because there are strong biological constraints on the development of the systems that are used to process semantic information, or it may be that semantic processing is governed by more general cognitive experience, which is more similar in deaf and hearing Ss than is experience with the grammar of English.

These results are of interest in view of studies of language development that show that the open class elements of language are acquired earlier than are the closed class words. Of additional interest are reports that variations in maternal speech have virtually no effect on the time of acquisition of open class elements

ENGLISH SENTENCES

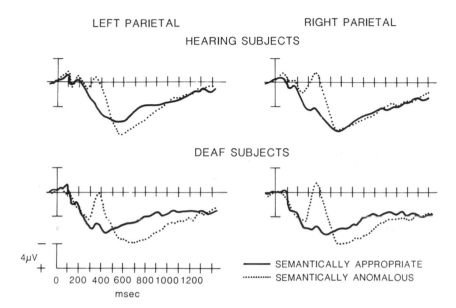

FIG. 11.11.   ERPs elicited to semantically appropriate and anomalous terminal words in English sentences. Responses from over left and right parietal regions of normally hearing and congenitally deaf Ss.

of the language but that they do affect the rate of acquisition of closed class items (Newport, Gleitman, & Gleitman, 1977). Moreover, it is of interest that deaf children who have not been exposed to a sign language nor have acquired speech invent their own signs for objects and events in the world (open class items), and the age of acquisition of these language milestones occurs at the same time as in normal hearing children. In contrast, these children display little evidence of acquiring any grammar (i.e., they do not invent closed class items) (Goldin-Meadow, 1979). Thus, it appears that whereas the acquisition of lexical semantics is not dependent on language input, some grammatical input is necessary in order for the systems that mediate the acquisition of grammar to unfold.

ASL Sentences

We further tested the hypothesized role of grammatical encoding in the development of left-hemisphere specialization and the hypothesis that similar neural systems mediate the acquisition of all formal languages by recording ERPs to the presentation of signed sentences. We translated the sentences utilized in the study of English described previously into ASL and digitized films (8 frames per sign)

ERPs TO CLOSED CLASS ITEMS

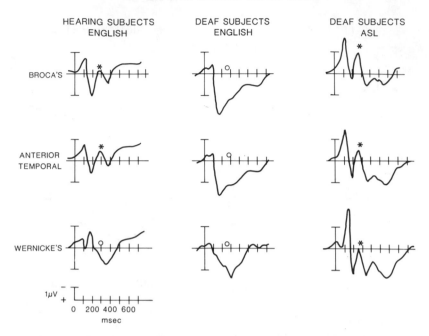

FIG. 11.12.   ERPs elicited by closed class items in English and ASL sentences. Responses from over frontal (Broca's area), anterior temporal, and parietal (Wernicke's area) brain regions.

of a person signing these sentences. Signs were classified (by U. Bellugi) as either open or closed class. Figure 11.12 shows the prominent negative peak (N280 — marked by the asterisk) elicited over anterior regions of the left hemisphere in response to closed class English words in hearing but not in the deaf subjects (left and middle panels). In contrast as seen in the right panel, ERPs elicited by the closed class items in the signed sentences *did* elicit a negative potential in the deaf subjects. This component was similar in morphology and latency to the potential evident in the hearing Ss responses to English. However, it extended more posteriorly in the deaf Ss, in whom it was recorded over parietal brain regions. This posterior extension could be the result of increased activity of posterior visual areas secondary to auditory deprivation (or compensatory hypertrophy/hyperactivity), a phenomenon we have reported in deaf adults in non-language tasks. (Neville, Schmidt, & Kutas, 1983; Neville & Lawson, 1987b). Alternatively, it could be accounted for by an increased role of parietal cortex in the perception of a language in which the lexicon and the grammar rely strongly on the perception of motion. We are currently assessing these two alternatives by studying the HD Ss on this paradigm. If auditory deprivation is the critical factor, their ERPs should not display the posterior distribution. However, if the second alternative holds, then the deaf and HD should show similar patterns. In summary, these results suggest that similar but nonidentical systems within the left hemisphere mediate grammatical encoding of spoken and signed languages.

Semantic Processing

In order to compare semantic processing in English and ASL, we also presented semantically appropriate and anomalous sentences as described previously. Semantically anomalous signs in ASL sentences elicited a large N400 response over parietal regions bilaterally which was very similar to that observed in response to the anomalous English sentences (see Fig. 11.13). Thus, these results suggest that there are strong similarities in the systems that mediate semantic processing in signed and spoken languages.

Phonological Processing

In view of recent evidence suggesting that phonological information is not necessarily obtained through the auditory modality and that some congenitally and profoundly deaf individuals display evidence of sensitivity to the phonology of English (Hanson & Fowler, 1987; Hanson & McGarr, 1989) the strong claim that syntactic competence is necessary and sufficient for the specialization of the

ASL SENTENCES

LEFT PARIETAL   RIGHT PARIETAL

DEAF SUBJECTS

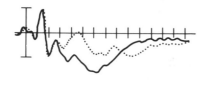
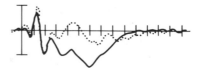

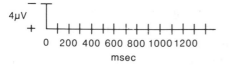

SEMANTICALLY APPROPRIATE
SEMANTICALLY ANOMALOUS

FIG. 11.13. ERPs elicited to semantically appropriate and anomalous terminal signs in ASL sentences. Responses from over left and right parietal regions of congenitally deaf Ss.

language hemisphere needs to be examined in other paradigms. For example, knowledge of the abstract rules that specify how meaningless linguistic units—for example, phonemes (English) and hand shape, motion and location (ASL)—are combined may be a critical factor. Phonological skills have been linked to left-hemisphere function in normally hearing persons for English and in congenitally deaf individuals for ASL (Milberg, Blumstein, & Dworetzky, 1988; Bellugi, Klima, & Poizner, 1988). If our deaf Ss who scored well on tests of English grammar also had good knowledge of English phonology, and if knowledge of the phonology of English is mediated by the left hemisphere in deaf individuals, this would suggest that grammatical processing, including both phonological and syntactic processing are critical variables in the development of left hemisphere specialization for language. We are currently testing this hypothesis utilizing the combined behavioral-electrophysiological approach in a paradigm similar to that employed by Hanson and Fowler (1987).

Nonlanguage Processing

In several experiments, beginning with the study of picture perception referred to at the beginning of the chapter, we have observed a pattern of results that suggests the roles of the hemispheres in processing certain nonlanguage material is in part determined by the modality and specific processing demands imposed by an individual's first language. Thus, for example, we compared deaf and hearing Ss in a study of visual attention (Neville & Lawson, 1987a, 1987b, 1987c). The Ss task was to perceive the direction of motion of a white square presented 20° out in the left or right visual field. Behavioral data and ERPs from hearing Ss suggested a greater role for the right hemisphere in this task (consistent with a large clinical literature). However, deaf Ss displayed strong behavioral and electrophysiological evidence of left-hemisphere specialization. We proposed that the increased role of the left hemisphere in the deaf Ss might arise from the temporal coincidence of motion perception and the grammar of ASL; this temporal correlation may result in these functions becoming organized together within the province of the language-specialized left hemisphere. We tested this hypothesis against an alternative view (that the increase in left-hemisphere activity might occur secondary to auditory deprivation) by testing the HD Ss, for whom there also exists a strong temporal correlation between the grammar of their first language, ASL, and the perception of motion. These subjects, like the deaf Ss, also displayed superior detection of the direction of motion in the RVF and increased attention-related activity over the left hemisphere. It is conceivable that this type of explanation can account for the reports of left-hemisphere superiority in the perception of the temporal order of nonlanguage stimuli in hearing individuals who have acquired an oral-aural language. That is, perhaps because the perception and production of speech co-occurs with and critically depends on the ability to make fine temporal discriminations, the left hemisphere comes to mediate the perception of temporal sequences of nonlanguage material as well.

Summary and Conclusions

The results presented in this chapter concerning the effects of language experience on cerebral organization can be considered within a framework like that suggested by Changeux (1985) and others (e.g., Edelman, 1987) in discussing the development of the sensory systems. According to this view, there is an initial period of growth that is genetically influenced. In the visual system, this includes, for example, the growth of retinal afferents to primary visual cortex, where they form ocular dominance columns. Those initial biases are strongly determined (e.g., they can occur in the absence of visual experience), but they are not immutable, as they can be substantially altered by visual experience (e.g., monocular deprivation). Following the early period of initial growth, there is a transient period of redundancy or exuberance of connections that has been documented in several species, in several brain regions both in humans (Huttenlocher, 1979; Huttenlocher, Courten, Garey, & Van Der Loos, 1982) and in animals (Cowan, Fawcett, O'Leary, & Stanfield, 1984). This transient redundancy may underlie the ability of inputs from an experienced eye to take over neurons that would normally receive input from an unexperienced eye as occurs following monocular deprivation. It has also been shown that there are early, transient connections between different sensory modalities, for example, from the retina to the ventro-basal (somatosensory) nucleus of the thalamus (Frost, 1984) and between primary auditory and visual cortex (Innocenti & Clark, 1984). Such redundant connections are present in the neonate but are normally eliminated early in postnatal development. Additionally, there is an early period when the callosal fibers that join the two hemispheres are considerably more numerous than in the mature animal (Innocenti, 1981). Therefore, during this time, which is probably different for different brain regions, there is maximal diversity of connections. The subsequent pruning of these diverse connections occurs in a few well-documented cases as a direct consequence of activity that selectively stabilizes certain connections, whereas others that do not receive input are eliminated or suppressed. It is further hypothesized that, in addition to competition between inputs, the temporal patterning between inputs is an important variable in setting up neuronal systems or groups; that is, neurons that are active together tend to aggregate. We have reported behavioral and ERP data during visual processing by congenitally deaf Ss that are compatible with the idea that in the absence of auditory input to auditory and/or polysensory temporal brain regions, visual afferents to these regions are stabilized, and in some cases their activity is increased. This would account both for our observations of increased visual ERP amplitudes over temporal cortex (Neville et al., 1983) and over posterior brain regions of both hemispheres following congenital auditory deprivation (Neville & Lawson, 1987b).

Our studies of the functional specializations of the two hemispheres can be viewed within the same framework. The results showing a greater role for the left hemisphere in the processing of both spoken and signed languages (by competent users of the language) indicate a strong initial bias for the left hemisphere to mediate language. This bias may also underlie the anatomical asymmetry in the planum temporal, observed by Geschwind and colleagues, where the left side is larger than the right by 28 weeks gestation (Geschwind & Levitsky, 1968). Later on in postnatal development, at least until 10 years of age as shown by clinical data on hemispherectomy cases, there is considerable redundancy such that each hemisphere can support many aspects of both language and visuospatial processing. This redundancy may be supported by extensive callosal fibers, which at least in other species are more abundant in the immature than the mature animal (Innocenti, 1981).

Our work suggests that one factor that is important in establishing or maintaining the specialization of the left hemisphere for language is the acquisition of competence in the grammar of language. This would account for the data showing that only hearing and deaf subjects that know the grammar of English display left-hemisphere specialization for English and for the data showing both deaf and hearing subjects that are native signers show left-hemisphere specialization for ASL.

Furthermore, our studies of nonlanguage processing raise the hypothesis that the fact and the nature of the language specialization also determines aspects of hemispheric specialization for nonlanguage material.

References

Bellugi, U., Klima, E., & Poizner, H. (1988). Sign Language and the brain: In F. Plum (Ed.), *Language, communication, and the brain* (pp. 30–56). New York: Raven.

Changeux, J. P. (1985). *Neuronal man*. New York: Pantheon.

Conrad, R. (1977). The reading ability of deaf school-leavers. *British Journal of Educational Psychology, 47,* 138–148.

Cowan, W. M., Fawcett, J. W., O'Leary, D. D. M., & Stanfield, B. B. (1984). Regressive events in neurogenesis. *Science, 225,* 1258–1265.

Edelman, G. (1987). *Neural Darwinism: The theory of neuronal group selection*. New York: Basic Books.

Frost, D. O. (1984). Axonal growth and target selection during development: Retinal projections to the ventrobasal complex and other "nonvisual" structures in neonatal Syrian Hamsters. *Journal of Comparative Neurology, 230,* 576–592.

Geschwind, N., & Levitsky, W. (1968). Left–right asymmetry in temporal speech region. *Science, 161,* 186–187.

Goff, W. R., Allison, T., & Vaughan, H. G. (1978). The functional neuroanatomy of event-related potentials. In E. Callaway, P. Tueting, & S. Koslow (Eds.), *Event-related brain potentials in man* (pp. 1–81). New York: Academic Press.

Goldin-Meadow, S. (1979). Structure in a manual communication system developed without a conventional language model: Language without a helping hand. In H. Whitaker & H. A. Whitaker (Eds.), *Studies in neurolinguistics* (vol. 4, pp. 125–209). New York: Academic Press.

Hanson, V., & Fowler, C. (1987). Phonological coding in word reading: Evidence from hearing and deaf readers. *Memory and Cognition, 15,* 199–297.

Hanson, V., & McGarr, N. (1989). Rhyme generation by deaf adults. *Journal of Speech and Hearing Research, 32,* 2–11.

Hillyard, S. A., & Kutas, M. (1983). Electrophysiology of cognitive processing. *Annual Review of Psychology, 34,* 33–61.

Hillyard, S. A., Picton, T. W., & Regan, D. (1978). Sensation, perception, and attention: Analysis using ERPs. In E. Callaway, P. Tueting, & S. Koslow (Eds.), *Event-related brain potentials in man* (pp. 223–323). New York: Academic Press.

Huttenlocher, P. R. (1979). Synaptic density in human frontal cortex—developmental changes and effects of aging. *Brain Research, 163,* 195–205.

Huttenlocher, P. R., Courten, C., Garey, L., & Van Der Loos, D. (1982). Synaptogenesis in human visual cortex—evidence for synapse elimination during normal development. *Neuroscience Letters, 33,* 247–252.

Innocenti, G. M. (1981). Growth and reshaping of axons in the establishment of visual callosal connections. *Science, 212,* 824–827.

Innocenti, G. M., & Clark, S. (1984). Bilateral transitory projection to visual areas from auditory cortex in kittens. *Developmental Brain Research, 14,* 143–148.

Klima, E. S., & Bellugi, U. (1979). *The signs of language.* Cambridge, MA: Harvard University Press.

Kutas, M., & Hillyard, S. A. (1980). Reading senseless sentences: Event-related brain potentials reflect semantic incongruity. *Science, 207,* 203–205.

Kutas, M., & Hillyard, S. A. (1984a). Brain potentials during reading reflect word expectancy and semantic association. *Nature, 307,* 161–163.

Kutas, M., & Hillyard, S. A. (1984b). Event-related potentials in cognitive science. In M. S. Gazzaniga (Ed.), *Handbook of cognitive neuroscience* (pp. 387–409). New York: Plenum.

Kutas, M., Neville, H. J., & Holcomb, P. (1987). A preliminary comparison of the N400 response to semantic anomalies during reading, listening and signing. *The London Symposia* (EEG suppl.), *39,* 325–330.

Liberman, A. M. (1974). The specialization of the language hemisphere. In F. O. Schmitt & F. G. Worden (Eds.), *The neurosciences third study program* (pp. 43–56). Cambridge, MA: MIT Press.

Milberg, W., Blumstein, S., & Dworetzky, B. (1988). Phonological processing and lexical access in aphasia. *Brain and Language, 34,* 279–293.

Neville, H. J. (1985). Biological constraints on semantic processing: A comparison of spoken and signed languages. *Psychophysiology, 22(5),* 576.

Neville, H. J. (in press). Neurobiology of cognitive and language processing: Effects of early experience. In K. Gibson & A. C. Peterson (Eds.), *Brain maturation and cognitive development: Comparative and cross-cultural perspectives* (Formerly *Brain maturation and behavioral development: Biosocial dimensions*). Hawthorne, NY: Aldine de Gruyter.

Neville, H. J., Kutas, M., Chesney, G., & Schmidt, A. (1986). Event-related brain potentials during initial encoding and recognition memory of congruous and incongruous words. *Journal of Memory and Language, 25,* 75–92.

Neville, H. J., Kutas, M., & Schmidt, A. (1982a). Event-related potential studies of cerebral specialization during reading. I. Studies of normal adults. *Brain and Language, 16,* 300–315.

Neville, H. J., Kutas, M., & Schmidt, A. (1982b). Event-related potential studies of cerebral specialization during reading. II. Studies of congenitally deaf adults. *Brain and Language, 16,* 300–315.

Neville, H. J., Kutas, M., & Schmidt, A. (1984). Event-related studies of cerebral specialization during reading: A comparison of normally hearing and congenitally deaf adults. In R. Karrer, J. Cohen, & P. Tueting (Eds.), *Brain and information: Event-related potentials* (pp. 370–376). New York: New York Academy of Sciences, Monograph #12.

Neville, H. J., & Lawson, D. (1987a). Attention to central and peripheral visual space in a movement detection task: An event-related potential and behavioral study. I. Normal hearing adults. *Brain Research, 405,* 253–267.

Neville, H. J., & Lawson, D. (1987b). Attention to central and peripheral visual space in a movement detection task: An event-related potential and behavioral study. II. Congenitally deaf adults. *Brain Research, 405,* 268–283.

Neville, H. J., & Lawson, D. (1987c). Attention to central and peripheral visual space in a movement detection task. III. Separate effects of auditory deprivation and acquisition of a visual language. *Brain Research, 405,* 284–294.

Neville, H. J., Schmidt, A., & Kutas, M. (1983). Altered visual-evoked potentials in congenitally deaf adults. *Brain Research, 266,* 127–132.

Newport, E. L. (1988). Constraints on learning and their role in language acquisition: Studies of the acquisition of American Sign Language. *Language Sciences, 10,* 147–172.

Newport, E. L., Gleitman, H., & Gleitman, L. R. (1977). Mother I'd rather do it myself: Some effects and noneffects of maternal speech style. In C. E. Snow & C. A. Ferguson (Eds.), *Talking to children: Language input and acquisition* (pp. 109–149). Cambridge, MA: Cambridge University Press.

Wapner, W., Hamby, S., & Gardner, H. (1981). The role of the right hemisphere in the apprehension of complex linguistic materials. *Brain and Language, 14,* 15–33.

Chapter 12

Neural Mechanisms of Binaural Fusion

Masakazu Konishi

Division of Biology, California Institute of Technology

Abstract

Neurons selective for complex acoustic signals in animals provide useful insights into the possible neural mechanisms of speech recognition. The stimulus selectivity of "complex" neurons may be the result of many processes that take place in the networks converging on the neurons. The networks are specialized for the creation of specific auditory percepts from particular signals. Systematic distribution of complex neurons such as those found in the auditory cortex of bats and in the owl's midbrain suggest that different percepts are separately mapped.

Human beings can perceive a single phantom source by listening to dichotic stimuli. The sounds that go to the two ears may differ from each other in phase, amplitude, or both, yet the subject perceives neither two separate sources nor the difference between the two but one source and one sound. Thus, the percept of a sound source based on binaural fusion is an example of a heteromorphic percept, as defined by Mattingly and Liberman (1988). Binaural fusion occurs not only in localization but also in pattern recognition and has served as a powerful tool in the study of speech perception (Broadbent, 1954; Mattingly & Liberman, in press; Studdert-Kennedy & Shankweiler, 1970). The term "percept" appears to be reserved for the description of human sensory experience. This restriction largely precludes the possibility of finding the neural mechanisms of percepts. Localization by binaural fusion is, however, one of the few auditory behaviors that can be demonstrated in animals. This fact means that the neural substrates for binaural fusion can be elucidated. This chapter describes how binaural fusion occurs in the barn owl's brain and discusses how similar principles of neural processing may underlie the perception of speech sounds.

Translation of Interaural Time Difference to Location

The barn owl can use sounds to localize prey in total darkness. A noise releases a quick turning of the head in the direction of the sound source. Dichotic stimuli presented by earphones cause the owl to turn its head in a direction other than the loci of the two sources (Moiseff & Konishi, 1981). This behavior suggests that sound localization by the owl is based on binaural fusion. Experiments show that the owl's brain translates a combination of interaural time difference (ITD) and

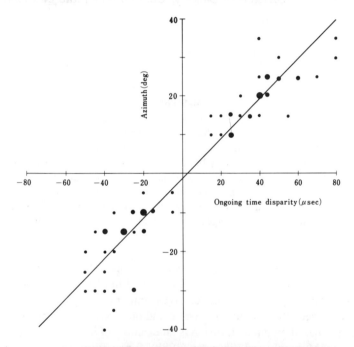

FIG. 12.1.   Translation of interaural time difference to location.
The owl wore special earphones for the delivery of dichotic stimuli consisting of time-shifted noises. Such stimuli induced the owl to turn its head in the direction of the perceived sound source. The orientation of the head was measured by the search coil technique. The owl derives interaural time differences from interaural phase differences in noise spectral components, which are collectively referred to as ongoing time difference. Interaural intensity difference was kept zero in all tests. Dots of different sizes show the different numbers of trials, the smallest dot indicating one trial (from Moiseff & Konishi, 1981. Reprinted by permission of the *Journal of Neuroscience.*

interaural intensity difference (IID) into a location in space. The perceived azimuthal position varies with ITD(see Fig. 12.1) and the elevational position with IID, although the separation of the two coordinate axes by these cues appears to be incomplete (Moiseff & Konishi, 1981; Moiseff, 1989a, 1989b; Olsen, Esterly & Knudsen, 1989). The use of IID for elevation depends on vertical assymetries in the directionality of the two ears (Payne, 1971; Knudsen & Konishi, 1978a).

Localization of Real and Phantom Targets by Neurons

Neurons that respond only to sounds coming from a restricted area in space, termed space-specific neurons, occur in the forebrain and midbrain auditory nuclei of the owl (Knudsen, Konishi, & Pettigrew, 1977; Knudsen & Konishi, 1978a, 1978b). These neurons have "receptive fields" in the same sense that is used in the visual system (see Fig. 12.2). However, whereas the retina registers the spatial location of stimuli, the cochlea does not. Therefore, spatial receptive fields in the auditory system must be synthesized by the central nervous system (Konishi & Knudsen, 1982; Konishi, 1986).

Space-specific neurons respond to a combination of ITD and IID as if a single real source were present in space (Moiseff & Konishi, 1981). They respond only to a particular combination of ITD and IID. Signals containing inappropriate ITD and IID, including monaural stimuli, are ineffective. The location of a space-specific neuron's receptive field corresponds to the area of space in which broadcasting of sound produces the range of ITDs and IIDs required by the neuron (Olsen et al., 1989). These findings show that neural circuits underlying the response of space-specific neurons translate a combination of ITD and IID into a spatial locus.

Parallel Pathways for Time and Intensity

The stimulus selectivity of a higher-order neuron may derive from lower-order neurons, it is therefore, essential to determine where and how the selectivity appears in the pathway leading to the higher-order neuron. The owl's auditory system processes ITD and IID in separate pathways (see Fig. 12.3) (Moiseff & Konishi, 1983; Konishi, Sullivan, & Takahashi, 1985). Each primary auditory fiber divides into two branches, one innervating the nucleus magnocellularis and the other the nucleus angularis. These cochlear nuclei are spatially separate and different from each other in both physiology and anatomy. Neurons of the nucleus angularis are sensitive to variation in sound intensity and insensitive to phase, whereas those of the nucleus magnocellularis are sensitive to phase and insensitive to intensity (Sullivan & Konishi, 1984). The phase sensitivity is manifested in a neuron's ability to fire spikes at or near a particular phase angle

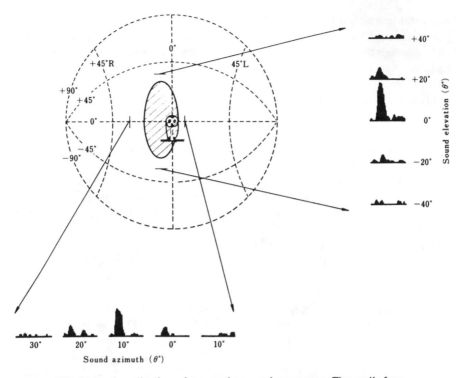

FIG. 12.2.   Localization of a sound source by neurons. The owl's forebrain and midbrain auditory nuclei contain space-specific neurons that
respond only to sound emanating from a restricted area in space. In
this example, the owl's head occupies the center of an imaginary
sphere. The histograms on the right of and below the sphere show the
numbers of spikes elicited from a neuron by a noise source at different
azimuthal and elevational angles. The shaded area on the sphere indicates the receptive field of the neuron (from Knudsen et al., 1977,
copyright 1977 by the AAAS).

of the stimulus tone. The owl's auditory system uses phase-locked spikes for the
measurement of ITD. The cochlear nuclei project to separate sets of pontine and
midbrain nuclei or their parts. The two pathways converge upon each other in the
inferior colliculus (Takahashi & Konishi, 1988a, 1988b). A simple way to show
independent processing of ITD and IID is to inject a local anaesthetic (lidocaine)
into one of the cochlear nuclei while recording from a space-specific neuron
(Takahashi, Moiseff, & Konishi, 1984). An injection into the nucleus magnocellularis causes a temporary change in the neuron's selectivity for ITD, although
its selectivity for IID remains largely unaffected. Conversely, an injection into
the nucleus angularis alters only the IID selectivity of the neuron.

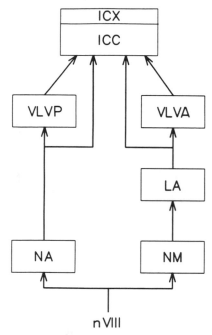

FIG. 12.3. Parallel processing of time and intensity. The owl's brain-stem auditory system consists of two anatomically and physiologically separate pathways starting from the cochlear nuclei, nucleus angularis (NA) and nucleus magnocellularis (NM). The diagram presents only the nuclei and connections discussed in this article. Each primary auditory fiber (nVIII) divides into two branches, one innervating NA neurons and the other, NM neurons. The NA pathway processes intensity, and the NM pathway, time. Nucleus laminaris (LA) is the first binaural nucleus where neuronal sensitivity to interaural time difference appears. VLVP and VLVA are nuclei of the lateral lemniscal complex. The VLVP is the first station where binaural sensitivity to interaural intensity difference emerges. The two pathways reunite in the inferior colliculus, which is composed of the central (ICC) and external nuclei (ICX). All auditory neurons of the ICX are space-specific.

Neural Circuits for the Measurement of Interaural Time Difference

Higher-order neurons may show stimulus selectivities that are lacking among lower-order neurons in the same pathway. The origin of a new selectivity is likely to involve a special neural circuit. Complex neurons, that is, those requiring complex stimulus configurations, tend to be refractory to the kind of analysis

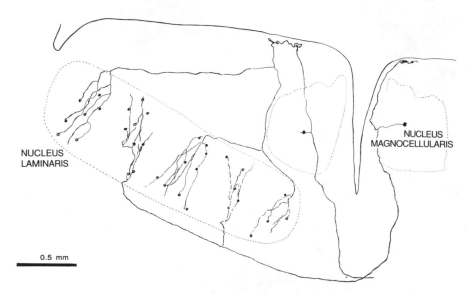

FIG. 12.4.   Neuonal circuits for binaural fusion in the time pathway. A coronal section of nucleus laminaris is shown with two axons from the ipsi- and contralateral magnocellular nuclei entering nucleus laminaris, respectively from its dorsal and ventral surfaces. The axons divide into several collaterals, and these interdigitate as they run almost straight to the opposite surface. The collaterals innervate laminaris neurons, which have large somata and very small dendrites (From Carr & Konishi, 1988).

necessary for the elucidation of the circuits underlying their stimulus selectivity. Space-specific neurons are a notable exception, because we have been able to identify the neural circuits for their ITD selectivity (Sullivan & Konishi, 1986; Carr & Konishi, 1988).

In the time-processing pathway, the first site of binaural convergence is the nucleus laminaris, the presumed avian homolog of the medial superior olivary

FIG. 12.5.   Axons as delay lines. Electrophysiological recordings from the interdigitating collaterals in nucleus laminaris show that spike conduction delays vary systematically as a function of distance from the entry points of the axons. Period histograms were used to measure the arrival of phase-locked spikes with respect to the beginning of each tonal cycle. Shifts in the distribution of spikes indicate changes in conduction time. When such shifts are plotted as a function of the depth of recording sites, systematic variations in conduction time with depth become apparent. A and B show contralateral and ipsilateral fibers, respectively. Different symbols indicate neurons recorded in different penetrations. C shows ipsilateral (open circles) and con-

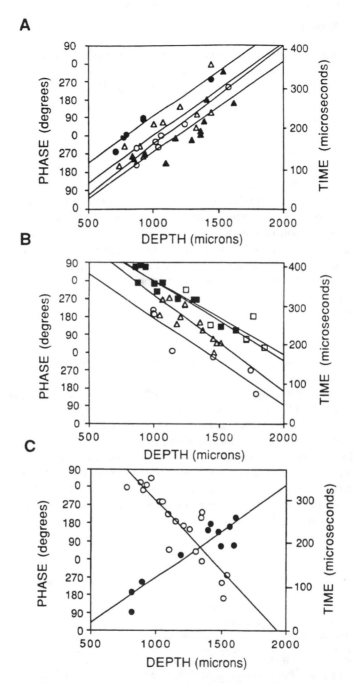

tralateral (closed circles) fibers recorded during one penetration across the nucleus. Conduction time to a given depth was independent of neuron's best frequency, indicating that time is mapped (from Carr & Konishi, 1988).

nucleus. Jeffress (1948) put forth a model circuit for the measurement of ITD using the principles of delay lines and coincidence detection. The nucleus laminaris appears to operate on the same principles (Sullivan & Konishi, 1984; Carr & Konishi, 1988). The mammalian auditory system also uses similar methods (Yin, Chan, & Carney, 1987). Axons from the nucleus magnocellularis divide into two branches, one innervating the ipsilateral nucleus laminaris and the other the contralateral nucleus (see Fig. 12.4). The ipsilateral axons enter the nucleus laminaris from its dorsal surface and the contralateral ones from the ventral surface. These axons divide further into collaterals near the entry point, and the collaterals run almost straight from one surface to the other. As the axon collaterals from the two sides interdigitate, they innervate laminaris neurons, which have few very short dendrites.

Recordings from these collaterals show that the arrival of phase-locked spikes varies systematically as a function of distance from the point of entry (see Fig. 12.5). As expected from the anatomical arrangement described previously, the ipsilateral and contralateral afferents show opposing gradients of delays; conduction delays become longer for the ipsilateral axons and shorter for the contralateral ones as the recording electrode traverses the nucleus from dorsal to ventral. Thus, the afferent axons work as delay lines.

If laminaris neurons function as coincidence detectors, they should fire maximally when spikes from the two sides arrive simultaneously. The opposing gradients of delays suggest that, for many laminaris neurons, phase-locked spikes from the two sides do not arrive simultaneously when the timing of the stimulus is identical in the two ears. Laminaris neurons are selective for ITD, although they respond to monaural stimuli. Period histograms made separately for ipsilateral and contralateral stimulation can show a disparity in the arrival of phase-locked spikes at a laminaris cell. The optimal ITD for a neuron exactly counteracts the disparity in its neural delays (see Fig. 12.6). These findings show that laminaris neurons are coincidence detectors. Also, the systematic variation in delay disparities along the dorso-ventral axis of the nucleus suggests a map of ITD's.

FIG. 12.6.   Neurons as coincidence detectors. Laminaris neurons respond to both monaural and binaural stimuli. Each pair of period histograms in A shows an interaural difference in the phase angle at which a neuron fired the largest number of spikes in response to monaural stimulation. When the phase differences obtained for different frequencies are converted to time, they all equal to 40 microsec. This difference is due to a left–right asymmetry in spike conduction time; in this case, the left side is faster than the right side. B shows binaural responses of the same neuron. The rate of spike discharge varied with interaural time difference and the maximal rate occurred when the right ear led the left ear by 40 microseconds. Thus, when the asymmetry in conduction time was exactly compensated for by the imposed interaural time difference, the neuron fired maximally (from Sullivan & Konishi, 1986, with permission).

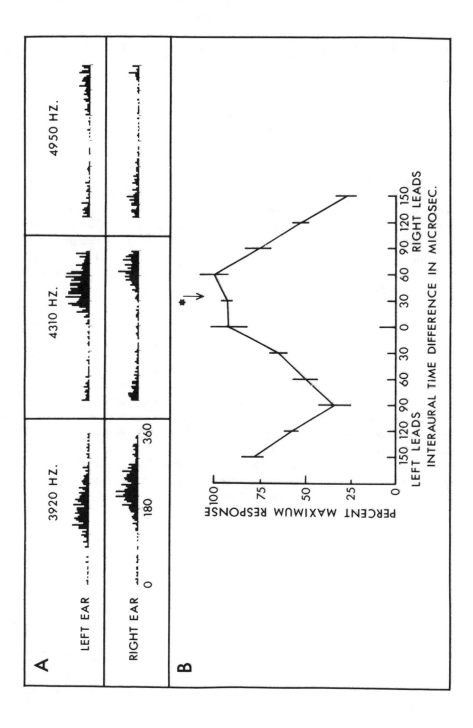

Further Processing of Interaural Time Difference

The nucleus laminaris projects to the inferior colliculus and the nucleus ventralis lemnisci lateralis, pars anterior (VLVa), one of the lateral lemniscal nuclei (cf. Fig. 12.3). Little is known about the VLVa, thus, the following discussion deals only with the inferior colliculus. The owl's inferior colliculus contains two major areas, the central nucleus (ICc), which receives direct inputs from medullary and pontine nuclei, and the external nucleus (ICx), which receives inputs only from the ICc (Knudsen, 1983; Takahashi & Konishi, 1988a, 1988b). All ITD-sensitive neurons of the time-processing pathway below the level of the ICx are narrowly tuned to frequency, and they show the same ITD tuning to tones and to broadband noises. These neurons respond not only to one ITD, which does not vary with stimulus frequency, but also to other ITD's, which are separated by integer multiples of the period (nxT) of the stimulus tone. The invariant ITD is termed the characteristic delay (CD) (Rose, Cross, Geisley, & Hind, 1966). The multiple ITD selectivity is termed "phase ambiguity," and it is due to the use of phase-locked spikes for the measurement of ITD. The auditory system does not distinguish a phase difference occurring during one tonal cycle from the same occurring during another cycle. Space-specific neurons also fire maximally for the CD and CD + nxT in response to a tone, if they respond at all, but they do not show phase ambiguity in response to a noise. The mechanisms for the elimination of phase ambiguity involve inhibitory interactions between different frequency channels. (Takahashi & Konishi, 1986; Fujita, 1988).

Another process that takes place between the nucleus laminaris and the ICc is the improvement of ITD selectivity. Neurons of the nucleus laminaris and VLVa are relatively broadly tuned to ITD. The enhancement of ITD selectivity occurs mainly in the ICc. This process also involves inhibition. An injection of a substance that blocks inhibition onto an ICc neuron causes a temporary broadening of its ITD-response curve (Fujita, 1988).

The Intensity-Processing Pathway

Little is known about the mechanisms of IID selectivity, although a recent study suggests the nucleus ventralis lemnisci, pars posterior (VLVp), one of the lateral lemniscal nuclei, is the initial site of IID selectivity. Stimulation of the contralateral ear excites and that of the ipsilateral ear inhibits VLVp neurons. Binaural stimuli can produce responses intermediate between excitation and inhibition. The neurons are sensitive to IID, because their excitatory and inhibitory responses vary differently as a function of different sound intensities in the two ears. Differences in preferred IIDs obtain, because some neurons are more easily inhibited than others. Furthermore, the strength of inhibition varies systematically along the dorso-ventral axis of the nucleus, resulting in a map of IID's (Manly, Koeppl, & Konishi, 1988).

A Map of Auditory Space

The ICx, the site of space-specific neurons, is the terminal stage of processing space information within the owl's auditory system. Although the exact locus of convergence between the time and intensity pathways is not known, all neurons of the ICx are selective for a combination of ITD and IID, which defines a location in the owl's auditory space. Space-specific neurons are arranged systematically according to the spatial coordinates of their receptive fields (see Fig. 12.7). The map is two-dimensional, azimuth and elevation, but the third dimension or distance does not appear to be encoded. The sensory epithelium of the ear does not register stimulus location, thus, the map of auditory space must be centrally synthesized (Konishi & Knudsen, 1982; Konishi, 1986; Knudsen, du Lac, & Esterly, 1987).

General Discussion

Speech can be studied at different levels of organization. To discover universal rules is the goal of the study at any level. These rules must be ultimately linked to brain mechanisms, because the brain controls speech and speech perception. The aspect of speech science that appears most conducive to neurobiological discussion is the study of precognitive perception of speech sounds, because the rules at this level are likely to be identical to the biological rules. A similar approach to the study of "preattentive" visual pattern recognition by Julesz (1984) has produced observations that appear eminently suitable for neurobiological analysis by techniques available today.

Suga, O'Neill, Kujirai, and Manabe (1983) and Sussman (1989) pointed out the possibility and desirability of using animal models in the discussion of speech sound perception. Liberman and Mattingly (1985) and Mattingly and Liberman (1988, in press) have used the examples of the mustached bat, the owl, and the songbird to support their claim for the existence of neural systems specialized for speech sounds. In the owl's auditory system, almost all stages of the neural processes leading to the determination of source location are known (review in Konishi, Takahashi, Wagner, Sullivan, & Carr, 1988). This knowledge enables us to address how signals like speech sounds may be processed, what specializations in the nervous system mean, and how they are achieved.

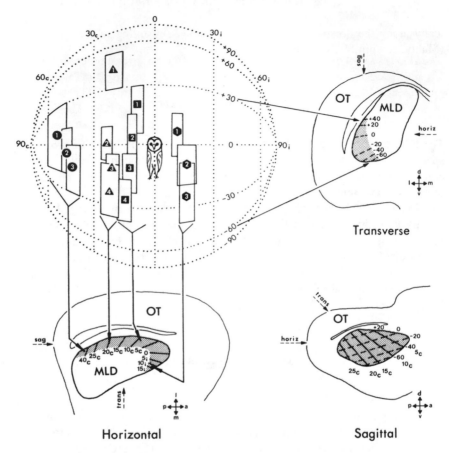

FIG. 12.7. A neural map of auditory space. Space-specific neurons
are systematically arranged in the external nucleus of the inferior colliculus so as to form a map of auditory space. Along the dorsoventral
axis of the nucleus, the receptive fields of neurons have similar azimuthal coordinates whereas their elevational coordinates change systematically. The map covers mostly the contralateral hemifield and a
small ipsilateral segment. Rectangles indicate the areas of receptive
fields where neurons fired maximally; symbols indicate neurons recorded in different penetrations, and numbers show the order in which
the neurons appeared. Coordinates are expressed in degrees: Subscripts c and i denote contralateral and ipsilateral, respectively, and
"+" and "−" denote above and below eye level, respectively. Abbrevi-
ations: MLD refers to nucleus mesencephalicus lateralis, pars dorsalis,
the avian homolog of the inferior colliculus. OT is optic tectum (From
Knudsen & Konishi, 1978b, copyright 1978 by the AAAS).

Hierarchical Schemes of Sensory Processing

The ITD selectivity of a space-specific neuron is due to several processes including phase locking in the ear, the imposition of delays by magnocellular axons, coincidence detection in the nucleus laminaris, the sharpening of ITD selectivity in the ICc, and the elimination of phase ambiguity in the ICx. The intensity pathway also contains several processes before the final form and degree of IID sensitivity is produced. Convergence of the time and intensity pathways allows space to be encoded by a combination of ITD and IID. Although the initial detection of ITD and IID occurs in the third-order station, the convergence occurs in the fifth- or sixth-order station. Thus, these processes occur in a hierarchically organized network in which space-specific neurons occupy the highest position. A similar hierarchical scheme is found in the jamming avoidance system of electric fish, Eigenmannia (Heiligenberg, 1986; Rose, Kawasaki, & Heiligenberg, 1988).

Analysis of complex signals such as speech sounds may involve a hierarchy of neurons (Sussman, 1988, 1989). Different variables of speech sounds are likely to be processed by different parallel pathways before the pathways converge to produce neurons selective for different combinations of the variables. The neurons at the top of the hierarchy are likely to be selective for stimulus configurations that produce percepts of speech sounds. Some of these configurations should be predictable from the study of speech sound perception. In the barn owl, the mustached bat (Suga, 1984), and the electric fish, Eingenmannia (Heiligenberg, 1986), the stimulus configurations that are effective for exciting higher-order neurons are also those that are behaviorally relevant to the animals. The behavioral relevance in these cases was either directly shown, as in the owl and the electric fish, or predicted from behavioral observations, as in the bat. Adaptations of sensory systems for processing of behaviorally relevant stimuli are well known in a wide variety of animals.

Space-specific neurons that are at the top of the hierarchy not only represent but also "map" the output of the network. Space-specific neurons are selective for combinations of ITD and IID, therefore, what is mapped is these combinations. Behavioral experiments show that the owl translates these combinations into spatial locations. It follows that the percept of space resulting from hearing ITD and IID is mapped. Similarly, the auditory cortex of mustached bats consists of separate areas containing neurons selective for different attributes of sonar signals. Neurons selective for delays between emitted sounds and their echoes form a map of delays (Suga & O'Neill, 1979). The bat presumably translates echo delays into distances, thus, the map of delays becomes a map of perceived distances. These maps of percepts are perhaps not isolated examples but represent the principles by which the brain's perceptual systems are organized.

The Nature of Specializations

The time and intensity processing pathways in the owl illustrate the nature of specializations in the brain. The owl's ear encodes amplitude, phase, and frequency of sound; amplitude is represented by the rate of spike discharge, phase by the timing of spikes, and frequency by the site of innervation on the basilar membrane. The spike codes arrive at both cochlear nuclei, but neurons of the nucleus angularis fail to accept the time code, whereas neurons of the nucleus magnocellularis are insensitive to the amplitude code. Large calycine synapses on the somata of magnocellular neurons are suitable for accurate transmission of phase information as seen in the ability of these neurons to phase lock. The connections between auditory fibers and angular neurons are by bouton-type synapses, located on dendrites and somata. Angular neurons fail to phase lock, presumably because variations in dendritic space and time constants make transfer of phase information inaccurate or impossible. These seemingly simple mechanisms are responsible for the initial physiological specializations of the two pathways. Thus, the ability to "preempt" one kind of information is built into the anatomy and physiology of neurons in each cochlear nucleus. Selection of phonological information by the brain may not be based on such simple cellular mechanisms, but it is conceivable that specialized neural circuits like the circuits for the measurement of ITD extract such information. When single neurons represent the output of specialized circuits as in the nucleus laminaris, the neurons confer their stimulus selectivity on higher-order neurons by connections, thus creating pathways specialized for one kind of information.

The Question of Modular Organization

The speech module, as characterized by Mattingly and Liberman (1988, in press) is supposed to contain neural structures and processes unique to speech sounds. What the brain receives from the ear is codes for frequency, amplitude, and phase. Frequency is line-labeled, and amplitude and phase are encoded, respectively in spike rate and timing. This coding scheme applies to both speech and nonspeech sounds. It is, therefore, higher-order neural circuits that must be specialized for different functions. Besides the specializations mentioned before, the inferior colliculus appears to be the site where the system for localization segregates from the rest of the auditory system. Space-specific neurons of the ICx exit the auditory system to join the visual system in the optic tectum, where they form an auditory-visual map of space (Knudsen, 1982), which in turn appears to be directly or indirectly linked to the motor system for head orientation (du Lac & Knudsen, 1987). Thus, the extension of the auditory system may be specialized for sound localization. The main problem with this interpretation is that we do not have any evidence for the exclusive use of the extension for sound localization. Thus, although it is possible to show neural specializations, neither neurophysiological nor neuroanatomical methods alone can show their exclusive use for a particular behavioral task. A behavioral demonstration that combinations of ITDs and IIDs are used exclusively for localization would prove the modular nature of the whole localization system.

Conclusions

If any study of human beings is to be called ethological, it is the analysis of speech perception by Liberman and his associates. Just as early ethologists were impressed by animals' selective responses to sign stimuli, so were Liberman and his associates by the human's special sensitivity to certain aspects of speech sounds (Tinbergen, 1951; Liberman, Cooper, Shankweiler, & Studdert-Kennedy, 1967). The ethologists were aware that the response of an animal to a stimulus varied with the context in which the stimulus was presented. For example, an egg in the next causes a broody gull to incubate it, but an egg outside her nest induces her to eat it. Similarly, Liberman and his associates found that the same sound may be perceived as a speech or a nonspeech sound, depending on the context. This finding led them to the hypothesis of a special brain mechanism for speech perception. Ethologists also hypothesized brain mechanisms for recognition of releasing stimuli. These mechanisms are specialized for each releaser. Neuroethologists endeavor to discover the anatomical and physiological substrates for such mechanisms. To establish a link between speech percepts and their brain mechanisms ultimately requires a combination of psychological and neurobiological methods. As the resolution of various brain scan methods improves, they will play crucial roles in establishing the link.

Acknowledgments

I thank Dr. Susan Volman for reading the manuscript. This work was supported by NIH grant 14617.

References

Broadbent, D. J. (1954). The role of auditory localization in attention and memory span. *Journal of Experimental Psychology, 47,* 191–196.

Carr, C. E., & Konishi, M. (1988). Axonal delay lines for time measurement in the owl's brainstem. *Proceedings of the National Academy of Science, 85,* 8311–8315.

du Lac, S., & Knudsen, E. I. (1987). The optic tectum encodes saccade magnitude in a push–pull fashion in the barn-owl. *Society for Neuroscience Abstracts, 13,* 393.

Fujita, I. (1988). The role of GABA mediated inhibition in the formation of auditory receptive fields. *Uehara Memorial Life Sciences Foundation Research Report* 2, 159–161 (in Japanese).

Heiligenberg, W. (1986). Jamming avoidance responses. In T. H. Bullock & W. Heiligenberg (Eds.), *Electroreception* (pp. 613–649). New York: Wiley.

Jeffress, L. A. (1948). A place theory of sound localization. *Journal of Comparative and Physiological Psychology, 41*, 35–39.

Julesz, B. (1984). Towards an axiomatic theory of preattentive vision. In G. M. Edelman, W. E. Gall, & W. M. Cowan (Eds.), *Dynamic aspects of neocortical function* (pp. 585–612). New York: Wiley.

Knudsen, E. I. (1982). Auditory and visual maps of space in the optic tectum of the owl. *Journal of Neuroscience, 2*, 1177–1194.

Knudsen, E. I. (1983). Subdivisions of the inferior colliculus in the barn owl (Tyto alba). *Journal of Comparative Neurology, 218*, 174–186.

Knudsen, E. I., du Lac, S., & Esterly, S. D. (1987). Computational maps in the brain. *Annual Review of Neuroscience, 10*, 41–65.

Knudsen, E. I., & Konishi, M. (1978a). Space and frequency are represented separately in auditory midbrain of the owl. *Journal of Neurophysiology, 41*, 870–884.

Knudsen, E. I., & Konishi, M. (1978b). A neural map of auditory space in the owl. *Science, 200*, 795–797.

Knudsen, E. I., Konishi, M., & Pettigrew, J. D. (1977). Receptive fields of auditory neurons in the owl. *Science, 198*, 1278–1280.

Konishi, M. (1986). Centrally synthesized maps of auditory space. *Trends in Neuroscience, 4*, 163–168.

Konishi, M., & Knudsen, E. I. (1982). A theory of neural auditory space. In C. N. Woolsey (Ed.), *Cortical sensory organization. Vol 3. Multiple auditory areas* (pp. 219–229). Clifton, NJ: Humana Press.

Konishi, M., Sullivan, W. E., & Takahashi, T. T. (1985). The owl's cochlear nuclei process different sound localization cues. *Journal of the Acoustical Society of America, 78*, 360–364.

Konishi, M., Takahashi, T. T., Wagner, H., Sullivan, W. E., Carr, C. E. (1988). Neurophysiological and anatomical substrates of sound localization in the owl. In G. M. Edelman, W. E. Gall, & W. M. Cowan (Eds.), *Auditory function: Neurobiological bases of hearing* (pp. 721–745). New York: Wiley.

Liberman, A. M., Cooper, F. S., Shankweiler, D. P., & Studdert-Kennedy, M. (1967). Perception of the speech code. *Psychological Review, 74*, 431–461.

Liberman, A. M., & Mattingly, I. G. (1985). The Motor Theory of Speech Perception Revised. *Cognition, 21*, 1–36.

Manley, G. A., Koeppl, C., & Konishi, M. (1988). A neural map of interaural intensity difference in the brainstem of the barn owl. *Journal of Neuroscience, 8*, 2665–2676.

Mattingly, I. G., & Liberman, A. M. (1988). Specialized perceiving systems for speech and other biologically significant sounds. In G. M. Edelman, W. E. Gall, & W. M. Cowan (Eds.), *Auditory function: Neurobiological bases of hearing* (pp. 775–792). New York: Wiley.

Mattingly, I. G., & Liberman, A. M. (in press). Speech and other auditory modules. In G. M. Edelman, W. E. Gall, & W. M. Cowan (Eds.), *Signal and sense: Local and global order in perceptual maps*. New York: Wiley.

Moiseff, A. (1989a). Binaural disparity cues available to the barn owl for sound localization. *Journal of Comparative Physiology, 141*, 629–636.

Moiseff, A. (1989b). Bi-coordinate sound localization by the barn owl. *Journal of Comparative Physiology, 164*, 637–644.

Moiseff, A., & Konishi, M. (1981). Neuronal and behavioral sensitivity to binaural time difference in the owl. *Journal of Neuroscience, 1*, 40–48.

Moiseff, A., & Konishi, M. (1983). Binaural characteristics of units in the owl's brainstem auditory pathway: Precursors of restricted spatial receptive fields. *Journal of Neuroscience, 3,* 2553–2562.

Olsen, J., Esterly, S., & Knudsen, E. I. (1989). Neural maps of interaural time and intensity differences in the optic tectum of the barn owl. *Journal of Neuroscience, 9,* 2591–2605.

Payne, R. S. (1971). Acoustic location of prey by barn owls (Tyto alba). *Journal of Experimental Biology, 54,* 535–573.

Rose, J. E., Cross, N. B., Geisler, C. D., & Hind, J. E. (1966). Some neural mechanisms in the inferior colliculus of the cat which may be relevant to localization of a sound source. *Journal of Neurophysiology, 29,* 218–253.

Rose, G. J., Kawasaki, M., & Heiligenberg, W. (1988). "Recognition units" at the top of a neuronal hierarchy? Prepacemaker neurons in Eigenmannia code the sign of frequency differences unambiguously. *Journal of Comparative Physiology, 162,* 759–772.

Studdert-Kennedy, M., & Shankweiler, D. (1970). Hemispheric specialization for speech perception. *Journal of the Acoustical Society of America, 48,* 579–594.

Suga, N. (1984). The extent to which biosonar information is represented in the bat auditory cortex. In G. M. Edelman, W. E. Gall, & W. M. Cowan (Eds.), *Dynamic aspects of neocortical function* (pp. 315–373). New York: Wiley.

Suga, N., & O'Neill, W. E. (1979). Neural axis representing target range in the auditory cortex of the mustached bat. *Science, 206,* 351–353.

Suga, N., O'Neill, W. E., Kujirai, K., & Manabe, T. (1983). Specificity of combination-sensitive neurons for processing of complex biosonar signals in auditory cortex of the mustached bat. *Journal of Neurophysiology, 49,* 1573–1627.

Sullivan, W. E., & Konishi, M. (1984). Segregation of stimulus phase and intensity in the cochlear nuclei of the barn owl. *Journal of Neuroscience, 4,* 1787–1799.

Sullivan, W. E., & Konishi, M. (1986). Neural map of interaural phase difference in the owl's brain stem. *Proceedings of the National Academy of Science, 83,* 8400–8404.

Sussman, M. H. (1988). The neurogenesis of phonology. In H. Whitaker (Ed.), *Phonological processes and brain mechanisms* (pp. 1–23). New York: Springer-Verlag.

Sussman, M. H. (1989). A bird brain approach to language. *Asha, 31*(5), 83–86.

Takahashi, T. T., & Konishi, M. (1986). Selectivity for interaural time difference in the owl's midbrain. *Journal of Neuroscience, 6,* 3413–3422.

Takahashi, T. T., & Konishi, M. (1988a). Projections of the cochlear nuclei and nucleus laminaris to the inferior colliculus of the barn owl. *Journal of Comparative Neurology, 274,* 190–211.

Takahashi, T. T., & Konishi, M. (1988b). Projections of nucleus angularis and nucleus laminaris to the lateral leminiscal nuclear complex of the barn owl. *Journal of Comparative Neurology, 274,* 212–238.

Takahashi, T. T., Moiseff, A., & Konishi, M. (1984). Time and intensity cues are processed independently in the auditory system of the owl. *Journal of Neuroscience, 4,* 1781–1786.

Tinbergen, N. (1951). *The study of instinct.* London: Oxford University Press.

Yin, T. C. T., Chan, J. C. K., & Carney, L. H. (1987). Effects of interaural time delays of noise stimuli on low-frequency cells in the cat's inferior colliculus. III. Evidence for cross-correlation. *Journal of Neurophysiology, 58,* 562–583.

Chapter 13

Gestural Structures: Distinctiveness, Phonological Processes, and Historical Change

Catherine Browman
Louis Goldstein

Haskins Laboratories

Abstract

Liberman and Mattingly (1985) stated that "gestures . . . have characteristic invariant properties . . . as the more remote structures that control the [peripheral] movements" (p. 23). In this chapter, we show that such gestures not only can characterize the movements of the speech articulators, but also can act as phonological primitives.

Gestures can serve to distinguish lexical items, by their presence or absence in a lexical entry, by differences among their individual attributes, and by the amount of overlap among different gestures in a lexical item, which can vary from complete through partial to minimal. Given this description of a lexical item, the development of a number of phonological alternations and sound changes can be seen as resulting from variability normally occurring during the act of talking—reductions in magnitude of the gestures and increase in the overlap of gestures. Additional cases of historical change, both assimilatory and dissimilatory, can be analyzed as a reassignment of gestural attributes in cases where two gestures overlap. Such reassignment is, in effect, a failure of the listener's normal ability to correctly identify which of two overlapping gestures is the source of some aspect of the acoustic signal.

In this chapter, we present a particular view of phonology, one in which lexical items are construed as characterizing the activity of the vocal tract (and its articulators) as a sound-producing system. Central to this characterization is the concept of dynamically defined articulatory gestures. Such gestures are, we argue, useful primitives for characterizing phonological patterns as well as for analyzing the activity of the vocal tract articulators. Gestural structures can function as lexical representations because distinctiveness is captured by these structures and phonological processes can be seen as operating on them. In addition, the gestural approach has two benefits: It serves to *analyze* phonological patterns according to their source (articulatory, acoustic, perceptual, etc.), and it captures the underlying *unity* among apparently disparate patterns, not only within phonology but also among phonology, perception, and production. These benefits lead to a simpler, more general account of a number of phenomena.

A gestural lexicon is part of the computational model of speech production that we are currently developing with Elliot Saltzman, Philip Rubin, and others at Haskins Laboratories (Browman, Goldstein, Kelso, Rubin, & Saltzman, 1984; Browman, Goldstein, Saltzman, & Smith, 1986; Saltzman, Rubin, Goldstein, & Browman, 1987). Our notion of gesture is based on the concept of coordinative structures (Fowler, Rubin, Remez, & Turvey, 1980) as developed in the task dynamic model (Saltzman, 1986; Saltzman & Kelso, 1987), and is consistent with the view of Liberman and Mattingly (1985) that "gestures . . . have characteristic invariant properties . . . as the more remote structures that control the [peripheral] movements" (p. 23). Briefly, the basic assumptions are: (a) that a primary task in speaking is to control the coordinated movement of groups of articulators (rather than the individual movements of individual articulators), and (b) that these coordinated movements can be characterized using dynamical equations. Each gesture has its own characteristic coordinative pattern.

The hypothesis that the lexicon is composed of dynamically specified gestures has several implications for the Motor Theory and Modularity claims. First, because the same lexicon is assumed to be accessed whether an individual is speaking or listening, the hypothesis implies that a listener ultimately recovers the set of gestures that are part of a given lexical entry. However, the Motor Theory is a specific proposal about the *mechanism* of recovery (among several possible proposals; see for example, Fowler and Rosenblum, chapter 3 this volume) and the arguments for a gestural lexicon should not be construed as supporting this or any other specific proposal. Second, we should note that the use of dynamical equations is not restricted to the description of motor behavior in speech but has been used to describe the coordination and control of skilled motor actions in general (Cooke, 1980; Kelso, Holt, Rubin, & Kugler, 1981; Kelso & Tuller, 1984a, 1984b; Kugler, Kelso, & Turvey, 1980). Indeed, in its preliminary version the task dynamic model we are using for speech was exactly the model used for controlling arm movements, with the articulators of the vocal tract simply substituted for those of the arm. Thus, in this respect the model is not consistent with Liberman and Mattingly's (1985) concept of language or speech as a separate module, with principles unrelated to other domains. However, in another respect, the central role of the task in task dynamics captures the same insight as the "domain-specificity" aspect of the Modularity hypothesis— the way in which the vocal tract articulators are yoked is crucially affected by the task to be achieved (Abbs, Gracco, & Cole, 1984; Kelso, Tuller, Vatikiotis-Bateson, & Fowler, 1984).

In this chapter, in which we focus on larger language patterns (lexical and phonological structure), we will be demonstrating how many of the patterns observed both in inventories and in alternations can be understood in terms of their articulatory and dynamic structure. The general principles governing motor behavior also interact with other principles, such as articulatory-acoustic relations, in a task-specific way to give rise to a variety of different patterns.

Lexical Organization

In this section, we discuss how gestural structures can fulfill one of the most important functions of lexical representation—distinctiveness. We will examine how contrastive words (or morphemes) differ from one another in terms of their component gestures and their organization. In addition, the same gestural structures have an inherent physical meaning: They directly (without mediation of any implementation rules) characterize the articulatory movements of those words.

Gestures and Distinctiveness

A dynamically defined articulatory gesture characterizes the formation (and release) of a constriction within the vocal tract through the movement of (a) a particular set of articulators, (b) towards a particular constriction location, (c) with a specific degree of constriction, and (d) in a characteristic, dynamically described manner. Gestures are not the movements themselves, but rather abstract characterizations of the movements. (See Browman & Goldstein, 1987, and Saltzman et al., 1987, for more detailed descriptions of gestures.) Contrastive gestures can be distinguished on the basis of the values of these four attributes.

Because the gestures characterize movements within the vocal tract, they are effectively organized by the anatomy of the vocal tract. For example, at the coarsest level, gestures may differ in the major articulatory subsystems (velic, laryngeal, and oral) employed (attribute a). These choices correspond to contrasts in nasality, voicing, and place. The oral subsystem can be further divided into three distinct articulator sets (or synergies), one for the lips, one for the tongue tip, and one for the tongue body. This (hierarchical) articulatory organization is also incorporated in a number of recent approaches to phonological features (e.g., Clements, 1985; Ladefoged & Halle, 1988; Sagey, 1986). Contrasts in the familiar oral place of articulation dimension involve one of these articulator sets moving to a particular constriction location (attribute b). Gestures may also contrast in the degree of such constriction (attribute c), corresponding, for example, to stop–fricative–approximant contrasts. Within our computational

tract variable	articulators involved
LP lip protrusion	upper & lower lips, jaw
LA lip aperture	upper & lower lips, jaw
TTCL tongue tip constrict location	tongue tip, body, jaw
TTCD tongue tip constrict degree	tongue tip, body, jaw
TBCL tongue body constrict location	tongue body, jaw
TBCD tongue body constrict degree	tongue body, jaw
VEL velic aperture	velum
GLO glottal aperture	glottis

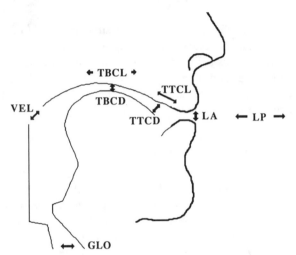

FIG. 13.1. Tract variables and associated articulators used in the computational model of phonology and speech production described in the text.

model, these three attributes determine the set of "tract variables" (see Fig. 13.1). Each oral gesture is represented as a pair of tract variable dynamical equations (one for constriction location, the other for constriction degree), each for the appropriate articulatory synergy. Velic and glottal gestures involve single tract variable equations (Saltzman et al., 1987; Browman & Goldstein, 1987). These dynamical equations include (in addition to specification of target value) dynamic descriptors such as stiffness (related to the rate of movement) and damping. Contrasts in these parameters (attribute d) may be relevant, for example, to the distinction between vowels and glides.

Thus, contrasts among gestures involve differences in the attributes a–d. We may ask, however, how the discreteness associated with lexical contrasts emerges from these differences in attributes. First, it should be noted that gestures involving movements of different sets of articulators (attribute a) differ in an inherently discrete way and are, thus, automatically candidates for distinctiveness (Liberman, Cooper, Shankweiler, & Studdert-Kennedy, 1967). The importance of this anatomical source of distinctiveness can be seen in the fact that, for the 317 languages reported in Maddieson (1984), 96.8% have nasals, and about 80% use voicing differences among consonants. Moreover, 98.4% have a contrast among gestures of the lips, tongue tip, and tongue body.

With respect to the other attributes, however, gestures may not differ discretely from an articulatory and/or dynamic perspective (although our knowledge about possible principles governing the control and coordination of speech gestures is, at present, quite limited). In these cases, other forces will tend to create discrete differences (and, hence, the automatic potential for distinctive use). For example, as Stevens (1972) argued, the potential continuum of constriction degree can be partitioned into relatively discrete regions that produce either complete closure or turbulence based on aerodynamic considerations. The stability of these regions is reflected in the fact that all the languages discussed in Maddieson (1984) have stops; 93.4% have fricatives. For wider constriction degrees, as well as for constriction location (for a given set of articulators), articulatory-acoustic relations (Stevens, 1972) and the predisposition to maximally differentiate the gestures and sounds of a language (e.g., Lindblom, MacNeilage, & Studdert-Kennedy, 1983) will help to localize the distinctive values of these variables in fairly well-defined, stable regions for any one language. These regions may, in fact, differ from language to language (e.g., Disner, 1983; Ladefoged, 1984; Lindblom, 1986), indicating that there is some nondeterminacy in the distribution of these regions. Thus, the distinctiveness of individual gestures is a confluence of general articulatory, acoustic, and perceptual pressures towards discreteness, with a certain amount of arbitrariness resolved in language-particular ways.

Gestural Organization and Distinctiveness

Gestures capture distinctiveness not only individually but also in their organization with respect to each other. Here the fact that gestures are both spatial and temporal becomes crucial. That is, because gestures are characterizations of spatiotemporal articulatory events, it is possible for them to overlap temporally in various ways. This fact of overlap, combined with the underlying anatomical structure, gives rise to different organizations that can be used contrastively and also leads to a variety of phonological processes. The distinctive use of overlap will be discussed in this section, its role in phonological processes later.

Gestural Scores.   A lexical item typically consists of a characteristic organization of several gestures. Within the computational model being developed, the concept of phase relations (Kelso & Tuller, 1985) is used to coordinate the set of gestures for a given lexical item. This results in a representation that we call a gestural score (Browman et al., 1986). Figure 13.2a shows a schematic gestural score for the item *spam*. The five separate rows can be thought of as "tiers": one each for the velic and glottal subsystems, and three for the oral subsystem, representing the three articulatory synergies. Each box represents a single gesture, its horizontal extent indicating the interval of time during which it is active. (For more details on gestural scores and their use, see Browman & Goldstein, 1987.)

Figure 13.2 compares two hypothesized gestural scores, one for *spam* (a) and one for *Sam* (b). There are two additional aspects of distinctiveness that appear when these scores are compared. The only difference between the scores is the

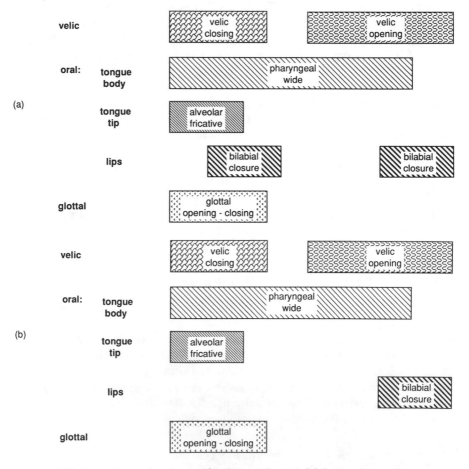

FIG. 13.2.   (a) Gestural score for the word *spam*. (b) Gestural score for the word *Sam*.

presence of the first bilabial closure gesture in *spam*. The first implication of this is that distinctiveness can be conveyed by the presence or absence of gestures (Browman & Goldstein, 1986a; Goldstein & Browman, 1986), which is an inherently discrete property. The second implication is that distinctiveness is a function of an entire constellation of gestures and that more complex constellations need not correspond to concatenated segment-sized constellations. That is, the difference between *spam* and *Sam* is represented by the difference between two oral gestures (alveolar fricative and bilabial closure) versus one oral gesture (alveolar fricative), in each case co-occuring with a single glottal gesture. This contrasts with a segment-based description of the distinction as two segments versus one segment, where each segment includes both a glottal and an oral constriction specification (see Browman & Goldstein, 1986a, for further discussion). In this sense, the gestural structures are topologically similar to autosegmental structures postulated on the basis of evidence from phonological alternations (e.g., Clements & Keyser, 1983; Hayes, 1986). Note that, in contrast with segment-based theories, which effectively require simultaneous coordination among all the features composing a segment, there are no *a priori* constraints on intergestural organization within the gestural framework. The relative "tightness" of cohesion among particular constellations of gestures is a matter for continuing research.

Gestural Overlap.   The gestural scores in Fig. 13.2 show substantial temporal overlap among the various gestures. In this section, we examine how differences in degree of overlap might be used distinctively in the case of two gestures, each with approximately the same extent in time as could occur with some "singleton" consonants, for example [n] (velic and oral gestures) and [t] (glottal and oral gestures). The different possibilities for overlap of such gestures are exemplified in Fig. 13.3, where (as in the gestural scores of Fig. 13.2) the horizontal extent of each rectangle represents the temporal interval during which a particular gesture is posited to be active. There is a potential continuum ranging from complete synchrony—displayed in row (a)—through partial overlap (row b) to minimal overlap (row c). Depending on the particular articulatory subsystems involved (shown in the different columns), as well as the amount of overlap, these gestural combinations would be categorized (by phonologists and phoneticians) as being very different phenomena, as indicated by the labels for each example. Various, and in some cases *ad hoc,* phonological features have been employed to capture these contrasts (see Browman & Goldstein, 1986a for discussion of this point). We would propose, however, that direct analysis of these contrasts in terms of degree of overlap could lead to a simpler and more explanatory description of the distribution of these structures in phonological inventories.

The simplest example of overlap would be the case in which two gestures

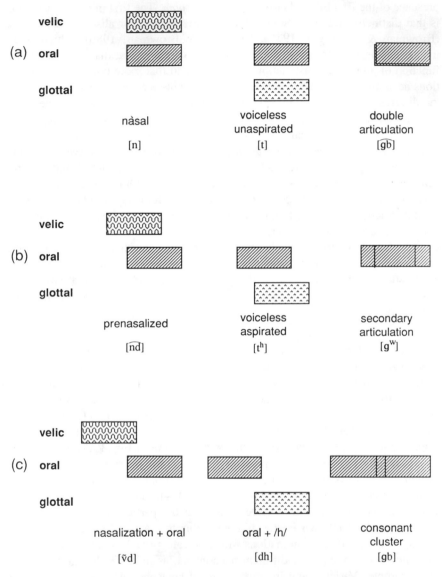

FIG. 13.3. Examples of gestural overlap. Each box represents the temporal interval during which a particular gesture is posited to be active. (a) Complete synchrony. (b) Partial overlap. (c) Minimal overlap. The leftmost column contrasts degrees of overlap for velic plus oral gestures, the middle column for glottal plus oral gestures, and the rightmost column for two oral gestures.

from different articulatory subsystems overlap completely, both having approximately the same extent in time (Fig. 13.3a, left and middle). This case, which (in some sense) maps in a 1:1 fashion onto a segmentation of the acoustic signal, is often analyzed as a segmental unit, for example, (initial) nasal stops or voiceless unaspirated stops (velic plus oral or glottal plus oral, respectively).

What would happen to this simple case, however, when one of the gestures is slid slightly so that the overlap is partial rather than complete (Fig. 13.3b, left and middle)? An aspirated rather than unaspirated stop, for example, maps onto a sequence of two distinct acoustic events—voiceless stop and aspiration—leading to difficulties, in purely acoustic segmentation, in assigning the aspiration to the preceding stop or the following vowel. From a gestural point of view, however, the difference between unaspirated and aspirated stops may be that two gestures are simply organized slightly differently such that there is no longer complete synchrony between the two (see Lisker & Abramson, 1964; Löfqvist, 1980). About 50 languages in Maddieson's (1984) survey contrast voiceless unaspirated with voiceless aspirated stops—these languages, thus, may demonstrate a contrast between the two overlap patterns. The similar overlap differences between the velic and oral gestures may underlie the contrast between prenasalized and nasal stops that occur in 15 of the 18 languages with prenasalized stops (see also Herbert, 1986; Browman & Goldstein, 1986a).

The status of overlap between two gestures within the same articulatory subsystem (oral-oral: Fig. 13.3, right column) differs in several respects from that of overlap between gestures from different articulatory subsystems (oral-glottal or oral-velic). Overlapping oral (consonant) gestures are relatively rare and seem to be restricted to two types. First, nearly synchronous double oral articulations (Fig. 13.3a, right) involving stops are possible, although they occur in only 6.3% of the languages surveyed by Maddieson (1984); moreover, they are apparently restricted to labial and velar closure gestures. Relatively synchronous alveolar and velar closure gestures also occur, albeit rarely, but appear to be associated with a different airstream mechanism—velaric suction—that produces clicks (Traill, 1985). In fact, Marchal (1987) suggested the possibility that the suction associated with clicks could develop automatically from the increased overlap of sequential velar and alveolar closures, as he observes currently in French. Labial-alveolar double articulations have been reported for such languages as Bura and Margi, but the data of Maddieson (1983) show that the gestures involved display at most only partial overlap (however, cf. Sagey, 1986, for further discussion of the phonological status of these structures). Second, stops may show at least partial overlap with a gesture of constriction degree wider than stop or fricative (Fig. 13.3b, right). For example, labialization of stops is observed in about 13% of the languages in Maddieson (1984), and roughly the same proportion of languages show palatalization. Other than these cases, the possibilities for overlap of oral closure gestures with other constriction degrees (e.g., fricatives) is controversial (see Sagey, 1986). Thus, although it is clear that languages can have two (nearly) synchronous oral closure gestures and can also have two such gestures with minimal overlap (that is, consonant clusters as in Fig. 13.3c, right), the status of other kinds of contrastive degrees of overlap involving oral stops and fricatives requires further investigation.

Thus, when we examine contrast in terms of gestures and their organization, we find restrictions or "gaps" in phonological inventories. These restrictions involve the distinctive use of overlap among oral gestures (compared to the relatively freer use of overlap contrasts across articulatory subsystems) and can probably be accounted for by a combination of anatomical and acoustic factors. Labials and velars, for example, use different sets of articulators (lips and tongue) so that it is possible to produce them simultaneously (see Halle, 1982); they also have similar, mutually reinforcing effects on the acoustic signal, both having comparatively more energy in the lower rather than upper end of the spectrum (Jakobson, Fant, & Halle, 1969). Ohala and Lorentz (1978) argued that no other combination of constrictions formed with independent articulators shows this type of acoustic compatibility and that this could account for the predominance of labiovelars among "double" articulations. Constraints on overlapping of gestures with different constriction degrees can also be understood in terms of the aerodynamic or acoustic interaction of the two gestures. It is simply not possible to have the oral tract simultaneously completely closed and also open enough to permit, for example, frication, even if the two constrictions involve different articulator sets and different locations. The acoustic consequences of the oral tract as a whole will be dominated by the narrowest constriction. Note that this points up an inherent difference between the use of two gestures within the same or within different articulatory subsystems. It is perfectly possible, for example, to have the oral tract closed while the nasal tract remains open: The acoustic consequences of the open nasal tract will not be obscured. As Mattingly (1981) pointed out, this type of conflict may constrain the organization of oral gestures in order to maintain the perceptual recoverability.

More generally, we may ask, as we did in the case of gestural attributes, how the potential continuum of intergestural overlap (particularly when involving different articulatory subsystems) might be partitioned into the three discrete contrasting overlap patterns suggested in Fig. 13.3. Although the answer here is quite speculative, again a combination of dynamic articulatory and acoustic factors may be involved. Recent research on bimanual rhythmic movements has demonstrated discrete, stable coordinative modes (in-phase versus out-of-phase) whose properties can be understood in terms of differential coupling of nonlinear oscillators (e.g., Kay, Kelso, Saltzman, & Schöner, 1987; Turvey, Rosenblum, Kugler, & Schmidt, 1986). To the extent that the coordination of different speech gestures can be analyzed in a similar way, it may be possible to discover analogous coupling modes that correspond to contrastive patterns of gestural overlap. In addition, although the overlap between two gestures may form an articulatory continuum, certain qualitative acoustic events may emerge at some critical degree of overlap. For example, as the glottal gesture slides further to the right between rows (a) and (b) of Fig. 13.3 (middle column), at some point perceptible aspiration will be generated. Such emerging acoustic properties could also contribute to the partitioning of the overlap continuum.

In summary, lexical distinctiveness can be represented in gestural structures in three different ways: differences in gestural attributes, presence versus absence of particular gestures, and differences in gestural overlap. In many cases, the gestural framework provides a natural basis for discrete categorization, particularly when supplemented with additional aerodynamic, acoustic, and perceptual principles. In addition, certain general tendencies found in the phonological inventories of human languages can be rationalized when the elements of these inventories are described as gestural structures.

Phonological Processes

The role of gestures and gestural overlap in phonology is not limited to their ability to capture the distinctions among lexical items. Gestural overlap, in particular, can help explain much variability observed during speaking. For example, as argued in the early formulation of the Motor Theory (Liberman et al., 1967), much coarticulation can be explained in terms of the overlap of vowel and consonant gestures ("parallel transmission"), and this idea has been incorporated into our gesture-based computational model (Saltzman et al., 1987; Browman & Goldstein, 1987). In addition, as will be exemplified below, simple changes in gestural overlap can account for more extreme forms of variation such as apparent segment assimilations, deletions, and insertions (Browman & Goldstein, 1987). The explanatory power of gestural overlap springs from the fact that gestures are abstract characterizations of the actual movements of the articulators, movements that occur in space and over time. When two gestures using the same articulator set co-occur, the movements of the articulators will be affected by both gestures. Even when two co-occurring gestures use different sets of articulators, the nature of their overlap can lead, as we will see, to interesting discontinuous effects in the acoustic signal.

The consequences of overlapping gestures are particularly clear in casual speech (Browman & Goldstein, 1987), where casual speech is defined as that fluent subset of fast speech in which reductions typically occur (Lindblom, 1983; Gay, 1981). Indeed, Browman & Goldstein (1987) proposed that all variability in casual speech may be due to gestural reduction and/or changes in gestural overlap. The same patterns that occur in casual speech are also observed in "natural" phonological processes (e.g., Sloat, Taylor, & Hoard, 1978) and in many types of historical change (Pagliuca, 1982; Browman & Goldstein, 1986b). In the following section, we discuss these common patterns, exemplifying how gestures and gestural overlap can contribute to our understanding of the patterns in each of these areas. Next, we discuss synchronic and diachronic patterns (i.e., phonological alternations and historical change) that do not correspond to casual speech processes, showing how in many cases the gestural framework also clarifies the emergence of the patterns.

Synchronic and Diachronic Patterns Attributable To Casual Speech Processes

If we assume that a speaker's knowledge of a lexical item includes a specification of its gestures and their organization, it is possible to provide an explanatory account for many (synchronic and diachronic) patterns of phonological and phonetic variation. First, many kinds of variation that have been described by allophonic or low-level phonetic rules can be modeled as the automatic consequence of talking in which overlapping gestures are produced concurrently. Second, additional kinds of variation can be modeled as consequences of two general principles governing the realization of gestures in casual speech: reduction and increase in overlap. For both of these types of variation, no explicit changes in the talker's representation of the items needs to be assumed. Third, for many kinds of variation that cannot be modeled in this way, we can nevertheless establish a relationship between specific casual speech processes and the development (over historical time) of parallel changes in the talker's representation of the gestural structures themselves (how this might occur is discussed following). Such changes to the gestural structures may either be limited to only some of the environments in which a morpheme occurs, leading to a synchronic alternation that can be described by a gestural phonological rule, or the change may affect an item in all its environments, leading to lexical change in a gestural structure. In this section, therefore, we will discuss patterns that might plausibly originate in the speech production mechanism. We will look first at reduction of individual gestures and then at consequences of overlapping gestures, noting different consequences for overlap when gestures employ the same or different sets of articulators. Each type of pattern will be exemplified in casual speech, phonological alternation, and historical (lexical) change.

Brown (1977) discussed a class of weakenings, or *lenitions,* in casual speech in English, where typical examples involve stop consonants weakening to corresponding fricatives: *because* pronounced as [pxəz], *must be* pronounced as [mʌsβɪ]. These changes are *reductions* in the magnitude of individual stop gestures such that there is incomplete closure and are an instance of the general tendency in some types of fast speech to reduce the movement amplitude (e.g., Lindblom, 1983). Such reductions can occur as regular alternations and, therefore, they can be identified as phonological rules in noncasual speech. For example, Spanish voiced stops are pronounced as fricatives when they occur intervocalically: *diccion* ("diction") pronounced with [ð] in *la diccion; guerra* ("war") pronounced with [ɣ] in *la guerra* (Sloat, Taylor, & Hoard, 1978). Finally, such reductions may occur not just as alternants but as the sole pronunciation of the word, thereby changing the constriction degree of the gesture in the lexical item. For example, Latin intervocalic /b/ is lenited to a fricative in modern Romance languages, as seen in Latin *habere* ("have"), Italian *avere*, French *avoir* (Lass, 1984).

We may inquire specifically how the articulatory or acoustic output of a casual speech process (in this case, reduction) might lead to more permanent or regular changes in the gestural structures that underlie the articulatory movement. One possibility is that some speakers become attuned to particular instances of casual speech variation (e.g., reduction in the output magnitude of some gesture) and actually shift (slightly) the value of the constriction degree parameter (CD) for that gesture in that direction. In the stop/fricative cases noted above, reducing the CD of a stop gesture will increase the likelihood that casual speech processes will result in an output that would be categorized as a fricative as opposed to a stop. The greater preponderance of fricative outputs could lead to a further reduction in CD, and, in general, to a systematic drift in this parameter value until a new stable value is reached (the value for a fricative, in this case), and, thus, an effective recategorization is achieved. Such stable values would coincide with the discrete parameter ranges discussed previously. Although appeals to drift have been made in other accounts of sound change (e.g., the "allophone" drift of Hockett, 1965), the interaction of this mechanism with the nature of gestural structures increases the range of phenomena to which it may be relevant. In particular, drift may be found not only in the parameters of individual gestures but also in their overlap, leading to a variety of different articulatory and acoustic consequences. These consequences can be related to phonological processes.

Gestural *overlap* plays a large role in the formation of phonological patterns. (Indeed it is conceivable that gestural reduction of consonants is partly due to their overlap with vowels, with their opposite requirements for constriction degree.) The consequence of gestural overlap when two gestures involve the same pair of (oral) tract variables (or, as described in Browman and Goldstein, 1987, they occupy the same articulatory tier) follows automatically from the fact that both use the same set of articulators, leading to blending of the movements of the two. This kind of *assimilation* occurs in the following examples of casual speech (some from British English): *eight things* pronounced as [ɛ⁺ǐt̪'θɪŋz]; *come from* pronounced as [kʌɱfrəm]; *this year* pronounced as ['ðɪʃjɪə] (Catford, 1977; Brown, 1977). Such blendings may also occur in the canonical form of words, particularly because the initial consonant and vowel gestures of a syllable may overlap (Browman & Goldstein, 1987; Fowler, 1983; Öhman, 1966). Such canonical blendings are traditionally described phonologically as instances of allophonic variation, for example, between front and back /k/ in English—*key* vs. *caw* (Ladefoged, 1982)—and can contribute to sound changes: (pre)Old English *ceap* (presumed to begin with [k]) becoming Modern English *cheap*, but Old

English *cuman* (also presumed to begin with [k]) becoming Modern English *come* (Arlotto, 1972).

When overlapping gestures use different tract variables (and, therefore, different sets of articulators), they do not affect each other's movements, but rather both contribute to the overall vocal tract shape, acoustic output, and perceptual response. One consequence of increasing the overlap between oral gestures from different articulatory tiers (i.e., using different tract variables) is (perceptual) assimilation. Various authors (Kohler, 1976; Barry, 1985; Browman & Goldstein, 1987) have presented articulatory evidence that alveolar articulations can occur (possibly reduced in magnitude) in assimilations such as "seven plus" pronounced as ['sɛvm̩plʌs] (Browman & Goldstein, 1987). In this example, the following labial gesture overlaps the alveolar gesture to such a degree that the alveolar gesture is effectively "hidden" in the acoustic signal. In addition, the labial gesture also partially overlaps the velic lowering gesture. The result is an apparent assimilation of the place of the nasal to the following consonant (from [n] to [m]—an assimilation that may involve no change in the individual gestures but simply increased overlap among gestures.

Another more striking consequence of increasing the overlap between gestures is the percept of *deletion* rather than assimilation. Apparent deletions, which are common in syllable-final position in fluent speech (Brown, 1977), can result from two gestures, on different articulatory tiers, sliding with respect to each other so that one gesture is effectively hidden. Articulatory evidence for sliding has been observed in the utterances *perfect memory* pronounced as ['pɚfək'mɛməri] and *nabbed most* pronounced as ['næbmows] (Browman & Goldstein, 1987). In these utterances, all the gestures were present: The final alveolar closures in *perfect* and *nabbed* were observed in the movements of the tip of the tongue. However, because of the increased overlap between *perfect* and *memory* (and *nabbed* and *most*), these final alveolar closures were acoustically hidden by the initial labial closures of the following word, resulting in an apparent deletion—acoustically and perceptually but not articulatorily.

In addition to these casual speech examples, increased overlap of gestures using different tract variables may also be the source of regular phonological alternations and lexical simplifications. In particular, we hypothesize that an oral gesture may be hidden an increasing proportion of the time through drift in the parameter(s) controlling intergestural phasing. Eventually, a regularly hidden gesture may be deleted from the lexical item, either in particular environments (leading to a synchronic rule) or from the lexicon entirely. Oral gesture deletion may occur regardless of whether, from a strictly segmental point of view, the perceptual consequences of the increased overlap are partial (i.e., corresponding to casual speech assimilations) or total (i.e., corresponding to apparent deletions). Examples of both types of gesture deletion can be found, where the likely motivation for the deletion is in all cases hiding due to increased gestural overlap.

An example of oral gesture deletion associated with assimilation involves the assimilation of nasals to the place of the following consonant. Such regular synchronic alternations occur commonly in languages of the world: e.g., Yoruba (a Nigerian language) [o ɱ fo] "he is jumping," [o n lo] "he is going," [o ŋ ke] "he is crying" (Bamgbose, 1969, in Sagey, 1986). Nasal place assimilation can also be seen in lexical changes in English, for example, in the change from Old French *conforter* to Modern English *comfort* (Arlotto, 1972). Oral gestural deletion of the total type may be seen in phonological rules that delete word-final consonants. For example, in Lardil, an Australian language, all nontongue tip consonants are deleted word-finally: [ŋalu] ("story") versus [ŋaluk-in] ("story" + nonfuture suffix) (Kenstowicz & Kisseberth, 1979). Word-final deletions may also occur in lexical simplifications, for example, Ancient Chinese /fap/ ("law") and /pat/ ("eight") becoming Mandarin /fa/ and /pa/ (Arlotto, 1972).

The hypothesized association between increased overlap and oral gesture deletion can also be seen as underlying the inventory restrictions on the distinctive use of overlapping oral consonantal gestures noted previously. Although units consisting of two oral obstruent gestures can arise from overlap, for example, in Margi (Hoffman, 1963, in Sagey, 1986), it is clear that there is a strong tendency against such a phenomenon in languages of the world.

Finally, variation in overlap among a whole constellation of gestures can lead to a percept of segment *insertion*. Several authors (e.g., Ohala, 1974; Anderson, 1976) have analyzed the epenthetic stop in nasal-fricative sequences such as *something* ['sʌmpθɪŋ] and *Samson* ['sæmpsən] as arising from variation in the relative timing of the velic closure gesture and the oral closure gesture. In particular, if denasalization precedes the release of the closure gesture, then a short interval of oral closure will be produced. Such variation can lead to historical change, as in the Old English θymle becoming Modern English *thimble*. Note that in these cases, no gesture is ever added. Rather, the categorical historical change involves drift in the gestural organization to a different stable pattern of overlap.

Other Types of Synchronic and Diachronic Patterns

In the previous section, we discussed synchronic and diachronic patterns whose explanation required reference only to the mechanism of speech production, as indicated by their correspondence to casual speech patterns. In this section, we explore some synchronic and diachronic patterns that do not correspond to casual speech variation; that is, they cannot be completely accounted for by the principles of gestural reduction and increase in overlap. A number of these cases have been analyzed as being acoustically or perceptually based. Yet, as we will see, these factors do not appear to operate independently of the articulatory and gestural structures involved but rather interact with these structures to produce the change (or synchronic alternation). In particular, two additional principles are hypothesized to account for these cases: reassignment of gestural parameters among temporally overlapping gestures and misparsing of articulatory movements into their underlying discrete gestural regimes.

Reassignment of Gestural Attributes.   The ability of listeners to recover the intended gestures from the "single aspect of the acoustic signal" (Liberman et al., 1967, p. 455) that results from gestural overlap is as important in its occasional failure as in its more frequent success. That is, whereas in the normal course of events, as Fowler (1984) wrote, "listeners use coarticulatory information as information for the influencing segment, and . . . do not integrate it into their perceptual experience of the segment with which it co-occurs in time" (p. 365), the failure of this ability can lead to changes in the lexical gestural structure. Such a failure may be exemplified by the change from [x] to [f] in English words such as "cough" and "tough," whose vowels were diphthongs with rounded offglides at the time these changes took place. This sound change has typically been attributed solely to the acoustic similarity of labials and velars (e.g., Jonasson, 1971). However, Pagliuca (1982) showed that most such [x]–[f] changes are not purely acoustic but rather are conditioned by labial and velar articulations occurring in close proximity prior to the change. That is, in many cases the [x]–[f] change consists of a change in the overlap and constriction degree of the gestures rather than the insertion of a completely new articulation.

For the English examples like *cough* and *tough,* Pagliuca (1982) described the change as due to "the gradual coarticulation of decaying x with the adjacent rounded diphthong" (p. 171). For words undergoing the [x]–[f] change, the rounded diphthong apparently changed to an unrounded monophthong at the same time that the [x] was changing to [f] (Dobson, 1968, in Pagliuca, 1982). In the gestural framework, all these changes might result simply from an increase in overlap (drifting over time) between the second element of the diphthong ([ʊ]) and the following velar fricative. Figure 13.4a shows the hypothesized gestural score before the change, for the VC portion of the word. Both [o] and [ʊ] comprise two gestures: a tongue body gesture (uvular narrow or velar narrow, respectively), and a narrow bilabial gesture for rounding. Increasing overlap, as shown in Fig. 13.4b, would automatically shorten the preceding vowel from a diphthong to a monophthong. As shown in the figure, it would also mean that the lip-rounding gesture for [ʊ] co-occurred with the frication from the velar gesture. Only one additional step would then be needed: the attribution of the frication (presumably on the part of the listener) to the labial gesture rather than to the tongue body (velar) gesture. This reassignment of the constriction degree parameter value appropriate for frication would result in a bilabial fricative (and a velar gesture that subsequently is deleted), leaving the structure in Fig. 13.4c. The monophthongal vowel also lowers at some point to [ɔ], and the bilabial fricative becomes [f], neither of which is shown in the figure.

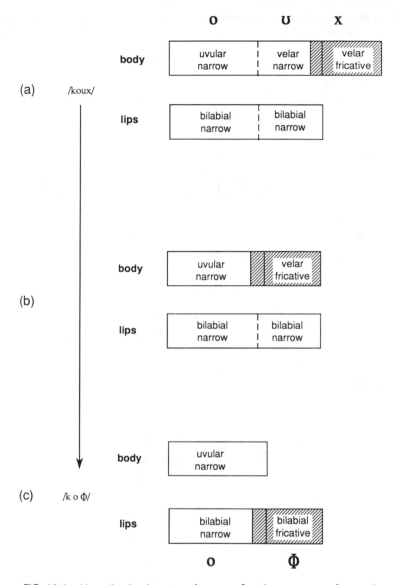

FIG. 13.4. Hypothesized gestural scores for three stages of sound change for English *cough.* Only the VC portion of the word is shown. (a) is the earliest stage, and (c) is the latest shown.

Ohala (1981) also argued for the importance of (partially) overlapping articulations in historical change, although his emphasis is on the explanatory role of
the listener rather than of articulatory overlap, *per se*. For example, Ohala (1981)
attributed many examples of assimilation to the (mis)attribution of some acoustic
effect to the segment temporally coincident with the effect rather than to segments in the environment: eighth century Tibetan /nub/ "west" becoming /nuː/,
but /lus/ "body" becoming /lyː/ (Michailovsky, 1975, in Ohala, 1981). In this

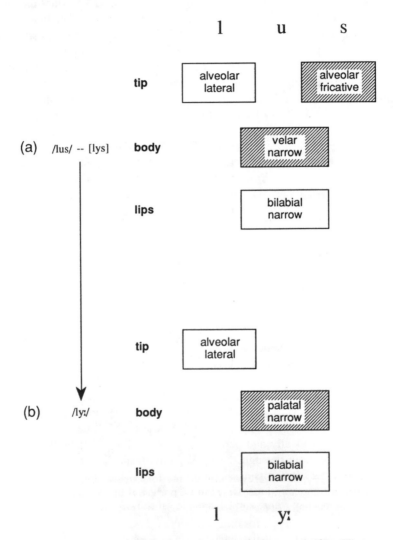

FIG. 13.5. Hypothesized gestural scores before and after Tibetan
sound change: /lus/ → /lyː/.

example, Ohala proposed that, because of coarticulation, /lus/ is auditorily [lys], and, therefore, the lexical change to a front vowel in /lyː/ results from a reassignment of the acoustic effects of the overlapping /s/ to the vowel articulation, as the /s/ is deleted. (An analysis along these same lines for similar changes in the history of Lisu is also presented in Javkin, 1979.) In gestural terms, the situation in Tibetan can be represented as in Fig. 13.5. As the alveolar fricative gesture in (a) is deleted in (b), the constriction location of the tongue body gesture is recategorized as palatal rather than velar in order to account for effects that were originally due to the overlapping alveolar gesture. As Ohala noted, the acoustic effect on the vowel in [lys]—in (a)—need not result from an articulatory fronting of the tongue body itself—a partially overlapping tongue tip constriction will produce the same auditory effect as a fronted tongue body constriction. This is consistent with the analysis of overlap presented previously. That is, because the alveolar and vowel gestures are on separate tiers, they interact through the acoustic effect of the gestures occurring simultaneously rather than through actual blending of constriction targets. Finally, note that the increased length of the vowel in /lyː/ is also automatically accounted for by this analysis. As shown in Fig. 13.5, the duration of the vowel gestures (tongue body and lips) is assumed to not change—from (a) to (b)—but the part of their duration that is hidden by the overlapping alveolar gesture at the earlier stage is uncovered when the alveolar is deleted. This type of explanation for "compensatory lengthening" phenomena was proposed by Fowler (1983).

Thus, although acoustic and perceptual factors are relevant in accounting for the changes described in this section, the overlapping of two gestures and their interaction are also crucial to the account. Note that these changes do not involve adding articulations that were not there to begin with; rather they involve changes in the parameters of gestures that are already present.

Gestural Misparsing.   Other examples of historical change appear to involve introduction of a gesture that was not present at an earlier stage. One such apparent example is the historical introduction of nasalized vowels in words without a nasal consonant in the environment: Sanskrit sarpa ("snake") becoming Hindi /sãp/, Sanskrit švãsa ("breath") becoming Hindi /sãs/ (Ohala & Amador, 1981). As analyzed by Ohala & Amador (1981), such "spontaneous" nasalization is acoustically and perceptually based. The acoustic effects on the vowel of high air flow through the open glottis (especially for fricatives) are reinterpreted by the listener as nasalization, leading to the introduction of a velic opening gesture (in gestural terms). However, there is an alternative (or perhaps complementary) articulatory account suggested by Ignatius Mattingly (personal communication). In general, for oral constriction gestures that are not nasalized, the associated velum height has been found to vary directly with the gesture's constriction degree, decreasing in the series obstruents—high vowels—low vowels (Bell-Berti, 1980). A relatively low velum position is found during non-nasalized low vowels, even in a language (such as Hindi) that contrasts nasalization on low vowels (Henderson, 1984). Thus, in the normal production of utterances like /sa/, the velum will lower rapidly from the consonant to the vowel of this utterance. This rapid change in velum position may be misinterpreted by a listener (or by a child learning the language) as an explicit velic lowering gesture. This account would be most plausible in the case of low vowel nasalization (as in the cited Hindi examples), and to accept it, we would need to know how often such spontaneous nasalization is associated with low versus high vowels. To summarize this proposal, if we hypothesize that the continuous articulatory movement (velum lowering) associated with a word is parsed by the language learner into the discrete gestures (and organization) of the gestural score, then this case involves a misparsing: Velum lowering is assigned to an explicit gesture. Note however, that in this view, the added gesture is based on an articulation that is already present rather than being suddenly introduced by listeners with no articulatory basis.

This kind of misparsing is very similar to that proposed by Ohala (1981) to account for various kinds of historical dissimilations. An acoustic (or articulatory) effect is attributed to coarticulation with segments in the environment rather than to the segment itself. For example, in the case of pre-Shona /kumwa/ becoming Shona /kumɣa/ (Guthrie 1967–1970 and Mkanganwi, 1972, in Ohala, 1981), Ohala proposed that listeners attribute the labiality of the /w/ to the preceding labial consonant, and, therefore, factor it out, leaving the velar component /ɣ/. Ohala's analysis, translated into gestural terms is shown in Fig. 13.6. In (a), the superimposed curve illustrates the waxing and waning of lower lip raising (over time) that might be expected when the lips are under the control of the two successive lip gestures shown in the score. In (b), we see that roughly the same lip movement curve would be expected, even if there is only a single bilabial gesture. As in the nasalization case previous, we can view this change in terms of how the observed articulatory movements are parsed into the gestures that could give rise to them. The pattern of lip movement is attributed to a single gesture rather than to a pair of overlapping lip gestures. In this case, the misparsing results in too few gestures (thus deleting one), whereas in the nasalization case, the misparsing results in an additional gesture.

A related pattern of labial dissimilation occurs synchronically in Cantonese. As described by Yip (1988), labial dissimilation in Cantonese operates on both labial consonants and rounded vowels, that is, on gestures involving the lips. A co-occurrence restriction prevents more than a single gesture using the lips from occurring in the same syllable (except that a back rounded vowel may co-occur with a preceding, but not following, labial consonant). Moreover, this co-occurrence restriction is used productively in a Cantonese "secret language" called La-mi. As discussed in Yip (1988), this secret language uses a form of reduplication in which /$C_1V(C_2)$/ becomes /$1V(C_2) C_1i(C_2)$/ (/yat/ → /lat yit/, /kei/ → /lei

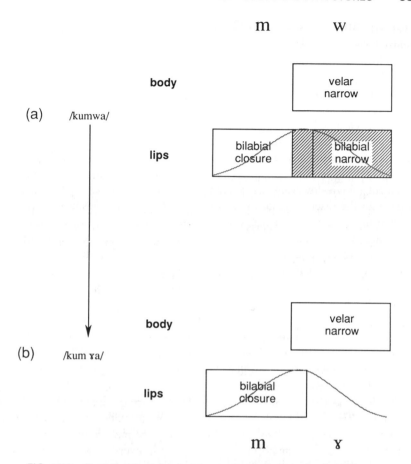

FIG. 13.6. Hypothesized gestural scores before and after Shona sound change: /kumwa/ → /kumɣa/. Only the medial consonants are shown. The curve superimposed on the bilabial gestures shows the expected lower lip movement over time resulting from these gestures.

ki/). However, /sap/ does not become /lap sip/ but rather /lap sit/; similarly, /t′im/ becomes /lim t′in/. That is, the co-occurence restriction includes the entire two syllables in this secret language so that a final labial stop is replaced with an alveolar stop in order to preserve the general restriction on labial gestures within a unit. Note that in this secret language, a distinctive gesture is neither deleted nor added (as in earlier examples of this section) but rather is replaced by another oral gesture that uses a different set of articulators (i.e., is on a different tier). Moreover, the example shows that a dissimilatory pattern, once set up, can be extended beyond the original misparsed environments that presumably led to the change.

Patterns not Attributable to Gestures
or Gestural Overlap

Some phonological alternations are so complex as to not permit an adequate description using gestural principles (even with the acoustic and perceptual interactions described in the previous sections). Kenstowicz and Kisseberth (1979) described a morphophonemic process in Chimwi:ni (a Bantu language spoken in Somalia) that exemplifies the degree of complexity that languages can attain. The process involves an interaction between the perfective suffix for verbs and the final consonant of the stem. The form of the perfective suffix for verbs either contains a liquid [ɫ] "that is phonemically distinct from both l and r" (Kisseberth & Abasheik, 1975, p. 250), or, if the stem-final consonant is [s,z,š,ñ], it contains a [z]. This appears to be a kind of assimilatory process. However, the class of [s,z,š,ñ], is not a natural class articulatorily: Although they are all central, and all use the front part of the tongue, other central tongue tip consonants ([d], [n]) occur with [ɫ] rather than [z].

The behavior of the stem-final consonant adds to the eye-glazing complexity of the perfective form. Stem-final consonants that are stops in the infinitive form generally correspond to the central alveolar fricatives [s] and [z] in the perfective form. That is, the oral gesture can use different articulators in the two forms (for example, [p]/[s]), as well as having a different constriction degree (voicing is unchanged). However, [k] corresponds to [š] not [s], thereby showing some slight hint of articulatory conditioning, either of the specific articulator or front/back constriction location.

Although the Chimwi:ni example displays a certain amount of articulatory patterning, it is not possible to provide a general statement of the patterns contributing to the alternations, even using highly abstract projections of gestures (or their acoustic consequences). At some point in every language, the patterns begin to take on a life of their own, loosened from their articulatory and/or acoustic underpinnings and perhaps respecting other sets of principles (cf. Anderson, 1981). Phonologists have attempted to describe these patterns (e.g., "crazy rules," Bach & Harms, 1972) as emerging from the interaction of a number of independent rules, each of which by itself can be simply understood. Rule telescopy (Wang, 1969) and rule inversion (Vennemann, 1972) are examples of such interaction.

In summary, we have attempted to show how lexical representations can be viewed as gestural structures and that to view them thus contributes to an understanding of phonological inventories and processes. Although other principles and sources of constraint are no doubt required to completely explicate patterns in phonology, we have been surprised by the range of phenomena that can be handled with the relatively simple assumptions that we are making: That phonological structures consist of temporally overlapping, dynamically defined gestural units, that the output of these structures may be systematically altered (in highly constrained ways) in casual speech, and that variations in output of these structures can lead (historically) to changes in the values of gestural parameters—both through drift and through mechanisms such as reassignment and misparsing. Indeed several of the cases that we present in this chapter were initially chosen by us to illustrate where the gestural approach would fail. Once the gestural analyses were made explicit, however, they were more insightful than even we expected. We suggest that it is interesting and important to see just how much such simple structures and principles can contribute to understanding phonological patterns.

Acknowledgments

This work was supported by NSF grant BNS 8520709, and NIH grants HD-01994 and NS-13617, to Haskins Laboratories. Our thanks to Margaret Dunn, Alice Faber, Ignatius Mattingly, Elliot Saltzman, and Douglas Whalen for helpful comments on a previous manuscript.

References

Abbs, J. H., Gracco, V. L., & Cole, K. J. (1984). Control of multimovement coordination: Sensorimotor mechanisms in speech motor programming. *Journal of Motor Behavior, 16,* 195–231.
Anderson, S. R. (1976). Nasal consonants and the internal structure of segments. *Language, 52,* 326–344.
Anderson, S. R. (1981). Why phonology isn't "Natural." *Linguistic Inquiry, 12,* 493–540.
Arlotto, A. (1972). *Introduction to historical linguistics.* Boston: Houghton Mifflin.
Bach, E., & Harms, R. T. (1972). How do languages get crazy rules? In R. P. Stockwell & R. K. S. Macaulay (Eds.), *Linguistic change and generative theory* (pp. 1–21). Bloomington: Indiana University Press.
Bamgbose, A. (1969). Yoruba. In E. Dunstan (Ed.), *Twelve Nigerian languages.* New York: African Publishing.
Barry, M. C. (1985). A palatographic study of connected speech processes. *Cambridge Papers in Phonetics and Experimental Linguistics, 4,* 1–16.
Bell-Berti. F. (1980). Velopharyngeal function: A spatio-temporal model. In N. J. Lass (Ed.), *Speech and language: Advances in basic research and practice* (vol. IV, pp. 291–316). New York: Academic Press.
Browman, C. P., & Goldstein, L. (1986a). Towards an articulatory phonology. *Phonology Yearbook, 3,* 219–252.
Browman, C. P., & Goldstein, L. (1986b). Dynamic processes in linguistics: Casual speech and historical change. *PAW Review, 1,* 17–18.
Browman, C. P., & Goldstein, L. (1987). Tiers in articulatory phonology, with some implications for casual speech. *Haskins Laboratories Status Report on Speech Research, SR-92,* 1–30. To appear in J. Kingston & M. E. Beckman (Eds.), *Papers in laboratory phonology I: Between the grammar and the physics of speech.* Cambridge: Cambridge University Press.
Browman, C. P., Goldstein, L., Kelso, J. A. S., Rubin, P., & Saltzman, E. (1984). Articulatory synthesis from underlying dynamics. *JASA, 75,* S22–S23. (Abstract).

Browman, C. P., Goldstein, L., Saltzman, E., & Smith, C. (1986). GEST: A computational model for speech production using dynamically defined articulatory gestures. *Journal of the Acoustical Society of America, 80,* S97 (Abstract).

Brown, G. (1977). *Listening to spoken English.* London: Longman.

Catford, J. C. (1977). *Fundamental problems in phonetics.* Bloomington, IN: Indiana University Press.

Clements, G. N. (1985). The geometry of phonological features. *Phonology Yearbook, 2,* 225–252.

Clements, G. N., & Keyser, S. J. (1983). *CV phonology: A generative theory of the syllable.* Cambridge, MA: MIT Press.

Cooke, J. D. (1980). The organization of simple, skilled movements. In G. E. Stelmach & J. Requin (Eds.), *Tutorials in motor behavior* (pp. 199–212). Amsterdam: North-Holland.

Disner, S. F. (1983). Vowel quality: The relation between universal and language specific factors. *UCLA Working Papers in Phonetics, 58.*

Dobson, E. J. (1968). *English pronunciation 1500–1700.* (2nd ed.). Oxford: Clarendon Press.

Fowler, C. A. (1983). Converging sources of evidence on spoken and perceived rhythms of speech: Cyclic production of vowels in sequences of monosyllabic stress feet. *Journal of Experimental Psychology: General, 112,* 386–412.

Fowler, C. A. (1984). Segmentation of coarticulated speech in perception. *Perception and Psychophysics, 36,* 359–368.

Fowler, C. A., Rubin, P., Remez, R. E. & Turvey, M. T. (1980). Implications for speech production of a general theory of action. In B. Butterworth (Ed.), *Language production* (pp. 373–420). New York: Academic Press.

Gay, T. (1981). Mechanisms in the control of speech rate. *Phonetica, 38,* 148–158.

Goldstein, L., & Browman, C. P. (1986). Representation of voicing contrasts using articulatory gestures. *Journal of Phonetics, 14,* 339–342.

Guthrie, M. (1967–1970). *Comparative Bantu* (vols. 1–4). Farmborough: Gregg.

Halle, M. (1982). On distinctive features and their articulatory implementation. *Natural Language and Linguistic Theory, 1,* 91–105.

Hayes, B. (1986). Assimilation as spreading in Toba Batak. *Linguistic Inquiry, 17,* 467–500.

Henderson, J. (1984). *Velopharyngeal function in oral and nasal vowels: A cross-language study.* Unpublished doctoral dissertation, University of Connecticut.

Herbert. R. K. (1986). *Language universals, markedness theory, and natural phonetic processes.* Berlin: Mouton de Gruyter.

Hockett, C. F. (1965). Sound change. *Language, 41,* 185–204.

Hoffman, C. (1963). *A grammar of the Margi language.* London: Oxford University Press.

Jakobson, R., Fant, C. G. M., & Halle, M. (1969). *Preliminaries to speech analysis: The distinctive features and their correlates.* Cambridge, MA: The MIT Press.

Javkin, H. (1979). Phonetic universals and phonological change. *Report of the Phonology Laboratory, 4.*

Jonasson, J. (1971). Perceptual similarity and articulatory reinterpretation as a source of phonological innovation. *STL-QPSR, 1,* 30–42.

Kay, B. A., Kelso, J. A. S., Saltzman, E. L., & Schöner, G. (1987). Space-time behavior of single and bimanual rhythmical movements: Data and limit cycle model. *Journal of Experimental Psychology: Human Perception and Performance, 13,* 178–192.

Kelso, J. A. S., Holt, K. G., Rubin, P., & Kugler, P. N. (1981). Patterns of human interlimb coordination emerge from the properties of nonlinear limit cycle oscillatory processes: Theory and data. *Journal of Motor Behavior, 13,* 226–261.

Kelso, J. A. S., & Tuller, B. (1984a). A dynamical basis for action systems. In M. Gazzaniga (Ed.), *Handbook of cognitive neuroscience* (pp. 321–356). New York: Plenum.

Kelso, J. A. S., & Tuller, B. (1984b). Converging evidence in support of common dynamical principles for speech and movement coordination. *American Journal of Physiology: Regulatory, Integrative and Comparative Physiology, 246*, R928–R935.

Kelso, J. A. S., & Tuller, B. (1985). Intrinsic time in speech production: Theory, methodology, and preliminary observations. *Haskins Laboratories Status Report on Speech Research, SR–81*, 23–39.

Kelso, J. A. S., Tuller, B., Vatikiotis-Bateson, E., & Fowler, C. A. (1984). Functionally specific articulatory cooperation following jaw perturbations during speech: Evidence for coordinative structures. *Journal of Experimental Psychology: Human Perception and Performance, 10*, 812–832.

Kisseberth, C., & Abasheik, M. I. (1975). The perfect stem in Chi-Mwi:ni and global rules. *Studies in African Linguistics, 6*, 249–266.

Kenstowicz, M., & Kisseberth, C. (1979). *Generative phonology*. Orlando, FL: Academic Press.

Kohler, K. (1976). Die Instabilitat wortfinaler Alveolarplosive im Deutschen: eine elektropalatographische Untersuchung [The instability of word-final alveolar plosives in German: An electropalatographic investigation.] *Phonetica, 33*, 1–30.

Kugler, P. N., Kelso, J. A. S., & Turvey, M. T. (1980). On the concept of coordinative structures as dissipative structures: I. Theoretical lines of convergence. In G. E. Stelmach & J. Requin (Eds.), *Tutorials in motor behavior* (pp. 3–47). New York: North-Holland.

Ladefoged, P. (1982). *A course in phonetics* (2nd ed.). New York: Harcourt Brace Jovanovich.

Ladefoged, P. (1984). "Out of chaos comes order": Physical, biological, and structural patterns in phonetics. In M. P. R. van den Broecke & A. Cohen (Eds.), *Proceedings of the Tenth International Congress of Phonetic Sciences* (pp. 83–95). Dordrecht, Holland: Foris.

Ladefoged, P., & Halle, M. (1988). Some major features of the International Phonetic Alphabet. *Language, 64*, 577–582.

Lass, R. (1984). *Phonology*. Cambridge: Cambridge University Press.

Liberman, A. M., Cooper, F. S., Shankweiler, D., & Studdert-Kennedy, M. (1967). Perception of the speech code. *Psychological Review, 74*, 431–436.

Liberman, A. M., & Mattingly, I. G. (1985). The Motor Theory of Speech Perception Revised. *Cognition, 21*, 1–36.

Lindblom, B. (1983). Economy of speech gestures. In P. F. MacNeilage (Ed.), *The production of speech* (pp. 217–245). New York: Springer-Verlag.

Lindblom, B. (1986). Phonetic universals in vowel systems. In J. J. Ohala & J. J. Jaeger (Eds.), *Experimental phonology* (pp. 13–44). Orlando, FL: Academic Press.

Lindblom, B., MacNeilage, P., & Studdert-Kennedy, M. (1983). Self-organizing processes and the explanation of phonological universals. In B. Butterworth, B. Comrie, & O. Dahl (Eds.), *Explanations of linguistic universals* (pp. 182–203). The Hague: Mouton.

Lisker, L., & Abramson, A. S. (1964). A cross-language study of voicing in initial stops: Acoustical measurements. *Word, 20*, 384–422.

Löfqvist, A. (1980). Interarticulator programming in stop production. *Journal of Phonetics, 8*, 475–490.

Maddieson, I. (1983). The analysis of complex phonetic elements in Bura and the syllable. *Studies in African Linguistics, 14*, 285–310.

Maddieson, I. (1984). *Patterns of sounds*. Cambridge: Cambridge University Press.

Marchal, A. (1987). Des clics en francais. *Phonetica, 44*, 30–37.

Mattingly, I. G. (1981). Phonetic representation and speech synthesis by rule. In T. Myers, J. Laver, & J. Anderson (Eds.), *The cognitive representation of speech* (pp. 415–420). Amsterdam: North-Holland.

Michailovsky, B. (1975). On some Tibeto–Burman sound changes. *Proceedings of the Annual Meeting, Berkeley Linguistics Society, 1*, 322–332.

Mkanganwi, K. G. (1972). The relationships of coastal Ndau to the Shona dialects of the interior. *African Studies, 31*, 111–137.

Ohala, J. J. (1974). Experimental historical phonology. In J. M. Anderson & C. Jones (Eds.), *Historical linguistics* 2 (pp. 353–389). Amsterdam: North-Holland.

Ohala, J. J. (1981). The listener as a source of sound change. In C. S. Masek, R. A. Hendrick, & M. F. Miller (Eds.), *Papers from the parasession on language and behavior* (pp. 178–203). Chicago: Chicago Linguistic Society.

Ohala, J. J., & Amador, M. (1981). Spontaneous nasalization. *Journal of the Acoustical Society of America, 69,* S54–S55 (Abstract).

Ohala, J. J., & Lorentz, J. (1978). The story of [w]: An exercise in the phonetic explanation for sound patterns. *Report of the Phonology Laboratory, 2,* 133–155.

Öhman, S. E. G. (1966). Coarticulation in VCV utterances: Spectrographic measurements. *Journal of the Acoustical Society of America, 39,* 151–168.

Pagliuca, W. (1982). *Prolegomena to a theory of articulatory evolution.* Doctoral dissertation, SUNY at Buffalo. Ann Arbor: University Microfilms International.

Sagey, E. C. (1986). *The representation of features and relations in non-linear phonology.* Unpublished doctoral dissertation, Massachusetts Institute of Technology.

Saltzman, E. (1986). Task dynamic coordination of the speech articulators: A preliminary model. In H. Heuer & C. Fromm (Eds.), *Generation and modulation of action patterns* (Experimental Brain Research Series 15) (pp. 129–144). New York: Springer-Verlag.

Saltzman, E., & Kelso, J. A. S. (1987). Skilled actions: A task dynamic approach. *Psychological Review, 94,* 84–106.

Saltzman, E., Rubin, P. E., Goldstein, L., & Browman, C. P. (1987). Task-dynamic modeling of interarticulator coordination. *Journal of the Acoustical Society of America, 82,* S15 (Abstract).

Sloat, C., Taylor, S. H., & Hoard, J. E. (1978). *Introduction to phonology.* Englewood Cliffs, NJ: Prentice-Hall.

Stevens, K. N. (1972). The quantal nature of speech: Evidence from articulatory-acoustic data. In E. E. David & P. B. Denes (Eds.), *Human communication: A unified view* (pp. 51–66). New York: McGraw Hill.

Traill, A. (1985). *Phonetic and phonological studies of !X00 Bushman.* Hamburg: Helmut Buske Verlag.

Turvey, M. T., Rosenblum, L. D., Kugler, P. N., & Schmidt, R. C. (1986). Fluctuations and phase symmetry in coordinated rhythmic movements. *Journal of Experimental Psychology: Human Perception and Performance, 12,* 564–583.

Vennemann, T. (1972). Rule inversion. *Lingua, 29,* 209–242.

Wang, W. (1969). Competing changes as a cause of residue. *Language, 45,* 9–25.

Yip, M. (1988). The Obligatory Contour Principle and phonological rules: A loss of identity. *Linguistic Inquiry, 19,* 65–100.

Chapter 14

Reading and the Biological Function of Linguistic Representations

Ignatius G. Mattingly

Haskins Laboratories

Abstract

The processes of reading and writing present a problem for those who claim that linguistic processing is modular. How is it that the language module, specialized to respond only to speech-like acoustic patterns, can apparently respond also to optical patterns of arbitrary form? It is proposed that cognitive linguistic representations such as those that the module creates can also drive the module, even if these representations are incomplete, and even if they are actually of cognitive origin. Thus, given a convention for transcribing such incomplete representations (an orthography), it is possible to exploit the language module in reading and writing. But what is the biological function of an arrangement in which cognitive linguistic representations and not just semantic ones can be modular inputs as well as modular outputs? Not communication, which could have been managed more straightforwardly without linguistic representations external to the module. The function of this arrangement is rather to bring about language change and diversity and thus, as Nottebohm has proposed, to facilitate subspeciation.

Liberman and I (1985) have embraced Fodor's (1983) proposal that language is the business of a module. We have also, however, repeatedly urged that the "secondary" processes of reading and writing are closely related to and dependent on the "primary" processes of speaking and understanding speech (e.g., Mattingly, 1972; Liberman, Liberman, Mattingly, & Shankweiler, 1980). It would seem to follow that reading and writing must somehow make use of the language module. In some ways, this seems quite plausible: Many of the properties that, according to Fodor (1983, Part III), characterize the modular input processes generally and the understanding of spoken language in particular hold also for reading, at least (and this is obviously a significant reservation) in the case of the mature, experienced reader. Thus, reading is "mandatory" (cf. III. 2); one can't look at a word without reading it. "Central access" is limited (cf. III. 3): One has no intuitions about the module's computations and internal representations. Reading is fast (cf. III. 4)—even faster than listening. Reading is "informationally encapsulated" from "top-down" cognitive influences (cf. III. 5), at least to the same extent as understanding speech. If reading has these modular properties, and if we exclude the possibility that there is a separate reading module, it must be that the language module is used in reading.

There is, however, a difficulty. A module is supposed to be "domain specific" (III. 1), and as long as attention is restricted to the understanding of speech, the language module appears to meet this requirement: Its domain is the domain of phonetic events, clearly a significant natural class, and the only acoustic signals to which it attributes linguistic structure are those that are (or could have been) produced by human vocal tract movements. But if we are going to claim that the linguistic module operates in reading, then we apparently have to say that the module can also attribute linguistic structure to signals that result from various sets of arbitrary optical patterns: the signs of writing systems. (A superficially similar problem is posed by manual sign language: see, in this volume: Poizner, Klima, & Bellugi, chapter 7; Neville, chapter 11; and Studdert-Kennedy, chapter 4 comments). These written signs (unlike manual signs) do not inherently constitute a natural class of any interesting kind, and if they specify phonetic events, it is only by convention.

I believe that there is a way out of this difficulty and that we can continue to view language as modular, but it will be necessary to elaborate the account of the language module presented in Fodor (1983). I hope to do so in a way that cannot be dismissed as ad hoc. The revised language module that results, however, seems at first sight rather peculiar. It therefore becomes necessary to explain why this kind of language module is reasonable from an evolutionary viewpoint.

According to Fodor's account, the language module is an "input system." When an utterance is understood, the module provides to central cognition a representation of its linguistic form—that is, its phonetic, phonological, morphological, and syntactic structure. It is also suggested that "logical form" is represented, but whether (and if so, how) the speaker's "message" (in the sense of Fodor, Bever, & Garett, 1974) is represented or centrally derived from logical form is problematic.

The first way in which I want to elaborate Fodor's account is to regard the production of utterances, as well as their perception, as modular. I'm going to assume also that one module is responsible for both processes, and not two distinct modules, but this is really a separate issue (see Liberman & Mattingly, 1985; chapter 18, this volume). This assumption requires that the language module be able to operate in different modes, the input in one mode perhaps being the output in another, although the same internal computations go on in all modes. As will be seen, this assumption is required on other grounds, anyway.

The input to the module, in its production mode, is the speaker's message (or its logical form). The output is the neuromotor commands to the speech articulators. But what is of present interest is that there is a second output, a linguistic representation of the utterance that is cognitively accessible to the speaker. Although he did not choose his words (the module did), he knows what he said as well as what he meant.

A further elaboration is that although in perception and production linguistic representations are outputs of the module, they can also be inputs. This is most obvious in the case of short-term rehearsal. The linguistic representation of an utterance just heard or spoken decays; in order to retain what has been said verbatim, one requires the module to recompute the utterance, thus creating a fresh linguistic representation. (Thus, for the modularist, linguistic processes support short-term memory processes and not the other way around; see Ren & Mattingly, 1989.) The input to this computation cannot be the original signal, which is long since lost; nor is it the message, for such an input would lead to a series of increasingly inaccurate paraphrases as rehearsal continued; it is the decaying linguistic representation itself. Because this representation is highly redundant, it can be accurately refreshed by the language module.

Next, and crucially for my account of reading, I claim that linguistic representations sufficient to drive the language module need not themselves have been produced by the module; they may be synthetic, that is, of purely central origin. A speaker-hearer can decide to think of words that begin with *b,* or words that rhyme with June, or he can rearrange a sentence in the active voice as a sentence in passive voice. That linguistic representations can be thus centrally devised and manipulated is hardly surprising; they are mental objects and can be freely analyzed into their component parts and these parts recombined. Inventing pseudowords is no different, in principle, from inventing centaurs and griffins. What is significant is that these purely synthetic representations can then be modular inputs: We hear the corresponding utterances in the mind's ear. Indeed, it is impossible to synthesize a word without so hearing it: The mandatoriness of the module is still evident when the input is synthetic.

The kinds of mental acts I have just been talking about have sometimes been called "metalinguistic." From the modularist's point of view, however, this term is misleading. When I think of some phonological sequence and use the language module to compute its full linguistic representation, this is still natural, first-order linguistic behavior. But there is nevertheless an important difference between such mental acts and producing and understanding speech: Awareness of the structure of linguistic representations (Mattingly, 1972) is needed. Cognitive representation in itself does not guarantee such awareness; it merely makes it possible. Linguistic representations are quite complex, and one has to learn to attend to particular aspects of these representations, just as the painter learns to attend to details of visual representations. On the other hand, linguistic awareness does not imply access to representations internal to the module.

Synthetic linguistic representations are usually incomplete; it would take a lot of mental effort to synthesize a complete one. But this does not prevent them from serving as inputs to the module. The module seems quite happy to produce a complete linguistic representation that will consist with whatever sort of partial representation the speaker-hearer has synthesized. For example, the speaker-hearer can compose candidate sentences just by mentally concatenating arbitrarily chosen words represented as strings of segmental phonemes. If a candidate happens to be actually grammatical, the phrase-structure and prosody as well as the segmental structure will be computed by the module and cognitively represented. Note also that, for a speaker, the input can be a message together with a partial linguistic representation: A speaker *can* choose his words, if he wants to. Similarly, he can formulate an utterance under systematic phonological constraints; that is, write verse.

We have now postulated several sorts of input to the language module: acoustic signals, "messages," and linguistic representations, both modular and synthetic. That the module seems able to accept so many different forms of input has implications about the sort of processing that must go on inside it. Some form of analysis-by-synthesis, in which any of several forms of input may serve as a filter specification, may be indicated. However, I will not pursue this issue here.

It should now be pretty obvious how my account of writing and reading goes. The writer uses the language module to produce an utterance corresponding to his message. This yields a linguistic representation. Because he has mastered a system for partially transcribing linguistic representations—that is, an orthography—he can write down the text of the utterance. The reader, who also knows the orthography, uses the text to synthesize a partial linguistic representation. From this, the module computes a complete linguistic representation, plus logical form, and the text is understood.

This account of reading and writing is not very different from others that have been presented in nonmodular terms; it makes these activities dependent on the mechanisms for spoken language, but it recognizes that written symbols and speech signals stand in a quite different relation to the linguistic structure of the utterance and are differently processed. The special role of central processes in reading and writing is accommodated. The paradox I began with is avoided, for it is not the arbitrary orthographic symbols themselves that turn the language module on but rather the linguistic representations cognitively derived from these symbols.

It has, however, been necessary to complicate the language module considerably. It no longer looks like your garden-variety input system (stereopsis, scene analysis, echo ranging), having acquired various alternative modes and inputs that it did not have in Fodor's original version. I have tried to show that these elaborations could be justified independently of the requirements of reading and writing, but this may just make things worse for the devout modularist.

Before trying to sort this out, I want to indicate some other little puzzles that arise even with the basic Fodor version of the language module. First, why is there a linguistic representation at all? Only logical form is directly pertinent to the speaker's message. But the listener is nevertheless presented by the module with a wealth of syntactic, morphological, phonological, and phonetic information. Compare the actual language module with a hypothetical one that would encode from mentalese to neuromotor commands and decode from the acoustic signal to mentalese, with no linguistic representations external to the module. Why must the language module trouble us with all these linguistic details?

Note that this is not a problem for nonmodular accounts, which regard this "extra" information as a byproduct of perceptual processes. Thus, phonetic representations are supposed to be there, because they were used by working memory to support the parser's computations (Baddeley & Hitch, 1974). But the modularist cannot resort to this sort of explanation, for intermediate representations, internal to a module, are supposedly inaccessible. Therefore, all externally available representations that the module produces are true outputs and have to be explained and biologically justified as such.

Secondly, there is the redundancy of the linguistic representation. It includes, for example, both a systematic phonemic level and a phonetic level. Yet the latter is more or less predictable from the former. That both should be computed is unsurprising, but why should both be centrally represented?

Finally, there is the problem of language change. Why should there be language change and thus linguistic diversity? It is often thought that language change results from drift, or noise in the system. However, this explanation seems inconsistent with the modularity of language. Central processes are supposed to be sloppy, imprecise, imperfect, but not modular ones. If a stable scene analysis module could evolve, why not a stable linguistic module?

I suggest that these puzzles can be satisfactorily answered only if we revise our ideas about the biological function of language. We are apt to suppose that this function is primarily the communication of messages. Is it not the superior ability of our species to communicate that put it at the top of the tree? If only something could be done about linguistic diversity, which can interfere seriously with communication, the situation would be ideal.

There is, however, another possible account, according to which communication of messages is just the come-on. On this account, the true function of language is to divide the species into isolated subpopulations. So much, indeed, is implied by the myth of Babel. Nottebohm (1970), however, made the idea more precise: Genetically isolated subpopulations can adapt rapidly to local environmental conditions. Dialects, of bird song or of language, facilitate such isolation. However, because the dialects are learned, the isolation can be accomplished without irrevocable commitment to actual subspeciation.

We can now begin to understand some of the peculiarities of the language module and, in particular, the function of the linguistic representation. It is there, in the first place, to tell the listener what dialect group the speaker belongs to.

This is the information that is really important to communicate. It is of some interest to note how the module does this. Given input in a dialect different from the listener's, the language module does not simply halt (another fact with implications about linguistic processing that I will not pursue here). It is, as they say, "user-friendly." It makes the best analysis it can and at the same time indicates discrepancies between phonological and phonetic levels that the listener is instantly aware of, as if to say: "This word is doubtless supposed to be /pil/, but the [p] is not sufficiently aspirated." Of course, the more different the speaker's dialect is from the listener's, the less coherent the module's analysis will be, but even under conditions of total mutual unintelligibility, the module provides *some* pattern of discrepancies, and this pattern is what specifies the speaker's dialect for the listener. The point is that the method of indicating the discrepancies depends on their being multiple levels in the linguistic representation. These levels are redundant from the standpoint of grammatical description, but not in the actual ecological situation, in which the dialects of speaker and listener cannot be assumed to be identical.

The linguistic representation, therefore, gives the listener information about the dialect of the speaker. But at this point, some one might raise the objection that there is still no reason for this information to be centrally represented. Consider another hypothetical language module, in which a sufficient amount of dialect discrepancy leads automatically and subdoxastically to an aversive reaction by the listener without central access to the linguistic details. But, though things might work in just this way for white-crowned sparrows, the case is different with human beings. It may be true that "Every time an Englishman opens his mouth, he makes some other Englishman despise him," but this is not the inevitable result of an automatic, mandatory, domain-specific, subdoxastic, and so forth, process. It depends rather on the political and social beliefs and attitudes of the listener. Having perceived that the speaker's dialect is different from his own, the listener might indeed decide to avoid the speaker or to attack him. On the other hand, if the listener regards the speaker's dialect group as prestigious, he may make quite a different decision: to imitate or adopt the speaker's dialect.

Whether the difference between the dialects of speaker and listener is large or small, this decision of the listener's entails some form of second-language acquisition, and, as a consequence, the linguistic representation comes into play in another way. Both first-language acquisition and second-language acquisition entail modification of the language module. But one difference between the two is that whereas first-language acquisition depends on the acoustic input during the critical period and is mandatory, second-language acquisition (setting aside "infant bilingualism") occurs only when the speaker-hearer has the appropriate beliefs and attitudes, and requires central synthesis of linguistic representations to drive the language module. That is, practice is required, not merely immersion. The language learner attends to his linguistic representations of native speaker's utterances, synthesizes similar representations of his own, produces the corresponding utterances, and compares the resulting output representation with the native model. From the module's point of view, the synthetic input is discrepant, in the sense suggested earlier. The only way for the module to make sense of it is to revise its internal algorithms. Second-language learning can be viewed as series of such forced revisions.

It has often been suggested that bilingual speakers play a crucial role in changes that result in new dialects and languages. Having learned a second language, L2, their first language, L1, is to some degree altered, or perhaps we should say that the algorithms of their language modules are partly consistent and partly inconsistent with both L1 and L2, and they really specify a third language, L3. If there are a large number of such speakers, the way is open for language change, for the next generation of speakers will be acquiring a version of L3 rather than of L1.

Linguistic representations thus have two functions in the system for genetic isolation that the language module supports. On the one hand, they allow individuals to identify the subgroups to which other individuals belong. On the other hand, by virtue of their role in second-language acquisition, they facilitate the emergence of new dialects and languages in response to changing social and political conditions.

Viewed primarily as a genetic isolation system, rather than primarily as a system for communicating messages, the revised language module appears somewhat less bizarre. We have a way to think about certain linguistic activities—reading and writing and also second-language acquisition—in which central processes clearly have an important role. Furthermore, although it has acquired some more inputs, the language module still retains its original endearing properties. It is still domain-specific, fast, mandatory, and so on, and although central processes can provide input, they cannot tamper with the processing of such input by the module. In this sense, the criterion of "limited central access" is still satisfied.

Acknowledgment

Support from NICHD grant 01994 to Haskins Laboratories is gratefully acknowledged.

References

Baddeley, A. D., & Hitch, G. B. (1974). Working memory. In G. H. Bower (Ed.), *The psychology of learning and activation* (vol. 4, pp. 47–90). New York: Academic Press.

Fodor, J. A. (1983). *The modularity of mind.* Cambridge, MA: MIT Press.

Fodor, J. A., Bever, T. M., & Garrett, M. (1974). *The psychology of language.* Cambridge, MA: MIT Press.

Liberman, A. M., & Mattingly, I. G. (1985). The Motor Theory of Speech Perception revised. *Cognition, 21,* 1–36.

Liberman, I. Y., Liberman, A. M., Mattingly, I. G., & Shankweiler, D. (1980). Orthography and the beginning reader. In J. F. Kavanagh & R. L. Venezky (Eds.), *Orthography, reading, & dyslexia* (pp. 137–153). Baltimore: University Park Press.

Mattingly, I. G. (1972). Reading, the linguistic process, and linguistic awareness. In J. F. Kavanagh & I. G. Mattingly (Eds.), *Language by ear and by eye: The relationships between speech and reading* (pp. 133–147). Cambridge, MA: MIT Press.

Nottebohm, F. (1970). Ontogeny of bird song. *Science, 167,* 950–956.

Ren, N., & Mattingly, I. G. (1989). *Short-term serial recall performance by good and poor readers of Chinese.* Manuscript submitted for publication.

Comment: Writing Systems and the Modularity of Language

Daniel Holender
Université libre de Bruxelles

In their recent case for the revised, modular version of the Motor Theory of Speech Perception, Liberman and Mattingly (1985; Mattingly & Liberman, 1985, 1988, in press) sometimes alluded to an idea that, although pervading their whole thinking, is so tangentially touched on that a careless reader could have missed it altogether. This idea is that not only speech processing but language processing as a whole is best conceived of as modular in J. A. Fodor's (1983) sense. In the chapter I am discussing, Mattingly attempts to work out some of the consequences of this idea. He is more specifically concerned with the way the relationships between the written and the spoken modes of communication should be construed, if language is modular. For dealing with this problem, Mattingly is led to formulate four basic assumptions; these are: (a) The language module can operate in both an input and an output mode, (b) the linguistic representation delivered by the module is extremely elaborated, (c) linguistic representations can also be synthesized centrally and used as inputs to the language module, (d) the primary biological function of language is to promote the isolation of subpopulations in the human species.

What I purport to do in this discussion is to invite you to consider a view of language that is less radically modular than that entertained by Mattingly. In the course of doing so, I shall have a good deal to say about assumptions (a), (b), and (c), but nothing relevant to my purposes about assumption (d).[1]

---

[1]As one of the major forces promoting the development of very complex human societies, language has also generated as a byproduct a new form of selection that is sociocultural rather than biological. It is allegedly extremely difficult to evaluate the respective roles played by the selection of initial conditions and by epigenesis in the development of a complex, multifunctional faculty such as

347

The basic tenet of the Motor Theory is that the object of speech perception is better specified in articulatory than in acoustical terms. Both speech perception and speech production are, thus, assumed to share the same motoric invariants. In its modular version, the theory claims that in listening, the conversion of the speech flow into the underlying intended articulatory gestures is not mediated by the same processes as those involved in analysing auditory events in general. Hence, in being both computational and domain specific, speech perception qualifies as a Fodorean module.

Other properties of the computations performed by a module, such as speed of operation, mandatoriness, cognitive impenetrability, and informational encapsulation are probably transferable to theoretical frameworks different from that of J. A. Fodor. I suppose, for example, that theorists adopting an event approach to speech perception (e.g., Fowler, 1986; Fowler & Rosenblum, chapter 3 this volume), although rejecting the thesis of the poverty of the speech stimulus and the computational and inferential character of speech perception it entails, would nevertheless agree that the perception of speech has the four properties just mentioned or at least something akin to these reformulated in noncomputational terms. I presume that these four properties would also be taken for granted by theorists denying the domain specificity of speech perception but adhering to the computational approach.

Whatever the ultimate truth may be, I cannot help feeling sympathetic with the revised version of the Motor Theory of Speech Perception because of the range of facts it can elegantly accommodate. For the time being, I am just as attracted by the computational form of the theory developed by Liberman and Mattingly (1985) as I am by the direct-realist perspective promoted by Fowler (1986). For the sake of the present discussion, however, I assume that the computational approach is correct, which allows me to discuss Mattingly's proposals from his own vantage point. This much being agreed upon, I am extremely reluctant to extrapolate, as Mattingly has done, to the view that the full language faculty is modular in pretty much the same way speech processing is.

According to J. A. Fodor, a module is a special-purpose computational system having its own database and programs allowing for autonomous computation of mental representations. A module can, thus, compute an output mental representation by relying exclusively on its internal, very limited knowledge base without using the general background information available to cognition. It is assumed

---

language. One can hypothesize that natural selection should have played some role in the shaping of the initial anatomical and neuronal modifications necessary for the development of at least two functions of language: subserving propositional thinking and communicating about propositional thinking. If Mattingly is right in thinking that another function of language is to promote the isolation of subpopulations through language diversification, I surmise that what controls this function are sociocultural selective forces whose origin ultimately lies in the language faculty itself; this function cannot, thus, be primary, if the view presented here is correct.

by Fodor that perceptual systems are modular in this sense and that only the final output representation, not the intermediate representations generated in processing, becomes an object of conscious experience. This conception is quite reasonable as far as it applies to unitary input systems mediating between proximal stimulation and cognition, but its extension to language as a whole is much more problematic.

One obvious difficulty is that the language module cannot be just an input system; it has to deal with both the perception and the production of linguistic messages. I fully concur with Mattingly in assuming that, if language is indeed modular, the same single module should be endowed with both perceptual and production modes of operation. In spite of the surface similarity between (a) the assumption that language processing shares the same primitives in its input and output modes, and (b) the basic assumption of the Motor Theory according to which speech perception and production share the same motoric invariants, one should not be misled in thinking that the latter is the only thread leading to the former. By this, I mean that theorists believing neither in the Motor Theory nor even in the specialness of language would probably postulate that language perception and production should share a fair amount of common knowledge and processes.

Another obvious difficulty faced by the hypothesis of the modularity of language stems from the fact that, contrary to unitary input systems, language as it is conceptualized in current linguistic theories comprises a collection of modular subcomponents that are themselves composed of other modular subcomponents. What kind of processing architecture do we have to postulate for accounting for the exchanges of information between cognition, language, and its submodules?

There is, I think, only one solution to this question that is compatible with a strict modular view of language; it has two main characteristics:

1. Any submodule should have access only to the output of one other submodule—or maybe to the respective outputs of several other submodules; it should have no access either to the intermediate representations computed by any other submodule or to the general background information available to cognition.

2. Cognition should have access only to a final resultant representation computed by the interacting submodules of the language module; it should have no access either to the intermediate or to the output representations computed by each submodules.

If I understand Mattingly correctly, (1) and (2) should constitute accurate statements of the architecture he has in mind, although he does not say anything about the interfaces between the various submodules of the language module. Before discussing Mattingly's claims about the language/cognition interface, I would like to make a few remarks on some formal and empirical aspects of characteristic (1).

On the formal side, there has been a clear tendency in generative linguistics to postulate various components and subcomponents of the language faculty that are as autonomous and informationally encapsulated as my formulation of (1) implies. Yet after perusing some of the recent linguistic literature, I wonder whether, although remaining basically modularists, many linguists are not already trading the absolute form of modularity for a more relative one. If, in those complex and controversial matters, there is more to this claim than a mere projection stemming from my skepticism about strict modularity, it implies that we can now envisage a certain degree of interpenetrability between some subcomponents of the language faculty; a certain degree of access to background central knowledge seems also required for accounting for the modulation of language processing by some pragmatic aspects of communication (e.g., Lindblom & MacNeilage, 1986).

On the empirical side, the demonstration of the modularity of the subcomponents of the language faculty is facing its own difficulties. With respect to the autonomy of lexical access, for example, the claim made by J. A. Fodor (1983) that "associations are the means whereby stupid processing systems manage to behave as though they were smart ones" (p. 81) is critically dependent on the validity of the interpretation of the semantic contextual effects in terms of spreading activation in a semantic associative network. Indeed, an associative network needs to be postulated in any account of the semantic priming effect, but spreading activation can probably be dispensed with completely. During the last few years, the aspects of the semantic contextual effects amenable to a spreading activation interpretation have progressively shrunk to a point where they finally disappeared completely from at least some theoretical accounts. Were it not for her belief, which I cannot share (see Holender, 1986), in the reality of the unconscious semantic priming effects, de Groot (1985) would have left no role for spreading activation in her account of associative priming effects in lexical decision and naming tasks. This final step has now been accomplished by Ratcliff and McKoon (1988), although for reasons different from those of de Groot, in their retrieval theory of priming in memory. Although I have no space to develop this point, I submit that the alternatives to the spreading activation account of the semantic priming effect promoted by de Groot and by Ratcliff and McKoon (1988) both attribute the cause of the effect to cognition only. If this interpretation of their proposals is correct, the initial argument for the intralexical origin of some aspects of the semantic contextual effects is no longer valid. This, of course, does not imply that lexical access is not autonomous; it simply means that semantic priming effects do not constitute evidence that it is so.

With respect to the modularity of syntax, very strong positive claims have been made during the last few years. It should be remembered that in the dedication of *The Modularity of Mind,* J. A. Fodor said that it was Merrill Garrett's assimilation of parsing to a reflex that promoted the reflections leading to the thesis of the book. J. A. Fodor should, therefore, have been pleased by the claim made by Lyn Frazier during this conference, according to which almost none of the evidence contrary to the modularity of syntax can resist careful analysis. Unfortunately, my very limited knowledge about syntax does not allow me to formulate a valuable personal assessment of the extent to which the empirical data support the autonomy of parsing. Judging from the penetrating discussion provided by J. D. Fodor (1988), however, I gather that the interpretation of these data is less straightforward than is sometimes assumed.

Let us now turn towards the problems raised by finding a satisfactory account of the exchanges of information between cognition and language. In fully endorsing characteristic (2), Mattingly has had to make some radical assumptions about the interface between the language module and cognition; they can be summarized as follows. Cognition has access to a single representation delivered by the language module; it is structurally complex and very rich in linguistic details. As an object of thought, this output representation is amenable to whatever kind of analyses, from the simplest to the more sophisticated, we know cognition is capable of. Among the various cognitive activities based on the output of the language module, such as punning, versification, and comprehending or generating what has been called "secret" or "play" languages (e.g., pig Latin), one can single out as a case in point the invention of writing systems. The efficient use of orthographies for reading and writing is readily accounted for, because cognition can use its derived linguistic knowledge for synthesizing linguistic representations that, although incomplete, approximate, and eventually clumsy, are nevertheless able to turn on the language module; it alone is responsible for automatically filling in the missing details and making the adjustments needed for running smoothly.

There are two major problems—one empirical and the other conceptual—with the foregoing account of the relationships between modular and nonmodular linguistic knowledges. The empirical problem is that a good deal of the experimental data leading first—in the early 1970s—to the idea of automatic processing and later—in the early 1980s—to that of modular processing, has been gathered with written letters and words. In its ability to synthesize linguistic representations on the basis of linguistic units derived from the analysis of the output of the language module, cognition, thus, seems to be as efficient as the language module is in the processing of its internal linguistic information. Hence, as far as the comparison between the written and the spoken modes of language comprehension is concerned, there is no empirical content to the distinction between modular and cognitive linguistic knowledges (see Jusczyk & Cohen, 1985, for a similar claim).

The conceptual problem is this. If writing systems are built on the cognitive linguistic representations derived from the analysis of the output of the language module, and, considering the usual creativity of cognition, why are writing systems not much more diverse than they actually are? Moreover, why do all the written symbols actually in use always map onto one or another of the linguistic levels we have to postulate to account for the performance of the presumably modular language faculty?

However, are writing systems so little diverse in the first place? Well, written symbols representing phonemes (classical or systematic), syllables, moras, and morphemes can be found either singly or in combination in all the orthographies of the world and nothing else (Holender, 1987a; Mattingly, 1984, 1985, 1987). For example, no practical orthography is based on phonetic segments, and none maps its symbols onto speech units of half-syllable length, although the mere concatenation of half syllables,[2] unlike concatenation of phonetic segments, requires no, or very little, boundary adjustment to yield intelligible speech (Peterson, Wang, & Sivertsen, 1958). Although Chinese, with its moderately complex syllables, could have been written efficiently with a relatively small number of symbols mapping onto half syllables, it never resorted to this solution.

Assume, with Studdert-Kennedy (1987), that a written symbol is a conventional representation of the information needed to *indicate* how to pronounce something, as opposed to the information *specifying* pronunciation conveyed by a spoken utterance (see Turvey & Kugler, 1984, for a clear statement of the distinction between these two forms of information.) Assume further, with Mattingly, that the origin of such convention rests in the cognitive analysis of the rich output of the language module. Then to reiterate my initial question, how can it be that neither the phone, nor the half syllable, nor any other more exotic but perfectly efficient cognitive ways of indicating how to pronounce something were ever used in writing? The answer lies, I suspect, in the fact that the basic linguistic information used for generating practical orthographies is to be found in the internal representations of the language module itself.

It should be acknowledged that, taken alone, the lack of diversity in the principles used for the visual representation of linguistic messages is equally compatible with a strict modular view of language. It suffices to assume that among all the cognitive possibilities, only those leading to efficient, rapid synthesis of linguistic representations sufficient to turn on the language module have been selected for practical writing purposes. If, however, it can be shown that only linguistic units used by the language module itself have been elected for writing, then it seems to me that the cognitive penetrability hypothesis would receive more support than the strict modular view of language.

Until very recently, the debate about which units are or which units should ideally be represented in writing has taken place within theoretical frameworks admitting only the classical phoneme, the morphophoneme (or the systematic phoneme), and the morpheme as units relevant for the analysis of language. Therefore, because syllables and moras played no role in these linguistic theories, one could argue that only a subset of the cognitive linguistic representations used by writing systems happened to coincide with the linguistic representations requested for accounting for the language competence, a view that is perfectly

---

[2]By half syllables, I mean the stretches of speech that would result from cutting a syllable somewhere in the middle of the nucleus vowel. This is quite different from a linguistically motivated analysis of the syllable into constituents such as the onset and the rhyme.

compatible with Mattingly's present modular conception of language. With the recent developments in the phonological and morphological theories, however, there is not a single unit used in any orthography that is not also considered as a unit of language processing. That this is so can be best appreciated by using Halle's (1985) metaphor of the spiral-bound notebook to refer to the geometry of the lexical representations we now have to postulate.

The spine of the spiral-bound notebook represents unspecified phonemic time slots. The notebook should be visualized as open in a way allowing for seeing the edges of several pages, the edge of each page standing for a different autosegmental tier in the representation. There are, for example, one tier (page) for phonemic segments, another one for syllabic segments, still others corresponding to various morphemic constituents. The successive segments occupying the edge of each page are connected to one or more than one time slots on the skeleton represented by the spine of the notebook. The spiral-bound notebook analogy is intended to capture the idea that each tier is autonomous in terms of the processes that can act upon it but that the temporal overlaps between the autosegments on each tier are constrained by their associations with the timing units of the skeleton. With respect to phonemes, postulating only a single phonemic tier suffices for describing the lexical entries in most languages, but one has to assign the vowels and the consonants to separate tiers for accounting for the morphology of the Semitic languages (McCarthy, 1981). Likewise, no language can do without a syllabic tier, but only a subset of the languages of the world requires an additional moraic tier—Japanese being a case in point (Yoshiba, 1981).

In limiting the discussion to the writing systems still in use today, how do the linguistic levels represented by the orthographies relate to the multi-tiered lexical representation just postulated? For the Chinese script, one has the choice between the syllabic and the morphemic tiers. I do not wish to discuss here the different implications of this dual description for the development of Chinese writing, but I just want to point out that what is often described as the only complete logographic script ever used can be equally considered syllabic writing, although it is not technically speaking a syllabary. Notwithstanding the logographic component that is more historically than linguistically motivated, the Japanese script started being a syllabic script at a time at which the simple CV structure of the language made syllables and moras fully confounded. In its present state, Japanese has evolved an independent moraic structure that requires an additional tier in the morphological description; written symbols are now mapping onto this moraic tier. Semitic scripts map their letters onto one of the two independent phonemic tiers, the consonantal one, required for their description, whereas all the other alphabets basically map onto a single, complete phonemic tier comprising both consonants and vowels. Sometimes an alphabetic orthography, such as English, may considerably depart from this basic principle in keeping the visual make-up of morphemes constant in spite of the pronunciation modifications determined by different morphological environments, thereby allowing for an alphabet to map onto the morphemic tier (see Holender, 1987a, and Mattingly, 1984, for partially different views on this topic and references therein).

This brief survey of the relationships between the written and the spoken modes of language communication shows that there is not a single level of orthographic representation that is not also a level of representation that has to be postulated for accounting for the processes subserving the language faculty. Conversely, very efficient, purely cognitive codes for indicating how to pronounce something have been invented that have no relevant counterparts in linguistic theories, the half syllable and the phonetic segment being two cases in point.

The Chinese people came close to using the half syllable for indicating the pronunciation of an unknown character by means of two known characters (Downer, 1963). This, however, is a late development stemming from the original *fanqiè* principle resting on the analysis of the syllable into two constituents: the onset and the rhyme. Although these constituents are now playing a role in some theories of language processing, the half syllable remains a pure invention of cognition. Similarly, the phonetic code is an extremely efficient means of indicating the pronunciation of an utterance. Yet phonetic segments, in addition to having no acoustical or articulatory counterparts in the speech flow (e.g., Browman & Goldstein, 1986, chapter 13 this volume; Studdert-Kennedy, 1987), are now denied any linguistic relevance as well (e.g., Mohanan, 1986). Phonetic segments are, thus, pure cognitive psychological entities playing no role in language processing.

Two important conclusions can be drawn from the foregoing analysis. First, contrary to the widespread use of traditional orthographies resting on units relevant to both cognition and language, those codes based on units relevant to cognition only have always been used by a very limited number of scholars and trained specialists. Second, for elaborating the traditional writing systems, cognition has relied exclusively on linguistic representations subserving language processing, which I take as incontrovertible evidence of the partial cognitive penetrability of the language module.

Partial cognitive penetrability of the language module is also assumed by Mohanan (1986) when he suggests that "the representation that is input to the implementational module in terms of the lexical alphabet of a language is what a speaker of a language thinks he is saying or hearing" (p. 194). As the units of the lexical alphabet roughly correspond to the classical phonemes, Mohanan's claim amounts to saying that the phonemes are readily accessible to speakers of any language of the world, whether they know an alphabet or not.[3] Support for this

---

[3]This claim is not necessarily in contradiction with the data showing a lack of phonemic awareness in preliterates, illiterates, or readers of nonalphabetic orthographies (see Bertelson & de Gelder, chapter 17 this volume and references therein). In assuming that some linguistic levels of representation subserving processing are easy to access cognitively, one does not imply that no training at all is needed nor that the relative salience of each of these levels is not language dependent.

assumption can be found in the way Indian would-be-linguist priests of the first millennium B.C. faced the problem of preserving the exact pronunciation of the Vedas. As I argued elsewhere (Holender, 1987b), they achieved a fully phonemic description of their language well before they developed a phonemic script that was entirely based on their orally acquired phonological knowledge.[4]

To conclude and to summarize, I think Gardner (1985) was right in proposing to range the cognitive processes on a continuum, putting at one end the strongly modular processes and at the other end the strongly isotropic ones. According to this view, perceptual input systems would probably remain as modular as in J. A. Fodor's account. If it turns out that Alvin Liberman has been right all along in claiming that the input system dealing with speech delivers to cognition a percept that is best characterized in terms of the intended articulatory gestures retrieved through processing the auditory signal in a special way, then this module is assuredly "vertically unparalleled" to use this beautiful image of Mattingly and Liberman (1985).

With respect to language as a whole, and without even willing to relinquish the idea that language is special, I do not think, however, that it can be as strictly modular as Mattingly assumes in his chapter. After reviewing a series of empirical and formal difficulties one has to face for sustaining this idea, I have argued that the language faculty should be more cognitively penetrable, thereby less modular, than Mattingly implies. I have offered as a tentative argument for this claim the fact that all the cognitive, linguistic representations ever used for generating traditional orthographies are a subset of the linguistic representations we have to postulate for accounting for the performance of the language faculty.

In making this argument, I am simply adhering to a position that was held by Mattingly before and that is still held by Studdert-Kennedy (1987) when he claimed that the "possibility of the alphabet was discovered, not invented" (p. 69). In adopting a strong modular view of language, Mattingly is now forced to espouse the less likely possibility that the alphabet or any other orthographic principles simply are invented by cognition rather than being the discovery of possibilities implicit in the language faculty.

Acknowledgments

This work has been supported by the Belgian "Fonds de la Recherche fondamentale collective" (Convention 2.4537.88) and the Belgian Ministry of scientific Policy (Action de Recherche concertée "Processus cognitifs dans la Lecture" and National Incentive Program for Fundamental Research in Artificial Intelligence).

---

[4]In spite of its underlying syllabic design, the Brahmi script was really the most theoretically motivated phonemic written representation of language ever used before the advent of modern linguistics.

I am very grateful to Ignatius G. Mattingly for helping me in better understanding his position through friendly discussions after the conference. I feel fully responsible for any remaining misinterpretations.

References

Browman, C. P., & Goldstein, L. M. (1986). Toward an articulatory phonology. *Phonology Yearbook, 3,* 219–252.

de Groot, A. (1985). Word-context effects in word naming and lexical decision. *Quarterly Journal of Experimental Psychology, 37A,* 281–297.

Downer, G. B. (1963). Traditional Chinese phonology. *Transactions of the Philological Society,* 127–142.

Fodor, J. A. (1983). *The modularity of mind.* Cambridge, MA: MIT Press.

Fodor, J. D. (1988). On modularity in syntactic processing. *Journal of Psycholinguistic Research, 17,* 125–168.

Fowler, C. A. (1986). An event approach to the study of speech perception from a direct-realist perspective. *Journal of Phonetics, 14,* 3–28.

Gardner, H. (1985). The centrality of modules. *Behavioral and Brain Sciences, 8,* 12–14.

Halle, M. (1985). Speculations about the representation of words in Memory. In V. A. Fromkin (Ed.), *Phonetic linguistics* (pp. 101–114). Orlando, FL: Academic Press.

Holender, D. (1986). Semantic activation without conscious identification in dichotic listening, parafoveal vision, and visual masking: A survey and appraisal. *Behavioral and Brain Sciences, 9,* 1–23, 50–66.

Holender, D. (1987a). Synchronic description of present-day writing systems: Some implications for reading research. In J. K. O'Regan & A. Levy-Schoen (Eds.), *Eye movements: From physiology to cognition* (pp. 397–420). Amsterdam: North-Holland.

Holender, D. (1987b). *Phonemic awareness and nonalphabetic literacy.* Unpublished manuscript.

Jusczyk, P., & Cohen, A. (1985). What constitutes a module? *Behavioral and Brain Sciences, 8,* 20–21.

Liberman, A. M., & Mattingly, I. G. (1985). The Motor Theory of Speech Perception Revised. *Cognition, 21,* 1–36.

Lindblom, B., & MacNeilage, P. (1986). Action theory: Problems and alternative approaches. *Journal of Phonetics, 14,* 117–132.

Mattingly, I. G. (1984). Reading, linguistic awareness, and language acquisition. In J. Downing & R. Valtin (Eds.), *Language awareness and learning to read* (pp. 9–25). New York: Springer.

Mattingly, I. G. (1985). Did orthographies evolve? *RASE, 6,* 18–23.

Mattingly, I. G. (1987). Morphological structure and segmental awareness. *Cahiers de Psychologie Cognitive, 7,* 488–493.

Mattingly, I. G., & Liberman, A. M. (1985). Verticality unparalleled. *Behavioral and Brain Sciences, 8,* 24–26.

Mattingly, I. G., & Liberman, A. M. (1988). Specialized perceiving systems for speech and other biologically significant sounds. In G. M. Edelman, W. E. Gall, & W. M. Cowan (Eds.), *Functions of the auditory system* (pp. 775–792). New York: Wiley.

Mattingly, I. G., & Liberman, A. M. (in press). Speech and other auditory modules. In G. M. Edelman, W. E. Gall, & W. M. Cowan (Eds.), *Signal and sense: Local and global order in perceptual maps.* New York: Wiley.

McCarthy, J. (1981). A prosodic theory of nonconcatenative morphology. *Linguistic Inquiry, 12,* 373–419.

Mohanan, K. P. (1986). *The theory of lexical phonology.* Dordrecht, Holland: Reidel.

Peterson, G. E., Wang, W. S. Y., & Sivertsen, E. (1958). Segmentation techniques in speech synthesis. *Journal of the Acoustical Society of America, 30,* 739–742.

Ratcliff, R., & McKoon, G. (1988). A retrieval theory of priming in memory. *Psychological Review, 95,* 385–408.

Studdert-Kennedy, M. (1987). The phoneme as a perceptuomotor structure. In A. Allport, D. MacKay, W. Prinz, & E. Scheerer (Eds.), *Language perception and production* (pp. 67–84). London: Academic Press.

Turvey, M. T., & Kugler, P. N. (1984). A comment on equating of information with symbol strings. *American Journal of Physiology, 246,* 925–927.

Yoshiba, H. (1981). The mora constraint in Japanese phonology. *Linguistic Analysis, 7,* 241–262.

Chapter 15

Panel Discussion: The Modularity of Speech and Language

Ursula Bellugi
The Salk Institute

Sheila Blumstein (Chairman)
Department of Linguistics, Brown University

Jerry Fodor
Department of Philosophy, City University of New York

Virginia Mann
Department of Cognitive Sciences,
University of California, Irvine

Arthur Samuel (Reporter)
Department of Psychology, Yale University

BLUMSTEIN: Among the very critical current issues is the extent to which language and speech are modular. There are multiple forms of modular views of language and speech, with the weakest view claiming that speech and language are distinct from all other cognitive behavior, but the claims of Fodor and Liberman, I think, are much richer than that. In their view, language is built out of autonomous subsystems with certain very definite traits that meet the conditions of modularity, such as impenetrability, information encapsulation, and mandatory operations.

What we are going to be addressing today is whether speech is special and to what extent it is modular. I would like us to consider such questions as "What evidence can be brought to bear on the issue that speech is special or speech is modular?" and "To what extent does it meet the constraints that have been suggested by Fodor (1983) that would show it is in fact a modular system?"

BELLUGI: In regard to the first issue, whether speech is special, and to what extent it is modular, it seems to me that research on linguistic systems that are independent of speech and the vocal apparatus is relevant. It has been found that the structure of signed and spoken languages is remarkably similar at all linguistic levels: there is the equivalent of phonology and phonological processes, a rich system of morphological processes, and a syntax that is essentially spatialized. Nonetheless, we find that the way in which linguistic levels are instantiated is heavily influenced by the modality in which the language develops. For example, signed languages contrast with spoken languages in their elaborated use of multilayering and spatial contrasts at all linguistic levels. Yet, signed and spoken languages share fundamental principles of organization that are uncharacteristic of other cognitive systems (Bellugi & Studdert-Kennedy, 1980; Klima & Bellugi, 1988; Poizner, Bellugi, & Klima, this volume). From this vantage point, it is "Language", not "Speech" itself, that is special. Moreover, studies of the effects of left hemisphere lesions in deaf signers show that components of sign language are selectively impaired, reflecting differential breakdown along linguistically relevant lines. This suggests that the organization of sign language in the brain may turn out to be modular (Bellugi, Poizner, & Klima, 1989).

I would like to mention a new line in our research that may shed a different light on the issue of modularity. We have been investigating a population of children who exhibit an unusual fractionation of higher cortical functioning: severely impaired cognition together with remarkably spared grammatical capacity. These children have Williams Syndrome, a rare metabolic disorder which is manifested in characteristic facial features, an unusual heart defect, and mental retardation. We match adolescent Williams Syndrome children with Down Syndrome children on age and IQ, and contrast the two groups on linguistic and cognitive tasks (Bellugi, Bihrle, Trauner, Jernigan, & Doherty, in press; Bihrle, Bellugi, Delis, & Marks, 1989).

Common to their low IQ, both groups fail across the board on cognitive tasks such as reasoning, conservation of weight, number, and quantity, and problem solving. In contrast to their severe impairment in conceptual reasoning, Williams Syndrome adolescents, unlike their Down Syndrome counterparts, are surprisingly flawless in their syntactic production and over a wide range of formal grammatical processing tasks. Indeed, Williams Syndrome adolescents exhibit a decoupling between spared syntactic capacities and purported cognitive underpinnings that is unusual. Moreover, our studies suggest that the semantic organization of children with Williams Syndrome may turn out to be deviant. We are currently pursuing the hypothesis that the most autonomous aspects of language, namely syntax, are spared in this neurodevelopmental disorder whereas those aspects which interact more with cognitive systems —for example, semantics— are impaired. Thus, this is another way of approaching the modularity issue (Bellugi, Marks, Bihrle, & Sabo, 1988).

FODOR: As I pointed out in *Modularity of Mind* (1983), the view of a language as a modularized system for the production and perception of linguistic signals implies a departure from the traditional view of cognitive architecture. The traditional picture was: language and thought on one hand, and perception and action on the other. The modularity view breaks that up. What it says is: You have thought, and then language, perception, and action, with language being just some sort of specialized transponder.

At the heart of the traditional view—that language and thought came in a package—is the idea that language is not just the medium of the expression and communication of thought but also the medium in which we think: So we have two ways of looking at the relation between linguistic and other psychological mechanisms—one that stresses relations between language and thinking and one that stresses relations between language and perception and action systems. The question is, which one of these ways of looking at things is right.

There is a line of argument on this issue in Chomsky's work that goes like this: Natural language must be the vehicle of thought, not just the medium in which it is expressed, because only that assumption would explain a characteristic difference between the cognitive capacities of verbal organisms on the one hand and the cognitive capacities of infraverbal organisms on the other (Chomsky, 1968, 1988). Namely, that only in the case of verbal organisms is thought productive. Only verbal organisms, in this view, have unbounded conceptual capacities. The idea is that the productivity of thought literally derives from the productivity of language. In particular, the productivity of thought exploits the combinatorial syntactic and semantic structure of natural language representation. This arrangement is perfectly intelligible on the assumption that we think in language. Contrapositively, infraverbal organisms have access to no productive representational systems and, therefore, exhibit inherently bounded cognitive capacities. Thus, on this view, combinatorial syntactic and semantic structure explains the productivity of natural language, which in turn explains the productivity of thought, but it does so only on the assumption that we think in language—so language is a cognitive faculty; so it's wrong to think of language as an input/output system; so there is something wrong with the modularity picture of language.

Notice that it is central to this argument that only verbal organisms have productive cognitive capacities: If the thought of infraverbal organisms is ever productive, it can't be the combinatorial structure of natural language that explains the productivity of their cognitive capacities. It's essential to this picture that a certain coextension exists between organisms with productive cognitive capacities and organisms that talk.

Pylyshyn and I (1988) have been pushing the view that infrahuman and, a fortiori, human thought, has a property other than productivity that presupposes a combinatorial medium of mental representation. This property is what we call *systematicity*. Consider a very general property of minds, both infrahuman and human: The ability to think a thought with a certain semantical content seems under very general conditions to be lawfully connected to the ability to think other thoughts with related semantical context. That's true not only of human minds but of the minds of anything anybody has ever bothered to try to study the psychology of. Examples: If an organism can learn to prefer the red triangle to the green circle, it can learn to prefer the green triangle to the red circle. If an organism can learn to prefer the configuration with the circle over the triangle, it can learn to prefer the configuration of the triangle over the circle. To put it more generally, if an organism can learn something which depends upon representing a state of affairs in which A bears a certain relation to B, then it can learn to represent a corresponding state of affairs in which B bears the same relation to A.

The point of this observation is that systematicity, like productivity, apparently requires combinatorial structure of the mental representation for its explanation. If the ability to mentally represent a state of affairs A r B implies the ability to represent a state of affairs B r A, that is presumably because the two representations are constructed from the same parts in the same semantically significant arrangement. So, systematicity is phylogenetically at least as widespread as productivity, and like productivity, it seems to require combinatorial structure in mental representation for its explanation.

What are the morals? First, combinatorial structure in mental representation apparently does not require verbal capacity. Second, combinatorial structure in mental representation is phylogenetically quite early; its presence can't be what makes us smarter than infraverbal organisms. It is very often suggested that the reason we have what passes for civilization, and rats and turtles and pigeons don't, is that we have minds which exploit representational capacities that are productive and combinatorial, and they don't. Our minds are productive and involve combinatorial syntax and semantics, their minds are lists or something of that sort. That seems perfectly plausible and perfectly reasonable, but considerations about systematicity suggest that it can't be true. Third, since complex mental representation does not, in general, presuppose verbal capacity, its presence in humans does not argue that we think in our natural languages, contrary to the line of argument that it seems to me Chomsky has wanted to endorse. Finally, since there is, thus far, no argument that we think in natural language, there is, thus far, no argument for viewing language as a cognitive system rather than an input/output system. So the modularly picture is o.k.—so far.

MANN: Speech perception meets every one of Fodor's nine criteria for modularity, but since I've got limited time, I thought I would just choose three, the ones that my data happen to support the most clearly: domain specificity, cognitive impenetrability, and characteristic breakdown patterns.

First, in a study I did with Al Liberman (Mann & Liberman, 1983) on the duplex phenomenon, we showed very clearly that perception of nonspeech chirps is quite different from the categorical perception of speech. Many other studies have shown this. Context effects show it very nicely. So I think domain specificity is one of the tried and true statements that we can make about speech perception.

A study I conducted in Japan gave me an opportunity to study people whose behavior was influenced by something they could not report. Many Japanese cannot distinguish [l] and [r]. What I discovered in my experiment on context effects—once again, something that we argue to be a domain-specific property of speech—was that subjects who confuse [l] and [r] in a normal labeling test, show a difference between [l] and [r] in a context-effect situation. With English speakers (who distinguish between [l] and [r]), preceding a [da]–[ga] continuum with the syllable [al] shifts the labeling of the [da]–[ga] relative to their labeling when preceded by the syllable [ar]. Japanese listeners (who do not discriminate [l] and [r]) nevertheless show the context effect, a domain-specific context effect (Mann, 1986). This certainly argues for a lack of cognitive penetrability. Otherwise, Japanese listeners wouldn't have an [l]–[r] discrimination problem.

The final case I want to talk about is a child with a learning disability. (To avoid making Gall's mistake, I'm not going to think of him as being individually different: I'm going instead to think of him as having a specific breakdown). What we have found is that the problems of such a child are best characterized within the domain of speech perception. For example, Sue Brady, Don Shankweiler, and I (1983) compared good and poor readers' ability to perceive two different kinds of material: speech and environmental sounds. In the case of speech, good readers made more correct responses than poor readers when the stimuli were masked. That is, they show superior perception of speech in noise. However, when we go to noise-masked environmental sounds, there is no difference. So, speech alone shows a perceptual impairment for the poor reader. Nonspeech sounds do not show this at all. We see this in other cases: In an experiment I did with Isabelle Liberman and Don Shankweiler and some of their students, we find a short-term memory impairment for poor readers when we look at nonsense syllables, but not when we look at faces and nonsense designs (Liberman, Mann, Shankweiler, & Werfelman, 1982). So once again, in the case of memory, something that might be a central process, we find an impairment that is specific to language memory, a characteristic breakdown pattern. So, I think that modularity has offered us a very nice perspective on problems in reading disability and problems in speech perception.

SAMUEL: Of the various properties Jerry Fodor (1983) lists for modular systems, let me emphasize, in order of their importance for Fodor, information encapsulation, domain specificity, and then neurobiological specialization and innateness. Fodor's claim is that input systems are modules, and language should be included as one of the input systems. I am a little concerned about the loose usage of the term "modularity." Several examples: In the BBS commentary on modularity, someone suggested that the lexicon itself is a module, rather than being part of the language module (Seidenberg, 1985). Similarly, yesterday we heard assertions that perhaps there is a module for the grammar and maybe one for the phonetics. Again, this usage of modularity seems to defeat the point of Fodor's claim for information encapsulation: If we separate these pieces, then the data in hand say that they are not informationally encapsulated, which defeats the purpose. A third example: It was mentioned in passing that there may be a module for ASL. On the one hand, there seems to be some very interesting evidence coming out that might be taken that way. On the other hand, Sign language seems to be a system like the one Ignatius [Mattingly] mentioned—reading—that has appeared only recently in an evolutionary scale. That seems to be a problem for biologically motivated considerations.

These kinds of misuses or stretchings of the term aside, I personally have a few problems that I hope will get ironed out here today: (a) I generally agree with Jerry Fodor's claims, (b) I generally disagree with Al Liberman's claims, and (c) Jerry Fodor and Al Liberman generally agree with each others' claims. I hope there is a resolution here. It might be the case that Fodor's claims of modularity, particularly with respect to speech and language, may be more extreme than I really can believe or even than he has led us to believe. Similarly, Liberman's claims for modularity in speech and language may in fact be even more extreme than Fodor can believe. I hope this all gets worked out today.

When all else fails, it seems to me that we can try to resolve problems by considering the facts. In this spirit, I'd like to offer two facts from my lab that seem to me something we might want to consider in terms of language modules. Briefly, fact one: In *Modularity* (1983), Jerry Fodor cited some of my earlier work on phonemic restoration. In two sentences, it said: (a) It appears that lexical information is used perceptually to increase the illusory perception of missing speech sounds, and (b) sentential predictability appears to exert its effects postperceptually. The modularity moral is that the lexicon is included in the language module, whereas higher level semantic processing may not be. The fact and problem here is some recent work that Lucinda DeWitt and I have been doing with musical stimuli (DeWitt & Samuel, 1990) which show: (a) Well-established musical structures like scales and chords are used perceptually to increase the illusory perception of missing notes, and (b) melodic predictability appears to exert its effects postperceptually. In short, the pattern of information encapsulation appears to be exactly the same for musical and speech stimuli. So either we have two modules with precisely the same architecture or, more parsimoniously, the same processing system is at work. If so, domain specificity may be in jeopardy.

Fact two: Hearing a musical tone (the pluck), which is a thoroughly nonspeech sound, can induce reliable changes in the perception of speech sounds. If you're labeling /ba/-/wa/ syllables, hearing the pluck played repeatedly reduces report of /ba/. A standard out for this result is to say that this is just some sort of low-level auditory effect, and as speech scientists we don't care about audition. The problem is some recent data which show that this effect is undiminished if the syllables are whispered speech, such that there is a really serious acoustic mismatch between the plucked string and speech (Samuel, 1989). Moreover, the effect remains intact, even if the tone is presented to one ear, and the whispered /ba/–/wa/ syllables are presented contralaterally. In other words, this decidedly nonspeech sound is causing changes in speech behavior under conditions that are very hard to account for in terms of some uninteresting peripheral auditory kind of effect. I'm hoping that the two leading modularity proponents here can address these apparent breaches of domain specificity.

FODOR (to SAMUEL): I agree with you—I wish I'd taken out a patent on the term "module" so I can stop people from using it the way they do. It doesn't produce clarity to use the term, as it's often used in the literature to mean just any functionally specifiable system—a very strong claim is being made about a subclass of such systems. It's an empirical claim, and one doesn't want to blur it. On the other hand, I don't think that the notion of a domain, as understood in the claim that linguistic or other modular processes are domain specific, has to be taken psychophysically. In fact, I would be very surprised in the general case, if it could be taken psychophysically. It might turn out in the case of language that there is some particular connection between being in the linguistic domain and having a certain psychophysical acoustical structure, but it also might not. Facts about reading and facts about signing and so on suggest it probably isn't. Most certainly I wouldn't want to suppose that the kind of domain specificity or impenetrability that's characteristic of language (if there is such a thing) should predict that phonetic processes should be insensitive to the acoustic environment.

SAMUEL: I quite agree. My point is that in the adaptation results that you are addressing here, the commonalities of the acoustics are at best obscure. The suggestion is that there are no acoustic explanations for this sort of effect. Instead it's something structural that the representation of /ba/ shares with the canonical plucked string. What makes the data interesting to me is that when you transform the /ba/ into a whispered form so it no longer has its canonical form and, therefore, does not have the acoustic match to the pluck, you nevertheless keep the effect.

FODOR: The only way you could prohibit such phenomena is if you required that no parameter which is assigned to a signal in a structural description ever be assigned to anything that's not a linguistic object, and that seems wildly too strong. For example, you have to mark the intensity of utterances, because they convey all sorts of information about the affect, state of the speaker, and so on, but nobody would claim that no signal other than speech signals gets marked for intensity.

SAMUEL: It's the confluence though that I think . . . .

FODOR: Any modularity thesis which is remotely close to being sane is going to have to allow such cases, because the properties of the things that get structural descriptions are not disjoint with the properties that other things in the world have. The idea that there should be an inside/outside distinction for whole lots of different kinds of perceptual systems, that is, a distinction between the kind of information that the system is allowed to exploit on-line and the kind that it is not, is an idea I find extremely congenial. The more of that there is, the more argument there is for modular kinds of systems. That's only an interesting line to take if there are other reasons to suppose (independent reasons) that systems that exhibit such dualities are modular—I don't know what the case is with music.

SAMUEL: You get a lot of common findings in music, if you look for the kinds of things you find in speech. One of the things that strikes me about these data is that in detail you see the same sort of architectural arrangement. That is, low-level things seem to impact perceptually. Higher level things—if we can use that kind of description—don't.

FODOR: I think that's a law of perception.

SAMUEL: I hope it is.

FODOR: If you do find it with music or with the perception of visual form, that in itself is not an embarrassment to the modularity theory nor does it require that one redraw the boundaries of modules. It just says look, and you'll find this kind of exclusion. It looks like you may find that kind of boundary drawing going on, because you're dealing with a fixed kind of architecture governing the interface between perceptual and other sorts of systems.

SAMUEL: Right. If that's the case—and I tend to believe that it is—are we reduced to the phrase, "speech is special, but so is everything else?" (cf. Mattingly & Liberman, 1985).

FODOR: Not everything else. I think that's a good way to look at things. Not everything else is special. Thought isn't special—not in that kind of way—but it may well be that just about everything that gets information into and out of the head is special in that kind of way.

ALVIN LIBERMAN: I would be happier to try to answer Arty [Samuel]'s comments about the pluck, if I better understood what selective adaptation is all about.

SAMUEL: At one level, I quite agree that we don't understand it. At another level, it seems to me that we don't have to understand to see the regularities that are in the world and in the data. To simply say, "Well, we don't understand the technique," misses the point that there is a regularity in the data, and it's one that is very difficult to account for either in terms of the acoustics or in terms of a speech mode or a speech module. Jerry [Fodor]'s account is: "Well, we're using the same acoustic material in both speech and music, and somehow that's going to lead us to have this kind of effect showing up across modules," but I'm not convinced that that accounts for the results.

FERNANDO NOTTEBOHM: I think it would be very useful for a neurobiologist to know how we could equate modules as they are used by linguists with modules as they are organized by people who worry about circuits. A function that seems modular in its product can be composed of smaller components that are shared by many other functions; at some unknown point the product becomes different from others. Yet you give the idea that there is a whole module that is behind that product. What happens if you throw away the notion of module as you have been using it, and you stay with a more particular description of each of the functions that makes language particular? Do you gain something by saying, "Ah, it's the language module that is involved?"

FODOR: I think you do. As Art Samuel said, I think the basic fact is information encapsulation. Suppose you have a system which may be what the language system is like, which has different subcomponents for phonetics, syntax, lexical information, and so on. One question is, do they talk to one another? I actually am rather ecumenical about that. I don't take strong views about the flow of information inside the system. I also don't have very strong views about whether or not this system could be overlapped with some other device. I don't know of any really clear case of that, but maybe it could happen. What do you get by drawing a big box around all these small boxes? The answer is one of expressing or claiming a generalization which is not implicit in the inventory of interacting subsystems. Namely, that there is a common constraint at least on the inputs to these systems. You can't have information input to one subcomponent but not to another. Whatever sharing of information subcomponents may do among themselves, there is a generalization about the sources of their contacts with extrasystematic information. That's an empirical claim, obviously. If it turns out that a subcomponent has general free access to background information that others don't, the modularity story about the system is just false.

DANIEL MARGOLIASH: I'd like to pursue Fernando [Nottebohm]'s question. It seems to me that we have a system we don't have to discuss in theoretical terms—the barn owl system. Everyone has agreed that sound localization is a modular system. That system has two inputs. There are two ascending pathways in it that don't communicate—time and intensity systems. In that sense, it seems to me that it doesn't fit your description of what you need for a modular system unless you want to include the ear as part of the module, in which case I'm not sure how useful that concept is.

FODOR: There is a degree of freedom which I simply don't have any views about, namely, can these various systems talk to one another? But what's striking about the kind of systems we see in the barn owl is that there is no other source of informational access which operates differentially in these systems. That is, the flow of information to these systems is straightforwardly bottom-up. That's what's characteristic of modular systems—constraints on the way that their subprocesses can exchange information with other cognitive systems. A good way of putting the modularity question for cognitive systems in human beings is whether or not they are as rigidly modular as the data about the barn owl suggest. So we must be having a terminological difference.

MARGOLIASH: I'm saying that in the module for sound localization, there are two inputs. There's a time input and an intensity input. The boxes that are associated with the time input don't have access to the intensity input information and vice versa.

FODOR: I don't think that raises an empirical issue. Draw the boxology like this: There's a time system. There's an intensity system. Then they converge at a neuron or class of neurons.

MARGOLIASH: So is this whole thing one module then?

FODOR: It doesn't matter.

MARGOLIASH: It does matter for a neurobiologist who's trying to figure out whether a system is a module or not.

FODOR: That's terminological. The empirical question is whether or not there are systems that are constrained in the kinds of sources of informational access that they have. You can count one or two in this case—I don't care.

PETER JUSCZYK: I'm a little surprised at what I've seen you do with respect to the box here. I agree that it would be ridiculous to go to the extreme of saying nothing that ever appears in one module can ever appear in any other system, but it seems to me that we should think of a system that develops. There's a bunch of parts around, and you put the parts together into some sort of system. The system becomes automatized in some sense and then functions more or less on its own as an automatic system. If you make that kind of move, it would probably get you out of some of the problems with reading. Also, it probably would allow you to handle some of the sign language stuff. If somebody says, "How could you have a module for sign language?" you can say, "Look, you have some spare parts around, and you build this sort of thing," and the parts are basically innate, because all the systems function innately separately. This does suggest a slightly more constructivist kind of approach to this sort of thing than I thought you might be willing to take.

FODOR: There are two questions. One question is: "What do you think is right?" The other question is: "What's the minimum you have to claim to have an empirical thesis?" The minimum you have to claim to have an empirical thesis is that the nervous system is parsable in terms of uniformities of informational access. That is, there are subsystems of the nervous system around which you can draw boxes and say if there is a constraint on the information available to one part, it's also a constraint on the information available to the other parts. That's the minimum you could claim and still have a substantive thesis. I'm not suggesting there's any positive reason to believe that this kind of system, for example, is at the disposal of other kinds of psychological mechanisms. I know of no reasons for believing that. I don't think the data about reading or sign suggest that, because they can be treated in the sort of way that Ignatius [Mattingly] suggests—that the coupling is very low down—it's at the level of pairings of psychophysically specified objects with phonetically specified objects. Whether or not that's true, there is a residual thesis left, one that's a serious question about cognitive architecture, and it's this question which distinguishes modular kinds of systems from highly interactive kinds of systems. There are questions about domestic affairs and about foreign affairs. The question about foreign affairs is the one that is at the core of the modularity thesis.

PATRICK HAGGARD: I think you're right that the minimum requirement to make this an empirical view is to ask whether things within the box can only take one kind of input, but I think you let yourself off the hook by suggesting earlier that one type of input could incorporate things on different psychophysical dimensions. It seems to me if you say there's one type of input, but one type can include multiple psychophysical dimensions, you could, for example, say the data Summerfield was talking about yesterday were either consistent or inconsistent with the modularity thesis. I'd like you to get back on the hook.

FODOR: I think it is not only possible but entirely likely that the notion of domain that you want for specification for domain specific systems would be quite abstract. In fact, it's more interesting, if it turns out that way. You can imagine a possible world in which there aren't any psychophysical constraints on linguistic exchanges at all. People can do them with little rubber balls, by waving their hands, or making noises in the back of their throats, or by doing songs and dances. It doesn't matter. Would it follow from that that there is no modularity thesis for language in that world? No, not at all. In fact, it would be fascinating if out of all this wide variety of psychophysical displays some mental mechanism could latch onto displays that have a certain abstract structure. That wouldn't be the death of the modularity thesis; that would be extremely interesting.

SAMUEL: I'd like to return to a question that I would like both Ursie [Bellugi] and you to address, which is—rather than bouncing rubber balls about—hands moving about. It seems to me that this is in some sense an embarrassment of riches for the modularity view. What do you think?

FODOR: I would just be inclined to say over again what I did say. If it turns out that the human communicative system is specialized for a certain class of abstract object and doesn't give beans about the psychophysical realization, it is highly platonic. It just looks for geometrical and algebraic relations in the world. If they are in clouds, that's fine. If they are in hands, that's fine. If it grabs them and says, "This is a special class of signals, which I am required to treat in a special kind of way," that would be fascinating.

JANET WERKER: I'd like to address this question to Al [Liberman]. Supposing there is a phonetic module and supposing also that Louis [Goldstein] and Cathe [Browman]'s theory of articulatory phonology turns out to be accurate, and supposing that all parts of it including the idea that the lexicon is specified according to articulatory parameters turn out to be accurate, and that this articulatory phonology can account for both production and perception, then how would you define the bounds of the phonetic module?"

LIBERMAN: I'm not sure. I guess the right answer to that is that in the end that's an empirical question. We have to work on that.

JACQUES MEHLER: I want to come back to this platonic rules system—the bouncing ball, signers and speakers, and so on. We have to acknowledge that the data we have about babies is not fabulously reliable, but most of the data I know of points to the fact that infants seem to have functional specialization for speech in the left hemisphere with no training at all but not for other acoustic stimuli. Given that, don't you want to make some more specific claims about what you think is at the initial state and what is necessary to compile a system that is predisposed, somehow, but is influenced by experience?

BELLUGI: I think the kind of data we presented and Helen Neville presented bears indirectly on the issue of initial state. The research shows that humans are predisposed to create specifically linguistic, and equivalently abstract, complex systems out of alternative raw materials (whether sounds in the vocal tract, and/or hands moving in space). In the absence of hearing from birth, but without linguistic input, rudimentary systems may develop, as Goldin-Meadow (1979) and her group have shown. In the hands of young deaf children of deaf parents, sign language emerges by the same stages, the same maturational time-table as does spoken language, reflecting its biological basis (Bellugi, 1988; Newport & Meier, 1986). Studies of sign language, its formal architecture and its representation in the brain are revealing. Importantly, patterns of breakdown in left and right hemisphere lesioned deaf signers show that the left hemisphere is specialized for signed as well as spoken language, and that sound is not critical to such specialization. This suggests that the left hemisphere in humans has an innate predisposition for language, regardless of modality (Bellugi, Poizner, & Klima, 1989; Poizner, Bellugi, & Klima, chap. 7 in this volume). Both in acquisition and brain organization, language clearly transcends its medium of expression.

FODOR: Jacques [Mehler], it seems to me plausible that when the dust settles, there will be a special relationship between language and certain kinds of sounds. You also have to remember that the most plausible proposals around for what kinds of language universals there could be are blissfully unconcerned with how these structures are realized. They say things like: "You can't have a first language that has the syntacticals, and for that matter, semantical structure, of first order logic." But they don't care whether it's realized in monopoly chips as far as the statement of the universals is concerned.

LIBERMAN: Did I understand you correctly, Jacques, to be asking something about the effect of experience?

MEHLER: I wasn't questioning that much of language is abstractly structured. What I was suggesting is that there are now some data indicating that infants seem to be specialized to treat speech sounds in a specific way at birth—weeks or months thereafter—and they do not seem to be with other acoustic sounds. Do you think there is equivalent specialization that we could show for treating signs or visually presented scenes, and if not, to what extent is one system symbiotic on the other and dependent on the properties of the other.

EDWARD KLIMA: I'm cautious about ascribing the same type of modularity to Sign as I would to some of the aspects of speech. I happen to feel that ASL is a part of the language module. There are certain things that suggest that that is probably very likely. If one of the characteristics of the language module is that it has a particular neural architecture, brain organization, and if it's the case that the findings from sign aphasia pertain to that, then it seems to be becoming more and more suggestive.

372   BELLUGI et al.

LIBERMAN: I think the answer to Jacques' question about signers is "no." I would doubt that the one week old infant can distinguish those hand movements and shapes and so forth that are relevant to sign and those that are not. I would expect it to be the case, because of the richness of the sign system—there doesn't have to be a specialization at the phonetic level, even though there may be a phonetics of sign and certainly a phonology. You don't need anything special in order to handle it, and there isn't anything special that handles it at that level—but what you're looking at in the case of the infants who are responding differently to speech sounds and to other acoustic events is a reflection of the phonetic specialization. They distinguish between sounds that carry phonetic information and sounds that do not. That's very important, if they are going to learn to talk.

LILA GLEITMAN: Everything we've seen in the last decade or so about Sign and its learning makes it premature at best to suppose that when the infancy work is done, we're not going to find specialization for sign. Not anything can be a sign. I think the reason you tend to think about Sign this way from the outside is you think that it's not a special system, and any old thing you could do with your hands could be part of the sign system—but everything we know so far about the learning functions for Sign, which is not just onset data but what the whole internal function looks like, looks identical to the facts about learning a spoken language. When people get around to the infancy data, I would bet that you're going to find the same thing: You're going to get responsiveness to gestures that are within the sign system, and you're not going to get the same kind of response to ambient motor activity, even when done by animate beings like your mother.

References

Bellugi, U. (1988). The acquisition of a spatial language. In F. Kessell (Ed.), *The development of language and language researchers: Essays in honor of Roger Brown* (pp. 153–185). Hillsdale, NJ: Lawrence Erlbaum Associates.

Bellugi, U., Bihrle, A., Jernigan, T., Trauner, D., & Doherty, S. (in press). Neuropsychological, neurological, and neuroanatomical profile of Williams Syndrome. *American Journal of Medical Genetics.*

Bellugi, U., Marks, S., Bihrle, A., & Sabo, H. (1988). Dissociation between language and cognitive functions in Williams Syndrome. In D. Bishop & K. Mogford (Eds.), *Language development in exceptional circumstances* (pp. 177–189). Edinburgh: Churchill Livingstone.

Bellugi, U., Poizner, H., & Klima, E. S. (1989). Language, modality and the brain. *Trends in Neurosciences, 10,* 380–388.

Bellugi, U., & Studdert-Kennedy, M. (Eds.). (1980). *Signed and spoken language: Biological constraints on linguistic forms.* Dahlem Konferenzen. Weinheim/Deerfield Beach, FL: Verlag Chemie.

Bihrle, A., Bellugi, U., Delis, D., & Marks, S. (1989). Seeing either the forest or the trees: Dissociation in visuospatial processing. *Brain and Cognition, 11,* 37–49.

Brady, S., Shankweiler, D., & Mann, V. A. (1983). Speech perception and memory coding in relation to reading ability. *Journal of Experimental Child Psychology, 35,* 345–367.

Chomsky, N. (1968). *Language and mind.* New York: Harcourt Brace Jovanovich.

Chomsky. N. (1988). *Language and problems of knowledge: The Managua lectures.* Cambridge, MA: MIT Press.

DeWitt, L. A., & Samuel, A. G. (1990). The role of knowledge-based expectations in music perception: Evidence from musical restoration. *Journal of Experimental Psychology: General, 119,* 123–144.

Fodor, J. A. (1983). *The modularity of mind.* Cambridge, MA: MIT Press.

Fodor, J. A., & Pylyshyn, Z. (1988). Connectionism and cognitive architecture. *Cognition, 28,* 3–71.

Goldin-Meadow, S. (1979). Structure in a manual communication system developed without a conventional language model; Language without a helping hand. In H. Whitaker & H. A. Whitaker (Eds.), *Studies in Neurolinguistics,* New York: Academic Press.

Klima, E. S., & Bellugi, U. (1988). *The signs of language.* Cambridge, MA: Harvard University Press.

Liberman, I. Y., Mann, V. A., Shankweiler, D., & Werfelman, M. (1982). Children's memory for recurring linguistic and nonlinguistic material in relation to reading ability. *Cortex, 18,* 367–375.

Mann, V. A. (1986). Distinguishing universal and language-dependent levels of speech perception: Evidence from Japanese listeners' perception of English "l" and "r." *Cognition, 24,* 169–196.

Mann, V. A., & Liberman, A. M. (1983). Some differences between phonetic and auditory modes of perception. *Cognition, 14,* 211–235.

Mattingly, I. G., & Liberman, A. M. (1985). Verticality unparalleled. *Behavioral and Brain Sciences, 8,* 24–26.

Newport, E., & Meier, R. (1986). Acquisition of American Sign Language. In D. I. Slobin (Ed.), *The crosslinguistic study of language acquisition.* Hillsdale, NJ: Lawrence Erlbaum Associates.

Samuel, A. G. (1989). Central and peripheral representation of whispered and voiced speech. *Journal of Experimental Psychology: Human Perception and Performance, 14,* 379–388.

Seidenberg, M. S. (1985). Lexicon as module. *Behavioral and Brain Sciences, 8,* 31–32.

Chapter 16

Modularity and Learning to Read

Stephen Crain
Donald Shankweiler
Haskins Laboratories

Abstract

This chapter explains how a limitation in phonological processing gives rise both to word decoding and sentence comprehension difficulties in poor readers. The explanation rests on several assumptions about the architecture of the language apparatus. Most generally, the language apparatus is viewed as an autonomous system in the sense that its operations are sealed off from the general purpose cognitive systems concerned with inference making and real world knowledge. More specifically, to explain how a single deficit at one level can give rise to problems at other levels, we propose that the language apparatus consists of hierarchically organized subcomponents: the phonology, the lexicon, syntax, and semantics. These submodules are seen to function independently of each other, with information flowing unidirectionally from lower to higher levels. The flow of information between levels is regulated by the "executive component" of verbal working memory, which is grounded in phonological operations. Poor readers are deficient in setting up and organizing phonological structures, thus, sentence comprehension is compromised, because inefficient working memory creates a "bottleneck" that constricts information flow to higher levels of language processing.

In our search for the causes of reading disorder in children, several considerations have led us to believe that the origin of the difficulties should be sought in the language domain, and not in some other perceptual or cognitive system.[1] The

---

[1]The search in many ways reflects the influence of Alvin Liberman's views on the nature of speech and language and his guidance on the central issues concerning the problems of reading. Basic

first observation is that reading is largely parasitic upon primary language acquisition. The child who is learning to read does not have to acquire a new communication system but can rely on pre-existing language structures that have long been exploited in spoken communication by the time instruction in reading begins.

Apart from general considerations concerning the nature of reading and its relation to primary language, many empirical findings support the contention that the source of the difficulties in reading is in the language domain. For example, poor readers have been found to be impaired relative to good readers in identification of acoustic stimuli masked by noise, but only when the stimuli are speech. Other kinds of sounds presented in noise are perceived as accurately by poor readers as by good readers (Brady, Shankweiler, & Mann, 1983). Further evidence indicates that poor readers are reliably worse in memory for pictures of familiar objects, letters, nonsense syllables, and strings of unrelated words, but they are equivalent to good readers in memory for unfamiliar faces and nonsense designs (Katz, Shankweiler, & Liberman, 1981; Liberman, Mann, Shankweiler, & Werfelman, 1982; Liberman, Shankweiler, Liberman, Fowler, & Fischer, 1977).

From further consideration of the internal organization of the language faculty and the nature of alphabetic writing, researchers at Haskins Laboratories were led to expect that some limitation in the management of phonological structures might be the specific source of decoding problems. It seemed obvious that mastery of reading requires the learner to discover how the segments of the orthography represent the phonological segments of the language. It also seemed obvious that until the would-be reader has explicit awareness of phonological structure, it would prove impossible to grasp the orthographic code, let alone become skilled in its use (I. Y. Liberman, 1973; Mattingly, 1972). What was not obvious was whether preschool children would find phonemic segmentation of spoken words difficult to apprehend. Following the original study on English-speaking children (Liberman, Shankweiler, Fischer, & Carter, 1974), this has been found in a variety of language communities (Cossu, Shankweiler, Liberman, Katz, & Tola, 1988; Morais, Cluytens, & Alegria, 1984; Lundberg, Olofsson, & Wall, 1980).[2]

---

to the whole enterprise of reading research at Haskins Laboratories is the idea, so often expressed in his writings and conversation, that the language apparatus forms a coherent system of biological specializations, not a mere collection of parts, fashioned for other purposes and only coincidentally brought together to serve the goals of communication. Beyond the idea of coherence, Alvin Liberman has emphasized the importance of distinguishing between primary and secondary processes in language, and he has stressed the biological implications of the fact that speech is a universal human possession, whereas reading and writing are far more limited.

[2]Evidence that the source of the difficulty is linguistic and does not stem from the general cognitive demands of these phonological tasks comes from several studies that fail to find reader group differences on nonlinguistic counterparts of these tasks (Morais et al., 1984; Pratt & Brady, 1988).

Given the evidence that the segments on which alphabetic writing is based are not automatically available to consciousness, the next step in our diagnosis of specific reading difficulties was to ask whether good and poor readers are regularly distinguished on tests that require explicit awareness of the internal structure of spoken words. The answer is now clear. In fact, measures of phonological awareness have emerged time and again as the best predictors of reading success (for reviews, see Bryant & Bradley, 1985; Liberman & Shankweiler, 1985; Stanovich, 1986).

Several observations have led us to think that the problem in poor readers is not limited simply to awareness of phonological structure. The difficulties in phoneme segmentation may be symptomatic of a pervasive underlying deficit in phonological processing. Other difficulties commonly encountered by these children point to this possibility. Among the relevant findings, we may take note of a mild deficiency in extracting the speech signal from noise (Brady et al., 1983) and the tendency to err on tests of object naming (Denckla & Rudel, 1976; Jansky & de Hirsch, 1973; Wolf, 1981). Analysis of errors reveals that the mistakes are often based on phonological confusions rather than on semantic confusions (Katz, 1985). Children with reading difficulty also display impaired performance on tests of ordered recall of linguistic stimuli (see Liberman et al., 1977; Wagner & Torgesen, 1987). Differences in recall have been obtained with a variety of verbal materials, including words and spoken sentences, but differences were not typically found with materials that cannot be coded linguistically.

Because the verbal working memory system exploits phonologic structure, poor readers' difficulties in ordered recall can be regarded as an additional symptom of a phonologic deficit (Conrad, 1972). There is, moreover, direct evidence from memory experiments that poor readers in the beginning grades are less affected by phonetic similarity (rhyme) than age-matched good readers. This has been taken to indicate their failure to fully exploit phonologic structure in working memory (Mann, Liberman, & Shankweiler, 1980; Olson, Davidson, Kliegel, & Davies, 1984; Shankweiler, Liberman, Mark, Fowler, & Fischer, 1979). Our current research, which we will discuss presently, has explored possible implications of a phonological processing deficit for performance by poor readers on spoken language tasks and on reading.[3]

To summarize the discussion so far, our guiding assumptions about the relation between reading and the language apparatus led to studies that uncovered

---

[3]An important source of evidence in support of the conclusion that poor readers utilize phonologic structure less effectively than good readers comes from studies of congenitally deaf readers. Among the several indications that good and poor readers among the deaf, as among the hearing, can be distinguished on a variety of tasks that tap phonologic abilities, it has been shown in a short-term memory experiment that successful deaf readers were more affected by phonetically confusable words than by those that were orthographically confusable or confusable in formation as signs (Hanson, Liberman, & Shankweiler, 1984).

poor readers' difficulties in the language domain but not in visual processing or in other cognitive domains. Within language, it was found that a prominent source of problems for poor readers lies at the level of phonological processing. Several symptoms of the complex were seen to be tied to a deficiency in phonologic processing, including problems in word segmentation, object naming and verbal working memory.

Other findings, however, cannot be so readily assimilated to the view that a phonological processing deficit accounts for all of the symptoms of reading disability. Persistent indications that poor readers do not perform as well as good readers on some tests of comprehension of spoken sentences seem, at first glance, to resist an explanation in phonologic terms (e.g., Byrne, 1981; Mann, Shankweiler, & Smith, 1984). However, appearances may be deceiving, and an important priority of our recent research has been to discover whether or not these differences are related to phonological processing or whether they point to a second set of problems in poor readers that possibly originate in the syntactic component of language.

To explain how the difficulties of poor readers in understanding spoken sentences might be derived from deficient phonological processing, the following paragraphs contain an overview of our conception of the architecture of the language apparatus. Within this framework, it is explained how the failures of poor readers to comprehend sentences can be directly related to their limitations in processing at the phonological level. Then we turn to the laboratory to present evidence that bears on the possibility that the differences between good and poor readers in spoken language comprehension are a manifestation of their differences in phonological processing.

The Language Apparatus

We hold the position that language processing is accomplished by a biologically coherent system that is isolated from other cognitive and perceptual systems. In contemporary terms, language forms a "module" (Fodor, 1983). We would extend this notion of modularity to differentiate subcomponents of the language faculty. As we conceive of it, the language apparatus is composed of a hierarchy of structures and processors. The structures include the phonology, the lexicon, syntax, and semantics. Each level of structure is served by a special-purpose parsing mechanism. A parser consists of algorithms for accessing the rules used to assign structural representations, and it may also contain mechanisms for resolving ambiguities that may arise. We assume that the transfer of information within the language apparatus is unidirectional, beginning at the lowest level with phonological processing and proceeding upward to the syntactic and semantic parsers (for discussion, see Crain & Steedman, 1985; Fodor, 1983; Forster, 1979; Shankweiler & Crain, 1986). We assume, moreover, that in the course of sentence processing, the entire system works on several levels in parallel, with the operations of the various components interleaved in time rather than in strict sequence. This permits the system to function "on-line."

Like Mattingly and Liberman (1988), we assume that the possibility of interfacing phonetic, phonological, syntactic, and semantic information arises only because these components have important properties in common, despite their inherent formal differences. The components form a coherent system that nature has fashioned specifically for language processing. This permits the tightly coordinated flow of information that is so necessary for efficient processing. The responsibility of synchronizing the transfer of information between levels is relegated to the verbal working memory system. Given the prominent role that this system plays in explaining the symptom complex of disabled readers, it will be worthwhile to describe our conception of working memory in slightly more detail.

We assume, along with other researchers, that the verbal working memory system has two parts (Baddeley & Hitch, 1974; Daneman & Carpenter, 1980). First, there is a storage buffer where rehearsal of phonetically coded information takes place. This buffer has the properties commonly attributed to short-term memory.[4] It can hold linguistic input only briefly, perhaps only for a second or two, in the order of arrival, unless the material is maintained by continuous rehearsal. The limits on capacity of the buffer mean that information must be rapidly encoded in a more durable form, beginning with phonological processing, if it is to be retained for subsequent higher level analysis.

The second component of working memory is a control mechanism, whose primary task is to relay the results of lower-level analyses of linguistic input upward through the system. To keep information flowing smoothly, the control mechanism must avoid unnecessary computation that would forestall the rapid extraction of meaning. We would speculate that the language faculty has responded to the limited working memory capacity by evolving special-purpose parsing mechanisms (e.g., the syntactic parser) to organize and shunt information rapidly upward to the next level of the system, allowing their previous contents to be abandoned. Rapid on-line parsing, in turn, explains how individuals with drastically curtailed working memory capacity—capable of holding only two or three items of unstructured material—are sometimes able to comprehend sentences of considerable length and complexity (Martin, 1985; Saffran, 1985).

To see what is most costly of memory resources, we have found it useful to consider situations that are amenable to straightforward transfer of information between levels (see also Hamburger & Crain, 1987). In the simplest case, (a) each well-formed fragment of language code at lower levels of representation is associated with a single constituent of code at higher levels, (b) the fragments of code at each level can be concatenated to form the correct representation of the

---

[4]It is this aspect of working memory that most comparisons of good and poor readers consider, but in our recent research we have given more weight to the second component.

input, (c) the fragments can be combined in the same order that they are accessed, and (d) each fragment is processed immediately after it is formed, permitting the source code to be discarded. These four conditions form a straightforward translation process of sequential look-up-and-concatenation familiar in the compiling of programming languages. However, all these conditions are rarely met in ordinary language. Furthermore, when they are not, the computations involved in reaching the target code (e.g., the semantic interpretation of a sentence), could stretch the resources of verbal working memory.

To make our view more concrete, the remainder of the paper will focus on one of the ways that linguistic input can deviate from the best-case scenario—by violating condition (c). Let us call any violation of this condition a *sequencing problem*. A sequencing problem arises, for example, when subjects are asked to act out the meanings of sentences containing temporal terms such as *before* and *after*. These terms explicitly dictate the conceptual order of events, but they may present problems of sequencing, if the order in which events are mentioned conflicts with the conceptual order (i.e., the most appropriate order of execution in acting out the events depicted by the sentence). This kind of conflict is illustrated in sentence (1).

(1) Jabba the Hutt flew away in an X-Wing fighter after Hans Solo sped away in the Millennium Falcon.

It is reasonable to suppose that such a conflict exacts a toll on the resources of working memory, because both clauses must remain available long enough to enable the perceiver to formulate a response plan that represents the conceptual order. The conceptually correct response requires the formation of a two-slot template and a specification of the sequence in which the two actions are to be carried out. The information in both clauses must be held in memory long enough to put the first-mentioned action into the second slot, which would violate condition (c) in the simple translation process.

Evidence that these suppositions are correct comes from research on language acquisition. It has been found that young children frequently misinterpret sentences like (1) by acting out their meanings in an order-of-mention fashion (Clark, 1970; Johnson, 1975). This response presumably reflects a simple look-up-and-concatenate translation process that serves as a default procedure for interpreting sentences that exceed children's memory capacity. Consistent with this interpretation is the observation that they often begin to act while the sentence is still being uttered.

Explaining the Symptom Complex of Poor Readers

We are now prepared to show how the various difficulties manifested by poor readers can be explained in terms of the functional architecture of language. A modular view of the language apparatus raises the possibility that a single component may be the source of the entire symptom complex that characterizes reading disability. Specifically, we appeal to the modular architecture of the language apparatus to explain how a deficit in phonologic processing may masquerade as a deficit in spoken language comprehension. As we saw, the other features of the symptom complex of reading disability stem from a phonologic-based deficiency. Therefore, if the difficulties poor readers encounter in spoken language comprehension also implicate the phonological component, we could offer a unitary account of a set of symptoms that might otherwise appear unrelated.[5]

Put simply, our account is as follows. As we saw, the regulatory duties of working memory begin at the lowest level by bringing phonetic (or orthographic) input into contact with phonological rules for word level analysis. In our view, this is the site of constriction for poor readers. One thing leads to another: A low-level deficit in processing phonological information creates a bottleneck that impedes the transfer of information to higher levels in the system (see also Crain, Shankweiler, Macaruso, & Bar-Shalom, 1990; Perfetti, 1985; Shankweiler & Crain, 1986). In other words, the constriction arises because in language processing the "bottom-up" flow of information from the phonologic buffer is impeded by the difficulties in accessing and processing phonological information. Therefore, all subsequent processes in the language system will be adversely affected.

In research on reading, it is sometimes assumed that the transient character of speech would force greater reliance on working memory in comprehending spoken sentences in comparison to reading text, because the latter is fixed and, therefore, available for re-examination. We would stress the relevance of the reader's skill in making any such comparison, noting that the advantage of text permanence can be exploited only by the skilled reader. The opportunity to look back confers no advantage on the unskilled reader, because the demands of orthographic decoding consume all the available memory resources. Therefore, until the reader is skilled, reading is often more demanding of working memory than listening.

In spoken language comprehension, the deficient use of phonologic structure by poor readers should be revealed only in comprehension of sentences that place heavy demands on verbal working memory, for example, by presenting a sequencing problem. On sentences that are less taxing of memory resources, poor readers should display successful comprehension. The early emergence of grammatical competence by both good and poor readers follows in part from our

---

[5]To our knowledge, Kean (1977) was the first to argue that these architectural features of the language apparatus could explain how a deficit in a single component can have widespread manifestations throughout the system. This possibility was explored by Kean in her research on Broca-type aphasia. She pointed out that one consequence of the hierarchical architecture of the language apparatus is that a lower-level deficit could give rise, in principle, to a variety of symptoms involving higher levels of processing.

adherence to the theory of Universal Grammar, which maintains that the basic organizational principles of linguistic structure are innately specified. We contend that acquisition of primary language structures is essentially complete by the time instruction in reading and writing begins. The early emergence of syntax is seen to be a consequence of the innate specification of many syntactic principles which either come "prewired" or are subject to rigid system-internal innate constraints on grammar construction (see, e.g., Chomsky, 1965, 1981). Because syntactic structures are largely built into the blueprint for language acquisition, it follows that inherent complexity of grammatical structures as such will not be a source of reader-group differences (Crain & Shankweiler, 1988). Poor readers will be at a disadvantage, however, in contexts that stress verbal working memory.

There is an alternative hypothesis, however. The limitations of poor readers in sentence comprehension could be independent of their deficits in analyzing phonological structures. Poor readers could simply lag behind good readers of the same age in the acquisition of those linguistic constructions that they find difficult to comprehend. We will refer to this as the *structural lag hypothesis* (SLH). The SLH is tied to an implicit assumption about the course of language acquisition as well as to an assumption about linguistic complexity. It supposes that some linguistic structures develop before others, with the course of development determined by the relative complexity of the structures. Our research has been directed to a version of the structural lag hypothesis that holds that some poor readers suffer from a developmental lag in *syntactic* knowledge.[6]

This version of the SLH appears to draw support from some classical studies in language acquisition that find the late emergence of certain constructions; for example, temporal terms, relative clauses, and adjectives with exceptional control properties, such as *easy*, as in *The doll is easy to see* (see C. Chomsky, 1969; Clark, 1970; Sheldon, 1974). On the SLH, the differences between good and poor readers on spoken language comprehension are readily explained: Comprehension problems appear on late emerging structures that are beyond their developmental level. It is important to recognize, however, that by allowing at least two basic deficits in poor readers, this hypothesis abandons a unitary explanation of reading disability. Our own proposal, by contrast, attempts to tie together the entire symptom complex of poor readers as a consequence of deficient phonological processing. Let us refer to our account as the *processing limitation hypothesis* (PLH).

---

[6]If the SLH were upheld, it would be appropriate to ask, further, whether the poor readers had failed to acquire some of the structures needed for comprehension, or whether instead the good readers had advanced beyond their age-matched classmates, because their greater experience in reading has enhanced their knowledge of critical grammatical structures. Either eventuality poses a challenge to our efforts to tie together the observed differences between good and poor readers at the sentence level and at the level of the phonology.

Testing Between Competing Hypotheses

Much of our recent research has centered on testing between these alternative explanations for the sentence comprehension problems of poor readers. Our research strategy has two components. First, we have chosen to investigate structures that are known to emerge late in the course of normal language acquisition. Then, for each construction we designed a pair of tasks that vary memory load while keeping syntactic structure constant. If reading disability stems from a structural lag, then children who have reading problems should perform poorly on both tasks. However, according to the PLH, poor readers should have greater difficulty than their age-matched controls only in tasks that place heavy demands on working memory, whatever the inherent complexity of the linguistic structure being investigated. When the same test materials are presented in tasks that minimize processing load, poor readers should do as well as good readers.[7] We now review the findings from studies adopting this research strategy with several linguistic constructions.

Temporal Terms

Sentences containing temporal terms have been found to pose problems for children, as we have seen. Not surprisingly, the difficulty they encounter with such sentences has been explained in the literature in two ways. Consistent with the SLH is the proposal that temporal terms are mastered late in childhood, because younger children lack certain structural knowledge that is essential to sentences with subordinate syntax, such as temporal terms and relative clauses. This interpretation is buttressed by the finding that children have difficulty with temporal term sentences like (2) following, which pose conflicts between order of mention and conceptual order, and not with sentences with similar meaning but with "simpler" syntax such as the coordinate structure sentences in (3) following (Amidon & Carey, 1972).

(2) Push the motorcycle after you push the helicopter.
(3) Push the motorcycle last; push the helicopter first.

Other research has questioned the assumption that sentences (2) and (3) are equivalent in meaning, suggesting, contrary to the SLH, that the earlier studies

---

[7]There is another way to address the question of a processing limitation versus a structural deficit, by examining the pattern of errors across constructions for each reader group. Elsewhere, we propose that a processing limitation and not a structural deficit can be inferred if: (a) there is a decrement in performance by poor readers, as compared to good readers, but (b) both reader groups reveal a similar pattern of errors across sentence-types, and (c) poor readers manifest a sufficiently high rate of correct response on a subset of the sentences.

may have obtained differential responses to (2) and (3) because they failed to control for a presupposition that is present just in sentences like (2) (Crain, 1982; Gorrell, Crain, & Fodor, 1989). The presupposition associated with this sentence is that the hearer intends to push a helicopter. To satisfy this presupposition, the subject should have established this intention *before* the command in (2) is given. A procedure that allows subjects to establish in advance their intent to perform the action mentioned in the clause introduced by the temporal term was incorporated into a study by Crain (1982). Children are asked, before each test sentence is presented, to identify one object they want to play with in the next part of the game. The experimenter subsequently incorporates this information in the subordinate clause introduced by the temporal term. For instance, sentence (2) would have been presented only after a subject had selected the helicopter, which makes the use of the temporal term *felicitous*.

When young children were given this contextual support, they displayed unprecedented success in comprehending sentences with temporal terms. Thus, the mistake in research that resulted in high error rates was to present sentences like (2) in the "null context," (i.e., in violation of the presupposition inherent in the use of temporal terms). In the null context, unmet presuppositions must be "accommodated" into the listener's mental model of the discourse setting (Lewis, 1979). Compensating for unmet presuppositions requires the hearer to revise his/her current mental model (to make it match the mental model of the speaker). The process of revising one's mental model of the discourse is seen to be highly taxing of processing resources (see Crain & Steedman, 1985, and references therein).

If this reasoning is sound, children's grammars should be exonerated from responsibility for the errors that occurred in research that failed to satisfy the presuppositions of the test sentences. It would also seem reasonable to suppose that children's limitations in working memory would contribute to their difficulties in processing sentences in the null context. In light of these considerations, the PLH would anticipate that both good and poor readers would display a high rate of successful comprehension in felicitous contexts, but that the performance of the poor readers would suffer appreciably in contexts that are more taxing of working memory. The SLH, on the other hand, would anticipate the same differences between good and poor readers both with and without contextual support, because lightening the burdens imposed on working memory would not result in comprehension of a structure, if the structure were not present in the internal grammar.

Subsequently, we investigated these questions in a study of poor readers' comprehension of sentences with temporal terms (Macaruso, Bar-Shalom, Crain, & Shankweiler, 1989). We will report on one experiment in which we tried to exacerbate the processing load on both reader groups by including an additional prenominal modifier in half of the test sentences. As exemplified in (4) following, the main clause of these sentences contained "complex NPs" with an ordinal quantifier (*second*) and a superlative adjective. Adjectives combine to introduce added complexity to the plan that one must formulate in order to respond accurately to the sentence. The remaining test sentences contained "simple NPs" (i.e., with no additional ordinal modifier in the main clause) as in (5) following.

(4) Push the *second smallest horse* before you push the blue car.
(5) Pick up the *largest truck* after you pick up the blue horse.

The stimuli consisted of 16 sentences with temporal terms *before* and *after*. Four sentences were presented in which the order of mention of events was the same as the conceptual order, as in (4). In the remaining twelve sentences, the order of mention was opposite to the conceptual order, as in (5).[8] Children encountered the test sentences in two contexts: one that satisfied the presupposition associated with the use of temporal terms and one that did not (i.e., the null context).

As anticipated, poor readers performed less well overall than good readers in acting out temporal terms sentences. However, satisfying the felicity conditions and thereby reducing memory demands resulted in a significant reduction in errors for both groups combined. Moreover, the satisfaction of presuppositions benefited poor readers more than good readers. This lends credence to the hypothesis that, without contextual support, poor readers' limitations in working memory are exacerbated. However, the poor readers performed at a success rate of 82.4% when the felicity conditions were satisfied, even when half of the test sentences contained complex NPs. This calls into question the claim of the SLH that poor readers lag in their mastery of complex syntactic structures.

Further support for a processing interpretation of poor readers' comprehension difficulties comes from the finding that poor readers were more adversely affected by changes in NP complexity than good readers. The special problems that poor readers had with the complex NP sentences presumably reflect the fact that

---

[8]For sentences that present a conflict between order of mention and conceptual order, the presence of a temporal term in the initial clause eases the burden on working memory by indicating in advance that a two-slot template is required, as in (A):

(A) Before you push the helicopter, push the motorcycle.
(B) Push the motorcycle after you push the helicopter.

Here, the use of *before* in the initial clause forestalls execution. This contrasts with the corresponding sentences with *after,* such as (B), because there the temporal conjunction is delayed until the second clause. On the account of memory difficulties we have proposed, we would predict the sentences with *after* to be harder, because the subject has no warning that information should be maintained in memory while awaiting subsequent material. As expected, poor readers in the Macaruso et al. study were least successful in responding to *after* sentences that presented a conflict between order of mention and conceptual order, and no contextual support in the form of satisfied presuppositions. Good readers, on the other hand, were not as handicapped by the memory demands imposed by these sentences.

these sentences are more taxing on working memory resources, as mentioned earlier. Taken together, the findings of this experiment indicate that as processing demands are increased, poor readers' performance involving temporal terms sentences is eroded much more than good readers' performance. Decreasing processing demands, either by satisfying the felicity conditions or by using less complex NPs, elevates performance by poor readers such that group differences diminish. In the best case, both reader groups perform at a high level of success.

Relative Clauses

The relative clause has often been the focus of studies in normal language acquisition as well as in studies on reading disability. Relative clauses have been found to evoke difficulties in interpretation for preschool children (Tavakolian, 1981) and for older children who are poor readers (Byrne, 1981; Stein, Cairns, & Zurif, 1984). Early research with each population led some to the conclusion that children's poor performance was due to a lack of syntactic knowledge. Others have stressed the processing difficulties that can arise with certain sentences containing relative clauses. One source of processing difficulty, involving a sequencing problem, was demonstrated in a study by Hamburger and Crain (1982), who found that many preschool children who performed the correct actions associated with OS relatives like (6) often failed, nevertheless, to act out these events in the same way as adults.

(6) The cat scratched the dog that jumped through the hoop.

Most 3-year-olds and many 4-year-olds acted out this sentence by making the cat scratch the dog first and then making the dog jump through the hoop. Older children and normal adults act out these events in the opposite order, the relative clause *before* the main clause. Intuitively, acting out the second mentioned clause first seems conceptually more correct, because "the dog that jumped through the hoop" is what the cat scratched. Presumably, the difference between children and adults reflects the more severe limitations in children's working memory in coping with the sequencing problem.

As this discussion shows, both the SLH and the PLH have a stake in discovering why poor readers have more difficulties understanding relative clauses than good readers. To test between these hypotheses, Mann et al. (1984) had good and poor readers in the third grade act out sentences containing relative clauses. In this study, four types of relative clauses were presented. As illustrated in (7) following, each set of sentences contained exactly the same ten words to control for vocabulary and sentence length.

(7) a) The sheep pushed the cat that jumped over the cow.
     b) The sheep that pushed the cat jumped over the cow.
     c) The sheep pushed the cat that the cow jumped over.
     d) The sheep that the cat pushed jumped over the cow.

It was found that the type of relative clause structure had a large effect on comprehensibility. Sentences of type (a) and (d) evoked the most errors in keeping with the findings of earlier research on younger children (e.g., Tavakolian, 1981). Good and poor readers did not fare equally well, however. The Mann et al. study confirms the earlier findings that poor readers have more difficulty than good readers in understanding complex sentences, even when these are presented in spoken form. However, in several respects, the findings of this study invite the inference that poor readers' problems with these sentences reflect a deficit in processing. First of all, the poor readers were worse than the good readers in comprehension of each of the four types of relative clause structure that were tested. However, the poor readers did not appear to lack any type of relative clause structure entirely. In fact, their pattern of errors closely mirrored that of the good readers; they simply did less well on each sentence type.

Further support for the view that poor readers' difficulties with relative clauses reflect performance factors comes from a later study of good and poor readers' comprehension of relative clauses by Smith, Macaruso, Shankweiler, and Crain (1990). This study was based on a methodological innovation of Hamburger and Crain (1982), who studied preschool children's grammatical knowledge. The change in methodology was motivated by the observation that many restrictive relative clauses are used felicitously only in contexts that introduce a set of objects corresponding to the head noun phrase of the relative clause. Hamburger and Crain (1982) found that most preschool children produced and understood relative clause sentences when this condition was satisfied, suggesting that failure to meet this condition interfered with children's comprehension of the test sentences in previous work. In the case of poor readers, the findings in the literature of impaired performance on comprehension of relative clause sentences might also be tied to excessive processing demands imposed by failure to meet felicity conditions.[9]

To explore this possibility, the study by Smith et al. made two objects available in the experimental workspace corresponding to the head noun of the relative clause. For example, for sentence (8) following, two sheep were placed in the experimental workspace, where only one had appeared in earlier studies.

(8) The sheep that the cat pushed jumped over the cow.

With this change in place, Smith et al. compared their findings on good and poor readers in the second grade with those of the Mann et al. study, in which the same subject selection criteria were used but in which the pragmatic presuppositions

---

[9]An additional experiment with the same children investigated how well good and poor readers could recover from a variety of "garden path" sentences. It was found that poor readers had significantly more difficulty reanalyzing a sentence that they had initially misparsed, and the greatest difference between reader groups appeared on sentences involving relative clauses (Crain et al., 1990).

associated with restrictive relative clauses was not met. The data of the new study support the PLH decisively. Both good and poor readers made far fewer errors than in the earlier relative clause study (despite the fact that subjects were nearly a year younger than in the earlier study).

Detection and Correction of Ungrammatical Sentences

An attempt by Fowler (1988) to disentangle structural knowledge and processing capabilities in beginning readers yielded striking results. In preliminary tests used to assess children's metaphonological awareness, working memory, and spoken sentence understanding, once again there were clear-cut correlations with measures of reading. In addition, children were compared on a grammaticality judgment task and a sentence correction task. The grammaticality judgment task was used to establish a baseline on the structural knowledge of the subjects for comparison with the correction task. The judgment task is presumed to place minimal demands on working memory. This expectation is motivated in part by recent research on aphasia showing that agrammatic aphasic patients with severe memory limitations were able to judge the grammaticality of sentences of considerable length and syntactic complexity (Linebarger, Schwartz, & Saffran, 1983; Saffran, 1985; Shankweiler, Crain, Gorrell, & Tuller, 1989). The findings from aphasia suggest that this task taps directly the syntactic analysis that is assigned. In the correction task, subjects were asked to change ungrammatical sentences (taken from the judgment task) to make them grammatical. Clearly, correcting grammatical anomalies requires the ability to hold sentences in memory long enough for reanalysis.

According to the PLH, both good and poor readers should do equally well on the grammaticality judgment task, but differences should occur on the correction task. This is exactly what was found. Reading ability was significantly correlated with success on the correction task but not with success on the judgment task. This is further support for the view that processing complexity and not structural complexity is a better diagnostic of reading disability. Two additional findings bear on the competing hypotheses about the causes of reading failure. First, the level of achievement on grammaticality judgments was well above chance for both good and poor readers, even on complex syntactic structures (e.g., Wh-movement and Tag Questions). Second, results on a test of short-term recall (with IQ partialed out) were more strongly correlated with success on the sentence correction task than with success on the judgment task.

Conclusion

We began by stating the basic theoretical assumptions that relate reading to our conception of the language apparatus. The manner in which reading is erected on preexisting linguistic structures led us to predict that the causes of reading disability would lie within the language domain. Accordingly, seemingly normal school children who fail to make the expected progress in learning to read were found to have language-related difficulties, including problems in meta-phonological awareness and unusual limitations in verbal working memory. Both of these problems are arguably grounded in phonology, therefore, one of our central concerns has been to determine if all the language-related difficulties evinced by poor readers might stem from a single deficit in processing phonological information.

The observation that poor readers have difficulties in correctly interpreting some spoken sentences seemed at first to threaten the phonological deficit account. However, in the context of our assumptions about the architecture of the language apparatus and in view of the phonological nature of the working memory code, we argued that a processing deficit might also explain this problem. If so, it would obviate the need to attribute the comprehension difficulties of reading disabled children to a developmental lag in structural competence over and above their well-attested deficiencies in phonological processing. In order to tease apart the alternatives, tasks were constructed that stress processing in varying degrees, holding syntactic structure constant.[10] We reviewed a set of interlocking studies that demonstrates large differences between good and poor readers in comprehending certain spoken sentences in contexts that stress working memory, but much smaller differences when the same materials are presented in ways that lessen memory load. Contrary to the expectations of the SLH, in contexts that minimize memory demands, both reader groups achieve such a high level of accuracy that competence with the constructions under investigation would seem guaranteed. Inefficient use of verbal working memory resources in processing phonological information was identified as the proximal cause of poor readers' sentence comprehension problems. Because faulty word decoding also reflects phonological deficiencies, it is likely that, as a consequence of modular organization, both problems derive from the same source.

References

Amidon, A., & Carey, P. (1972). Why five-year-olds cannot understand *before* and *after*. *Journal of Verbal Learning and Verbal Behavior, 11*, 417–423.

---

[10]It is pertinent to note also that the experimental results we have summarized were predicted by a theoretical framework that is itself supported by a substantial literature in other areas of psycholinguistic investigation, including language acquisition, language breakdown in aphasia, and normal sentence processing. We were guided by this theoretical and empirical base in selecting materials and tasks for our studies of reading disability. For instance, in order to provide support for the supposition that working memory is the cause of performance failures in poor readers, we chose structures that were known to be problematic for other groups with working memory limitations: for example, very young children (Tavakolian, 1981), mentally retarded adults (W. Crain, 1986), aphasics (Caramazza & Berndt, 1985), and in some cases even normal adults, when spoken sentences are presented in a way that stresses memory (see Crain & Fodor, 1985).

Baddeley, A. D., & Hitch, G. B. (1974). Working memory. In G. A. Bower (Ed.), *The psychology of learning and motivation* (vol. 8, pp. 47–89). New York: Academic Press.

Brady, S., Shankweiler, D., & Mann, V. A. (1983). Speech perception and memory coding in relation to reading ability. *Journal of Experimental Child Psychology, 35,* 345–367.

Bryant, P., & Bradley, L. (1985). *Children's reading problems.* Oxford: Blackwell.

Byrne, B. (1981). Deficient syntactic control in poor readers: Is a weak phonetic memory code responsible? *Applied Psycholinguistics, 2,* 201–212.

Caramazza, A., & Berndt, R. (1985). A multicomponent view of agrammatic Broca's aphasia. In M.-L. Kean (Ed.), *Agrammatism* (pp. 27–63). New York: Academic Press.

Chomsky, C. (1969). *The acquisition of syntax in children from 5 to 10.* Cambridge, MA: MIT Press.

Chomsky, N. (1965). *Aspects of the theory of syntax.* Cambridge, MA: MIT Press.

Chomsky. N. (1981). *Lectures on government and binding.* Dordrecht: Foris.

Clark, E. V. (1970). How young children describe events in time. In G. B. Flores d'Arcais & W. J. M. Levelt (Eds.), *Advances in psycholinguistics* (pp. 275–284). Amsterdam: North-Holland.

Conrad, R. (1972). Speech and reading. In J. F. Kavanagh & I. G. Mattingly (Eds.), *Language by ear and by eye: The relationships between speech and reading* (pp. 205–240). Cambridge, MA: MIT Press.

Cossu, G., Shankweiler, D., Liberman, I. Y., Katz, L., & Tola, L. (1988). Awareness of phonological segments and reading ability in Italian children. *Applied Psycholinguistics, 9,* 1–16.

Crain, S. (1982). Temporal terms: Mastery by age five. In *Papers and Reports on Child Language Development: Proceedings of the Fourteenth Annual Stanford Child Language Research Forum* (pp. 33–38). Stanford, CA: Department of Linguistics, Stanford University.

Crain, S., & Fodor, J. D. (1985). On the innateness of Subjacency. In *The Proceedings of the Eastern States Conference on Linguistics* (vol. 1, pp. 191–204). Columbus, OH: Ohio State University.

Crain S., & Shankweiler, D. (1988). Syntactic complexity and reading acquisition. In A. Davison & G. M. Green (Eds.), *Linguistic complexity and text comprehension: Readability issues reconsidered* (pp. 167–192). Hillsdale, NJ: Lawrence Erlbaum Associates.

Crain, S., Shankweiler, D., Macaruso, P., & Bar-Shalom, E. (1990). Working memory and comprehension of spoken sentences: Investigations of children with reading disorder. In G. Vallar & T. Shallice (Eds.), *Neuropsychological impairments of short-term memory* (pp. 477–508). Cambridge, UK: Cambridge University Press.

Crain, S., & Steedman, M. (1985). On not being led up the garden path: The use of context by the psychological syntax processor. In D. Dowty, L. Karttunen, & A. Zwicky (Eds.), *Natural language parsing* (pp. 320–358). Cambridge, UK: Cambridge University Press.

Crain, W. (1986). *Restrictions on the comprehension of syntax by mentally retarded adults.* Unpublished doctoral dissertation, Claremont, CA: Claremont Graduate School.

Daneman, M., & Carpenter, P. A. (1980). Individual differences in working memory and reading. *Journal of Verbal Learning and Verbal Behavior, 19,* 450–466.

Denckla, M. B., & Rudel, R. G. (1976). Naming of object-drawings by dyslexic and other learning disabled children. *Brain and Language, 3,* 1–15.

Fodor, J. A. (1983). *The modularity of mind.* Cambridge, MA: MIT Press.

Forster, K. (1979). Levels of processing and the structure of the language processor. In W. E. Cooper & E. Walker (Eds.), *Sentence processing: Psycholinguistic studies presented to Merrill Garrett* (pp. 27–85). Hillsdale, NJ: Lawrence Erlbaum Associates.

Fowler, A. E. (1988). Grammaticality judgments and reading skill in grade 2. *Annals of Dyslexia, 38,* 73–84.

Gorrell, P., Crain, S., & Fodor, J. D. (1989). Contextual information and temporal terms. *Journal of Child Language,* 16, 623–632.

Hamburger, H., & Crain, S. (1982). Relative acquisition. In S. Kuczaj (Ed.), *Language develop-*

ment Volume 1: Syntax and semantics (pp. 245–274). Hillsdale, NJ: Lawrence Erlbaum Associates.

Hamburger, H., & Crain, S. (1987). Plans and semantics in human processing of language. *Cognitive Science, 11,* 101–136.

Hanson, V. L., Liberman, I. Y., & Shankweiler, D. (1984). Linguistic coding by deaf children in relation to beginning reading success. *Journal of Experimental Child Psychology, 37,* 378–393.

Jansky, J., & de Hirsch, K. (1973). *Preventing reading failure.* New York: Harper & Row.

Johnson, M. L. (1975). The meaning of *before* and *after* for preschool children. *Journal of Experimental Child Psychology, 19,* 88–99.

Katz, R. B. (1985). Phonological deficiencies in children with reading disability: Evidence from an object-naming task. *Cognition, 22,* 225–257.

Katz, R. B., Shankweiler, D., & Liberman, I. Y. (1981). Memory for item order and phonetic recoding in the beginning reader. *Journal of Experimental Child Psychology, 32,* 474–484.

Kean, M. -L. (1977). The linguistic interpretation of aphasic syndromes: Agrammatism in Broca's aphasia, an example. *Cognition, 5,* 9–46.

Lewis, D. (1979). Scorekeeping in a language game. *Journal of Philosophical Logic, 8,* 339–359.

Liberman, I. Y. (1973). Segmentation of the spoken word and reading acquisition. *Bulletin of the Orton Society, 23,* 65–77.

Liberman, I. Y., Mann, V. A., Shankweiler, D., & Werfelman, M. (1982). Children's memory for recurring linguistic and nonlinguistic material in relation to reading ability. *Cortex, 18,* 367–375.

Liberman, I. Y., & Shankweiler, D. (1985). Phonology and the problems of learning to read and write. *Remedial and Special Education, 6,* 8–17.

Liberman, I. Y., Shankweiler, D., Liberman, A. M., Fowler, C., & Fischer, F. W. (1977). Phonetic segmentation and recoding in the beginning reader. In A. S. Reber & D. L. Scarborough (Eds.), *Toward a psychology of reading: The proceedings of the CUNY conferences* (pp. 207–225). Hillsdale, NJ: Lawrence Erlbaum Associates.

Liberman, I. Y., Shankweiler, D., Fischer, F. W., & Carter, B. (1974). Explicit syllable and phoneme segmentation in the young child. *Journal of Experimental Child Psychology, 18,* 201–212.

Linebarger, M., Schwartz, M., & Saffran, E. M. (1983). Sensitivity to grammatical structure in so-called agrammatic aphasia. *Cognition, 13,* 361–392.

Lundberg, I., Olofsson, A., & Wall, S. (1980). Reading and spelling skills in the first school years predicted from phonemic awareness skills in kindergarten. *Scandinavian Journal of Psychology, 21,* 159–173.

Macaruso, P., Bar-Shalom, E., Crain, S., & Shankweiler, D. (1989). Comprehension of temporal terms by good and poor readers. *Language and Speech, 32,* 45–67.

Mann, V. A., Liberman, I. Y., & Shankweiler, D. (1980). Children's memory for sentences and word strings in relation to reading ability. *Memory and Cognition, 8,* 329–335.

Mann, V. A., Shankweiler, D., & Smith, S. T. (1984). The association between comprehension of spoken sentences and early reading ability: The role of phonetic representation. *Journal of Child Language, 11,* 627–643.

Martin, R. C. (1985, October). *The relationship between short-term memory and sentence comprehension deficits in agrammatic and conduction aphasics.* Paper presented at the annual meeting of the Academy of Aphasia, Pittsburgh, PA.

Mattingly, I. G. (1972). Reading, the linguistic process, and linguistic awareness. In J. F. Kavanagh & I. G. Mattingly (Eds.), *Language by ear and by eye: The relationships between speech and reading* (pp. 133–147). Cambridge, MA: MIT Press.

Mattingly, I. G., & Liberman, A. (1988). Specialized perceiving systems for speech and other biologically significant sounds. In G. M. Edelman, W. E. Gall, & W. M. Cowan (Eds.), *Auditory function: Neurological bases of hearing* (pp. 775–792). New York: Wiley.

Morais, J., Cluytens, M., & Alegria, J. (1984). Segmentation abilities of dyslexics and normal readers. *Perceptual and Motor Skills, 58,* 221–222.

Olsen, R. K., Davidson, B. J., Kliegl, R., & Davies, S. E. (1984). Development of phonetic memory in disabled and normal readers. *Journal of Experimental Child Psychology, 37,* 187–206.

Perfetti, C. A. (1985). *Reading ability.* New York: Oxford University Press.

Pratt, A., & Brady, S. (1988). Relation of phonological awareness to reading disability in children and adults. *Journal of Educational Psychology, 80,* 319–323.

Saffran, E. M. (1985, October). *Short-term memory and sentence processing: Evidence from a case study.* Paper presented at Academy of Aphasia, Pittsburgh, PA.

Shankweiler, D., & Crain, S. (1986). Language mechanisms and reading disorder: A modular approach. *Cognition, 24,* 139–168.

Shankweiler, D., Crain, S., Gorrell, P., & Tuller, B. (1989). Reception of language in Broca's aphasia. *Language and Cognitive Processes, 4,* 1–33.

Shankweiler, D., Liberman, I. Y., Mark, L. S., Fowler, C. A., & Fischer, F. W. (1979). The speech code and learning to read. *Journal of Experimental Psychology: Human Learning and Memory, 5,* 531–545.

Sheldon, A. (1974). The role of parallel function in the acquisition of relative clauses in English. *Journal of Verbal Learning and Verbal Behavior, 13,* 272–281.

Smith, S. T., Macaruso, P., Shankweiler, D., & Crain, S. (1990). Syntactic comprehension in young poor readers. *Applied Psycholinguistics, 10,* 429–454.

Stanovich, K. E. (1986). Matthew effects in reading: Some consequences of individual differences in the acquisition of literacy. *Reading Research Quarterly, 21,* 360–407.

Stein, C. L., Cairns, H. S., & Zurif, E. B. (1984). Sentence comprehension limitations related to syntactic deficits in reading-disabled children. *Applied Psycholinguistics, 5,* 305–322.

Tavakolian, S. L. (1981). The conjoined-clause analysis of relative clauses. In S. Tavakolian (Ed.), *Language acquisition and linguistic theory* (pp. 167–187). Cambridge, MA: MIT Press.

Wagner, R. K., & Torgesen, J. K. (1987). The nature of phonological processing and its causal role in the acquisition of reading skills. *Psychological Bulletin, 101,* 192–212.

Wolf, M. (1981). The word-retrieval process and reading in children and aphasics. In K. Nelson (Ed.), *Children's language* (vol. 3, pp. 437–493). New York: Gardner Press.

Chapter 17

The Emergence of Phonological Awareness: Comparative Approaches

Paul Bertelson
Beatrice de Gelder

*Université Libre de Bruxelles
and Tilburg University*

Abstract

The notion that the capacity to represent explicitly some aspects of the phonological structure of utterances is an important condition of the acquisition of alphabetic literacy has been, since its introduction by the Libermans and their coworkers, a cornerstone of research on reading acquisition. The capacity is generally referred to by the term "phonological awareness." With attention focused mainly on its role in the acquisition process, the question of the conditions under which phonological awareness itself develops has been somewhat neglected. One central issue is whether phonological awareness develops spontaneously, through maturation or sheer experience of speech communication, or whether it requires specific learning opportunities. In 1977, Liberman, Shankweiler, Liberman, Fowler, and Fischer proposed to approach the question through comparisons of the metaphonological abilities of populations with different educational experiences. Arguments favorable to a nonspontaneity view derive from the fact that illiterate adults, and also some readers of nonalphabetic scripts, show poor ability to manipulate utterances at the level of phonetic segments. The strength of the argument is being critically examined. The necessity to distinguish between different levels of phonological awareness is stressed and illustrated with some so far unpublished results. In spite of some contradictions, the bulk of the available evidence is compatible with the view that the capacity to appreciate phonological similarity and awareness of some submorphemic units, like syllables and rimes, develops spontaneously, but command of segmental units generally requires deliberate instructional help. Contrary to an often expressed opinion, this view is in no way inconsistent with the notion of an important role of phonological awareness in reading acquisition. Finally, it is suggested that the conception of phonological awareness as resulting from "access" to intermediate stages of speech processing has created unnecessary difficulties for the kind of modular view advocated by Alvin Liberman and should be avoided.

Alvin Liberman on Reading

In the classical paper on "The perception of the speech code," Liberman, Cooper, Shankweiler, and Studdert-Kennedy (1967) mentioned written language at several places. That was mainly to emphasize by contrast some specific features of speech that reading/writing does not possess, and these were features that were later going to be called *modular*. On one hand, speech is "a complex code," whereas the written representation is "a simple cipher" (p. 433). Technology was called to the bar on that point: "If speech were a cipher, like print, it would be no more difficult to build a speech recognizer than a print reader" (p. 445). On the other hand, for human beings, the opposite order of difficulty holds. "In the history of the race, as in the development of the individual, speaking and listening come first; writing and reading come later, if at all. . . . Perceiving the complex speech code is thus basic to language, and to man, in a way that reading an alphabet is not" (p. 434).

Liberman developed these ideas further the following year in the discussions that took place at a symposium organised by Kavanagh (1968) and that was a sort of precursor to the famous "Language by ear and by eye" conference (Kavanagh & Mattingly, 1972). One aspect of the difference in difficulty between reading and listening, he noted, is that "Listening doesn't really need to be taught. One only needs to bring up a child in something other than a dark closet. Reading needs to be taught" (in Kavanagh, 1968, p. 119). One possible reason why the maturation of the speech machinery does not allow reading was alluded to in a later passage discussing the psychological reality of phonemes. It was noted (p. 127) that if phonemes "are real psychologically, they are not necessarily real at a very high level of awareness. That is to say, it does not follow from anything I have said that the man in the street can tell you about phonemes, or that he can even tell you how many phonemes there are in particular utterances". That Liberman was thinking of this lack of awareness of phonemes as a possible source of the difficulty of reading is shown by the immediately following remark that "if phonemes existed at a higher level of awareness than they do, then it wouldn't have taken so long for man to invent the alphabet."

Thus, the essential point that Liberman was stressing is that the development of reading capacity does not display the autonomy of a process under mainly endogenous control. This aspect makes reading a sort of test case in the framework of current discussions of modularity. In the fluent adult reader, written word recognition presents several of the Fodorean modular features (Fodor, 1983): (a) Its functioning is mandatory, as demonstrated by Stroop interference and semantic priming, (b) it proceeds through largely unaccessible intermediate representations, (c) it is fast and probably encapsulated and, (d) it shows highly specific breakdown patterns after brain lesions, but its development is strongly dependent on intentional learning and on contributions from central cognitive processes. The case of reading, thus, suggests that the relation between the candidate modular features is more complex than one of necessary coexistence.

Reading Acquisition and Phonological Awareness

Liberman's notion that the acquisition of reading requires some explicit representation of the phonological structure of utterances—now generally referred to by the term "phonological awareness"—that is not necessary for speech communication has been elaborated in well-known papers by Mattingly (1972), Isabelle Liberman (1973), Rozin (1976, 1978), Gleitman and Rozin (1977), and Rozin and Gleitman (1977). It has exerted a decisive influence on empirical studies of reading acquisition.

We tried elsewhere (Bertelson & de Gelder, 1989) to summarize the existing support for the notion, and we can limit ourselves here to a brief recapitulation. Early arguments were based largely on logical analyses of the principle of alphabetic representation and of the task it was supposed to set to students, and on evidence from the history of writing systems. Direct empirical evidence consisted first of demonstrations of correlation between success in reading and performance on tasks involving the analysis of utterances into submorphemic units— syllables or phonetic segments. More recently, evidence for properly causal effects of forms of phonological awareness on progress in reading has been provided by both experimental training studies (e.g., Bradley & Bryant, 1983, 1985; Fox & Routh, 1984) and applications of partial correlation methodology (e.g., Bradley & Bryant, 1983, 1985; Stanovich, Cunningham, & Cramer, 1984; Perfetti, Beck, & Hughes, 1987). Taken together, these studies support reasonably well the notion that at least some forms of phonological analysis competence contribute to success in reading acquisition.

With attention focused mainly on its role in reading acquisition, the question of how phonological awareness itself develops has been rather neglected. One reason might be the fact that reading has often been lumped together under such unitary headings as metalinguistic abilities or "secondary linguistic activities" with achievements like appreciation of rhyme, generation of puns, or speech repairs, which clearly need not be taught. Examination of the literature of the 1970s reveals a good deal of hesitation concerning the conditions for the emergence of phonological awareness.

A Comparative Approach

A critical step was initiated by Liberman, Shankweiler, Liberman, Fowler, and Fischer (1977) in a discussion of possible interpretations of their earlier finding that counting the number of segments a spoken word is made of is virtually impossible for kindergarteners but well within reach of first-graders. One possibility was that maturation made children aware of phonemes at about that age, the other that awareness of the phonological structure of words is something that is brought about by alphabetic reading acquisition. They suggested that one way to decide between the alternatives would be to find out whether a similar change with age occurs when it is a logographic script, Chinese for instance, that is acquired. Then, in a footnote, they remarked that the test was probably no longer feasible, because reading instruction in the People's Republic of China now starts with teaching of an alphabetic script, the Hanyu Pinyin. Nevertheless, the authors' suggestion was essential in pointing to a comparative approach to the effects of reading instruction experience.

Granted that the evidence from Chinese readers was no longer available, an alternative way to examine the question was to assess phonological awareness in adult illiterates. One difficulty for that approach is that in societies where reading instruction is generally available, those who do not profit from the opportunity might well be a selected sample. The problem is less acute where illiteracy is still a normal fact of life. Portugal is one of the countries of Europe with a high rate of illiteracy, and we had several former students working there. One of them, Luz Cary, obtained access to an agricultural area where schools were normally not available, but some inhabitants had attended adult literacy classes. She administered a task to both illiterate and "ex-illiterate" subjects in which they had either to delete the initial consonant from a spoken word or pseudoword, or add a consonant at the beginning. These tasks had already been run on Belgian school children (Alegria & Morais, 1979). The results show that illiterates performed at the same floor-level ($\pm$ 20%) as Belgian first-graders tested at the beginning of the year, and ex-illiterates at a comfortable 70% correct level, similar to that of second-graders (Morais, Cary, Alegria, & Bertelson, 1979). The low performance of illiterates or semiliterates on phonetic manipulations has since been confirmed in several studies from our group and from others (Byrne & Ledez, 1983; Liberman, Rubin, Duques, & Carlisle, 1986; Morais, Bertelson, Cary, & Alegria, 1986; Read & Ruyter, 1985; Bertelson, de Gelder, Tfouni, & Morais, 1989).

These observations are of course consistent with the notion that some competence necessary for manipulating phonetic segments does rarely develop spontaneously, and it generally requires some specific learning experience that the literacy classes provide. However, they are not sufficient by themselves to establish the point. Any performance difference between the two populations cannot be immediately attributed to the direct effect of reading instruction per se. Other possibilities are: (a) differences before enrollment in the literacy program; for instance, the individuals who took advantage of the existence of literacy training could have been on the average brighter or better motivated than the ones who did not; (b) general cognitive or attitudinal changes induced by class attendence (e.g., familiarity with test situations, understanding of instructions, capacity to infer a rule from examples); (c) wider life experiences—access to books and printed information in general, better jobs—made available by literacy. We do not think one can control for these confounding factors completely. However, it is possible to obtain an estimate of their respective contributions by adequate use of the comparative method (i.e., by extending both the types of populations and the range of tasks on which the populations are compared). In the rest of the paper, we examine how the interpretation of the basic finding can, thus, be narrowed down.

Before embarking on that examination, we must note that there need not be a contradiction between the notion of the nonspontaneity of some aspects of phonological awareness and the possibility that those aspects facilitate reading acquisition. We have argued (Bertelson, 1986; Bertelson & de Gelder, 1989), as have our colleagues (Morais, Alegria, & Content, 1987a), that the "chicken and egg" question, "Is phonological awareness a prerequisite of reading acquisition or one of its consequences?" is not one that could ever allow a single yes or no answer. The reason is that notions such as phonological awareness and reading acquisition are too global. Reading acquisition is very likely an interactive process involving a succession of quantal steps, some in the sphere of phonological ability and some in other domains of the skill (de Gelder, 1987, in press). A full understanding of the process would involve identification of those steps, and only on that level could one expect to identify simple unidirectional causal links.

Specific Effect of Literacy Training versus General Cognitive Influence of Schooling

The performance difference between illiterates and ex-illiterates might be linked to general cognitive or attitudinal effects of schooling that would affect a wide range of activities. Many early studies of the influence of literacy have been flawed by failure to control for such effects. A nice demonstration has been provided by Scribner and Cole (1981), in their famous study of the Vai people of Liberia, where they could study users of different writing systems living together with complete illiterates in otherwise similar socioeconomic circumstances: readers of the Vai script, a local syllabic writing taught only through private tuition, readers of Arabic writing learned at Koranic school, and readers of the alphabet learned at western-type schools. Only the latter subjects were found superior to illiterates at solving logical problems, namely syllogisms. Although the finding shows the necessity of distinguishing between general effects of schooling and specific effects of literacy, it certainly does not imply that the same pattern of influence must hold for all domains of competence. Logical thinking is in fact not a sort of capacity one would expect to be influenced directly by reading instruction. Regarding the more relevant metalinguistic capacities, Scribner and Cole's exploration, which was limited to asking their subjects to name "a long word," was not adequate to detect the specific effects of the particular orthographies they had learned.

Some recent data directly address the question of the generality of the effect observed in segmental analysis. Kolinsky, Morais, Content, and Cary (1987) compared subjects from the same two populations on a visual part-probe task (Palmer, 1977) consisting of deciding if a pattern of lines contains a particular subpattern. The task bears some formal resemblance to a consonant detection task (finding the word in a sentence that begins with a particular target consonant) in which ex-illiterates have been found much superior to illiterates (Morais et al., 1986). In the visual task, only a nonsignificant difference in performance was obtained between ex-illiterates (65.1% correct) and illiterates (61.6%). Clearly, the superiority of ex-illiterates in segmental analysis does not mean that they are better at analyzing all sorts of things into parts. In a similar vein, ex-illiterates showed no significant superiority relative to illiterates in a musical tone deletion task consisting of playing back a short melody on a simplified xylophone without its initial note (Morais et al., 1986).

The visual part-probe task has also been administered to Belgian children in kindergarten, first, and second grade. The performance of kindergarteners was comparable (59% correct responses) to that of unschooled illiterate and ex-illiterate Portuguese subjects, but first- and second-graders reached higher levels (74.5% and 89.0% respectively). These results suggest that the critical ability involved in the task is one that, like syllogisms and unlike segmental analysis, is promoted not by reading instruction proper but rather by other school activities.

Distinguishing among Metaphonological Capacities

As we have noted already, in many early presentations, phonological awareness was conceived as an homogeneous achievement. Yet many data were available that pointed in the direction of dissociable levels. Prereading children appreciate nursery rhymes and engage in word games that involve attending to the form rather to the meaning of the items. Illiterate societies have poets who rely on phonological relations like assonance, rhyme and alliteration in their work. In the classical study demonstrating that prereaders cannot count phonemes, Liberman, Shankweiler, Fischer, and Carter (1974) found that the same children performed substantially better on syllable counting. Similarly, Alegria and Morais (1979) found that kindergarteners were much better at manipulating syllables, that is, at adding a syllable to an utterance or deleting the initial syllable of an utterance, than at performing the same manipulations on phonetic segments. These data suggested that the incapacity of illiterates with consonants might not extend to all submorphemic units or all sorts of phonological properties.

The suggestion has been supported by the results of a new study again with Portuguese illiterates and ex-illiterates but using a wider range of tasks (Morais et al., 1986). Illiterates performed very poorly in all tasks in which they had to deal with segments, irrespective of the form of the task: in consonant deletion, detection of a consonant target in a spoken sentence, or free segmentation of an utterance into smaller units. They attained more substantial levels of performance, although still inferior to those of ex-illiterates, in rhyme judgment (choosing a picture with a name rhyming with a target) and in tasks involving the manipulation of syllabic targets (deleting the initial syllabic vowel of an utterance and detecting a syllabic target in a spoken sentence).

Interestingly, there was no significant difference in the effect of phonological similarity on short-term retention of picture names between the groups: Rhyming names created the same relative degree of interference in illiterates and in ex-illiterates. The result adds to a body of data that cast doubt on the existence of a strong relation between the use of speech-based codes in short-term retention— the correlate of reading acquisition on which the presentation of Crain and Shankweiler (chapter 16 this volume) is focused—and explicit segmental analysis (see e.g., Content, Morais, Kolinsky, Bertelson, & Alegria, 1986).

A more recent study with Brazilian adults, some illiterate and some with rudimentary reading capacity resulting from school attendence in second-grade at most, has produced results that agree with a multicomponential view of phonological awareness (Bertelson et al., 1989). The subjects were tested successively on rhyme judgment (deciding if two words pronounced by the experimenter—*cola-mola, mito-fama*—rhyme or not), syllabic vowel deletion (*ako →
ko*), and consonant deletion (*fin → in*). The instructions were conveyed exclusively by examples (e.g., "When I say *ako*, you say *ko;* when I say *asur,* you say *sur,*" etc.), and corrective feedback was provided throughout each test whenever the subject failed to produce the expected response ("I said *afir;* you should have said *fir*"). For rhyme judgment and vowel deletion, testing continued to a criterion of six successive correct responses. The criterion was reached by all readers in both tasks, and by 12 out of 16 illiterates in rhyme judgment and 10 in vowel deletion. In the consonant deletion task, which involved 24 trials, irrespective of results, the criterion was reached by 7 out of 9 readers and by only 3 out of 16 illiterates. Overall percent correct was 77 for readers and 33 for illiterates. Thus, illiterates can infer a phonological manipulation rule from examples, when it applies to rhyming or to syllabic units, but not when it involves phonetic segments.

These results suggest the existence of a dissociation from the point of view of developmental history between segmental analysis proper and other manifestations of phonological awareness.

Evidence from Nonalphabetic Literates

Charles Read discovered that in China one can still find readers of the traditional logograms who never learned to read the alphabetic Pinyin introduced after the revolution. Thus, the investigation contemplated by Liberman et al. (1977) was still feasible. Together with Chinese colleagues, Read applied the consonant addition and deletion tasks to two groups of Chinese subjects, a group of alphabetic readers who could read both the logograms and the pinyin, and a group of pure logographic readers who had attended school before the revolution (Read, Zhang, Nie, & Ding, 1986). Mean percent correct responses over the two tasks for the trials with pseudowords was 21 in the logographic subjects and 83 in the alphabetic ones. The difference is, thus, as large as the one obtained between illiterates and literate subjects.

An important implication of this result concerns the possible role of factors other than literacy training in the causation of the difference between literates and illiterates. Two of the factors we have considered, pre-existing difference in ability or motivation, and general cognitive benefits of class attendance, should play a lesser role for the Chinese subjects: The introduction of Pinyin instruction was an administrative decision that presumably applied to whole groups of children irrespective of preference or ability; the logographic subjects had been to a regular school. We are not claiming, of course, that the effects of the schooling enjoyed by the two groups were necessarily equivalent but simply that whatever difference there may be between the learning opportunities available to these two groups must be smaller than the one between literacy training and no school instruction at all.

One can ask if the differential profile of performance obtained in the comparison between illiterates and ex-illiterates would hold also for the present contrast. In a pilot study carried out in Tilburg with Jean Vroomen, we had the opportunity to examine Chinese adults, all of whom could read logograms, but some of whom had learned to read Dutch and the others not.[1] All understood spoken Dutch. They were tested on rhyme judgment (with Dutch words), initial consonant deletion (Dutch pseudowords) and on separate enunciation of the initial phoneme of a pseudoword, either a vowel or a consonant. As appears in Table 1, non-alphabetic subjects were virtually as good as alphabetic ones on rhyme judgment, but much poorer on consonant deletion. The profile of differences found with illiterates and ex-illiterates is thus reproduced. In phoneme enunciation, a task that has not been used so far with illiterates, the non-alphabetic subjects performed poorly with both consonants and vowels.

Results by Mann (1966) might create difficulties for the view that acquiring a

---

[1]The majority of the subjects came from Hongkong and had never been exposed to Pinyin. However, even a few who came from mainland China reported no knowledge of that system. Pinyin instruction might be less universal than has been reported.

Table 17.1
Chinese Logographic Monoscriptals and Chinese-Dutch Biscriptals:
Mean Percent Correct Responses on Metaphonological Tasks
(Unpublished Data of de Gelder, Vroomen, & Bertelson)

Task	Monoscriptals N = 15	Biscriptals N = 16
Reading Dutch words	13.3	87.7
Reading Dutch pseudowords	0.3	58.1
Rhyme judgment	76.3	78.4
Deletion of initial consonant	21.7	56.9
Enunciation of initial segment:		
vowel	17.3	77.5
consonant	1.3	51.3

non-alphabetic orthography does not promote segmental analysis. She tested Japanese school children in different grades on initial segment deletion and initial mora deletion.[2] The first graders were much inferior to American contemporaries on the segment tasks (24% correct responses against 56%) and slightly superior on the mora task. This profile of performance that corresponds to the school experiences of the two groups is consistent with the data described so far. The discrepant result is that Japanese fourth graders, who in principle had been taught no alphabetic reading,[3] gave 63% correct responses. A segment counting and a mora counting task were also applied and gave similar results, which might, however, be contaminated to an unknown degree by the fact that many subjects were found to use an orthographic strategy based on counting kanas and applying a correction to the count.

There is, for the time being, no ready-made interpretation for these results. Mann considered the possibility that experience of any *phonological orthography* promotes the development of speech analysis up to the segmental level, but then rejected it on the basis of the results of Read et al. (1986) with nonalphabetic Chinese readers. The Chinese "phonetic compound" characters are composed of a "radical," which refers to the meaning, and of a "phonetic," which refers to the pronunciation, hence, she reasoned, Chinese orthography is phonological. There is, however, an important difference between reading Chinese phonetic compounds and either kanas or alphabetic characters: The phonetics represent whole morphemes and do not engage the reader in submorphemic segmentation. Thus, a viable hypothesis that Mann did not consider is that learning a *sub-*

[2]Japanese moras are the rhythmic units of speech that kana characters represent. The majority are CV syllables, but the phoneme /n/ in isolation or in final position, and the final segment of double vowels, count also as moras.

[3]Japanese children begin learning the Romaji, an alphabetic orthography, in the second part of the fourth year of school.

morphemic orthography is sufficient to start the reader on the road to full segmental analysis.

It is also possible that some particular features of the kanas facilitate the
discovery of segments. The kanas are actually not pure syllabaries. First, some
characters represent single segments: the five vowels "a/, /ε/, /i/, /o/ and /u/,
and the consonant /n/. Also, the fact that different kana stand, for instance, for
/pa/, /ta/, /ka/, /ma/, and /a/ may indirectly draw attention to the consonants.
The probability of such discovery is increased, because the kanas are usually
presented to the pupils in matrix arrangement with columns corresponding to the
initial consonant of the represented mora and the rows corresponding to the
vowel. Another important factor may be that foreign names and terms are spelled
by using katakana to represent the initial segments of the corresponding moras.

Finally, we have to consider the more trivial possibility of straightforward
teaching of Romaji in the family before it is officially taught at school. The
competitive Japanese society, with its high premium on school achievement, is
one in which we could expect such factors to play an important role. Mann
unfortunately did not examine knowledge of alphabetic characters in her subjects. Any progress along this line of investigation will require the collection of
data on out of school training as well as on the possible influence of educational
television programs. We shall have to return to these issues in the next section.

The Evidence from Preschool Children

In the Morais et al. (1979) study, an important comparison was one between
illiterate adults and Belgian prereaders. The fact that both groups performed at
about the same low level on consonant manipulation was considered as suggesting that maturation and experience of speech communication have little influence
on the development of segmental analysis. More detailed examination of the
literature, however, raises some difficulties for that conclusion. Many studies
have confirmed that, consistent with a multicomponential view of phonological
awareness, preschool children are better at judging phonological similarity and at
manipulating syllables than at dealing with segments (Lundberg, Olofsson, &
Wall, 1980; Alegria, Pignot, & Morais, 1982; Stanovich et al., 1984). However,
on the other hand, there are reports of nonnegligible ability to manipulate the
latter units in some preschool children (Fox & Routh, 1975; Lundberg et al.,
1980; Bradley & Bryant, 1983; Stanovich et al., 1984). To interpret that evidence, one must consider two points, which concern respectively the possible
origin of the reported performance and the tasks that have been used.

In developed countries, preschool children can have already benefited from
various forms of informal training, ranging from word games (see "Geography"
as described by Mann, 1986) to tuition in reading proper provided by the family
(parents, school-attending siblings) or television (see programs such as "Sesame

Street"). Information regarding these factors is difficult to obtain and is generally not provided in the papers.

One case where information is available illustrates how serious the problem can be. About two-thirds of the Swedish kindergarteners tested by Lundberg et al. (1980) in their well-known longitudinal study had some elementary reading capacity, which was correlated with performance on both measures of phonemic analysis and synthesis and with later achievement in reading. On the basis of information provided by the authors, Valtin (1984) showed that these subjects were largely responsible for the substantial average performance of the whole group on phonemic tests. As appears in Table 17.2, the performance of the nonreaders on segment-level tasks was in the range previously obtained with illiterates, with the exception of a segment detection task on which they reached an appreciable 47%. It was better on syllable-based tasks and came close to ceiling on a rhyme production task. Thus, when the effect of preschool reading ability is controlled for, real prereaders have a profile of performance comparable to that of most other alphabet illiterates who have been examined so far.

The extent to which informal preschool tuition may have influenced the performances reported in other studies (especially Stanovich et al., 1984) is difficult to establish. The importance of the data from illiterate adults living in low-literacy environments is that these subjects are much less exposed to experiences likely to promote phonological awareness. Regarding kindergarteners, efficient use of data from such populations would require more attention than has been usual to assessment of out of school instruction.

Table 17.2
Performance on Metaphonological Tasks of Kindergarteners
With and Without Elementary Reading Ability
(Data of Lundberg et al., 1980, after Valtin, 1984)

Task	Non-readers N = 48	Readers N = 85
Rhyme production	75	86
Fusioning syllables into words[1]	65	92
Analyzing words into syllables	50	52
Fusioning segments into syllables[2]	20	82
Analyzing syllables into segments	35	89
Inversing segments	5	60
Detecting segment[3]	47	89

[1]task SYNSYLC;
[2]task SYNPHONC;
[3]task ANPHONPOS.
The descriptions of the tasks are based on Lundberg et al. (1980) and the figures are recalculated from those in Table 12.4 of Valtin (1984, p. 245).

Turning to tasks, it is clear that some of those that have been used to measure phonemic analysis are more difficult than others. We have already noted that the nonreaders of the Lundberg et al. (1980) study performed much better on segment detection than on any of the other segment-based tasks. In the study by Stanovich et al. (1984), deletion of the initial consonant was more difficult than various syllable-matching tasks (e.g., finding the syllable among three that has the same initial sound as the target syllable). Two kinds of interpretation of such differences have been developed.

One consists of invoking particular cognitive operations that the more difficult tasks may impose in addition to speech analysis. In that way, the differences can be explained without abandoning the notion of phonological awareness as an homogeneous attribute. Bryant and Bradley (1985), for instance, proposed that prereaders' inability in phoneme counting and in phoneme deletion or addition reflects the difficulty of the counting, deletion, or fusion operations that these tasks impose in addition to analysis into individual segments. The "sound classification task," which the subjects of their longitudinal study already performed reasonably well in kindergarten, consists of identifying that item among three or four CVC words presented by the experimenter that differs from the others at the level of either the first, the medial, or the final segment. That task would not require additional difficult operations, and that would be the reason why it is within the reach of prereaders. One problem for that interpretation is that the counting or deletion operations do not create similar difficulties when the target is a syllable or a syllabic vowel instead of a segment.

The other interpretation is based on the notion that different tasks tap different levels of metaphonological ability. For instance, one can question that Bradley and Bryant's sound classification task specifically taps segmental analysis. If we consider the conditions with initial and with final consonantal target, the presented words always had the medial vowel in common. A typical trial would involve quartets such as *pig, pit, pill, fin* or *fat, pat, cat, man*. The authors interpret the task as implying the identification of the consonant by which the odd item differs from the distractors. As a matter of fact, what the distractors have in common is either the initial CV- or the final -VC, and identifying such strings might be easier than identifying consonants. As part of a study in progress, Content and Bertelson have administered five-year-old prereaders both the initial and the final consonant conditions of Bradley and Bryant, which will be called here the "constant vocalic context" task, and a "variable vocalic context" task. In the latter, the four words presented on a trial have different vowels. To succeed in that task, it is, thus, necessary to focus on the critical consonant itself. Examples of the four types of trials we ran appear in Table 17.3, together with the results of the 56 children tested so far. They found the variable vocalic context tasks very difficult. Actually only 12 (18%) scored better than chance on these tasks. In comparison, 23 (41%) performed above chance in the constant vocalic context conditions. Thus, the relative easiness of Bradley and Bryant's sound classifica-

Table 17.3
**Word Classification Tasks: Mean Percent Correct Responses in Each
Condition (Unpublished Data of Content & Bertelson)**

Vocalic context	Critical segment	Example	Percent correct
Constant	Initial	DUC, DUNE, DUR, CHUTE /dyk, dyn, dyʀ, ʃyt/	38.2
	Final	GUIDE, VIDE, RIDE, FICHE /gɪd, vɪd, ʀɪd, fɪʃ/	37.9
Variable	Initial	DATE, DOUZE, DONNE, CHEF /dat, duz, dɔn, ʃɛf/	32.0
	Final	RONDE, CHAUDE, SOUDE, MECHE /ʀõd, ʃod, sud, mɛʃ/	32.4

tion task might be due to the fact that it does not require attention to segments proper.

It would be worthwhile to examine whether other differences in difficulty reported in the literature might also be interpreted in terms of degree of explicitness of the segmental analysis that the task requires. The question has actually two aspects. One concerns the size of the critical phonological string. It was the focus of the preceding example. The other aspect is whether the task requires explicit identification of that critical string. For instance, one can wonder whether judging rhyme (deciding, e.g., that one word rhymes with a target word and that another does not) implies, as has often been assumed, identification of the string common to the rhyming items, the rime. It is equally possible that such a judgment could be carried out on the basis of a global impression of phonological similarity.

There are for the time being few data on which to base a decision. However, one observation goes strongly in the direction of the similarity view. With Jose Morais and Luz Cary, we have examined a Portuguese illiterate poet (for more details, see Morais, Alegria, & Content, 1987b, and Bertelson & de Gelder, 1989). He could produce rhymes with great facility and was 100 percent correct in all the rhyme judgment tasks we submitted him to, including the discrimination between full rhymes (*capa-papa*) and other forms of phonological resemblance such as assonances (*gola-cota*) or quasi-rhymes (*cara-raro*). However, he failed in spite of repeated attempts on our part to enunciate the "part" that the rhyming items had in common. When we asked him to explain his (correct) judgment that *miro* did not rhyme with *cola*, he would typically provide examples of rhyming items.

The distinction between explicit analysis of utterances and judgment of phonological similarity requires more systematic study. This might help us to understand the recurring finding that segment detection and classification tasks are easier than segment manipulation ones.

Nature of the Critical Experience

Reading instruction, whether at school, at literacy classes, or at home, could conceivably influence phonological awareness by two different routes. One, that can be called *direct,* is through teaching of the alphabetic principle and exercises in speech analysis. The other, *indirect* route is through the availability of orthographic representations.

That the way literate people represent spoken language is influenced by orthographic knowledge is illustrated by many examples, such as the fact that linguistic change often goes in the direction of adaptation to spelling, or the phenomenon of "spelling pronunciation", in which the pronunciation of words with inconsistent spelling is modified in the direction of a better match with the orthographic representation (Kerek, 1976).

An effect described by Seidenberg and Tanenhaus (1979) offers a striking demonstration of the use of orthographic representations when effecting operations on heard words. These authors found that the time it takes to decide that two spoken words rhyme is shorter when the spelling of the rime is identical (*pie-tie*) than when it is different (*pie-guy*).

One can also cite a phenomenon demonstrated by one of us some time ago. In the click location task, in which the subject must judge at what time in a spoken sentence an extraneous sound was produced, the judgment is influenced by the spatial relation between click and sentence: With English or French material, the click is reported as coming earlier when it is delivered to the left ear and the sentence to the right one than with the opposite arrangement. We have shown that the polarity of the effect depends on the direction of writing of the language used in the task. French-Hebrew bilinguals showed the usual pattern when tested with French sentences and the mirror one with Hebrew sentences (Bertelson, 1972). That phenomenon would seem to imply the use of some orthographic image in relating the click to the sentence.

More specific examples of the influence of orthography have been reported in the context of tests of segmental analysis. Ehri and Wilce (1980) reported that in the segment counting task readers would for instance count one unit more for *pitch* than for *rich,* and Mann (1986) described similar errors in the segment counting performance of her Japanese subjects. It is true that these results are linked to the ambiguity of the instructions. They nevertheless have the important implication that once available, the orthographic representation is considered a reliable source of information about phonological structure.

Our present problem is of course to know if the effect of reading instruction on phonological awareness is completely mediated by orthographic knowledge. This extreme hypothesis can apparently be excluded. A number of studies have now shown that performance on segment manipulation can be trained in preschool children independently and prior to reading acquisition (Content, Morais, Alegria, & Bertelson, 1982; Olofsson & Lundberg, 1983, Fox & Routh, 1984;

Content, Kolinsky, Morais, & Bertelson, 1986; Lundberg et al., 1988). Recently, we have shown that even illiterates can make progress in the consonant deletion task when provided with continuous corrective feedback plus some limited tuition in segmental analysis (Morais, Content, Bertelson, Cary, & Kolinsky, 1988).

However, a question one can ask about such acceleration studies is whether the type of segmental awareness they promote is equivalent to that which results from full reading acquisition. Some unpublished experiments by Alain Content (Content, 1985) are relevant. Content examined in kindergarteners the transfer that training on initial consonant deletion produced on performance on two other classical segmental awareness tasks: the segment counting task (Liberman et al., 1974) and a syllable classification task (Treiman & Baron, 1981) in which the child decides which of three CV syllables are closest and can choose on the basis of either a common segment or of overall similarity. In a way, the latter task measures the degree of salience of segments compared to overall similarity. The results were not completely clear-cut, but, on the whole, little transfer was apparent. It is, thus, possible that training promotes locally efficient procedures specific of the particular task rather than full segmental awareness.

Comparisons of the effects of different teaching methods could bring useful evidence about the present issue. Alegria et al. (1982) compared, on a segment inversion task, first-graders taught by a strict look-say and by a phonic method, and found a strong superiority of the latter. That result might indicate that the direct effect is important. The authors unfortunately did not measure the reading performance attained by their subjects, so that the possibility that some of the obtained difference in the inversion task might result from differences in level of literacy cannot be excluded. One can remark, however, that the differences in reading achievement induced by different teaching methods, as reviewed by Chall (1967), are much smaller than the effects observed at the level of segmental analysis.

Relevant also is the fact mentioned by Read et al. (1986) that some of their alphabetic subjects who could no longer read Pinyin, nevertheless performed well on segmental analysis. Similar observations were made in our Brazilian study.

Access or Discovery?

Thus far, we have hardly considered the two most fundamental questions concerning phonological awareness. They are: (a) Why would awareness of segments be so rarely attained without external help? and (b) what is the nature of the change that occurs when it is attained? The two questions are of course closely related and are best considered together.

Although it was not couched in modularist language, the dominant answer, as expressed during the 1970s by several theorists (Mattingly, 1972; Rozin, 1976,

1978; Rozin & Gleitman, 1977), referred essentially to the nonaccessibility to conscious inspection of the internal workings of the speech module. Phonemes, they reminded us, have no separate physical correlates in the acoustic stream. They are computed within the speech module, but at a preconscious stage. In other words, they are not represented as such in the final output of the module, available for ulterior cognitive elaborations. Finally, the intermediate phonemic representations can be accessed by some deliberate effort.

For the sake of historical accuracy, one should note that there was some hesitation concerning the exact object of access. Some formulations, clearly influenced by the Chomskyan conception of linguistic competence as consisting of propositional knowledge, were in terms of tacit or implicit knowledge that, when accessed, became explicit. Rozin (1978), for instance, wrote: "A significant portion of human learning can be described, along with the alphabetic insight, as gaining access to knowledge already in the head" (p. 434). Other formulations were in terms of processes. Mattingly (1972) made the distinction between "primary linguistic activity" and "awareness of that activity". Rozin and Gleitman (1977) proposed that "the use of an alphabet requires . . . gaining access to the machinery in the head which analyzes and produces sound segments" (p. 56).[4]

Beyond these differences in formulation, the important emphasis was on retrieval of some representations inherent in the preformed linguistic equipment. This notion of acquisition as retrieval had of course axiomatic status in generativist thinking.

The notion of a module that is normally not accessible but becomes so, if sufficient insistence is applied, is somehow unsatisfactory and creates difficulties for the modular view. Modularity is being invoked to account for both inaccessibility and access—eating the cake and having it. Serious application of the notion would require some specification of the conditions under which a typically "closed" module (following the terminology of Mattingly & Liberman, in press), such as the phonetic module, can be accessed.

It would, thus, be worth giving more consideration to possible alternatives. One candidate is discovery of implicit properties of things at the level of conscious postperceptual representations. A good deal of our important intellectual insights consist of discovering new properties of objects or concepts. Such discoveries can occur without implying the perceptual processes in any way. We can, for instance, realize that a square's diagonals cross at right angles, and

---

[4]It is worth noting that "access" and "accessibility" have sometimes been used in the more neutral sense of reaching a particular level of linguistic description. When Klima (1972), for instance, wrote that "the various levels of language structure may, by their very nature, not be equally accessible" (p. 59), he was not committing himself to a particular assumption regarding location in a sequence of processes.

nobody will presumably propose that when we do so, we have accessed the operation of diagonal analyzers in the visual system. Similarly, the discovery of the phonological structure of linguistic objects might proceed completely at the post-perceptual level. The proposal is consistent with the stimulating speculations of Mattingly (1987) concerning the way an illiterate speaker could gain some understanding of phonology by applying paradigmatic analysis to morphologically related tokens. The proposal, which should presumably not be construed as a realistic description of how children usually become aware of segments, has the important property that it implies no reference to the way language is being processed.

Other theorists have already proposed that awareness of segments might be the result of a process of discovery without link to what happens at the level of speech processing (Warren, 1976; Marcel, 1983). For these authors, however, the proposal was part of a conception following which phonemes play no role in speech processing proper. Our position is that the question of the role of phonemes in perception and that of segmental awareness are orthogonal. Phonemes could play no role in perception and emerge only in postperceptual elaborations. Alternatively, they could be detected within the module, then be integrated into a holistic percept in which they are not represented separately and finally be rediscovered as a result of postperceptual analysis of the latter.

Evidence relevant to the latter question has been provided by a study of selective dichotic listening in illiterates and ex-illiterates by Morais, Castro, Scliar-Cabral, Kolinsky and Content (1987). These authors found no difference between the two groups of subjects in the tendency to commit "feature blendings" (i.e., to attribute to a segment of the attended utterance a feature of the corresponding segment of the nonattended utterance). This type of mistake would seem to reveal extraction of information at the segmental level. The result is consistent with the notion that segments are extracted on-line during speech processing irrespective of degree of awareness.

This kind of finding is important also regarding the wider question of the origin of phonological awareness. If phonological awareness effectively resulted from access to representations within the speech module, we should expect at the same time to observe some degree of cognitive penetration of the operation of the module. Speech processing might be modified by the availability of explicitly segmented representations, for instance, in the way considered by Mehler, Morton and Juscyk (1984). There is for the time being very little relevant evidence, apart from the result of Morais and his collaborators. The data showing correlations between accuracy of speech recognition and reading ability (Brady, Shankweiler, & Mann, 1983; Werker & Tees, 1987) are ambiguous to the extent that the differences in speech recognition performance may have arisen at the postperceptual level. We clearly need systematic comparative studies of on-line speech processing in subjects with different literacy statuses.

Acknowledgments

This work has been supported by the Belgian "Fonds de la Recherche fondamentale collective" (Convention 2.4562.86), the Belgian Ministry of scientific Policy (Action de Recherche concertée "Processus cognitifs dans la Lecture" and National Incentive Program for Fundamental Research in Artificial Intelligence) and by Tilburg University (Research Grant VF 595). The scientific responsibility of the paper is assumed by the authors. Thanks are due to Ignatius Mattingly, Bob Crowder, Alexander Pollatsek, José Morais, Daniel Holender, Jesus Alegria and Alain Content for fruitful discussions of the present issues. Correspondence to: Paul Bertelson, Laboratoire de Psychologie expérimentale, U.L.B., 117, av. Adolphe Buyl, 1050 Bruxelles (Belgium), E-mail: R072Ø1@BBRBFUØ1 (Bitnet).

References

Alegria, J., & Morais, J. (1979). Le developpement de l'habileté d'analyse consciente de la parole et l'apprentissage de la lecture [The development of explicit speech analysis ability and reading acquisition]. *Archives de Psychologie, 183,* 251–270.

Alegria, J., Pignot, E., & Morais, J. (1982). Phonetic analysis of speech and memory codes in beginning readers. *Memory & Cognition, 10,* 451–456.

Bertelson, P. (1972). Listening from left to right vs. right to left. *Perception, 1,* 161–165.

Bertelson, P. (1986). The onset of literacy: Liminal remarks. *Cognition, 24,* 1–30.

Bertelson, P., & de Gelder, B. (1989). Learning about reading from illiterates. In A. Galaburda (Ed.), *From reading to neurons.* Cambridge, MA: MIT Press.

Bertelson, P., de Gelder, B., Tfouni, L. V., & Morais, J. (1989). Metaphonological abilities of adult illiterates: New evidence of heterogeneity. *European Journal of Cognitive Psychology, 1,* 239–250.

Bradley, L., & Bryant, P. E. (1983). Categorising sounds and learning to read: A causal connection. *Nature, 301,* 419–421.

Bradley, L., & Bryant, P. E., (1985). *Rhyme and reason in reading and spelling.* Ann Arbor, MI: University of Michigan Press.

Brady, S. A., Shankweiler, D., & Mann, V. (1983). Speech perception and memory coding in relation to reading ability. *Journal of Experimental Child Psychology, 35,* 345–367.

Bryant, P. E., & Bradley, L. (1985). *Children's reading difficulties.* Oxford: Blackwell.

Byrne, B., & Ledez, J. (1983). Phonological awareness in reading-disabled adults. *Australian Journal of Psychology, 35,* 185–197.

Chall, J. (1967). *Learning to read: The great debate.* New York: McGraw-Hill.

Content, A. (1985). *L'analyse segmentale de la parole chez l'enfant.* Unpublished doctoral dissertation, Université libre de Bruxelles.

Content, A., Kolinsky, R., Morais, J., & Bertelson, P. (1986). Phonetic segmentation in prereaders: Effect of corrective information. *Journal of Experimental Child Psychology, 42,* 49–72.

Content, A., Morais, J., Alegria, J., & Bertelson, P. (1982). Accelerating the development of phonetic segmentation skills in kindergartners. *Cahiers de Psychologie Cognitive, 2,* 259–269.

Content, A., Morais, J., Kolinsky, R., Bertelson, P., & Alegria, J. (1986). Explicit speech segmentation ability and susceptibility to phonological similarity in short-term retention: No correlation. *Perceptual and Motor Skills, 63,* 81–82.

de Gelder, B. (1987). Awareness and abilities. *Cahiers de Psychologie Cognitive, 7,* 465–471.

de Gelder, B. (in press). Phonological awareness, misidentification and multiple identities. In J. A. Edmondson, P. Mühlhäuser, & C. Feagin (Eds.), *Development and diversity: Linguistic variations across time and space*. Berlin: Springer.

Ehri, L. C., & Wilce, L. S. (1980). The influence of orthography on readers' conceptualization of the phonemic structure of words. *Applied Psycholinguistics, 1*, 371–385.

Fodor, J. A. (1983). *The modularity of mind*. Cambridge, MA: MIT Press.

Fox, B., & Routh, D. K. (1975). Analyzing spoken language into words, syllables, and phonemes: A developmental study. *Journal of Psycholinguistic Research, 4*, 331–342.

Fox, B., & Routh, D. K. (1984). Phonemic analysis and synthesis as word attack skills: Revisited. *Journal of Educational Psychology, 76*, 1059–1064.

Gleitman, L. R., & Rozin, P. (1977). The structure and acquisition of reading I: Relations between orthographies and the structure of language. In A. S. Reber & D. L. Scarborough (Eds.), *Toward a psychology of reading* (pp. 1–53). Hillsdale, NJ: Lawrence Erlbaum Associates.

Kavanagh, J. F. (Ed.). (1968). *Communicating by language: The reading process*. Bethesda, MD: National Institute of Child Health and Human Development.

Kavanagh, J. F., & Mattingly, I. G. (1972). *Language by ear and by eye*. Cambridge, MA: MIT Press.

Kerek, A. (1976). The phonological relevance of spelling pronunciation. *Visible Language, 10*, 323–338.

Klima, E. S. (1972). How alphabets might reflect language. In J. F. Kavanagh & I. G. Mattingly (Eds.), *Language by ear and by eye* (pp. 57–80). Cambridge, MA: MIT Press.

Kolinsky, R., Morais, J., Content, A., & Cary, L. (1987). Finding parts within figures: A developmental study. *Perception, 16*, 399–407.

Liberman, A. M., Cooper, F. S., Shankweiler, D. P., & Studdert-Kennedy, M. (1967). Perception of the speech code. *Psychological Review, 74*, 431–461.

Liberman, I. Y. (1973). Segmentation of the spoken word and reading acquisition. *Bulletin of the Orton Society, 23*, 65–77.

Liberman, I. Y., Rubin, H., Duques, S. L., & Carlisle, J. (1986). Linguistic skills and spelling proficiency in kindergarteners and adult poor spellers. In J. F. Kavanagh, D. Gray, & D. Pearl (Eds.), *Dyslexia: Biology and behavior* (pp. 163–176). Parkton, MD: York Press.

Liberman, I. Y., Shankweiler, D., Fischer, F. W., & Carter, B. (1974). Explicit syllable and phoneme segmentation in the young child. *Journal of Experimental Child Psychology, 18*, 201–212.

Liberman, I. Y., Shankweiler, D., Liberman, A. M., Fowler, C., & Fischer, F. W. (1977). In A. S. Reber & D. L. Scarborough (Eds.), *Towards a psychology of reading* (pp. 207–226). Hillsdale NJ: Lawrence Erlbaum Associates.

Lundberg, I., Frost, J., & Petersen, O.-P (1988). Effects of an extensive program for stimulating phonological awareness in preschool children. *Reading Research Quarterly, 23*, 263–284.

Lundberg, I., Olofsson, A., & Wall, S. (1980). Reading and spelling skills in the first school years predicted from phonemic awareness skills in kindergarten. *Scandinavian Journal of Psychology, 21*, 159–173.

Mann, V. (1986). Phonological awareness: The role of reading experience. *Cognition, 24*, 65–92.

Marcel, A. J. (1983). Conscious and unconscious perception: An approach to the relations between phenomenal experience and perceptual processes. *Cognitive Psychology, 15*, 238–300.

Mattingly, I. G. (1972). Reading, the linguistic process, and linguistic awareness. In J. F. Kavanagh & I. G. Mattingly (Eds.), *Language by ear and by eye* (pp. 133–147). Cambridge, MA: MIT Press.

Mattingly, I. G. (1987). Morphological structure and segmental awareness. *Cahiers de Psychologie Cognitive, 7*, 488–493.

Mattingly, I. G., & Liberman, A. M. (in press). Speech and other auditory modules. In G. M. Edelman, W. E. Gall, & W. M. Cowan (Eds.), *Signal and sense: Local and global order in perceptual maps*. New York: Wiley.

Mehler, J., Morton, J., & Jusczyk, P. W. (1984). On reducing language to biology. *Cognitive Neuropsychology, 1,* 83–116.

Morais, J., Alegria, J., & Content, A. (1987a). The relationship between segmental analysis and alphabetic literacy: An interactive view. *Cahiers de Psychologie Cognitive, 7,* 415–438.

Morais, J., Alegria, J., & Content, A. (1987b). Authors' response. Segmental awareness: Respectable, useful, and almost always necessary. *Cahiers de Psychologie Cognitive, 7,* 530–556.

Morais, J., Bertelson, P., Cary, L., & Alegria, J. (1986). Literacy training and speech segmentation. *Cognition, 24,* 45–64.

Morais, J., Cary, L., Alegria, J., & Bertelson, P. (1979). Does awareness of speech as a sequence of phones arise spontaneously? *Cognition, 7,* 323–331.

Morais, J., Castro, M. S. L., Scliar-Cabral, L., Kolinsky, R., & Content, A. (1987). The effects of literacy on the recognition of dichotic words. *The Quarterly Journal of Experimental Psychology, 39A,* 451–465.

Morais, J., Content, A., Bertelson, P., Cary, L., & Kolinsky, R. (1988). Is there a sensitive period for the acquisition of segmental analysis? *Cognitive Neuropsychology, 5,* 347–352.

Olofsson, A., & Lundberg, I. (1983). Can phonemic awareness be trained in kindergarten? *Scandinavian Journal of Psychology, 24,* 35–44.

Palmer, S. E. (1977). Hierarchical structure in perceptual representation. *Cognitive Psychology, 9,* 441–474.

Perfetti, C. R., Beck, I., & Hughes, C. (1987). Phonemic knowledge and learning to read are reciprocal: A longitudinal study of first grade children. *Merrill-Palmer Quarterly, 33,* 283–320.

Read, C., & Ruyter, L. (1985). Reading and spelling in adults of low literacy. *Remedial and Special Education, 6,* 43–52.

Read, C. A., Zhang, Y., Nie, H., & Ding, B. (1986). The ability to manipulate speech sounds depends on knowing alphabetic reading. *Cognition, 24,* 31–44.

Rozin, P. (1976). The evolution of intelligence and access to the cognitive unconscious. In J. M. Sprague & A. N. Epstein (Eds.), *Progress in psychobiology and physiological psychology* (vol. 6, pp. 245–280). New York: Academic Press.

Rozin, P. (1978). The acquisition of basic alphabetic principles: A structural approach. In C. A. Catania & T. A. Brigham (Eds.), *Handbook of applied behavior analysis* (pp. 410–453). New York: Irvington.

Rozin, P., & Gleitman, L. R. (1977). The structure and acquisition of reading II: The reading process and the acquisition of the alphabetic principle. In A. S. Reber & D. L. Scarborough (Eds.), *Toward a psychology of reading* (pp. 55–141). Hillsdale, NJ: Lawrence Erlbaum Associates.

Scribner, S., & Cole, M. (1981). *The psychology of literacy.* Cambridge, MA: Harvard University Press.

Seidenberg, M. S., & Tanenhaus, M. K. (1979). Orthographic effects on rhyme monitoring. *Journal of Experimental Psychology: Human Learning and Memory, 5,* 546–554.

Stanovich, K. E., Cunningham, A. E., & Cramer, B. B. (1984). Assessing phonological awareness in kindergarten children: Issues of task comparability. *Journal of Experimental Child Psychology, 38,* 175–190.

Treiman, R., & Baron, J. (1981). Segmental analysis ability: Development and relation to reading ability. In T. G. Waller & G. E. McKinnon (Eds.), *Reading research: Advances in theory and practice* (vol. 2, pp. 159–198). New York: Academic Press.

Valtin, R. (1984). Awareness of features and functions of language. In J. Downing & R. Valtin (Eds.), *Language awareness and learning to read* (pp. 227–260). New York: Springer.

Warren, R. M. (1976). Auditory illusions and perceptual processes. In N. J. Lass (Ed.), *Contemporary issues in experimental phonetics* (pp. 389–417). New York: Academic Press.

Werker, J. F., & Tees, R. C. (1987). Speech perception in severely disabled and average reading children. *Canadian Journal of Psychology, 41,* 48–61.

Comment: Linguistic Awareness and Metalinguistic Control

Edward S. Klima

Department of Linguistics, University of California, San Diego

Introduction

In May 1971, there was a conference on the relationships between reading and speech perception. This was one of the many seminal interdisciplinary meetings that Alvin Liberman was instrumental in organizing. It was truly seminal in that it engendered a totally new area of inquiry. It was also by necessity interdisciplinary; for in no case did the work of any of the participants deal directly with the sort of comparison between speech perception and reading that was the subject of the conference. The proceedings were published as *Language by Ear and by Eye*, (1972) edited by James Kavanagh and Ignatius Mattingly. As general discussant of the papers presented at that conference, George Miller made a remark that has direct relevance to the contribution by Bertelson and de Gelder to the present conference. Miller remarked that, in addressing the issue of literacy, one of the things that should be kept in mind is what possible cognitive differences are introduced (other than the ability to make the right sound when you see the right squiggle) in the process of learning to read. You think about words very differently, he suggested, when you know how to read and write them.

Orthographic Effects on Language Processing

In fact, considerable evidence has emerged which suggests strongly that not only phonological, but also orthographic, representations are accessed when certain operations are carried out on the "heard" word (and not just when you are reading and writing). As Bertelson & de Gelder point out, among the experimental studies addressing this issue are ones showing an orthographic effect on monitoring for rhyme, even under *auditory* presentation. Orthographically similar rhymes presented auditorily were detected more rapidly than orthographically dissimilar rhymes: *goat* as rhyming with *boat* versus *vote* as rhyming with *boat* (Donnenworth-Nolan, Tanenhaus, & Seidenberg, 1981). Results such as these suggest that the two representations are highly interactive if not strictly integrated. It should be borne in mind, however, that rhyme detection is a metalinguistic operation and not, it would seem, a pairing that automatically rings a bell in most mortal ears without talent, training, or special attention.

In addition to results from experiments, there are quotidian glitches in linguistic performance that suggest an orthographic effect on lexical retrieval in the course of the production of speech. The Tip-of-the-Tongue State, so dubbed by Brown and McNeill (1966), and more recently considered by Schachter (1988) on the basis of extensive data collected and analyzed by Browman (1978), appears to provide such performance data. When a word or a name is "at the tip of your tongue," candidate words often come into consciousness that, although readily recognized as not being the elusive sought-after target, are felt nonetheless to be somehow related to it. One common way that a candidate may be related to a target is phonological. Aside from sharing other characteristics, they may both start with the same phoneme: "Rock Hudson," a candidate for the sought-after "Rex Harrison;" "Karen," for "Kathe." However, there are also cases where the relationship between candidate and target is more purely orthographic: "Peg," a candidate for "Phyllis" (phonologically [p-] versus [f-]; "Charles," a candidate for "Chris."

I gather that it has come to be considered self-evident that phonological representations are involved in reading and in learning to read. However, it appears that a complementary situation also holds: The network of connections that is involved in the interpretation and production of language can include orthographic information. What is not yet clear is whether there are special circumstances that promote orthographic effects. It is also not clear just when, during the time course of language processing, orthographic effects occur.

Phonemic Awareness and Alphabetic Literacy

At that same NIH-sponsored meeting on reading and speech perception, Mattingly (1972) elaborated the notion of "linguistic awareness"—which I take to mean conscious awareness—on the part of the language user of linguistic units (phonemes, syllables, morphemes, lexemes, words, etc., or whatever the correct mental constructs turn out to be) and the structures in which they occur. Presumably, individuals differ in linguistic awareness and in their proclivity to exercise that awareness. Moreover, it is probable that not all linguistic units and structures are equally amenable to awareness. The syllable might well turn out to be more amenable than the phonemic segment, and perhaps differences in structural properties among languages affect amenability to linguistic awareness. I would expect syllables to be more amenable to linguistic awareness in a language in which syllable structure is constrained to the open syllable CV type than in one like English where, at the intersyllabic juncture in such a word as *planet,* a single unit at the level of phonemic segments, the segment /n/, maps onto two separate syllable constituents, the coda of the first syllable and the onset of the second.

Some of the difficulty that even literate speakers of English encounter in mastering the conventions for hyphenating English words may be due, in part (but only in part), to a lack of appreciation not only of mappings like these between phonemic segments and units of intrasyllabic structure, but also of how such mappings interact with how a word is spelt: *gan-net,* but *plan-et* and not *pla-net; plac-ard,* but *pla-cate; moth-er,* but *fa-ther.* In *placate* and *father,* the stressed syllable closes with the vocalic segment (which is tense); hyphenation mirrors syllable structure. Stressed syllables in English can close with a tense vowel but not with a lax vowel. (The quality of the vowels in the stressed syllables of *gannet, planet, placard,* and *mother* is lax.) Stressed syllables with a lax vowel can, however, close with a single consonantal segment, but then that single segment is both coda of the stressed syllable and onset of the following syllable. When the single segment is represented orthographically by a single letter or digraph (as in *planet* and *mother* respectively), hyphenation after that letter or digraph shows the required closing of the syllable. However, when that single segment is represented orthographically by a doubled letter (as in *gannet*), then the hyphenation also mirrors the bifurcation in the segment's function in syllable structure. Hyphenation, thus, requires more than knowledge of the grapheme–phoneme correspondences and other conventions of English orthography, for the sequence of letters representing a word does not in all cases tell you where the hyphens go. Correct hyphenation must at least be facilitated by a grasp of the constituents of syllabic structure and the mapping between those constituents and the phonological segments represented by the letters.

Phonemic Segments and Syllable Constituents

One of Bertelson and de Gelder's concerns is to explore the notion that different tasks tap different levels of metaphonological ability (and reveal, in turn, different levels of phonological awareness) and that among factors that crucially differentiate tasks are the size of the critical phonological string involved and the extent to which explicit identification of the individual phonological segments (phonemes) is demanded, as contrasted to judgment carried out on the basis of "a global impression of phonological similarity," as Bertelson and de Gelder (in their article in this volume) put it. In their paper for this volume, Bertelson and de Gelder present some relevant new data from work in progress by Content and

Bertelson. In the latter work, a "sound classification" task used by Bryant and Bradley (1985) has been refined by focusing on the ability of prereading children to selectively analyze out an individual phonemic segment in a word—and specifically, a consonant. The Bryant & Bradley study included auditorily presented quadruplets such as *pig, pit, pill, fin*. In *fin*, it was apparently assumed by Bryant and Bradley that the pattern was violated by the initial consonant segment *f-*. (Quadruplets were also presented in which the pattern is broken in the other CVC positions.) The subjects (prereaders and children who had just begun to read) were to specify the pattern-breaking word in each of the quadruplets. Bryant and Bradley found that kindergarten prereaders performed reasonably well even in spotting the words in which the pattern is broken by the initial consonant. Accordingly, it would appear from one interpretation of these data that awareness of the phonemic segments of a word (even individual consonant segments) precedes reading acquisition and presumably does not require the particular types of instruction typically associated with learning to read an alphabetic script or even the "fair-fit" of a model of phoneme-level segmentality that alphabetic script appears to provide. However, Bertelson and de Gelder argue that when subjects search for the odd-ball in quadruplets like *pig, pit, pill, fin*, they may be making their judgment not by selectively focusing on the individual word-initial consonant segment itself but rather on the basis of the longer auditory string *pi-* as a whole. (This would constitute a sort of "reverse rhyme.") A critical property of such a string could be that it contains a vowel, and not merely that it is longer (two segments rather than one). For, as Bertelson and de Gelder mention, there is considerable independent evidence that prereading children and illiterate adults have a relatively easier time identifying and operating on units that contain a vowel, such as rhymes and syllables. Content and Bertelson's refinement consisted in systematically varying the vowels in the quadruplets, e.g., in something like *pit, peg, pull, fan*, so that in three of the words, the initial consonant segment alone sets up the similarity pattern broken by the odd word, *fan*. (The English examples are mine; the words actually used were French.) Bertelson and de Gelder report that their results so far show a great increase in difficulty for prereaders when the vowel segment (and not only the final consonant) is also systematically varied.

   Thus, it appears that among phonological units, the syllable is most amenable to linguistic awareness; rhyme next, along with other strings like *pi-* and *fi-* above in which a consonant "leans" on a vowel; and then finally the individual, isolated consonant segment. However, what sort of unit, from a phonological point of view, is the string *pi-* in the word *pig?* Although phonological models differ as to what they posit as the constituents of the syllable, there is no model I know of that treats the vowel and a preceding consonant, in *pig*, for example, as a constituent in syllable structure. There are models that recognize the prevocalic consonants as forming a constituent (the onset), the vowels and semivowels after the onset as forming another constituent (the nucleus or peak), and the consonants after the nucleus as another distinct constituent (the coda). Some of these models also treat the nucleus and coda as a higher-order constituent (the syllable's so-called "rhyme" constituent). However, none of the models posit that the onset and the nucleus are a constituent in syllable structure. If Bertelson and de Gelder's reinterpretation of the subject's judgments in the Bryant and Bradley study is correct, then the basis for comparison within the quadruplets is not a unitary phonological constituent but rather a chunk that contains all the phonetic material from the beginning of the syllable up through the vowel. Although apparently not significant from the point of view of phonological structure, the chunk is, nonetheless, significant from an acoustical-phonetics perspective in that it is the stretch along which essential information about the identity of the consonants preceding the vowel is provided by the form of the sound wave.

The refinement that Content and Bertelson introduced by allowing only the initial segment, the consonant, to be the same in the three words setting the similarity pattern in, e.g., *pit, peg, pull, fan,* was intended to show which groups of subjects focus specifically on the consonant segment itself. However, if none of the words used as stimuli have more than one consonant before the vowel, the results will be ambiguous. For *p-,* in *pit,* is at one and the same time the first phonemic segment of the word and the onset of the syllable. Thus, effects associated with *p-* could be attributable directly to its status as a phonemic segment or alternatively to its status as an onset (that only coincidentally is represented by a single phonological segment). *p-* shares this onset function with initial strings consisting of more than one consonant segment (e.g., *spit* and *split).*

The Structure of Alliteration in Anglo-Saxon
Oral Poetry

The play between phonemic structure and syllable structure, along with the scale of amenability to phonological awareness (with isolated consonants toward the bottom), raises interesting questions when we consider the role and structure of alliteration in certain poetic traditions—and, in particular, in so-called "oral poetry." "Oral poetry is verse composed *in*" (and not *for*) "oral performance, by people who do not read or write" (Preminger, 1974, p. 591). The experience that leads to becoming an oral poet is that of having heard other oral poets.

In many traditions of oral poetry, one of the main linguistic devices that creates verse structure is alliteration, the strictly patterned rather than incidental and merely ornamental repetition of the same initial sounds (e.g., consonants or consonant clusters) in two or more words in a verse-line. The same pattern of repetitions occurs systematically, verse-line after verse-line. ("Verse-line" here refers to a division motivated by poetic structure and not by typography.) In some oral traditions, the pattern of repetitions is so regular and so essential to overall verse structure that such poetry is fittingly described as being composed in alliterative *meter*. Thus, in nonliterate cultural contexts such as the Anglo–Saxon oral tradition, units that are crucial for establishing verse structure—namely, the consonantal segments that form the alliterative pattern—are the very units that have emerged, from studies like Bertelson and de Gelder's on illiterates and prereaders, as least amenable to operations that would indicate phonological awareness at the level of phonemic segments. Recall that Bertelson and de Gelder suggest that the identification and manipulation of consonant segments may be a more accurate diagnostic of phonemic awareness than handling longer stretches of sound such as in rhyme. In fact, in English, rhyme (*start/part*, but also multisyllabic *nation/inflation*) appears to be based not directly on identity between certain strings of phonemes in two words, but rather on identity between specific constituents of intrasyllabic structure; words that rhyme are distinct from one another in the onset of the stressed syllable but identical in stressed nucleus and everything that follows.

Let me use a few lines from *Beowulf* (Klaeber, 1950) to sleuth out some of the niceties of alliterative meter in Anglo–Saxon oral poetry and to provide a basis for arguing that a particular phonologically motivated structuring of strings of consonants that occur before the stressed vowel of a word accounts for the constraints on well-formedness of alliteration in this preliterate poetic tradition. (To be sure, there is no way to ascertain whether the particular oral poet who composed the version of *Beowulf* handed down to us was actually illiterate, but there is ample reason to believe that the alliterative meter represented in the poem developed when the society was still preliterate.)

210 a) Fýrst fórd gewat; / b) flóta waes on ýthum,
The time went forward;   the ship was in the
                                          waves,

212 a) On stéfn stígon, / b) stréamas wúndon,
Aboard they climbed,   currents eddied,

1147 a) Swéord-bealo slíthen / b) aet his sélfes hám,
A cruel death-by-sword   at his own home

Each verse-line has, I think appropriately, been analyzed as consisting of two half-lines, each of which has two heavy beats that fall on two stressed syllables that are long in quantity. (These have been given an acute accent in the examples; the line numbers are those in Klaeber, 1950.) In addition, differing numbers of unstressed syllables may occur. In the second half-line of each line, one of the two stressed syllables alliterates with at least one, but much more usually with both, of the stressed syllables of the first half-line. (The alliterating units are underlined.) This strict pattern of alliteration is maintained relentlessly, line after line, for the 3,182 verse-lines of *Beowulf*.

As the lines in the examples abundantly illustrate, words in Old English could begin with consonant clusters, but a three-consonant string, *skr-, spr-* or *str-* as in *streamas* (212b), was the maximum in word-initial position before the vowel(s). The presence of such word-initial consonant clusters brings up the following issues: What are the basic alliterating units in this preliterate oral poetic tradition? Further, to what extent are those units strictly phonemic segments—rather than representing, for example, distinct constituents of the syllable such as syllable onset?

The examples show that the basic unit of alliteration (the minimal strings that must be identical in form in order to count as alliterating) is not the whole string of consonants (the syllable onset) occurring before the vowel (V). For *fV-* alliterates not only with itself, as in (210a), but with *flV-* in (b) i.e., *flota* does not demand another word beginning in *flV-* for purposes of alliteration; *fV-* suffices). Similarly, in (1147) *swV-, slV-,* and *sV-* all alliterate. All this makes a difference in deciding at what structural level alliteration is operating. For if the whole string of initial, prevocalic consonants had to be identical, then this situation would call for treating alliteration of that variety as operating on a higher-level constituent of the syllable (its onset) rather than directly on individual phonemic segments, even in the degenerate case where the shared syllable onset happens to contain only one consonant segment. Incidentally, in the most common form of Pig Latin, a language game played by English-speaking children, it is in fact the onset that is the unit operated on: *igpay atinlay=Pig Latin,* but *eestray artsmay=street smart.* However, alliterative meter in the tradition of Anglo–Saxon oral poetry appears not to treat syllable onset as the minimal unit of alliteration.

Common to most informal characterizations of alliteration in the Anglo–Saxon oral tradition and of alliteration in general is that an initial consonant (of a stressed syllable) alliterates with itself only and alliterates with itself freely (Preminger, 1974, p. 587). (We will not be concerned here with vowel alliteration.) According to such a characterization, a necessary and sufficient condition for alliteration is that the initial consonant in each of two or more stressed syllables be identical, but this too does not adequately characterize alliteration in Anglo-Saxon oral poetry. For *spV-, skV-,* and *stV-* never alliterate with one another, or with *sV-,* despite the initial *s* in common; *spV-, skV-,* and *stV-* alliterate only with *spV-, skV-,* and *stV-* respectively, as in line 212, or with the same sequence but with a liquid preceding the vowel as in *streamas* in the same line. Many students of Anglo–Saxon prosody have observed this exceptional characteristic in these particular clusters that have an initial *s*. Initial *s* in such consonant clusters appears to lose its unit-status with respect to alliteration. However, not so in all consonant clusters, for *swV-, slV-,* and *sV-* (and also *s* followed by a nasal) all alliterate with each other, as in line 1147, and each with itself. In this environment, an identical initial *s* is sufficient as the minimal unit of alliteration.

At first glance then, it would appear that the prosody of Anglo–Saxon oral poetry includes a special poetic convention that arbitrarily requires a two-segment sequence consisting of an *s* followed by a stop to count alliteratively as a single unit. Before other consonants then, *s* would count as a separate unit. More or less arbitrary conventions are, after all, not unheard of in poetic traditions. However, research in theoretical phonology that has recently been focusing on syllable structure suggests that the apparent ambivalence of *s* in alliteration may well reflect basic phonological processes brought into play by properties of *s* and the relation of that sound to the sounds around it. Several phonologists, including Selkirk (1984), have suggested that the syllable can be defined and distributional constraints on phonological segments accounted for by considering the sonority ("loudness") of sounds relevant to one another, with stress, pitch, and length the same, a characterization of sonority due to Ladefoged (1982, p. 221). Here is a sampling relevant to our concerns from highest to lowest on the sonority scale: vowels $> r > l > m,n > s > p,t,k$ (adapted from Hogg & McCully, 1987). What is found in general in English syllable structure is that as you move to the left from the vowel, the sonority value of the phonemic segments gets progressively lower as in *print, treat, tart;* in *print,* for example, going to the left from the vowel, *r* is lower than *i* and *p* is lower than *r.* (The same progressive lowering in sonority is found going to the right from the vowel.) The pattern is violated, however, by the initial *s* in *sprint, street, start,* where *s* is higher in sonority, rather than lower, than the preceding *p* or *t.* This violation in sonority patterning has led some pho-nologists to posit that initial *st-, sp-* and *sk-,* as consonant clusters, each functions as a unit, at least in terms of higher-level constituents of intrasyllabic structure. Such a hypothesis is bolstered by the fact that in English words that have three consonants before the vowel (e.g., *sprint*), the only consonant that occurs as first consonant is *s.*

These hypotheses about the nature of the internal structure of the syllable in English, tentative though they may be, begin to illuminate some of the con-straints on Anglo–Saxon alliteration (Hogg & McCully, 1987). The environ-ments in which initial *s* functions as a minimal alliterative unit (*sw-, sl-, sm-, sn-,* and *s-* alone followed directly by a vowel) are precisely those environments in which the segments that follow *s* are higher than *s* on the sonority scale. When followed by a segment lower on the sonority scale (as in *sk-, sp-,* and *st-*), initial *s* is not free to alliterate by itself; the clusters themselves each become a separate minimal alliterating unit. The minimal alliterating unit of a stressed syllable, thus, is the phonological segment (to the left of the vowel) with the lowest sonority value plus any segment that precedes it.

Hence, the phonological basis for Anglo–Saxon alliteration is more finely articulated than just syllable onset; the basis is also not merely the syllable's first phonemic segment. Anglo–Saxon alliteration, at least from a frankly structural-linguistic point of view, is an operation on a structured sequence of phonemic segments—structured, I have argued here, by a sonority hierarchy. The finely articulated nature of the constraints on what counts as a minimal alliterative unit and the regularity with which pairs of alliterating words occur line after line are all the more interesting when we recall that oral poetry such as this was not memorized and then recited; it was composed orally on the spot—by "stand-up" poets, if you will—to commemorate past but also present events. Furthermore, originally it was not written down in letters, for it developed in an unlettered, preliterate society.

The central issue of much of the research cited by Bertelson and de Gelder has to do with the relation between literacy and phonological awareness, or more precisely, I would say, between alphabetic literacy and phonemic awareness. Several of the researchers mentioned by Bertelson and de Gelder have argued that the development of phonemic awareness is dependent on knowledge of an alphabetic orthography. This view is compatible with the results of studies that used, as a diagnostic for segmental awareness, subjects' ability to operate on phonemic segments (to delete an initial consonant, for example). However, other views are also compatible with the experimental results (e.g., that learning an alphabetic orthography merely promotes phonemic awareness or that the metaphonological operations involved in learning an alphabetic orthography assist in grappling with operations such as those involved in the experimental tasks designed to tap phonemic awareness). I suggest that manipulating words in an utterance in such a way that alliteratively appropriate segments occur in the correct places is an operation comparable to those mentioned previously. If so, the analysis of Anglo–Saxon oral poetry presented in this chapter shows phonemic awareness in the absence of knowledge of any orthography. It seems to me that, in general, much more will be learned about illiterates, preliterates, prereaders and other special groups by undertaking studies that focus on their competencies rather than their deficits.

Acknowledgments

This research was supported in part by the National Institutes of Health, grants #NS 15175, #NS 19096, #HD 13249, and National Science Foundation grant #BNS86-09085.

References

Browman, C. (1978). Tip of the tongue and slip of the ear: Implications for language processing. *UCLA Working Papers in Phonetics, 42,* 1–149.

Brown, R., & McNeill, D. (1966). The "tip of the tongue" phenomenon. *Journal of Verbal Learning and Verbal Behavior, 5,* 325–337.

Bryant, P. E., & Bradley, L. (1985). *Children's reading difficulties.* Oxford: Blackwell.

Donnenworth-Nolan, S., Tanenhaus, M., & Seidenberg, M. (1981). Multiple code activation in word recognition: Evidence from rhyme monitoring. *Journal of Experimental Psychology: Human Learning and Memory, 7,* 170–180.

Hogg, R., & McCully, C. B. (1987). *Metrical phonology.* Cambridge: Cambridge University Press.

Kavanagh, J. F., & Mattingly, I. G. (Eds.) (1972). *Language by ear and by eye.* Cambridge, MA: MIT Press.

Klaeber, F. (Ed.) (1950). *Beowulf.* Boston: D. C. Heath.

Ladefoged, P. (1982). *A course in phonetics.* New York: Harcourt Brace Jovanovich.

Mattingly, I. G. (1972). Reading, the linguistic process, and linguistic awareness. In J. F. Kavanagh & I. G. Mattingly (Eds.), *Language by ear and by eye* (pp. 133–147). Cambridge, MA: MIT Press.

Preminger, A., (Ed.). (1974). *Princeton encyclopedia of poetry and poetics.* Princeton: Princeton University Press.

Schachter, P. (1988). What's in a name? Inferences from tip-of-the-tongue phenomena. In L. M. Hyman & C. N. Li (Eds.), *Language, speech and mind* (pp. 295–321). London: Routledge.

Selkirk. E. O. (1984). *Phonology and syntax: The relation between sound and structure.* Cambridge, MA: MIT Press.

Chapter 18

Panel Discussion: Sentence Perception and Sentence Production

Janet Fodor
Department of Linguistics, City University of New York

Lyn Frazier
Department of Linguistics, University of Massachusetts

Merrill Garrett
Department of Psychology, University of Arizona

Paul Gorrell (Reporter)
Linguistics Program, University of Maryland

Jacques Mehler (Chairman)
Laboratoire de Psychologie, Paris

Alvin Liberman and his colleagues (e.g., Liberman & Mattingly, 1985) proposed that speech production and speech perception are "different modes of the same mechanism." The focus of the panel discussion is whether this proposal can be extended to sentence production and sentence perception. Such an extension was a goal of initial research into the relationship of production and perception to a generative grammar. In the earliest conceptualization of this relationship, the production of a sentence was viewed as essentially identical to its grammatical derivation. Sentence perception was simply the reverse of this process. Thus, sentence production and sentence perception were initially viewed as different modes of the same mechanism; that mechanism being the application of the grammar.

More recently, theories of sentence perception have incorporated "parsing strategies" to account for intuitive and experimental evidence concerning "garden-path" phenomena and the parser's response to structural ambiguity. These strategies are not part of the grammar, nor is ambiguity a grammatical concept. The investigation of parsing strategies is best exemplified in the work of Lyn Frazier and her colleagues (Frazier, 1978; Frazier & Fodor, 1978).

Although such an approach has clearly increased our understanding of the mechanisms underlying sentence perception, it has also served to obscure the relationship between the parser and the grammar. In turn, this has made it more difficult to relate theories of sentence production to theories of sentence perception.

Fodor noted that although the fundamental problems of relating the production and perception mechanisms for speech are quite similar to those that exist at the syntactic level, researchers in the two domains have opted for different approaches. For example, the Motor Theory of Speech Perception states that the units of the speech code are determined by the production system (i.e., that natural classes of sounds are determined as those sounds that are produced by similar vocal gestures). This requires that the perception mechanism be suitably enriched with a special speech-recognition mechanism. If the natural classes of sounds were determined by the perception system, we would have required a richer production mechanism. As it stands, the perception system must contain within it a model of the production system. This allows perception of a particular speech sound in terms of what it would have taken to produce it. Thus, within the Motor Theory, speech perception is viewed as essentially analysis-by-synthesis.

Fodor pointed out that there is a similar production/perception asymmetry at the syntactic level, and as with speech, the asymmetry was resolved in favor of the production mechanism. This is most clearly seen in the case of structural ambiguity, where a particular word string is compatible with more than one structural analysis. Such ambiguities, which, although largely unnoticed, are quite common in natural language, result from the fact that the production system does not incorporate constraints that prohibit ambiguity. This may be because such constraints would require transderivational power (i.e., the ability to check for other possible derivations of a particular string).

As with speech, the result is that the perception system bears the burden of coping with idiosyncratic properties of the production system. Here, Fodor noted, it is interesting that models of sentence perception that appealed to analysis-by-synthesis routines were soon abandoned. This was largely due to the fact that such routines were hopelessly inefficient, involving numerous false starts and guesswork.

The question that Fodor posed is whether it would be possible for the Motor Theory to give up analysis-by-synthesis, relying instead on analytic strategies as proposed for sentence perception, but to retain its reliance on the production system by allowing this system to define the units for perception.

Ignatius Mattingly commented that analysis-by-synthesis, if taken literally, cannot be the correct answer, if we are to explain how speech is perceived in real time. Instead, it may be useful for speech perception researchers to think in terms of parsing strategies such as those proposed by Lyn Frazier for sentence perception. Frazier responded that much of the progress in parsing theory is due to assuming the grammar as the data base for processing routines. Similarly, it might prove profitable for researchers into speech perception and production to think in terms of a grammatical (i.e., phonological) data base.

Within the framework of Liberman and Mattingly's (1985) Motor Theory of Speech Perception, the connection between perception and production is closely tied to the view of modularity outlined in Jerry Fodor (1983). Frazier addressed three questions that seek to shed additional light on these issues. The first question concerns modularity directly by asking if the sentence comprehension system is modular in the sense that purely structural information is used to identify the initial syntactic analysis. For example, the parsing strategy, Late Closure (Frazier, 1978), states that, at choice points, new lexical items will be incorporated into the phrase currently being processed. In sentence (1) following, this would cause the NP, *the sock,* to be analyzed as the object of the verb, rather than as the subject of a new clause (e.g., *the sock fell off her lap*).

(1) While Mary was mending the sock . . . .

In (1), the choice results from the fact that a verb such as *mend* may occur with or without an object. Recent work by Cuetos and Mitchell (1988) appears to offer evidence that Late Closure does not guide the parsing of sentences in Spanish. Using stimuli such as sentence (2a) following, where Late Closure would predict attachment of the relative clause to *del coronel* and not to *la hija,* Cuetos & Mitchell's results suggest that their subjects prefer the high attachment for the relative clause (i.e., to *la hija*). Sentence (2b) is the literal translation of (2a).

(2) a. El periodista entrevisto a la hija del coronel que tuvo el accidente.
     b. The journalist interviewed the daughter of the colonel who had had the accident.

Moreover, Frazier reported that recent work with Chuck Clifton indicates that the Cuetos and Mitchell results are not peculiar to Spanish but are evident in English as well. This work shows that there is a "relevance constraint" at work that prefers a phrase to modify the main assertion of the sentence. In (2), this would result in a preference for attaching the relative clause to *la hija.*

The question for modularity is whether the nonstructural relevance constraint is used to identify the initial analysis of the sentence or if it is used at some later point to check the initial analysis. Frazier and Clifton used a self-paced reading study to try to answer this question. Using stimuli such as those in sentence (3) following, they used reflexive pronouns to syntactically disambiguate the sentence (i.e., to indicate the initial attachment preference for the relative clause).

(3) a. The doctor called in the son of the pretty nurse who hurt herself.
     b. The doctor called in the son of the pretty nurse who hurt himself.

If the relevance constraint is used to determine the initial analysis of the sentence, then we would expect to find a preference for the high attachment of the relative clause, (i.e., to the NP *the son* rather than to *the pretty nurse*). This would then result in faster reading times for the masculine reflexive as compared to the feminine reflexive. If, in fact, the attachment of the relative clause is determined solely by structural information (i.e., by Late Closure), then we would expect faster reading times for the feminine reflexive. The results indicate that initially only structural information is used, confirming the prediction of a modular sentence processing mechanism. Thus, the relevance constraint comes into play at a point subsequent to the construction of the initial syntactic analysis of the sentence.

The second question Frazier addressed is whether specifically production-based knowledge is used in the comprehension process. If this is the case, then a third question arises as to how it is used. That is, is it used in a modular fashion or as part of a *post hoc* checking mechanism?

The phenomenon of blocking illustrates this issue. Aronoff (1976) observed that novel words are not derived, if there exists a morphologically related word that is synonymous. Thus, the existence of *gloriousness* blocks the derivation of *gloriosity,* just as the irregular past tense *went* blocks the derivation of *goed.* There are also syntactic cases of blocking. For example, in null subject languages, there appears to be a restriction on the interpretation of overt pronouns: They can only be interpreted emphatically, if they occur in a position where a null pronoun is permitted.

Turning to comprehension, it is interesting that in a sentence such as *Grapes are more good than bananas,* we notice that the speaker did not use the correct comparative form *better*. The question here is what knowledge underlies this perception. Given that it is permissible for the comparative *more* to modify adjectives, and that *good* is an adjective, why does the comprehension system simply not compute the meaning of *more* + *good?* That is, why do we notice that *better* was not used?

A plausible account of this is that part of the comprehension process is to check the input against what linguistic form we would (or could) have produced to convey the computed message. Further, assuming that it is specifically production-based knowledge that allows detection of blocked forms would permit us to postulate a very simple mechanism: When you have a narrowly specified form, you check for that form first, and only if it does not exist do you use some more general means.

This may well be a specific instance of the general process of lexicalization. If we ask how is it that speakers locate lexical items, it appears that they must take a conceptual specification of what they want to say and check to see if a lexical item exists that permits them to convey that message.

If this simple production mechanism were to be incorporated directly into the comprehension system, we would need to incorporate extremely powerful mechanisms that are otherwise unnecessary. The reasoning here is similar to Janet Fodor's account of the difficulty of incorporating constraints that prohibit ambiguity into the comprehension system. In both cases, enriching the comprehension system in this way would require giving it transderivational power. Thus, the most parsimonious account of our ability to notice blocked forms is that we are using specifically production-based knowledge in the comprehension process.

We can now consider the issue of whether this type of knowledge is used to guide the initial parse or as a *post hoc* checking mechanism. The following discussion describes an experiment in progress. The results are not yet available. Consider sentences (4) and (5):

(4)   When I arrived, I talked to Jim and Alexander went home.
(5)   When I arrived, I talked to Alexander and Jim went home.

There is independent evidence that producers will order conjuncts with the shorter element first (i.e., S + L). This is not a grammatical restriction, S + L and L + S are both perfectly grammatical conjuncts. For sentences (4) and (5), Late Closure would predict a garden-path effect (i.e., an initial analysis of *Jim and Alexander* and *Alexander and Jim* as conjoined NPs).

The question is whether the relative length of the two nouns in the conjunct is important to the comprehension system. If it is, we would expect the S + L conjuncts to reinforce the garden-path effect. Conversely, would the L + S order lessen the garden-path effect (by serving as a checking mechanism) or perhaps eliminate the effect (by guiding the initial parse)?

If it turns out that there is less of a garden-path effect in (5) than in (4), then we would have evidence that this production-based knowledge is used by the comprehension system. However, to answer the additional question of how this knowledge is put to use, we need to compare sentences similar to (4) and (5), but where the resolution of the ambiguity is in accord with Late Closure. That is, if the unexpected L + S order does not induce a garden-path effect where one would not ordinarily occur, but does serve to speed reanalysis in those cases where Late Closure predicts a garden-path, we would then have evidence that this type of production-based knowledge is used as a *post hoc* check.

Garrett considered the problem of generalizing the Motor Theory of Speech Perception to lexical and syntactic processing. Concerning lexical processing, the issue is to what extent lexical access in the production and perception systems might overlap.

One of the interesting things to emerge from the study of language production processes at lexical and phrasal levels is the case for a multistage lexical retrieval process. The first stage is driven by semantic representations and yields a lexically specific, grammatically coded but *nonphonologically* interpreted record. A second stage accesses the abstract phonological records in the lexicon for purposes of developing pronounceable phrasal representations.

It is the second stage that is an obvious candidate for production/perception convergence. There are a number of empirical reasons to accept something like this two-stage account, not the least of this evidence are the patterns observed in word substitution errors, for example, meaning-related errors (e.g., *listen/speak; finger/hand; sword/arrow*) as well as form related errors (e.g., *modern/modest; considered/consisted*), but not much overlap in the two sets (e.g., *read/write*). These and related facts prompted Fay and Cutler (1977) to suggest that both the production and the comprehension systems used the same inventory of word forms. The similarity between the effective access parameters for the two systems is quite apparent. For example, consider the effects of segmental similarity at different serial positions, and the effects of stress, length, and morphological structure on the access processes.

This account of a common form inventory for comprehension and production is just an empirical elaboration of what most people are inclined to believe. The stronger claim would be that one enters the space of lexical form possibilities by the very same means in the two systems. This does not seem so likely, partly due to the observation that on-line recognition processes may normally reach phonological records via lexical mediation, and partly due to the fact that it might *pay* the system to have more than a single access route on error checking principles.

This brings us to the issue of modularity. The central empirical challenge to the modularity thesis for language processing has been the need to maintain plausible real-time models that are form driven, while at the same time providing for the very rapid and powerful interpretive constraints on sentence processing. For example, for a sentence such as *I saw the Grand Canyon flying to New York,* we appear to compute only the plausible reading of the ambiguity (i.e., we normally do not become aware of the silly reading where *the Grand Canyon* is the subject of *flying*).

Despite this type of intuitive data, the major burden of experimental evidence from parsing and word recognition studies has been precisely to display the processing independence for semantic, syntactic, and lexical systems. The basic processes seem to be insulated from their interpretive consequences. The effects of context are, thus, accounted for by interpretive filtering of the products of the lexical and phrasal systems.

However, what is the source of this meaning-driven filter? One general suggestion has been that the products of the lexical access system are routed not only to the parsing system but to the production system for the generation of plausible construals of the sentence's lexical content that are associated with a syntactic structure by the operation of the normal production machinery. This provides a mechanism for comparing the comprehension systems's purely syntactically generated analyses with the representations generated by the production system.

This model of an interpretive checking system requires that the production system be fast, flexible, and potentially multicomponential. The evidence supports such a view. Also, a limited degree of parallelism may be required to plausibly account for some of the relations between parsing and interpretation, as well as some parsing internal details. Thus, the proposed filter system must be able to deal with this, and there is good reason to claim such parallelism for the production system. For example, during the panel discussion, Ignatius Mattingly noted that we have the capacity for on-line stylistic adjustment of sentence form. This capacity requires the ability to filter the output of our production system through our comprehension system in order to pick the precise details of form that we require.

Based on these observations, Garrett here concludes that the notion of a common mechanism for production and perception at the lexical and syntactic levels runs counter to the symbiotic relationship between the systems with regard to modularity. Each is the means of protecting against the error or indeterminacy that may arise from the modular function of the other.

Gorrell here points out that, as we search for correspondences between the processes used in production and those used in perception, we need to distinguish between *representational* correspondence and *procedural* correspondence. Most current models of production and perception are characterized by: (a) distinct levels of representation, and (b) a set of procedures that map from one level to another. Given this, we can define representational correspondence as the claim that models of production and perception incorporate similar, if not identical, levels of representation. Procedural correspondence is the claim that, in addition to a representational correspondence, mappings between levels incorporate similar mechanisms.

To date, the empirical evidence does not support the stronger claim of procedural correspondence, although as this panel discussion has made clear, there is general support for some form of representational correspondence. One reason for this is that mapping procedures will necessarily involve idiosyncratic properties designed to overcome the particular informational and temporal constraints inherent in moving from one level to the next. Related to this is the fact that the empirical support for proposed mapping procedures is often the detection of mapping errors (e.g., speech errors or garden paths).

What this suggests is that if we are to accept the challenge of generalizing the Motor Theory to include the lexical and syntactic domains, we will need to formulate theories of production and perception that incorporate abstract principles that are not so closely tied to the particular data of either production or perception. If this approach proves successful, then we will be in a better position to view production and perception as, in Liberman and Mattingly's phrase, "different modes of the same mechanism."

References

Aronoff, M., (1976). *Word formation in generative grammar.* Cambridge, MA: MIT Press.

Cuetos, F., & Mitchell, D. (1988). Cross-linguistic differences in parsing: Restrictions on the use of the Late Closure strategy in Spanish. *Cognition, 30,* 73–105.

Fay, D., & Cutler, A. (1977). Malapropisms and the structure of the mental lexicon. *Linguistic Inquiry, 8,* 505–520.

Fodor, J. A. (1983). *The modularity of mind.* Cambridge, MA: MIT Press.

Frazier, L. (1978). *On comprehending sentences: Syntactic parsing strategies.* Unpublished doctoral dissertation, University of Connecticut.

Frazier, L., & Fodor, J. D. (1978). The sausage machine: A new two-stage parsing model. *Cognition, 6,* 291–326.

Liberman, A. M., & Mattingly, I. G. (1985). The Motor Theory of Speech Perception Revised. *Cognition, 21,* 1–36.

Chapter 19

Summary of the Conference: Speech is Special

James J. Jenkins

Department of Psychology, University of South Florida

It is my pleasant duty in beginning this final session to thank Ignatius Mattingly, Patrick Nye, and Alice Dadourian for arranging this conference for all of us. It has been a very pleasant three days, with interesting discussions, good arguments, and pleasant comradeship. All of us have had wonderful time at this conference, and we are grateful to the Haskins personnel who set it up and arranged that everything should run so smoothly. (Applause).

In a general sense, most of us owe a debt to Haskins Laboratories. Many of us have worked and studied here, have sent our students here, and have seen our students' students come here in turn. We are several generations deep in our relationships with this unique institution. We owe a debt to this institution itself, to Frank Cooper, Al Liberman, and Caryl Haskins for creating such a place and endowing it with a cooperative and collaborative atmosphere, which is both remarkable and rare. This institution (often with the help of James Kavanagh and the NICHD) has opened its doors to young investigators and given them an opportunity to do remarkable research projects that they could not do anywhere else. By such actions, it has not only produced research but also has recruited many talented investigators to research in speech perception. The work performed here and the researchers who have been trained here have made enormous contributions to the field. As one distinguished linguist put it when a committee was engaged in evaluating Haskins Laboratories, "Gentlemen, we must keep in mind that we are dealing with a national treasure."

Finally, of course, I want to give thanks to Alvin Liberman. When one visits Haskins, the first thing one does is to go to lunch or dinner with Al and hear "the list." The list is a compendium of all the interesting things that are going on in the world of speech perception. If one is very lucky and works very hard, one

431

may earn a place on the list . . . perhaps the highest honor one can get. Dr. Strange and I believed that our vowel research had "arrived" when we learned that Al was telling people about it when they came to visit the lab. He is a unique part of this unique institution, and we all owe him a considerable debt.

Liberman's Background (Apocryphal)

I decided that it would be appropriate for me to do a little research to discover what had determined the course of Liberman's career . . . in addition to his "sainted grandmother," of course. I believe that I have uncovered a little-known influence on his life.

Alvin Liberman was born, as we all know, in St. Joseph, Missouri, a little town on the Missouri River. If one traces the course of the river, one will find that it flows just a little south of Columbia, Missouri, the home of the University of Missouri. At the time Al was born, the University employed a distinguished psychologist named Max Meyer, a former student of Stumpf. Like Stumpf, Meyer was very much concerned with hearing and with the ear and speaking apparatus. He was a staunch behaviorist and wrote a book called, *The psychology of the other-one*. This book was published in 1922 when Al was a wee infant and, thus, according to Janet Werker, very susceptible to outside influence. I am happy to report that I now know the path of such influence.

There are chapters in Meyer's book that reflect his interest in speech. For example, there is a chapter called "The Other-One is equipped with a sense organ particularly suited to signals" (by this he meant the ear). This chapter is immediately followed by a chapter, "The Other-One's talking machinery." In the second of these chapters, Meyer discussed speech production from the point of view of phonetics and mentioned the perceptual difficulties caused by coarticulation and changes in the rate and stress of speech. He then proceeded to the question of how speech is acquired. Although in general he argued against imitation in this book, he wrote: "But it seems that to a certain extent Nature has equipped the Other-One with reflex responses to auditory signals which repeat with some accuracy auditory stimulation" (p. 328). Furthermore, he wrote: "auditory imitative actions are virtually the only class of imitative reactions which are inherited and for whose inheritance there is some need" (p. 329). His most general argument is that the human ear has evolved in the way that it has just in order to perceive the "great variety of resonating air volumes" that the mouth can produce. "not only a variety from moment to moment, but a variety of several air volumes at the same moment . . . each having its proper tone" (p. 318). (Obviously, Meyer anticipated formants.) His overall argument is that the mouth and the ear are the way they are, and interconnected in the reflex way that they are, just so speech can be learned and take place. In short, he makes the case that *speech is special*.

That message drifted up the Missouri river, floated by St. Joseph and imprinted itself on a baby who later went to the University of Missouri and on to Yale and who is the first person most of us heard say, "Speech is special." And now we know where that conviction really came from.

Progress in Research in Speech Perception

When Liberman began doing research on speech (more than a few years after Max Meyer, of course), one must remember how impoverished the field was with respect to both information and instrumentation. There were a few specially built speech spectrographs, but nothing on the commercial market. There were a few synthesizers. (Klatt, 1987, has recently memorialized the development of synthesizers and has provided recorded samples of them.) There were no convenient means of recording speech: no tape recorders, no wire recorders. (Today's students blanch when they learn this fact.) One had to make phonograph disks on cumbersome machines. These were not only unhandy for field work, they permitted no editing or manipulation (except for rate). A recording was either right or wrong; there was no way to patch it up. There was no way to randomize a series of stimuli or change their timing. There were no computers or even electronic calculators. Research was painfully more difficult than it is today.

In psychology, learning theory was "the theory" of psychology; the only controversies revolved around whose learning theory one should believe. Psychology was behavioristic, operationalistic, and reductionistic. American linguistics was in pretty much the same state. It was behavioristic and positivistic and heavily biased toward description as its only goal. The notion of language universals was scorned and subjectivism was denied. Linguistic giants like Bernard Bloch would tell a class (in the 1950s) that it was possible (in principle) to take some large corpus (say 40 books of fine-grained description of Choctaw), put the corpus into a computer (if one's university had one) and *automatically* determine the phonology of the language on distributional principles alone. Further, if one put the resulting phonology back in the computer, one could determine the morphology, and, by reiteration in turn, one could arrive at the immediate constituents. The process was said to require no judgment; it was "untouched by human hands." (Of course, no one actually did things that way, but it was believed that it was possible in principle.) Linguistic results were justified by the method that produced them; they needed no other rationalization or justification. Linguistics was said to be the complete (and perfect) science. It did not need any changes, and it was not going to change.

It is apparent, however, that things have changed radically. Our instrumentation, our philosophies of science, our theoretical orientations, and the disciplines themselves have changed in extraordinary ways. None of the papers that have been given at this conference could have been given even 30 years ago. The data that we talk about so familiarly did not exist. The knowledge about speech and language that is common to everyone here was unknown. The amazing auditory capabilities of other species like bats, dolphins, and whales that we now take for granted were not even suspected.

The goal of building a reading machine (then just a dream) has been achieved; we have text-to-speech machines that are of very high quality. We have new understanding of alternative communication systems, such as Sign language. We have totally reversed our opinions about infant perception. Whereas we used to think that infants had to work incredibly hard in order to achieve discrimination of sounds, we now believe that they are born into the world with these sensitivities readily available. We have a wealth of tools, computers, synthesizers, brain scans, and new experimental paradigms. We have a psychology today that is frankly cognitive, speculative, and adventurous. We now have a linguistics that is much more open, varied, and exciting than the linguistics of the 1940s and 1950s.

In my reconstruction of history, I see two crucial facts that combined to drive the Haskins tradition. The first was their rediscovery of the fact that an arbitrary collection of sounds could not substitute for the sounds of speech, although these had been viewed by conventional psychology as essentially arbitrary in themselves. The second was the discovery of categorical perception. These facts marked the end of traditional approaches for the Haskins researchers. The first fact meant that speech was not simply an arbitrary collection of unrelated sounds—the implication being that these sounds were processed in some unique fashion. The second fact, categorical perception, implied that there was something different about this signal that was not true of stimuli in other sensory-perceptual domains such as colors, or tones, or the length of lines. This phenomenon argues that there really is something special about speech: As Max Meyer hinted, one could both hear and produce the sounds of speech. That, in turn, I think, led to the Motor Theory. Of course, my reconstruction may be wrong, but that is the way I saw it when I met Al in the 1950s.

Motor Theory

The original Motor Theory played to a very critical audience. Almost no one believed it. In one sense, it seemed to be a hangover from the days of learning theory, a kind of Hullian solution to a difficult problem. As good behaviorists, psychology students were taught that the only entities in the psychological world were stimuli and responses. If one faced a collection of acoustic stimuli that were supposed to be signals of the same phonetic class, and if one could not find common elements or some common properties of the stimuli, one had to explain the existence of the class via the responses associated with the particular members of the collection. (This was called "acquired stimulus equivalence.") The

Motor Theory solved the problem of diversity of acoustic stimuli by playing the stimulus back through the system and seeing what response it took to produce it. In essence, when it came out of one's mouth, one could understand what it meant. This solution is complicated and clumsy. It is also not economical of effort or time, but what else could do the job?

Judged by the usual canons of science, however, the Motor Theory was a certified success, because it sparked all kinds of subsequent research in speech perception and in psychoacoustics. The acousticians argued that one did not need the theory. If one just gave them enough time, they said, they would explain what was going on via acoustic analysis. Liberman, of course, said, "We can't wait for you. We have to do speech now." So he pressed on, whereas the psycho-acousticians tried to show that categorical perception was some kind of artefact and that speech was not special, so a great deal of psychoacoustics was done, and hundreds of articles were written, in an attempt to demolish categorical perception and the Motor Theory. The result was that we came to know more and more about the psychoacoustics of speech and speech-like acoustic complexes.

Nor was psychoacoustics the only area to profit. Work in electromyography of the speech production systems was practically nonexistent before the advent of the Motor Theory. The Motor Theory provided the impetus for doing this work either to support the theory or to refute it. At first, of course, the findings did not fit the simple Motor Theory. As we have heard at this conference, the elec-tromyographic records were neither simpler nor more cohesive; they showed just as much complexity and ambiguity as the acoustic stimulus. This in turn gener-ated more research to try to make sense out of these recalcitrant facts. Surely, researchers said, one end or the other of speech ought to make sense, otherwise speech production would have the same problems as speech perception. Every-one believed that there must be some solid ground somewhere and tried to find it. The theory furnished a target to be attacked or a claim to be substantiated.

Revised Motor Theory

How did the content of the original theory fare? As MacNeilage told us, the content suffered. Research could not find the nice clear muscle signals that were supposed to solve the invariance problem, so the theory had to retreat, to become more abstract, and to marry itself to other views. Today the received Motor Theory is a distant, abstract form of its former self, but it is not doing badly. Consider what we have heard here in the last three days. It is clear that we can put together *a nice story*.

Of course, we must attend to the fact that a good story is not a proof. What we are hearing is "compatible with" but not "proof of," because there are a host of other possible explanations for any of the results that we have heard here. I think that a good story is a major achievement, and the best we can do until a "better story" is invented. I am contented to believe that TRUTH may always evade us. My hope is that we can develop better and better stories to tell.

The story runs something like this:

1. *There is a neural locus for language systems.* How inclusive it is, is not clear as yet. It may be that the specialization includes the phonological level, that is, that it begins with the ear and the mouth, or it may be that it is not activated until a higher level of language is reached. We do know that the left hemisphere is highly specialized for language, regardless of the *form* of the language, regardless of whether it is a *first* or a *second* language, and regardless of whether it is *sign* or *speech.* There is a locus, and Neville, Poizner, Belugi, and Klima have given us fascinating information about that.

2. *Speech-language specialization begins very early in life.* We now have behavioral characterizations that we did not have before. The work with infants has had a profound impact. The original work by Eimas and his colleagues (Eimas, Siqueland, Jusczyk, & Vigorito, 1971) has led to a whole research tradition. We see from Eimas, Jusczyk, Kuhl, Miller, and now Werker's beautiful cross-language work, that the acoustic environment of the human infant is *pre-structured;* it already has discernable seams. The baby does not have to "break in" to the acoustic stream in some magical fashion to get into speech; the child is already sensitive to the phonetic universals. Then, very rapidly in the first year of life, the sensitivities are selectively enhanced or suppressed to yield a pattern that selects the speech sounds that the child hears in the community. Either peaks are forming, or valleys are being pushed down, to use Pisoni's metaphor. There is, overall, a sharpening of distinctions that count, and a grouping together or collapsing of the sounds that are not important in the child's environment. These findings are surprising in the light of our knowledge of 10 years ago and totally unexpected in the light of our knowledge of 20 years ago.

3. *Speech production is regularized during early vocalizations.* As long ago as the 1920s, people wrote that babbling was important to the development of speech and language, but there were very few data. Most data that existed were naturalistic observations of a child or two. In more extreme cases, there were no data at all, just claims. For example, Floyd Allport in his famous *Social Psychology* (1924) claimed that the child could not imitate anything that he or she had not gained control of through babbling. The assertion is clear, but there are neither data in his text to support it nor any data to support his entire scheme of the child's acquisition of speech. Nevertheless his scheme was repeated for 50 years in general psychology texts and taken for granted by many generations of psychologists. Max Meyer and Allport agreed that there had to be some kind of mouth–ear connection (a reflex in Meyer's case, conditioned acquisition in Allport's case). Now Vihman has shown us that it is possible to trace the regulariza-

tion of that relationship. The phenomenon can be studied and observed as it comes into play. One can specify the ways in which deaf children are different. One can see that there is surprising variety among the hearing children in a community and then observe that with further development there is increasing convergence on the units that are going to be in the child's language. There are data now that substantiate the claim that children do not imitate sounds that they have not established in some way by babbling. Children in different language environments develop in different directions. We now have concrete evidence for developmental processes that were only speculative a few years ago.

4. *Vision plays a role in speech development and speech perception.* Research with infants finds that blind children do not give the precedence to bilabials that sighted children do. Research with adults discloses the impact of vision on speech perception, even overriding audition, as in the McGurk–MacDonald effect. Summerfield showed us some of the power and limits of lip reading. Indeed, research from many laboratories reinforces the important fact that there is more than one route into the language system. What this says is that information about what the mouth is doing is important to speech perception, and such information can be obtained in any one of several ways. This should remind us of the success of the TADOMA method of speech reading, which is done entirely by touch with the hands placed on the speaker's articulators in such a way as to feel the vibrations of the larynx, the movements of the lips and jaw, and the stream of air from the mouth and nose. These findings are impressive evidence that the visual information available on the face and the vibratory and tactual information of the neck and face can communicate language.

5. *Speech is separated out of the acoustic world and treated separately.* I heard a welcome concern here with the relationships of speech to the general acoustic surround. Bregman's work on scene analysis and Darwin's work on ongoing noises and how they are "taken out" of speech, if they are present when speech begins, are important contributions. They tell us that the speech perceptual system is playing with the whole acoustic domain around us. Obviously we can never see these phenomena or appreciate their role, if we restrict ourselves to working in a sound-controlled laboratory. These studies originate in concerns with natural settings in which speech normally takes place. Such concerns are coming more to the fore as we struggle with problems of speech understanding mechanisms and with the possibilities of machines that can listen to what we say.

6. *Speech sounds may function by telling us about speech gestures.* Fowler and Rosenblum tell us that sounds specify their sources. I am very sympathetic with this view (see Jenkins, 1985), so I can get carried away with Fowler's exegesis. Surely this is one of the more promising generic facts about the world of sound. Sounds in general do specify their sources, and our hope is that we can find out how the sounds of speech specify the gestures of the vocal tract that

produce them. Is there a way to put this together with all the information that we have about what the mouth and the head are doing to give us a key with which to unlock the system?

Some Cautions

There are some serious problems confronting the Motor Theory. The fundamental content of the theory is as yet undemonstrated. No one has yet done what is promised; that is, no one has recaptured the gestures from the acoustic stream. Browman and Goldstein are working on the brave attempt to deliver on this promissory note. They are trying to specify the dynamics that will produce the right kinematics on the articulatory synthesizer to make speech come out of it. That would be an enormous accomplishment. In discussion, Dennis Klatt has issued a challenge to the "true believers." If you really believe this, he said, then you ought to write a gestural score to go with speech and see if your computer can extract it; see if it can find the invariants that you think are hiding there at a deep and abstract level. Obviously that is a crucial step in advancing the Motor Theory and one that must be tried.

The more abstract the theory gets, the more danger there is that there will not be any substance, that it will not be able to make contact with data. On the other hand, the more abstract it gets, the more powerful it will be, if all of these postulated relationships are correct. The real possibility exists that there may be a "unitarian" ground that Al keeps talking about instead of the "trinitarian" view that so many of us lapse back into.

Lindblom cautions us not to get overly concerned with the speaker. He urges us to examine what listeners have been doing. Janet Fodor appears to give the case away to the production side, but if one goes back to the writings of George Kingsley Zipf (1949) and the "Principle of Least Effort," it is apparent that the argument goes both ways. The listener insists that the speaker makes certain distinctions. If the speaker does not make them, the listener does not get the message, so the listener has a kind of negative control over what the speaker is doing. The speaker on his part (Zipf supposed) tries to do as little as possible but is constantly constrained by the listener.

The speech communication system that gets established in just such interaction between the speaker and the listener is the system that Lindblom is talking about. He argues that there must be dispersal in the acoustic space. There must be some optimal distribution for perceptual reasons (and the more items one is talking about, the more crucial is the optimal dispersal), but obviously the items cannot be perceptually distributed, unless the speaker can produce them within the range of "reasonable" effort. As Max Meyer would have argued in the 1920s, the joint constraint of production and perception is an important and fundamental fact about the speech system. Lindblom's suggestion that we employ what we know about linguistic systems to inform ourselves about the resultants of the tension between production and perception is extremely useful.

As To Modularity

So far, I have not said anything about modularity. My feeling is that modularity took a beating in the last discussion period. When people try to discuss how sentences really work and how language actually works, modularity seems to vanish from the discussion. It is remarkable that on the one hand we talk about modularity and then on the other hand go on to list multiple variables to which the system must be responsive in order for communication to take place. Fodor says that the units within the system can all "talk to each other." Garrett says that these are pretty much modules in their own right and urges us to be careful not to run them all together. Each subsystem may have different inputs and use different kinds of information. They must be responsive to different kinds of constraints from other parts of the system.

I think modularity of the total language system is a lot to ask for, and I see no reason to suppose that we can support such a view. It seems to me that some variety of Garrett's position is going to be more productive for us. If we treat these components as subunits, we can direct our attention to what the inputs and outputs are and try to determine how the units influence one another. At the limit, of course, if one makes the modules small enough and the interaction great enough, the whole notion of modularity disappears from the scene.

I am reminded of my early naive assumptions when I first began to work with aphasic patients. In accord with the linguistic view of the time, I supposed that the language system of the aphasic would come apart in terms of the various analytic linguistic levels: features, phonetics, phonology, morphophonemics, morphology, syntax, and semantics. I supposed that these were arranged in a vast layer cake and that the layers were independent. Our research work (Jenkins, Jimenez-Pabon, Shaw, & Sefer, 1975) showed that this view was almost entirely incorrect.

Aside from the fact that these partitions are our academic levels of analysis, why would one suppose that language would be organized in the individual in this fashion? The more one works with real language in context, the more one finds that the layer cake picture is incorrect. The levels interpenetrate each other and persist in doing so in spite of our best efforts. Reflection suggests that an interdependence is likely to be correct on developmental grounds at least. Children do not learn language one piece at a time: first learning phonetics, then phonology, then morphology, and so on. All of these levels are intricately interwoven in the child's experience; children simultaneously acquire behavior at all levels. Similarly, one does not teach (or learn) a foreign language in the layer cake fashion. If one tried, I suspect that one would fail dreadfully. All of this suggests to me that it would be a real mistake to let the modules be closed up tightly, if we think that the modules correspond at all with our analytic notions.

The best described module that we have heard about at this conference, the beautiful analysis that Konishi presented of the localization apparatus in the barn owl, is tremendously impressive, but we should notice even in this case that Konishi finds separation of the neural pathways for different aspects of information; separation and then a convergence again. The common signal is stripped apart initially; the components are processed separately and then recombined at a later point. Although that appears complex enough, we are surely not going to see anything nearly that simple with respect to language. It is conceivable that we might find something like that at an auditory level (if we are lucky), but I cannot imagine that we will ever see a system that can be described in that way at the language level.

If one postulates a modular system at the speech level, one runs into the problems that we discussed this morning, namely how does the reading and writing system get hold of the information so that it can make use of it? If the information is encapsulated, how does reading break into it? I asked that question of Shankweiler last night, and he said, "Well, that is why reading is hard, and that is why reading is easy. It is because language is modularized. It is hard to break into, but once you break into it, the whole system works." Surely this argues that there is some penetrability at some point. Mattingly gives us a plan for breaking into the module, which is to convert reading material into whatever the speech code is, and then let the speech code enter the system and behave itself as usual.

Problems for Further Discussion

In closing, let me say some of the things that I am still curious about. First, I have not heard anyone talk about the great plasticity of the human nervous system. We know that as we move up the animal chain, we see more and more plasticity in nervous system function. It is true, for example, that the left hemisphere in humans is privileged for language. It is also true, however, that if a small child has a left hemispherectomy (because of trauma or disease), the child will still acquire language in the remaining right hemisphere. The predisposition of the left hemisphere for language does not mean that the left hemisphere is the only place that language can be supported. The system is more plastic than that.

Secondly, I think there are indications that the modules must be somewhat "leaky." That is to say that although they are somewhat modular, they are not really modules in the *strict* sense of the term as Fodor uses it. We know that the "innards" of some modules can become available to us under some conditions. For example, trained phoneticians can in fact hear things that the average person cannot hear. The modules must be able to accommodate some kinds of inquiries or interrogations. There are some ways to get in and out of the closed boxes. Those of you who have conducted visual experiments with distorting or colored goggles or those who have studied the McCullough effect know that one can alter the functioning of the visual system by approaching it through these peripheral manipulations. We do not necessarily understand what happens, but it is apparent that the performance of this presumably closed system can be altered in some fairly basic ways.

Third, I have been surprised by the neglect of "soft-wired" systems. There is a lot of concern in many branches of psychology these days with how behaviors become automated. Some behaviors that are fragmentary and voluntary at the beginning of experience can be made automatic; the behavior can be given, if you like, an encapsulation. Have such behaviors been modularized? This question has been mentioned once or twice during the conference, but no one has pursued the idea. Is it possible that some of the systems that we are talking about here are soft-wired? They may appear "hard-wired" when we examine them in adults (after years and years of practice), but that does not mean that they are innate. Practice and automatization are important issues for us to consider.

Fourth, I think there is a too-easy dichotomy between modularization and general thought. It would be convenient to think that everything is modularized except general thought. Fodor would not go so far as to claim that, but I think he would be sympathetic to such a division. I would suppose on the other hand that we may observe a continuum, with some behaviors more modularized and other less so. This view is compatible, of course, with my thoughts about plasticity and my concerns with soft-wired modules.

Final Comments

Finally, I must comment on some aspects of this meeting that were particularly constructive. The atmosphere here, like the atmosphere at Haskins Laboratories, has been incredibly reasonable. People disagree with one another without rancor and with respect. If one looked for the "monolithic Haskins position," one looked in vain. That monolith is mythical. Almost all of the Haskins people began their talks by saying, "Well, Al and I disagree on . . . ." In fact, one speaker roused the whole group when he said, "This is different from other talks, because we agree with Al." This is the impressive atmosphere that pervades not only the institution but the conference itself.

The second thing that I liked about the conference was the biological orientation. We all agree that it is healthy to recognize that we are dealing with real organisms living in a real world and that the organisms have many of the same tasks to accomplish as our brethren lower on the evolutionary scale. We recognize that there is a biological continuity as well as a discontinuity.

Third, I have been impressed with the welcome atmosphere that has been set up for a variety of kinds of data. At this conference, we have heard neurological data, behavioral data, acoustical data, linguistics systems data, diachronic linguistic data, data from ethological and ecological points of view, and data concerning alternative communication systems. There is an openness here for enlightenment from any source that is available to us. This is admirable.

Postscript

If Alvin Liberman's sainted (though previously unrecognized) Godfather, Max Meyer, were with us today, I think he would be grateful to his fellow Missourian for advancing so ably the fundamental idea with which he was imprinted. I am sure that he would predict that the next few years may see even more enlightenment as we continue to press forward toward an even better story about the special nature of speech.

Acknowledgment

Support from NICDC Grant DC 00323 to Winifred Strange and James Jenkins is gratefully acknowledged.

References

Allport, F. H. (1924). *Social psychology*. Boston: Houghton Mifflin.

Eimas, P. D., Siqueland, E. R., Jusczyk, P., & Vigorito, J. (1971). Speech perception in infants. *Science, 171*, 303–306.

Jenkins, J. J. (1985). Acoustic information for objects, places and events. In W. H. Warren Jr. & R. E. Shaw (Eds.), *Persistence and change* (pp. 115–138). Hillsdale, NJ: Lawrence Erlbaum Associates.

Jenkins, J. J., Jimenez-Pabon, E., Shaw, R. E., & Sefer, J. W. (1975). *Schuell's Aphasia in adults* (2nd ed.). Hagerstown, MD: Harper & Row.

Klatt, D. H. (1987). Review of text-to-speech conversions for English. *Journal of the Acoustical Society of America, 82*, 737–793.

Meyer, M. F. (1922). *Psychology of the other-one* (2nd ed.). Columbia, MO: Missouri Book.

Zipf, G. K. (1949). *Human behavior and the principle of least effort*. Reading, MA: Addison-Wesley.

Chapter 20

Afterthoughts on Modularity and the Motor Theory

Alvin M. Liberman
Haskins Laboratories

I am deeply grateful to all of you for having come here to talk about modularity and the Motor Theory, two notions that are dear to some of my colleagues and me. You do these notions and us great honor.

Naturally, I think modularity and the Motor Theory deserve the careful attention you've given them. I have often said why I think that, but my reasons have most commonly arisen out of particular and circumscribed experiments; they have connected only spottily to the more general considerations that have strongly influenced my thinking. Fortunately for me, these considerations have figured in the provocative discussions we've had here; as a result, they have come to be uppermost in my mind, and I have been stimulated to reconsider them. Perhaps it is appropriate, then, that I take this opportunity to say how I see them now.

The first consideration is a fact—at least, I take it to be a fact—that must seem the best kept secret in speech research: Only the sounds of speech are efficient vehicles for phonetic structures; no other sounds, no matter how artfully contrived, will work better than about one tenth as well. As Frank Cooper said in his opening remarks, this is the conclusion he and I arrived at in the mid-forties, when, in connection with the enterprise he described, we tested to see at what rates consonants and vowels could be perceived if nonspeech sounds were substituted for the real things. Of course, we did not then and could not now test all possibilities. But we were nevertheless convinced of the validity of our conclusion, and we remain so today, not just because our various nonspeech patterns failed, but because they failed in ways that made it clear why we ought never to have expected them to succeed. At all events, it was this (to us) surprising and enlightening experience that raised in our minds the question that has guided our research ever since: What is special about speech that it works uniquely well?

The general answer some of us have been led to is that speech perception is managed by a specifically phonetic adaptation (a module) and that a critically important property of this adaptation is a common set of gestural primitives for perception and production (the Motor Theory). This answer is an alternative to what seems the more conventional view, which is that perception of speech rests on the same processes and primitives that underlie perception of all sounds, and that these processes and primitives are wholly distinct from those of speech production.

But if the conventional view is correct, then it ought to be possible, even easy, to find nonspeech substitutes for speech. Consider the alphabet. Surely, there is nothing special about its characters; they simply conform to those general principles that govern the perception of any optical shapes. The obvious consequence is that a large number of shapes can be made to do the job. Moreover, such shapes can be designed even though the relevant principles of visual perception are not in hand. Now, if in like manner the sounds that can be used for phonetic communication need only conform to the principles that govern perception of nonspeech sounds, then a similarly large number should prove suitable. But can such sounds be found? I think not, so I accept that speech is special and try to figure out how and why.

The second consideration is no secret: Only human beings produce phonetic structures; nonhuman animals, including our closest relatives among the primates, do not and can not. Though obvious and, one might think, obviously important, this invidious fact seems not to count for much in theories about speech. A consequence is that, just as so many believe there is nothing special about the perception of speech, so, too, do they seem to believe there is nothing special about its production. Taking principles gleaned from the study of systems that don't talk, they therefore apply them to the only system that does. Of course, speech must at some level have much in common with other modes of action, but it must also have properties specifically adapted to its species-specific function. In this connection, some of us think that a special set of gestures evolved to serve phonetic communication, together with special controls that overlap and merge the gestures so as to produce high rates of communication and yet preserve information about the underlying phonetic structure. Indeed, a primary constraint on the evolution of the specialized phonetic gestures must have been the extent to which they lent themselves to being coarticulated. But whatever the conditions of their evolution, these gestures (or their intentional antecedents) are, in our view, the primitives of an action module that is specifically phonetic, not generally motor.

The third consideration, which, like the first, was prefigured by Frank Cooper's opening remarks, looks to a requirement that is imposed on all communication systems: Sender and receiver must be bound by a common understanding that certain signals have communicative significance. For convenience, Mattingly and I have referred to this as the requirement for "parity." In speech, parity exists when that which counts as phonetic structure for the speaker counts also for the listener. One asks then how parity was established as speech developed in the race and as it develops anew in each child.

On the conventional view that there is no phonetic specialization, parity can hardly have come about by normal evolutionary processes. For if there is no phonetic specialization, then there are no specifically phonetic primitives, hence, nothing that is specifically marked for communicative purposes. In that case, people who might have wanted to communicate phonetically must first have agreed to assign phonetic significance to some arbitrarily chosen patterns of primitives. This is to say that speech would have had to be invented.

Alternatively, one can assume, still on the conventional view, that some things in speech are destined, by virtue of genetic endowment, to be specifically phonetic, but that these exist only at the cognitive level, where they take the form of phonetic prototypes, labels, or ideas; they are not to be found among the primitives of action and perception. But that is either to beg the question or to answer it in an unparsimonious way. Indeed, the answer is more unparsimonious than one might at first think, because it not only introduces such uncertain concepts as innate prototypes, labels, or ideas, but, in so doing, rounds out a troika of modes—a specifically phonetic one, a generally motor one, and a generally auditory one—and so creates the need for a cognitive process of some kind to form the three into a functional unit.

Development in children would necessarily follow an equally cognitive course. If speech were an invention, then children would have to master it, as they might an invention of any other kind, by trial and error, inference, or instruction. If there were innate phonetic ideas or prototypes to head them in the right direction, they would still have to establish the connections to the non-phonetic modes of action and perception needed to make communication of these phonetic things possible. In either case, they would have to puzzle out the complex relation between the phonetically unmarked movements and sounds of speech, on the one hand, and, on the other, the special-purpose phonetic structures they convey. That done, the children woud have to set about firmly fixing this relation in mind, using for this purpose the same cognitive learning processes they would recruit in becoming proficient with Morse code or the alphabet.

Because it has these implications for phylogenetic and ontogenetic development, the conventional view of speech, or its equivalent, is patently unacceptable as an account of intraspecies communication among nonhuman animals. Small wonder then that such communication is generally understood to rest on specializations narrowly adapted to, and distinctively marked for, their communicative function. It does not matter, for this argument, that the communicative signal is variously acoustical, optical, chemical, or electrical and that the relevant processes vary accordingly. What does matter is that the signals are dealt with by specializations, for it is only then that communication can evolve in each species by appropriately precognitive processes and only then that it can redevelop in each individual member in a similarly precognitive way. Are we to suppose that human beings, alone among Nature's creatures, are not similarly specialized? Have we somehow risen above the modules that control communication in other species, and is that why we so often refer to language as a higher mental function? If I believed that, I should feel obliged to explain how this most unparsimonious state of affairs came about, and to defend the notion that phonetic communication is an achievement of cultural, not biological, evolution. I would far rather suppose that we are like other creatures in having a communication module, and that we differ from them in that our module, but only ours, is phonetic. My concern then is to learn more about our module.

But specialization for communication takes care of only part of the parity requirement. It gets matters off to a good start, to be sure, since it provides for communication without somebody having to get everybody else to agree about what counts as communicative. Still, it leaves open the possibility that there are two specializations, one for production and one for perception, that must then be harmonized. Unfortunately for parsimony, such harmony can only be brought about by processes of a very cognitive sort: All who would communicate must learn—for example, by trial and error—which special speech sounds go with which special speech movements. In that case, the two sides of the communication system cannot coevolve. Yet coevolution must have occurred, certainly in the nonhuman case, which is why one finds there evidence that production and perception of communication signals have genetic and neurobiological roots in common. Surely it is reasonable to assume a similar arrangement for phonetic communication in humans. The Motor Theory is a step in that direction, for it assumes that production and perception are simply different faces of the same module, sharing a common set of (gestural) primitives and, to the extent possible, a common set of processes. There is then no need in phylogenetic or ontogenetic development to establish by cognitive procedures the connection between production and perception that must exist; this necessary connection is a fundamental property of the phonetic module.

Thus, modularity and the Motor Theory set speech apart from other motor and perceptual processes, but not from the biology that underlies communication in the rest of the animal kingdom. Like birdsong, speech is a specialization; in my view, it is not to be understood except in that light.

These, then, are the general considerations that our symposium has moved me to reconsider. I look forward to some future symposium, when I might want to reconsider them yet again.

Author Index

Subject Index

457

QP 399 .M63 1991

Modularity and the motor
  theory of speech perception